# Lecture Notes in Computer Science

T0237869

*Commenced Publication in 1973*
Founding and Former Series Editors:
Gerhard Goos, Juris Hartmanis, and Jan van Leeuwen

Nabil Abdennadher   Dana Petcu (Eds.)

# Advances in Grid and Pervasive Computing

4th International Conference, GPC 2009
Geneva, Switzerland, May 4-8, 2009
Proceedings

 Springer

Volume Editors

Nabil Abdennadher
University of Applied Sicences
Western Switzerland (HES-SO)
Geneva, Switzerland
E-mail: nabil.abdennadher@hesge.ch

Dana Petcu
Computer Science Department
West University of Timisoara
Timisoara, Romania
E-mail: petcu@info.uvt.ro

Library of Congress Control Number: Applied for

CR Subject Classification (1998): C.2, D.1, D.2, F.1, F.2, D.4, C.4, H.4, K.6

LNCS Sublibrary: SL 1 – Theoretical Computer Science and General Issues

ISSN        0302-9743
ISBN-10     3-642-01670-7 Springer Berlin Heidelberg New York
ISBN-13     978-3-642-01670-7 Springer Berlin Heidelberg New York

springer.com

© Springer-Verlag Berlin Heidelberg 2009
Printed in Germany

Typesetting: Camera-ready by author, data conversion by Scientific Publishing Services, Chennai, India
Printed on acid-free paper        SPIN: 12662647        06/3180        5 4 3 2 1 0

# Preface

Grid and Pervasive Computing (GPC) is an annual international conference devoted to the promotion and advancement of all aspects of grid and pervasive computing. The objective of this conference is to provide a forum for researchers and engineers to present their latest research in the fields of grid and pervasive computing.

Previous editions of the Grid and Pervasive Computing conference were held in: Kunming (China) May 25-28, 2008, Paris (France) May 2-4, 2007, and Taichung (Taiwan) May 3-5, 2006.

The fourth edition took place in Geneva, Switzerland during May 4-8, 2009. It was organized by members of the University of Applied Sciences Western Switzerland (Haute Ecole de Paysage, d'Ingénierie et d'Architecture - hepia), in collaboration with colleagues from various places around the world.

The conference spanned a full week, including a three-day technical program where the papers contained in these proceedings were presented. The conference was followed by two tutorial days where attendants had the opportunity to discuss a variety of topics related to the fields covered at the conference, at both introductory and advanced levels. The technical program also included an industrial session, with contributions illustrating challenges faced and solutions devised by industry. Furthermore, the conference offered an opportunity for vendors and researchers to present their products and projects at an exhibition (Grid Village) where solutions supporting the development of grid and pervasive computing were displayed.

Three workshops were held in conjunction with the conference:

- The Third International Symposium on Service, Security and Its Data Management Technologies in Ubi-comp (SSDU 2009)
- The 4th International Workshop on Workflow Management (ICWM 2009)
- The First International Workshop on Grids, Clouds and Virtualization (IWGCV 2009)

The proceedings of these workshops are not included in this volume but are published in a separate book.

The conference featured four distinguished invited speakers, who delivered state-of-the-art information on the conference topics:

- Exa-Scale Volunteer Computing by David P. Anderson (University of California, Berkeley, USA)
- Towards a Sociology of the Grid by Ian Foster (Computation Institute at Argonne National Laboratory, USA)
- The Swiss National Grid (SwiNG) project by Heinz Stockinger (Swiss Institute of Bioinformatics, Switzerland)

- Successful Industry Use of Grid and Cloud Technology by Bernhard Schott (Platform Computing GmbH, Germany)

We would like to express our sincere gratitude to these distinguished speakers for sharing their insights with the conference participants.

Exactly 112 papers were submitted, from as many as 34 different countries. The Program Committee worked hard to review them (at least three reviewers per paper), and the selection process proved to be difficult, since many papers had received excellent reviews. The Program Committee finally selected 42 papers for the conference and these proceedings.

The conference also includes an interesting selection of tutorials, featuring international experts who presented introductory and advanced material in the domains of grid and pervasive computing:

- Grid Metadata Management by Sandro Fiore (Euro-Mediterranean Centre for Climate Change and University of Salento, Lecce, Italy)
- An Introduction to Volunteer Computing Using BOINC, by Nicolas Maire (Swiss Tropical Institute, Basel, Switzerland)
- Building a Condor Desktop Grid, by Michela Thiémard, Pascal Jermini (Ecole Polytechnique Fédérale de Lausanne, Domaine IT)
- Trusted Computing for Trusted Infrastructures, by Andrew Boris Balacheff (HP Labs) and Andrew Martin (University of Oxford, UK)

The first Swiss Grid School (SGS 2009) was also held in conjunction with the conference. This school, organized by the Swiss National Grid (SwiNG) association, aimed at transferring grid knowledge to academia, research and industry. It provided lectures and practical lab sessions that illustrated the current state of the art in grid computing in various domains such as grid architecture, security and middleware, resource management, data management and workflow management. It also focused on a variety of practical case studies (applications).

The fourth edition of GPC was made possible through the generous support and diligent work of many individuals and organizations. A number of institutional and industrial sponsors also made important contributions and participated in the industrial exhibition. Their names and logos appear on the GPC website (http://gpc09.eig.ch). We gratefully acknowledge their support.

Various Program Committee members were assigned to shepherd some of the papers. We are grateful to all those who contributed to the technical program of the conference. We would also like to thank the members of the Organizing Committee for their valuable effort in taking care of all the organizational details, which led to a smooth ride of the conference. Finally, we also thank the authors of the contributions submitted to the conference and to all the participants who helped achieve the goal of the conference: to provide a forum for researchers and practitioners for the exchange of information and ideas about grid and pervasive computing.

May 2009                                          Nabil Abdennadher
                                                  Dana Petcu

# Organization

## Steering Committee Members

| | |
|---|---|
| Hai Jin | Huazhong University of Science and Technology, China |
| Christophe Cérin | University of Paris XIII, France |
| Sajal K. Das | University of Texas at Arlington, USA |
| Jean-Luc Gaudiot | University of California - Irvine, USA |
| Kuan-Ching Li | Providence University, Taiwan |
| Cho-Li Wang | University of Hong Kong, China |
| Chao-Tung Yang | Tunghai University, Taiwan |
| Albert Y. Zomaya | University of Sydney, Australia |

## Conference Chair

| | |
|---|---|
| Nabil Abdennadher | University of Applied Sciences, Western Switzerland |

## Program Co-chairs

| | |
|---|---|
| Nabil Abdennadher | University of Applied Sciences, Western Switzerland |
| Dana Petcu | West University of Timisoara, Romania |

## Tutorial Chair

| | |
|---|---|
| Krishna Madhavan | Clemson University, USA |

## Exhibition Chair

| | |
|---|---|
| Claude Evequoz | University of Applied Sciences, Western Switzerland |

## Publicity Chairs

| | |
|---|---|
| Brian Yunes Univa UD | USA |
| Wenbin Jiang Huazhong | University of Science and Technology, China |
| Raphaël Couturier | University of Franche Comte, France |

## Local Chair

| | |
|---|---|
| Régis Boesch | University of Applied Sciences, Western Switzerland |

# Program Committee

| | |
|---|---|
| Abawajy Jemal | Deakin University, Australia |
| Abdennadher Nabil | University of Applied Sciences, Western Switzerland |
| Albuquerque Paul | University of Applied Sciences, Western Switzerland |
| Arabnia Hamid R. | University of Georgia, USA |
| Arantes Luciana | LIP6, France |
| Baker Mark | The University of Reading, UK |
| Banicescu Ioana | Mississippi State University, USA |
| Barker Ken | University of Calgary, Canada |
| Belli Fevzi | University of Paderborn, Germany |
| Cérin Christophe | Université de Paris XIII, France |
| Chang Hsi-Ya Jerry | NCHC, Taiwan |
| Chang Ruay-Shiung | National Dong Hwa University, Taiwan |
| Chung Yeh-Ching | National Tsing Hua University, Taiwan |
| Cirne Walfredo | UFCG, Brazil |
| Couturier Raphaël | LIFC, University of Franche Comte, France |
| Damon Shing-Min Liu | National Chung Cheng University, Taiwan |
| De Mello F. Rodrigo | University of Sao Paulo, Brazil |
| De Roure David | University of Southampton, UK |
| Di Martino Beniamino | Second University of Naples, Italy |
| Du David H.C. | University of Minnesota, USA |
| Evequoz Claude | University of Applied Sciences, Western Switzerland |
| Foukia Noria | University of Otago, New Zealand |
| Grigoras Dan | University College Cork, Ireland |
| He Xiangjian | University of Technology Sydney, Australia |
| Hobbs Michael | Deakin University, Australia |
| Hsiao Hung-Chang | National Cheng Kung University, Taiwan |
| Hsu Hui-Huang | Tamkang University, Taiwan |
| Hu Bin | University of Central England at Birmingham, UK |
| Huang Kuo-Chan | National Taichung University, Taiwan |
| Hussain Sajid | Acadia University, Canada |
| Jemni Mohamed | ESSTT, Tunisia |
| Jeong Young-Sik | Wonkwang University, South Korea |
| Jia Weijia | City University of Hong Kong, China |
| Jiang Hai | Arkansas State University, USA |
| Jiannong Cao | Hong Kong Polytechnic University, China |
| Katz Daniel S. | Louisiana State University, USA |
| Kim J. Moon | IBM, USA |
| Lau C.M. Francis | University of Hong Kong, China |
| Li Kuan-Ching | Providence University, Taiwan |

Liu Hai                          Hong Kong Baptist University, Hong Kong
Malyshkin Victor                 Russian Academy of Sciences, Russia
Manneback Pierre                 Faculty of Engineering, Mons, Belgium
Margalef Burrull Tomás           Universitat Autónoma de Barcelona, Spain
Medeiros Pedro                   New University of Lisbon, Portugal
Müller Henning                   University of Applied Sciences,
                                   Western Switzerland
Navaux Philippe                  Federal University of Rio Grande do Sul,
                                   Brazil
Olmedilla Daniel                 Telefonica R&D, Spain
Omer Rana                        Cardiff University, UK
Panetta Jairo                    INPE, Brazil
Paprzycki Marcin                 IBSPAN, Poland
Pautasso Cesare                  University of Lugano, Switzerland
Perrott Ronald                   Queen's University, UK
Petcu Dana                       West University of Timişoara, Romania
Pinotti Cristina                 Universitá degli Studi di Perugia, Italy
Podvinec Michael                 Biozentrum, University of Basel, Switzerland
Raad Wasim                       King Fahd University of Petroleum and
                                   Minerals, Saudi Arabia
Ranka Sanjay                     University of Florida, USA
Ro Won-Woo                       Yonsei University, Korea
Sadjadi Masoud                   Florida International University, USA
Sato Matsumoto                   Liria New University of Lisbon, Portugal
Sato Mitsuhisa                   University of Tsukuba, Japan
Shi Yuanchun                     Tsinghua University, China
Stockinger Heinz                 Swiss Institute of Bioinformatics, Switzerland
Talbi El-Ghazali                 INRIA Lille - Nord Europe, France
Tcaciuc Sergiu                   University of Siegen, Germany
Thulasiram K. Ruppa              University of Manitoba, Canada
Wang Zhigang Frank               Cranfield University, UK
Wendelborn Andrew                University of Adelaide, Australia
Wu Jan-Jan                       Academia Sinica, Taiwan
Wu Song                          Huazhong University of Science and
                                   Technology, China
Xiao Nong                        National University of Defense Technology,
                                   China
Xue Jingling                     University of New South Wales, Australia
Yang Caho-Tung                   Tunghai University, Taiwan
Yu Zhiwen                        Kyoto University, Japan
Zeadally Sherali                 University of the District of Columbia, USA
Zhou Yuezhi                      Tsinghua University, China
Zhu Yanmin                       Imperial College London, UK

# Table of Contents

# Middleware

# Scheduling

## Load Balancing

## Pervasive Computing

## Sensor Networks

# Peer-to-Peer

# Fault Tolerance

# Capacity Planning in Economic Grid Markets

Marcel Risch[1] and Jörn Altmann[2]

[1] International University in Germany, School of Information Technology
Campus 3, 76646 Bruchsal, Germany
`marcel.risch@i-u.de`
[2] TEMEP, School of Industrial and Management Engineering
College of Engineering, Seoul National University,
San 56-1, Sillim-Dong, Gwanak-Gu, Seoul, 151-742, South-Korea
`jorn.altmann@acm.org`

**Abstract.** Due to the few computing resource planning options currently available in Grid computing, capacity planning, an old discipline for analyzing resource purchases, is simple to perform. However, once a commercial computing Grid is established, which provides many different resource types at variable prices, capacity planning will become more complex and the user will require support for handling this difficult process. The support could come from an online Grid Capacity Planning Service, which helps users with little IT expertise to make use of the Grid in a cost-effective manner. This Grid Capacity Planning Service is a stand-alone service, enabling companies to outsource their capacity planning task. This paper describes the Grid Capacity Planning Service and demonstrates the workings of the service through simulations.

**Keywords:** Grid Economics, Grid Capacity Planning, Service-Oriented Computing, Grid Computing, Resource Allocation, Utility Computing.

## 1 Introduction

Capacity planning is being applied in many variations in companies. The more the company depends on capacity planning decisions, the more effort is allocated to it. For example, in data centers, capacity planning is extensively used to determine the computing resource needs. To ensure that all applications run with the required QoS and none of the computing resources becomes overloaded, the IT staff continuously monitors system data and resource usage, forecasts the future demand of applications and, thus, predicts their resource requirements. This requirements list can then be turned into an allocation plan and, if the existing resources are insufficient, into a list of required resources which need to be purchased.

At present, the computing capacity planning process of companies is fairly simple, since required computing resources can only be purchased or leased. With the advent of commercial Grids, however, capacity planning becomes more involved. Any company that requires additional resources now is offered a new option for satisfying its computing resource needs: purchasing Grid resources from the commercial Grid. This

N. Abdennadher and D. Petcu (Eds.): GPC 2009, LNCS 5529, pp. 1–12, 2009.

additional option adds additional complexity to the resource purchase decision making process, since three issues have to be addressed: Firstly, it needs to be decided which applications are suitable to run on the Grid. Secondly, since a Grid market is expected to be competitive, prices will fluctuate with changes in supply and demand. Thus, if the overall cost of Grid usage has to be determined, the price for Grid resources has to be predicted accurately. Finally, the demand fluctuations have to be predicted accurately, since the benefit from using the Grid comes from selling spare capacity on the Grid and buying additional resources at times of peak demand times. From these three issues, it can be seen that, while capacity planning is vital to using computing resources in an economically efficient manner, it is extremely difficult to perform it properly.

Because of this difficulty, we propose a new service in the commercial Grid environment: the Grid Capacity Planning Service (GCPS). The remainder of the paper is organized as follows. Section 2 gives an introduction to capacity planning, while section 3 elaborates on the difference between traditional capacity planning and Grid capacity planning. Our capacity planning model is introduced in section 4 and expanded in section 5. The workings of the model are then demonstrated with the use of simulations in section 6.

## 2   An Introduction to Capacity Planning

The term "capacity planning" is often used but rarely defined. To avoid any ambiguity, we follow the definition given by IBM [1]: *"Capacity Planning encompasses the process of planning for adequate IT resources required to fulfill current and future resource requirements so that the customer's workload requirements are met and the service provider's costs are recovered."*

This definition allows us to categorize the users of capacity planning into two groups: customers and providers. Current research has largely taken the stance that the provider's problem in Grids is a resource allocation problem to which economic mechanisms can be applied [2, 3, 4, 5, 6, 7]. Other researchers have taken a more long-term view of capacity planning which works with reservations [8] while still others have applied the problem to specialized fields, such as phased workloads [9].

However, there is, as of yet, no research being done on the customer's need for capacity planning in a utility computing environment. We will remedy this situation by focusing solely on the customer's capacity planning problem, which is at least as challenging as the provider's.

The following three tasks are at the heart of the capacity planning process, according to the definition given above: (1) monitoring of the current resource utilization, (2) estimation of future resource requirements of applications and, finally, (3) cost estimation to ensure that a company does not overspend.

### 2.1   Capacity Planning Tasks

Before the introduction of commercial Grids, capacity planning had only been a long-term approach. Data center staff had to analyze the current application-to-resource mapping, the monitoring data, and some economic data, such as the income generated by certain applications. Using this input, the data center staff then had to determine whether the resource pool is able to run all applications at the required QoS. If this had not been the case, the data center staff had to determine which additional resources have to be purchased or leased and then create a migration plan for the applications that have to be migrated.

With the advent of commercial Grid offers, capacity planning can also be used to solve short-term capacity problems. In this case, the data center staff can purchase additional Grid resources if the applications no longer run at the required QoS. Since this decision can be implemented within minutes, the capacity planning process now takes on a short-term aspect as well. However, as has been shown in [10], using the Grid excessively is also not to be encouraged, as the Grid becomes more expensive than in-house resources in the long run.

We can therefore say that the capacity planning process for utility computing consists of two parts: The short-term capacity planning process and the long-term capacity planning process which has been used in datacenters before the introduction of utility computing environments. This idea is illustrated in the figure below.

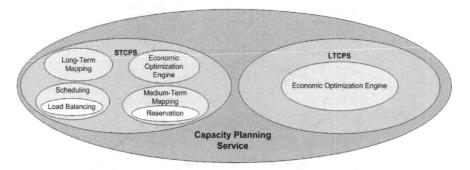

**Fig. 1.** Capacity Planning Structure for Utility Computing

Each of the two capacity planning sub-services, the Short-Term Capacity Planning Service (STCPS) and the Long-Term Capacity Planning Service (LTCPS), has a number of tasks to perform. For the STCPS, the main task is the scheduling of applications to resources that are available. A further subtask of scheduling is load balancing which ensures that all resources are used evenly. Furthermore, the STCPS has the capability to perform medium-term mapping of applications to resources (i.e. resource reservation). This is useful in the case of daily demand peaks which can then be planned for. Such a module reserves utility computing resources (e.g. on a day-ahead basis) to ensure that the scheduler has sufficient resources to schedule all applications. Lastly, the STCPS also has to take the economics of Grid usage into account. Not only can the Grid usage become expensive over time, it can also be more expensive than letting an application run slower. To determine whether using the Grid is economically efficient, the STCPS has to have an economic optimization module.

The LTCPS, on the other hand, is mostly concerned with the economics of resource purchases. In other words, its focus lies on the question of which resource purchase is the most economically efficient one. This procedure has to take into account the current mapping of application to resources, the performance of each application and the costs incurred by using Grid resources. Furthermore, the user's budget constraints and economic requirements (e.g. importance of applications to the user's business, the expected long-term benefits of providing good QoS) have to be considered when developing a new application mapping.

Especially, the LTCPS also has to consider risks. Some risks are inherent to the system, such as resource failures or provisioning issues. To avoid these problems, the Economic Optimization Engine has to take into account the risks inherent to using in-house and Grid resources and has to determine which course of action (e.g. fault tolerance mechanisms) can minimize these risks.

## 2.2 Capacity Planning Inputs and Outputs

To perform their tasks, both capacity planning services require a number of inputs which are shown together with the outputs of the capacity planners in the following figure.

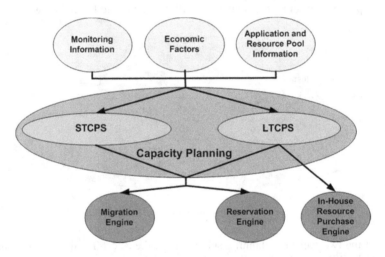

**Fig. 2.** Capacity Planning Inputs and Outputs

The first input parameter is the monitoring information. In this case, monitoring refers to three types of actions: measuring the utilization rates of resources, response time analysis of applications, and traffic analysis. In the utilization rate measuring process, the IT staff analyzes to which percentage any given resource is used. Once the utilization approaches a critical level, the resource is classified as overloaded.

The response time analysis determines the response time of applications. The rise of the response time over a certain threshold level indicates that the application has insufficient resources available.

The traffic analysis is used to determine traffic flows within the data center and the traffic flows into and out of the data center. This data can then be used to determine whether individual resources need to be connected differently. The traffic flow information can also be used to determine whether the infrastructure is able to handle all data transmissions.

The second type of input is the economic factors which are stated by the user. These can include requirements (e.g. certain applications have to run in-house) and restrictions. Restrictions can be categorized into financial restrictions or into purchasing restrictions. Furthermore, the user may have a certain budget which has to be considered when creating a new capacity plan.

The third type of input is the information about the resource and application pool. In particular, the capacity planning service has to know which applications are running and what they are being used for, since the use can have a big impact on the resource requirements. For example, a Web server for text-based Web pages has a different load pattern than a Web server which is used for streaming videos.

Furthermore, the capacity planning service has to know which resources are available. This includes not only in-house resources but also resources that have been purchased on the Grid and resources that are available on the Grid.

Based on these inputs, the capacity planning service creates a number of outputs which can either be used by automated programs or by the data center staff. The former is the Migration Engine which is responsible for either migrating applications according to the resource allocation plan generated by the capacity planning service.

The second output consists of a recommendation list for making reservations of computing capacity on the Grid. These can be either short-term reservation recommendations which come from the STCPS or long-term reservation recommendations from the LTCPS. The actual reservations, based on the recommendation list, can be made on behalf of the user by an automated Reservation Engine. Alternatively, the reservations can also be made by the user.

Lastly, the Long-Term Capacity Planning Service can also create a plan for purchasing in-house resources. Since this task cannot be performed automatically, the LTCPS only gives out human-readable list of resources that have to be purchased and the store at which to purchase them.

## 3   Grid Capacity Planning and Traditional Capacity Planning

There are a number of differences between traditional capacity planning as it is performed today and Grid capacity planning. This section will illustrate these differences and thereby demonstrate the need for a Grid Capacity Planning Service.

### 3.1   Resource Selection

The outcomes of traditional capacity planning are fairly limited, since there are only three courses of action: purchasing in-house resources, renting or leasing in-house resources, or doing nothing. This lack of fine-grained options does not require a long-winded capacity planning process for small and medium-sized companies. Therefore, the decisions of those companies that can be made can be made quickly, optimizing the costs for the capacity planning procedure [11].

While capacity planning is not an attractive tool in non-utility computing environments, it becomes more important in commercial Grids due to the wider range of options: purchase Grid resources, purchase in-house resources, lease resources, any combination of the previous, sell spare computing capacity, or do nothing. This increased number of options leads to the problem that an optimal capacity planning solution is not obvious anymore. For example, users willing to sell computing resources must consider the expected income during the capacity planning process.

Overall, due to the increased complexity, the capacity planning staff requires more time, which makes the capacity planning process more expensive and, thus, a utility computing environment less attractive.

## 3.2  Price Volatility and Demand Fluctuation

The prices of the current computing resource market are static, i.e. resource prices do not change frequently. Differences only occur because of special offers or economies of scale. This means that the capacity planning team does not need to rush the process to avoid rising prices, since even the currently available utility computing resource prices remain constant (e.g. Amazon [12], Tsunamic Technologies [13]).

With the advent of commercial Grids in which companies can purchase and sell resources according to their needs, the changes in supply and demand will lead to fluctuating prices [14, 15, 16, 17]. These varying prices must be taken into account in the capacity planning process.

Furthermore, taking fluctuations of demand into account, it becomes necessary to predict how prices will develop in the future, and thus, the timing of purchases may become a relevant parameter in the capacity planning process. To achieve a precise prediction, the capacity planner must consider the past behavior of the market with respect to the available resources. This means that the capacity planner should not only look at the average demand but also at peak demand times on the utility computing market, which can occur when many Grid users require additional resources. Furthermore, the own demand must be seen in comparison to the peak demand. If there are regular demand peaks on the utility computing market and the own demand peaks occur at the same time, the required Grid resources might only be available at very high prices, which might cause budget problems. On the other hand, if the own demand is anti-cyclical to the market demand, Grid resource prices should not be an issue.

## 3.3  Application Mapping

Optimizing the mapping of applications to resources also becomes more convoluted in a Grid market environment. In traditional capacity planning scenarios, companies only have to find a mapping of applications to their in-house resources and, if necessary, purchase additional resources for in-house installation. This approach, while not trivial, is manageable, since the number of possible mappings and the resource diversity are fairly small. In fact, once a company knows which resources have to be purchased, the suitable products can be ranked according to their cost.

On the other hand, optimizing the application mapping in a utility computing environment is also more involved. The application-to-resource mapping depends on the resources that could potentially be purchased on the Gird. Therefore, for each application, two groups of options have to be considered: running the application on one of the suitable in-house resources, or running the application on one of the suitable Grid resources. Each of the Grid options has its own price, since the pricing structures differ between resource types and resource providers.

**Table 1.** Comparison of Traditional and Grid Capacity Planning

|                      | Traditional Capacity Planning | Grid Capacity Planning |
|----------------------|-------------------------------|------------------------|
| Resource Selection   | Few courses of action         | Many courses of action |
| Price Volatility     | Small                         | Large                  |
| Application Mapping   | Small                         | Large                  |

Furthermore, applications have to be sorted according to whether they are suitable to run on the Grid or not. Some applications may not run on the Grid because of several reasons, such as applications that require sensitive information for their calculation which is not allowed to be transmitted to external resources.

### 3.4 Comparison

Grid capacity planning is more elaborate than traditional capacity planning due to the additional options available in computing resource markets. These differences are summarized in Table 1. This increased complexity will mean that companies with little or no IT expertise that are new to the Grid will either not use it or overspend.

However, all companies participating in the Grid need to perform the same capacity planning steps and many run similar applications with similar loads. Therefore, it would be useful if the capacity planning process could be outsourced to an external entity which specializes in providing a capacity planning service. This service, the Grid Capacity Planning Service (GCPS), would allow companies to benefit from utility computing by optimizing companies' Grid resource purchases at low costs. Therefore, this service would be a Grid market enabler.

## 4   A Capacity Planner Model

Following the general model introduced in section 2, the GCPS consists of two parts working in concert. Their workings and interaction is illustrated in more detail in this section.

### 4.1 The Long-Term Capacity Planning Service

The Long-Term Capacity Planning Service (LTCPS) performs the long-term data analysis as described in section 2. Since its main task is to analyze the current data center computing resource pool and the current application mapping, it must be given this information, in addition to economic information, such as the budget of customer (both for Grid and in-house resource purchases), the relative importance of each application and whether the customer would be willing to sell resources on the Grid market.

The next step of the LTCPS is to analyze how the applications which have to run in-house (so-called in-house applications) can be mapped to existing resources. The outcome of this analysis can fall into the following categories: (1) the user has to purchase additional in-house resources, (2) the user has idle in-house resources, (3) the user has idle in-house resources but also has to purchase additional resources to satisfy the demand, or (4) the user has no idle in-house resources and all applications have been mapped. In cases 1 and 3, the user has to purchase additional in-house resources. In the remaining cases, the LTCPS can continue the capacity planning process. This is illustrated in the following figure.

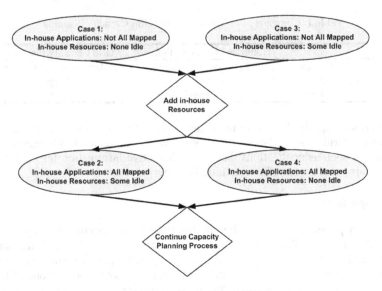

**Fig. 3.** Initial Steps of the LTCPS

In the next step, the LTCPS will have to consider the costs and benefits of using Grid resources. In general, it has to weigh (1) using in-house resources versus using Grid resources, (2) purchasing new in-house resources versus using Grid resources and (3) whether the user is willing to sell resources on the Grid and if so, which resource configuration would be the best selling option. All these factors then have to be analyzed with regards to the market issues that have been described previously, namely demand fluctuation and price fluctuations.

The result of this step will be an optimal or near-optimal mapping of applications to resources such that all user requirements are met and that the resources are used as efficiently as possible. The result can fall into one of the following categories: Purchase Grid resources, purchase in-house resource, and purchase both in-house and Grid resources. The purchase of Grid resources could be implemented in the form of a purchasing plan. To avoid high prices, such Grid purchases could be done far in advance by using the Reservation Engine. For regularly occurring demand peaks, peaks could be covered by using Grid resources in addition to in-house resources.

## 4.2 The Short-Term Capacity Planning Service

The Short-Term Capacity Planning Service (STCPS) performs measurements on the in-house resources to determine their load and the response time of applications. To ensure that these tests do not affect the system adversely, STCPS will only do so periodically. Should it notice that either a resource is being used to maximum capacity or that an application response time is decreasing, it will determine which Grid resource can take up the additional demand.

Furthermore, the STCPS will consider the number of times a similar Grid resource has been purchased in the past. This will allow the STCPS to monitor two important issues: On one hand, it can determine whether these Grid purchases are necessary at regular intervals. If so, it can determine when the Grid resources will be required again and can then suggest reserving Grid resources.

The STCPS will inform the LTCPS of the Grid resource purchase. This allows the LTCPS to determine whether the total cost for these Grid resources approaches the costs of an in-house resource. If this is the case, the LTCPS can warn the user, since this may be a sign that the capacity plan is outdated.

The purchasing information also allows the LTCPS to determine whether Grid resource purchases are occurring at regular intervals. If this is the case, the next purchasing date can be predicted without difficulty and Grid resources can be purchased in advance.

## 5  Implementation and Validation

An initial test of the performance of both components has been implemented. The services are expected to function within a continuous double auction (CDA) setting, which was implemented using Repast [18]. The simulation environment consisted of 500 agents, which traded resources within this market for 500 days. At the beginning of the day, each agent determines its demand. If the demand is larger than the number of in-house resources, the agent will bid for resources on the Grid market. Should the number of required resources be lower than the number of in-house resources, the agent would attempt to sell the excess resources. The traded resources were made available the following day.

Using this setup, we developed two scenarios: In the first scenario, the agents used their current demand level to purchase or sell resources. The result of this simulation can be seen in Fig. 4, which shows the number of available resources. A negative value shows that the agent has fewer resources than required, while a positive value shows that the agent has more resources than it requires.

The spikes in the graph show that the agent rarely has the correct number of resources available. This fact shows that this very basic capacity planning approach is far from optimal when it comes to predicting the resource.

The second scenario worked with a more complex capacity planning approach: The agents' capabilities were expanded to allow predicting their demand based on past resource requirements. The requirements prediction was implemented using the linear regression tool of the Apache Commons Math Toolbox [19]. The linear regression used the demand from the past 30 days to predict the demand for the next day. This information was then used to buy or sell resources. The result of this simulation is shown in Fig. 5 below.

**Table 2.** Simulation Parameters Overview

| Parameters | Value |
|---|---|
| Number of agents | 500 |
| Number of in-house resources (per agent) | 20-40 |
| Market mechanism | CDA |
| Number of simulated trading days | 500 |
| Offer expiration time | 1 day |
| Demand distribution | Normal |
| Distribution Mean | 30 |
| Distribution Variance | 30 |

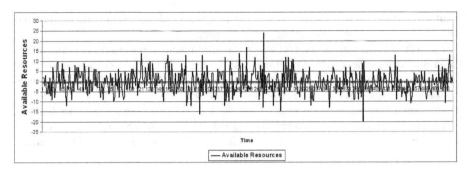

**Fig. 4.** Resource Availability with Basic Capacity Planning

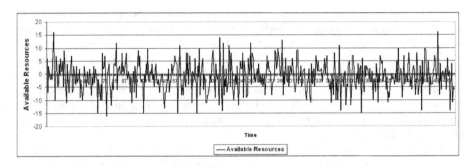

**Fig. 5.** Resource Availability with More Advanced Capacity Planning

Fig. 5 shows that the peaks are no longer as large as before and that the extreme peaks no longer occur with the agents. While this is not a marked improvement, it should be noted that the prediction algorithm is still fairly basic.

The simulations demonstrated that the GCPS is indeed a valuable tool in a Grid market environment in which price volatility and demand fluctuation have to be considered. The GCPS can ensure that a company will have sufficient resources at its disposal in such an environment. Since these comparisons are also computationally fast, the entire capacity planning process in this environment took only a few milliseconds per agent. However, the simulations also showed that much remains to be done to improve the predictive capabilities of this service.

## 6  Conclusion

In this paper we defined capacity planning for utility computing and placed it in context with load balancing, scheduling, and reservations. Furthermore, we have shown that capacity planning is more complex in a Grid environment than traditional capacity planning. Due to the complexity, we believe that a Grid Capacity Planning Service is required for a successful Grid usage, since performing capacity planning using in-house staff is costly and would negate the benefits of utility computing.

The GCPS described in this paper consists of two distinct parts: the Short-Term Capacity Planning Service and the Long-Term Capacity Planning Service. This structure reflects the fact that capacity planning in a commercial Grid environment has to be used to solve short-term and long-term problems. The first is responsible for ensuring that all applications and resources are running as required by the user and will give advice regarding additional resources if necessary. The latter is responsible for long-term planning of data centers and takes into account the resource requirements of all applications, the available in-house resources, prices, demand fluctuations, and the user requirements. Using this information, a mapping of all applications is found and (if necessary) recommendations for resource purchases are made.

Furthermore, the GCPS has been implemented and initial tests have shown that the performance overhead is low. Future work will center on refining the capacity planning algorithms of the two components, since the simulations have also shown that the demand prediction has to be improved.

# References

1. IBM: A Statistical Approach to Capacity Planning for On-Demand Computing Services, http://domino.watson.ibm.com/comm/research.nsf/pages/ r.statistics.innovation2.html
2. Li, C., Li, L.: Competitive proportional resource allocation policy for computational grid. Future Generation Computer Systems 20(6), 1041–1054 (2004)
3. Yu, J., Li, M., Ying, L., Hong, F., Gao, M.: A Framework for Price-Based Re-source Allocation on the Grid. In: Liew, K.M., Shen, H., See, S., Cai, W., Fan, P., Horiguchi, S. (eds.) PDCAT 2004. LNCS, vol. 3320, pp. 341–344. Springer, Heidelberg (2004)
4. Li, C., Li, L.: Dynamic resource allocation for joint grid user and provider opti-misation in computational grid. International Journal of Computer Applications in Technology 26(4), 242–250 (2006)
5. Wolski, R., Brevik, J., Plank, J.S., Bryan, T.: Grid Resource Allocation and Control Using Computational Economies. In: Berman, F., Fox, G., Hey, T. (eds.), pp. 747–771. John Wiley & Sons, Hoboken (2003)
6. Pourebrahimi, B., Bertels, K., Kandru, G.M., Vassiliadis, S.: Market-Based Resource Allocation in Grids. In: Second IEEE International Conference on e-Science and Grid Computing, pp. 80–88. IEEE Press, New York (2006)
7. Afzal, A., McGough, A.S., Darlington, J.: Capacity planning and scheduling in Grid computing environments. Future Generation Computer Systems 24(5), 404–414 (2008)
8. Siddiqui, M., Villazon, A., Fahringer, T.: Grid Capacity Planning with Negotiation-based Advance Reservation for Optimized QoS. In: SC 2006, pp. 21–37. IEEE Press, New York (2006)
9. Borowsky, E., Golding, R., Jacobson, P., Merchant, A., Schreier, L., Spasojevic, M., Wilkes, J.: Capacity planning with phased workloads. In: Proceedings of the 1st international Workshop on Software and Performance, pp. 199–207. ACM, New York (1998)
10. Risch, M., Altmann, J.: Cost Analysis of Current Grids and its Implications for Future Grid Markets. In: Altmann, J., Neumann, D., Fahringer, T. (eds.) GECON 2008. LNCS, vol. 5206, pp. 13–27. Springer, Heidelberg (2008)
11. Risch, M., Altmann, J., Makrypoulias, Y., Soursos, S.: Economics-Aware Capacity Planning for Commercial Grids. In: Collaborations and the Knowledge Economy, vol. 5, pp. 1197–1205. IOS Press, Amsterdam (2008)
12. Amazon Elastic Compute Cloud (Amazon EC2), http://www.amazon.com/gp/browse.html?node=201590011

13. Tsunamic Technologies Inc., http://www.clusterondemand.com/
14. Regev, O., Nisan, N.: The POPCORN market—an online market for computational resources. In: Proceedings of the First international Conference on information and Computation, pp. 148–157. ACM, New York (1998)
15. Waldspurger, C.A., Hogg, T., Huberman, B.A., Kephart, J.O., Stornetta, W.S.: Spawn: A Distributed Computational Economy. IEEE Transactions on Software Engineering 18(2), 103–117 (1992)
16. Buyya, R., Abramson, D., Giddy, J.: An economy grid architecture for service-oriented grid computing. In: 10th IEEE International Heterogeneous Computing Workshop. IEEE Computer Society Press, Los Alamitos (2001)
17. Lai, K., Rasmusson, L., Adar, E., Zhang, L., Huberman, B.A.: Tycoon: An implementation of a distributed, market-based resource allocation system. Multiagent and Grid Systems 1(3), 169–182 (2005)
18. Repast Simulation Environment, http://repast.sourceforge.net/
19. Apache Commons Math Libraries, http://commons.apache.org/math/

# A Financial Option Based Grid Resources Pricing Model: Towards an Equilibrium between Service Quality for User and Profitability for Service Providers*

David Allenotor**, Ruppa K. Thulasiram, and Parimala Thulasiraman

Department of Computer Science,
University of Manitoba
Winnipeg, MB R3T 2N2.
Canada
{dallen,tulsi,thulasir}@cs.umanitoba.ca

**Abstract.** In this paper, we design and develop a financial options-based model for pricing grid resources. The objective is to strike and maintain an equilibrium between service satisfaction of grid users and profitability of service providers. We explain how option theory fits well to price the grid resources. We price various grid resources such as memory, storage, software, and compute cycles as individual commodities. We carried out several experiments and provide a mapping of our research results based on the spot prices to the expected cost of utilizing the resources from three real grids that reflects their usage pattern. We further enhance our model to achieve the objective of equilibrium between Quality of Service (QoS) and profitability from the perspectives of the users and grid operators respectively.

## 1 Introduction

Grid computing aims at providing high resource availability [1]. The applications cut across areas of Science, Engineering, and Business where computational needs incrementally exceed the available capacity. Some of the advantages of the grid include free access to compute resources and government funding. As a result of the government funding, there are little or no efforts towards pricing the grid resources. Instead, research efforts in recent years have focused mostly on issues such as security [3], middleware and grid infrastructure [1], and Grid resource management [4]. Even if the grid users are not charged, to quantify the services provided in terms of actual money, it is necessary to price these resources for their use. This is because doing so will justify the government efforts and will

---

* This research was done with partial financial support from the Natural Sciences and Engineering Research Council (NSERC) Canada through Discovery Grants and with the University Research Grants Program (URGP) of the University of Manitoba.
** Corresponding author.

serve as a mechanism to report to the government agency on the value of the
services provided. The grid resources characteristically exist as compute cycles
(refereed here to as grid compute cycles). We call grid resources grid compute
commodities (*gcc*). The *gcc* distribution cuts across wide geographical regions.
They are non-storable, and ownership is by different organization whose rights
and policies vary as widely as the spanned regions. To price the grid resources,
we treat the *gcc* as real assets. The *gcc*-s include CPU cycles, memory, network
bandwidths, computing power, disks, processor times, and various visualization
tools, software and specialized instrumentation. Since *gcc*-s are transient, their
availability for use varies between "now" (that is, life of the contract to use gcc
resources) and "later"[1] (contract expiration). The availability variations account
for uncertainty and are measured as a fuzzy quantity $(\tilde{u})$, where $gcc : \alpha \rightarrow [0, 1]$.
To control the flexibility qualities of the *gcc* we apply real option (see the next
subsection for the definition of an option) defined in a fuzzy domain $[0, \cdots, 1]$
(also called membership function) [5].

In the current study, to ensure that we capture the users' varied behavior,
we obtain trace data from three real grids: one commercial grid (Grid3 [6]), one
experimental platform grid Grid5000, and one research grid (SHARCNET [7]).
We evaluate our proposed model and provide a justification by comparing real
grid behavior to simulation results obtained using some base spot prices for the
commodities. In particular, we strive to provide service guarantees measured
as Quality of Service (QoS) and profitability from the perspectives of the users
and grid resource providers respectively. The objective is to strike and keep a
balance between a given service, expected profitability, and satisfaction for using
grid resources.

**Financial Options:** A financial option is defined (see, for example [9]) as the
right to buy or to sell an underlying asset that is traded in an exchange for
an agreed-on sum. The right to buy or sell an option may expire if the right
is not exercised on or before a specific time and the option buyer loses the
premium paid at the beginning of the contract. The exercise price *(strike
price)* mentioned in an option contract is the stated price at which the asset
can be bought or sold at a future date. A *call option* grants the holder the
right (but not obligation) to buy the underlying asset at the specified strike
price. On the other hand, a *put option* grants the holder the right to sell the
underlying asset at the specified strike price. An *American option* can be
exercised any time during the life of the option contract; a *European option*
can only be exercised at expiry. Since options are instruments derived from
some underlying assets, they are also called derivative securities. They are
risky securities because the price of their underlying asset at any future time
may not be predicted with certainty. This means the option holder has no
assurance that the option will bring profit before expiry.

**Real Options:** To hold a real option means to have a certain possibility for a
given time to either choose for (exercising, deferring), or against (abandon,

---

[1] See Section 3.4 for the notion of "now" and "later".

wait, find other alternative) investment decision. A real option provides a choice from a set of alternatives.

**Fuzzy Logic Concept:** We capture these alternatives using fuzzy logic and express the choices as a fuzzy number. A Fuzzy number is expressed as a membership function that exists in the range $[0, 1]$ and we apply it for the development of QoS guarantee for the benefit of the grid users and operators.

The rest of this paper is organized as follows. In Section 2 we review related work. Section 3 we provide the model theory and architecture, methodology, assumptions, and the underlying pricing architecture. Section 4 we describe the simulation environment and the discussion of results of our experiments. We end the Section 5 with directions for future work.

## 2   Related Work

Besides the focus on security related issues [3] and middleware and grid infrastructure [1], most of the current research in grid resource pricing focus on market based economy approaches (for example [10] and [23] ) and contingent bids in auctions [11]. The research efforts highlight a common goal that involves the use of economic principles to decide a fair share of grid resources that involves resources redistribution and scheduling. Currently, there is no charge for using grid resources. However, a trend is developing because of large interest in grid for public computing. Therefore, a sudden explosion of grid use is expected in near future. Iosup et al. [2] obtain traces of grid resources utilization. Their results show possibility for a future increase in resources use. They concluded that the grid resources use will reach a peak value soon and this could lead to one of the grid problems. To avoid the problem of sudden explosion of computing resource, Amazon has introduced a Simple Storage Service (S3) [12].

Several other research efforts that explores the possibilities of bringing resources pricing into the grid infrastructure include Sang et al. [14], Tan and Gurd [15], and Juheng et al. [24]. Researchers under these forums, have followed two distinct approaches that is, either to extend the existing standardized grid middleware or to present some novel work with focus on grid economy referencing resources share and management. In [24], a real option valuation scheme was developed using Monte Carlo simulation. However, this scheme did not consider the effects of critical technological changes as considered in [17]. Resources management is actually not only about scheduling large and compute-intensive applications (or resources), or some form of advanced reservations. It also involves the manner of putting compute resources to work for the benefit of the user and owner [8]; that is, "profitability". In a similar study Chunlin and Layuan [16] presented an optimization-based resources pricing algorithm that focus on increasing the grid providers' effective gain. In another related study, Sulistio et al., [18] evaluate the effectiveness of grid revenue management using resource reservations as a focus. They show that by charging customers with differentiated prices will increase the effective total revenue for the resource in question. They also showed that their scheme guarantees a fare share of the resources applications with highest computing priorities. The focus of the study given in [14], [15], [18] is on resource sharing and resource scheduling with references to market economy. Mutz et al. [13] have some interesting schemes that points to our current research. Mutz et al. modeled a job priority model using efficient design mechanism in [19]. They based their proposal on a compensation function that schedules jobs for a time $t_i$. Their objective realizes a compensation function $d$ paid by job at $t_{n-1}$ that wishes to gain access to computation at $t_n$. The compensation may be disbursed as incentives (say more gcc) to the waiting jobs.

Bhargava and Sundaresan in [11] model a computing utility and examine the possibility to extend the pay-as-you-go pricing, using the auction system. In a recent study [17], we focused on balancing the grid profits as seen from the perspectives of the grid resources provider. In our current model, we introduce concepts for such a purpose (i) option with dividend paying underlying asset and (ii) a penalty function – the price variant factor (pvf) (Section 3.2 provides details). The work that we present in this paper is the performance evaluation using real data to test our previously proposed model [17] on grid resources pricing.

# 3   Model Assumptions and Theory

Several schemes exist in the literature to price financial options. Some of these approaches include application of the Black-Scholes (BS) model [20]. The BS model captures the price movements continuously and requires solution of a partial differential equation. Binomial lattice captures the underlying asset price discretely [21] still under BS risk neutral model. The binomial lattice is one of the most commonly used methods. In our simulation we use the trinomial model (see [9]) to solve the real option pricing problem to enhance the accuracy. This is a discrete time approach to calculate the discounted expectations in a trinomial-tree. We develop the grid resources pricing model using the following set of assumptions. First, we set some base prices for the $gcc$-s, as discussed in Section 4. Second, since the resources exist in nonstorable states, and various opportunities are presented to the user in exercising the option to use the resources, we value them as real assets. This assumption qualifies them to fit into the general stream of investment included in the real option valuation approach. An option in the current context means a holder has the right to use some grid resources mentioned in the option contract, during the contract period. Consider a $gcc$ whose price is initially $S_0$ and an option on this $gcc$. Suppose the option has a lifetime of $T$. It can either move up from $S_0$ to a new level $S_0u$ with a payoff value of $f_u$ or move down from $S_0$ to a new level, $S_0d$ and with a payoff value of $f_d$ where $u > 1$ and $d < 1$. This is a one-step binomial model. Splitting the contract period into various steps leads to multi-step binomial model. We define a job on the grid as a service that needs one or more of the $gcc$-s from start to finish.

## 3.1   Model Architecture

Figure 1 shows an abstract representation of our model architecture (see [8] for a detailed description). The architecture comprises of a four-level price-based infrastructure model. Level-0 contains the pools of available grid compute commodities $gcc$. Level-1 Resource modeling: The grid infrastructure provides a description of the available resources, application capabilities, and defines inter-component relationships between the various clusters that comprise the grid. The grid resources modeling approach facilitates resource discovery, provisioning, and QoS management. Level-2 Monitoring and Notification: At any time during a grid computation, the infrastructure ensures that it provides updates regarding the state of use of resources. These include notifications for changes in projected utilization levels and application notification regarding services changes. The monitoring capability also helps to maintain resource discovery and maintain QoS needed to support accounting and billing functions on resources pricing. Following notification and resources monitoring, resources may be re-deployed to ensure resource availability using some form of reservation. Level-3 Accounting and auditing: The accounting and auditing level of the grid provides a log for the usage of shared resources. Level-3 also transforms resources usage into cost for charging resource use by applications and users.

In our model architecture, we focus on Level-3 – the application layer where a larger part of resource usage and cost transformation is done. For this integration, we set service classes as immediate, non-immediate, and delay-allowable computations. An immediate utilization service requires haste and has high priority. The non-immediate utilization service requests require resources at a relatively lesser priority (computations that can wait for a later time). The delayed utilization services may take hours, days, or even months to process. In either of these service classes, we match the requested service with the SLA conditions to obtain the QoS. Consider some user requests such as $R_i$ for resources $j_i$ for $i = 1, \cdot, n$ waiting to be granted resources. If the requests were made in sequence, $R_i$ receives service before $R_{i+1}$ if all conditions of Service Level Agreement (SLA)-QoS remain equal. However, the reverse could be the case if requests made by $R_{i+1}$ belongs to the immediate service class. In this scenario, a penalty function computed as $p_f$ is applied to $R_{i+1}$ and $R_i$ gets a compensation.

## 3.2   Price Variant Factor

An important functionality of our model is the price variance factor $(p_f)$. The $p_f$ is a fuzzy number, a multiplier and based on the fuzziness (or uncertainty in changes in technology) given as $0 \leq p_f \leq 1$. The value depends on changes in technological developments such as new and faster algorithms, faster and cheaper processors, and changes in access rights and policies. The certainty in predicting the effects caused by these is hard using crisp schemes. As a result, we capture the resultant changes using fuzzy logic and treat $p_f$ as a fuzzy number. For a use time of $(t_{ut})$, we express a fuzzy value of $p_f$ as a fuzzy membership function that is, $\mu(p_f)$. For example, the grid resources may become under used if users

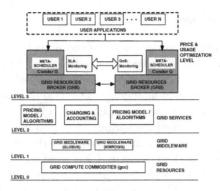

**Fig. 1.** Pricing Infrastructure [8]

find better and faster ways to solve their computing problems. Therefore, to increase the grid resources usage with more capacity for computations under same technology, we set the value of $p_f(ut)$ to 0.1 and with new technology, the $p_f = 1.0$. Our model therefore, adjusts the price in the use of grid resources by $(p_f(ut))^{-1}$ while providing QoS set at the SLA of the contract.

### 3.3   Discretized Real Option

We apply the trinomial-tree model [22] to price mainly American-style and European-style options on a single underlying asset. Binomial model is a discretized approach of BS model [20]. To compute option prices, we build a discrete time and state trinomial model of the asset price and then apply discounted expectations. Suppose $S$ is current asset price and $r$ is the riskless and continuously compounded interest rate, the risk-neutral Black-Scholes model of an asset price paying the continuous dividend yield of $\delta$ for each year [9] is given by $dS = (r - \delta)Sdt - \sigma Sdz$. For convenience, let $x = lnS$, this equation can be written as $dx = vdt + \sigma dz$, where $v = r - \delta - \sigma^2/2$. Consider a trinomial model of asset price movement in a small interval $\delta t$ as shown in Figure 2a. The price could remain same at $x$ or move up or down by $\delta x$ with probability $p_m$, $p_u$, and $p_d$ respectively, during a small interval $\delta t$. The drift (because of known reasons) and volatility ($\sigma$, because of unknown reasons) parameters of the asset price can be obtained in the simplified discrete process using $\delta x, p_u, p_m$, and $p_d$. In a trinomial lattice the price step (with a choice) is given by $\delta x = \sigma\sqrt{3\delta t}$. By equating the mean and variance over the interval $\delta t$ and imposing the unitary sum of the likelihoods, we obtain a relationship between the parameters of the continuous time and trinomial as

$$E[\delta x] = p_u(\delta x) + p_m(0) + p_d(-\delta x) = v\delta t \tag{1}$$

where $E[\delta x]$ is the expectation as mentioned before. From Equation (1),

$$E[\delta x^2] = p_u(\delta x^2) + p_m(0) + p_d(\delta x^2) = \sigma^2\delta t + v^2\delta t^2 \tag{2}$$

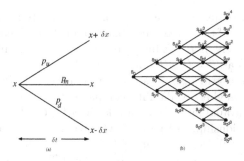

**Fig. 2.** Trinomial Lattice

where the unitary sum of probabilities $p_u$, $p_m$, and $p_d$ equal 1, are probabilities of
the price going up, down or remaining same respectively. Solving Equations (1),
(2), and the summed up probabilities, yields the transitional probabilities;

$$p_u = 0.5 * ((\sigma^2 \Delta t + v^2 \Delta t^2)/\Delta x^2 + (v \Delta t)/\Delta x) \tag{3}$$

$$p_m = 1 - ((\sigma^2 \Delta t + v^2 \Delta t^2)/\Delta x^2) \tag{4}$$

$$p_d = 0.5 * ((\sigma^2 \Delta t + v^2 \Delta t^2)/\Delta x^2 - (v \Delta t)/\Delta x) \tag{5}$$

The trinomial process of Figure 2(a) could be repeated several times to form
an $n$-step trinomial tree. Figure 2(c) shows a four-step trinomial. For number of
time steps (horizontal level) $n = 4$, the number of leaves (height) in such a tree
is given by $2n + 1$. We index a node by referencing a pair $(i, j)$ where $i$ points
at the level (row index) and $j$ shows the distance from the top (column index).
Time $t$ is referenced from the level index by $i : t = i \Delta t$. From Figure 2(c), node
$(i, j)$ is thus connected to node $(i + 1, j)$ (upward move), to node $(i + 1, j + 1)$
(steady move), and to node $(i + 1, j + 2)$ (downward move). The option price
and the asset price at node $(i, j)$ are given by $C[i, j] = C_{i,j}$ and $S[i, j] = S_{i,j}$
respectively. The number of up and down moves required to reach $(i, j)$ from
$(0, 0)$ estimates the asset price and is given as $S[i, j] = S[0, 0](u^i d^j)$.

## 3.4 Fuzzy Logic Framework and QoS

To fuzzify the utility of $gcc$, we express the quality of the $g_{cc}$ availability as
a function of the time when gcc is needed and the time the resources become
available for use as $g_{cc} = f(t_{ut}, t_n)$, where $t_n$ is the life of the contract and is
given as $0 \leq t_n \leq 1$, and $t_{ut}$ is the actual utilization time. A best scenario is
when $t_n = t_{ut}$ i.e., when the resources are available when gcc is needed or $t_n = 0$
(no wait time). If $t_n = 0$, $g_{cc}$ use is "now" otherwise, $t_n = 1$ and usage is in the
future until the end of the contract period (say 6 months). Users often request
and use $g_{cc}$ for computation and expects a best scenario where service provided
meets expectations or when $t_{ut} - t_n \approx 0$ for a high QoS. In this instance, it is hard
to guarantee provision of the $g_{cc}$ on-demand and satisfy the users' QoS without
additional $g_{cc}$ to satisfy the conditions named in the Service Level Agreements

(SLAs) document. To capture the fuzziness of the parameters $t_n, t_{ut}$, and QoS, we express them in terms of their fuzzy membership functions. That is, $\mu(t_n), \mu(t_{ut})$, and $\mu(QoS)$ respectively. If $T$ is a fuzzy set, the membership function is defined (see for example [5]) as $T = (t, \mu(t)), \mu_T(t) \in [0, 1]$.

To price one of the grid resources, we consider SHARCNET CPU time because of its relative higher availability compared to other grids in our study. Therefore, the 80% availability of CPU cycles in SHARCNET is considered normal. Using this relationship, in Figure 3, we have a 75% normalized CPU time availability in Grid5000. Hence, we use CPU time availability index set at 0.75 for SHARCHNET in our simulation. This index (CPU time availability) will provide a user with an initial idea to select a particular grid, or certain *gcc* from certain grid depending on the resource requirement which the user knows best. To obtain a balance between service and cost for using the grid resources, we express the generated indices $i$ as a membership function $\mu_i(p_n)$ of the prices $p$. Our simulation calibrates prices as $p_1, p_2, \cdots, p_n$ and the corresponding membership function $\mu_i(p_n)$ using fuzzy values in a range of $[0, 1]$.

## 4    Experiments and Results

We setup base prices for the various *gcc*-s using real market and current market values and charge $\$95.89 \times 10^{-6}$/day/MB for a 2GB storage, $\$68.49 \times 10^{-8}$/day/MB for a 200GB hard disk, and $\$68.49 \times 10^{-6}$/day/MHz for CPU cycles.

### 4.1    Real Grid Trace Data Collection and Analysis

We collect resources usage pattern from SHARCNET, Grid5000, and Grid-3 between January 01, 2007 till December 31, 2007 (without any date assigned). The collected traces include number of processors, memory, CPU time, run time, and wait time. The collected traces have no cost components, however, we associate monetary values from the collected usage patterns (more details provided latter). For instance, Figure 3(a) and (b) shows the used CPU time against number of jobs for SHARCNET and Grid5000 respectively. Despite SHARCNET supports a larger part of jobs, it also experiences a sharp drop in the number of jobs it served in the later part of the year. Similarly, Grid500 supports a larger number of jobs after the middle of the year. We deduce that these two grids for instance serves as a better blend to offer resources since they complement each other deficiencies in the possible number of jobs supported. More jobs taking larger CPU time results in larger wait time especially when the grid job is resource intensive. We do not rule out the possibility for most number of jobs to take larger CPU time than required. The early (before middle of the year) part of Grid5000 is a typical example of waste of compute cycles. It can be said that the times of low CPU availability which causes the jobs to stay longer is because of either waste, wait or priority jobs served by the grid or any combination of these.

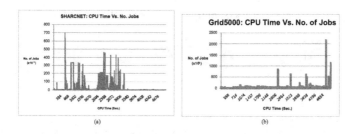

**Fig. 3.** CPU Time Vs. Number of Jobs: (a) SHARCNET (b) Grid5000

## 4.2   Grid Resources Pricing Using Financial Options Theory

We price the *gcc*-s by running a one-step trinomial using the parameters: strike price ($K$ = \$0.70), resources price ($S$ = \$0.80), expiration time ($T$ = 0.5 in years), interest rate ($r$ = 0.06), volatility ($\sigma$ = 0.2), and the number of time steps ($N_j$ = $2N + 1$). We extend our study by varying the volatility $\sigma$ in steps of $0.0, 0.1, \cdots, 0.7$ and $N = 4, 8, 16, 24$. For a 6 month contract, for example, $N = 3$ means a 2 months step size and $N = 12$ mean a 2 weeks step size. For a call option, we simulate the effects of time of use of one of the *gcc*-s (memory (RAM)), hard disk (HD), and CPU. We start with memory (one of the *gcc*-s) using the following parameters: $S = \$6.849.00 \times 10^{-7}$, $T = 0.5$, $r = 0.06$, $N = 4, 8, 16, 24$, $\sigma = 0.2$, and $N_j = 2N + 1$. We run our experiments with various strike prices. Figure 4 (a) shows option value for RAM for $K$ = \$0.70 while Figure 4 (b) shows option value for RAM for $K$ = \$0.90 call. Over the number of step sizes, the option value reaches a steady state.

Similarly, we obtain from our simulation the option values for CPU using the parameters $S$ = \$68.49 and $K$ = \$68.47 and \$80.47 (all values scaled at ($\times 10^{-6}$)) and simulated for a varying time step of $4, 8, 16, 24$. Figure 5 (a) shows the option value for CPU at $K$ = \$68.47. The option values for other *gccs* under our current study include RAM in Figure 4 (a) and HD in Figure 6. Figure 6 shows the option for HDD which increases with the number of time steps. This behavior implies that at any given time, a consumers' cost for using the grid resources is the base cost and the extra cost which depends on the time of use of the *gcc*. Therefore, deciding the exact price of *gcc* in real life is uncertain and hard to predict. However to achieve an equilibrium between users-service

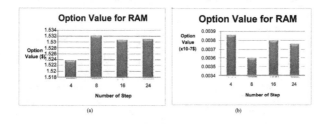

**Fig. 4.** Option Value for RAM: (a) At $K$ = \$0.70 (b) At $K$ = \$0.90

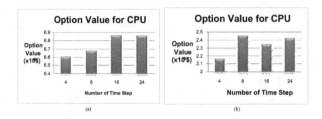

**Fig. 5.** Option Value for CPU: (a) At $K = \$68.47$ (b) At $K = \$80.47$

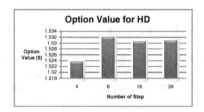

**Fig. 6.** Option Value for HD At $74.90

satisfaction and provider-profit opportunities, we have imposed a price modula-
tor called price variant factor $p_f$ which depends on changes in the technology
of the grid infrastructure or changes in the grid resources usage requirements.
These variations are unknown before exercising the options to hold the right
to use of grid resource. Hence, to increase *gcc* utilization ($ut$) with more computing facilities and with existing technology, we set the value of $p_f(ut)$ to 0.1
and with new technology, the $p_f = 1.0$. Fuzzified boundary value of $p_f$ is set up
as $p_f(ut) = [0.1, 1.0]$ to simplify fuzzification. Our model, therefore, adjusts the
price in the use of grid resources by $(p_f(ut))^{-1}$ while providing quality service
to the user. What was an unfavorable condition initially for the user was turned
into a favorable situation through the $p_f$, with an early exercise. Figure 5 (b)
shows a corresponding option value for option value for CPU at $K = \$80.47$.
We repeat this for various *gcc*-s of the grid. Figure 7 (a) shows execution time
for HD, CPU, and RAM at various time steps. The option values captured the

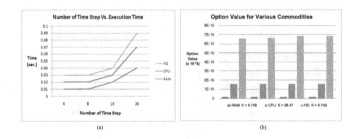

**Fig. 7.** Various Commodities: (a) Execution Time (b) Option Value

experiments show that they converge (error level set at 0.1% for academic purpose) in 24 steps. Increasing the computation beyond 24 steps did not yield better solution for the option values, instead, it increase the cost of computation. This is in contrast to the finance market where the stock prices are highly volatile and for convergence one needs to go for very small step sizes. Since the time required to achieve a steady state in option value increases with the number of steps (number of nodes in the trinomial tree) as shown in Figure 7 (a) without yielding better solution, we stopped at 24 steps. Figure 7 (b) shows our evaluation for various commodities computed individually.

## 5   Conclusions

We have analyzed the usage pattern of resources in three grids and fit our pricing model to compute on these resources. Our two important contributions are: (i) option value computation for grid resources usage and to select the best time to exercise an option to utilize grid resources. This helps the user as well as the grid resources provider to optimize resources for service and profitability respectively; in other words, we achieve an equilibrium; (ii) our study also incorporate a price varying function $p_f$ which controls the price of the resources and ensures the grid users get the resources at best prices and the resources provider also make reasonable revenue at the current base price settings. Future work will focus on the larger problem of pricing grid resources for applications that use diverse resources across varied grids simultaneously.

## References

1. Ian, F., Kesselman, C., Tuecke, S.: The Anatomy of The Grid: Enabling Scalable Virtual Organizations. Intl. Journal of Supercomputer Applications 15(3), 200–222 (2001)
2. Iosup, A., Dumitrescu, C., Epema, D., Li, H., Wolters, L.: How are Real Grids Used? The Analysis of Four Grid Traces and its Implications. In: Proc. 7th IEEE/ACM Intl. Conf. on Grid Computing, Barcelona, Spain, pp. 262–269 (2006)
3. Ian, F., Kesselman, C., Tsudik, G., Tuecke, S.: A security Architecture for Computational Grids. In: ACM Conf. on Comp. and Comm. Security, pp. 83–92 (1998)
4. Sim, K.M.: Grid Commerce, Market-Driven G-Negotiation, and Grid Resource Management. Systems, Man, and Cybernetics 36(6), 1381–1394 (2006)
5. Bojadziew, G., Bojadziew, M.: Fuzzy Logic for Business, Finance, and Management Modeling, 2nd edn. World Scientific Press, Singapore (1997)
6. GRID3 International (retrieved January 02, 2009), http://www.grid3.com/
7. SHARCNET – Shared Hierarchical Academic Research Computing Network (SHARCNET) (retrieved January 02, 2009 ),
   http://www.sharcnet.ca/Performance/curperf.php
8. Allenotor, D., Thulasiram, R.K.: G-FRoM: Grid Resources Pricing A Fuzzy Real Option Model. In: Proc. 3rd Intl. Conf. on e-Science and Grid Computing (eScience 2007), Bangalore, India, December 10-13, pp. 388–395 (2007)
9. Hull, J.C.: Options, Futures, and Other Derivatives, 6th edn. Prentice-Hall, Englewood Cliffs (2006)

10. Buyya, R., Abramson, D., Venugopal, S.: The Grid Economy. IEEE Journal 93(3), 698–714 (2005)
11. Bhargava, H.K., Sundaresan, S.: Contingent Bids in Auctions: Availability, Commitment and Pricing of Computing as Utility. Journal of Management Info. Systems 21(2), 201–227 (2004)
12. Palankar, M., Onibokun, A., Iamnitchi, A., Ripeanu, M.: Amazon S3 for science grids: A viable solution? In: DADC 2008: Proceedings of the 2008 Intl. workshop on Data-aware distributed computing, pp. 55–64 (2008)
13. Mutz, A., Wolski, R., Brevik, J.: Eliciting Honest Value Info. in a Batch-Queue Environment. In: The 8th IEEE/ACM Intl. Conf. on Grid Computing, Austin, Texas, USA, September 1921, pp. 291–297 (2007)
14. Kang, W., Huang, H.H., Grimshaw, A.: A highly available job execution service in computational service market. In: The 8th IEEE/ACM IntI Conf. on Grid Computing, Austin, Texas, USA, September 1921, pp. 275–282 (2007)
15. Zhu, T., Gurd, J.R.: Market-based grid resource allocation using a stable continuous double auction. In: The 8th IEEE/ACM Intl. Conf. on Grid Computing, Austin, Texas, USA, September 1921, pp. 283–290 (2007)
16. Chunlin, L., Layuan, L.: Pricing and resource allocation in computational grid with utility functions. In: Intl. Conf. on Info. Tech.: Coding and Computing (ITCC 2005), vol. II, pp. 175–180 (2005)
17. Allenotor, D., Thulasiram, R.K.: Grid resources pricing: A novel financial option-based quality of service-profit quasi-static equilibrium model. In: The 9th IEEE/ACM IntI Conf. on Grid Computing (Grid 2008), Tsukuba, Japan, September 29-October 01, pp. 75–84 (2008)
18. Sulistio, A., Schiffmann, W., Buyya, R.: Using revenue management to determine pricing of reservations. In: Proc. 3rd Intl. Conf. on e-Science and Grid Computing (eScience 2007), Bangalore, India, December 10-13, 2007, pp. 396–405 (2007)
19. Krishna, V., Perry, M.: Efficient mechanism Design, 1998 (2007), http://ratio.huji.ac.il/dp/dp133.pdf
20. Black, F., Scholes, M.: The Pricing of Options and Corporate Liabilities. Journal of Political Economy 81(3), 637–654 (1973)
21. Cox, J.C., Ross, S., Rubinstein, M.: Option Pricing: A Simplified Approach. Journal of Financial Economics 7, 229–263 (1979)
22. Boyle, P.P.: Option Valuing Using a Three Jump Process. Intl. Options Journal 3(2), 7–12 (1986)
23. Yeo, C.S., Buyya, R.: Integrated Risk Analysis for a Commercial Computing Service. In: Proc. of the 21st IEEE Intl. Parallel and Distributed Processing Symposium (IPDPS 2007), pp. 1–10. IEEE CS Press, Los Alamitos (2007)
24. Juheng, Z., Subhajyoti, B., Selwyn, P.: Real option valuation on grid computing. Decission Support Systems Journal 46(1), 333–343 (2001)

# Negotiating and Enforcing QoS and SLAs in Grid and Cloud Computing

Vladimir Stantchev[1,2,3] and Christian Schröpfer[2]

[1] International Computer Science Institute, Berkeley CA 94704, USA
vstantch@icsi.berkeley.edu
[2] Technische Universität Berlin, Berlin, Germany
[3] FOM Fachhochschule fuer Oekonomie und Management, Berlin, Germany

**Abstract.** Emerging grid computing infrastructures such as cloud computing can only become viable alternatives for the enterprise if they can provide stable service levels for business processes and SLA-based costing. In this paper we describe and apply a three-step approach to map SLA and QoS requirements of business processes to such infrastructures. We start with formalization of service capabilities and business process requirements. We compare them and, if we detect a performance or reliability gap, we dynamically improve performance of individual services deployed in grid and cloud computing environments. Here we employ translucent replication of services. An experimental evaluation in Amazon EC2 verified our approach.

**Keywords:** QoS and SLA Negotiation, Assurance, Service-oriented computing.

## 1 Introduction

Service-oriented architecture (SOA) is an architecture that combines elements of software architecture and enterprise architecture. It is based on the interaction with autonomous and interoperable services that offer reusable business functionality via standardised interfaces. Services can exist on all layers of an application system (business process, presentation, business logic, data management). They may be composed of services from lower layers, wrap parts of legacy application systems or be implemented from scratch. Typically, services at the business process layer are described as *business services*, while services at the lower implementation level are described as *technical services*.

### 1.1 Emerging Grid Computing Infrastructures for Services

Datacenters and cloud computing environments are grid computing infrastructures that are emerging as platforms for provision of technical services. An example for such an environment is Amazon EC2, recently evaluated from the user perspective at Harvard [1]. The development and extension of tools to monitor and control such infrastructures is part of large research projects, e.g., at Stanford and UC Berkeley [2]. On the other side, the mapping of business process requirements at the infrastructure level in such environments is rarely addressed.

N. Abdennadher and D. Petcu (Eds.): GPC 2009, LNCS 5529, pp. 25–35, 2009.

## 1.2   Challenges

A successful service offering has two main objectives: to provide the needed functionality and to provide the needed Quality of Service (QoS). QoS parameters are part of the run-time related nonfunctional properties (NFPs) of a service and present one of the main research challenges in service-oriented computing [3]. Contrary to design-time related NFPs (e.g., language of service or compliance), run-time related NFPs are performance oriented (e.g., response time, transaction rate, availability). They can change during runtime – when times of extensive concurrent usage by many users are followed by times of rare usage, or when failures occur.

An approach to measure and dynamically adapt service performance in grid and cloud computing environments to such changes can ensure continuous meeting of service levels defined at the business level. This is an even more challenging task in such IT infrastructures that are not owned or controlled directly by the enterprise. Specifically, such approach should consider service reconfiguration at runtime, as changes in service implementation are not realistic.

NFPs of services (both technical and human, as well as their combinations) are typically specified in Service Level Agreements (SLAs). They are typically defined at the level of a business process but need to be addressed at the level of IT infrastructures. Thereby several technical services are orchestrated in order to provide business services for a business process. SLAs are negotiated between the process owner and the service provider who have to agree upon them.

This work proposes a straightforward way to negotiate business process SLAs between a process owner and a service provider and to enforce these SLAs at the level of grid and cloud computing infrastructures – if we formalize both the service level requirements of the process owner and the capabilities of the technical services in the grid (cloud) using a similar structure, we can compare them in an automated way. Based on such comparisons, we can negotiate and provide optimized service configurations in the grid (cloud) and thereby enforce the SLAs of the business process in the QoS characteristics and the service levels of these technical services.

## 1.3   Work Structure

The remainder of this work is structured as follows: Section 2 gives an overview of our proposed approach and puts it in the context of related research in the areas of service-oriented computing, QoS-aware platforms and grid workflow optimization. Section 3 describes the formalization of service and QoS levels as a main precondition for the negotiation of SLAs. Section 4 deals with performance and availability as NFPs that are representative for the approach and their enforcement in grid and cloud computing environments. In Section 5, we present an experimental evaluation of the approach. Thereby our solution was deployed in Amazon EC2 and demonstrated the viability and applicability of SLA formalization and subsequent QoS enforcement in cloud computing infrastructures.

## 2   An Approach for SLA Mapping

When a company is in control of its internal IT infrastructure, business analysts and developers can define service level requirements during design time and can actively select and influence components in order to meet these requirements. However, in cloud computing environments SLAs are typically provided for basic platform services (e.g., system uptime, network throughput). Business processes typically expect service levels for the technical services they integrate (e.g., order submission in less than 1 second). How can we bring these two worlds together?

This work proposes an approach for SLA mapping between business processes and IT infrastructures. It is based on a method for the assurance of NFPs and includes three major tasks (see Figure 1): (i) Formalization of business process requirements at the business side and of service capabilities at the IT infrastructure. Both are specified in a formal way, using a predefined service level objective structure and predefined NFP terms. (ii) Negotiation of service capabilities at the IT infrastructure that correspond to the formalized business process requirements: Here, we assess whether the aggregated technical services provide the expected service levels to meet business process requirements under different load hypotheses. Within this comparison we also calculate the aggregated service level, using the performance metrics of the individual technical services. Based on the result of this comparison we can decide where to apply replication in the next step. A reasoner or comparing unit must understand both structure of the statements and used NFPs on the business and the infrastructure side. (iii) Enforcement of business process SLAs at the IT infrastructure level: Here, we apply translucent parallelization of service processing using multiple nodes in a datacenter environment [4]. Replication can be enacted to improve service levels regarding response time, transaction rate, throughput and availability, respectively reliability.

### 2.1   Related Work

The SOA-specific aspects of major architectural concerns, such as service visualization [5], integration [6], and service selection [7] have been consistently

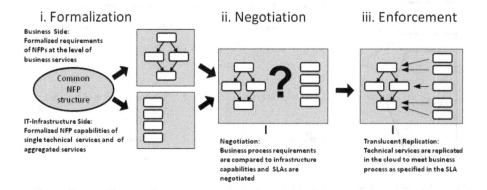

**Fig. 1.** Approach Overview

addressed by researchers. The existing standards for specification of QoS characteristics in web service environments can be grouped according to their main focus: software design/process description (UML Profile for QoS and QML - QoS Modeling Language [8]), service/component description (WS-Policy) and SLA-centric approaches (WSLA - Web Service Level Agreements [9], WSOL - Web Service Offerings Language [10], SLAng - Service Level Agreement definition language [11] and WS-Agreement [12]).

Much work has been done in the area of QoS-aware web service discovery [13], QoS-aware platforms and middleware [14,15,16,17], and context-aware services [18]. However, all of these approaches do not address adaptive enforcement of NFPs, but rather deal with the composition of services where the aggregation of predefined NFP levels would satisfy a specific requirement. Of particular interest are approaches that allow the "gridification" of specific applications, e.g., in [19] where a set of programs for inferring evolutionary trees is ported to the grid platform XtremWeb-CH [20]. Approaches such as shared memory have also been proposed for such tasks [21]. There is ongoing research in the area of adaptive optimization, more specifically in the areas of grids (e.g., grid workflow optimization [22]) and parallel database operations [23].

## 3    Formalization and Negotiation of SLAs

Figure 2 shows the structure we have recently proposed [24,25] for formalization of business process service level objectives (SLOs) and technical service capabilities. The figure also contains sample service level statements about response time, throughput and transaction rate. These statements are then stored with the service description (service capabilities) respectively with the business process definition (business process SLO) and are the starting point for the negotiation of SLAs. An example for a statement about the service capability is "The transaction rate of the service is higher than 90 transactions per second in 98% of the cases as long as throughput is higher than 500 kB/s." An example for a

| SLO pattern | NFP | Predicate | Metric (Value, Unit) | Percentage | Qualifying conditions (QC) | | |
|---|---|---|---|---|---|---|---|
| | | | | | NFP | Predicate | Metric |
| SLO examples | Response time | less than | 100 ms | in 95 % of the cases | if transaction rate | less than | 10 tps |
| | Throughput | higher than | 1000 kB/s | in 95 % of the cases | if transaction rate | less than | 10 tps |
| | Transaction rate | higher than | 90 tps | in 98 % of the cases | if Throughput | higher than | 500 kB/s |

**Fig. 2.** Structure of Service Level Objectives (SLOs) and Examples (tps - Transactions per second)

requirement business process level is "The transaction rate of the process should be higher than 50 transactions per second in 97% of the cases while throughput is higher than 500 kB/s."

In this work we deal with the negotiation and the enforcement of performance-related NFPs as part of SLAs and therefore focus on their formalization. However, our scheme can also be used to describe further aspects of SLAs, e.g., design-time related NFPs, such as cultural (e.g. language), legal (e.g. Sarbanes-Oxley-Compliance, Basel-II-Compliance), organizational (partner list), service usage-related (e.g. GUI simplicity) and trust-related (e.g. Customer rating, experience of provider).

In our proposed approach, the process owner specifies service level requirements as expected from the business perspective. At the IT infrastructure side we evaluate different replication configurations of technical services in grid and cloud computing environments such as Amazon EC2. Both requirements and service capabilities of the different configurations are then formalized and compared. Furthermore, we can start a negotiation between process owner and service provider based on this comparison. Thereby, the replication configuration that meets (or is closest to) the business requirements is selected and is the starting point for the actual SLA. The transparent cost model of Amazon Web Services allows us to put different price tags for the required service levels (e.g., a business process that needs higher transaction rates has to pay more), thus allowing for real activity-based IT costing. Furthermore, we can use the SLO structures in a supply-oriented way, contrary to the demand-oriented approach we present here. Thereby, we can specify combinations of NFP levels that represent different generic SLAs (e.g., "Gold", "Standard"', "Cost-optimized" [26], or "Time-Critical", "Load-Critical", "Dependability-Critical").

## 4  QoS Enforcement of SLAs in Grid and Cloud Computing Environments

In order to satisfy the SLAs of a business process we should look at ways to represent and control NFPs at the level of a technical service. While cloud computing environments specify service levels for basic platform operations (e.g., system uptime), we focus on the improvement of service levels for specific technical services that are composed to provide the needed business service. One example is the composition of the technical services `GetOrder()` and `ClearPayment()` to provide the business service *Order Placement*. In this work we show exemplary how we can improve performance-oriented NFPs, particularly response time and transaction rate, as well as dependability for single and composed technical services.

### 4.1  Performance

A general and broadly accepted definition of performance is to observe the system output $\omega(\delta)$ that represents the number of successfully served requests (or transactions) from a total of input $\iota(\delta)$ requests during a period of time.

$$\omega(\delta) = f(\iota(\delta)) \tag{1}$$

This definition of performance corresponds to transaction rate as NFP – the system guarantees to process $n$ requests during time period $t$. The performance of a serial composed service chain is determined by the performance of the service with the lowest performance. Let us assume that we compose a service chain from Service 1, Service 2 and Service 3. If Service 1 and Service 3 are providing high transaction rate (e.g., 500 requests per second) and Service 2 is providing a much lower transaction rate (e.g., 50 requests per second), our composed service will only serve 50 requests (or actually less than 50 requests) per second overall. We can easily calculate the average response time from the transaction rate by dividing the time period through the number of requests. Furthermore, we can also measure further performance metrics, such as worst-case execution time (WCET) if we need to specify them in the SLA.

When we introduce parallelism through functional replication we can ideally double the processing performance. The replication of the service with the lowest transaction rate (Service 2) leads to an overall increase of the transaction rate for the composed service. Therefore, replication has advantageous effects on service chain performance when no replica synchronization is required. This includes transaction rate, throughput and response time as parameters of SLAs.

## 4.2  Dependability

Dependability integrates several attributes: availability, reliability, safety, integrity, and maintainability. These are defined as follows [27]:

– availability denotes the readiness to provide a correct service,
– reliability denotes the continuity of service provision,
– safety is an attribute that assures there are no catastrophic consequences on the user and the environment.
– integrity denotes that there are no improper changes of the system.
– maintainability denotes that a system can undergo changes and repairs.

There are four categories of approaches to attain dependability [27]: fault prevention, fault tolerance, fault removal, and fault forecasting. In the context of this work we focus on availability as attribute and on fault tolerance as approach to attain it.

Availability needs to be quantified in the SLAs so that we can negotiate and enforce it. It has been defined traditionally as a binary metric that describes whether a system is "up" or "down" at a single point of time. A common extension of this definition is to compute the average percentage of time that a system is available during a certain period – this is a typical availability measure that describes a system as having 99.999% availability, for example.

There are several extended definitions of availability that address the inherent limitations of the traditional definition – availability should be considered as a spectrum, rather as a binary metric, as systems can have various degraded, but operational, states between "up" and "down". Furthermore, the definition does not consider QoS aspects.

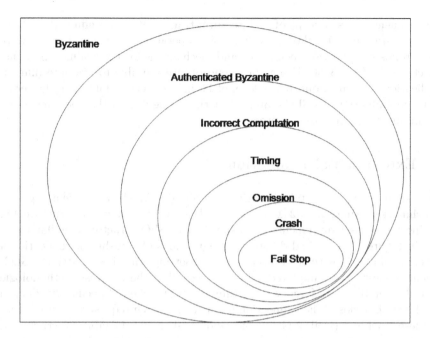

**Fig. 3.** Fault Model used in the SLO Structures

One possibility is to measure availability by examining variations in system QoS metrics over time [28]. The authors state that the particular choice of QoS metrics depends on the type of system and suggest performance and degree of fault tolerance as obvious metrics for server systems. In this case, performance would mean requests satisfied (successfully served) per second. This corresponds to our definition of performance in the previous subsection. In order to specify degrees of fault tolerance we need an underlying fault model. We use a model that was also used in [29] (see Figure 3). The model was originally proposed in [30] and extended in [31]. It incorporates several aspects that are typical for technical services in cloud computing environments, as compared to traditional distributed systems (e.g., trust issues).

One recent adaptation of traditional methods for better availability to the world of SOA is proposed in [32]. It involves replication of technical services across multiple, wide-area sites. Typically, we need to provide strong consistency between the replicas in order to provide better availability. This makes the application of the approach problematic, particularly in cloud computing environments - the overhead we introduce to ensure strong consistency generally has a negative impact on performance.

### 4.3 Evaluation and Improvement of IT Infrastructure Capabilities

While these general aspects of replication are hardly surprising, there are different ways *where* and *how* we can replicate technical services in cloud computing environments. The concept of architectural translucency [4] defines three levels for replication in SOA platforms (hardware, operating system, and serviceware) and proposes replication techniques and mechanisms for the evaluation of their effects on NFPs [33,34]. Using such concepts we are able to evaluate different replication configurations at the level of IT infrastructure, formalize the results of these evaluations as SLOs, and select the configuration that best meets the requirements of the business process.

## 5   Experimental Evaluation

For a series of experimental evaluations we deployed WSTest 1.1 [35] as a generic benchmark in Amazon EC2 [1] as a grid and cloud computing infrastructure. Our business process requirements were specified in SLO structures similar to the one in Figure 2. We tested different configurations of translucent replication as specified in [34,33] with the objective to find settings that best match the SLOs. Client requests were simulated using the second of the two test methodologies described in [35] and Mercury LoadRunner's SOAP client. Specifically, 25 client machines that closed the connection at the end of each request were used. Each of these machines (Dell, 2 GHz Core Duo, 2 GB RAM, Gigabit Ethernet) runs Mercury LoadRunner agents and can generate approx. 2000 concurrent requests. Every replication setting was tested for 120 minutes with 1 second think time before a request. This corresponds to some 7200 requests that were sent to each setting. These 120 minutes tests were automated and repeated 10 times on 21 consecutive days. Figure 4 shows an overview of the results. All replication settings provided better service levels as the original configuration. Furthermore, there were two replication settings (3 and 4) that satisfied the requirements of the

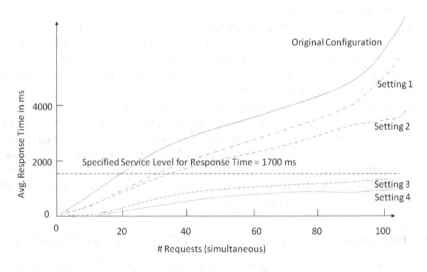

**Fig. 4.** Overview of Results

business process and thus allowed the mapping of its SLAs at the level of the IT architecture. These two settings caused only marginally higher costs compared to the original configuration in Amazon EC2.

## 6   Conclusion and Outlook

We presented an approach for negotiation of SLAs of business processes and the corresponding QoS enforcement at the level of IT infrastructure. It consists of three main tasks. The formalization of NFPs allows us to compare required and existing service levels. Using translucent replication we can meet expected service levels by automatically reconfiguring service replicas in cloud computing environments. The experimental evaluation demonstrated that we could improve service levels by over 50 % under certain load hypotheses. Furthermore, it demonstrated that we are able to keep business process service levels as specified in the SLAs continuously. Providers of cloud computing environments typically offer very flexible and detailed cost accounting, so the costs of providing and enforcing different service levels for business processes are transparent. This allows us to taylor QoS levels to the specific requirements of every business process and we support concepts such as activity-based costing in an enterprise. We are currently working on a user interface that will allow process owners to set their expected preferences regarding NFPs in an easy and convenient way. Thereby, a predefined set of service levels for response time, availability and other NFPs will correspond to a simple description (e.g. gold, standard, cost-optimized). Users will be able to select a setting using a simple user interface such as a slider and the infrastructure will automatically adapt to this setting. Furthermore, we are currently investigating ways to derive such preferences from existing processes and incorporate them in the process model repository as SLOs which will ultimately result in the automatic provision of service compositions that best meet the functional and nonfunctional requirements of the business process. Furthermore, we also plan to address limitations of distributed replication of services with respect to availability and particularly the trade-off communication vs. availability [32].

## References

1. Garfinkel, S.: An evaluation of amazon's grid computing services: Ec2, s3 and sqs. Technical report tr-08-07, School for Engineering and Applied Sciences, Harvard University, Cambridge, MA (July 2007)
2. Bodık, P., Fox, A., Jordan, M.I., Patterson, D., Banerjee, A., Jagannathan, R., Su, T., Tenginakai, S., Turner, B., Ingalls, J.: Advanced Tools for Operators at Amazon.com. In: The First Annual Workshop on Autonomic Computing (2006)
3. Papazoglou, M.P., Traverso, P., Dustdar, S., Leymann, F.: Service-oriented computing: State of the art and research challenges. Computer 40(11), 38–45 (2007)
4. Stantchev, V., Malek, M.: Architectural Translucency in Service-oriented Architectures. IEE Proceedings - Software 153(1), 31–37 (2006)

5. Eicker, S., Spies, T., Kahl, C.: Software Visualization in the Context of Service-Oriented Architectures. In: Proceedings of the 4th IEEE International Workshop on Visualizing Software for Understanding and Analysis (Vissoft 2007), pp. 108–111. IEEE, Los Alamitos (2007)

6. Zhang, J., Chang, C.K., Chung, J.-Y., Kim, S.W.: Ws-net: a petri-net based specification model for web services. In: IEEE International Conference on Web Services, 2004. Proceedings, July 6-9, 2004, pp. 420–427 (2004)

7. Reinicke, M., Streitberger, W., Eymann, T.: Evaluation of Service Selection Procedures in Service Oriented Computing Networks. Multi Agent and Grid Systems 1(4), 271–285 (2005)

8. Frolund, S., Koistinen, J.: Quality of services specification in distributed object systems design. In: COOTS 1998: Proceedings of the 4th conference on USENIX Conference on Object-Oriented Technologies and Systems (COOTS), Berkeley, CA, USA, p. 1. USENIX Association (1998)

9. Ludwig, H., Keller, A., Dan, A., King, R.P., Franck, R.: Web Service Level Agreement (WSLA) Language Specification. IBM Corporation (2002)

10. Tosic, V., Patel, K., Pagurek, B.: WSOL-Web Service Offerings Language. In: Bussler, C.J., McIlraith, S.A., Orlowska, M.E., Pernici, B., Yang, J. (eds.) CAiSE 2002 and WES 2002. LNCS, vol. 2512, pp. 57–67. Springer, Heidelberg (2002); (revised papers)

11. Lamanna, D.D., Skene, J., Emmerich, W.: SLAng: A Language for Defining Service Level Agreements. In: Proc. of the 9th IEEE Workshop on Future Trends in Distributed Computing Systems-FTDCS, pp. 100–106 (2003)

12. Andrieux, A., Czajkowski, K., Dan, A., Keahey, K., Ludwig, H., Pruyne, J., Rofrano, J., Tuecke, S., Xu, M.: Web Services Agreement Specification (WS-Agreement). Global Grid Forum GRAAP-WG, Draft (August 2004)

13. Makripoulias, Y., Makris, C., Panagis, Y., Sakkopoulos, E., Adamopoulou, P., Pontikaki, M., Tsakalidis, A.: Towards Ubiquitous Computing with Quality of Web Service Support. Upgrade, The European Journal for the Informatics Professional VI(5), 29–34 (2005)

14. Yau, S.S., Wang, Y., Huang, D., Hoh, P.: Situation-aware contract specification language for middleware for ubiquitous computing. In: The Ninth IEEE Workshop on Future Trends of Distributed Computing Systems, 2003. FTDCS 2003. Proceedings, May 28-30, 2003, pp. 93–99 (2003)

15. Zeng, L., Benatallah, B., Ngu, A.H.H., Dumas, M., Kalagnanam, J., Chang, H.: QoS-aware middleware for Web services composition. IEEE Transactions on Software Engineering 30(5), 311–327 (2004)

16. Canfora, G., Di Penta, M., Esposito, R., Villani, M.L.: An approach for QoS-aware service composition based on genetic algorithms. In: Proceedings of the 2005 conference on Genetic and evolutionary computation, pp. 1069–1075 (2005)

17. Solberg, A., Amundsen, S., Aagedal, J.Ø., Eliassen, F.: A Framework for QoS-Aware Service Composition. In: Proceedings of 2nd ACM International Conference on Service Oriented Computing (2004)

18. Tokairin, Y., Yamanaka, K., Takahashi, H., Suganuma, T., Shiratori, N.: An effective qos control scheme for ubiquitous services based on context information management. cec-eee, 619–625 (2007)

19. Abdennadher, N., Boesch, R.: Deploying phylip phylogenetic package on a large scale distributed system. In: IEEE International Symposium on Cluster Computing and the Grid, pp. 673–678 (2007)

20. Abdennadher, N., Boesch, R.: A scheduling algorithm for high performance peer-to-peer platform. In: Lehner, W., Meyer, N., Streit, A., Stewart, C. (eds.) Euro-Par Workshops 2006. LNCS, vol. 4375, pp. 126–137. Springer, Heidelberg (2007)
21. Ibach, P., Stantchev, V., Keller, C.: Daedalus a peer-to-peer shared memory system for ubiquitous computing. In: Nagel, W.E., Walter, W.V., Lehner, W. (eds.) Euro-Par 2006. LNCS, vol. 4128, pp. 961–970. Springer, Heidelberg (2006)
22. Wanek, H., Schikuta, E., Haq, I.U.: Grid workflow optimization regarding dynamically changing resources and conditions. Concurrency and Computation: Practice and Experience (2008)
23. Schikuta, E., Mach, W.: Optimized workflow orchestration of parallel database aggregate operations on a heterogenous grid. In: The 37th International Conference on Parallel Processing (ICPP 2008), Portland, Ohio, USA. IEEE Computer Society, Los Alamitos (2008)
24. Stantchev, V., Schröpfer, C.: Techniques for service level enforcement in web-services based systems. In: Proceedings of The 10th International Conference on Information Integration and Web-based Applications and Services (iiWAS 2008), pp. 7–14. ACM, New York (2008)
25. Krallmann, H., Schröpfer, C., Stantchev, V., Offermann, P.: Enabling autonomous self-optimization in service-oriented systems. In: Proceedings of The 8th International Workshop on Autonomous Systems - Self Organisation, Management and Control, Berlin, New York, pp. 127–134. Springer, Heidelberg (2008)
26. Schropfer, C., Binshtok, M., Shimony, S.E., Dayan, A., Brafman, R., Offermann, P., Holschke, O.: Introducing preferences over NFPs into service selection in SOA. In: International Conference on Service Oriented Computing - International Workshop on Non Functional Properties and Service Level Agreements in Service Oriented Computing (2007)
27. Avizienis, A., Laprie, J.-C., Randell, B., Landwehr, C.: Basic concepts and taxonomy of dependable and secure computing. IEEE Transactions on Dependable and Secure Computing 1(1), 11–33 (2004)
28. Brown, A., Patterson, D.A.: Towards Availability Benchmarks: A Case Study of Software RAID Systems. In: Proceedings of the 2000 USENIX Annual Technical Conference (2000)
29. Polze, A., Schwarz, J., Malek, M.: Automatic generation of fault-tolerant corba-services. Tools, 205 (2000)
30. Cristian, F., Aghili, H., Strong, R., Dolev, D.: Atomic broadcast: from simple message diffusion to byzantine agreement. Inf. Comput. 118(1), 158–179 (1995)
31. Laranjeira, L.A., Malek, M., Jenevein, R.: Nest: a nested-predicate scheme for fault tolerance. Transactions on Computers 42(11), 1303–1324 (1993)
32. Yu, H., Vahdat, A.: The costs and limits of availability for replicated services. ACM Trans. Comput. Syst. 24(1), 70–113 (2006)
33. Stantchev, V.: Effects of Replication on Web Service Performance in WebSphere. Icsi tech report 2008-03, International Computer Science Institute, Berkeley, California 94704, USA (February 2008)
34. Stantchev, V., Malek, M.: Addressing Web Service Performance by Replication at the Operating System Level. In: ICIW 2008: Proceedings of the 2008 Third International Conference on Internet and Web Applications and Services, pp. 696–701. IEEE Computer Society, Los Alamitos (2008)
35. Microsoft. Comparing Web Service Performance: WS Test 1.1 Benchmark Results for .NET 2.0, NET 1.1, Sun One/ JWSDP 1.5 and IBM WebSphere 6.0 (2006), http://www.theserverside.net/tt/articles/content/NET2Benchmarks

# Dynamic and Secure Data Access Extensions of Grid Boundaries

Yudith Cardinale, Jesús De Oliveira, and Carlos Figueira

Universidad Simón Bolívar,
Departamento de Computación y Tecnología de la Información,
Apartado 89000, Caracas 1080-A, Venezuela
{yudith,jdeoliveira,figueira}@ldc.usb.ve

**Abstract.** Grid technology provides a suitable platform for resource sharing, offering users the possibility of accessing large-scale controlled environments across different organizational boundaries through a virtualized single environment. In order to control accesses to those resources, a unique and global security infrastructure is needed, such as a PKI and Virtual Organizations. Hence, in order to process data in the grid, it must be first uploaded to a suitable resource belonging to the grid. We propose mechanisms to extend the grid data space boundaries by securely integrating data located in the client local file system or in external repositories. The proposed extensions only take place during execution of an application on the grid, preserving privacy and other security properties. We explain their implementation in SUMA/G, a middleware built on top of Globus, and show some experiment results.

## 1  Introduction

Grids [1, 2] provide transparent access to remote resources, secure resource management through a global safe platform, and access control through *Virtual Organizations* (VO) [3–5]. Each VO is granted access to a subset of available resources in the grid. We call *VO Working Space* (VOWS) the set of computing and data resources accessible by members of a particular VO. A VOWS is mainly composed of the computing platforms that can be used by the VO and the file systems accessible by that VO. For instance, in gLite, there are *Storage Elements* (SE) which can store the files to be processed. These files are usually directly uploaded by a data provider, or by users from their local host. In the latter case, the set of file systems in a VOWS is composed of the file systems directly accessed from computing platforms (*Execution Nodes*), and the SE's accessible to that VO, typically through gridFTP [6] or GFAL [7].

In most Globus-based platforms, when a user wants to process some data files stored in her/his local workstation, she/he must upload those files into her/his VOWS before the data can be processed within a grid. In other words, the data files have to be transferred from the user's local host into the file systems accessible by the grid's Execution Nodes before the execution starts. Storage Elements can always be used as intermediate data containers in the grid.

N. Abdennadher and D. Petcu (Eds.): GPC 2009, LNCS 5529, pp. 36–47, 2009.

There are contexts in which data sources are not part of the grid, but should be accessed from grid's Execution Nodes, during the execution of applications. Some scenarios require a high level of confidentiality because of business reasons, sensibility of private information, or even national security. For example, some data have privacy requirements, such as patient records or data that could be used for medical and research purposes. In this case, the privacy requirement is related to the *trust* factor and legal issues. An alternative for this kind of organizations could be not to belong to the grid; however, this alternative deprives organizations of the advantages of using a huge computational power available in other organizations. Due to the fact that the data could be processed in a different platform from that on which they are located, it is necessary to transfer files to computing resources, leaving a gap for possible *uncontrolled* access to confidential information. Resource access in a grid, including data repositories access, is typically supported by a Public Key Infrastructure (i.e., X.509 certificates). However, in these scenarios this basic security mechanism may not be sufficient. Thus, using the grid could be easier for most users if the file systems accessible from the local workstation and private repositories were part of the VOWS, at least during the execution of the application.

In this paper, we propose mechanisms that extend the VOWS by securely integrating data located on the client local file system or external repositories. The main advantages of the proposed extensions are: i) preserve the privacy and other security grid standards; ii) eliminate the necessity of explicitly uploading the data files to the grid, which helps to meet the grid goal of achieving seamless access to distributed resources; iii) eliminate the necessity of specifying location dependent file accesses into the application, thus, the programs designed for local file system access do not have to be modified for grid execution; they are programmed as if all accesses were local, regardless of location, in a secure way; and iv) Users have better control over their data, even private ones. Moreover, the extensions take place only during execution of an application on the grid. We explain their implementation in SUMA/G, a middleware built on top of Globus for execution of Java applications on the grid. With these extensions, SUMA/G execution model allows a user to launch Java applications that will run on a grid from her/his machine without requiring this machine to be part of the grid.

## 2 Related Work

Secure access to remote private data has been the focus of a number of works. In [8, 9], a secure global network file system with decentralized control, called *Self-certifying secure file system* (SFS), is presented. It implements the Network File System protocol for communicating with the operating system, while also providing transparent encryption of communications as well as authentication. SFS uses cryptography to provide security over untrusted networks. Thus, clients can safely share files across administrative realms without involving administrators or certification authorities. Servers have a public key and clients use the server public key to authenticate servers and to establish a secure communication channel. To allow clients to authenticate unknown servers, SFS introduces the concept of a *self-certifying pathname*. A self-certifying pathname contains a server's public-key hash, so that the client can verify that she/he is actually talking to a legitimate server. Once the client has verified a server, a secure channel is established and the actual file access takes place. This method is appropriate when applications run on specific machines under the user control, but it is not easily adaptable to grid environments where the application execution is delegated to some middleware component.

GSI-SFS [10] is a secure distributed file system with a single sign-on functionality. GSI-SFS is developed by extending SFS with GSI. It allows users to access files on the grid as if these files were local. Furthermore, all data transferred over network are automatically encrypted and verified by SFS. [11] describes an access control mechanism, called *Sygn*, implemented on $\mu$ *Grid*, an experimental grid platform specially oriented to medical applications. Because of the sensitivity of data, Sygn allows fine-grain access control by defining access permissions to data for authorized users. The OGSA Data Access and Integration Project (OGSA-DAI) [12] is developing software for integrating different and heterogeneous data sources on grids. OGSA-DQP [13] is an extension of OGSA-DAI that provides a service-based distributed query processor. *gLite Secure Storage Service* [14] is a service for storing, in a secure way (encrypted) confidential data (e.g. medical or financial data) on the grid SE's. The *gLite Secure Storage Service* consists of modified versions of user-space data access tools (including replica management, transparent I/O APIs and file transfer commands), which encrypts the data before it leaves the user security perimeter. In this sense, sensible data is always stored and transferred encrypt, making impossible for a third party to access it, even if she/he has sufficient privileges on the storage system where it is located (which is the case of system administrators), or gains access to the communication network. The data is encrypted using randomly generated keys. These keys are associated with the user, who is identified by her/his GSI X.509 certificate, ensuring that she/he will be the only one that can access the keys used to secure her/his data. All of these platforms consider only scenarios in which data sources belong to the grid. Additionally, they require establishing complex additional components to the Grid and specifications from the user. In contrast, our approaches implemented in SUMA/G emphasize transparency and usability at the expense of coping with more complex data access contexts.

# 3   SUMA/G Architecture Overview

SUMA/G[1] (Scientific Ubiquitous Metacomputing Architecture/Globus) [15, 16] is a grid middleware that transparently executes both sequential and parallel Java applications on remote machines. SUMA/G uses the Globus Security Infrastructure (GSI) [17], through the Java CoG Kit [18], to implement security and resource management. The SUMA/G architecture is depicted in Figure 1.

---

[1] http://gryds.net/suma

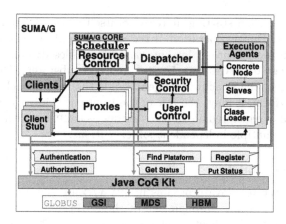

**Fig. 1.** SUMA/G Architecture

## 3.1 SUMA/G Components

SUMA/G services are accessible through local clients as command line and graphic interfaces, or through a web interface [19]. SUMA/G components, and their role in the execution of applications, are shown below.

**Client Stub.** Creates the application object, retrieves results and performance profiling data, and serves `Execution Agent` requests (callbacks) to load classes and data dynamically. It is executed on the user machine (for command line and graphic interfaces) or on a SUMA/G entry server, such as the web server for `GiPS`. In any case, the user must have a valid certificate installed on that machine.

**Proxy.** Receives an object from `Client Stub`, containing application information such as the name of the main class, scheduling constraints (optional), and number of CPUs. After checking user permissions, the `Proxy` asks the `Scheduler` for a suitable execution platform, then sends the application object to the selected one. In case of off-line jobs submission, the `Proxy` keeps results until the user requests them.

**Scheduler.** Responds to `Proxy` requests based on the application requirements and status information obtained from the grid platform. Using the Globus MDS service, the `Scheduler` learns of grid resources, obtaining information about available execution platforms (including memory size, available libraries and average load), data sets hosted at specific locations, and so on. With this information, the `Scheduler` selects a suitable resource satisfying the application requirements, while looking for load balance in the grid.

**User Control.** Is in charge of user registration and authentication.

**Security Control.** Serves all GSI certificates generation and verification requests.

**Execution Agent.** On starting, it registers itself at the `Scheduler` as a new available resource. During operation, it receives the application object from the `Proxy` and launches execution, loading classes and files dynamically from the client through the SUMA/G-`Class Loader` and I/O subsystem. Once the application has finished, the `Execution Agent` sends the results back to the client. In a parallel platform, it plays the role of the front-end. Only the front-end of a parallel platform is registered on SUMA/G either as a MPIJAVA enabled platform or as a farm, for multiple independent job executions.

## 3.2   Execution Model

The basics of executing Java programs in SUMA/G are simple. Users can start the execution of programs through one of these `Client`: a shell or a graphic interface running on the client machine, or through `GiPS`, the SUMA/G portal. They can invoke either `Execute`, corresponding to the on-line execution mode, or `Submit`, which allows for off-line execution (batch jobs). At this time a proxy credential is generated (by using GSI) that allows processes created on behalf of the user to acquire resources, without additional user intervention. Once the SUMA/G `CORE` receives the request from the client machine, it authenticates the user through GSI, transparently finds a platform for execution by querying the MDS, and sends a request message to that platform. An `Execution Agent` at the designated platform receives an object representing the application and starts, in an independent JVM, an `Execution Agent Slave`, who actually executes the application. The SUMA/G- `Class Loader` is started in that new JVM, whose function is to load classes and data during execution.

To execute an application, either on-line or off-line, the user has only to specify the main class name. In the case of `Execute` service, the rest of the classes and data files are loaded at run-time, on demand, without user intervention. Standard input and output are handled transparently, as if the user were running the application on the local machine. For the `Submit` service, SUMA/G `Client Stub` transparently packs all classes together with input files and delivers them to SUMA/G `CORE`; the output is kept in SUMA/G until the user requests it.

# 4   Extending Data Access

Access control to grid resources on Globus-based grids is based on VO and the GSI security infrastructure. Site administrators configure the access control list to the site's resources for the relevant VO's. Whenever a resource access request arrives to the site, a valid certificate must be provided; then, the VO for that particular user is resolved and access rights for the VO are granted to the user's request. Concerning data access, most Globus-based grids consider two possible scenarios:

1. A user wants to process some data files stored in her/his local workstation. In this case, she/he must upload those files into her/his VOWS before the data can be processed in the grid. For example, in `gLite`, the data files should be

transferred from the *User Interface* (UI-the entry point to the grid) into the file systems accessible by the Execution Nodes before execution starts; and
2. A user wants to process some data files already stored inside the grid (e.g. in the Storage Elements). In this case she/he has to specify the access through special instructions (such as GridFTP) from her/his application and, if it is necessary, to manually manage the replicas.

We present mechanisms for incorporating external data sources into the grid during the execution of a Java application. We consider two kinds of sources: file systems (local or remote) accessed from the client machine and private data repositories. In both cases, these data sources are not part of the grid.

### 4.1   Access to User Local File Systems

In order to avoid the previous uploading of data into the grid, we propose a mechanism where files are loaded on demand from the user's machine to the Execution Node. All data file requests issued by Java applications are transparently redirected to the client (with *callbacks*), which in turn connects to local file systems (i.e., at the client machine) or remote file systems specified by the user (e.g., at machines in which the user has an account) to serve requests during the execution. This scheme follows the Java execution model where classes and data are loaded on demand.

SUMA/G uses GSI for user authentication, authorization, and delegation, as well as a mechanism for including all SUMA/G components into the grid security space. For privacy, all SUMA/G components exchange messages through encrypted channels using SSL. The main SUMA/G components involved in the security model are the **User Control** and the **Security Control**.

The **User Control** is in charge of user registration and authentication. SUMA/G users must have a valid certificate installed on their machines. Certificates have to be signed by a SUMA/G Certification Authority. Users must register with the **User Control**, providing the VO they belong to. VOs are specially important for users authorization. One or more VOs for SUMA/G users should be registered at the **User Control**. The **User Control** authentication relies on the **Security Control** certificates verification. The **Security Control** serves all GSI certificates generation and verification requests. This module's design follows a General Responsibility Assignment Software Patterns (GRASP).

Figure 2 shows the authentication and authorization processes to gain access to resources. The **Client** uses the **Security Control** API to get the **Security-Message** signed with the user's private key, which contains at least a X.509 credential with a VO attribute assertion (step 1). The **SecurityMessage** is sent through CORBA to the **User Control** (step 2). The **User Control** verifies the SecurityMessage with the **Security Control** API and matches the X.509 credential to a VO group to authorize access to a subset of grid resources, that includes the file system of the client machine (step 3). Thus, during the execution the client machine is in the realm of the GSI security and the remote accounts are accessed with secure protocol such as scp, sftp or https.

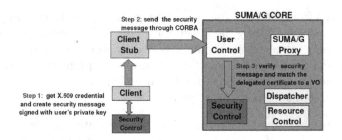

**Fig. 2.** SUMA/G security model to access user local file systems

## 4.2    Access to External Data Repositories

The grid access control scheme, based on VO's and GSI, is supported by a grid common trust domain, which allows for secure user authentication in the grid. However, when dealing with sensitive data, a more restricted access control could be enforced by the data keepers. In such scenario, the repository administrators may not agree to include it as part of the grid's realm of trust: the grid certificates are not accepted by the data repositories.

We present a mechanism based on a *Session Authentication Key (SAK)*, which allows grid users to obtain access rights to the repository for temporarily incorporating, into the grid, their data stored on external repositories.

In the following description, we consider three components: i) A data repository server, not belonging to the grid. The user is entitled an account on this repository, and access rights to a particular data area in the file system; ii) A client machine, where the user accesses grid services from, including job submission; and iii) A grid.

Data repository server and client machines use a Public Key Infrastructure. In order to submit a job for data processing from the external repository in the grid, a user must previously send a request to a data repository server in order to obtain a SAK. Then, the user submits her/his job to the grid, specifying the data repository URL and the SAK. The `Scheduler` will select an Execution Node in order to execute the job. During execution, the application running on the Execution Node requests data accesses to the repository, presenting the SAK in order to obtain the appropriate permissions. Figure 3 depicts this process. Note the whole external repository data access process remains in control of the user, who is granted access permission according to the server administrator policy. Data is moved through a secure channel established between Execution Node and the repository.

*a) SÂK components:* A SAK is composed by:

- An *ID*, the user identification at the repository server. It depends on the authentication mechanism used by the server (e.g., a login name);
- A *ticket* called Temporary Authentication Number (*TAN*). It is randomly generated by the server and stored for later access authentication. The TAN is locally allocated an expiration time; and
- A *Hash*, (e.g., SHA-2) of the previous components.

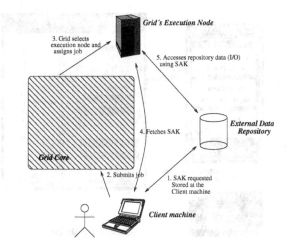

**Fig. 3.** External Repository access from the grid using a SAK

These three components are concatenated and encrypted using the server public key to make up a SAK, such that only the server can later process the thus generated SAK, and validate accesses during execution.

*b) Accessing the repository using a SAK:*
When the user submits a job to the grid, she/he provides along the SAK, using a secure connection, as given by GSI. During execution, every application's input/output operation to the repository server carries along a SAK, using a secure channel. The remote repository server then:

- Decrypts the SAK with its private key;
- Verify that the TAN is valid, i.e., it exists in the registry and has not expired;
- If the TAN is valid, verify that the owner (corresponding to the user ID in the SAK) has permission for the requested operation; and
- If it failed to present a valid SAK or to have permission for the requested operation, an access denied code is returned. Otherwise, the request is fulfilled.

## 5   Implementation in SUMA/G

In SUMA/G, classes and files are loaded on demand from the user's machines, which means that it is not necessary either previous installation of the user's Java code on the Execution Node nor packing all classes for submission. Bytecode and data files servers may be located on machines belonging to the grid, or on user controlled external servers by incorporating local file systems into a VOWS.

Supported classes, input files sources, and output destinations include:

- client machine where the application execution command is run and,
- remote file servers on which the user has an account. A pluggable schema allows for implementing several protocols for remote files access. Currently, schemes for CORBA and sftp are available.

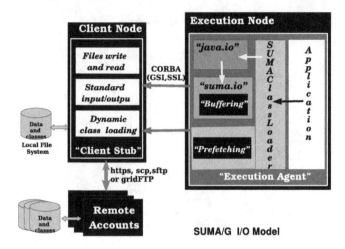

**Fig. 4.** SUMA/G I/O Subsystem

Figure 4 shows current SUMA/G I/O subsystem, which allow the incorporation of users' file systems into the grid during the execution of an application. The remote data and classes access mechanisms are:

1. Dynamic class loading. The `Execution Agent` in charge of the execution of an application instantiates a SUMA/G-`Class Loader`, which handles the dynamic class loading from the user's local machine up to the `Execution Agent` at run time by using *callbacks* to the `Client Stub`.
2. Standard input, output and error redirection. For interactive applications, the execution environment is modified such that the standard input, output and error are connected to the user's machine issuing the execution request, thus behaving as if it were a local execution.
3. `java.io` redirection. A new package, called `suma.io`, overloads the basic classes in `java.io`, such that, at run time, every invocation of a `java.io` method made by the application actually uses its modified version in `suma.io`. `suma.io` methods use *callbacks* to the `Client Stub` to access data files at the client machine. If the required data is not present at the user machine, the `Client Stub` locates and accesses the remote file system keeping the data. Data is transferred from the remote file system to the user machine, through a secure channel (by using https or sftp), and then to the `Execution Agent`, under GSI realm. Note that files are not transferred as a whole but in blocks, reducing the risk of obtaining a copy of the file.
4. Buffering and prefetching. Remote file accesses use buffering to improve performance, by reading or writing blocks, hence reducing the number of *callbacks* to data sources. The kind of buffering support provided in SUMA/G is different from that provided by buffer cache components commonly found in file system implementations. It rather resembles file prestaging, in the sense that it consists of a single block, which could actually be the whole

file. At execution time a block size is specified and the data transfer is performed on demand, when the application executes a read on a file. The data block transferred from the remote file system starts at the first byte accessed by the application. If the application tries to access a byte not contained in the transferred data block, another data block is transferred, overwriting the previous block. Prefetching techniques are used for transfer delay masking, by overlapping class loading with computation. The idea is to prefetch classes from the client machine to the `Execution Agent`, as early as possible to reduce the delay when the actual reference to a class is made [20].

The possibility of accessing external data repositories is an alternative mechanism of SUMA/G that bypasses the client, by directly connecting applications to data repositories (only for data files). As explained before, SUMA/G I/O subsystem provides redirection of I/O to access local file systems. The same mechanism (redefinition of `java.io`) was used to implement secure access to external data repositories. The modifications to the SUMA/G platform comprise:

- A new set of `suma.io` redefinition classes to transparently handle accesses to external data repositories. Every I/O method includes a new parameter, the SAK. Currently, communication between the `Execution Agent` and the repository is implemented using RMI with SSL; and
- The SUMA/G Client and the intermediate SUMA/G components accept a new parameter, the SAK, which travels along with the request.

Additionally, a client-server system for the SAK generation and communication was developed, as well as the repository server side for the I/O requests. The file name containing the SAK is passed as an argument of job submission commands. Next Section presents the SAK details.

## 6   Experiment Results

The goal of these experiments is to address concerns about performance overhead incurred by the newly added data handling functionnalities. We selected a simple application which stresses file transfer mechanisms, by copying (read/write) a 21 MB file. This application is executed in the three scenarios depicted below.

- The file is in the client machine's file system, the application is executed with SUMA/G. The source and destination files are directly accessed from/to the client's file system.
- The file is located at a remote repository (i.e., outside the grid), the application is executed with SUMA/G. The source and destination files are accessed from/to the remote repository.
- The file is in a User Interface machine and the application is executed with `gLite`. The `gLite` job input sandbox mechanisms imply to transfer the source file to the Execution Node during the job submission, then transfer back the destination file upon job completion.

**Table 1.** Wall clock time for three test scenarios, with a 21 MB file copy application

| Scenarios | Client's File System in SUMA/G | Remote Repository in SUMA/G | Transferred Files in gLite |
|---|---|---|---|
| **Wall Clock Time** | 31.06s | 590.43s | 71.22s |

For each scenario, 10 experiments were performed, taking the best case. All scenarios were run over the same execution platform, namely dedicated nodes of PC's dual core 3.4 GHz Pentium-IV, 1 GB RAM, interconnected through a 100 Mbps LAN network, running Debian GNU/Linux etch 4.0r5. All grid components (SUMA/G and gLite components), client machine, and data repository were each executed on different nodes.

As shown on table 1, the best performance is obtained when files are located on the client's machine. This is due to the prefetching and buffering mechanisms built in SUMA/G, not present in gLite. However, the flexibility of securely accessing a remote repository, comes at a considerable penalty; overhead is due to the SSL handshake and encryption/decryption at both sides of the connection established between the `Execution Agent` and the remote repository.

## 7   Conclusions

Security is the key issue when dealing with resource sharing and collaboration. While current grid middleware provides a standard common security infrastructure, which certainly suits many contexts of use, it can not correctly handle some others where special requirements on confidentiality, for instance, are imposed by organizations, such as medical or business private data.

The mechanisms introduced in this work offer a solution for using grid power to process data located on repositories outside the grid. This data is temporarily accessed by applications on the user behalf. Session keys and block data transfers helps on preserving the data confidentiality. Together with the middleware I/O subsystem that includes file systems accessible from the client during application execution, the grid boundaries are actually extended in a secure and dynamic way. An implementation of these mechanisms in a grid middleware SUMA/G, was also presented. We are currently working on incorporating GlusterFS [21] as an alternative source to be incorporated into the grid.

## References

1. Foster, I., Kesselman, C., Nick, J., Tuecke, S.: The Physiology of the Grid: An Open Grid Services Architecture for Distributed Systems Integration. Open Grid Service Infrastructure WG document, Global Grid Forum (2002)
2. Abbas, A.: Grid Computing: A Practical Guide to Technology and Applicactions. Charles River Media (2004)
3. Foster, I., Kesselman, C., Tuecke, S.: The Anatomy of the Grid: Enabling Scalable Virtual Organizations. Int'l. Journal of High Perfor. Computing Apps. 15 (2001)

4. Baduel, L., Baude, F., Caromel, D., Contes, A., Huet, F., Morel, M., Quilici, R.: Programming, Deploying, Composing, for the Grid. In: Grid Computing: Software Environments and Tools. Springer, Heidelberg (2006)
5. Laurence Field: Getting Grids to work together: interoperation is key to sharing (2006), http://cerncourier.com/articles/cnl/3/11/10/1
6. Allcock, W., Bresnahan, J., Foster, I., Liming, L., Link, J., Plaszczac, P.: GridFTP Protocol Specification. Technical report, Global Grid Forum (2002)
7. GFAL: Gfal (2003), http://grid-deployment.web.cern.ch/grid-deployment/gis/GFAL/gfal.3.html
8. Mazieres, D.: Security and decentralized control in the SFS global file system, MIT Master's thesis (1997)
9. Mazières, D.: Self-certifying file system. PhD thesis, Massachusetts Institute of Technology (2000)
10. Kido, Y., Date, S., Takeda, S., Hatano, S., Ma, J., Shimojo, S., Matsuda, H.: Architecture of a grid-enabled research platform with location-transparency for bioinformatics. Genome Informatics 15, 3–12 (2004)
11. Seitz, L., Montagnat, J., Pierson, J.M., Oriol, D., Lingrand, D.: Authentication and autorisation prototype on the microgrid for medical data management. In: Health Grid 2005 (2005)
12. OGSA: The OGSA Data Access and Integration Project (2008)
13. Alpdemir, M.N., Mukherjee, A., Gounaris, A., Paton, N.W., Fernandes, A., Sakellariou, R., Watson, P., Li, P.: Using OGSA-DQP to support scientific applications for the grid. In: Herrero, P., S. Pérez, M., Robles, V. (eds.) SAG 2004. LNCS, vol. 3458, pp. 13–24. Springer, Heidelberg (2005)
14. Scardaci, D., Scuderi, G.: A Secure Stora Service for the gLite Middleware. In: Proc. of the Third Inter'l. Symp. on Information Assurance and Security (2007)
15. Cardinale, Y., Curiel, M., Figueira, C., García, P., Hernández, E.: Implementation of a CORBA-based metacomputing system. In: Hertzberger, B., Hoekstra, A.G., Williams, R. (eds.) HPCN-Europe 2001. LNCS, vol. 2110, p. 629. Springer, Heidelberg (2001)
16. Cardinale, Y., Hernández, E.: Parallel Checkpointing on a Grid-enabled Java Platform. In: Sloot, P.M.A., Hoekstra, A.G., Priol, T., Reinefeld, A., Bubak, M. (eds.) EGC 2005. LNCS, vol. 3470, pp. 741–750. Springer, Heidelberg (2005)
17. The Globus Alliance: The Globus Toolkit (2006), http://www.globus.org/
18. von Laszewski, G., Foster, I., Gawor, J., Smith, W., Tuecke, S.: CoG Kits: A Bridge between Commodity Distributed Computing and High-Performance Grids. In: ACM Java Grande 2000 Conf., pp. 97–106 (2000)
19. Cardinale, Y., Figueira, C.: GiPS: A Grid Portal for Executing Java Applications on Globus-based Grids. In: Stojmenovic, I., Thulasiram, R.K., Yang, L.T., Jia, W., Guo, M., de Mello, R.F. (eds.) ISPA 2007. LNCS, vol. 4742, pp. 669–682. Springer, Heidelberg (2007)
20. Cardinale, Y., De Oliveira, J., Figueira, C.: Remote class prefetching: Improving performance of java applications on grid platforms. In: Guo, M., Yang, L.T., Di Martino, B., Zima, H.P., Dongarra, J., Tang, F. (eds.) ISPA 2006. LNCS, vol. 4330, pp. 594–606. Springer, Heidelberg (2006)
21. Z-Research: GlusterFS (2007), http://www.gluster.org/docs/index.php/GlusterFS

# Proxy Restrictions for Grid Usage

Joni Hahkala[1], John White[1], and Ákos Frohner[2]

[1] Helsinki Institute of Physics, FIN-00014 Helsingin Yliopisto, Finland
{Joni.Hahkala,John.White}@cern.ch
[2] CERN European Organization for Nuclear Research, CH-1211 Geneve 23,
Switzerland
Akos.Frohner@cern.ch

**Abstract.** The scale and power of Grid infrastructures makes them
an inviting target for attack. Even if the Grid software is secure the
Grid infrastructure is vulnerable via operating system vulnerabilities and
misconfiguration. One of the worst results of the exploit of these vulnerabilities is user proxy credential compromise. This paper describes a
pragmatic and simple way, using proxy certificate extensions, to mitigate
the damage in case of credential compromise. The potential damage is
limited by restricting the range of hosts that the credentials can be used
to open connections to and be accepted from. This paper also describes
a way to help investigate credential delegation problems.

## 1 Background

### 1.1 Certificates

A user on a Grid must be trusted on all services and resources of the infrastructure that he accesses or uses. Therefore some form of credential must be
presented to the Grid services in order for it to authenticate and eventually authorize a user to perform an action. Many of today's Grid middleware systems
authenticate users with Public Key Infrastructure (PKI) certificates that follow
the X.509 [7] format. This X.509 certificate is used to establish the chain of trust
that is needed for a user to access a remote Grid resource or service.

In this identification scheme a user obtains an X.509 certificate from a recognized certificate authority (CA). In order to do this the user simultaneously
generates a public and private key pair and puts the public key into a certificate
request. The signed certificate request is sent to the CA and the identity of the
requester is verified using an out of band method such as a telephone call to the
requester's employer. After the verification, the CA signs the request creating
a certificate that can be used by the user in conjunction with their previously
generated private key to prove that he is the person who requested the certificate
from the CA.

At this stage a trust relationship has been established between the Grid user
and the CA. The Grid user has declared his identity to the CA, the CA has
verified this and it has issued a credential asserting this fact. The services and

N. Abdennadher and D. Petcu (Eds.): GPC 2009, LNCS 5529, pp. 48–56, 2009.

users that trust the CA in question can now trust the owner of the certificate if he can prove he has the private key corresponding to the public key in the certificate.

## 1.2  Proxy Certificates

In order for a user to allow Grid services to act on his behalf, which is usually needed, the services must present the user's credentials to a resource they need to access in order to be authenticated and authorized as the user. To first order, this can be accomplished by sending his CA-signed certificate and private key to the service giving it the power to authenticate as the user. This has an obvious security flaw in that anyone in possession, through interception, of this pair could pretend to be the user.

This security problem is avoided by allowing the user to delegate their security rights to Grid services by using a different type of certificate. This is the proxy certificate which, as the name indicates, is an authorized credential derived from the original credential or intermediate proxies that is allowed to act on behalf of the Grid user. In order to generate a proxy certificate a new public/private key pair is generated and used to create a request for a proxy certificate. This request is subsequently signed using the private key of the user's original CA-issued certificate or by an intermediate proxy.

Therefore, the proxy certificate is a credential that contains the identity and provenance of the owner. These certificates usually have a short validity time, usually 24 or 12 hours as opposed to CA-issued credentials that have a lifetime of months. As the proxy certificate is generated locally by the owner of the credential and the private key it is based on and not by a CA, the trust is provided by the original user and possible intermediate proxy credentials. As the private key of previous credentials is used for the signing, the chain of trust is extended from the CA to this proxy credential. In theory this proxy chain can be extended infinitely, but in practice software implementations and size constraints limit the number of proxies in a chain. In this document extensions to the basic proxy certificate, as can be currently used in the EGEE gLite middleware, are discussed.

## 2  Problem Definition

The main usage of proxy credentials in a Grid is the authorization of the user's rights through the job submission system to the worker node (WN) of the cluster where the user's actual computation takes place, and the data access from the WN.

To achieve this without transferring the full credentials with private key over the network, thus exposing it to attacks, the credentials have to be delegated through the job submission system. Each move between services entails at least one delegation and thus one more proxy certificate in the certificate chain.

As the services need to use the credentials for authentication on behalf of the user, the private key in the proxy credentials has to be in plain text, unencrypted and thus unprotected. This leads to the vulnerability that if any machine or service in the job submission chain is compromised, the attacker can harvest these proxies that pass through or are stored on that host. The vulnerability is especially apparent on the WN where code submitted by the user is run or at least a program is run with input data provided by the user. A rogue Grid user has more possibilities to exploit vulnerabilities on that WN host and access the credentials of other jobs running on that host. Furthermore, if a shared file system is used, possibly all credentials in the shared file system and thus in the site can be compromised. Another possibility is to start processes on the WN that harvest incoming credentials, unless rigorous cleaning of processes is done after the job ends.

After the attacker has obtained credentials, he can impersonate the owner of the credentials and e.g. access the owner's files and run jobs under the owner's identity.

These problems are already mitigated through some limitations on proxies. Firstly, the proxies should have a short lifetime, typically they are limited to 24 hours, but for various reasons this limitation is sometimes ignored and longer proxies are used e.g. a week or 10 days. Another limitation is to use a limited proxy. When a proxy is delegated to the WN with the user's job it is marked in the process as limited proxy. Subsequent job submissions using limited proxies are refused at the workload management system (WMS) and computing elements (CEs). Thus proxies harvested from a WN cannot be used to submit more jobs, but they can still be used to access data and other services. Limited proxies can still be used by an attacker by submitting jobs to another site using their own credentials and then within those jobs use the compromised credentials to access data and do other damage.

## 3    Proxy Restrictions

To mitigate the possibilities for causing damage with compromised proxies, the amount of damage that can be caused by compromised proxies and to control the compromised proxies two proxy restrictions will be described.

### 3.1    Source Restriction

This restriction is used to limit the source network address space from which the proxy can be used for authentication when opening connections. If a proxy is limited using this extension to an address space, Grid services will only accept the proxy as authentication credentials when the connection is opened from that specific address space.

When the address spaces where the proxy will be delegated to in the future are known this restriction can be used to limit the credentials and the further delegations derived from these credentials to only work from those address spaces. As the restriction is inherited, meaning that if there is this extension a proxy certificate in the chain the further proxies derived from this proxy are also restricted. Therefore, the restriction cannot be bypassed by generating a new sub-proxy.

This extension should, at least in the beginning be non-critical to allow gradual migration even on the production services. After enough systems support it, it should be marked critical to make sure the restriction is honored.

Two examples of usage of this type of restriction:

1. A job is submitted by the WMS into a CE in a site. If it is known that the job runs only in the CE site without needing to delegate rights to any service to act on behalf if it and that the job will stay in the site, the proxy can be restricted to the CE site during the delegation of the credentials from the WMS to the CE. If the CE site is compromised, the credentials harvested from these hosts can only be used on that site. Thus, if there is a compromise in a site, isolating the site from the rest of the Grid will ensure that the problem is isolated. After waiting the maximum allowed proxy lifetime and after the centre has fixed the damage and cleaned the machines, the site can be taken back to the Grid with knowledge that the compromised credentials have expired and are thus unusable.

2. A job is submitted by a CE into the WN. Again, if it is known that the job only operates from that WN and does not need to delegate rights elsewhere, this restriction can be put into the credentials during the delegation from the CE to the WN thus tying the credentials to that specific WN. This way if the WN is compromised, it can simply be taken offline stopping possibility of abuse of the credentials. After the vulnerability has been fixed and after waiting that the compromised credentials have expired, the WN can be safely returned to use.

Without this restriction, compromised credentials may be used anywhere in the Grid and thus the only way to recover from the incident is to ban all the users that had credentials in the compromised machines, which can be hard to determine. Thus, this restriction greatly eases the recovery from an incident and allows the users to continue working using other sites.

## 3.2 Target Restriction

This restriction is used to limit the target network address space where the proxy can be used to authenticate connections to. If a proxy is limited using this extension to an address space, the services will only accept the proxy as an authorized credential when the service resides in that specific address space. As above, when the address spaces where the proxy will be delegated to and what services need to be contacted using these credentials are known, this restriction can be used to limit the further delegations derived from these credentials to only work as credentials in those address spaces. Also as above the same considerations for criticality of this extension has to be taken into account.

An example of the usage of the extension: If a CE knows the storage elements that a user's job will contact to get the data it needs and the possible storage elements (SEs) where the job will store the results, it can, during the delegation to the WN, limit the proxy to be acceptable only when contacting those services.

This way if the credentials are compromised, they can only be used to contact those specific storage elements. The other Grid storage elements and services outside of the address spaces are protected and the attacker cannot cause damage to them using these credentials. Thus the possibility for damage is greatly reduced.

### 3.3  Identifiers

The object identifiers (OID) for these restrictions have been requested from the International Grid Trust Federation and await approval. The requested OIDs are iGTFProxyRestrictSource (1.2.840.113612.5.5.1.1.2.1) for the source restriction and iGTFProxyRestrictDestination (1.2.840.113612.5.5.1.1.2.2) for the target restriction.

### 3.4  Data Structure

Both of the extensions need to define a list of 0 to n namespaces containing a single internet protocol (IP) address or IP address range. RFC 5280 [2] already defines a data structure with similar properties, the NameConstraints extension. Instead of defining a new data structure and implementing it the NameContraints data structure is used and the software implementations for it are reused. The data structure contains a list of permitted subtrees and a list of excluded subtrees. The lists consist of GeneralName structures that each define a single address space. Use of three possible fields of the GeneralName have been considered: the dNSName, iPAddress and uniformResourceIdentifier. The iPAddress is a strongly preferred solution as that avoids the interaction with the DNS system when verifying the IP address with the extension. This way speed is increased by avoiding the calls to the DNS system, the reliability is increased as a crashed or slow DNS server does not affect the verification. Also the possibility to use DNS spoofing attacks is removed.

For example when the WMS submits a computing job into a CE in a site, it knows that the job will run in that site and that the proxy will not need to be delegated into another site. Therefore, as the WMS knows that the network addresses of the site are in the address space e.g. 137.138.0.0/16, it can add the source restriction using iPAddress field in the GeneralNames structure and this address space. When a service is contacted and a proxy certificate chain containing this restriction is presented as credentials, the service can find this restriction and reject the authentication attempt if the connection was opened from any other network address than the one allowed in the restriction.

## 4   Proxy Tracing

The proxy delegation tracing extensions [4] are used to add to the proxies the information where they were delegated from and where they were delegated to. Currently, when a proxy is examined, there is no way to tell where the proxy has been and how it got here, except looking at all the delegation service logs and comparing the timestamps of the delegation logs. These extensions make the tracking of the delegations through the delegation chain a trivial task and thus help to resolve the problems.

Each time there is a delegation, a new proxy is created. During this process, the source and target service unified resource identifiers (URIs) [1] are added to the proxy using these extensions. This way, whenever a proxy is looked at, the path it has traveled via delegation can be seen. This helps in debugging possible problems with credentials. It can also be used informally when investigating compromises. But it is trivial to fake long additional delegation chains that do not reflect the true delegation path and thus implicate services that have not been compromised. This can simply be done by generating new proxies locally and putting the URIs of those services as the source or target service. Thus, the extensions are not fully useful for auditing and compromise investigations as the information in them is not trustworthy.

The tracing extensions can be used to reject certificates that have passed through a compromised site. When a proxy is delegated into a site, the new delegated proxy contains a trace that was put there by the previous service that delegated it, and the services in the site that receives it does not have means to remove it. Thus, assuming a situation where the previous service is not compromised and the site is, the proxy that passed through the site contains the trace that it has been in the site and can thus be rejected as possibly compromised. There is, though, the proxy renewal service [8], that can defeat this tracing unless the renewal service carefully re-applies the trace extensions to the new proxy.

The OIDs for these extensions have been approved by the IGTF. The OIDs are iGTFProxyTracingIssuerName (1.2.840.113612.5.5.1.1.1.1) that determines where the delegation came from and the iGTFProxyTracingSubjectName (1.2.840.113612.5.5.1.1.1.2) that defines where the proxy was delegated to.

The data structure of the extensions is the GeneralNames ASN.1 structure as used in e.g. RFC 5280 [2]. While iPAddress and dNSName can be used, the URI field is the most useful of the choices. As there can be several services running in a host, even in the same TCP port, each with their own delegation system, the URI can identify the exact service that performed the delegation and thus it is the only choice that provides the exact and correct information. For the user client to the service delegation step a special URI format has been proposed. The URI is formed by using the client program name as the scheme and, as normally for HTTP URLs, the machine DNS name as the authority. The URI can then still be further completed by using the user account as the path. But the user account must be omitted e.g. in case a pseudonymity service [6] is used.

A delegation from a WMS client to a WMS service would add both the iGTFProxyTracingIssuerName and iGTFProxyTracingSubjectName extensions to the proxy being generated to identify the client and the service. The iGTFProxyTracingIssuerName and iGTFProxyTracingSubjectName could have the URIs, for example, of "WMS-client://clienthost/johndoe" and "WMS-server://wmshost:8443/examplewms" respectively.

To avoid the problem of the possibility to fake delegations locally a solution has been proposed. This solution would add a signature to this extension made by the host or service credentials. Adding this signature would prove that the proxy actually passed by that host. This way the tracing extension could be used for auditing and investigating compromises. But, so far the increase of proxy size caused by the additional signature and the performance hit caused by the signature calculations have been considered too big compared to the advantages brought by adding it.

Using the signature algorithm and signature structure in RFC 5280 [2], the signature with 2048 bit RSA key and SHA1 would add 260 bytes without counting the additional data structures needed to include it, while the actual extension without signature is 27 bytes for the data structure overhead and OID in addition to the bytes the URI string takes to encode (39 bytes in the WMS client example above).

## 5   Discussion

In the current Grids the proxies are limited when they come to the WN. Thus, the proxies that get compromised in the WN, which is the most vulnerable place for the proxies, cannot be used to submit jobs. That means that the biggest possibility of launching a massive number of jobs, which use compromised credentials to attack some services, is already prevented. But if a CE or WMS is compromised, the bigger number of credentials in these services can be used to launch attacks limited only by the capacity of the system.

Even if the proxies are limited as in the WN, they are still usable to access the SEs, information systems and other services and thus the potential for damage is great. The most valuable of these vulnerable services are the data management (DM) systems as the data in the infrastructure is the most valuable part. Thus, the implementation of these limitations should be started from the DM services giving the best return for the effort and biggest additional protection.

The RFC 3820 [10] defines an proxyInfoExtension with the possibility to define own policy languages. But this cannot be used for this work for two reasons. First, many infrastructures like EGEE still use legacy proxies and do not support the RFC 3820 proxies yet. Thus they do not understand this extension and adding this extension, which has to be critical by definition, would make the proxies fail as they fail the critical extension checks. Second, defining a policy language and using it would mean that the default inherit-all and limited policies could not be used. But these policies are the only ones implemented and supported in the current systems. Thus, using a policy language would break the interoperability with existing systems.

UNICORE [5] jobs, including input data, are signed by the client's private key providing protection from changes in the job description by intermediate gateways and avoiding the delegation of a proxy certificate at all. In respect of protection against hijacked credentials UNICORE is clearly in advantage.

The SAML-based authorization token system [9] preserves the pre-defined nature of the UNICORE system (the user has to pre-scribe which resources can be accessed and which actions can be invoked). However it already empowers the submitted job to act on the user's behalf, for example to access remote files.

The other end of the palette is the Globus style delegation model [3] with full identity delegation through proxies. It allows the usage of highly dynamic jobs, where for example the input and output data does not have to be submitted with the job but can be dynamically accessed on demand from any convenient location using the proxy credential.

Our approach tries to find a middle-ground among these models by balancing security with the ease of usability. It provides protection against the most obvious credential hijacking problem of full delegation. Furthermore, these restrictions would be automatically introduced by the job submission and delegation chain, with no explicit action from the user, but still with almost the same level of protection that a SAML-based system can provide.

## 6 Conclusion

The extensions in this paper greatly reduce the damage caused by a compromised machine, a virtual machine or a site. The extensions also help in management and recovery from a compromise providing a way to avoid user and Virtual Organization (VO) banning and thus makes the Grid more resilient to interruptions. The tracing extension is useful for debugging and a way to make it valid for auditing and compromise investigation is described.

## References

1. Berners-Lee, T., et al.: Uniform Resource Identifier (URI): Generic Syntax. IETF RFC (January 2005), http://www.ietf.org/rfc/rfc3986.txt
2. Cooper, D., et al.: RFC 5280 Internet X.509 Public Key Infrastructure Certificate and Certificate Revocation List (CRL) Profile, IETF RFC (May 2008), http://www.ietf.org/rfc/rfc5280.txt
3. Demchenko, Y., Mulmo, O., Gommans, L., de Laat, C., Wan, A.: Dynamic security context management in Grid-based application. Future Generation Computer Systems 24(5) (May 2008)
4. Groep, D.: OID for Proxy Delegation Tracing, International Grid Trust Federation OID registry (February 28, 2008), http://www.eugridpma.org/documentation/OIDProxyDelegationTracing.pdf
5. Goss-Walter, T., Letz, R., Kentemich, T., Hoppe, H.-C., Wieder, P.: An Analysis of the UNICORE Security Model, Open Grid Forum, Grid Final Document (July 18, 2003), http://www.ogf.org/documents/GFD.18.pdf
6. Hahkala, J., Mikkonen, H., Silander, M., White, J.: Requirements and Initial Design of a Grid Pseudonymity System. In: Proceedings of the 2008 High Performance Computing & Simulation Conference (HPCS 2008), Nicosia, Cyprus, June 3-6 (2008)

7. ITU-T: X.509 Information Technology - Open Systems Interconnection - The Directory: Public-key and attribute certificate frameworks (August 2005),
   http://www.itu.int/rec/T-REC-X.509-200508-I
8. Kouril, D., Basney, J.: A Credential Renewal Service for Long-Running Jobs. In: Proceedings of the 6th IEEE/ACM International Workshop on Grid Computing, November 13-14, 2005, pp. 63–68 (2005)
9. Snelling, D., van den Berge, S., Li, V.: Explicit Trust Delegation: Security for Dynamic Grids. Fujitsu Scientific & Technical Journal (FSTJ) - Special Issue on Grid Computing 40(2) (December 2004)
10. Tuecke, S., et al.: RFC 3820 Internet X.509 Public Key Infrastructure (PKI) Proxy Certificate Profile, IETF RFC (June 2004),
    http://www.ietf.org/rfc/rfc3820.txt

# An Account Policy Model for Grid Environments

David Aikema, Cameron Kiddle, and Rob Simmonds

Department of Computer Science, University of Calgary
2500 University Drive NW, Calgary, AB, Canada
{aikema,kiddlec,simmonds}@cpsc.ucalgary.ca

**Abstract.** To manage jobs in multi-institutional grid environments, an automation tool needs to know not only the characteristics of resources, but also whether
a job's credentials will be mapped to accounts on them. Credentials may be
mapped to an existing dedicated or shared account on a resource, or a new account may be created. Existing information models provide little account policy
information, even though the development of virtual organization and account
management tools means that account policies may be increasingly dynamic.
Without automation tools being able to understand account policies, projects are
unable to take full advantage of modern virtual organization and account management systems. Using advertised account policies, automation tools could consider
whether the account creation, access, expiry, and cleanup policies of a service
provider make it a good candidate for running particular jobs. Additionally, account renewals could be managed automatically using information in an expiry
policy model.

## 1 Introduction

Organizations face many challenges gaining access to sufficient computing resources.
Grid computing [1] addresses this by creating infrastructure to enable the sharing of
heterogeneous resources across institutional boundaries, and models [2, 3] have been
developed to describe the capabilities of grid resources. However, in addition to models
of resource capabilities, it is desirable to have a policy model to make service providers'
account access and lifecycle management policies clear. A model of these policies will
enable automation tools to manage accounts through their entire lifecycle and make
better, more-informed decisions about where to submit particular jobs for execution.

In the past, or in projects where few parties are in a relatively-static relationship, account policy information could be communicated offline in an informal manner. However, as projects involve larger numbers of parties, and the relationships between these
parties become more dynamic, there is an increasing need for a formal model of account
policy. A formal, machine-interpretable model also enables the creation of general-
purpose automation tools.

Signed attribute assertions, supplied to users through a service run by a virtual organization, have been used to enhance the flexibility of the authentication and authorization process [4, 5]. Attribute assertions are short-lived credentials which describe
the membership of a user in a virtual organization, as well as their role(s) and other
properties of their membership. Virtual organizations (VOs) are groups of users united

N. Abdennadher and D. Petcu (Eds.): GPC 2009, LNCS 5529, pp. 57–68, 2009.

by a common goal or a shared entitlement to access a particular set of resources. VOs also may recursively include other virtual organizations amongst their membership. Attribute-based authentication and authorization enables new accounts to be allocated without requiring manual administrative intervention. It also enables users to be mapped to differing accounts based on their active role, and aids in the revocation of access to users leaving a project or organization [6].

This paper introduces an account policy model exposing policies governing the creation of, access to, expiry of, and cleanup of accounts. The job submission process is enhanced as the model information may be used to locate service providers offering both sufficiently powerful resources and satisfactory account policies. This enables more powerful and flexible resource discovery tools to be developed. Such a model could be used by an automation tool to create accounts on grid resources in which to run a user's jobs. At present, the user would be required to inquire about a service provider's policies for establishing accounts prior to being able to employ automation tools.

Before introducing our account policy model, we first set the stage by describing existing virtual organization and account management systems in Section 2. In the same section, we also consider existing models designed for grid environments. After introducing a series of requirements in Section 3, Section 4 then describes the policy model which we created. This is followed in Section 5 by an example of how this model could be used. Finally, the paper concludes in Section 6 and suggests areas for future work.

## 2   Background

Prior work has considered ways to increase the flexibility of account management using virtual organizations. Useful tools have been developed, and we introduce some of these in Section 2.1, as examples of the sort of systems whose policies we wish to model. Then, in Section 2.2, we examine existing models that have been developed for grid environments to determine whether or not these provide a model of account creation, access, renewal, and revocation processes.

### 2.1   Virtual Organization and Account Management Software

Grid environments often use X.509 certificates [7] for authentication without requiring the presenter of the certificate to have a prior relationship with a service provider. This has resulted in the development of systems which use template accounts. Template accounts [6] are accounts that are dynamically assigned to users logging into the system. It allows groups of users to access the system, without requiring that accounts be pre-created for all users who might attempt to connect to this system. Tools such as gridmapdir [8] allow users with certificate distinguished names listed in a configuration file to gain access to a template account on a system. Other tools integrate with virtual organization management systems to provide more-generic attribute-based authentication and authorization. VOMS, the Virtual Organization Membership Service [9], can be used to administer a virtual organization, adding users, placing them in groups, and associating them with role and capability information. The Grid User Managment System (GUMS) [4] can be used to provide users access to a system based upon an assertion signed by a VOMS server, containing VO attributes.

In addition to VOMS and GUMS, other tools have also been developed for attribute-based authentication and authorization in grid environments. Shibboleth [10] which has been widely deployed in academic institutions to provide attribute-based access to web databases has been the target of numerous extensions to grid environments [11]. Of these, the most promising is GridShib [5]. Other projects including CAS [12], PRIMA [13], Akenti [14], and PERMIS [15] have also been developed. These software packages use a variety of techniques to encode attributes, including SAML [16] and XACML [17] as well as various proprietary mechanisms.

## 2.2  Existing Models

Creating models for grid environments has been the focus of some prior work. However, the resulting models focus on resource capabilities rather than authentication and authorization. Nordugrid [18] developed an LDAP-based model providing basic information such as account names and a fixed lifetime for job session directories. The Japanese NAREGI project [19] extended DTMF's Common Information Model (CIM) [2] to grid environments, but the broad focus of CIM makes it complex to work with. CIM allows an abstract "Account Management Service" to be assigned as controller of accounts but provides no information about account lifecycles beyond a boolean flag to indicate whether an idle account might be deactivated. The GLUE schema [3] was developed specifically for grid environments, and it focuses on describing sites, services, and computing and storage resources, rather than access control and lifecycle information. In earlier work we introduced the GRC model [20] which includes information about file lifetimes, allowing both rigid and flexible lifetime representations. However, this model is also lacking information regarding credentials required to access systems.

The Enterprise Grid Alliance (EGA) model [21] is the grid model most focused on lifecycle information. It focuses on the provisioning of resources, and describes a number of states in which resources can be, but it does not describe how the transitions between the states might be initiated. This abstract model is being extended by the OGF Reference Model Working Group in order to produce a concrete, formal lifecycle schema. However, this work is in an early stage, and also does not include information about how to initiate lifecycle transitions or the credentials required to access systems.

# 3   Requirements

An account policy model addresses a number of challenges. Knowledge of the policies connected with an account to which a job is mapped may determine whether this account is suitable for use. At present, account policies must be manually determined by users of a system. By introducing an account policy model, automation tools may be built which are able to determine these policies without manual intervention. Thus, access to resources may be improved while lessening complexity for the end-user.

Many aspects of account policy are relevant to managing job submissions. What credentials are required to gain access to an account? Will an existing account be used or a new one created? Will privacy concerns require the use of a dedicated account, or is an account shared by multiple users and/or projects sufficient? Will tasks, such as renewal or the creation of a backup copy, need to be scheduled? Can the account renewal process be automated? Will an account be active long enough to complete a job? These are some of the questions we formalize in the following requirements.

First, it is necessary to know what credentials are needed to create accounts and, later, to access them. A user may be part of several groups in a VO and may also be able to assume one of several distinct roles, e.g., production, testing, or postanalysis. What combination of attributes will map to a particular account?

Second, it must be known whether it is possible to create an account on a new resource that is a good candidate for a job. Service providers may own multiple resources but may provide a particular user with access to only a subset, leaving certain resources off-limits. As well, the account management system in use must support dynamic account creation to allow new accounts to be created on the fly. It must be possible to determine on which of the service provider's systems accounts may be created, as well as the properties of such accounts.

Third, the relationships between accounts should be understood. Distinct accounts on a system may have access to shared storage through membership in a common system group, thus minimizing duplication of common files. On the other hand, an account may give a user simultaneous access to multiple systems with no common filesystem.

Fourth, to ensure that a job can be completed and its output be retrieved prior to being deleted, details of account expiration policies should also be known. An expiration policy may also provide a means by which accounts can be renewed. Doing so may require that a renewal service be contacted, or information at a service be updated. This service may be periodically queried to determine whether to extend account lifetimes.

Finally, knowledge of how account cleanup occurs may determine what tasks will be performed near an account's expiry date. An expiration policy may be soft, providing minimum guarantees, or hard, with a fixed lifetime, and the system may treat each of these cases differently. The service provider may also take action. For example, it could create an archival copy of the account's contents and upload it to a VO-managed data repository or make it available for download by the former account holder.

In order for effective use to be made of its resources, a service provider should make available information describing its systems. It must be clear how accounts may be created and what credentials are required to create and access them. Knowledge of the relationships between accounts enables efficient resource sharing, and descriptions of expiry processes ensures that expiry will not unexpectedly occur. When an account eventually expires, however, a model of the service provider's cleanup processes will ensure that appropriate actions may be taken to preserve key data. With a formal model of these processes, automation tools may be developed which make more effective use of resources.

## 4    Model Overview

This section introduces a model created to fulfill the requirements outlined in Section 3. An overview of the key classes in the model, and their relationships, are found in Figure 1. The model is intended to act in conjunction with existing resource models, augmenting them with account policies. It builds on some of our earlier work [22, 23].

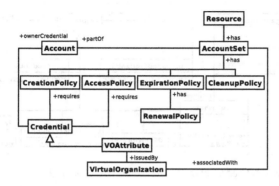

**Fig. 1.** Overview of the account policy model

All figures throughout the paper are presented in the form of UML class diagrams. In these diagrams classes in the model are represented by boxes. A line joining two boxes indicates a relationship between the classes which is described by a label. For example, in Figure 1 a *VOAttribute* is part of a relationship, being "issuedBy" a *VirtualOrganization*. Lines with an open triangle at one end indicate a subclass relationship. In Figure 1, for example, a *VOAttribute* is a subclass or type of *Credential*.

The following sections provide more information about many of the classes in Figure 1. In Section 4.1 we first present a credential model. This credential model is able to describe attributes that a virtual organization may issue, and we also represent the virtual organizations themselves. Then, in Section 4.2, we address the question of how to represent accounts. We also address the issue of how to describe connections between accounts. Finally, in Section 4.3, we discuss the policies which apply to the account lifecycle, including creation, access, expiry, and cleanup.

## 4.1  Credentials and VOs

To gain access to a resource, credentials must be submitted alongside job requests. These credentials, in combination with other attributes of the job request, may result in the job being mapped to an existing account. Alternatively, a new account may be created under which to execute the job.

A variety of types of credentials may be represented in the model. We illustrate our credential model in Figure 2. The model describes X.509 certificates, signed by a certificate authority, in an instance of the *X509Certificate* class. Using an instance of the *VOAttribute* class, attributes issued by a virtual organization may also be represented as credentials. Other types of credentials such as usernames, passwords, as well as credentials stored in MyProxy [24], or other credentials management services, may also be represented. Any combination of these credentials may be required.

Attributes signed by a virtual organization are represented as (name, value) pairs and associated with an explicitly modelled virtual organization, which is responsible for issuing the attribute assertion. As mentioned in Section 2, different virtual organization management systems represent attributes in different ways, but (name, value) pairs are

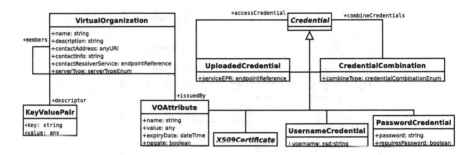

**Fig. 2.** Credential model, including virtual organizations

a way in which each of these representations may be encoded. The virtual organization model is presented in Figure 2 alongside the credential model.

The model allows for flexibility in the modelling of virtual organizations. VOs may be composed hierarchically, as in the case of a Shibboleth federation, or lack such a structure, as in a virtual organization using a VOMS servers. New VO management systems may be integrated into the model by extending the *serverType* enumeration in the *VirtualOrganization* class. Properties of these systems, such as the server location from which attribute assertions may be obtained, are stored in instances of the *KeyValuePair* class.

## 4.2   Accounts and Account Grouping

When a job is executed on a system, it may be mapped to a preexisting account. Alternatively, it may execute in a new account if submitted to a system which supports template accounts. In systems which do not preserve state or usage history in account form, access to the system may be seen as analogous to having a freshly-created, short-lived account assigned to each job submitted.

In Figure 3 we present a model of accounts and account grouping. In this model, the *Account* class contains basic information about an account. This includes a name as well as a set of credentials to represent the primary owner of the account. In Section 4.1 we introduced a credential model to represent these credentials. In order to minimize the amount of redundant information published, the model associates most account policy

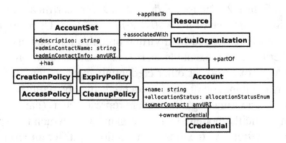

**Fig. 3.** Account and Account Grouping classes

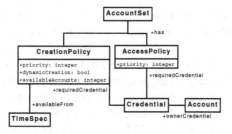

**Fig. 4.** Creation and Access Policy classes

information with an account set, rather than with the individual accounts themselves. We will discuss these policies in greater detail in the next section.

### 4.3   Account Policies

As mentioned in Section 4.2, our model pushes much of the complexity of account modelling into an account policy class. In this section we focus on how to describe the policies relating to key aspects of an account's lifecycle. First account creation is discussed, and then the issue of who can access the account is addressed. Following this, we focus on expiry policies and then on how to describe cleanup actions that a service provider may initiate when an account is revoked.

**Creation.** The account creation policy class is illustrated in Figure 4. An account may be allocated when the set of user credentials specified in an instance of the creation policy class are presented to the system, possibly by an automation tool. The ordering with which the account management system used by the service provider evaluates account creation and access policies may be specified by setting the priority value of the policies. If a user requires two accounts, e.g. one for production use and another for development purposes, he or she may be able to override the mapping of a job to an existing account by explicitly requesting a new account.

This creation policy instance may also specify additional information about the availability of accounts. It may describe whether accounts can be created dynamically to meet user demand, whether accounts are drawn from a pool, or, if no accounts are listed as available, that a new account cannot be automatically assigned. An additional *availableFrom* attribute may specify the time at which the agreement that established this account set begins. Alternatively, a future date may be set if a new account cannot currently be allocated.

Like several other policy classes, the creation policy employs a model called *Time-Spec* [22] which we developed to provide a very flexible, yet comprehensible, means of describing the timing of events. The model allows event times to be specified both in absolute terms or relative to the time of some other event. A time may also be computed from the minimum, maximum, or average of other times. Times may be calculated based upon the end of a renewal policy or the expiry of another account on the system, optionally padded with an additional time interval. Times may also be calculated based upon statistics or metrics associated with various model elements such as resources or account sets. Event times, numbers, and time intervals may all be recorded as statistics.

**Access.** The *AccessPolicy* class is illustrated in Figure 4. It contains information about the credentials needed to access an existing account. Based on the credentials found in the model, an automation tool could determine which of its available credentials to present to the system in order to gain access. It could also discover whether the account is a shared account, requiring only that a set of VO attributes be presented to access it, or if the account is dedicated, requiring an X.509 certificate with a particular distinguished name to access.

The credentials of an account owner are represented in the *Account* class as an attribute. A special instance of the *Credential* class, *OwnerCredential*, exists which represents these credentials in access policies. Thus, it is possible for a compact access policy representation in the access policy class, while retaining significant flexibility. By using this special *OwnerCredential* instance when specifying access policies, the amount of redundant information published is reduced and the consistency of policy across an account set is indicated.

As mentioned in the previous section, creation and access policies are evaluated in the specified priority order.

**Expiry.** The expiration policies, and associated renewal mechanisms, are illustrated in Figure 5. Soft and hard accounts lifetimes can both be specified indicating, respectively, minimum and maximum lifetime guarantees. The ability to request account termination is modelled as a revocation service. This allows behaviours, similar to the immediate and scheduled termination operations in the WS-ResourceLifetime standard [25], to be specified.

A large portion of our expiry model addresses ways of renewing accounts. There are two types of renewal processes which are represented in our model. The first of these, a *ManualRenewal*, indicates that a user or automation tool can contact a grid service to request an extension of a defined length. It also defines a list of input parameters to be

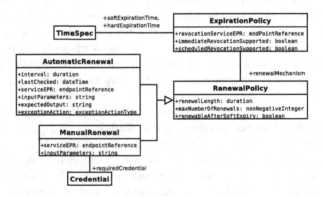

**Fig. 5.** Account Expiration and Renewal Policies

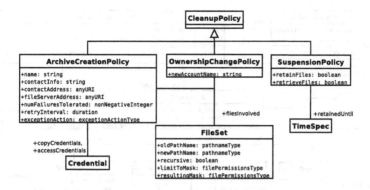

**Fig. 6.** Cleanup Policy model

passed to the service to represent the account and the parameters of the extension. We also model *AutomaticRenewal*s, a second type of renewal mechanism. An *AutomaticRenewal* occurs, transparent to the user, as an activity initiated by the service provider. A service provider could query a grid service, typically operated by the virtual organization, at a defined interval, as outlined in the model, to determine whether or not the grid service's output indicates that the account is still needed.

The renewal policy information published by a service provider may be used by an automation tool to request account extensions, as described in the *ManualRenewal* class. It could also inform an automation tool that it should update the information published by a grid service to ensure that accounts which are still needed will remain active when the service provider performs an *AutomaticRenewal*.

**Cleanup.** When an account on a system is about to expire, often users perform certain actions. When users receive notice that their account is about to expire they will typically login to the system to make a backup of their files or transfer files to another account on the system which still needs them. Rather than requiring that the user perform these typical actions, a service provider might provide better service by performing such actions themselves and describing these actions using the *CleanupPolicy* model.

The cleanup policy model which we propose describes actions which the service provider will initiate at the time of expiry. We provide three options, although these may be applied in different combinations to different directories in which the user has files stored. We include a model to describe ownership change actions, in which a service provider may change the ownership of some or all of the files contained in an account being revoked. This may preserve key files, used by other members of the virtual organization, when an account is revoked. In addition, we also model how a service provider may create an archive of the files in the account. This archive may potentially either be made available to the user for download, or may be uploaded to a server managed by the user's virtual organization. A third option which we allow for is account suspension. When an account is suspended, files may be retained, and potentially made available for download, but jobs may no longer be executed in the account.

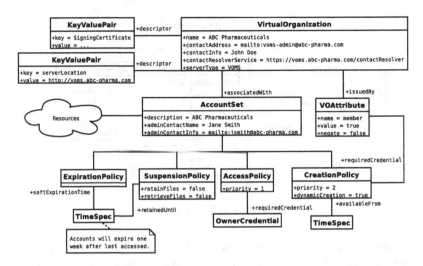

**Fig. 7.** Example of a service provider offering "permanent" user accounts

## 5   Example

One example of a situation in which the model may be used is depicted in Figure 7. It illustrates how a service provider may use the model to describe its policy wherein accounts are available to any member of a particular virtual organization but will expire after a period of inactivity. In the figure, a virtual organization is shown, using a VOMS server to sign attributes. In order to access the specified resources, an attribute assertion indicating that the requester is a member of the virtual organization must first be signed by the specified VOMS server.

When an automation tools uses the credentials of a new user to submit a job to the system, a new account will be assigned as the creation policy in the lower right of the diagram indicates that accounts are dynamically created. The resulting account will inherit account policy from the account set, described at the centre of the diagram. The user's credentials will be assigned as the owner of the account and the same credentials will be required to access the account. When future attempts are made to access the system using the same credentials supplied with the initial job submission, these will be mapped to the existing account, as the access priority defined in the access policy is higher than the creation priority.

Following a week-long period of inactivity, as specified by the *TimeSpec* instance [22] in the lower right of the diagram, accounts may be suspended and the files contained within them deleted. As specified in the *SuspensionPolicy* on the right-hand side of the diagram, files will not be retained for later retrieval.

## 6   Conclusion and Future Work

The model presented here facilitates the sharing of information about account policies and renders the timing of account lifecycle transitions understandable. It also describes the authentication and authorization mechanisms used to secure access to accounts. Using the information presented in this model, account creation, access, renewal, and revocation policies are expressed in such a way that tools can be developed which are able to parse this information and use it to make better resource selection decisions. Thus the ability of automation tools to discover suitable resources can be extended. In addition, automation tools are able to address a larger scope than simply resource discovery. For example, tools could be developed which automate periodic account renewals and initiate appropriate actions as an account is nearing expiry.

Future work could expand the model to address virtualization. Explicit modelling of virtual machine managed environments could be incorporated into the model, as this is a topic which has gained much attention in the past few years. The use of virtualization removes the need for a fixed mapping between accounts and physical resources. The challenges of modelling policies governing virtual machine provisioning closely parallel those encountered in account creation and access policies.

In addition, development work could extend the capabilities of existing tools which perform resource discovery to incorporate the policies described in this model such that they can make better resource selections. Additionally, incorporating elements in the model to describe the cost incurred by holding an account may also be worthy of further exploration.

# References

[1] Foster, I., Kesselman, C. (eds.): The grid: blueprint for a new computing infrastructure. Morgan Kaufmann Publishers Inc., San Francisco (1999)
[2] Distributed Management Task Force, Inc. CIM Schema version 2.20 (November 2008), http://www.dmtf.org/standards/cim
[3] Andreozzi, S. (ed.): GLUE specification v2.0 (revision 4 after public comment) (February 2009), http://forge.ggf.org/sf/projects/glue-wg
[4] Baker, R., Yu, D., Wlodek, T.: A model for grid user management. In: Computing in High Energy and Nuclear Physics (2003)
[5] Welch, V., Barton, T., Keahey, K., Siebenlist, F.: Attributes, anonymity, and access: Shibboleth and globus integration to facilitate grid collaboration. In: 4th Annual PKI R&D Workshop (2005)
[6] Hacker, T.J., Athey, B.D.: A methodology for account management in grid computing environments. In: Proceedings of the 2nd International Workshop on Grid Computing, pp. 133–144 (2001)
[7] Foster, I., Kesselman, C., Tsudik, G., Tuecke, S.: A security architecture for computational grids. In: Proceedings of the 5th ACM Conference on Computer and Communications Security, pp. 83–92 (1998)
[8] gridmapdir (2002), http://www.gridsite.org/gridmapdir/
[9] Alfieri, R., Cecchini, R., Ciaschini, V., dell'Agnello, L., Frohner, A., Lorentey, K., Spataro, F.: From gridmap-file to VOMS: Managing authorization in a grid environment. Future Generation Computer Systems 21(4), 549–558 (2005)
[10] Scavo, T., Cantor, S.: Shibboleth architecture technical overview (June 2005), http://shibboleth.internet2.edu/docs/draft-mace-shibboleth-tech-overview-latest.pdf

[11] Gietz, P., Grimm, C., Groper, R., Haase, M., Makedanz, S., Pfeiffenberger, H., Schiffers, M.: IVOM work package 1: Evaluation of international Shibboleth-based VO management projects (v 1.2) (June 2007), http://www.d-grid.de/

[12] Pearlman, L., Welch, V., Foster, I., Kesselman, C., Tuecke, S.: A community authorization service for group collaboration. In: Proceedings of the 3rd International Workshop on Policies for Distributed Systems and Networks, pp. 50–59 (2002)

[13] Lorch, M., Adams, D.B., Kafura, D., Koneni, M.S.R., Rathi, A., Shah, S.: The PRIMA system for privilege management, authorization and enforcement in grid environments. In: Proceedings of the 4th International Workshop on Grid Computing, pp. 109–116 (2003)

[14] Thompson, M., Essiari, A., Keahey, K., Welch, V., Lang, S., Liu, B.: Fine-Grained Authorization for Job and Resource Management Using Akenti and the Globus Toolkit. ArXiv Computer Science e-prints (June 2003)

[15] Chadwick, D., Otenko, A.: The PERMIS X.509 role based privilege management infrastructure. Future Generation Computer Systems 19(23), 277–289 (2003)

[16] Cantor, S., Kemp, J., Philpott, R., Maler, E. (eds.): Assertions and protocols for the oasis security assertion markup language. OASIS Standard (March 2005)

[17] Moses, T. (ed.): eXtensible Access Control Markup Language (XACML) Version 2.0. OASIS Standard (2005)

[18] Nordic Testbed for Wide Area Computing and Data Handling. Nordugrid information system (September 2002),
http://www.nordugrid.org/documents/ng-infosys.pdf

[19] Hitachi Ltd. NAREGI Resource Description Schema Specification and Relational Data Model (2007),
http://forge.ogf.org/sf/docman/do/downloadDocument/
projects.glue-wg/docman.root.background.specifications/
doc14300

[20] Kiddle, C., Kivi, D., Simmonds, R.: Model-driven automation in grid environments. In: Proceedings of the 4th International Symposium on Frontiers in Networking with Applications (2008)

[21] Enterprise Grid Alliance. Reference Model and Use Cases v1.5 (2006),
http://www.ogf.org/gf/docs/egadocs.php

[22] Aikema, D.: VO-centric account management. M.Sc. thesis, University of Calgary (2007)

[23] Aikema, D.: A model of account access control and lifecycle management. Technical Report 2007-885-37, Department of Computer Science, University of Calgary (December 2007)

[24] Novotny, J., Tuecke, S., Welch, V.: An online credential repository for the grid: MyProxy. In: Proceedings of the 10th IEEE International Symposium on High Performance Distributed Computing, pp. 104–111 (2001)

[25] Srinivasan, L., Banks, T.: Web Services Resource Lifetime 1.2 (WS-ResourceLifetime) (January 2006), http://docs.oasis-open.org/
wsrf/wsrf-ws_resource_lifetime-1.2-spec-os.pdf

# Providing Security of Real Time Data Intensive Applications on Grids Using Dynamic Scheduling

Rafiqul Islam, Toufiq Hasan, and Md. Ashaduzzaman

Computer Science and Engineering Discipline,
Khulna University, Khulna-9208, Bangladesh
{dmri1978,toufiq_riad1045,ashaduzzaman29}@yahoo.com

**Abstract.** In this paper we have proposed a dynamic real time scheduling algorithm named SARDIG, which is capable of scheduling real time data intensive applications and provides security for real time data intensive applications running on grids. We have presented a grid architecture, which describes the scheduling framework of the security attentive real time data intensive applications running on data grids. In addition, we have introduced a mathematical model for the scheduling policy to provide optimum security for real time data intensive applications. The time complexity of the SARDIG algorithm has been analyzed to show the efficiency of the algorithm. Simulation result shows that the SARDIG algorithm provides better performance and security than two existing scheduling algorithms.

**Keywords:** Security, algorithm, data grid, scheduling, real time, application.

## 1 Introduction

A grid is a collection of geographically dispersed computing resources, providing a large virtual computing system to users [3]. Data Grid is a grid computing system that deals with the sharing and management of large amounts of heterogeneous data and data intensive applications are those, which use large data storages distributed on data grids. Nowadays it becomes crucial to use scheduling strategies to manage and schedule the real time data intensive applications running on grids because grids are emerging as future platforms for large-scale computation and solving data intensive problems.

Real time applications are those, which depend on deadlines. In real time systems each job has a deadline before or at which it should be completed. In this system completion of a job after its deadline is considered useless. Thus, it is critical to meet the deadline requirements for real time applications.

Real time data intensive applications with security requirements are emerging in various fields including government, science, and business. Data grids often deal with large amount of sensitive data, which requires special protection against unauthorized access and various security threats. In addition, real time data intensive applications running on data grids require protection to meet their security needs, so it is highly important to fulfill security requirements of both data and application. Example of

N. Abdennadher and D. Petcu (Eds.): GPC 2009, LNCS 5529, pp. 69–78, 2009.

real time data intensive application is the Real-time Observatories, Applications, and Data management Network (ROADNet) [8].

There had been some previous efforts to ensure security of real time applications on grids through dynamic scheduling proposed by Xie and Qin [2] and ensuring security of the data intensive applications running on data grids [7]. SAHA [7] is designed to schedule data intensive application but does not consider real time applications. SAREG [2] provides solutions for real time applications but does not fully consider data intensive application scheduling. Unfortunately, it is not possible to simply combine these two algorithms to support both data intensive applications and real time scheduling so there is no way to readily accomplish both tasks by directly extending either. Furthermore, neither algorithm provides sufficient consideration for security for real time data intensive applications.

To provide security with proper scheduling for real time data intensive applications on data grids we have proposed a security attentive real time data intensive scheduling algorithm for grids called SARDIG, which schedules the real time data intensive applications and provides security by enhancing the security level. To demonstrate this, we have introduced a security gain function to measure the security level enhancement afforded for a job on a grid site.

The time complexity of our SARDIG algorithm is shown to be bounded by the product of the number of site ($m$), the number of jobs ($n$), and the log of the number of possible security levels ($k$) (i.e. $O(mnlogk)$). Finally, our simulation result shows that SARDIG algorithm provides better performance and enhanced security.

## 2   Other Related Work

Recently grid security services have drawn much attention because security has become a baseline requirement. The task scheduling algorithm MINMIN [2] provides security by randomly selecting security service levels. Like the MINMIN algorithm, SUFFERAGE [2] and EDF [5] algorithms randomly choose security service levels. So security quality cannot be optimized with these algorithms.

Xie and Qin [6] propose a security middleware model for real-time applications on Grids. The security middleware model creates a platform to exploit various security services to enhance the grid application security. This middleware model implements the SAREG algorithm.

Another algorithm named JobRandom [4] is a data grid scheduling algorithm where security services are not considered. This algorithm only considers random site selection for job allocation. Another data grid scheduling algorithm named JobData-Present [4] differs from JobRandom algorithm by submitted each job to the site that holds the job's data set.

## 3   Grid Architecture for Security Attentive Real Time Data Intensive Jobs

Here we propose a grid architecture that will consist of $n$ sites. Each site is denoted by $M_i$, where $1 \leq i \leq n$. They are connected with a wide area network. Each site consists

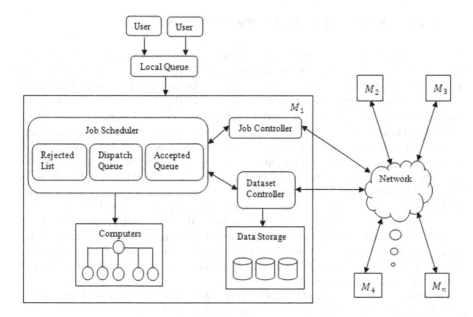

**Fig. 1.** Grid architecture for a data grid

of a job scheduler, job controller, dataset controller, data storage infrastructure, and computers. Each job scheduler is comprised of an accepted queue, dispatch queue, and rejected list. Figure 1 shows the architecture of our data grid. To provide security for the job and data grid's data sets each site has three security services. The security services are confidentiality, integrity, and authentication.

In the grid each site has a local queue, where incoming jobs from local users are listed and which transfers the jobs to the job scheduler of the local site one by one. The job scheduler checks whether the incoming job can be completed within its deadline while meeting the security requirements at each site on the data grid. If the job's deadline can be met, then the job scheduler uses the security gain function to measure the enhancement of security level achieved by each site that is capable of meeting the deadline. The job scheduler will schedule the job to the accepted queue of the site, capable of achieving highest (most enhanced) security level. The job scheduler will send the job to the rejected list on the job's submission site, if the job cannot be completed within its deadline on any site on the data grid. After scheduling the job, the job scheduler will move it from accepted queue to the dispatch queue. In the dispatch queue the security level of the accepted job is enhanced and dispatched to the designated site on the grid. The function of the job controller is to transfer the job to the remote site or fetch the job from the remote site according to the job scheduler's policy. The dataset controller transfers the data to the remote site from the local data storage or fetches the data from the remote site's data storage conformant to the job scheduler's policy.

## 4 Security Services for Real Time Data Intensive Jobs

Security is achieved at the cost of performance degradation [2]. It is necessary to measure the security level of various security services in such a way that overall security is maximized without degrading performance. Xie and Qin [2] proposed the security overhead model where security overhead is denoted as a function of security level and indicates the time required to provide security for a certain amount of data.

Three security services are considered to provide security for real time data intensive applications. They are confidentiality, integrity, and authentication. Confidentiality can be provided with cryptographic algorithms. There are nine cryptographic algorithms considered for each site. These cryptographic algorithms are SEAL, RC4, Blowfish, Knufu/Khafre, RC5, Rijndael, DES, IDEA, and 3DES [2]. Each cryptographic algorithm is assigned a corresponding security level from 0.1 to 0.9. For example security level 0.9 denotes the cryptographic algorithm 3DES, which is defined to be the maximum security level and provides the strongest security among all the cryptographic algorithms. Conversely, the security level 0.1 denotes the cryptographic algorithm SEAL, which is the minimum security level and providing the weakest security among these algorithms.

To provide integrity related security service for each site on grids, there are ten hash functions considered. These hash functions are MD4, MD5, RIPEMD, RIPEMD-128, SHA-1, RIPEMD-160, Tiger, Snefru-128, MD2, and Snefru-256 [2]. Each hash function is assigned a corresponding security level from 0.1 to 1.0 where security level 0.1 denotes the weakest hash function (MD4) and security level 1.0 denotes the strongest hash function (Snefru-256).

To provide authentication related security service for each site on grids various authentication methods are considered. These are HMAC-MD5, HMAC-SHA-1, and CBC-MAC-AES [2]. Corresponding security level for each authentication method are defined to be at 0.3, 0.6, and 0.9 respectively; where security level 0.3 denotes the weakest authentication method (HMAC-MD5) and security level 0.9 denotes the strongest authentication method (CBC-MAC-AES).

The SARDIG algorithm provides optimum security by enhancing the security level for the real time data intensive applications. The SARDIG algorithm enhances the security by selecting the optimum security level that will successfully meet the deadline. Security services demanding higher security levels requires more time than those with lower demands. Thus, for real time data intensive applications, it is not always possible to naively select the maximum security level for each security service without considering its impact on meeting the deadline.

## 5 Scheduling Strategy of Real Time Data Intensive Jobs for Security Enhancement

A security attentive real-time data intensive job can be specified as a set of vector parameters such as, $J_i = (e_i, p_i, d_i, l_i, SC_i, SD_i)$, where $J_i$ denotes the $i$th job, $e_i$ is the execution time, $p_i$ is the number of machines required for the job $J_i$, $d_i$ is the deadline, and $l_i$ denotes the amount of data (measured in KB) to be protected, $SC_i$ measures the security level for job's application, $SD_i$ measures the security level for job's data set, and $1 \leq i \leq n$. Fortunately, $e_i$ can be estimated by code profiling and statistical prediction [1].

The security level for a job's application can be expressed by a vector, $SC_i = (sc_i^1, sc_i^2, \ldots sc_i^q )$, where $q$ is the number of required security services and $sc_i^v$ denotes the security level of the $v^{th}$ security service for the $i^{th}$ job. Similarly, the security level for the job's data set can be expressed by a vector, $SD_i = (sd_i^1, sd_i^2, \ldots sd_i^q )$, where $sd_i^v$ denotes the security level of the $v^{th}$ security service for the $i^{th}$ job.

We introduce the security value function, $SV$ to measure the security level for a job on a site. The security value function, $SV$: $sc_i$, $sd_i \rightarrow R$, where $R$ is the set of positive real numbers can be expressed by the following equation:

$$SV(sc_i, sd_i) = \sum_{v=1}^{q} (w_i^v sc_i^v + w_i^{v+q} sd_i^v) . \tag{1}$$

$$\text{where } 0 \leq w_i^v \leq 1, \sum_{v=1}^{q} w^v = 1, \text{ and } v\epsilon\{a,c,g\}.$$

Here $w_i^v$ is the weight of the $v^{th}$ security service for the $i^{th}$ job's application, $w_i^{v+q}$ is the weight of the $v^{th}$ security service for the $i^{th}$ job's data set and $a$, $c$, $g$ denotes authentication, confidentiality, and integrity. Weights are used to assign relative priorities to the required security services.

To compute the optimum security level for a job on the site we can use the security value function in the following form:

$$SV_{opt}(sc_i, sd_i) = maximize \left\{ \sum_{v=1}^{q} (w_i^v sc_i^v + w_i^{v+q} sd_i^v) \right\}. \tag{2}$$

$$\text{subject to } \begin{cases} sc_i^v \leq \max(sc_i^v), \\ sd_i^v \leq \max(sd_i^v), \\ f_i \leq d_i . \end{cases}$$

where $SV_{opt}(sc_i, sd_i)$ denotes the optimum security value function, which calculates the highest possible security level within the deadline. Here $f_i$ is the finish time of job $J_i$ and $\max(sc_i^v )$ is the maximum security level of $i^{th}$ job's application and $\max(sd_i^v)$ is the maximum security level of $i^{th}$ job's data set.

Each job submitted to a grid site will have its minimum security level requested by the user for job's application and its data set. To calculate the requested minimum security value, $SV_{req}$ $(sc_i, sd_i)$ for a job on a site we can use the following equation:

$$SV_{req} (sc_i, sd_i) = \sum_{v=1}^{q} (w_i^v sc_i^v + w_i^{v+q} sd_i^v) . \tag{3}$$

$$\text{subject to } \begin{cases} sc_i^v = req(sc_i^v), \\ sd_i^v = req(sd_i^v), \\ f_i \leq d_i . \end{cases}$$

where $req(sc_i^v)$ is the requested minimum security level of $i^{th}$ job's application, and $req(sd_i^v)$ is the requested minimum security level of $i^{th}$ job's data set.

To measure the enhancement of security level for a job on a site we devise a security gain function, which calculates the difference between optimum security value provided by the site and the requested minimum security value for the job. The security gain function can be expressed as follows:

$$SG_i\,(sc_i, sd_i) = SV_{opt}(sc_i, sd_i) - SV_{req}(sc_i, sd_i).  \tag{4}$$

where $SG_i$ denotes the security gain function of job $J_i$.

## 6  Security Overhead of Real Time Data Intensive Jobs

Xie and Qin [7] propose four conditions when scheduling real time data intensive jobs. The *first condition* is that input data is locally available and processing is performed on the local site. The security overhead is calculated as the sum of the time spent in securing the application code and its data set. The security overhead can be denoted as $C_1^v$. The *second condition* considered is that locally executed jobs accessing a remote data sets via the networks. The security overhead is calculated as the sum of the time spent in securing the application code, its data set, and transferring the remote data set to local site. The security overhead is denoted as $C_2^v$. The *third condition* is to compute the security overhead of a remotely executed job that accesses its data set on a local site. Thus, the application code needs to be transmitted to the remote site where the data is stored. The security overhead is calculated as the sum of the time spent in securing the application code, its data set, and transferring the job to the remote site. The security overhead is denoted as $C_3^v$. Finally, the *fourth condition* calculates the security overhead of a job executed on a remote site to which the job's data set is moved. Thus, the application code and the data must be transmitted to the remote site. In this case, the security overhead is calculated as the sum of the time spent in securing the application code, its data set, and transferring both the data set and the job to the remote site. The security overhead is denoted as $C_4^v$. We can calculate the total security overhead for $i^{th}$ job using the following equation:

$$C_i = \sum_{v \in \{a, c, g\}} (X_1^v C_1^v + X_2^v C_2^v + X_3^v C_3^v + X_4^v C_4^v).  \tag{5}$$

where $X_1^v, X_2^v, X_3^v$ and $X_4^v$ are two step functions. $X_1^v = 1$ and others $= 0$ if the first condition is satisfied. $X_2^v = 1$ and others $= 0$ if the second condition is satisfied. $X_3^v = 1$ and others $= 0$ if the third condition is satisfied. Finally, $X_4^v = 1$ and others $= 0$ if the fourth condition is satisfied.

## 7  Deadline and Earliest Start Time

Xie and Qin [2] also described how to generate an appropriate randomly selected deadline. The deadline assignment is controlled by a deadline base or laxity, denoted as $\beta$. The Job's deadline is generated as follows:

$$d_i = a_i + e_i + c_i^{max} + \beta.  \tag{6}$$

where $d_i$ is the deadline, $a_i$ is the arrival time, $e_i$ is the execution time, $c_i^{max}$ is the maximum security overhead of the job. The maximum security overhead denotes the time required to provide security using the maximum security level.

The finish time $f_i$ is defined as the time required to complete the execution of the job. The finish time can be calculated as follows:

$$f_i = a_i + e_i + c_i . \tag{7}$$

where $a_i$ is the arrival time, $e_i$ is the execution time, and $c_i$ is the security overhead of the job.

The earliest start time $s_i$ of the job $J_i$ can be calculated as the sum of the finish time $f_j$ of the running job, the overall execution time $e_l$ and security overhead $c_l$ of the waiting jobs assigned to site $M_j$ prior to the arrival of job $J_i$. Thus, the earliest start time is calculated as:

$$s_i = f_j + \sum_{J_l \in M_j} (e_l + c_l) . \tag{8}$$

where the earliest start time $s_i$ denotes the starting time of a job $J_i$ at site $M_j$.

## 8  The SARDIG Scheduling Algorithm

The name SARDIG is derived from the term Security Attentive Real time Data Intensive application on Grids. The SARDIG algorithm schedules the real time data intensive applications and provides the highest possible security level.

| |
|---|
| 1.  **For** each job $J_i$ on site $M_j$ **do** |
| 2.       Compute the earliest start time of job $J_i$ on site $M_j$ |
| 3.       Compute the requested security overhead of job $J_i$ |
| 4.       **If** submitted job meets its deadline on site $M_j$ **then** |
| 5.            Compute requested security value of job $J_i$ |
| 6.            **For** each security service do |
| 7.                 Calculate security overhead of job $J_i$ |
| 8.                 Find optimum security level using binary search within the deadline. |
| 9.            **End for** |
| 10.           Use security level obtained from step 8 and Calculate security gain for job $J_i$ on site $M_j$ |
| 11.      **Else**  job $J_i$ is rejected from site $M_j$ |
| 12.  **End for** |
| 13.  **For** each job $J_i$ do |
| 14.       Find the site $M_j$ where security gain function $SG$ is maximum |
| 15.       Optimize the security level of the job $J_i$ |
| 16.       Dispatch job $J_i$ to the designated site $M_j$ |
| 17.  **End for** |

**Fig. 2.** The SARDIG scheduling algorithm

For each submitted job, the SARDIG algorithm checks whether the job meets its deadline and achieves the requested minimum security level. If the job can be completed within its deadline at the minimum security level, then the SARDIG algorithm selects the highest possible security level using binary search for each site on the grid while ensuring deadlines are met. It then calculates the security level enhancement for the job using security gain function.

If the job cannot be completed within its deadline, then SARDIG algorithm rejects the job from that site. The algorithm will apply this procedure to each site. After calculating the security level enhancement for each site for a particular job, the algorithm identifies the site where the security gain is highest. The algorithm then schedules the job to that site. After enhancing the security level and finishing the execution of the scheduled job, the SARDIG algorithm dispatches the job to the designated site. If the job cannot be completed within its deadline at any site on grid, the SARDIG algorithm rejects the job entirely.

## 9   The Performance Analysis

We evaluate the performance analysis of the SARDIG algorithm in term of time complexity. The time complexity in step 1 is $O(n)$, where $n$ is the number of sites in the grid. In step 2 the earliest start time is computed and the time complexity is $O(m)$, where $m$ is the number of jobs running on a site. In step 3 the security overhead is computed with a time complexity of $O(1)$. From step 6 to step 9, for each job, the security level is increased for the three security services using iterative binary search. Thus, the time complexity is computed as $O(3mlogk)$, where $k$ is the number of possible security levels for a particular security service. From step 13 to step 17 the time complexity is calculated as $O(n)$ so the time complexity of the SARDIG algorithm is as follows:

$$O(n)(O(m) + O(1) + O(3mlogk)) + O(n)$$
$$= O(nm) + O(n) + O(3mnlogk) + O(n)$$
$$= O(mnlogk)$$

where $n$ is the number of sites in a grid, $m$ is the number of jobs running on a site, and $k$ is the number of possible security levels for a particular security service.

The time complexity of SARDIG algorithm is $O(mnlogk)$ as compared to the SAREG algorithm [2], which has a time complexity of $O(knm)$ and SAHA algorithm [7], which has a time complexity of $O(knm)$. Thus, the performance of SARDIG algorithm is better than both SAREG and SAHA algorithms in terms of time complexity.

## 10   Simulation Results

We have conducted experiments based on the grid simulator GridSim [9]. The grid simulator is modified based on algorithm described in the previous section. The key system parameters in the experiment are given in the Table 1.

The performance metrics by which we evaluate system performance include *security value* and *average finish time*. Here *security value* is calculated using Equation 1

**Table 1.** Key System Parameters.

| Parameters | Value |
|---|---|
| Deadline Base or Laxity | (100 – 900) second |
| Network Bandwidth | 100 MB/Second |
| Number of sites | (4,8,16) |
| Number of jobs | (1000- ) |
| Size of data sets | (100-1000) MB |
| Job security level | (0.1-1.0) |
| Site security level | (0.1-1.0) |
| Weight of security services | Authentication=0.2; Confidentiality=0.3; integrity=0.5 |

and the finish time is calculated using Equation 7. The *average finish time* is the average value of all jobs' finish times.

To demonstrate the strength of SARDIG, we compared it with two well-known gird scheduling algorithms, namely SAREG [2] and SAHA [7].

Figure 3 shows the simulation results of the security value for the three algorithms. The security value is calculated as the deadline base or laxity is varied from 100 to

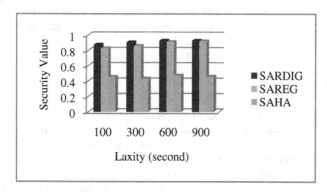

**Fig. 3.** Performance comparison in terms of security value

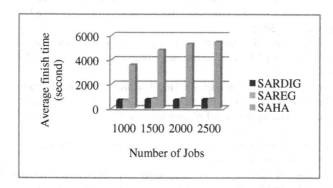

**Fig. 4.** Performance comparison in terms of average finish time

900 seconds. The proposed SARDIG algorithm shows better security values than the other two algorithms as the deadline base or laxity increases.

Figure 4 shows the simulation result of the average finish time for the three algorithms. Average finish time is calculated as the number of jobs is varied from 1000 to 2500. Small average finish times indicate better performance for a job on a grid site, as the job can provide quick service to the user. The proposed SARDIG algorithm shows better performance than the other two as the number of jobs increases.

## 11 Conclusion

In this paper, we have proposed a data grid architecture that supports real time data intensive applications. We have devised an algorithm named SARDIG for scheduling and enhancing the security of real time data intensive applications on data grids. The proposed algorithm provides three security services, which are authentication, integrity, and confidentiality. We also introduce the security gain function to measure the security level enhancement achieved by each site for a job. We showed that the SARDIG algorithm provides better performance than the SAREG and SAHA algorithm in terms of time complexity, schedules the real time data intensive applications running on data grids, and provides the best achievable security for the jobs. The simulation results show that the SARDIG algorithm provides better performance and security than the other two existing algorithms.

## References

1. Iverson, M.A., Ozguner, F., Potter, L.C.: Statistical prediction of task execution times through analytic benchmarking for scheduling in a heterogeneous environment
2. Xie, T., Qin, X.: Enhancing security of real-time applications on grids through dynamic scheduling. In: Feitelson, D.G., Frachtenberg, E., Rudolph, L., Schwiegelshohn, U. (eds.) JSSPP 2005. LNCS, vol. 3834, pp. 219–237. Springer, Heidelberg (2005)
3. Foster, I., Kesselman, C., Tuecke, S.: The anatomy of the grid: enabling scalable virtual organizations. Int. Journal Supercomput. Appl. 15(3), 200–222 (2001)
4. Ranganathan, K., Foster, I.: Decoupling computation and data scheduling in distributed data intensive applications. In: Proc. IEEE Int. Symp. High Performance Distributed Computing, pp. 352–358 (2002)
5. Stankovic, J.A., Spuri, M., Ramamritham, K., Buttazzo, G.C.: Deadline Scheduling for Real-Time Systems – EDF and Related Algorithms. Kluwer Academic Publishers, Dordrecht (1998)
6. Xie, T., Qin, X.: A Security Middleware Model for Real-Time Applications on Grids. In: Proc. The Institute of Electronics, Information and Communication Engineers (2006)
7. Xie, T., Qin, X.: Security-driven scheduling for data-intensive applications on grids. Journal of Cluster Computing (2007)
8. Real-time Observatories, Applications, and Data management Network,
   http://roadnet.ucsd.edu/
9. A Grid Simulation Toolkit for Resource Modeling and Application Scheduling for Parallel and Distributed Computing, http://www.gridbus.org/gridsim/

# Solving a Realistic FAP Using GRASP and Grid Computing

José M. Chaves-González, Román Hernando-Carnicero,
Miguel A. Vega-Rodríguez, Juan A. Gómez-Pulido, and Juan M. Sánchez-Pérez

Univ. Extremadura. Dept. Technologies of Computers and Communications,
Escuela Politécnica. Campus Universitario s/n. 10071. Cáceres, Spain
jm@unex.es, romanstrat@gmail.com,
{mavega,jangomez,sanperez}@unex.es

**Abstract.** In this work we describe the methodology and results obtained when grid computing is applied to resolve a real-world frequency assignment problem (FAP) in GSM networks. We havJose used a precise mathematical formulation for this problem, which was developed in previous work, where the frequency plans are evaluated using accurate interference information taken from a real GSM network. We propose here a newly approach which lies in the usage of several versions of the GRASP (Greedy Randomized Adaptive Search Procedure) metaheuristic working together over a grid environment. Our study was divided into two stages: In the first one, we fixed the parameters of different GRASP variants using the grid so that each version obtained the best results possible when solving the FAP; then, in the second step, we developed a master-slave model using the grid where the GRASP tuned versions worked together as a team of evolutionary algorithms. Results show us that this approach obtains very good frequency plans when solving a real-world FAP.

**Keywords:** FAP, Frequency Planning, Grid computing, GRASP.

## 1 Introduction

In this paper we study the usage of grid computing with different versions of GRASP (Greedy Randomized Adaptive Search Procedure) metaheuristic; first by their own, to adjust each GRASP version to the problem we deal with, and later working together over a real grid environment with the objective of solving in an optimum way a realistic-sized real-world frequency assignment problem (FAP). FAP is an NP-hard problem, so its resolution using metaheuristics has proved to be particularly effective [1]. However, the adjustment of evolutionary algorithms requires a great amount of experiments to fix their multiple parameters. Moreover, these experiments generally take in their execution from minutes to hours. Therefore, the usage of grid computing in these first stages is a very interesting option because it allows performing the high number of experiments which are necessary to obtain optimal solutions in a shorter period of time (in grid environments, this kind of applications is habitually called PSAs, Parameter Sweep Applications [2]). Furthermore, after the fine adjustment, we developed a master-slave approach using the grid and the different versions of the

N. Abdennadher and D. Petcu (Eds.): GPC 2009, LNCS 5529, pp. 79–90, 2009.

evolutionary algorithm tuned in the previous stage. The metaheuristics in this stage work together like a team of evolutionary algorithms with the aim to obtain the best frequency plan for a real-world GSM (Global System for Mobile communications) network. It is important to point that GSM is the most successful mobile communication technology nowadays. In fact, at the end of 2007 GSM services were in use by more than 3 billion subscribers [3] across 220 countries, representing approximately 85% of the world's cellular market. Besides, FAP is one of the most relevant and significant problems that can be found in the GSM technology, because it is a very important and critical task for current (and future) mobile communication operators. In fact, to deal with the realistic problem we work with, we use a complex formulation, proposed in [4], which takes in consideration the requirements of real-world GSM. FAP deals with many parameters [5], although we can state that the two more important elements in this problem are the transceivers (TRXs), which give support to the communication, and the frequencies, which make possible the communication. A mobile communication antenna includes several TRXs grouped in several sectors of the antenna and each TRX has to have assigned a specific frequency in the most optimum way to provide the widest coverage and minimizing the interferences produced in the network. The problem is that there are not enough frequencies (there are usually no more than a few dozens) to give support to each transceiver (there are generally thousands of them) without causing interferences. It is completely necessary to repeat frequencies in different TRXs, so, a good planning to minimize the number of interferences is highly required.

The rest of the paper is structured as follows: In Sect. 2 we present the fundamentals of the FAP solved and the mathematical formulation we use for its resolution. Section 3 describes the metaheuristic used to solve it: the GRASP algorithm. After that, our environment of grid computing is explained in Sect. 4. The experiments performed and the results obtained are detailed in Sect. 5. Finally, conclusions and future work are discussed in the last section.

## 2 Frequency Assignment Problem in GSM Networks

The two most relevant components which refer to frequency planning in GSM systems are the *antennas* or, as they are more known, base transceiver stations (BTSs) and the *TRX*. The TRXs of a network are installed in the BTSs where they are grouped in sectors, oriented to different points to cover different areas. The instance we use in our experiments is quite large (it covers the city of Denver, USA, with more than 500,000 inhabitants) and the GSM network includes 2612 TRXs, grouped in 711 sectors, distributed in 334 BTSs. We are not going to extend the explanation of the GSM network architecture but the reader interested in it can consult reference [5].

FAP lies in the assignment of a channel (or a frequency) to every TRX in the network. The optimization problem arises because the usable radio spectrum is very scarce and frequencies have to be reused for many TRXs in the network (for example, the instance we have used for this study, includes 2612 TRXs and only 18 available frequencies). However, the multiple use of a same frequency may cause interferences that can reduce the quality of service down to unsatisfactory levels. In fact, significant interferences will occur if the same or adjacent channels are used in near overlapping areas [6].

Although there are several ways of quantifying the interferences produced in a telecommunication network, the most extended one is by using what is called the *interference matrix* [7], denoted by *M*. Each element $M(i,j)$ of this matrix contains two types of interferences: the *co-channel interference*, which represents the degradation of the network quality if the cells *i* and *j* operate on the same frequency; and the *adjacent-channel interference*, which occurs when two TRXs operate on adjacent channels (e.g., one TRX operates on channel *f* and the other on channel *f+1* or *f−1*). An accurate interference matrix is an essential requirement for frequency planning because the final goal of any frequency assignment algorithm will be to minimize the sum of all the interferences. In addition to the requirements described above, frequency planning includes more complicating factors which occur in real life situations (see [5] for a detailed explanation).

Finally, in the following subsection we give a brief description of the mathematical model we use (for more information, consult references [4], [6]).

## 2.1 Mathematical Formulation

We can establish that a solution to the problem is obtained by assigning to each TRX $t_i$ (or $u_i$)$\in T = \{t_1, t_2,..., t_n\}$ one of the frequencies from $F_i. = \{f_{i1},..., f_{ik}\} \subset N$. We will denote a solution (or frequency plan) by $p \in F_1 \times F_2 \times ... \times F_n$, where $p(t_i) \in F_i$ is the frequency assigned to the transceiver $t_i$. The objective, or the plan solution, will be to find a solution *p* that minimizes the cost function (*C*):

$$C(p) = \sum_{t \in T} \sum_{u \in T, u \neq t} C_{sig}(p,t,u) \qquad (1)$$

The smaller the value of *C* is, the lower the interference will be, and thus the better the communication quality. In order to define the function $C_{sig}(p,t,u)$, let $s_t$ and $s_u$ be the sectors (from $S = \{s_1, s_2,..., s_m\}$) in which the transceivers *t* and *u* are installed, which are $s_t=s(t)$ and $s_u=s(u)$ respectively. Moreover, let $\mu s_t s_u$ and $\sigma s_t s_u$ be the two elements of the corresponding matrix entry $M(s_t,s_u)$ of the interference matrix with respect to sectors $s_t$ and $s_u$. Then, $C_{sig}(p,t,u)$ is equal to the following expression:

$$\begin{cases} K & if \ s_t = s_u, |p(t) - p(u)| < 2 \\ C_{co}(\mu_{s_t s_u}, \sigma_{s_t s_u}) & if \ s_t \neq s_u, \mu_{s_t s_u} > 0, |p(t) - p(u)| = 0 \\ C_{adj}(\mu_{s_t s_u}, \sigma_{s_t s_u}) & if \ s_t \neq s_u, \mu_{s_t s_u} > 0, |p(t) - p(u)| = 1 \\ 0 & otherwise \end{cases} \qquad (2)$$

$K>>0$ is a very large constant defined by the network designer to make undesirable allocating the same or adjacent frequencies to TRXs serving the same area (e.g., placed in the same sector). $C_{co}(\mu, \sigma)$ is the cost due to *co-channel interferences*, whereas $C_{adj}(\mu, \sigma)$ represents the cost in the case of *adjacent-channel interferences* [6].

## 3 The GRASP Metaheuristic

The Greedy Randomized Adaptative Search Procedure (GRASP) [8, 9] is an evolutionary algorithm used to solve optimization problems (such as the FAP). GRASP is a

**Algorithm 1**

1:  best_solution ← randomSolutionGenerator ()
2:  best_solution ← localSearch (best_solution)
3:  **while (not** time-limit)
4:      solution ← greedyRandomizedGenerator ()
5:      solution ← localSearch (solution)
6:      updateBestSolution (solution, best_solution)
7:  **endwhile**
8:  **return** best_solution

Fig. 1. Pseudo-code for the GRASP metaheuristic

multi-start metaheuristic in which each iteration basically consists of two stages: first, construction of a solution, and second, local search over that solution. In our case, at the end of the first stage, a valid frequency plan which solves the FAP is given, meanwhile during the second stage, this first approach is improved making a search in the neighborhood of this initial solution until a local minima is found. The obtained solution is an improvement of the original one. At the end of the process, the best overall solution (the best frequency plan) is returned as the final result. The pseudo-code for the GRASP main blocks can be observed in Fig. 1.

As we can see in Fig. 1, GRASP only works with a single solution –the best one till that moment– which is randomly generated (line 1) and improved (line 2) at the beginning of the algorithm. The process continues through an arbitrary number of iterations (line 3) creating, in each generation, a greedy randomized solution (line 4) which is improved (line 5) using a local search method carefully adapted to the FAP [10]. Finally, at the end of each iteration it is checked if the best solution (frequency plan with the smallest cost) found until that moment was improved by the new one, and in that case, the best solution is updated (line 6).

There are several variants of the GRASP algorithm, which basically depends on the method used in the greedy randomized generator (line 4) which is applied in each iteration to create a new solution (all the rest of the scheme drawn in Fig. 1 is the same). Moreover, the greedy generator method (line 4) can use as well different bias functions to create nicer solutions from the beginning. Fig. 2 illustrates the general structure of the greedy randomized generator method. At each iteration of this method, let the set of candidate elements be formed by all elements that can be incorporated to the partial solution under construction without destroying feasibility (in our

**Algorithm 2**

1:  solution ← ∅
2:  Evaluate the incremental cost of candidate elements
3:  **while** (solution is not complete)
4:      Build the restricted candidate list (RCL)
5:      Select an element *s* from RCL randomly
6:      solution ← solution ∪ {*s*}
7:      Reevaluate the incremental costs
7:  **endwhile**
8:  **return** solution

Fig. 2. Pseudo-code of the greedy randomized generator

case, the candidate elements are frequencies which can be assigned to a specific TRX within a sector). The selection of the next element for incorporation is determined by the evaluation of all candidate elements according to a greedy evaluation function specially adapted to our FAP according to the mathematical description given in Sect. 2. This function represents the increase in the cost function due to the incorporation of the specific frequency into the solution under construction. The evaluation of the elements by this function leads to the creation of a restricted candidate list (RCL) formed by the best elements, e.g. those whose incorporation to the current partial solution results in the smallest incremental costs (this is the greedy aspect of the algorithm). The element to be incorporated into the partial solution is randomly selected from those in the RCL (this is the probabilistic aspect of the heuristic). Once the chosen element is incorporated to the partial solution, the candidate list is updated and the incremental costs are re-evaluated (this is the adaptive aspect of the heuristic).

GRASP has two main parameters: one related to the stopping criterion (which in our case is a time limit) and another to the quality of the elements in the restricted candidate list. The construction of the RCL used in the greedy randomized generator (line 4, Fig. 2) will give us the different variants of the GRASP algorithm. Basically, the RCL can be limited either by the number of elements (cardinality-based, which is the first GRASP variant –type 1–) or their quality (value-based, the second variant – type 2). In the first case, it is made up of the $k$ elements (in our case, frequencies which can be assigned in a sector) with the best incremental costs, where $k$ is a parameter. In the second case, the RCL is associated with a threshold parameter $\alpha \in [0; 1]$ which determines the range of the RCL size (and its quality). However, there are more options for the creation of the RCL which define more GRASP variants. The third type in our study is the RG construction (first random and later greedy –type 3–) in which the first $k$ frequencies are taken from the RCL randomly and the rest to complete the sector are chosen greedily (the algorithm selects the best frequencies to build the best solution possible). Finally, the PG construction (first a perturbation function changes data and then the frequency is selected greedily from the data obtained after the perturbation –type 4–) creates a new solution using a perturbation operator (specified by the $k$ parameter, which is the perturbation grade).

In addition to the 4 variants explained above, it is possible to use a *bias operator* to modify the random selection of the elements which are taken from the RCL (line 5, Fig. 2). Without this parameter, the elements of the RCL have equal probabilities of being chosen. However, any probability distribution can be used to bias the selection toward some particular candidates (the ones which obtain better results). There are several bias functions [9], although we have used 3 variants in our study: random bias (bias = 0); linear bias (bias = 1) and exponential bias (bias = 2).

With all the information given in this section, we can summarize the variants of the GRASP metaheuristic according to three parameters which define its behaviour: the type used (types 1, 2, 3 and 4); the values taken by the $k \in \{1 - 18\}$ or the $\alpha \in [0; 1]$ parameters in each case; and the bias function used (random, linear or exponential). All these parameters will be referred in Sect. 5 of this paper, where the experiments and results obtained are explained.

## 4  Our Environment of Grid Computing

We have used grid computing to perform all the experiments in our study. The access to the grid resources has been granted through the EELA [11] virtual organization (VO), which includes several hundreds of working nodes. It is widely known that a middleware is necessary to use the resources of the grid and to execute applications. For this research, gLite 3.0 has been chosen as middleware. gLite is used in the EGEE project [12] and it allows a simple use of the resources of the grid. Besides, we used GridWay [13] as metascheduler because the final application we have developed with the variants of GRASP is based on a master-slave paradigm and this metascheduler manages in an efficient and easy way complex workflows. Thus, we have developed a master-slave model with the resources of the grid such as we can see in Fig. 3. The *Preprocessing Job* (executed in the UI, *User Interface*) creates the configuration files needed by the jobs to be submitted to the CE (*Computing Element*). These files indicate the arguments that a single job will use to find the best frequency planning possible with the algorithm used. The configuration files for job submission consist in commands describing the job, the requirements of the job and the dependencies among jobs. Some attributes of these files represent request-specific information and specify in some way actions that have to be performed by the metascheduler (in our case GridWay) to schedule the job or jobs of a complex request. The *Postprocessing Job* waits until all the processes (executing in their corresponding WNs –*Working Nodes*–) have ended and computes the results of these jobs, in our case, the best frequency plan found by that node to solve the FAP. More detailed information about how the master-slave model used works will be given in the next section.

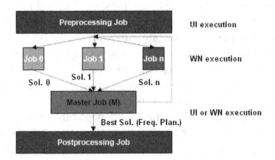

**Fig. 3.** Diagram of the jobs running in the system and data flows between jobs

## 5  Experiments and Results

In this section we are going to discuss the experiments performed and the results obtained with the grid and the GRASP versions. The experiments have been divided in two parts: first, we have used the grid for doing individual experiments in order to adjust the parameters of the different variants of the GRASP metaheuristic (see section 3) to obtain the best results when solving the FAP; and then we have developed a distributed master-slave approach (Fig. 3) with a team of evolutionary algorithms (the versions of the GRASP metaheuristic adjusted firstly) to improve the results obtained by the single sequential executions.

All experiments have been performed using the grid environment described in Sect. 4. It is important to highlight that the usage of the grid has been an essential requirement for our study, because all the experiments run sequentially would take over 2500 hours (more than 104 days) without the facilities of the grid.

### 5.1 Tuning the GRASP Parameters

Tuning the GRASP parameters for the different versions used was the first step in our study. The objective was that each GRASP variant gave us the best results when it has to solve our problem. Moreover, to obtain statistical and reliable results, all the experiments were repeated 30 times (so, we performed 30 independent executions using grid computing for each experiment), limiting each single execution to 1 hour and taking results every 2 minutes (to study the evolution curve for each experiment). It was important to study in depth the results obtained in this phase of the research, because the success in the following stage of our study (which will be described in Sect. 5.2) depended on the fine adjustment developed here. For this reason, only the best configurations and variants of the metaheuristic were used in the master-slave model we developed after tuning the GRASP parameters.

As we have said, we have used the grid resources to perform all our experiments, so we developed a script for the master job which run the different experiments in the grid and recovered the results of each single job. We have performed 4 blocks of experiments (one for each GRASP variant described in section 3 –types 1 to 4–):

– *Type 1 tests* (cardinality-based variant): It consists of 30 different experiments with 10 different values for the $k$ parameter ($k = \{1 - 10\}$) and three possibilities for the bias function (bias = 0, bias = 1 and bias = 2) –see Sect. 3 for the explanation of these parameters. All these experiments would have taken 900 hours of execution if they had been run sequentially (30 experiments × 30 independent executions × 1 hour each independent execution).
– *Type 2 tests* (value-based variant): It includes 21 different experiments with three different bias functions (bias = 0, bias = 1 and bias = 2) and the following values for the $\alpha$ parameter: 0.01, 0.02, 0.05, 0.07, 0.10, 0.25 and 0.50. All these experiments would have taken 630 hours if they had been executed sequentially.
– *Type 3 tests* (RG variant): 12 different experiments with the three different bias functions (the same as types 1 and 2) and 4 different values for the $k$ parameter ($k = \{1 - 4\}$). 360 hours are needed to run all these experiments sequentially.
– *Type 4 tests* (PG variant): 4 different experiments with random bias and 4 different values for the $k$ parameter ($k = \{1, 2, 3, 4\}$). 120 hours would have been necessary to run all these experiments sequentially.

Due to the limitation in the number of pages of this paper, we are not going to show the results obtained in all the experiments performed in this phase of our study, but a summary with the evolution in the mean results (in 30 runs) for the best configuration found for each of the variants of the algorithm is shown in Fig. 4. In that figure we can see how the evolution in the cost values (which represents the decrease in the interferences included in the GSM network) is quite significant for any variant of the

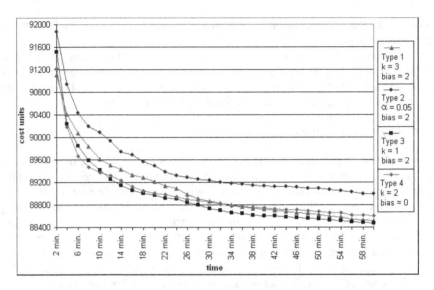

**Fig. 4.** Evolution results for the best versions of each GRASP variant

GRASP algorithm (without the metaheuristic, the costs in any frequency plan generated would be huge –millions of cost units).

The most important conclusion we can get from the study of all the experiments performed here is that the usage of a bias function in the GRASP metaheuristic provides a great improvement in all the tests run. This makes sense since the best frequencies have more probability to be taken when a new solution is created if the bias function is not random. In fact, the best results for types 1, 2 and 3 (type 4 does not use bias function) are obtained when the bias function is exponential (which provides the best probability distribution), such as we can see in Fig. 4. On the other hand, we can observe that for all the variants, the value of the $k$ or $\alpha$ parameter is quite low, which means that better results are obtained when the algorithm has not present a very random behaviour –or in case of type 4, there are not a lot of perturbation in the solutions. Therefore, we can state that not very random strategies (and quite greedy) work very well (they obtain the best results). Finally, we can see how the value-based variant (type 2) obtains the poorest results (though they are reasonable good as well). All in all, the four different versions (with its best configuration) were considered for the next phase of our study, because such as we can see in Fig. 4, all of them have a good evolution curve and moreover, with the inclusion of one version for each variant of the algorithm, we give more diversity (an important aspect) to our team of evolutionary algorithms.

## 5.2  Using Grid Computing

Once we had adjusted the different parameters of the GRASP variants that we have explained in the previous section, the following step was to choose the best candidates to perform a parallel algorithm in which the different variants work together (as a team of evolutionary algorithms) in order to improve the sequential results, that is, obtaining better frequency plans in the same period of time. For doing this, we developed a distributed master-slave approach with a selection of the best versions of the GRASP metaheuristic (the ones shown in Fig. 4), plus a very interesting variant (type 1, $k = 2$, bias = 0), because its results were pretty good and it had the particularity of obtaining such good results with a random bias function (which is not very common). Therefore, we added this fifth variant to include more diversity to the behaviour of our parallel team. On the other hand, the study has been performed making experiments with a different number of jobs in the master-slave model.

We have worked with 5 (the minimum number is one job for each of the 5 different variants chosen), 10, 15 and 20 jobs (we did not work with a bigger number of jobs, because the grid we used to do the experiments usually did not have more than 20-25 working nodes free in average). Besides, we want to emphasize that when we made the experiments with 10, 15 and 20 jobs, we launched versions replicated on the grid (more than one job for each GRASP variant), and this event created redundancy in the system, which is a good feature when we work in a real grid environment. Thus, we do not need that all the jobs have finished when the master job has to evaluate the best solution. For our master process, if the 40% of the jobs have finished, it considers the iteration successfully done (and it will kill the unprocessed slave-jobs, which probably are waiting to execution because the grid does not have enough free resources or there is some failure in the grid infrastructure). However, we have to point that in all our experiments, approximately the 90% of the jobs finished correctly their executions, returning in time their results. Moreover, each experiment has been repeated 30 times to obtain results with statistical confidence (like we did with the sequential study). Besides, to compare the results with the sequential versions, we have done experiments up to 1 hour, taking results every 2 minutes, such as we can see in Fig. 5.

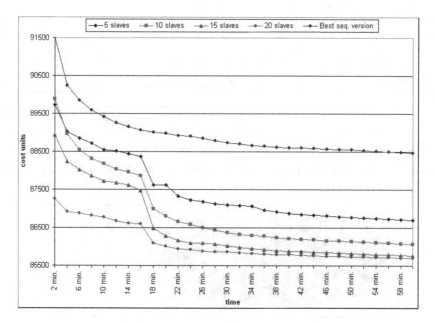

**Fig. 5.** Comparison between the evolution in the results of the different parallel experiments performed (master-slave model with 5, 10, 15 and 20 jobs) and the best sequential version

On the other hand, the master-slave application is based on the feedback which is applied over the slave jobs by using the best solution found every 16 minutes of execution. Therefore, there are synchronization points every 16 minutes. In those points, the slave jobs are restarted by the master, but they use the best individual found so far (by all the jobs in the team) as initial solution. Finally, the algorithm stops when 4 blocks of 16 minutes have been run.

As we can see in Fig. 5, all the parallel versions improve the results obtained by the best sequential variant. Besides, we can observe how the results are better when the number of slaves configured grows. In the graph we can also see that a great improvement occurs at minute 18. This gap is explained because in the minute 16 the first synchronization is performed, so all the jobs re-start their execution after minute 16 with the best solution found so far as initial solution, and this causes a great improvement in the next result output, which is in the minute 18.

Furthermore, we have studied the evolution of the system in longer executions (as we can see in Fig. 6). For doing this, we have performed an execution during 10 hours using the best parallel configuration found, which is the one with 20 jobs, as we can observe in Fig. 5. According to the obtained results, we can say that our algorithm does not stagnate its evolution in long executions, although the improvement obtained after 2 hours is very slow (see Fig. 6).

Moreover, we have studied the contribution that each GRASP variant used in the parallel model provides to the whole system. For doing this, we have studied which

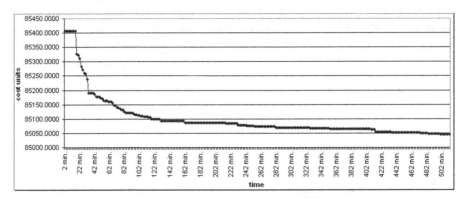

**Fig. 6.** Evolution in the mean results for the best parallel version (20 jobs running in parallel)

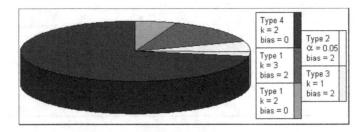

**Fig. 7.** Best solution hits for each version in the synchronizations of the parallel model

**Table 1.** Empirical results (in cost units) for different metaheuristics. It is shown the best, average and standard deviation of 30 executions.

| | 120 seconds | | | 600 seconds | | | 1800 seconds | | |
|---|---|---|---|---|---|---|---|---|---|
| | Best | Avg. | Std. | Best | Avg. | Std. | Best | Avg. | Std |
| ACO | 90736.3 | 93439.5 | 1318.9 | 89946.3 | 92325.4 | 1092.8 | 89305.9 | 90649.9 | 727.5 |
| SS | 91216.7 | 94199.6 | 1172.3 | 91069.8 | 93953.9 | 1178.6 | 91069.8 | 93820.4 | 1192.3 |
| DE | 92145.8 | 95414.2 | 1080.4 | 89386.4 | 90587.2 | 682.3 | 87845.9 | 89116.8 | 563.8 |
| LSHR | 88543.0 | 92061.7 | 585.3 | 88031.0 | 89430.9 | 704.2 | 87743.0 | 88550.3 | 497.0 |
| Seq. GRASP | 88857.4 | 91225.7 | 1197.2 | 87368.4 | 89369.6 | 1185.1 | 86908.4 | 88850.6 | 1075.2 |
| Parallel GRASP | **85313.0** | **87256.9** | 2309.2 | **85313.0** | **86772.1** | 1701.0 | **85259.4** | **85855.3** | 686.9 |

variant provided the best solution generated in every synchronization of the algorithm. We counted the number of the contributions given by each variant in all the experiments performed. To summarize this study, we show here the results provided by the best parallel execution, which is the model which works with 20 jobs. The results for 30 independent executions can be seen in Fig. 7. In the chart of that figure, we can see that all variants contribute to make the algorithm evolve, however, the best variant is the PG version (type 4), with a 71% of hits, meanwhile the rest of versions share their contribution to the evolution of the algorithm.

Finally, we want to emphasize that thanks to the parallel approach developed here, the results were significantly improved, mainly if we use more than 15 slaves in our distributed model. In fact, our results beat (or improve the lowest bound of the best cost of) other recent results obtained with other approaches (Ant Colony Optimization –ACO–, Scatter Search –SS–, Differential Evolution –DE–, and Local Search with Heuristic Restarts –LSHR–) using the same problem instance and measurements [4], [14], [15] (see Table 1).

## 6   Conclusions and Future Work

In this paper we study the usage of grid computing when solving a real-world FAP (2612 transceivers and only 18 frequencies) with several variants of the GRASP algorithm. According to the obtained results, the grid provides a double advantage: first, it provides a high computational power to perform the great number of experiments which are necessary to adjust the metaheuristics; and then, if the grid is used to develop a parallel system where the jobs work together, it was proved that the results are significantly improved.

Besides, our approach includes the combination of other interesting ideas: redundant jobs to compensate the leaks that can be produced in the grid, team of evolutionary algorithms, synchronization points in the parallel model, distributed master-slave model, etc.

Future work includes the development of a team of heterogeneous evolutionary algorithms (GRASP, SS, PBIL, ILS...) to be executed in parallel. Furthermore, we are working now to obtain more real-world instances, in order to evaluate the algorithms using different instances.

**Acknowledgments.** This work was partially funded by the Spanish Ministry of Education and Science and FEDER under contracts TIN2005-08818-C04-03 (the OPLINK project) and TIN2008-06491-C04-04 (the MSTAR project). José M. Chaves-González is supported by the research grant PRE06003 from Junta de Extremadura (Spain).

# References

1. Blum, C., Roli, A.: Metaheuristics in Combinatorial Optimization: Overview and Conceptual Comparison. ACM Computing Surveys 35, 268–308 (2003)
2. Berman, F., Hey, A., Fox, G.C.: Grid Computing. Making the Global Infrastructure a Reality. John Wiley & Sons, Chichester (2003)
3. GSM World, http://www.gsmworld.com/news/statistics/index.shtml
4. Luna, F., Blum, C., Alba, E., Nebro, A.J.: ACO vs EAs for Solving a Real-World Frequency Assignment Problem in GSM Networks. In: GECCO 2007, London, UK, pp. 94–101 (2007)
5. Eisenblätter, A.: Frequency Assignment in GSM Networks: Models, Heuristics, and Lower Bounds. PhD thesis, Technische Universität Berlin (2001)
6. Mishra, A.R.: Radio Network Planning and Opt. In: Fundamentals of Cellular Network Planning and Optimisation: 2G/2.5G/3G... Evolution to 4G, pp. 21–54. Wiley, Chichester (2004)
7. Kuurne, A.M.J.: On GSM mobile measurement based interference matrix generation. In: IEEE 55th Vehicular Technology Conference, VTC Spring 2002, pp. 1965–1969 (2002)
8. Feo, T.A., Resende, M.G.C.: Greedy Randomized Adaptive Search Procedures. Journal of Global Optimization 6, 109–134 (1995)
9. Resende, M.G.C., Ribeiro, C.C.: Greedy Randomized Adaptive Search Procedures. AT&T Labs Research Technical Report, pp: 1–27 (2001)
10. Luna, F., Estébanez, C., et al.: Metaheuristics for solving a real-world frequency assignment problem in GSM networks. In: GECCO 2008, Atlanta, GE, USA, pp. 1579–1586 (2008)
11. EELA Web, http://www.eu-eela.eu
12. EGEE Web, http://www.eu-egee.org
13. GridWay Web, http://www.gridway.org
14. Chaves-González, J.M., Vega-Rodríguez, M.A., et al.: SS vs PBIL to Solve a Real-World Frequency Assignment Problem in GSM Networks. In: Giacobini, M., Brabazon, A., Cagnoni, S., Di Caro, G.A., Drechsler, R., Ekárt, A., Esparcia-Alcázar, A.I., Farooq, M., Fink, A., McCormack, J., O'Neill, M., Romero, J., Rothlauf, F., Squillero, G., Uyar, A.Ş., Yang, S. (eds.) EvoWorkshops 2008. LNCS, vol. 4974, pp. 21–30. Springer, Heidelberg (2008)
15. da Silva Maximiano, M., et al.: A Hybrid Differential Evolution Algorithm to Solve a Real-World Frequency Assignment Problem. In: Proceedings of the International Multiconference on Computer Science and Information Technology, Wisła, Poland, pp. 201–205 (2008)

# The Swiss ATLAS Grid

Eric Cogneras[1], Szymon Gadomski[2], Sigve Haug[1], Peter Kunszt[3],
Sergio Maffioletti[3], Riccardo Murri[3], and Cyril Topfel[1]

[1] Center for Research and Education in Fundamental Physics, Laboratory for High
Energy Physics, Bern University, Sidlerstrasse 5, CH-3012 Bern, Switzerland
[2] DPCN, Geneva University, 24 Quai Ernest-Ansermet, CH-1211 Geneva 4,
Switzerland
[3] Swiss National Super Computing Center (CSCS), Galleria 2 - Via Cantonale
CH-6928 Manno, Switzerland

**Abstract.** In this paper the technical solutions, the usage and the future development of the Swiss ATLAS Grid are presented. In 2009 the Swiss ATLAS Grid consists of four clusters with about 2000 shared computing cores and about 250 TB of disk space. It is based on middlewares provided by the NorduGrid Collaboration and the EGEE project. It supports multiple virtual organisations and uses additional middleware, developed by the ATLAS collaboration, for data management. The Swiss ATLAS grid is interconnected with both NorduGrid and the Worldwide LHC Grid. This infrastructure primarly serves Swiss research institutions working within the ATLAS experiment at LHC, but is open for about two thousand users on lower priority. The last three years about 80 000 wall clock time days have been processed by ATLAS jobs on the Swiss ATLAS Grid.

## 1   Introduction

The Swiss ATLAS Grid (SAG) is a computing infrastructure serving Swiss ATLAS physicists. ATLAS is one of four large particle physics experiments at the Large Hadron Collider (LHC) in Geneva (CERN) [1][2]. The data from its detector is expected to answer fundamental questions about the universe, e.g. about the origin of mass and about the physical laws right after the *Big Bang*. The LHC will perform its first hadron collisions this year (2009). ATLAS will record, replicate, simulate and analyze the data from these collisions. Several tens of petabytes per year will be produced in this process. A large effort has been invested into the world wide distributed computing system, hereinafter called the ATLAS grid, with the SAG being the Swiss part of this system [3]. The SAG is realized as a collaboration between the Universities of Bern and Geneva, the Swiss National Super Computing Center (CSCS) and the Swiss Institute for Particle Physics (CHIPP).

In 2005 the prototype of the SAG was described in "The Swiss ATLAS Computing Prototype" [4]. Since then both infrastructure and usage have evolved. This is the first publication on this evolvement. In Sec. 2 we describe the job patterns and their requirements. Then we proceed in Sec. 3 with the infrastructure

N. Abdennadher and D. Petcu (Eds.): GPC 2009, LNCS 5529, pp. 91–97, 2009.
© Springer-Verlag Berlin Heidelberg 2009

and the technical solutions which have been chosen in order to meet the requirements. This is followed by Sec. 4 on monitoring and accounting, and finally, we conclude and sketch the prospects for the Swiss ATLAS Grid.

## 2    ATLAS Job Patterns

Particle physics computing is data-intensive, but naturally parallel. The data, both simulated and real, comes in fragments called events, which correspond to different collisions of particles. The data from different events is in general processed independently, which leads to easy parallelism. However, there are other challenges. In case of the LHC experiments the sheer data volume is one challenge. Another is the distribution and the availability of the data to a huge collaboration.

In ATLAS the computational jobs may be divided into two categories. One is the simulation of data. The other is the analysis of simulated and measured data. The simulation of the data is normally divided into four steps. The first generates the physical event in the LHC proton-proton collisions. The second takes the particles generated in the first step and simulates the transport in and the interactions with the detector. In a third step the information from the second is digitized. In the final step the digitized information is reconstructed. The reconstruction step in the simulation of the data is the same as the reconstruction of measured data. The output is then analyzed.

Jobs in both categories may be handled in two different ways, either by the central production system or by individual grid users. In the central production system a database is filled with job descriptions. These are picked up by so called executors, continuously running remote processes. They translate the job descriptions into the required grid flavor and submit them with the corresponding grid clients. These executors also supervise the jobs until their output is safely stored and registered in the respective databases.

When jobs from the executors enter the sites, they are properly designed and obey the guidelines for ATLAS jobs. These imply that one core takes one job, one job does not require more than 2 GB memory and last less than 24 hours. Furthermore the input and output is kept within 10 GB per job. The number of input and output files are normally not more than some tens and the file sizes within some GB. The SAG clusters are designed to handle this pattern. However, for clusters which handle more than 1000 simultaneous ATLAS jobs, filesystem limitations and non-distributed computing and storage elements tend to become an issue.

ATLAS jobs designed and submitted by individual users sometimes do not respect the guidelines above. Experience has shown that this can block various services. Their presence on the grid is expected to increase significantly, and sites will have to learn to protect themselves by removing jobs which threaten the system in time. In ATLAS there are more than 2000 collaborators and the majority possesses a grid certificate and consequently has access to the resources on the ATLAS grid.

# 3   Infrastructure

The ATLAS grid is described in the ATLAS "Computing Technical Design Report" [3]. It is a hierarchical grid with a so called *four-tier* structure. Data from the tier zero (T0) at CERN in Geneva is pushed through dedicated network hardware to about ten computing centers, so called "tier ones" (T1) around the world. They again replicate and push data to their associated "tier twos" (T2), normally national or regional computing centers. The "tier twos" serve their "tier threes" (T3) which typically are clusters owned by single universities or research groups. The final tier four is the desk- or laptop of an ATLAS physicist. The SAG has one T2 at the *Swiss Super Computing Center* (CSCS) in Manno which is connected to the T1 at the *Forschungszentrum Karlsruhe*, Germany. In Switzerland two T3, in Bern and Geneva respectively, are being served by CSCS. This hierarchical structure is enforced in order to avoid the break down which a totally flat and chaotic structure can cause on the services.[1]

The SAG sites are connected by the shared SWITCHlan dark fibre network, i.e. the bandwith can be adjusted by illuminating the optical fibres with multiple frequencies [5]. This shared network is currently operated with one 10 Gb/s channel, but more bandwidth is possible. The network map is shown in Fig. 1. The foreseen output from the ATLAS detector is about 2.4 Gb/s, thus the Swiss capacity of the network meets the estimated ATLAS requirements for connectivity. The international BelWu 1 Gb/s connectivity to the T1 in Karlsruhe may have to be increased, in particular because this connection is also not dedicated to ATLAS. However, the redundant topology shown in Fig. 1 does ensure a stable connectivity at the low level.

A speciality is a direct and dedicated network link between the T0 at CERN and the Geneva T3. As only a small fraction of the data can be processed in Geneva, this option is not of interest for final physics analysis of the data, which will need to start with large datasets at T1 sites. However, the direct line will enable the users of the Geneva T3 to participate more effectively in the commissioning of the ATLAS experiment. During regular data taking the direct line can be used for data quality monitoring, which can be done by processing of the order of 1% of the data.

Concerning the computation and storage resources in the SAG, about 2000 worker node cores and 250 TB disk space are comprised by four clusters. The cluster hardware is summarized in Tab. 1. In 2004 the sites *gridified* with some 32 bit one core desktop boxes and then evolved to the current, in the Swiss context, considerable resources made up by 64 bit four and eight core servers. Both Intel and AMD processors are represented. The storage systems are all disk based. All clusters use Gigabit ethernet for interconnections, and at least 2 GB RAM

---

[1] Admittedly this hierarchical structure is not fully respected. A considerable amount of horizontal and vertical data pulling between tiers is tolerated and crucial for the individual needs of the physicists.

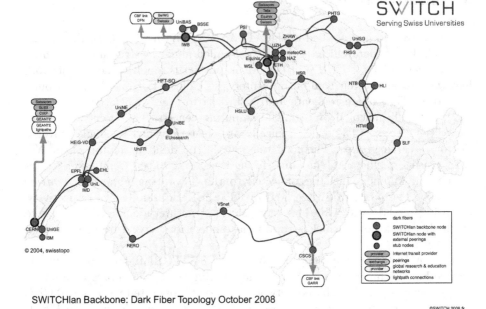

SWITCHlan Backbone: Dark Fiber Topology October 2008

**Fig. 1.** The SWITCHlan backbone. The SAG T2 is located at CSCS, while the T3s at UniBE and UniGE respectively.

is available per core. The size of the resources will be growing with the needs in ATLAS, along a timeline exceeding a decade.[2]

The choice of operating system and middleware has been a compromise between maintenance minimization and feasibility. The ATLAS software has a size of several hundred GB of which a so called "kit" is extracted, validated and pulled to the tiers. Kits are typically released several times a month and occupy about 10 GB each. They are developed, compiled and validated on Scientific Linux Cern (SLC) [6]. Experience has shown that the deployment of this software on other operating systems may imply a significant additional workload. Thus, the SLC has become the preferred operating system on the SAG clusters. However, on a shared cluster like Bern T3 B, which is running Gentoo, it is not possible for one project to determine the operating system. On such clusters the additional workload is accepted, e.g. by using *change root* environments. Similar is the situation for the choice of middleware. EGEE's gLite practically does not support other platforms than SLC or related operating systems [7]. Further, gLite has historically been quite worker node intrusive and manpower demanding. These are the reasons for the extended use of the NorduGrid

---

[2] This long timeline gives rise to many challenges, i.e. the transition from the 32 bit to the 64 bit infrastructure is not trivial. The applications still have to run in a 32 bit compatibility setup. Another example is the bankrupt of hardware suppliers and the related loss of warranties.

**Table 1.** The Swiss ATLAS Grid sites end 2008. The second column shows the worker node cores, the third the disk storage in terabyte (TB), the fourth the operating system (OS), the fifth the middleware (MW), the sixth the local resource management system (LRMS), and the seventh the storage element (SE). The $^s$ indicates that the resource is shared and not used by ATLAS only. The numbers typically undergo a 10% fluctuation following the actual status of the resources.

| Cluster | Cores | TB | OS | LRMS | MW | SE |
|---------|-------|-----|--------|-------------|-----------|-------------|
| Bern T3 A | 30 | 30 | SLC4 | Torque | ARC | ARC SE |
| Bern T3 B | 1000$^s$ | 0 | Gentoo | SGE | ARC | - |
| CSCS T2 | 1000$^s$ | 150 | SLC4 | Torque/Maui | ARC/gLite | dCache |
| Geneva T3 | 188 | 70 | SLC4 | Torque | ARC | ARC SE/DPM |

Collaboration's *Advanced Resource Connector* and for the rapid start up in 2005 as a light weight grid [8]. The only cluster also deploying gLite is the T2 at CSCS which is serving additional LHC experiments.

The distributed data management (DDM) system on the ATLAS grid requires some specific storage element features [9]. The system is a set of central databases at the T0 which organize files on the grid into data containers. Containers have locations which are file catalogs, gLite's LFC, deployed at the T1. These again contain the physical file names of the files stored on storage elements in their respective T2. The actual movements are issued by Python services at the T1 which in turn issue gLite's File Transfer Service (FTS) service with SRM endpoints. Virtual splitting of the storage into so called *space tokens* is extensively used. Until now this has effectively excluded the ARC SE as an option and the most used solutions are dCache and EGGE's DPM [10] [11]. Since the ATLAS DDM system normally does not contain T3 sites, only the Swiss T2 is connected. However, a DPM based storage element is now being installed in Geneva.

## 4   Monitoring and Accounting

The SAG monitoring is locally done with custom made scripts and Ganglia [12]. On the grid level the ARC monitor and the ATLAS dashboard are used. The ARC and gLite information systems, on which these web applications are based, provide sufficient data for identifying problems on an hourly basis. Concerning computational issues these solutions are sufficient. Monitoring of the data transfers still requires a lot of attention due to the immature state of the storage elements and the middleware services.

The usage is tracked in three ways and shows a non-linear growth. For the T3 clusters the Torque and SGE accounting files are analyzed. For the T2 cluster the EGEE accounting portal and the ATLAS dashboard are consulted [13] [14]. Both sources rely on EGEE's APEL database. In 2007 the T2 wall clock time from these sources were cross checked several times with the analysis of the local accounting. The numbers were consistent within 5%, which is the estimated uncertainty for the SAG accounting.

# Wall time days on the Swiss ATLAS Grid

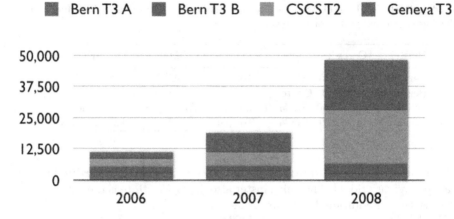

Fig. 2. Wall clock time days on the Swiss ATLAS Grid. The total wall clock time in 2008 corresponds to 1% of the world wide ATLAS wall clock time as accounted by the ATLAS dashboard.

Figure 2 shows the ATLAS usage of the clusters in wall clock time days. Compared to 2006 the usage increased by a factor of five to approximately 48000 wall clock time days in year 2008, i.e. 130 wall clock time years. This corresponds to more than 1% of all the accounted ATLAS computing [14].[3] Of the 220 sites which contributed to the 11 000 wall clock time years on the ATLAS Grid in 2008, only 10 sites (the number of T1) contributed with more than 2% and no site contributed with more than 10%. Considering the increase in the available worker nodes on the SAG the usage in 2009 is expected to double. However, the prediction is uncertain since the experiment will start recording collider data. On one hand it is likely that this will increase the usage further. On the other many more unexperienced users will submit jobs which eventually will cause new unforeseen challenges for the sites.[4]

On the SAG there is no automated disk space accounting. The storage is mostly inspected in an *ad hoc* and manual manner. An integrated storage element solution with detailed information of all disk operations down to the level of distinguished names is very much desired. However, such solutions are not yet provided by the middleware.

---

[3] Neither on the Swiss ATLAS Grid nor on the world wide ATLAS grid is all usage accounted, e.g. interactive work and usage by other projects are not contained in the numbers.

[4] Already now jobs with enormous inputs and outputs, i.e. several tens of GBs, output files with 40 GB size etc have been observed. Such usage may rapidly bring down the services.

# 5   Conclusions and Outlook

In 2009 the Swiss ATLAS Grid (SAG) consists of four clusters with about 2000 worker node cores and about 250 TB of disk storage. The ATLAS share of the cores is about 700. The sites are connected with the *Advanced Resource Connector* (ARC). The tier 2 cluster at CSCS is connected to the worldwide LHC Grid with gLite and all clusters are connected to NorduGrid with ARC. The storage elements are ARC SE, DPM and dCache. In 2008 about 130 wall clock time years were accounted. During the last three years about 210 wall clock time years have been processed.

The SAG is a hybrid light weight grid with a pioneering status within the Swiss context. It is recognized by the emerging Swiss national grid initiative (SwiNG) and will connect with resources and experience to a Swiss national grid infrastructure [15]. Within the next two years SAG is expected to approximately double its computing and storage capacity.

**Acknowledgments.** The indispensable work of the contributing resources' system administrators is highly appreciated. The resources on the Swiss ATLAS Grid are extensively funded by the Swiss National Science Foundation.

# References

1. The ATLAS Collaboration, Aad, G., et al.: The ATLAS Experiment at the CERN Large Hadron Collider, 2008 JINST 3 S08003 (2008)
2. Evans, L., Bryant, P. (eds.): The LHC Machine, 2008 JINST 3 S08001 (2008)
3. ATLAS Collaboration: Computing Technical Design Report, CERN-LHCC-2005-022, ATLAS-TDR-017
4. Gadomski, S., et al.: The Swiss ATLAS Computing Prototype, ATL-SOFT-PUB-2005-03, CERN-ATL-COM-SOFT-2005-07
5. SWITCH, http://www.switch.ch
6. Scientific Linux homepage, https://www.scientificlinux.org
7. Generic Installation and Configuration Guide for gLite 3.1, https://twiki.cern.ch/twiki/bin/view/LCG/GenericInstallGuide310
8. Ellert, M., et al.: Advanced Resource Connector middleware for lightweight computational Grids. Future Generation Computer Systems 23, 219–240 (2007)
9. Haug, S., et al.: Data Management for the World's Largest Machine. In: Kågström, B., Elmroth, E., Dongarra, J., Waśniewski, J. (eds.) PARA 2006. LNCS, vol. 4699, pp. 480–488. Springer, Heidelberg (2007)
10. dCache homepage, http://www.dcache.org
11. Disk Pool Manager, https://twiki.cern.ch/twiki/bin/view/LCG/DpmGeneralDescription
12. Chun, B.N., et al.: The Ganglia Distributed Monitoring System: Design, Implementation, and Experience. Parallel Computing 30(7) (July 2004)
13. EGEE Accounting Portal, http://www3.egee.cesga.es
14. ATLAS Collaboration's Dashboard, http://dashboard.cern.ch/atlas
15. The Swiss National Grid Association, http://www.swing-grid.ch

# Grid Based Training Environment for Earth Observation

Dorian Gorgan, Teodor Stefanut, and Victor Bacu

Technical University of Cluj-Napoca, Computer Science Department,
28 G. Baritiu Str., 400027, Cluj-Napoca, Romania
{dorian.gorgan,teodor.stefanut,victor.bacu}@cs.utcluj.ro

**Abstract.** The content of the satellite images supplies information on the earth surface, weather, clime, geographic areas, pollution, and natural phenomena. Unfortunately, the real time supervision and the teaching related techniques require high computation and massive spatial data storage resources. This paper presents the Grid oriented GiSHEO eLearning Environment (eGLE) supporting the training and experimental practice in Earth Observation (EO). eGLE facilitates specific access for the academic and scientific community to on-demand services related to specific EO applications. The teachers have the ability to easily create lessons for different topics, supporting both the knowledge presentation and Grid based processing. The eGLE environment is based on the gProcess platform developed through the MedioGrid national project. The gProcess platform consists of a set of tools supporting the flexible description, instantiation, scheduling and execution of the workflow based Grid processing.

## 1 Introduction

Satellite images encode information about the earth surface, weather, clime, geographic areas, pollution, and natural phenomena. The study and the real time supervision require high computation resources and the storage of massive spatial data. Meanwhile the Earth Observation (EO) related education needs real time experiments in order to prototype the real systems and natural phenomena. The main processing concerning the satellite images consists of segmentations and classifications of data, which is actually a search of information through combinations of multispectral bands of the satellite data. Moreover, the data exploration and interpretation depends on many variables such as satellite image type (e.g. MODIS, Landsat etc), geographical area, soil composition, vegetation cover, season, context (e.g. clouds, hydrothermal alterations, terrain configuration), and so on. All these specific and variable conditions require flexible tools and friendly user interfaces to support an optimal research within the space of solutions.

This papers aims to present an eLearning Platform, developed through the GiSHEO [1] project (On Demand Grid Services for Higher Education and Training in Earth Observation) funded through the PECS program of European Space Agency (ESA). It is a three year project starting in 2008 which intends to create a Web-based training platform for hands-on experimental practice in Earth Observation (EO). The overall technical objectives of the GiSHEO project are to: (a) Set-up and organize a virtual organization (VO) based on Grid technology for education, training and knowledge dissemination for EO and related activities; (b) Development of specific

N. Abdennadher and D. Petcu (Eds.): GPC 2009, LNCS 5529, pp. 98–109, 2009.

instruments dedicated to on-demand services for education activities based on EO data; (c) Facilitate specific access for the academic and scientific community to on-demand services related to specific EO applications; and (d) Correlation and harmonization of resources with national, European and ESA projects dedicated to services for EO, such as G-POD [2] and GENESI-DR [3].

The GiSHEO eLearning Environment (eGLE) will offer to the teachers the ability to easily create lessons for different topics, supporting knowledge presentation and assessment, and Grid based processing both for teachers and students. It is based on the gProcess [4] platform developed through the MedioGrid [5] national project. The gProcess platform consists of a set of tools supporting the flexible description, instantiation, scheduling and execution of the workflow based Grid processing.

The research reported by the paper concerns mainly with gProcess based eLearning Environment architecture, workflow based description and execution of the Grid processing, different lesson patterns supporting the real time and flexible experiments, and the developing of different EO related teaching materials.

## 2 Teaching Materials and Scenarios

eGLE involves three domains of eLearning, Earth Observation and Grid processing. The great possible number of users attends the lessons by exploring Earth Observation subjects by intensive computation of the huge spatial data distributed over the Grid. eGLE makes possible the following scenarios:

$1^{st}$ scenario. The teacher describes visually the processing workflow for some remote sensing data. The workflow considers as inputs three bandwidth channels of the satellite image and describes in the graph nodes a few specific operators or Grid services already available (e.g. provided by GENESI-DR system). The teacher builds up the content of the lesson, by combining a few available content patterns. He describes by text some theoretical notions and then visualizes in three figures two initial images and the resulted image processed through the workflow execution over the Grid. At runtime the student selects from a list the two input images and executes the workflow in order to check the resulted image.

$2^{nd}$ scenario. The teacher adds to the previous scenario a few features. For instance, the student can edit the workflow and experiments other processing algorithms for different available input data-sets.

$3^{rd}$ scenario. The teacher completes the text explanation by voice and adds to the previous scenario a movie about the last ten years evolution of the vegetation in Danube Delta. In order to make it possible, the teacher executes the simulation over the Grid by using a specialized graphics cluster. He visualizes the simulation remotely on his Internet-connected workstation and records the animation into a short movie. This movie is a lesson resource available for the students.

## 3 Related Works

In [6] Plaza et al. show that the development of fast techniques for transforming massive amounts of hyperspectral data into scientific understanding is critical for space-based Earth science and planetary exploration. So far, the Grid capabilities could be used only by technical trained personnel who conducted research activities based on massive data processing. Most of the efforts towards the eLearning development in the remote sensing area were focused on creating teaching materials and tutorials that present implementation techniques used in remote sensing and information about data acquisition, storage and processing [7].

In the last few years, the international community has become more interested in EO teaching activities, developing projects such as D4Science [8] – remote sensing data management on Grid infrastructures, and SEOS [9] – to support the integration of EO and remote sensing as an element of science education in high schools.

Actually there are only a few numbers of resources involved in educational activities in EO. One of the most complex projects is EduSpace [10]. Besides the current existing platforms that provides tutorials and training materials in EO, GiSHEO intents to be a dynamic platform mainly concerning with experimentation and extensibility. Moreover, GiSHEO is oriented towards EO skills, rather than GILDA [11], promoted and developed in frame of EGEE project [12].

Most of Grid workflow systems are using the direct acyclic graph as a solution for modeling processes. In the UNICORE [13] and Symphony [14] the DAG based description solution is chosen, while the Kepler [15] and Triana [16] are using direct cyclic graphs solution. Another available solution is related with the usage of Petri nets [17]. The description language of Grid workflows is using mainly the XML description, like the Grid Service Flow Language (GSFL) and Grid Workflow. Another description language is BPEL4WS; both BPEL4WS and GSFL allow the defining of complex workflows and modeling of different input data. Grid Workflow Execution Language (GWEL) [18] uses some concepts that were defined in the BPEL4WS in order to describe the interaction between services by using WSDL.

The Grid-Flow [19] system architecture consists of 3 levels: the user interface, the Grid-Flow engine and the data and process integration platform over the Grid. By interactive editing tools the user models the graph that lately is mapped to the Grid Flow Description Language (GFDL). In Pegasus [20] two types of workflows are defined, abstract and concrete workflows that can be executed using the Condor-G or the DAGMan.

## 4   GiSHEO eLearning Environment Architecture

The eGLE platform lays on gProcess toolset and consists of GiSHEO eLearning Environment and eLearning Oriented Level (see Fig.1). The platform implements both the user interaction tools and the components supporting the development, execution and the management of the teaching materials. Through eGLE the teacher develops lesson patterns and resources, and combines them through templates into the lessons. The teacher may use the Grid based execution both for testing the lesson already created, and for developing lesson resources such as processed images, and workflows as graph based process descriptions. The students just execute the lessons. They can also describe and experiment new workflows and input satellite images.

The gProcess platform defines an intermediate level between the eLearning Oriented Level and the Grid Infrastructure by creating a set of services and tools supporting the flexible description, instantiation, scheduling and execution of the workflows.

The databases include conceptual and particular workflow based descriptions, teaching materials and lesson resources, satellite and spatial data.

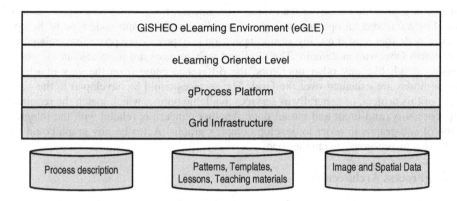

**Fig. 1.** Functional levels in the eGLE related architecture

# 5  gProcess Platform

The gProcess platform [4] provides a flexible diagrammatical description solution for image processing workflows in the EO. At the conceptual level the algorithms are described by processing acyclic graphs (Fig.2), in which the nodes represent operators, services, sub-graphs and input data (e.g. satellite image bandwidths), and the arcs represent the execution dependencies between nodes. The development of the processing graphs implies two steps. The first step describes the conceptual Process Description Graph (PDG), as pattern processing a satellite image type (i.e. MODIS, Landsat). The second step describes the Instantiated Process Description Graph (IPDG), by mapping the already created PDG pattern over a particular satellite image data. The IPDG description together with the input satellite data are actually the subject of Grid based execution.

## 5.1  Description of Grid Based Processing

Conceptually the algorithm is described as an acyclic graph (Fig.2). There are four types of nodes. The first type represents input data or data resources. Input data is an

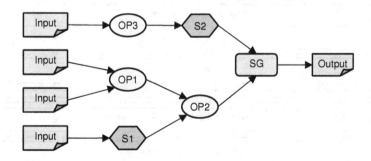

**Fig. 2.** Workflow describes the Grid based processing, by satellite image bandwidths (Input), operators (OP), Grid and Web services (S), sub-graphs (SG), and processed images (Output)

image (e.g. satellite images or data value – i.e. integer, float, string data types – that is used by some special operations (e.g. threshold). Another graph node type is the operator node that represents any atomic operation (i.e. processing procedure) related to the Earth Observation domain. The Grid and web services are integrated in the processing graph like any other operators; the difference came from the way in which these nodes are executed over the Grid. The services could be developed in the context of this project, or generally as services available online, which match the required functionality, and input and output data. Another concern is related with the integration of sub-graphs in order to develop complex graphs. Actually, any graph could be included as sub-graph in another one.

### 5.2  gProcess Architecture

The gProcess architecture (Fig.3) is based on the client-server model. At the server side the Grid Infrastructure supports the access to computing resources and distributed databases through a set of services such as EditorWS, ManagerWS, ExecutorWS, and ViewerWS.

The client side encapsulates Client Java API, User Oriented Application Level, and Applications. The Web and desktop applications access the gProcess services by the Client Java API level. A set of user interaction supporting components, such as EditorIC, ManagerIC, and ViewerIC are exposed through the User Oriented Application Level. It is the higher level of accessing the gProcess services through the Client Java API level as well. The last level of Applications combines the editor, manager, and viewer related functionality into complex user interaction tools.

### 5.3  Service Level

The following functionalities of the gProcess platform are exposed by services:

*EditorWS* provides relevant information on available resources (e.g. lists of operations, sub-graphs, satellite image types, data types). This information is then published by the EditorIC in some interaction components for designing and developing the graph editor's user interface;

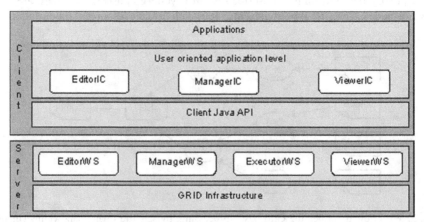

**Fig. 3.** gProcess Platform based architecture

*ManagerWS* provides information on workflows (i.e. PDG, IPDG), and fetches and uploads related resources (i.e. workflows, operators, services, sub-graphs, data). This service supports the main interaction with the gProcess operators, services, resources available in the database;

*ExecutorWS* executes the instantiated workflows (IPDG) over the Grid, and monitors the execution of the workflows. The service maps the workflow into an internal data structure, and analyzes and schedules the operators for sequential and parallel execution on the Grid;

*ViewerWS* gets and formats the input and output data (e.g. initial and processed satellite images). It supports the access and visualization functionality of the satellite images.

## 5.4  User Level

The components from the User Oriented Application Level support the complex user interaction functionality of the applications:

*EditorIC* provides the user editing operations of the workflow development. It supports features such as interactive design of the processing graph, specification of different graph node information, and visualization at different levels of details (e.g. auto expansion of sub-graphs);

*ManagerIC* instantiates the workflow for particular satellite data and administrates the model resources such as operators, services, sub-graphs, and satellite data;

*ViewerIC* displays in the application the input and output data (e.g. initial and processed satellite images), and gets and displays the monitoring data. The graphical user components implement specific user interaction techniques for manipulation of satellite images such as zoom, scroll, area selection etc.

## 5.5  Process Execution

The Executor service processes the IPDG file in order to accomplish the workflow processing over the Grid. The service parses the IPDG description and generates the appropriate internal data structure. The Executor expands the sub-graphs and considers for execution just atomic nodes such as operators, services and data resources. The consistency checking is performed at the processing graph editing phase and as well at the execution phase. The consistency concerns with data, operators and services. Data consistency is checked by the editor at the creation of links between graph nodes. The input data of some operator or service must match the output of another operator, service or resource node. The other type of consistency is related with operator or service accessibility at the execution time. It is possible that at execution time the operators (e.g. executable ones) or services are not available any more. In this case the system must look for another operator or service, which matches the required functionality.

The Condor job manager is responsible with the scheduling and execution of processing graph nodes, and every atomic node is submitted as a request to the job manager. The gProcess database stores graph nodes related real time data such as execution status, output resource location, and starting and final execution time, supporting the visualization of the execution progression in the graphical user interface.

## 5.6 Operators

The gProcess platform goal was to provide a toolset for a flexible description and execution of the processing graphs. In the EO domain different image processing operators were defined and described in the literature. The main image operations are common in many other domains. In this category we can include the basic operators like addition, subtraction, division, and so on. Histogram equalization, blurring, convolution, geometric transformations make part from the same category. A special case of operators are the ones that are related, for example, with the computation of vegetation and water indices. This is a special category that receives as input a multispectral satellite image and based on a processing algorithm returns some relevant information about the structure of vegetation and water. These operators can be integrated in gProcess like sub-graphs that are expanded at the execution time or just like atomic operators, in order to assure the execution of an operator on a single worker.

# 6 Teaching Material Development and Execution

As it was already mentioned before, eGLE provides tools and functionalities which support the development of the lessons based on GRID computing technology. The target community of users includes mainly non-technical users such as teachers specialized in different domains like Earth Observation, Environmental Studies.

The lesson development process consists of the following phases:

1. Acquire the lesson content
2. Organize and display the lesson content
3. Data binding and user interaction description
4. Lesson execution

### 6.1 Acquire the Lesson Content

Information that will be included into the lessons (e.g. text, images, videos, and sounds) through the GiSHEO platform is mostly stored in distributed databases over the network or is the result of different processing over the Grid (see Fig. 4).

As the acquiring process can thus become very complex, it is imperative that the interface provides functionalities that will reduce the complexity of operations for the user, without major restraints on Grid capabilities. The teacher must be able to browse the available resources without any knowledge about the location or storage mechanism and must have the ability to launch processing jobs over the grid in a non-technical manner.

### 6.2 Organize and Display the Lesson Content

After the data acquisition phase, the teacher must organize the information and specify all the necessary visual formatting (i.e. layout, fonts, colors, image size, video size) and interaction techniques used in the lesson (i.e. if the student may control a slideshow, modify data inputs for a processing description graph etc.). The display structure of a lesson in the GiSHEO platform has the following components:

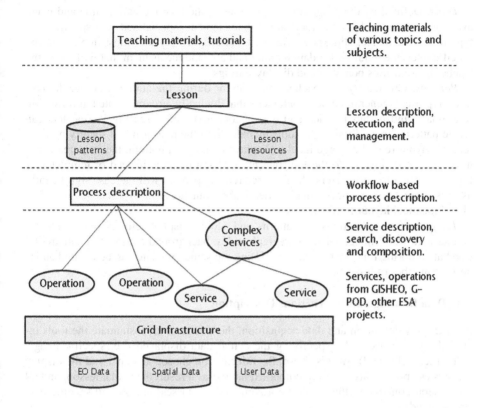

**Fig. 4.** Grid based teaching material composition

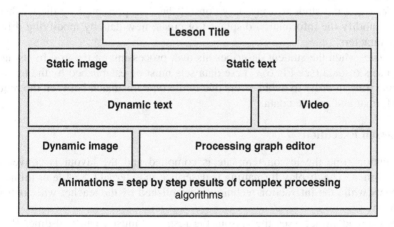

**Fig. 5.** Lesson Presentation Structure: different patterns gathered into the lesson template

*Tools.* Defined by the programmers previous to the lesson creation time and made available for the teachers, the tools are atomic elements specialized on a specific data type (e.g. text, image, slideshow, video, sound etc.). Every tool must implement the specific interface required for data binding and also the mechanism that will allow the teacher to control its behavior and display settings.

*Patterns.* Created by the teachers previous or during the authoring time, the patterns represent general layout containers that logically groups related information (e.g. image and its label, video and explanatory text etc.) – see Fig.5. Teachers can create patterns by combining the tools included into the platform and specifying their relative layout (e.g. the image label is displayed on top/on bottom, the text area is beneath the video area, or to the left/right etc.). Using patterns instead of templates as logical information organizers, the resource reusing percent will increase significantly as it is more likely to have smaller identical layout areas in different lessons than global identical layout for these.

*Templates* are collections of patterns and global display settings (e.g. fonts for regular text, titles, image labels, paragraph styles, background colors etc.) and are defined at authoring time by the teachers. Using the same template can be created an indefinite number of lessons.

## 6.3  Data Binding and Interactions Description

After display definition and data acquisition, the teacher must instantiate the tools included into the lesson by specifying the actual data displayed (i.e. specific image, video file, and sound). At this phase, the information chosen at step 1 and the display settings established at step 2 are combined having as a result the actual lesson, and all the general containers (that could be assimilated to classes) are bind to specific data (instantiated).

Depending on the interaction level allowed by the teacher for the students and on the ability of the formers to launch data processing on the Grid, the lesson scenarios can be classified as:

*Static,* when the students may only consult the data presented by the teacher but may not modify the information displayed or create new data by modifying different input parameters.

*Dynamic,* when the student describes his own processing on the grid by using predefined sets of data (see Fig.6). These data sets must be established by the teacher at authoring time in order to avoid errors due to the type mismatch between the required inputs format and selected data.

## 6.4  Lesson Execution

At execution time the lesson template is compiled and the layout is converted in HTML format. The display formatting is described in external CSS file or inline style statements while the interaction techniques established by the teacher will control the tools behavior.

When a student accesses the lesson, the response must be in real-time. Because there are situations when execution on the Grid can be a very time consuming operation, the teacher should include into the lessons materials that are stored into the

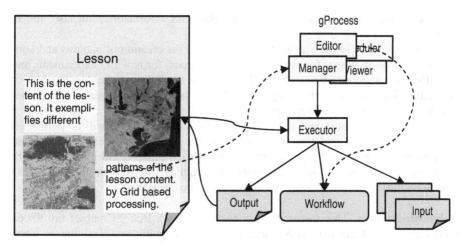

**Fig. 6.** Grid processing based lesson execution.

database. If any processing is required for some areas of the lesson it should be performed at authoring time and only the result included into the lesson. Nevertheless, this information preprocessing can be performed mostly for lessons based on static scenarios.

When comes to dynamic lessons, it can be very difficult to predict all the processing that might occur for all the possible datasets, especially for larger ones. The students may be granted the ability to use the same processing description graph with other input data or even to edit the graph using the operators and information chosen by the teacher at authoring time (Fig. 6). As the multiple requests of all the students consulting a dynamic lesson could overload the Grid and generate very big delays in answers retrieval, a safety mechanism should be adopted. When possible, the teacher should perform at authoring time all the processing that will be available through the lesson, having the ability to save also the intermediary results, if any. At runtime, the results of the processing chosen by the students will be in fact read from the database and thus the overload of the Grid network can be avoided.

# 7  Conclusions

The teachers are able to create complex lessons in EO without knowledge on Grid technologies, and the students may visualize and even execute operations on large amount of data, using transparently the Grid processing resources and facilities.

The development of training and teaching material based on complex EO services is an ongoing task. While simple services, as depicted in the paper, are already available, more complex ones will be built in the near future relying on these simple ones. The first category of targeted complex services is related to automated natural resource monitoring and management. Then the disaster management application services, involving more than just remote sensing data will be developed. Finally as main research challenge, innovative services for archeology will be built involving complex scenarios using not only satellite data and other GIS information, but also human intervention.

Another challenging activity is the one related to the creation of patterns and templates for platform usage, for new lessons and tutorials, for new EO experiments and for different categories of users. Intended to allow flexibility in the development of new educational services, the design of GiSHEO expresses the desire of its further development through user intervention.

Tests on the suitability and accessibility of the learning objects will be performed in the next period in real labs for master students in geography and environment. Training events open to the public will be organized in the second part of the three years project. The interest of public bodies for training activities in the field of EO will be established in parallel with the above described activities.

**Acknowledgments.** This research is supported by ESA PECS Contract no. 98061 GiSHEO – On Demand Grid Services for High Education and Training in Earth Observation.

# References

1. GiSHEO Consortium. On-demand Grid Services for High education and Training in Earth Observation (2009), http://gisheo.info.uvt.ro
2. Fusco, L., Cossu, R., Retscher, C.: Open Grid Services for Envisat and Earth observation applications. In: Plaza, A., Chang, C. (eds.) High Performance Computing in Remote Sensing, pp. 237–280. Chapman & Hall/CRC, Taylor & Francis Group (2008)
3. GENESI-DR project consortium (2009), http://www.genesi-dr.eu
4. Radu, A., Bacu, V., Gorgan, D.: Diagrammatic Description of Satellite Image Processing Workflow. In: Proc. Int. Symp. Symbolic and Numeric Algorithms for Scientific Computing (SYNASC 2007), pp. 341–348. IEEE Press, Los Alamitos (2007)
5. Petcu, D., Zaharie, D., Gorgan, D., Pop, F., Tudor, D.: MedioGrid: a Grid-based Platform for Satellite Images. In: Procs. IDAACS 2007, pp. 137–142. IEEE Press, Los Alamitos (2007)
6. Plaza, A.J., Chang, C.-I. (eds.): High Performance Computing in Remote Sensing. Computer and Information Science Series, vol. 16. Chapman & Hall/CRC, Boca Raton (2007)
7. Rees, P., MacKay, L., Martin, D., Durham, H. (eds.): E-Learning for Geographers: Online Materials, Resources, and Repositories. Idea Group Inc., (IGI) (2008)
8. D4Science Consortium, DIstributed colLaboratories Infrastructure on Grid ENabled Technology 4 Science (2009), http://www.d4science.org
9. SEOS Project - Science Education through Earth Observation for High Schools (2009), http://www.seos-project.eu
10. ESA. The European Earth observation Web Site for Secondary Schools (2009), http://www.eduspace.esa.int
11. Andronico, G., Ardizzone, V., Barbera, R., Catania, R., Carrieri, A., Falzone, A., Giorgio, E., Rocca, G.L., Monforte, S., Pappalardo, M., Passaro, G., Platania, G.: GILDA: the Grid INFN Virtual Laboratory for Dissemination Activities. In: Procs. 1st Internat. Conf. on Testbeds and Research Infrastructures for the Development of Networks and Communities, pp. 304–305 (2005)

12. EGEE-III Consortium, Enabling Grids for Science (2008),
    http://www.eu-egee.org
13. Erwin, D.W., Snelling, D.F.: UNICORE: A Grid Computing Environment. In: Sakellariou, R., Keane, J.A., Gurd, J.R., Freeman, L. (eds.) Euro-Par 2001. LNCS, vol. 2150, pp. 825–834. Springer, Heidelberg (2001)
14. Lorch, M., Kafura, D.: Symphony - A Java-based Composition and Manipulation Framework for Computational Grids. In: Proceedings of 2nd IEEE/ACM International Symposium on Cluster Computing and the Grid (CCGrid 2002), Berlin, Germany, May 21-24 (2002)
15. Altintas, I., Berkley, C., Jaeger, E., Jones, M., Ludaescher, B., Mock, M.: Kepler: Towards a Grid-Enabled System for Scientific Workflows. In: Proceedings of Workflow in Grid Systems Workshop in GGF 10, Berlin, Germany (2004)
16. Shields, M., Taylor, I.: Programming Scientific and Distributed Workflow with Triana Services. In: Proceedings of Workflow in Grid Systems Workshop in GGF 10, Berlin, Germany (2004)
17. Peterson, J.L.: Petri Nets. ACM Computing Surveys 9(3), 223–252 (1977)
18. Cybok, D.: A Grid Workflow Infrastructure. In: Proceedings of Workflow in Grid Systems Workshop in GGF 10, Berlin, Germany (2004)
19. Cao, J., Jarvis, S.A., Saini, S., Nudd, G.R.: GridFlow: Workflow Management for Grid Computing. In: Proc. 3rd IEEE/ACM Int. Symp. on Cluster Computing and the Grid, Tokyo, Japan, pp. 198–205 (2003)
20. Deelman, E., Blythe, J., Gil, Y., Kesselman, C., Mehta, G., Vahi, K., Blackburn, K., Lazzarini, A., Arbree, A., Cavanaugh, R., Koranda, S.: Mapping Abstract Complex Workflows onto Grid Environments. Journal of Grid Computing 1(1), 25–39 (2003)

# Improving Energy-Efficiency of Grid Computing Clusters

Tapio Niemi, Jukka Kommeri, Kalle Happonen, Jukka Klem,
and Ari-Pekka Hameri

Helsinki Institute of Physics, Technology Programme,
CERN, CH-1211 Geneva 23, Switzerland
{tapio.niemi,kommeri,kalle.happonen,jukka.klem,ari-pekka.hameri}@cern.ch

**Abstract.** Electricity is a significant cost in high performance computing. It can easily exceed the cost of hardware during hardware lifetime.
We have studied energy efficiency in a grid computing cluster and noticed that optimising the system configuration can both decrease energy
consumption per job and increase throughput. The goal with the proposed saving scheme was that it is easy to implement in normal HPC
clusters. Our tests showed that the savings can be up to 25%. The tests
were done with real-life high-energy physics jobs.

## 1 Introduction

Computing power is an important resource in many fields from basic science
to industry. In science, high energy-physics heavily depends on the computing
resources. For example the Worldwide LHC Computing Grid (WLCG), to be
used to analyse the data that the Large Hadron Collier will produce, includes
over 50 000 CPU cores. In this scale, even a small system optimisation can offer
noticeably energy savings.

By energy efficiency we mean how many similar jobs can be processed by
using the same amount of electricity. By computing efficiency, i.e. the system
throughput, we mean how many similar jobs can be processed in a time unit.
Optimising one of these two figures can sometimes lead to the other one getting
worse. In our study, the aim was to find the optimal energy efficiency without
decreasing the system throughput. Luckily, the tests indicated that – at least
in our test environment – these two aims are not contradictory, meaning that
optimising system throughput also improves its energy efficiency.

Improving energy efficiency in cluster and grid computing has mostly focused
on infrastructure issues such as cooling and buying energy efficient hardware. As
far as we know, there are not many studies focusing on optimising the system
configuration in grid computing. Basically the problem is similar to production
management in any manufacturing process.

N. Abdennadher and D. Petcu (Eds.): GPC 2009, LNCS 5529, pp. 110–118, 2009.

## 2 Background

### 2.1 Grid Computing Clusters

The common practice in HPC clusters is to configure the batch scheduler to run a single job per available processor core. As an example, the gLite [18] grid middleware by default configures the Torque scheduler [21] to have one job slot per core on the computing nodes (the Torque configuration variable is even called number of processors). Also, the ARC grid middleware [17] reports the available job slots as the number of cores in the cluster.

Common schedulers like Torque and Sun Grid Engine [6] have configuration options to specify how many CPUs/cores there are per machine. These numbers are used to calculate how many jobs are allowed to run at one time on that machine. These numbers can be overridden, but this is not often the case.

### 2.2 LHC Computing

The WLCG computing grid that is used for analysis of CERN LHC data has more than 140 computing centres around the world and each centre operates clusters typically with thousands of CPUs and storage devices that can store up to Petabytes of data.

In LHC computing there are centralised production teams that send up to millions of similar long simulation jobs. There are also thousands of scientists who will send analysis jobs in a more chaotic way. The two different applications used in our energy efficiency tests are based on these two use cases (simulation and analysis).

The production and analysis jobs are typically submitted as large sets of similar kinds of jobs and the execution time of an individual job can be estimated quite well. Especially in the case of centralised production, the execution time of one job is not as important as the total throughput of the system.

As conclusion the following special features of the WLCG computing can be taken into account when developing methos for optimising energy efficiency:

1. jobs are foreknown simulations or analysis jobs,
2. jobs are submitted as large sets of similar kinds of computing jobs,
3. the execution time of an individual job can be estimated quite well, and
4. the execution time of an individual job is not as important as the total throughput of the system.

## 3 Related Work

Ge et al. [11] have studied methods to decrease power consumption in HPC clusters. The method is based on Dynamic Voltage Scaling technology of microprocessors. The authors created a software framework to implement and evaluate their method. While, Kappiah et al. [14] have developed a method to decrease power consumption of parallel computation in power-scalable clusters. And Yuan and Nahrstedt [23] studied the same issues in mobile devices.

Venkatachalam and Franz [22] give a detailed overview on techniques that can be used to reduce energy consumption of computer systems. Essary and Amer [7] have studied how disk arm movements can be optimised and in this way save energy, while Zhu et al. [26] proposed a disk array energy management system. Li et al. [15] studied performance guaranteed control algorithms for energy management of disk and main memory. Conner et al. [5] studied how energy consumption can be reduced by dynamically disabling network links in super computing clusters. Zhang et al. [25] give compiler-based strategies to optimise cache energy consumption of microprocessors.

There are several studies on power saving in mobile devices and sensor networks (for example, [13,20,24,19]. Zhang et al. [24] studied cache architectures in embedded systems. Li et al. [16] studied how hand-held devices can be connected to a server as thin clients using WLAN and in this way save energy. Further, Chen et al. [4] have presented a method for saving energy in mobile devices by tuning garbage collection of Java systems, while An et al. [1] have studied a similar problem in spatial database applications. Barr and Asanovic [2] have studied energy saving in data compression for wireless transmission. Fei et al. [10] proposed four types of source code transformations to save energy in embedded software.

## 4    Method

We used a test cluster including one front-end and three computing nodes running Sun Grid Engine [6]. The nodes had single core Intel Xeon 2.8 GHz processors (Supermicro X6DVL-EG2 motherboard, 2048 kB L2 cache, 800 MHz front side bus) with 2 gigabytes of memory and 160 gigabytes of disk space. The operating system was Linux with the kernel version 2.6.24.4 and the cluster management system Rocks 5.0. The electricity consumption of the computing nodes was measured with the Watts Up Pro electricity meter.

We tested the accuracy of our test environment by running the heavy CRAFT analysis test several times with exactly the same settings. The differences between the runs were around +-1% both in time and electricity consumption.

The energy consumption of our test cluster (the computing nodes) was 0.46 kW when being idle and 0.77 kW with full power. The electricity consumption of a cluster can be presented: P = idle power + work power. In our case, the maximum work power was 0.77-0.46=0.31 kW. Since the power consumption of the idle state is 60% compared to running the system at the full power, it is straightforward to conclude that the system should be fully powered (but not over loaded) – or turned off – to get the best energy-efficiency. Therefore we focused on optimising the maximum throughput of the system, that is, minimising the average processing time of the job in a large set of jobs processed in parallel. This is not the same as minimising the processing time of a single job, which is a common practice in grid computing clusters.

Based on the observations explained above we made a hypothesis that running multiple jobs in parallel can increase both energy efficiency and system throughput.

## 5   Tests

We used two different real-world applications related to the CERN LHC accelerator and experiments. Our method was to run the set of identical jobs with different configurations of the test cluster and measure the consumed electricity and used time. In this way we were able to measure both the energy consumption and system throughput. The setting we changed was the amount of simultaneous jobs per processor. This setting was chosen since changing it would not require any software or hardware changes in computing clusters.

Our two test applications were:

- **Beam-beam simulation:** The executable used in the tests is a simulation that has been used in the design of the LHC collider. It simulates the beam-beam effect, i.e. the forces that act on the beam particles when bunches cross in the LHC interaction points. These simulations are important because beam-beam effect is one the major limitations to LHC collider performance [3,12].
- **CRAFT analysis:** CRAFT (CMS Running At Four Tesla) analysis uses cosmic ray data recorded with CMS detector at the LHC during 2008 [8]. During these measurements the CMS magnet was operated at four Tesla field and the detector was close to its final configuration. This analysis uses CMSSW software [9] and it is very close to the final data analysis which will be carried out when the LHC collision data is available.

Both of these programs were tested with two different size data sets. The tests with Beam-beam software used only a small input file that was stored on the local disk. The CRAFT analysis tests were done using two different input files: 98 MB and 360 MB. A part of these tests were done transfering input data from the front-end node of the cluster using encryption (Linux scp command) and the other part using only local disks of the computing nodes. To eliminate the influence of disk buffers, the input file was recreated for each job by copying it using the standard Linux cp command. The output files of the test applications were small. We performed, in total, five different test sets shown in Table 1.

**Table 1.** Summary of test executed

| Program | Input file size | Jobs run | Mem. usage | Output |
|---|---|---|---|---|
| Beam-beam simulation heavy | less than 1MB | 12-50 | some MBs | 1KB |
| Beam-beam simulation light | less than 1MB | 500 | some MBs | 1KB |
| CRAFT analysis heavy network disk | 360MB | 82 | 368MB | 1.6MB |
| CRAFT analysis heavy local disk | 360MB | 246 | 368MB | 1.6MB |
| CRAFT analysis light local disk | 98MB | 246 | 271MB | 60KB |

# 6 Results

The results, shown in Table 2 and Figures 1, 2 4, indicated that it is more efficient to run more than one simultaneous jobs in a processor. This improved

**Table 2.** Test results

| Description | Jobs/CPU | Jobs | Jobs/hour | Wh/job | Avg. kW |
|---|---|---|---|---|---|
| Beam-beam simulation heavy | | | | | |
| | 1 | 12 | 323 | 2.0 | 0.65 |
| | 2 | 12 | 246 | 2.8 | 0.69 |
| | 3 | 50 | 244 | 2.9 | 0.69 |
| | 4 | 50 | 263 | 2.6 | 0.68 |
| Beam-beam simulation light | | | | | |
| | 1 | 500 | 1433 | 0.343 | 0.49 |
| | 2 | 500 | 2894 | 0.177 | 0.51 |
| | 3 | 500 | 4255 | 0.126 | 0.54 |
| | 4 | 500 | 5806 | 0.097 | 0.56 |
| CRAFT analysis 360MB network disk | | | | | |
| | 1 | 246 | 119 | 5.92 | 0.704 |
| | 2 | 246 | 123 | 5.79 | 0.712 |
| | 3 | 246 | 123 | 5.83 | 0.716 |
| | 4 | 246 | 122 | 5.82 | 0.712 |
| CRAFT analysis 360MB local disk | | | | | |
| | 1 | 246 | 127 | 5.50 | 0.701 |
| | 2 | 246 | 127 | 5.49 | 0.699 |
| | 3 | 246 | 112 | 6.07 | 0.683 |
| | 4 | 246 | 100 | 6.60 | 0.663 |
| CRAFT analysis 98MB local disk | | | | | |
| | 1 | 246 | 239 | 2.89 | 0.691 |
| | 2 | 246 | 339 | 2.24 | 0.760 |
| | 3 | 246 | 351 | 2.19 | 0.768 |
| | 4 | 246 | 310 | 2.38 | 0.736 |

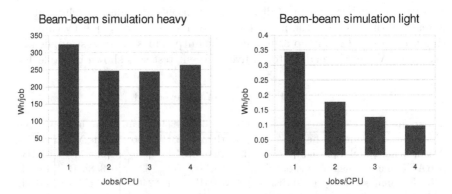

**Fig. 1.** Results of Beam-beam tests

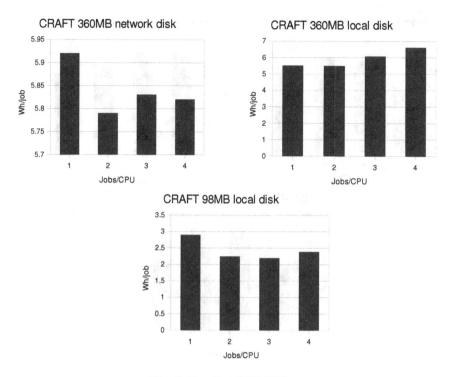

**Fig. 2.** Results of CRAFT tests

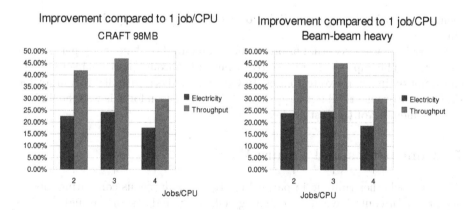

**Fig. 3.** Relative improvement compared to 1 job/CPU setting

both energy efficiency and system throughput. The amount of memory and I/O traffic seem to be the limiting factor, since with memory intensive jobs two or three jobs per CPU settings were most efficient. I/O was probably also the reason for the small unexpected peek in CRAFT 360MB tests. In the case of the less

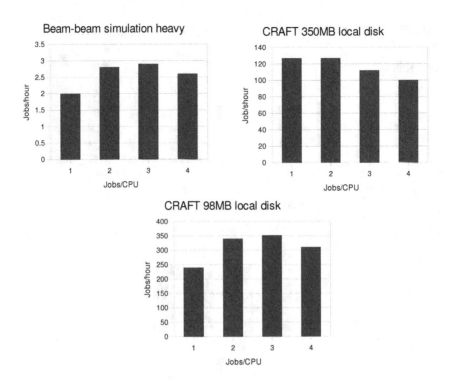

**Fig. 4.** System throughput in some tests

memory intensive Beam-beam light job even four jobs per CPU increased the efficiency.

Figure 3 shows percentual improvements compared to the one job per processor setting. The improvement is relatively bigger in throughput than in electricity consumption in these two test cases. In CRAFT analysis with 360 MB input file similar improvement did not happen. The obvious reason for this was the limited amount memory of the test cluster.

## 7   Conclusions and Future Work

We tested whether running in parallel multiple simultaneous computing jobs in one processor could have effect on energy efficiency and system throughput. We ran our tests in a dedicated test cluster and measured the used electricity and time. Our tests showed that the energy efficiency and system throughput increased when more than one job per processor were run simultaneously. Depending on the jobs, the optimal efficiency was two, three, or even four simultaneous jobs.

Our future plans include continuing testing with different applications and with different system settings. On the software side we are planning to test e.g. different Linux schedulers and on the hardware side large memory sizes, modern energy efficient processors and their energy optimisation possibilities.

# References

1. An, N., Gurumurthi, S., Sivasubramaniam, A., Vijaykrishnan, N., Kandemir, M., Irwin, M.J.: Energy-performance trade-offs for spatial access methods on memory-resident data. The VLDB Journal 11(3), 179–197 (2002)
2. Barr, K.C., Asanović, K.: Energy-aware lossless data compression. ACM Trans. Comput. Syst. 24(3), 250–291 (2006)
3. CERN. LHC Beam-beam Studies, http://lhc-beam-beam.web.cern.ch/lhc-beam-beam
4. Chen, G., Shetty, R., Kandemir, M., Vijaykrishnan, N., Irwin, M.J., Wolczko, M.: Tuning garbage collection for reducing memory system energy in an embedded java environment. Trans. on Embedded Computing Sys. 1(1), 27–55 (2002)
5. Conner, S., Link, G.M., Tobita, S., Irwin, M.J., Raghavan, P.: Energy/performance modeling for collective communication in 3-d torus cluster networks. In: SC 2006: Proceedings of the 2006 ACM/IEEE conference on Supercomputing, p. 138. ACM, New York (2006)
6. Sun Grid Engine. Gridengine - project home (2009), http://gridengine.sunsource.net
7. Essary, D., Amer, A.: Predictive data grouping: Defining the bounds of energy and latency reduction through predictive data grouping and replication. Trans. Storage 4(1), 1–23 (2008)
8. CMS Collaboration, Adolphi, R., et al.: The CMS experiment at the CERN LHC. Journal of Instrumentatio 3 (2008)
9. CMS Experiment. CMSSW Application Framework, https://twiki.cern.ch/twiki/bin/view/CMS/WorkBookCMSSWFramework
10. Fei, Y., Ravi, S., Raghunathan, A., Jha, N.K.: Energy-optimizing source code transformations for operating system-driven embedded software. Trans. on Embedded Computing Sys. 7(1), 1–26 (2007)
11. Ge, R., Feng, X., Cameron, K.W.: Performance-constrained distributed dvs scheduling for scientific applications on power-aware clusters. In: SC 2005: Proceedings of the 2005 ACM/IEEE conference on Supercomputing, Washington, DC, USA, p. 34. IEEE Computer Society, Los Alamitos (2005)
12. Herr, W., Zorzano, M.P.: Coherent dipole modes for multiple interaction regions. Technical report, LHC Project Report 461 (2001)
13. Jiang, C., Chen, G.: Convergent sparsedt topology control protocol in dense sensor networks. In: InfoScale 2007: Proceedings of the 2nd international conference on Scalable information systems, Brussels, Belgium, pp. 1–8. ICST (Institute for Computer Sciences, Social-Informatics and Telecommunications Engineering) (2007)
14. Kappiah, N., Freeh, V.W., Lowenthal, D.K.: Just in time dynamic voltage scaling: Exploiting inter-node slack to save energy in mpi programs. In: SC 2005: Proceedings of the 2005 ACM/IEEE conference on Supercomputing, Washington, DC, USA, p. 33. IEEE Computer Society, Los Alamitos (2005)
15. Li, X., Li, Z., Zhou, Y., Adve, S.: Performance directed energy management for main memory and disks. Trans. Storage 1(3), 346–380 (2005)
16. Li, Z., Wang, C., Xu, R.: Computation offloading to save energy on handheld devices: a partition scheme. In: CASES 2001: Proceedings of the 2001 international conference on Compilers, architecture, and synthesis for embedded systems, pp. 238–246. ACM, New York (2001)
17. NorduGrid (2009), http://www.nordugrid.org/middleware
18. EGEE project (2009), http://www.glite.org

19. Sadler, C.M., Martonosi, M.: Data compression algorithms for energy-constrained devices in delay tolerant networks. In: SenSys 2006: Proceedings of the 4th International Conference on Embedded Networked Sensor Systems, pp. 265–278. ACM, New York (2006)
20. Schiele, G., Becker, C., Rothermel, K.: Energy-efficient cluster-based service discovery for ubiquitous computing. In: EW11: Proceedings of the 11th workshop on ACM SIGOPS European workshop, p. 14. ACM, New York (2004)
21. Torque. Torque resource manager (2009), http://www.clusterresources.com/pages/products/torque-resource-manager.php
22. Venkatachalam, V., Franz, M.: Power reduction techniques for microprocessor systems. ACM Comput. Surv. 37(3), 195–237 (2005)
23. Yuan, W., Nahrstedt, K.: Integration of dynamic voltage scaling and soft real-time scheduling for open mobile systems. In: NOSSDAV 2002: Proceedings of the 12th international workshop on Network and operating systems support for digital audio and video, pp. 105–114. ACM, New York (2002)
24. Zhang, C., Vahid, F., Najjar, W.: A highly configurable cache architecture for embedded systems. SIGARCH Comput. Archit. News 31(2), 136–146 (2003)
25. Zhang, W., Hu, J.S., Degalahal, V., Kandemir, M., Vijaykrishnan, N., Irwin, M.J.: Reducing instruction cache energy consumption using a compiler-based strategy. ACM Trans. Archit. Code Optim. 1(1), 3–33 (2004)
26. Zhu, Q., Chen, Z., Tan, L., Zhou, Y., Keeton, K., Wilkes, J.: Hibernator: helping disk arrays sleep through the winter. In: SOSP 2005: Proceedings of the twentieth ACM symposium on Operating systems principles, pp. 177–190. ACM, New York (2005)

# GFS: A Distributed File System with Multi-source Data Access and Replication for Grid Computing

Chun-Ting Chen[1], Chun-Chen Hsu[1][2], Jan-Jan Wu[2], and Pangfeng Liu[1][3]

[1] Department of Computer Science and Information Engineering National Taiwan University, Taipei, Taiwan
{r94006,d95006,pangfeng}@csie.ntu.edu.tw
[2] Institute of Information Science, Academia Sinica, Taipei, Taiwan
wuj@iis.sinica.edu.tw
[3] Graduated Institute of Networking and Multimedia National Taiwan University, Taipei, Taiwan

**Abstract.** In this paper, we design and implement a distributed file system with multi-source data replication ability, called Grid File System (GFS), for Unix-based grid systems. Traditional distributed file system technologies designed for local and campus area networks do not adapt well to wide area grid computing environments. Therefore, we design GFS file system that meets the needs of grid computing. With GFS, existing applications are able to access remote files without any modification, and jobs submitted in grid systems can access data transparently with GFS. GFS can be easily deployed and can be easily accessed without special accounts. Our system also provides strong security mechanisms and a multi-source data transfer method to increase communication throughput.

## 1 Introduction

Large-scale computing grids give ordinary users access to enormous computing power. Production systems such as Taiwan UniGrid [1] regularly provide CPUs to cycle-hungry researchers in a wide variety of domains. However, it is not easy to run data-intensive jobs in a computational grid. In most grid systems, a user must specify in advance the precise set of files to be used by the jobs before submitting jobs. In some cases this may not be possible because the set of files or the fragments of file to be accessed may be determined only by the program at runtime, rather than given as command line arguments. In other cases, the user may wish to delay the assignment of data items to batch jobs until the moment of execution, so as to better schedule the processing of data items.

To cope with the difficulties in running data-intensive applications with runtime-dependent data requirements, we propose a distributed file system that supports Unix-like run-time file access. The distributed file system provides the same namespace and semantics as if the files are stored on a local machine. Although a number of distributed file systems have been developed in the past

N. Abdennadher and D. Petcu (Eds.): GPC 2009, LNCS 5529, pp. 119–130, 2009.

decade, none of them are well suited for deployment on a computational grid. Even some distributed file systems such as the Andrew File System [2] are not appropriate for use in grid computing systems because of the following reasons:

1. They cannot be deployed without intervention by the administrator at both client and server
2. They do not provide security mechanisms needed for grid computing.

To address this problem, we have designed a distributed file system for cluster and grid computing, called *Grid File System* (GFS). GFS allows a grid user to easily deploy and harness distributed storage without any operating system kernel changes, special privileges, or attention from the system administrator at either client or server. This important property allows an end user to rapidly deploy GFS into an existing grid (or several grids simultaneously) and use the file system to access data transparently and securely from multiple sources.

The rest of this paper is organized as follows. Section 2 describes the system architecture of GFS. Section 3 describes our security mechanisms for file access. Section 4 presents GFS's multi-source data transfer. Section 5 describes our implementation of GFS on Taiwan Unigrid, as well as experiment results on the improvement of communication throughput and system performance. Section 6 gives some concluding remarks.

## 2    Architecture of Grid File System

This section describes the functionality of the components of *Grid File System* (GFS), and how GFS utilizes theses components to construct a grid-enabled distributed file system. The Grid File System consists of three major components – a *directory server*, *file servers*, and *GFS clients*. The directory server manages all metadata for GFS. File servers are responsible for the underlying file transfers between sites, and a GFS client serves as an interface between a user and GFS; users manipulate and access files in the GFS via GFS clients.

### 2.1    Directory Server

The directory server contains five services – *File control service* that receives requests from GFS clients and relays requests to appropriate services, *Host management service* that manages host information, *File management service* that maps a physical file to a logical file and locates a logical file, *Metadata service* that manages metadata of files and searches a registered file, and *Replica placement service* that decides where to create a replica of a logical file.

**File Control Service.** The file control service is responsible for receiving requests from GFS clients and relaying them to appropriate services of the directory server. The file control service also updates the information in the host management service.

**Host Management Service.** The host management service maintains the available space and the status of the hosts. Each GFS host record contains the following information: the *host name*, *available/total disk space* and the *status* which indicates whether a host is on-line or not.

A participant host will update its host information periodically. The file control service marks the status of a host as off-line if it does not update its host information over a certain period of time.

**File Management Service.** The file management service manages files as *logical GFS files*. For each logical GFS file, the file management service records the following information: the *logical file number*, the *physical file information*, the *owner tag*, the *modifier tag* and the *status*.

The logical file number is a globally unique identifier for a logical GFS file, which is determined by the metadata service. The physical file information helps GFS clients to locate a logical file. It contains a *physical file name*, *physical file location*, *physical file tag*, and a *physical file status*. The physical file name consists of the logical file name and a version number. The physical file location is the host name of the node where the physical file is stored. The physical file tag indicates whether this physical file is the master copy or a replica. With these information the file management service allows a GFS client to register, locate, modify and delete physical files within GFS.

The File Management Service also maintains the owner tag, the modifier tag, and the status of a logical file. The owner tag of a logical file is the name of the user who owns the file. We identify a GFS user by a GFS user name, which consists of the local user account name and the local host name, e.g., user@grid01. In this way, each user has a unique identity in the Grid File System. The modifier tag of a logical file records the name of the last user who has modified this file. The status of a logical file indicates whether this physical file is the latest version of the logical file.

**Metadata Service.** The metadata service creates and manages the metadata of GFS files. For each GFS file, the metadata service records the following information: *logical file path name*, *logical file name*, *file size*, *mode*, *creation time*, *modified time* and *status*.

The logical file path name is the global space file path. The file size is the size of the logical file. The mode follows the traditional Unix access permissions mechanism, which contains information such as the type of this file, e.g., a regular file or a directory, and the file access permission for users. The creation time and the modified time are the times at which the logical file is created and latest modified. The status indicates the availability of the logical file.

**Replica Service.** The replica service determines where to place the replica of a logical file when it is created. The replica service may use the information provided by the host management service to decide the appropriate location.

## 2.2  GFS Clients and File Servers

**GFS Clients.** The GFS client on a host serves as an interface between user programs and the Grid File System. The GFS client follows the standard Unix file system interface. With this interface, users are able to transparently access files in the Grid File System as if they are accessing files from a local file system. The GFS client performs host registration and the users manipulate GFS files through the GFS client.

As we pointed out in Section 1, in most grid systems, users must specify in advance the precise set of files to be used by the jobs before submitting jobs, which makes it difficult to run data-intensive jobs in grid systems. Therefore, we want to deploy Grid File System with ease in existing Unix-like distributed systems, and ensure that the access to GFS files must be transparent. GFS achieves these two goals by following the standard Unix file system interface.

Another important function of GFS client is to notify the directory server when a host joins GFS. When a user mounts GFS on a local host, the GFS client first communicates with the directory server. The GFS client will send the host information, such as the available space of the host and the host location, to the directory server. The GFS client then updates the local host information with the directory server periodically.

**File Server.** The file server is responsible for reading and writing physical files at local hosts, and transferring them to/from remote hosts. Each file server is configured to store physical files in a specified local directory. The file server accesses files based on the requests from the local GFS client. The GFS client will pass the information of physical files of the logical file to the file server. The file server then looks up the specified local directory to see whether the requested physical file is available in the local host. If it is, the file server reads/writes data from/to the physical file and sends the acknowledgment back to the user through the GFS client. On the other hand, if the requested file is at remote hosts, the file server then sends requests to GFS file servers at those remote hosts that own the data, and then receives the data from those remote servers simultaneously.

### 2.3   A Usage Scenario

We use a usage scenario to demonstrate the interaction among GFS client, GFS directory server, and GFS file server. The scenario is illustrated in Fig. 1a and Fig. 1b. We assume that the user mounts a Grid File System at the directory "/gfs", and the file server is configured so as to store files in "/.gfs". We also assume that a user "John" at the host "grid01" wants to copy a file "fileA" from the local file system to GFS. i.e., John at grid01 issues a command, "cp fileA /gfs/dirA/fileA".

After receiving the command from John, the GFS client first sends a LOOKUP query to the directory server asking whether the logical file "/dirA/fileA" exists or not. Then the metadata service of the directory server processes this query. If the answer is no, the GFS client then sends a CREATE request to the metadata service to create a logical file record with the logical path set to "/dirA", and the logical name set to "fileA". Then the GFS client asks the file server to create a physical file in /.gfs/dirA/fileA, and writes the content of fileA into /.gfs/dirA/fileA, as illustrated in steps 1 ~ 12 in Fig. 1a.

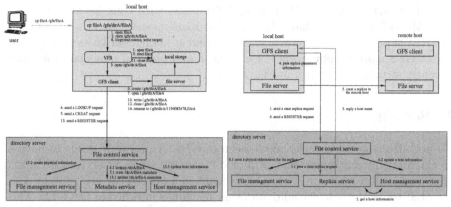

(a) Create a file at the local host.    (b) Place a replica to the remote host.

**Fig. 1.** The process of creating a file in GFS

After completing the creation, the GFS client sends a REGISTER request to the directory server. The metadata service updates the metadata information of fileA and the file management service creates a record for the new file such as the logical file number and the physical file information, as illustrated in steps 13 ∼ 14 in Fig. 1a.

Finally the GFS client sends a request for creating replicas of this logical file. The purpose of replication is to enhance fault tolerance and improve performance of GFS. The replica placement service decides where to put those replicas based on the information provided by the host management service. After receiving the locations of replicas, the GFS client passes this information to the file server, which is responsible for communicating with the remote file servers and creating replicas at those remote hosts. After successful replication, the GFS client sends a request to register those replicas with the file management service, which then adds the metadata of these replicas into physical file information database as the primary replicas of the physical file, as illustrated in Fig. 1b.

There are some notes about GFS naming convention. The first rule of GFS naming convention is that all GFS hosts must have the same mount point for

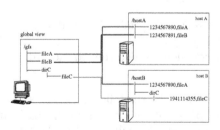

**Fig. 2.** The global view of GFS namespace

GFS. This restriction is due to compatibility issues with Unix file system interface. All GFS hosts can share the same logical namespace by this convention. The root of physical files, however, can be different in different hosts. The second rule of GFS naming convention is that logical and physical files share the same directory structure as shown in Fig. 2.

# 3   Security

We now describe the security mechanism of GFS. A user only needs to have a user account at any single host of a grid system in order to access GFS files. Therefore, a user who already has an account in a host of the grid system does not need to create new accounts on other machines in order to use GFS. This feature helps us deploy GFS to grid systems with ease since every user in a grid system can use GFS without extra effort from the system administrator.

## 3.1   Access Control

For each file, whether a user can access it or not depends on the *identity* of that user. The identity of a user is the concatenation of his/her *user account* and the hostname of *local machine*. For example, "john@grid01" is the identity of the user "john" at the host "grid01". In GFS, the owner of the logical file can modify the mode of the logical file.

GFS follows traditional UNIX permission mechanism with minor modification. We now discuss execution permission and read/write permission separately as follows. For execution permission we consider two cases. First, if the account that the system uses to run the executable is the user of the owner tag of the executable, i.e. "john@grid01" in our scenario, then the GFS client simply checks the GFS access permission of *owner* to determine whether it can run this executable or not. Second, if the account is *not* the user of the owner tag of the executable, the GFS client first checks the GFS access permission of *others*. If the permission is granted for *others*, the GFS client loads the executable for execution. If the execution permission by *others* is *denied*, then the GFS client will not load this executable file.

For read/write permission, we classify access to a file into two categories from the point of view of a GFS user:

- **Direct.** The permission is determined according to the GFS *owner/others* permission.
- **Indirect.** The permission is determined according to the GFS *group* permission.

This classification is motivated by the following usage scenario. We assume that John at grid01 wants to execute his program "progA" at two remote sites, "host1" and "host2", and "progA" will read his file "file1" as the input data. These two files, progA, and file1, are all created in GFS by John.

Now John wishes that "file1" can only be accessed by "progA". However, when a program is executed in a grid environment, it is usually executed by a *temporary account* in the remote host. That is, it is the administrators of the remote hosts that decide which account to use to execute the program and that decision is usually not predictable. The decision depends on the administration policies of the remote hosts. Thus, it is not possible to have "file1" accessible only to "progA" with the traditional UNIX permission mechanism.

Our solution is based on the fact that the program and the input files have the same owner tag, i.e., john@grid01, in GFS. When a user runs an executable file, "progA" in our scenario, as a process, the local GFS client will record the *owner tag* of this executable file and the *process ID* (PID) of this process. Note that here we assume that each process is associated with an executable file, and the process will not invoke other executables.

Now, when this process attempts to access a GFS file, the GFS client first gets the owner tag and the GFS access mode of this file from the directory server. If the user identity of this process is the owner of this GFS file, the GFS client simply checks the GFS *owner permission* to determine whether this process can *directly* access this file. Otherwise, the GFS client checks the *other* permission. If the permission is granted for others, this process can also *directly* access this file.

Next, we consider the case in which the permission by *others* is *denied*. In this case, the GFS client checks whether the GFS executable of that process has the same owner tag as the GFS file. The GFS client can simply check the PID and owner tag pair recorded when the process is created. If they have the same owner tag, the GFS client checks the GFS *group* permission to determine whether this process can *indirectly* access this file. If they do not have the same owner tag, the permission is denied.

## 4   Multiple Source Data Transfer Mechanism

In this section, we introduce the multiple source data transfer mechanism among GFS hosts. This mechanism improves both efficiency and reliability of file transfer by downloading a file from multiple GFS hosts simultaneously.

The data transfer mechanism works as follows. When a GFS client receives a user request for a logical GFS file, it sends a LOOKUP request to the file management service to find out where the physical files are. The file management service then returns the replica list to the GFS client, which contains "*on-line*" replicas of the requested file.

Then the GFS client passes the list to the file server at the local host. The file server first checks the list to find out whether a replica is available at the local host. If the local host is in the list, then GFS simply use the local replica. Otherwise, the file server sends a request to each of the hosts in the list to download the file simultaneously from those data sources. A GFS file is divided into blocks of equal size, and the file server requests/receives only blocks that are within the region requested by the user to/from the hosts in the replica list.

Note that data transfer can also improve the correctness of GFS host metadata. If a replica is not available, the GFS client will report it back to the file management service. The file management service then marks that replica as "off-line", to indicate that the replica is not functioning. Note that if the downloaded fragments constitute a complete file, the GFS client will register this physical file with the file management service as a *secondary replica* so that other file server can download the file from this host.

## 5    Performance Evaluation

We conduct experiments to evaluate the performance of GFS. We implemented a prototype GFS on Taiwan UniGrid system [1], a grid testbed developed among universities and academic institutes in Taiwan. The participating institutes of Taiwan UniGrid are connected by wide area network. The first set of experiments compare the performance of GFS with two file transfer approaches – SCP and GridFtp [3,4], both are widely used for data transfer among grid hosts.

The second set of experiments compare the performance of job execution with/without GFS. The third set of experiments test autodock [5], a suite of automated docking tools that predict how small molecules, such as substrates or drug candidates, bind to a receptor of known 3D structure.

### 5.1    Experiment Settings

Fig. 3 illustrates the system configuration in our experiments. Table 1 lists the hardware parameters of the machines.

Our prototype GFS implementation uses SQLite version 3.5.1 [6] and FUSE version 2.7.1 [7] without any grid middleware. SQLite is a database tool that GFS directory server management uses to keep track of metadata. FUSE is a free Unix kernel module that allows users to create their own file systems without changing the UNIX kernel code. The FUSE kernel module was officially merged

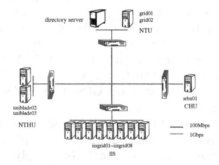

**Fig. 3.** An Illustration of the environment of our experiments. We use four sites in Taiwan UniGrid system. The directory server resides in host grid01 at National Taiwan University.

**Table 1.** Hardware configurations in GFS experiments

| Machine(s) | grid01 | grid02 | iisgrid01~08 | uniblade02,03 | srbn01 |
|---|---|---|---|---|---|
| CPU | Intel Core2 | Intel P4 | Intel Xeon | Intel Xeon | Intel P4 |
|  | 1.86GHz | 2.00GHz | 3.4GHz | 3.20GHz | 3.00GHz |
| Cache | 4M | 512K | 2M | 2M | 1M |
| RAM | 2G | 1G | 2G | 1G | 1G |

into the mainstream Linux kernel tree in kernel version 2.6.14. We used FUSE to implement GFS as a user-level grid file system.

The directory server was deployed on "grid01" (a machine located at National Taiwan University), which manages all metadata in our prototype GFS. Each of the other GFS hosts runs a GFS client and a GFS file server. File servers are responsible for the underlying file transfers between GFS sites, and GFS clients are interfaces between users (programs) and GFS, i.e., users manipulate and access GFS files via GFS clients.

## 5.2   Experiment Results

We now describe the experimental results from the three sets of experiments. The first set of experiments examine the effects of file length on the performance. The second set of experiments examine the performance of GFS file transfer. The final set of experiments examine the job success rate using GFS.

**Effects of File Length.** In the first set of experiments we perform a number of file copies from a remote site to a local site under different environment settings. Each experiment copies 100 files with size ranging from 5MB to 1GB, on the different Fast Ethernet switches. These file sizes are common in grid computing, e.g., the autodock tasks that we tested. Although it is possible to transfer task to where the data is located, it will be more efficient to transfer data to multiple sites so that a large number of tasks can run in parallel. This is particularly useful in running multiple tasks with different parameter setting.

The file transfer commands are different in SCP, GridFTP, and GFS. In GridFTP/SCP environment, one special command is invoked for each file in order to transfer data from a remote GridFTP/SSH FTP server to the local disk. On the other hand, after mounting GFS on the directory /gfs in each machine, we use the Unix copy command "cp" to transfer files. Each file has a master copy and a primary replica in the system. Each file is downloaded from its master copy and its primary replica simultaneously since GFS uses the multiple source data transfer mechanism to transfer files.

Table 2 shows that results from the first set of experiments. For files ranging from 100M to 1G, all three methods have about the same performance since the network overhead is not significant when compared to disk I/O overhead. However, when the size of files ranges from 5M to 50M, our approach has about the same performance with the SCP approach, and is 26%~43% faster than the popular GridFTP.

**Table 2.** Performance comparisons of SCP, GridFTP, and GFS. The numbers in the table are performance ratios compared to the transferring time of GFS.

|         | 5M   | 10M  | 50M  | 100M | 500M | 1G   |
|---------|------|------|------|------|------|------|
| SCP     | 1.10 | 1.13 | 0.93 | 0.98 | 0.99 | 0.98 |
| GridFTP | 1.26 | 1.39 | 1.43 | 1.02 | 1.03 | 1.02 |
| GFS     | 1    | 1    | 1    | 1    | 1    | 1    |

**GFS File Transfer.** The second set of experiments compare the performance of job execution with and without GFS multiple data file transfer mechanism. We run an MPI program StringCount that counts the number of occurrence of a given string in a file. The size of all input files are 1 GB. StringCount divides the input file into equal size segments and each computing machine is assigned one segment to count the occurrence of a given string in that segment.

In the first setting, we use the GFS file transfer mechanism. We put the executable file and its input files into GFS and execute the string counting MPI program. GFS file servers transfer these GFS files automatically. Note that the computing machines only receive the necessary segments of the input file from multiple file replicas simultaneously.

In the second setting, we do not use GFS file transfer mechanism. Instead, we follow the job submission mechanism of the Globus [3] system. Under Globus, the local machine transfers the executable and the entire input file to the computing machines before execution. Users *need* to specify the location of the input files and the executable file in a script file. GridFTP transfers the files according to the script.

The master copies of the executable file and its input files are in the host "iisgrid01" and the primary replicas are in the host "grid02". For the experiments that do not use GFS file transfer, the executable file and the input files are initially stored at the host "iisgrid01". The number of worker machines ranges from 2 to 10.

Fig. 4a shows the experimental results. The vertical axis is the execution time and the horizontal axis is the number of worker machines. From Fig. 4a we can see that the execution time of Globus increases as the number of hosts increases. This overhead is due to transferring the entire input file under Globus between worker machines and "iisgrid01", which has the input files. On the other hand, the execution time of GFS is much shorter because the worker machines only need to get the necessary segments of the input file rather than the entire file, which greatly reduces the communication cost.

Although it is possible for a programmer to use GridFTP API to transfer only the necessary parts of a input file, it takes extraordinary efforts for a programmer to learn the API and to modify the existing MPI programs. Another drawback is that once the program is modified, it cannot run in grid systems that do not have GridFTP, such as a cluster system without Globus. In contrast our GFS approach does not require a user to change his program since GFS is at the file system level.

**Job Success Rate.** The third set of experiments use autodock [5] to illustrate that GFS improves the success rate of submitted job under Taiwan Unigrid.

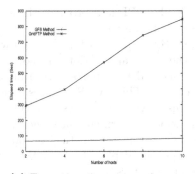 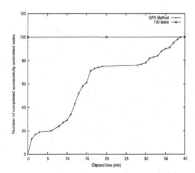

**(a)** Execution time comparison under Globus and GFS.

**(b)** The number of completed jobs with respect to elapsed time.

**Fig. 4.** Fig. 4a shows results of the second set of experiments and Fig. 4b shows results of the third set of experiments

When we submit a job into Taiwan UniGrid, the job may not be able to complete because jobs assigned to the same host may request input data or executable simultaneously. As a result the amount of simultaneous traffic may exceed the capacity of GridFTP at that site, and job fails to execute. In our experience, failure rate is about 18.44% when we submit 100 jobs with two GridFTP servers [8]. GFS solve this I/O bottleneck problem by bypassing GridFTP and using a more efficient mechanism to transfer data, so that job will execute successfully.

In a previous paper Ho et al. [8] reported that under the current Taiwan Unigrid Globus setting, the failure rate of an autoduck task is about 52.94% to 18.44%, depending on the methods of arranging executables and input files. The main reason of this high failure rate is the I/O bottleneck due to capacity limitation of GridFTP. Consequently, Globus GRAM jobs cannot stage in the executable program properly. This problem also occurred when tasks read the input files.

When we use GFS, the GRAM resource file "file.rsl" only specifies the executable and arguments, since the other information are implicitly implied by GFS file system. For example, the value of the executable is a local file path such as "/gfs/autodock" since GFS is treated as a local file system. The arguments of the executable file are specified as usual. The input data and the output data are accessible by GFS, so it is not required in "file.rsl".

Fig. 4b shows the results of virtual screening (a core computation of autoduck) by screening a 100 ligands database to avian influenza virus (H5N1) [9]. The job success rate is 100%, which means every task submitted completes successfully. In other words, GFS overcomes the I/O bottleneck problem while submitting multiple GRAM jobs, which cannot stage in the executable program due to the capacity limit of GridFTP.

## 6    Conclusion

To cope with the difficulties in running data-intensive applications with unknown data requirements and potential I/O bottleneck in Grid environment, we design

Grid File System (GFS) that provides UNIX-like API, and provides the same namespace and semantics as if the files are stored on a local machine.

GFS has the following advantages. First, GFS uses standard file I/O libraries that are available in every UNIX system; therefore, applications do not need modification to access remote GFS files. Second, GFS supports partial file access and replication mechanism for fault tolerance. Third, GFS accesses remote files with a multi-source data transfer mechanism, which improves data transfer rate by 26%~43% compared with GridFTP, which in turn enhances the overall system performance. Fourth, GFS is a user space file system that do not require kernel modification; therefore, it can be easily deployed in any Unix-like environments without the help of system administrators.

We also plan to integrate the authentication mechanisms such as GSI or PKI into our further release of GFS, and conduct more experiments to compare GFS with other grid-enabled distributed file systems, such as XtreemFS [10].

## Acknowledgement

The authors would like to acknowledge the anonymous reviewers for their valuable advises. This research is supported in part by the National Science Council, Republic of China, under Grant NSC 97-2221-E-002-128, and by Excellent Research Projects of National Taiwan University, 97R0062-06.

## References

1. Taiwan unigrid project, http://www.unigrid.org.tw
2. Howard, J., Kazar, M., Menees, S., Nichols, D., Satyanarayanan, M., Sidebotham, R., West, M.: Scale and performance in a distributed file system. ACM Transactions on Computer Systems (TOCS) 6(1), 51–81 (1988)
3. Globus toolkit, http://www.globus.org
4. Allcock, W., Foster, I., Tuecke, S., Chervenak, A., Kesselman, C.: Protocols and services for distributed data-intensive science. Advanced computing and analysis techniques in physics research 583, 161–163 (2001)
5. Autodock docking tools, http://autodock.scripps.edu/
6. Sqlite, http://www.sqlite.org/
7. Filesystem in userspace–fuse, http://fuse.sourceforge.net/
8. Ho, L.-Y., Liu, P., Wang, C.-M., Wu, J.-J.: The development of a drug discovery virtual screening application on taiwan unigrid. In: The 4th Workshop on Grid Technologies and Application (WoGTA 2007), Providence University, Taichung,Taiwan (2007)
9. Russell, R., Haire, L., Stevens, D., Collins, P., Lin, Y., Blackburn, G., Hay, A., Gamblin, S., Skehel, J.: Structural biology: antiviral drugs fit for a purpose. Nature 443, 37–38 (2006)
10. Xtreemfs, http://www.xtreemfs.org

# G2G: A Meta-Grid Framework for the Convergence of P2P and Grids

Wu-Chun Chung[1], Chin-Jung Hsu[1], Yi-Shiang Lin[1], Kuan-Chou Lai[2],
and Yeh-Ching Chung[1,*]

[1] Department of Computer Science,
National Tsing Hua University, Hsinchu, Taiwan, R.O.C.
{wcchung,oxhead,yslin}@sslab.cs.nthu.edu.tw,
ychung@cs.nthu.edu.tw
[2] Department of Computer and Information Science
National Taichung University, Taichung, Taiwan, R.O.C.
kclai@ntcu.edu.tw

**Abstract.** Grid systems integrate distributed resources to form self-organization and self-management autonomies. Recently, for large-scale computation requirement, the collaboration of different grid systems is one of the hot research topics. In this paper, we propose a meta-grid framework, called G2G framework, to harmonize autonomic grids for realizing the federation of different grids. The G2G framework is a decentralized management framework on top of existing autonomic grid systems. It adopts a super-peer network to coordinate distributed grid systems. A super-peer overlay network is constructed for the communication among super-peers in different grid systems. The contribution of this study is to propose a G2G framework for the Grid-to-Grid federation and to implement a preliminary system. Experimental results show that the proposed meta-grid framework could improve the system performance in the G2G system.

**Keywords:** Convergence, Peer-to-Peer (P2P), Super-peer, Grid Computing, Grid-to-Grid (G2G).

## 1 Introduction

The grid computing system is a distributed computing system for solving complex or high-performance computing problems, e.g., bioinformatics, medicare/healthcare, natural environment, large Hadron collider, and so on. The grid middleware enables the grid system to integrate large-scale distributed computing resources and to provide an abstract interface for system development. Then, the performance of distributed computing and data accessing could be improved by geographical distributed resources.

Many efforts adopt centralized or hierarchical architectures to develop grid systems based on the open grid service architecture (OGSA) [8]. In grid computing, a virtual

---

* The corresponding author.

N. Abdennadher and D. Petcu (Eds.): GPC 2009, LNCS 5529, pp. 131–141, 2009.
© Springer-Verlag Berlin Heidelberg 2009

organization is a self-organization and self-management group which shares the same computing resources [7]. Recently, for large-scale computation requirement, the collaboration of different grid systems (G2G grid system or meta-grid system) is one of hot research topics. The prospective cooperation is to integrate multiple autonomic virtual organizations through the federation of distinct grid systems. However, it is a challenge to harmonize grid systems without bringing a heavy burden on existing grid infrastructure.

In order to coordinate multiple grid systems, a grid system requires a middleware for the cross-grid convergence of diversely autonomic grid communities. This burdens a grid system with lots of efforts to harmonize with other grid systems; and moreover, there is no mature cross-grid middleware for integrating with distinct grid systems. In this paper, we present a meta-grid framework, called G2G framework, to federate with multiple institutional grid systems. The G2G framework could harmonize distributed grid systems over the Internet with seamless modification for existing grid systems.

The proposed decentralized G2G framework could realize the synergy between P2P networks and existing grid systems. This study utilizes a super-peer network [14] to develop our G2G framework for the coordination of multiple autonomic grid systems. To achieve the decentralization of G2G framework, the super-peer network adopts an overlay network for the communication among super-peers in different grid systems through the federation of wide area grids. Our contributions in this paper are to introduce a conceptual framework of the G2G system based on a super-peer network. We also present a preliminary implementation of the proposed G2G framework and develop a Grid-to-Grid network based on an overlay network in which each grid system communicates and negotiates with other grid systems.

The remaining of this paper is organized as follows. Section 2 discusses the related work. In Section 3, we present a conceptual overview of G2G framework and the implementation of G2G prototype. The experiment results of G2G system are shown in Section 4. We conclude this paper with future work in Section 5.

## 2   Related Work

As the grid size increases, the scalability of the large-scale grid systems becomes one of the challenges. There are some works that have discussed the practices adopting the P2P technique to improve the scalability of the grid system. Some similarities and differences between P2P computing and grid computing have been presented in [5], [13]. Several previous works are aimed to improve the centralized-based infrastructure using the P2P technique. These related works are introduced in this section.

The integration of a distributed event brokering system with the JXTA technology [16] to enable Peer-to-Peer Grids has been proposed in [9]. The authors utilize NaradaBrokering [12] based on the hierarchical structure in the broker network. By the integration of NaradaBrokering and JXTA, services are mediated by the broker middleware or the P2P interactions between machines on the edge. The main idea of NaradaBrokering aims to present a unified environment for grid computing with a P2P interaction. In addition, the overhead would be costly for NaradaBrokering to maintain the broker network of the hierarchical topology in a dynamically changed network.

A P2PGrid platform based on a two-layer model for integrating P2P computing into the Grid is presented in [1]. All grid services are provided within the grid layer in a standard manner while the P2P layer is used for grid services or ordinary PCs to participate in the grid activities. In this study, JXTA is adopted to develop JXTA Agents to create peers, deal with dynamics of peer groups, and communicate with peers on the underlying P2P network. By the implementation of the P2PGrid platform, resources on the edge of Internet are able to provide or consume services without the hassles of maintaining grid middleware packages. A separate layer from existing grid system is benefit since the original behaves of grid layer could be preserved without modifications, and the modification of the P2P manner would not affect the efficiency of the grid layer. The main idea of the P2PGrid is to provide a possible solution for integrating P2P computing with the grid environment. Peers in the P2P layer are created by the grid entities or common PCs without any grid system installed. Jobs are requested and dispatched to workers organized by created peers in the underlying P2P computing network.

In this study, we present a decentralized meta-grid framework on the top of existing autonomic grid systems from another perspective. The autonomic grids are coordinated based on the super-peer network to form a Grid-to-Grid collaborative computing environment. A super-peer in the G2G system stands for a grid system. In this study, a super-peer is able to provide/consume the grid services to/from other super-peers in remote grid systems. The autonomic grids are coordinated based on a unstructured super-peer overlay network to form a Grid-to-Grid collaborative computing environment. By adopting a separated layer, the G2G framework could integrate with existing grid systems without modifying the original mechanisms and policies. On the other hand, we not only concern the support of computation services and data services, but also propose a possible solution for the verification of accessing remote resources because of considering the security issues in the Grid-to-Grid environment.

## 3  G2G Framework and Prototype

Currently, most of the grid systems are deployed according to centralized or hierarchical management approaches. However, these approaches have poor performance in terms of scalability, resiliency, and load-balancing for managing distributed resources [11]. Centralization and hierarchy are the weaknesses of deploying large multi-institutional grid systems, let alone in the widely inter-networking G2G system. Some research work showed that the performance with adopting the super-peer model is generally more efficient and convenient than that without adopting the super-peer model in large-scale computing environments.

In our G2G framework, we utilize the super-peer network to coordinate the existing grid systems and adopt the P2P technique to coordinate grid systems. In this section, we describe the design concept for G2G system at first; and then, we introduce a basic conceptual overview of meta-grid framework. At the end of this section, we present a preliminary G2G prototype for the development of the G2G system.

### 3.1  Super-Peer Based G2G System

The super-peer network is proposed to combine the efficiency of centralized search as well as the features in terms of autonomy, load balance, and robustness of distributed search. A super-peer is a node that acts both as a centralized server to a set of ordinary nodes and as a coequality to negotiate with other super-peers.

Each super-peer in our G2G system acts a coordinator for a single grid system which is built in self-organization and self-management with the autonomy. A super-peer in the G2G system is responsible for coordinating a local autonomic Grid system and negotiating with other super-peers in remote Grid systems. For example, after obtaining a request for task execution, the super-peer firstly checks whether the request could be processed locally; otherwise, the request would be forwarded to other grid systems by cooperating with other super-peers.

Since there are multiple autonomic grid systems in the G2G system, we set up a P2P network on the grid systems to federate the super-peer in each grid system. In this way, the Grid-to-Grid interactions among distinct grid systems are by way of the P2P network. Based on P2P overlay networks, each grid in the G2G system could supply its resources and services to other grid systems and improve the resource utilization in the wide-area grids when some of the grids are overloaded and some of them are under-loaded.

In order to achieve the seamless integration of the grids in the G2G system, this study adopts the super-peer network on top of the existing grid systems, and harmonizes existing autonomous grids with each other without rebuilding/modifying any grid system. Each existent grid system could easily join the G2G system based on the super-peer network. The concept of the G2G system is shown in Fig. 1.

The G2G system consists of the Cross-Grid part, the Local-Grid part and the Meta-Grid interface. In the Local-Grid part, it consists of some autonomic grid systems which are built by the grid middleware to collaborate distributed resources. In the Cross-Grid part, the super-peers are deployed and the G2G layer is responsible to coordinate the super-peers in autonomic grids. These super-peers not only take charge of integrating the autonomic grids by the developed common interfaces but also handle the negotiation between grid systems in the G2G layer. The Meta-Grid interface is responsible to integrate the Cross-Grid part and the Local-Grid part. Using these common interfaces, the Cross-Grid part could acquire the resources and services from

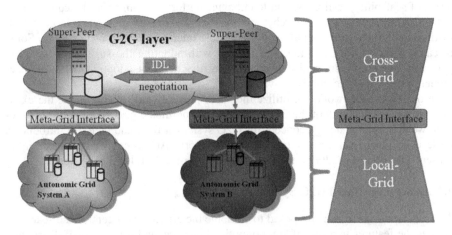

**Fig. 1.** Conception of the G2G system based on a super-peer network

the Local-Grid part without knowing the policies, mechanisms, or algorithms in the Local-Grid part. Since the Cross-Grid part and the Local-Grid part are independent, the Cross-Grid part doesn't need to be modified when the mechanisms in the Local-Grid part are modified or replaced.

### 3.2 G2G Framework

The G2G framework aims to support the seamless integration of the computing services and the data accessing services in the autonomous grids. Therefore, the super-peer in the Cross-Grid part consists of seven components: the Interactive interface, the security management, the network management, the task management, the data management, the resource management and the information service. The task management component takes care of the job computation, and the data management component is responsible for integrating the storage systems in the data grid [2]. The network management component handles the network topology and the G2G interaction between distinct grids. The resource management manages the distributed resources in grid systems according to the resource status supported by the information service component. The interactive interface component deals with the login process for users and the security management component is in charge of the authorization of using grids.

In this study, a meta-grid framework of the G2G system is proposed for federating multiple autonomic grid systems, as shown in Fig. 2. By cooperating these components in the G2G framework, we can apply grid applications on this framework. The detail notions of developing a G2G prototype are shown in the following.

### 3.3 G2G Prototype

This study uses JAVA to develop the proposed G2G framework in which the super-peers are connected by an unstructured overlay network. The developed components of the super-peer are deployed on top of each autonomic grid system to form the

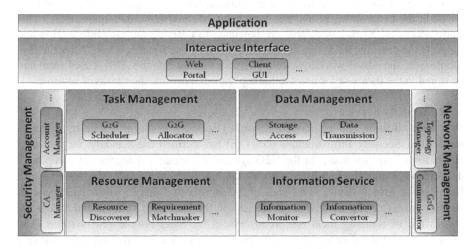

**Fig. 2.** Conceptual framework of components in the Cross-Grid part

federation environment. In this subsection, we describe the implementation and the cooperation of all components in the G2G computing system.

### 3.3.1 Portal and Single Sign-On

In general, a friendly interactive interface is important for users while using the grids. Therefore, this study develops a uniform web portal for users to easily enter a grid system and to utilize the authorized resources and services. There are two important functions for developing a uniform web portal: *Single Sign-On (SSO)*, and *workflow operation*.

Single Sign-On (SSO) is adopted for users to access the grids with only-once login. Each user could utilize grid resources/services after the successful verification through the proxy server and the security management. This study proposes a uniform web portal on top of each autonomous grid system. A redirection mechanism is also developed in the uniform web portal.

When a user logins the G2G system from this uniform web portal, the portal would determine which grid system the user should be entered according to the user's login information. The candidate grid system would verify whether the user's login information is valid or not. If the login is successful, the portal would deliver the user's login information to the local security service through the Meta-Grid interface. If the certificate of the user is also valid, the login process is successful and complete. Otherwise, it would be a failure one. Since the login process is accomplished through the integration of originally grid systems, the SSO in the G2G layer could be subsisted if the local grid supports the SSO mechanism.

The workflow operation in the G2G system supports the task submission. A workflow is composed of multiple stages and each stage is composed of multiple jobs. Jobs between distinct stages may be dependent. But jobs in the same stage are all independent, that is, all jobs within the same stage could be scheduled and allocated for simultaneous execution.

This study also develops a workflow editor in the uniform web portal. According to the resource status obtained from the information service component, users could not only edit the tasks on the portal, but also specify desired resource requirements. This study adopts an XML-based structure language to describe the task information and supports the resource discovery by multiple attributes with range query. After the task submission, the edited workflow would be transformed into the XML-based form and be stored in the database for users to lookup, cancel, or refine their tasks at anytime.

### 3.3.2 Security Service

Grid authentication and authorization are key services in the grid security management. Grid Security Infrastructure (GSI) [6] has defined the standard for the legal utilization of grid services. In the G2G system, the security management component deals with not only the certificate authorization locally, but also the admission request from remote grid systems. The issues of the secrecy and privacy in the G2G system have to guarantee the original legal services in the local grid systems and accept the permission of utilizing local resources/services for other remote grid systems. The security management component includes two primary parts: the passport manager for the authorized privilege and the account manager for the account management.

Passport manager takes care of the passport registration and the verification in the G2G system. A passport stands for the admission or verification of the request from remote grid systems. If one grid system wants to access resources in another grid system, it must get a visaed passport from the target grid system before accessing the resources. This study develops a distributed passport-interchange-mechanism in the G2G system. According to the maintenance of neighborhood relationship, each grid system could request a remote resource/service from its neighbors or neighbors' neighbors by forwarding the resource/service request along the overlay network. After discovering the available resource/service in remote grids, the requester would receive the visaed passports from the granted grid system; and then, the requester could submit tasks to the granted remote grids with legal permission.

Account manager is responsible for the account management. In this study, the function of the account authentication is used for a "local account" to login the grids. A local account indicates an originally user account in the local grid system. Once an account requests for a login from the portal, the portal would ask the account manager to verify its identification. Another important issue of the account manager is the account mapping mechanism. Account mapping is used to deal with requests issued by foreign users from remote grid systems. Every grid system which wants to use the resources in other grids must register to the granted grid system before accessing those resources. The register process acquires a passport and gets a temporary account. Once the register process is completed, every request with the visaed passport from remote grid systems would be treated as a local user account through the account mapping mechanism.

### 3.3.3  Data Service

In this study, the G2G system supports specific APIs for the transparent accesses of existent data storage in each local grid system and for the data transmission among different autonomic grid systems.

In the G2G system, the abstract APIs is responsible to contact a storage system in a local grid system or a general file system. Data accesses between the Cross-Grid layer and the Local-Grid layer adopt the general-defined data operations; otherwise, the data accesses from one grid to another grid adopt the G2G communication through super-peers. When a data transmission is necessary to communicate with remote grids, the super-peer takes care of the negotiation and communication with other super-peers in the G2G layer. We use the account manager to manage the foreign data files in this case. When the data files are accessed from remote grid systems, these data files could be stored in the storage system and then be mapped to local owners. After the data mapping and the account handling, the foreign data file could be accessible for local users.

### 3.3.4  Information Service

The main responsibilities of the information service include the resource indexing and monitoring for capturing the resource status in a grid system. Traditional Grid Information Service (GIS) generally adopts the centralized or hierarchical organization [3], [4]. Such architectures for the information service are hard to directly apply to the G2G system because of the single point of failure problem. To alleviate the failure problem, this study develops an information service for crossing the inter-grid systems on top of the existent information monitoring system. Our information service consists of two mechanisms: the information monitor and the information convertor.

This study also proposes an Information Description Language (IDL) in the form of the XML-based structure for describing the grid information in the Cross-Grid layer. The IDL is composed of many kinds of information such as task submission, task requirement, resource status, system utilization, and so on. Since the XML-based structure is wide used for information monitoring systems to record resource information, we also develop the information convertor to inter-transform other XML-based resource information into our IDL format.

### 3.3.5  Network Management

This study proposes a Grid-to-Grid overlay network based on the super-peer network. In the G2G system, the super-peer in each autonomic grid system takes responsible for the negotiation and communication with other super-peers over the G2G overlay network. The decentralized overlay network is adopted to construct the neighborhood relationship and to forward a request between super-peers.

In the cross-grid network management, we introduce the topology manager to maintain the overlay network with an adaptable mechanism for the neighborhood relationship or routing information. On the other hand, we also present the G2G communicator to take care of the network communication and message negotiation. In order to communicate with different autonomic systems, we not only apply IDL to describe the exchanged information but also design an application-level request format for message transmission. Every communication is accomplished by using the socket connection. The communication in-between two grid systems could be divided into sender- and receiver-modules. For the sender module, all the requests would be transformed into a predefined request format, and then the requests are sent to remote super-peers in serial. For the receiver module, remote super-peer de-serializes all the received requests and forwards to the corresponding components.

### 3.3.6  Task Management with Resource Discovery

The task management is in charge of the task submission through the interactive interface. A task would be a number of jobs executed in sequential or in parallel. In the G2G system, tasks are not only submitted from local users, but probably are requested from remote grid systems. The G2G scheduler and G2G allocator need to consider the job execution among the intra-grid submission as well as the inter-grid submission.

In the task management module, we adopt a workflow structure to organize jobs in a predefined order for execution. The workflow structure is constructed by stages and jobs. Those jobs in next stage must be waiting for execution until all jobs in current stage are finished because of considering the relations between stages are dependent. We also develop the workflow manager and the job manager to handle requested tasks. After a task is submitted to workflow manager, the manager schedules the order of jobs and decides where to execute these jobs. The decision of migrating the executable jobs to a local grid or a remote grid depends on the system performance or the current resource condition. Each job has its basic requirements of desired resources or the computing environment for execution. This study also applies a resource discovery mechanism [10] to explore distributed resources status over the Grid-to-Grid overlay network, and supports a matchmaking policy to provide candidate resources satisfied the specified requirements.

After a task is submitted to the waiting queue for execution, the G2G scheduler picks one of queuing jobs according to the First-Come-First-Served (FCFS) policy, and then checks whether local resources are sufficient or under loading at first. The decision of where to execute a job depends on not only checking whether local grid system is over loading, but also discovering whether local resources are satisfied with requirements through information service. If the local grid system is not busy and there are sufficiently available resources, the job would be migrated to the local grid system to be executed. Otherwise, the job manager would ask the distributed resource discovery module to search available resources over the overlay network. If there are sufficient resources in other super-peers, the job would be migrated to the remote grid system for execution. Otherwise, this job would be queued in the waiting queue for available resources.

## 4 Experimental Results

To evaluate the proposed G2G framework, two autonomic grid systems based on the framework of Taiwan UniGrid [15] are used. One autonomic grid system contains a cluster with 8 higher computational power CPUs. The other autonomic grid system contains a cluster with 32 lower computing power CPUs. We deploy the proposed super-peer network on top of each autonomic grid system to form a Grid-to-Grid federation environment. Each super-peer is responsible for coordinating the local autonomic grid system and for communicating with other super-peers over the Internet. By using the information converter, each grid system in the G2G system could extract resource information from the Information Service module. By using the IDL, the Cross-Grid layer could negotiate with the Local-Grid layer; and then the message could be exchanged between distinct grid systems.

We use a matrix multiplication program as the benchmark. Each job we used in the experiment is a parallel program written by MPI with C. The matrix size is 2048x2048. The number of required processors for each job is set to 2. The ratio of communication to computation of the test program is about 1 to 100. The task we used for performance evaluation is composed of five independent jobs. We estimate the average turnaround time for finishing all the jobs in three cases. The turnaround time of a task is defined as the time when a task is submitted to the waiting queue for processing in the Cross-Grid layer to the time when all the jobs are finished in the Local-Grid layer. In case 1, the task is submitted to the grid system with rich resources but lower computing power. In case 2, the same task is submitted to the grid system with fewer resources but higher computational power. For cases 1 and 2, all the jobs are only executed in the local grid system. In case 3, the same task is submitted to the G2G system that contains both grid systems. In this case, jobs will be executed in the local grid or the remote grid according to the decision made by the G2G scheduler and G2G allocator that we described in Section 3.3.6.

Fig. 3 shows the experimental results of three cases. The experimental results show that the proposed meta-grid framework could improve the system performance in the G2G system. In general, a grid system with rich resources could finish a task with less

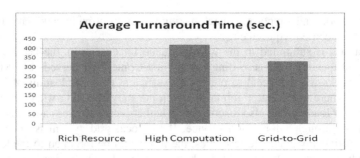

**Fig. 3.** Experimental results for finishing executing a task in three cases

turnaround time than that with higher computational power. The reason is that a job would be queued for a long time if local resources are all busy in a grid system with fewer resources. The longer time a job is queued, the more time the turnaround time would be consumed. When there are no available resources in a local grid system, the job would be migrated to a remote grid system with available resources for execution. Hence, a task in the G2G system would be finished with the least average turnaround time.

## 5   Conclusions and Future Work

Integrating the P2P technique with grid computing could improve the scalability of the large-scale grid system. This study proposes a meta-grid framework, named G2G framework, for the Grid-to-Grid federation of autonomic grid systems without modifying the original mechanisms and policies. Based on the super-peer network, we adopt a separated layer on top of existing grid systems to develop the Grid-to-Grid collaborative computing environment. A super-peer in the G2G system is responsible for coordinating an internally autonomic grid system and for communicating with other super-peers. The overlay network among super-peers is constructed by the unstructured approach.

A grid system is deployed with the capacity of the super-peer for coordinating the G2G system. With the well-defined APIs, the G2G system looks like an abstract layer separated from the existing grid systems. In our G2G system, an existing grid system could upgrade its G2G capability without upsetting original mechanisms. We not only take care of the support of computation services and data services, but also consider a possible solution for the grid security across different grid systems. To evaluate the performance of the G2G system, we implemented a preliminary system to show that the proposed system not only is workable but also improves the system performance.

We will continue to integrate with more autonomic grid systems and study on the efficiency of grid security across diverse grid systems. We also intend to integrate the G2G framework with the Service-Oriented Architecture (SOA) to develop a service-oriented G2G computing system in the future.

**Acknowledgments.** The work of this paper is partially supported by National Science Council, Ministry of Economic Affairs of the Republic of China under contract NSC 96-2221-E-007-129-MY3 and NSC 96-2221-E-007-130-MY3. We also thank all of the people for comments and advices.

# References

1. Cao, J., Liu, F.B., Xu, C.-Z.: P2PGrid: Integrating P2P Networks into the Grid Environment: Research Articles. Concurr. Comput.: Pract. Exper. 19, 1023–1046 (2007)
2. Chervenak, A., Foster, I., Kesselman, C., Salisbury, C., Tuecke, S.: The Data Grid: Towards an Architecture for the Distributed Management and Analysis of Large Scientific Datasets. Journal of Network and Computer Applications 23, 187–200 (2000)
3. Czajkowski, K., Fitzgerald, S., Foster, I., Kesselman, C.: Grid Information Services for Distributed Resource Sharing. In: 10th IEEE International Symposium on High Performance Distributed Computing, pp. 181–194. IEEE Press, New York (2001)
4. Fitzgerald, S., Foster, I., Kesselman, C., von Laszewski, G., Smith, W., Tuecke, S.: A Directory Service for Configuring High-Performance Distributed Computations. In: Sixth IEEE International Symposium on High Performance Distributed Computing, pp. 365–375. IEEE Press, Los Alamitos (1997)
5. Foster, I., Iamnitchi, A.: On Death, Taxes, and the Convergence of Peer-to-Peer and Grid Computing. In: Peer-to-Peer Systems II, pp. 118–128 (2003)
6. Foster, I., Kesselman, C., Tsudik, G., Tuecke, S.: A Security Architecture for Computational Grids. In: 5th ACM Conference on Computer and Communications Security, pp. 83–92. ACM, San Francisco (1998)
7. Foster, I., Kesselman, C., Tuecke, S.: The Anatomy of the Grid: Enabling Scalable Virtual Organizations. International Journal of High Performance Computing Applications 15, 200–222 (2001)
8. Foster, I., Kesselman, C., Nick, J.M., Tuecke, S.: The Physiology of the Grid: An Open Grid Services Architecture for Distributed Systems Integration. Technical Report. Global Grid Forum (2002),
   http://www.globus.org/alliance/publications/papers/ogsa.pdf
9. Fox, G., Pallickara, S., Rao, X.: Towards Enabling Peer-to-Peer Grids. Concurr. Comput.: Pract. Exper. 17, 1109–1131 (2005)
10. Mastroianni, C., Talia, D., Verta, O.: A Super-Peer Model for Resource Discovery Services in Large-Scale Grids. Future Generation Computer Systems 21, 1235–1248 (2005)
11. Mastroianni, C., Talia, D., Verta, O.: Evaluating Resource Discovery Protocols for Hierarchical and Super-Peer Grid Information Systems. In: 15th Euromicro International Conference on Parallel, Distributed and Network-Based Processing, pp. 147–154. IEEE Press, Los Alamitos (2007)
12. Pallickara, S., Fox, G.: NaradaBrokering: A Distributed Middleware Framework and Architecture for Enabling Durable Peer-to-Peer Grids. In: Endler, M., Schmidt, D.C. (eds.) Middleware 2003. LNCS, vol. 2672, pp. 998–999. Springer, Heidelberg (2003)
13. Talia, D., Trunfio, P.: Toward a Synergy between P2P and Grids. Internet Computing 7, 96–95 (2003)
14. Yang, B., Garcia-Molina, H.: Designing a Super-Peer Network. In: 19th International Conference on Data Engineering, pp. 49–60 (2003)
15. Po-Chi, S., Hsi-Min, C., Yeh-Ching, C., Chien-Min, W., Ruay-Shiung, C., Ching-Hsien, H., Kuo-Chan, H., Chao-Tung, Y.: Middleware of Taiwan UniGrid. In: 2008 ACM symposium on Applied computing, pp. 489–493. ACM, Fortaleza (2008)
16. JXTA Community Projects, https://jxta.dev.java.net/

# Distributed Asynchronous Iterative Algorithms: New Experimentations with the Jace Environment

Jacques M. Bahi, Raphaël Couturier, David Laiymani, and Kamel Mazouzi

Laboratoire d'Informatique de l'université de Franche-Comté
IUT Belfort-Montbéliard, Rue Engel Gros, 90016 Belfort - France
{bahi,couturier,laiymani,mazouzi}@univ-fcomte.fr

**Abstract.** Jace is a Multi-threaded Java environment that permits to implement and execute distributed asynchronous iterative algorithms. This class of algorithm is very suitable in a grid computing context because it suppresses all synchronizations between computation nodes, tolerates the loss of messages and enables the overlapping of communications by computation. The aim of this paper is to present new results obtained with the new improved version of Jace. This version is a complete rewriting of the environment. Several functionalities have been added to achieve better performances. In particular, the communication and the task management layers have been completely redesigned. Our evaluation is based on solving scientific applications using the french Grid'5000 platform and shows that the new version of Jace performs better than the old one.

## 1 Introduction

Many scientific programs require the solving of very large numerical problems. Due to their size, these problems cannot be processed by a single machine because of the lack of memory and computing power. So the use of a distributed architecture seems to be mandatory. In recent years, these architectures have greatly evolved. The development of fast and reliable networks coupled with the emergence of cheap and relatively powerful desktop computers have led to a wild use of new distributed platforms. These platforms are often almost as efficient as supercomputers and for a much smaller cost. Nevertheless, physicians define themselves as "gaseous users" which means that being given $x$ computing nodes at time $t$, they require $x + 1$ nodes at time $t + 1$. In this way, it appears that the local cluster architecture, composed of homogeneous computing nodes interconnected by a very fast local network, is no longer sufficient. Numerical computations need larger architectures composed of hundreds or thousands of heterogeneous nodes geographically distributed. We speak here of *distributed clusters* (when the architecture is composed of several interconnected remote clusters) or of *volunteer computing architecture* (when the architecture is composed of public unused stations connected to the Internet). Both architectures

N. Abdennadher and D. Petcu (Eds.): GPC 2009, LNCS 5529, pp. 142–152, 2009.
© Springer-Verlag Berlin Heidelberg 2009

provide large scale computing platforms able to (partially) tackle the size and the power requirements of many numerical applications. Unfortunately, the efficient parallelization of these applications on these platforms is not an easy task.

Indeed, there exist two main classes to solve numerical problems. The first is the class of *direct methods* which compute the exact solution of a numerical problem after a finite number of operations (we can cite here, LU or Cholesky algorithms). The second is the class of *iterative methods* which iterate many times the same instructions until reaching a good approximation of the solution. We say here that the algorithm has converged to the solution (we can cite here, the Jacobi or the Conjugate Gradient algorithms). In this paper we only focus on iterative methods since they are generally preferred over direct methods for large problems. Now, when studying the paralellization of iterative methods we can exhibit two main execution model: the *synchronous iteration model* and the *asynchronous iteration model*. In the *synchronous iteration model* all nodes are synchronized after each iteration in order to receive data dependencies from their neighbors. In this model, the number of required iterations is the same as in the sequential case. But the main drawback here are the numerous synchronizations which occur between iterations and during communications. These synchronizations can drastically reduce the overall performances especially in a large scale context with heterogeneous computing nodes (the slowest node slows down the overall platform). Now, the *asynchronous iteration model* [10], does not require any synchronization between each iteration. The computing nodes do not have to wait for data dependencies and can begin a new iteration using the last received data. The main drawback of this model is that the number of required iterations is generally greater than in the sequential case (and than in the synchronous iteration case also). Furthermore, this model is not suitable for all kind of iterative methods. Nevertheless, by suppressing synchronizations, this model allows to completely overlap communications by computations and is less sensitive to heterogeneity problems. Several works [5,6] have shown that the *asynchronous iteration model* is a very interesting execution model for the parallelization of iterative methods. These works underline the advantages of this model on large heterogeneous platforms with (medium to) high communication cost i.e. distributed clusters or volunteer computing platforms.

Unfortunately, the development and the deployment of *asynchronous iteration* applications is not straightforward. In [9], the authors show that the use of a dedicated middleware is almost mandatory for developers. To our knowledge, there exists only one development and execution environment dedicated to the *asynchronous iteration model*: Jace (Java Asynchronous Computing Environment) [8]. To tackle the heterogeneity of distributed clusters and to ensure an easy deployment over the computing nodes, Jace is a pure Java environment. It provides a message passing API (MPI-like style) allowing to use either RMI, NIO or Sockets. The actual version of Jace is 2.0.

The aim of this paper is to present the new developments and the new version of the Jace environment. We have rewritten Jace from scratch with a better objects model. This rewriting has allowed us to better apprehend the fundamental issues induced by the *asynchronous iteration model*. In particular, we have improved the communication layer and the threads management of the environment. We have also conducted an important new set of large scale experiments on the Grid'5000 testbed [1]. The experimental results show that our new developments allow to outperform the old version of Jace.

This paper is organized as follows. In section 2 we present the motivations and the context of our work. In particular, we present the actual version of the Jace environment. In section 3 we detail the improvements brought to Jace. We focus here on the communication layer and on the thread management layer. Section 4 presents the experimental results we obtain on the Grid'5000 platform. We end this paper in section 5 by some concluding remarks and future works.

## 2   Motivations and Context

As exposed in the introduction, the *asynchronous iteration model* seems to be a good execution model candidate for parallel numerical applications (especially when target architectures are distributed clusters or volunteer computing platforms). Nevertheless, the easy deployment of this model requires the use of a dedicated middleware. In this section we present the main features of the *asynchronous iteration model* and the Jace environment. We particularly point out the weaknesses of the actual version of Jace.

### 2.1   The Asynchronous Iterations Model

We focus here on the following kind of problems:

$$x = f(x) \tag{1}$$

Where $x$ is a $n$ dimension vector and $f$ is a $\mathbb{R}^n \rightarrow \mathbb{R}^n$ function. A sequential iterative algorithm can be expressed in the following way:

---
**Algorithm 1.** Sequential iterative algorithm model

---
Given $x^0$
**for** $k = 0, 1, \ldots$, until convergence **do**
  $x^{k+1} = f(x^k)$
**end for**

---

Algorithm 1 assumes the definition of a stopping threshold in order to stop computations. This threshold, also called *convergence criterion*, is generally defined from a norm computation. In the remainder we use the following norm criterion: $\max_{h \in 1..n} |x_h^{k+1} - x_h^k| < \varepsilon$ where $\varepsilon$ is the convergence criterion and $x_h^k$ is the $h$th component of vector $x$ at iteration $k$.

The parallelization of iterative algorithms have been extensively studied. An easy way to parallelize iterative algorithms is to decompose $x^k$ into $m$ blocks $X_i^k$ (for $i \in 1 \ldots m$). In the same way, $f$ can be partitioned into $m$ parts $F_i$ (for $i \in 1 \ldots m$). In this way: $x^k = (x_1^k, x_2^k, \ldots x_n^k) \equiv X^k = (X_1^k, X_2^k, \ldots X_m^k)$.

---

**Algorithm 2.** Parallel iterative algorithm model

---

Given $(X_1^0, \ldots X_m^0)$
**for** $k = 0, 1, \ldots$, until convergence **do**
  **for** $i = 0, 1, \ldots, m$ **do**
    $X_i^{k+1} = F_i(X_1^k, X_2^k, \ldots X_m^k)$
  **end for**
**end for**

---

Now, if each component $X_i^k$ is assigned to a computing node, each of them computes $X_i^{k+1}$ and sends it to all the other computing nodes in order for them to compute the next iteration. As mentioned in the introduction, the way these communications are performed can greatly influence the efficiency of the parallel algorithm. Indeed, synchronizations which occur during communication and between iterations can drastically decrease the overall performances of the algorithms. In this way, we can classify parallel iterative algorithms in two main classes (see [4] for more details):

- *The synchronous iterations model.* In this model, the iteration scheme is synchronous (as shown in Figure 1). The global behavior of the algorithm is the same as the sequential case. This strategy can be implemented by performing several asynchronous communications (data required on another processor are sent without stopping current computations) during the same iteration. We speak here of the *Synchronous Iterations Asynchronous Communications (SIAC) model.* Figure 1 illustrates this strategy with two processors. Here, the first half of data are sent as soon as updated (dashed arrows) while the second half is sent at the end of each iteration. Even if this model allows a partial overlapping of communications by computations, its performances can be poor, especially in a distributed clusters context. Indeed, as mentioned in the introduction, these architectures are composed of thousands of heterogeneous computing nodes interconnected with a generally high latency network (long distance links). In this context communications and interprocessors synchronization can drastically decrease the overall performances of the algorithm.

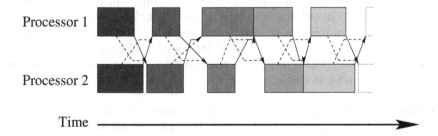

**Fig. 1.** The Synchronous Iterations - Asynchronous Communications model

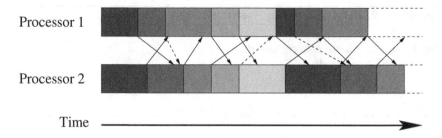

Processor 1

Processor 2

Time

**Fig. 2.** The Asynchronous Iterations - Asynchronous Communications model

– *The asynchronous iterations model.* Here, communications and iterations are performed asynchronously. We speak here of the *Asynchronous Iterations Asynchronous Communications (AIAC) model.* In this way, at step $k$, each processor updates its components by using their most recent values and not necessary the ones of iteration $k - 1$. With this model, communications and computations are well overlapped and there are no idle times anymore, due to inter-processor synchronizations between iterations (see figure 2). Unfortunately, in this model, the global iteration scheme is not the same as the sequential one. As a consequence, the number of iterations required before the convergence is generally greater than for the SIAC model. Nevertheless, in a distributed cluster context, the removal of inter-processors synchronizations allows to tackle the heterogeneity and long distance communications issues and thus to considerably improve the overall performances [5,4].

### 2.2   The Jace Environment

The implementation of AIAC algorithms is not a straightforward task [8,9]. Since this model relies on a full asynchronism paradigm, it is mandatory to be able to dissociate communications and computations. This property implies the use of multi-threaded environments and of dedicated message managers. In the remainder of this section we present Jace [8] a Java programming and executing environment especially designed to implement efficient AIAC algorithms. The choice of Java is an interesting point. Indeed, an important issue that must be addressed in a distributed clusters or volunteer computing context is the heterogeneity and the portability issue. In this way, and due to its execution model we think that the Java language is an interesting solution for developing distributed clusters applications [16,13] (even if its performances are not comparable to those of the C language for example).

**Architecture.** Jace builds a virtual machine composed of distributed interconnected nodes. Its programming interface is based on the message passing model (MPI-like style). Jace also provides primitives to implement algorithms based on the SIAC model. The Jace architecture is composed of the three following components: **the Daemon, the Spawner** and **the Worker.**

**The Daemon.** Daemons are launched on each node of the architecture and manage the whole Jace environment. They initialize the *workers* by continuously waiting for *spawner* requests (via TCP sockets). To achieve good scalability and efficient deployments, daemons are organized as a binomial tree [12]. This hierarchical organization allows to also optimize global communications inside the platform.

**The Spawner.** The spawner is the entity that starts the user application or *task*. A task is a computing unit which is executed as a thread. The spawner accepts a list of parameters: the number of tasks to be executed, the URL of the task byte-code, the parameters of the application, the list of target daemons, the mapping algorithm (round robin, best effort), the communication protocol etc. Daemons process spawner messages, by forwarding them to their neighbors (in the binomial tree) which starts workers to load and execute the user's tasks.

**The Worker.** *Workers* are structured into two layers (see figure 3): the *application layer* and the *communication layer*

- **The Application Layer**
  This layer allows tasks execution and global convergence detection. Jace is designed to control the global convergence process in a transparent way. Tasks only compute their local convergence state and call the Jace API to retrieve the global state. The application layer is also able to manage multiple tasks in order to reduce distant communications and to exploit new multi-core architectures.
- **The Communication Layer**
  This layer manages the inter-tasks communications. For this, waiting queues are created and managed by dedicated threads. For an execution in the SIAC

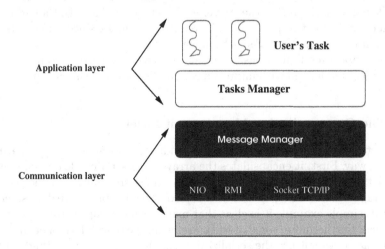

**Fig. 3.** The Jace worker architecture

mode, all messages sent by a task must be received by the other tasks. In the AIAC mode only the most recent version of a message is kept in the queue (the older ones must be deleted).

As exposed in the previous sections, it is very important that the communication layer provides an efficient device to transfer data. Jace allows to choose from the three following communication protocols: TCP/IP Sockets, NIO (New Input/Output) [3,15] and RMI (Remote Method Invocation). In [7] different series of tests have been conducted to evaluate the most efficient communication protocol. The socket protocol is generally the best protocol but the socket connections management of the NIO protocol allows it to be sometimes more efficient in a large scale context.

## 3   Improving Performances of the Jace Environment

### 3.1   Limitations of the Actual Version

In its actual version, the Jace environment suffers from two main drawbacks. First, it relies on the Java object serialization (rather than raw data) to transparently send objects. Second, its threads management layer may force implicit synchronizations and so may remove an important level of asynchronism.

The use of the Java serialization by Jace provides more flexibility but decreases overall performances. Many works [11] have shown that the object serialization is an important overhead added to communications. In a context of distributed clusters, where communications can rapidly become an important bottleneck, this serialization process must be avoided.

As exposed before, as Jace relies on a full asynchronism paradigm, it is mandatory to dissociate communications and computations through the use of a multithreaded architecture. Unfortunately, the management of these threads can be difficult, particularly during the convergence detection phase. But a bad threads management during this process can be really problematic since it may introduce (again) an important level of synchronism.

These important limitations forced us to rewrite Jace from scratch with a better object model and with improved communication and threads management levels.

### 3.2   The Communication Management Level

In its actual version Jace performs the sending of an array of `double` in the following way. First, it encapsulates the array into a serializable `Message` object. Then data are extracted and the sending routines are called. On the reception side, data are extracted again and then copied into an appropriate data structure. With this simple example it is clear that many memory copies are unnecessarily performed. Furthermore, some of them are in charge of the developer. In its new version Jace does not use the serialization anymore for the Java standard types (`float, double`...). Messages are now typed (`JACE.FLOAT, JACE.DOUBLE`...) and data copies are suppressed both on the sending and receiving sides. From an API point of view, the sending and receiving procedures are now very similar to the MPI ones i.e. JACE.send(Object, offset, lenght, DataType, receiver, Tag) and JACE.receive(Object, offset, length, DataType, sender, Tag, mode).

### 3.3 The Threads Management Level

Jace is a multi-threaded environment which runs three threads in parallel: the computation thread, the sender thread and the receiver thread. The new version of Jace totally redefines the threads management policy, in particular when several tasks runs on the same processor. This case becomes more and more relevant due to the generalization of multi-cores processors. So, to avoid synchronizations between the computation and the communications threads a unique sending queue is used. So, when $n$ tasks are running on a processor we get 1 sending queue and $n$ receiving queues.

The threads scheduling is also modified. Indeed, according to several experimentations it appears that AIAC algorithms are more efficient when the sender thread is of high priority. This can be explained by the fact that in this case, messages are more frequently updated and so the algorithm converges more quickly.

These optimisations have been implemented through the use of the java.util.concurrent package of the 1.5 Java JDK.

## 4 Experimentations

In this section, we report the experiments we have performed on the French Grid'5000 platform [1] (see figure 4). This platform is currently composed of about 5000 cores (mono-core bi-processors and bi-core bi-processors) that are located on 9 sites in France. Sites have Gigabit Ethernet Networks for local machines and links between the different sites range from 2.5 Gbps up to 10Gbps. Most processors are AMD Opteron and INTEL Xeon running the Linux operating system. For more details on the Grid'5000 architecture, interested readers are invited to visit the website: www.grid5000.fr.

### 4.1 The Test Application: The 3D Advection-Diffusion

The test application solves a three-dimensional advection-diffusion equation with a numerical parallel iterative algorithm. This system modeled the transport processes of pollutants, salinity, and so on, combined with their bio-chemical interactions can be mathematically formulated as a system of advection-diffusion-reaction equations. It follows an initial boundary value problem for a nonlinear system of PDEs, in which nonlinearity only comes from the bio-chemical inter-species reactions.

A system of 3D advection-diffusion-reaction equations has the following form:

$$\frac{\partial c}{\partial t} + A(c,a) = D(c,d) + R(c,t), \qquad (2)$$

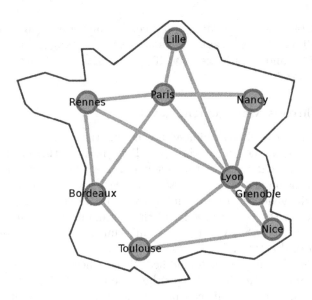

**Fig. 4.** Grid'5000 map

where $c$ denotes the vector of unknown species concentrations, of length $m$, and the two vectors

$$A\left(c, a\right) = \left[\mathbf{J}\left(c\right)\right] \times a^{T},\tag{3}$$
$$D\left(c, d\right) = \left[\mathbf{J}\left(c\right)\right] \times d \times \nabla^{T},\tag{4}$$

define respectively the advection and diffusion processes ($\mathbf{J}\left(c\right)$ denotes the Jacobian of $c$ with respect to $(x, y, z)$). For more details on the application readers can refer to [14].

## 4.2   Experimental Results

The experimentations have been performed on 60 nodes distributed over 4 clusters geographically located in three computer sciences Labs (Rennes, Bordeaux and Nancy). Nodes are quite heterogeneous (16 bi-processors AMD Opteron 246 2.0GHz, 20 bi-processors bi-core AMD Opteron 2218 2.6 GHz, 4 bi-processors bi-core Intel Xeon 5148 LV 2.33 Ghz, 20 bi-processors bi-core Intel Xeon 5110 1.6 GHz). The instance of the problem produces a sparse matrix of size $6,750,000 \times 6,750,000$. The number of non-zero elements is equal to 14 per row. The method we use, called the multisplitting method [5], allows us to execute the problem using either the synchronous or the asynchronous iteration model. It is an iterative method. Moreover, the multisplitting with non-linear problem has the particularity that each processor involved in the computation need to solve a local linear system at each iteration of the multisplitting process. In these experiments, we have used the MTJ library (Matrix Toolkit for Java) [2] with the

| Mode | Protocol | Old version | New version |
|------|----------|-------------|-------------|
| Synchronous | rmi | 855 | 710 |
| Asynchronous | rmi | 656 | 446 |
| Synchronous | socket | 631 | 555 |
| Asynchronous | socket | 457 | 352 |

**Fig. 5.** Comparison of the new and the old versions of Jace (time in s)

multi-threaded GMRES method. Consequently, each machine depending on its numbers of processors and cores and processing characteristics can solve more or less quickly a sparse linear system.

Results are presented in figure 5. From this table, several remarks can be made. First, it appears that for both versions i.e. old and new, synchronous and asynchronous, the socket protocol is clearly better than the RMI protocol. This is not surprising and confirms some previous works [7]. Second, we can see that in a distributed clusters context the AIAC model performs better than the SIAC model for both protocols i.e. RMI and socket. Again, these results are not surprising and confirm some previous works (see the introduction section). Finally, and most importantly, we can see that the new version of Jace outperforms the old one for both protocols and modes. The gain is important and varies from 12% (SIAC with Socket) to 32% (AIAC with RMI). As previously exposed, this can be easily explained by the optimizations brought to the communication and threads management layers.

In order to have a more precise idea of how the new version performs, we are currently running a new series of tests with more nodes and with various scientific applications.

## 5   Conclusion and Future Works

In this paper we have presented a new version of the Jace environment. This environment is dedicated to *Asynchronous Iterations Asynchronous Communications* algorithms and has proven its efficiency especially on a distributed clusters context. The new version of Jace is a complete rewriting of the environment (with a better object model). For this version, we have especially improved the threads and the communication management levels. Experimental results conducted on the Grid'5000 testbed, show that the new version performs better than the old one both in local and distributed clusters context.

Our future work include to test Jace in a large scale context (with more than 300 nodes) and with some other scientific applications. These tests will allow us to better characterised the behavior of Jace. Another interesting research track is to mix the asynchronous and synchronous models. In our idea, it seems to be interesting to study the use of synchronous solvers on local cluster and asynchronous solvers between distant sites. This approach seems to be able to gather the advantages of the both models.

# References

1. Grid'5000, http://www.grid5000.fr
2. MTJ: Matrix Toolkit for Java, http://mtj.dev.java.net/
3. New I/O API, http://java.sun.com/j2se/1.4.2/docs/guide/nio
4. Bahi, J.M., Contassot-Vivier, S., Couturier, R.: Performance comparison of parallel programming environments for implementing AIAC algorithms. Journal of Supercomputing 35(3), 227–244 (2006)
5. Bahi, J.M., Contassot-Vivier, S., Couturier, R.: Parallel Iterative Algorithms; From Sequential to Grid Computing. Chapman and Hall/CRC, Boca Raton (2007)
6. Bahi, J.M., Couturier, R., Laiymani, D.: Comparison of conjugate gradient and multisplitting algorithms of nas benchmark with the jace environment. In: IPDPS 2008. IEEE Computer Society Press, Los Alamitos (2008)
7. Bahi, J.M., Couturier, R., Laiymani, D., Mazouzi, K.: Java and asynchronous iterative applications: large scale experiments. In: IPDPS 2007, pp. 195–203. IEEE Computer Society Press, Los Alamitos (2007)
8. Bahi, J.M., Domas, S., Mazouzi, K.: More on jace: New functionalities, new experiments. In: IPDPS 2006, pp. 231–239. IEEE Computer Society Press, Los Alamitos (2006)
9. Bahi, J.M., Contassot-Vivier, S., Couturier, R.: Performance comparison of parallel programming environments for implementing AIAC algorithms. Journal of Supercomputing. Special Issue on Performance Modelling and Evaluation of Parallel and Distributed Systems 35(3), 227–244 (2006)
10. Bertsekas, D.P., Tsitsiklis, J.N.: Parallel and Distributed Computation: Numerical Methods. Prentice Hall, Englewood Cliffs (1989)
11. Carpenter, B., Fox, G., Ko, S.H., Lim, S.: Object serialization for marshaling data in a java interface to mpi. Concurrency: Practice and Experience 12(18), 539–553 (2000)
12. Gerbessiotis, A.V.: Architecture independent parallel binomial tree option price valuations. Parallel Computing 30(2), 301–316 (2004)
13. Huet, F., Caromel, D., Bal, H.E.: A High Performance Java Middleware with a Real Application. In: Proceedings of the Supercomputing Conference, Pittsburgh, Pensylvania, USA (November 2004)
14. Blom, J.G., Verwer, J.G., Hundsdorfer, W.: An implicit-explicit approach for atmospheric transport-chemistry problems. Applied Numerical Mathematics: Transactions of IMACS 20(1-2), 191–209 (1996)
15. Pugh, B., Spaccol, J.: MPJava: High Performance Message Passing in Java using Java.nio. In: Proceedings of the Workshop on Languages and Compilers for Parallel Computing, College Station, Texas, USA (October 2003)
16. van Nieuwpoort, R.V., Maassen, J., Kielmann, T., Bal, H.E.: Satin: Simple and efficient Java-based grid programming. Scalable Computing: Practice and Experience 6(3), 19–32 (2005)

# Predicting Free Computing Capacities on Individual Machines

Alek Opitz and Hartmut Koenig

Brandenburg Technical University Cottbus, Germany
{ao,koenig}@informatik.tu-cottbus.de

**Abstract.** The basic idea of grid computing is a better use of underutilized resources. Following this idea, desktop grids target ordinary workstations, which are very powerful today. However, due to the priority of the local users, it is impossible to exclusively reserve computing time for grid jobs on these machines. Consequently, an already running grid job might be delayed or even canceled. A forecast of future available computing capacities could alleviate this problem. Such a prediction would be especially useful for the allocation of the most appropriate machines and for making stochastic assertions on the completion of submitted jobs. In this paper we discuss suitable approaches for predicting the availability of computer resources. We develop measures to finally make a comparison of the approaches, which is based on empirical data from available workstations.

**Keywords:** grid computing, desktop grids, prediction, measures.

## 1 Introduction

In recent years a lot of work has been done to use idle computing resources distributed over the Internet. The idea of grid computing was born. It gives users the possibility to submit compute-intensive jobs to a grid that provides the required resources, whereas resource providers and users may belong to different organizations. The obvious motivation behind this idea is a possible reduction of the costs by achieving a substantial increase of the resource utilization, which is usually quite low for computing systems today [1].

The resources themselves can be resources dedicated to grid computing or, on the contrary, for instance ordinary workstations. Due to their permanently increasing capabilities the latter are becoming more and more important for the processing of even complex calculations. The development of new chips, for example, requires a lot of simulation runs to check the correctness of the logic and the performance of a new design [7]. The use of workstations is beneficial here because of the sheer mass of simulation runs, which are independent from each other. The runtimes of the simulations range from a few minutes to several days, sometimes even several weeks. Other examples for the possible use of ordinary workstations include simulations for the development of new drugs [2,5], the rendering of animation movies [5], or in-silico crash tests in the design of new automobiles [2].

N. Abdennadher and D. Petcu (Eds.): GPC 2009, LNCS 5529, pp. 153–164, 2009.

Despite the impressive computing power of today's workstations their use for grid computing is a challenging task, if the workstations are not exclusively dedicated to the grid. In case of using non-dedicated workstations the local users are usually prioritized. Hence, they can dramatically influence the availability of idle CPU cycles by starting new processes or by shutting down the machines. Thus, starting a job with a runtime of several hours on a desktop machine is a kind of a gamble without knowing the chances to win, i.e. without knowing the probability whether the job will be finished by a defined deadline. To alleviate this problem a prediction of the future available computing capacities might be useful. Such a prediction is the focus of the paper at hand. To specify precisely the measurement goal we use the following definitions:

**Definition 1.** The quantity $C_{cum}$ is defined for a single machine as the cumulated amount of unused computing capacity from now to the next shutdown or crash.

**Definition 2.** The quantity $C_{cum,h}$ is basically the same as $C_{cum}$, but considers only the next $h$ hours for the accumulation of the computing capacity.

The quantity $C_{cum}$ indicates, whether a job with a certain computational complexity can be finished on a given machine before it goes down (assuming that all the computing capacity not used by the local user can be consumed). Unfortunately $C_{cum}$ does not provide any information about an upper limit of the execution time. This motivates the introduction of $C_{cum,h}$, which sets the upper limit for the execution time to $h$ hours. In our experimental evaluations we scaled $C_{cum,h}$ to always achieve a value range from 0 to 100. For the usage of the values (or estimates) it is obviously necessary to incorporate the relative speeds of the considered machines.

We are interested in predictions for $C_{cum,h}$ to enable a reasonable selection of an appropriate machine for a given job (i.e. we want to select a machine capable to finish the job within the next $h$ hours). But, for this selection a single prediction value for $C_{cum,h}$ (e.g. the expectation value) is not a real aid because this single value can be very misleading. Actually, we are more interested in the machine with the highest probability to finish the job in the given time. Therefore, in this paper we concentrate on the prediction of the probability distribution for $C_{cum,h}$.

A discussion of conceivable prediction methods for probability distributions is useless without a reasonable empirical comparison. For this comparison we need suitable measures. Their derivation is not trivial at all, but has not been discussed in the literature up to now. Hence, the first contribution of this paper is the presentation of suitable measures to assess the accuracy of predicted probability distributions. The introduced measures are then applied to compare different methods for the prediction of available computing capacities. Based on empirical data from available workstations we are able to give indications for the relative accuracy of different approaches. These results are the second contribution of the paper.

The remainder of the paper is structured as follows. First, we give an overview of related work in Section 2. Thereafter, we introduce complementary measures for the assessment of different prediction methods. The subsequent Sections 4 and 5 discuss possible approaches for the prediction of available computing capacities. A summary of our empirical comparison is given in Section 6. Final remarks with an outlook on future work conclude the paper.

## 2 Related Work

The literature already contains quite a few papers about the prediction of the availability of computing resources. In this section we cover only the work most similar to ours. We do not discuss papers concentrating on the usage of predictions, since this is not the focus of the paper at hand.

The first category of possible availability prediction approaches models the behavior of groups of machines. For example, Nurmi et al. try to determine the statistical distributions for the idle times of workstations [10]. The authors conclude that Weibull and hyperexponential distributions fit the empirically determined distributions well. Mutka [8] attempts to predict the available computing power of ordinary workstations to enable the schedulers to meet given deadlines for individual jobs. The basic approach is the use of empirical distributions for a group of machines. Different distributions are constructed from values belonging to different times of the week. The author distinguishes weekdays from weekends and also several phases of a day. The main problem with both approaches is the aggregated consideration of different machines, which makes a sound selection of an individual machine for a certain job impossible. The application of the mentioned distributions for individual machines does not deliver reasonable results (comp. Section 6).

Approaches forecasting the availability of individual machines are closer to our prediction goal. One of these approaches is the Network Weather Service (NWS, see [10,15,16]). It predicts the availability of individual machines as well as the load of the network. A possible improvement of the NWS is discussed in [18]. The most important difference of these two approaches to our approach is the fact that they give predictions for only a few seconds in advance, whereas the methods discussed in the paper at hand aim at predictions for several hours in advance to support long-running jobs. Furthermore, the predictions deliver only point estimates, but no probabilities.

The approach closest to ours is that of Wyckoff et al. [17] who tries to determine the probability distributions for the idle times of workstations. The authors use one empirical distribution per machine derived from the results from one month. Based on this distribution they calculate the probability distribution for a machine in idle state by using conditional probabilities based on the current idle time of the machine. Although the basic approach is relatively similar to ours (comp. Section 4), there are some important differences. The first one is the item of the prediction itself. Whereas in [17] the length of the times is considered during that the local user does not actively use the machines, we consider the cumulated free computing power for the next hours. Consequently, the results from [17] cannot be simply assumed to be true for our analysis, especially because the forecast horizons in our investigation are much longer. Furthermore, Wyckoff et al. use a test for their proposed method that assumes the time series containing the idle times of a workstation to be stationary. That means, in their assessment they assume a probability distribution for the idle times that stays constant for at least one month. We do not see a justification for this assumption. Therefore we had to develop our own, more appropriate measures (Section 3). Last but not least, [17] mainly ignores the question of how to transform the empirical frequency distribution into the prediction distribution. As we will see in this paper, an appropriate transformation method has considerable consequences for the accuracy of the predictions (comp. Sections 5 and 6).

# 3   Measures for the Accuracy of Predictions

To compare various prediction methods we use empirical data observed on several workstations. For this comparison it is essential to use appropriate measures. This seemingly minor requirement is far from being trivial to fulfill. The problem becomes clearer when we consider the approach chosen in [10]. In this approach the empirical frequency distribution (EFD) of one time period is used for the predictions in the subsequent period. The accuracy of the predictions during this second period is assessed by comparing the EFDs of the two time periods. Obviously this assessment ignores varying probabilities, i.e. it is implicitly assumed that the probability distribution is constant during the chosen period. Similar consequences result from using standard fitting tests like the Chi-Square-Test or the Kolmogorov-Smirnov d-Test [7,12]. Since the mentioned stationarity assumption cannot be justified, we had to develop new measures for assessing prediction methods. Such measures are discussed next.

## 3.1   Accuracy on Average

The scenario behind the discussion in this paper is the use of computers provided by other organizations. In this case it seems appropriate to assume the existence of service level agreements (SLAs). Such an SLA usually contains some assertion about the availability of the resources. That means a user of the resources should get the assertion that she can submit a job with a certain computational complexity and this job will be finished by a certain deadline with a probability of $p$. To fulfill such stochastic assertions, the service provider needs an appropriate prediction method. For example, if this method makes $x$ predictions that a certain resource can finish the submitted job in the given time with a probability of 90 %, then the resource should really be able to finish the given jobs in $0.9 \cdot x$ cases. A prediction method having this property for each $p$ from the interval $[0,1]$ is called to be **accurate on average** in the rest of this paper.

   To assess the accuracy on average of a method, which gives estimations $F_i$ of the cumulated distribution functions (CDFs) for different times $t_i$, we exploit an interesting consequence of being accurate on average: It can be shown that for the finally measurable free computing capacities $C_{cum,h}(t_i)$ the values $F_i(C_{cum,h}(t_i))$ should be uniformly distributed between 0 and 1 – even if the underlying distribution of the observed values changes over time. (We omit the proof here due space constraints.)

   Obviously, this property will not be exactly fulfilled by a real prediction method. Hence, we have to assess how close a prediction method comes to this property. For doing so, we proceed as follows. For each point in time $t_i$ we use the considered method to predict the probability distribution of $C_{cum,h}$. After measuring the corresponding observable value (the measurement is possible $h$ hours after $t_i$) we determine the least percentile containing this value. For example, in Fig. 1 we have the observed value 9, which corresponds to the least percentile 36 %. Using the percentiles for the observed values (5, 9 (twice), and 16) we get the cumulated frequency distribution of the percentiles (the (red) step function in the right part of Fig. 1). Ideally, this function would match $f(x) = x$ in the interval $[0,1]$ (the (green) dotted line in Fig. 1). Now we define the measure $M_{avg}$ as the deviation between the two functions, i.e. the (yellow) shaded area in Fig. 1. Obviously, bigger values are worse than smaller values. The optimal value is 0. It should be noted that this measure does premise neither a constant distribution prediction nor the stationarity of the underlying time series.

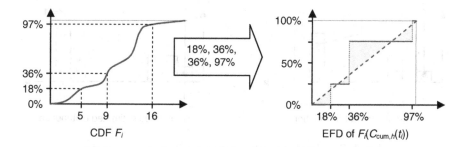

**Fig. 1.** Illustration of the measure $M_{\text{avg}}$

$M_{\text{avg}}$ gives a single assessment of the accuracy for all percentiles. Sometimes it might be more interesting to assess the accuracy for certain important percentiles. This leads to the more specific measure $\Delta(p)$, which considers only the percentile $p$:

$$\Delta(p) = \frac{\left|\left\{F_i(x_i)\middle|F_i(x_i) \leq p, i \in \{1,...,n\}\right\}\right|}{n} - p$$

For instance, if a resource provider assured $n$ times that the desired computing capacity will be available with at least 80% probability, then we could use $\Delta(20\%)$ to check the appropriateness of a given prediction method regarding the given promises.

### 3.2 Accuracy of Individual Predictions

The measure $M_{\text{avg}}$ gives an assessment of the accuracy on average, which is needed for the compliance with SLAs. Unfortunately, $M_{\text{avg}}$ does not assess the accuracy of individual predictions, i.e. it does not assess the ability of a prediction method to predict varying probabilities. The problem is depicted in Fig. 2 for an example with an alternating real distribution, but an unchanged prediction. Obviously, this prediction is far from being optimal, but it matches exactly the average distribution of the values. Therefore we need a further desirable property of a prediction method, the accuracy per prediction, whereas a method is said to be **accurate per prediction**, iff the predicted distributions match the real distributions of the corresponding points in time.[1]

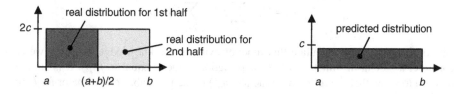

**Fig. 2.** Unchanged prediction for an alternating distribution

---

[1] With "real distributions" we mean the distributions chosen by a machine that knows all the data from the past and all existing relations between these data. Even such a hypothetical machine will not be able to predict the future values deterministically.

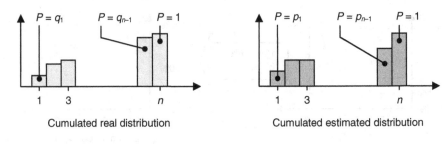

**Fig. 3.** Cumulated distribution functions with $n$ different classes

Again, it is practically impossible that a real prediction method fulfills this property. Consequently, we are not interested, whether this property is fulfilled, but how "far away" the prediction method is from fulfilling this property. For the assessment we use a measure, whose main idea is the use of intrinsically stochastic results, i.e. we propose a measure whose expectation value decreases with an improvement of the prediction. Hence, the measure applied on a single prediction is not significant but the sum of the measure values for different points of a long time series is.[2] The exact definition of this second measure (finally denoted by $M_{\text{exp}}$) is explained in the following.

**Discretization of Values**

Our measure requires a discretization of the value range into $n$ different classes (i.e. intervals) $I_1$ to $I_n$. Consequently, we have $(n-1)$ unknown probability values $q_1$ to $q_{n-1}$, where $q_i$ is the probability that a real value falls into a class $I_k$ with $k \leq i$ (see Fig. 3). The corresponding estimations for these probabilities are $p_1$ to $p_{n-1}$. For concise identifications, we introduce the two vectors $q = (q_1,\ldots,q_{n-1})^{\text{T}}$ and $p = (p_1,\ldots,p_{n-1})^{\text{T}}$.

We are now looking for a function $f_q(p)$ that is minimal for $p = q$, and that increases with increasing difference between $p$ and $q$. To create such a function we start with possible partial derivatives:

$$\frac{\partial f_q}{\partial p_i} = 2p_i - 2q_i \qquad \text{with} \qquad \frac{\partial^2 f_q}{\partial^2 p_i} = 2$$

An antiderivative for these partial derivatives is the following function $f_q(p)$, which is minimal for $p_i = q_i$ (if only $p_i$ is varied):

$$f_q(p) = C_q + \sum_{i=1}^{n-1} p_i^2 - \sum_{i=1}^{n-1} 2q_i \cdot p_i$$

Obviously, we cannot calculate this function without the knowledge of $q$, but we can construct a stochastic function whose expectation value is equal to $f_q(p)$. It is straightforward to show that the following function $s_q(p)$ is such an unbiased estimator for $f_q(p)$:

---

[2] Alternative assessment methods (compare the beginning of Section 3) collect the predictions and also the measured values to finally compare both sets. Hence there is no information about the accuracy per prediction. The method proposed here, on the contrary, evaluates the individual predictions at different points in time and finally averages the evaluations. This gives the desired information about the (average) accuracy per prediction.

$$
s_f(p) = \begin{cases} (n-k) + \sum_{i=1}^{n-1} p_i^2 - 2\sum_{i=k}^{n-1} p_i & \text{if the measured value belongs} \\ & \text{to class } k \ (1 \le k < n) \\ \\ (n-k) + \sum_{i=1}^{n-1} p_i^2 & \text{otherwise} \end{cases}
$$

Since a single value of $s_f(p)$ is not significant, we intend to add the values obtained for different points in time. To justify this summation, the expectation values of $s_f(p)$ must lie on an interval scale, whereas we have to define an appropriate scale for the deviations of the predictions in relation to the real distributions. For these deviations, we consider the sum of the quadratic deviations $(p_i - q_i)^2$ as a ratio scale, since such a scale is often (implicitly) used in similar cases, especially in regression methods based on the least square approach. Based on this view it can be shown that the expectation values of $s_f(p)$ lie on an interval scale, since the difference between $f_q(p)$ and $f_q(q)$ is simply this sum of the quadratic deviations $(p_i - q_i)^2$. Unfortunately, we do not have a ratio scale, because usually $f_q(q)$ is not equal to zero. Therefore we are not able to judge the percentage of the improvement of one prediction method in relation to another. But it should be clear that we cannot construct such a measure with a ratio scale. If we could, then we also could search for a $p$ with $f_q(p) = 0$ and thus we could exactly determine the real distribution $q$, which is impossible.

**The Measure $M_{exp}$**
We define the measure $M_{exp}$ as the average of the values of $s_f(p)$ calculated for the points of a time series, whereas we did not yet mention the choice of $n$. The introduction of any classification of the values is a simplification, as the actual distribution is continuous, but the consequences get more dramatic if the value of $n$ decreases. On the other hand, the complexity of the measure calculation increases with $n$. To trade-off these potential problems we chose the value $n = 100$ for our measurements.

### 3.3 Recapitulation of Proposed Measures

The discussion of desirable properties of a prediction method led to the introduction of the measures $M_{avg}$, $\Delta(p)$, and $M_{exp}$. The first two are used for the assessment of the average accuracy of the prediction method. This property is important for a service provider to avoid contract penalties. $M_{exp}$ assesses the ability of the method to predict the real distributions exactly on time. This property is desirable for a service provider to choose the most suitable machine for a certain job. A prediction method should be close to both properties, i.e. all measures should give good results.

## 4   Usage of Empirical Frequency Distributions (EFDs)

In our experiments we compared different approaches to make predictions. They all have in common to rely on empirical frequency distributions (EFDs) constructed from the (locally!) logged values of free computing capacities from the last time.

**Table 1.** Variants for the distinction of different EFDs

| Distinction criterion | Description |
|---|---|
| $D_{simple}$ | This variant uses only a single EFD. |
| $D_{uptime}$ | In this variant the uptime of the machine is used to distinguish between different distributions. There are 50 different EFDs, whereas the first one is used for uptimes less than an hour, the next one for less than two hours (but at least one hour), and so on. The last EFD contains the values of uptimes greater than 49 hours. |
| $D_{timeOfWeek}$ | This variant distinguishes the 168 different hours of the week. That means, for each of these hours a different EFD is used. |

The simplest model following this basic approach is the use of a single EFD per machine. A possibly better alternative is the distinction between different EFDs. For example, it might be useful to have separate distributions for different days of the week. In this case the values for Mondays are put into one EFD, the values for Tuesdays into a different one, and so on. For the prediction of $C_{cum,h}$ that EFD is used that corresponds to the current day of the week. The disadvantage of such a distinction is the lower count of values per EFD. This increases the influence of individual outliers, which might outweigh the advantage of the more specific EFDs (comp. Section 6).

The idea of a distinction between different EFDs is not new. The question is which distinction criterion is the most suitable one. Up to now, the literature does not compare possible alternatives. In this paper we give in Section 6 results for the three alternatives defined in Table 1. Originally, we experimented also with other alternatives, with slight variations, and with mixtures of the given three alternatives, but we could not gain further improvements.

# 5   Transformation of the EFD into the Prediction

Having the appropriate EFD for a certain machine is only the first step to get a prediction. The second is the transformation of the EFD into the prediction. In the literature several methods for this transformation can be found; the most important of these methods are described in the following subsection. Our own method to improve this derivation step is explained subsequently.

## 5.1   Transformation Methods Proposed in Literature

A very often applied transformation method is based on the construction of histograms [13]. The method divides the range of possible values into a certain number of intervals. For each of them the frequency of the values is counted. Then for an interval with frequency $f$ a probability of $f/n$ is assumed, where $n$ is the total number of values. Inside the intervals uniform distributions are assumed. This method is called $T_{histo}$ in the rest of the paper.

An alternative to $T_{histo}$ is the method to simply transform the EFD into a distribution of relative frequencies [13], i.e. for the empirically determined $n$ values $v_1$, $v_2$, ..., $v_n$ the predicted distribution function $F_{pred}(x)$ is constructed as follows:

$$F_{pred}(x) = \frac{\#\{i : v_i \leq x\}}{n}$$

We denote this approach $T_{1:1}$ here.

A further often used variant is the assumption of a certain standard distribution. In this case the values from the EFD are used to fit a parameterized distribution function of a certain type. The surveys indicating the existence of such a distribution consider always the aggregated values from groups of machines. In our opinion, these results cannot be used for individual machines. Nevertheless, the approach of fitting hyperexponential distributions was proposed in [11]. For this reason we included such a transformation method called $T_{hyperexp}$ in our experiments.

## 5.2  Transformation Method $T_{interval}$

Additionally to the approaches described so far, which are taken from literature, we introduce a further possible approach for the estimation of the real CDF. This approach, denoted here as $T_{interval}$, assumes uniform distributions in the intervals that are marked by neighboring values from the EDF.

Formally speaking, we consider the ascendingly sorted list of the $n$ observed values $v_i$. There are $(n+1)$ possible positions, where a new value $v$ could be inserted into this list. Without further information about the probability distribution the following assumption is the most reasonable one:[3]

$$P(v < v_1) = P(v_i < v < v_{i+1}) = P(v > v_n) = \frac{1}{n+1} \qquad (1 \leq i < n)$$

Thus we actually have $(n+1)$ intervals, but only one limit for the leftmost and only one limit for the rightmost interval. For the missing limits, we use the theoretical limits of the value range. Consequently, naming the lower limit $v_0$ and the upper limit $v_{n+1}$ we assume for each interval $(v_i, v_{i+1})$ a uniform distribution with probability $1/(n+1)$ for $0 \leq i \leq n$.

## 5.3  Adaptive Correction of Predictions

There is a possibility to correct the predictions created by the previously described transformation method $T_{interval}$ using the predicted percentiles for the finally measurable values of $C_{cum,h}$ (Fig. 4). For each point in time $t$ there is a prediction, which is essentially a CDF ($F$ in the figure). Not later than $h$ hours after $t$ the value of $C_{cum,h}$ at time $t$ can be determined and consequently also the percentile $p$ for this value, i.e. the predicted probability that $C_{cum,h}$ is not greater than this value $v$. The determination of these percentiles can be done for each measured value. Similarly to the discussion in Section 3.1 the percentiles should be uniformly distributed between 0 and 1.

---

[3] We simplify the discussion by assuming all the values to be different.

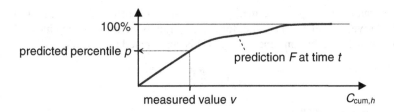

**Fig. 4.** Determination of predicted percentiles

Consequently, the prediction could be corrected depending on the deviation of the measured distribution of the percentiles and the uniform distribution. Having a distribution $F_P$ of the predicted percentiles (whereas we consider the predictions from all EFDs, i.e. ignoring the chosen distinction criterion) the original prediction $F$ can be corrected in the following way:

$$F_{\text{corr}}(x) = F_P\big(F(x)\big)$$

## 6   Experimental Results

To compare the discussed prediction methods we logged the use of CPU and main memory on different workstations for periods from several months to over a year.[4] We considered the unused CPU cycles only available if a certain minimum amount of main memory was free. We chose an exemplary limit at 256 MB.[5] Based on the log data we were able to test different prediction methods with exactly the same data.

We divided the logs into the disjoint sets A and B. Set A was quite small and only used for initial experiments with quite a lot of possible prediction approaches. The most promising of them have been described in Sections 4 and 5. The results of the experiments indicated that there is no clearly best classification criterion. However, the newly developed method $T_{\text{interval}}$ in conjunction with the adaptive correction $A_{\text{full}}$ delivered clearly better results than the transformation methods from the literature.

To verify the results regarding the transformation step we conducted measurements with the logs from set B. Despite the fact that such a separation between data for the development of new approaches and the assessment of new approaches is rarely done, it is very important to avoid an over-fitting to the given data by simply choosing the approach with the best results on the given data set.

---

[4] This does not mean that data from several months or even from a whole year are necessary to make a prediction. Instead we have chosen a sliding window of 10 weeks to construct the EFDs, whereas on a new machine predictions are also possible before the completion of the first 10 weeks. The long log periods have the sole purpose to get for each machine a lot of predictions. Hence, the assessment of the prediction quality on a certain machines does not depend on only a single prediction.

[5] For the application of the proposed predictions we consider the existence of several classes necessary that differ by the minimum amount of free memory. Then there are separate predictions needed for the different classes, whereas in dependence of the total amount of main memory on each machine only few classes should be supported.

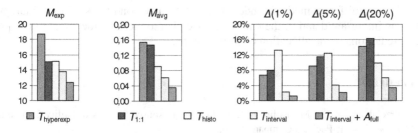

**Fig. 5.** Results of the different transformation methods

The mentioned set B consisted of 51 different machines. Roughly one-half of these are used as desktop machines in computer pools, offices, or at home. The other half are used as servers (for example as web servers). We examined the available computer capacity for 6, 12, and 24 hours ($C_{cum,6}$, $C_{cum,12}$, and $C_{cum,24}$). The results for the different transformation methods are depicted in Fig. 5.

According to theses results the recommended transformation method $T_{interval}$ in conjunction with the adaptive correction $A_{full}$ improves the accuracy of the predictions considerably. The significance tests of these results were done in two ways. First, the group of 51 machines was divided into four different homogenous sets, i.e. sets with machines with similar usage patterns. The advantage of the recommended combination could be observed for all four sets. Second, using the Bootstrap method [3] for the whole group the results could be confirmed at a significance level of 95%.

## 7 Conclusions

In this paper we have analyzed approaches to predict probabilities for the available computing capacities of individual machines within the next hours to support the selection of a suitable machine for a submitted grid job, whereas we focused on nonparallel jobs.

We first considered approaches for the assessment of potential prediction methods. The main problem with approaches found in the literature was the implicit assumption of stationary distributions. We introduced three complementary measures. $M_{avg}$ and $\Delta(p)$ are useful to assess the accuracy on average. As motivated in Section 3.1, this property is probably referenced in SLAs. The third measure, $M_{exp}$, is intended to assess the capability to predict the real distribution on time. This capability is needed to select a machine with a high probability to finish a given job.

Using the proposed measures we compared possible prediction methods. We focused on methods based on EFDs. Following this approach we identified two different problems. The first one is the selection of appropriate distinction criteria when using different EFDs for different points in time. Here we could not identify a clearly superior criterion. The second problem is the transformation of an EFD into a prediction. We introduced the new method $T_{interval}$, which delivered consistently better results than methods proposed in the literature. By enhancing this method with the newly developed adaptive correction $A_{full}$ we could even further improve the accuracy of the predictions.

Our next planned step is to test our prediction methods in running systems. So far our tests are based on log files. They contain real data and have the advantage to ease the analysis of different methods under exactly the same conditions. But to ensure not to miss an important detail of the real world, we plan to measure the effect of our proposed predictions in the allocation of workstations.

# References

1. Andrzejak, A., Arlitt, M., Rolia, J.: Bounding the Resource Savings of Utility Computing Models, Hewlett-Packard Company (2002),
   http://www.hpl.hp.com/techreports/2002/HPL-2002-339.html
2. Blumhardt, R.: Numerical optimization of the crash behaviour of automotive structures and components, Ph.D thesis. Shaker Verlag, Aachen (2002) (in German)
3. Good, P.I.: Resampling Methods. A Practical Guide to Data Analysis. Birkhäuser, Boston (1999)
4. Distributed Desktop Grid, PC Refresh Help Novartis Enhance Innovation, White Paper, Intel (2003), http://www.intel.com/ca/business/
   casestudies/pdf/novartis.pdf
5. Servicing the Animation Industry. HP's Utility Rendering Service Provides On-Demand Computing Resources, Hewlett-Packard (2004),
   http://www.hpl.hp.com/SE3D/whitepaper-urs.pdf
6. Keating, S.: No Processor Cycle Need Go to Waste, Drug Discovery & Development, 03/2004, Reed Business Information, Rockaway, NJ, USA, http://www.dddmag.com/
   PRArchivebyIssue.aspx?RELTYPE=INFE&YEAR=2004&MONTH=03
7. Mann, P.S.: Introductory Statistics, 4th edn. John Wiley & Sons, Chichester (2001)
8. Mutka, M.W.: An Examination of Strategies for Estimating Capacity to Share Among Private Workstations. ACM SIGSMALL/PC Notes 18(1-2), 53–61 (1992)
9. Nimmagadda, S., LeVasseur, J., Zahir, R.: High-End Workstation Compute Farms Using Windows NT. In: 3rd USENIX Windows NT Symposium, Seattle, Washington, July 12-13 (1999)
10. Nurmi, D., Brevik, J., Wolski, R.: Modeling Machine Availability in Enterprise and Wide-area Distributed Computing Environments. Technical Report CS2003-28, U.C. Santa Barbara, Computer Science Department (October 2003)
11. Nurmi, D., Wolski, R., Brevik, J.: Model-Based Checkpoint Scheduling for Volatile Resource Environments, University of California, Santa Barbara, Computer Science, Tech. Rep. TR-2004-25, November 6 (2004)
12. Pham, H.: Springer Handbook of Engineering Statistics. Springer, London (2006)
13. Rinne, H.: Handbook of Statistics, 3rd edn. Verlag Harri Deutsch, Frankfurt (2003) (in German)
14. Wolski, R.: Dynamically Forecasting Network Performance Using the Network Weather Service. Cluster Computing 1, 1 (1998)
15. Wolski, R., Spring, N.T., Hayes, J.: The Network Weather Service: A Distributed Resource Performance Forecasting Service for Metacomputing. Future Generation Computer Systems 15(5-6), 757–768 (1999)
16. Wolski, R., Spring, N., Hayes, J.: Predicting the CPU Availability of Time-shared Unix Systems on the Computational Grid. Cluster Computing 3 4, 293–301 (2000)
17. Wyckoff, P., Johnson, T., Jeong, K.: Finding Idle Periods on Networks of Workstations. Technical Report: TR1998-761, New York University New York, NY, USA (1998)
18. Yang, L., Foster, I., Schopf, J.M.: Homeostatic and Tendency-based CPU Load Predictions. In: International Parallel and Distributed Processing Symposium (IPDPS 2003) (2003)

# The Deployment and Maintenance of a Condor-Based Campus Grid

Dru Sepulveda and Sebastien Goasguen

Clemson University, Clemson SC 29634, USA
{dsepulv,sebgoa}@cs.clemson.edu

**Abstract.** Many institutions have all the tools needed to create a local grid that aggregates commodity compute resources into an accessible
grid service, while simultaneously maintaining user satisfaction and system security. In this paper, we present the strategy used at Clemson University to deploy and maintain a grid infrastructure by making resources
available to both local and federated remote users for scientific research.
Virtually no compute cycles are wasted. Usage trends and power consumption statistics collected from the Clemson campus grid are used as
a reference for best-practices. After several years of cyber-evolution, the
loosely-coupled components that comprise the campus grid work together
to form a highly cohesive infrastructure that not only meets the computing needs of local users, but also helps to fill the needs of the scientific
community at large. Experience gained from the deployment and management of this system may be adapted to other grid sites, allowing for
the development of campus-wide, grid-connected cyberinfrastructures.

## 1 Introduction

The act of pooling resources and sharing the computational weight of research
around the word is central to the idea of cyberinfrastructure (CI) [1] and is the
motivation for many grid programs at academic institutions [2]. Condor [4], a
high throughput batch system, provides a way of pooling resources into a usable
service without the cost of new machines and has the added benefit of being
well-maintained and well-documented by the Condor Research Group at the
University of Wisconsin at Madison. Condor provided more than enough computational power for research at Clemson University during its first year of use,
but due to excess computational power, machine cycles were left unused. To address the aforementioned idle time, Condor has been combined with the Berkley
Open Infrastructure for Networked Computing (BOINC) by using Condor Backfill, which donates the compute cycles that Condor does not used to projects
such as World Community Grid (WCG), Einstein@home and LHC@home. In
under six months Clemson University has become one of the top contributors
to BOINC projects in the world. As faculty and students at Clemson University
learned about the benefits of using High Throughput Computing (HTC) to accomplish their research goals the pools usage increased, but sometimes exceeded
the capacity of the Clemson Condor pool. A Condor Job_Router and Globus

N. Abdennadher and D. Petcu (Eds.): GPC 2009, LNCS 5529, pp. 165–176, 2009.

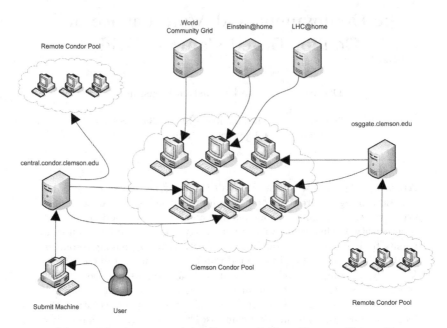

**Fig. 1.** The Anatomy of the Campus Grid at Clemson University

gatekeeper were deployed on the Condor pool to send overflow to other Condor pools on the Open Science Grid (OSG), and to better share our resources with others, respectively. Figure 1 shows how all of the middleware components work together at Clemson University to form the campus grid. The remainder of this paper is organized as follows: section 2 is a brief overview of Condor, section 3 presents Condor as a platform for a Campus Grid, section 4 presents challenges and solutions of deploying a Campus Grid, section 5 reviews the experiments that were conducted on the Clemson Campus Grid, section 6 explains future expansion, and section 7 concludes.

## 2   Condor

Condor is a high throughput batch system that provides job management and data handling for distributed compute resources. Condor was developed at the University of Wisconsin at Madison nearly thirty years ago with the goal of recovering idle cycles from commodity machines such as lab machines and work-stations. Condor centers its computing philosophy around high throughput computing versus high performance computing, which means that Condor is designed to reliably manage many computations over a long period of time [6]. Condor has been widely adopted by diverse Virtual Organizations (VO) in the grid community such as the Open Science Grid [7] and the Teragrid [8] and is capable of integrating with grid technologies. Clemson University is using the Condor Job_Router daemon and the Backfill function in Condor to meet its computational needs. The Job_Router allows for Condor jobs to be sent out to other

Condor pools that support a common VO, such as Engagement. The participating pools can be found by querying the Resource Selection Service (ReSS) for the Open Science Grid (OSG) [9]. Condor's Backfill function allows other distributed batch systems to run under Condor's management; currently the only supported Backfill system is BOINC. The following sections explain the motivation for creating the Clemson Condor Pool, the problems we encountered as well as the solutions we developed during setup and after deployment, discuss some statistics about Condor usage, and present the results from experiments that we have run on the Clemson Campus Grid.

# 3 Condor as a Way to Build a Campus Grid

Condor provides a comprehensive system for creating a Campus Grid, by managing distributed compute resources and providing remote Input/Output handling for staged jobs, as well as integrating with BOINC and OSG. Condor can only be a viable solution if there is some non-trivial amount of idle time. This key concern is discussed in the next section.

## 3.1 Motivation for the Clemson Condor Pool

Condor is only applicable if the amount of idle time on the machines is sufficiently great, so we took an informal survey in early 2007. All the labs that were visited were Windows machines, so it was reasonable to assume that if no one was sitting at the computer, then it was idle. We found from this study that the labs were unused after midnight and over the weekends, indicating that the public lab machines were idle nearly 45% of the time. In addition to the informal study of public labs, we reviewed the schedule for teaching labs and found that those machines were idle more than 90% of the time, on average, justifying a system that would make use of these unused cycles. The amount of backfill shown in Figure 2 below supports our original hypothesis concerning unused cycles.

|  | Total | Owner | Claimed | Unclaimed | Backfill |
|---|---|---|---|---|---|
| INTEL/LINUX | 4 | 0 | 0 | 4 | 0 |
| INTEL/WINNT51 | 946 | 280 | 3 | 375 | 288 |
| INTEL/WINNT60 | 1357 | 193 | 0 | 4 | 1160 |
| SUN4u/SOLARIS5.10 | 17 | 0 | 0 | 17 | 0 |
| X86_64/LINUX | 26 | 3 | 1 | 22 | 0 |
| Total | 2350 | 476 | 4 | 422 | 1448 |

**Fig. 2.** The output of Condor_status from a worker node on the Clemson Condor pool at 3:00pm on a class day

## 3.2   BOINC and Condor Backfill

"Berkeley Open Infrastructure for Network Computing (BOINC) is a platform for projects...that use millions of volunteer computers as a parallel supercomputer." [12] Institutions and individuals who use BOINC volunteer their free CPU cycles by joining BOINC projects. While we found the server side of BOINC to be complex, the client software is easy to install and will run with minimum administrative effort. Institutions abroad have successfully used BOINC to create a institutional cyberinfrastructure [3], but Clemson had three requirements: a system that has more fine grained control over how idle CPU cycles were donated, was already known by some of the faculty at Clemson, and uses a less complex API. Creating new BOINC projects involved using an API [5] that we felt would be restrictive given the lack of formal BOINC training among the Clemson faculty.

In early 2007, Condor version 6.7 [11] added a feature called Backfill to Condor that allowed it to schedule a secondary job scheduler which would utilize the idle time that Condor could not use. BOINC was the first and, at the time of this writing, only officially supported backfill program that Condor could schedule. The addition of the backfill functionality allowed Clemson to use Condor to manage both itself and BOINC with no negative interactions, essentially giving Clemson the ability to provide a usable resource for its faculty and students while donating CPU cycles to humanitarian causes.

## 3.3   Open Science Grid Expands Campus Grids

For the grid model of HTC to survive the ever growing demand for more computational power, there must be a concerted effort made to expand federated Condor pools through Embedded Immersive Engagement for Cyberinfrastructure (EIE-4CI), a NSF grant awarded to The Renaissance Computing Institute (RENCI) and Clemson University. EIE-4CI has created a ciTeam which helps to train future CI professionals on how to install and maintain grid middleware such as Condor and the OSG Virtual Data Toolkit (VDT), with the end goal of having the new virtual Organization join the Engagement VO until they mature as a grid site and move on to a VO that is tailored to their needs. Through this program, a half dozen new grid sites have been added to the Open Science Grid in the Engagement VO, which has not only increased the total number of machines available for HTC with Condor at Clemson, but has also allowed Clemson to share its Condor pool with others.

## 4   Campus Grid Implementation Challenges

While implementing and maintaining a Campus Grid at Clemson University several issues had to be resolved. Challenges included: deploying Condor to a heterogeneous set of lab machines, which created a Condor pool with independent administrative domains, discovering that the backfill system did not have dynamic control over which project BOINC joined and implementing a secure solution, deploying a Job-Router to the pool and finding a work around for a bug in the routing_config, and reviewing the effectiveness of the Job-Router to relieve congestion in the pool.

## 4.1  Deployment

After determining that Clemson would benefit from a Campus Grid, the next step was to create a campus wide Condor pool with the involvement of the local administrators and the central IT organization. Involving all of the stakeholders early in the process helped to alleviate future confusion and build group confidence. A small Condor pool was deployed on the lab computers in the computer science department and allowed to run for several weeks to show that Condor, when properly configured and managed, could be used to further scientific research, without imposing undue operational burden or compromising security [11]. After the testing period had expired, Clemson Computing and Information Technology (CCIT) agreed to install Condor to the public lab machines, and the Clemson Condor pool was created.

New versions of Condor are deployed to a test lab before being added to a new machine image that is pushed out to all of the labs. In our experience, the process of deploying grid technology can be divided into three sections: 60% human interaction, 35% software integration, and 5% luck, because most grid middleware is comprised of experimental technologies that follow the ebb and flow of scientific research. The very nature of grid technology [1] requires human to human interaction to establish trust, which can help to bring a department together for a common goal, or in the case of Clemson bring the historically separated computer science department and CCIT together to work on a joint project for the benefit of the University.

## 4.2  Backfill Configuration

Clemson donates CPU time to WCG through backfill, but wants the ability to change BOINC's project using Condor. A simple solution that securely updates the condor_config.local on each Windows machine and restarts Condor was engineered. A Linux Apache server with mod_ssl was configured to host a copy of the condor_config.dyn.local (a secondary local configuration file) file for each type of machine in the pool. Configuration based on machine type not only separated the machines into logical partitions, but also isolated configuration problems to a manageable subset of the pool. Each Windows machine in the pool has a configuration client, written in Python, that is run by the Windows scheduler every 30-35 minutes. The client is configured to use a X509 client certificate and base 64 encoded user name and password that allows it to run a secure HTTP_GET for the configuration file hosted on the Linux server. If a change has been made to the configuration file on the Linux server, the client replaces the local condor_config with the new configuration file pulled from the server and restarts Condor. If no changes have been made, the new unchanged file is dropped, and

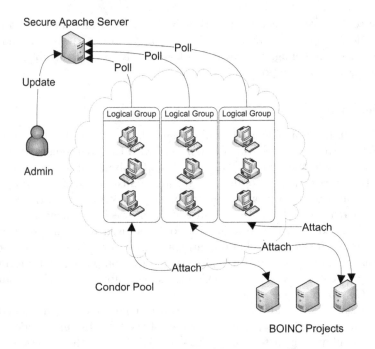

**Fig. 3.** Remote Configuration of Condor Backfill

the client waits another 30-35 minutes to poll the configuration server. This update system allows Clemson to change projects securely or alter other aspects of Condor quickly with little effort. Figure 3 shows how the individual components work together to form a secure polling update system.

### 4.3    Condor Job_Router

As use of Condor Pool spread, Clemson decided to expand the resources available through Condor to pools outside of the campus by adding a job_router to the central manager. The Condor job_router is a second "grid aware" scheduler, which has the ability to copy jobs from a local job queue to a federated off-site Condor pool with a Globus gatekeeper. The job_router at Clemson has been configured so that Engagement users can use their grid credentials to authenticate to the job_router. Clemson is a member of the Engage VO and obtaining a credential is a straight-forward process, which promote use of the job_router. Early tests with the job_router were not successful due to a bug in the configuration file format which caused the job_router to read the routing file in an loop. This issues was temporarily solved by the addition of static routes.

## 5    Results and Statistics

The cyberinfrastructure at Clemson has been successful at providing a compute resource for university research as well as giving back to the scientific community abroad. The following sections discuss collected statistics about the Clemson CI and present experiments which show a marked improvement in throughput with the job-router. We will also review the power consumption that Condor creates and what can be done to mitigate Condor's impact on the environment.

## 5.1   Condor Pool Usage and Administration

The Clemson Condor pool started with a single dual core Windows XP machine two years ago and now consists of nearly a thousand dual and quad core Windows XP and Vista SP2 machines. The increase in size and use of the Condor pool made it necessary to have a researcher monitoring the Condor pool and preparing updates, as well as added part-time administrators to train and provide assistance to users. The Condor pool is open to the faculty and students by allowing them to create and submit their own code with no oversite procedure. This was taken to be an acceptable risk to promote the Condor pool's user. Figure 4 shows Condor use during the month of May, and clearly shows the bursty use of Condor when over 40000 jobs were queued onto the pool by a single user on the first of the month. The user who submitted these jobs happened to be a industrial engineer, but jobs come from a diverse group of domains that range from business process simulations to deconvolution algorithms in biology. The largest number of jobs ever successfully submitted to Condor at one time is three hundred thousand. Job scaling problems occurred when five hundred thousand jobs were submitted to the pool and crashed the central manager. The central manager was rebooted and its scratch directory was deleted to rectify the problem. Node scaling problems occurred when the dual core machines were replaced with quad core machines last summer. The actual number of

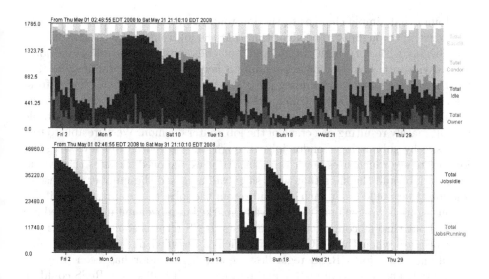

**Fig. 4.** Output From Condor View for the month of May 2008

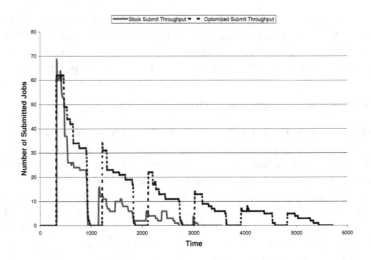

**Fig. 5.** Stock vs Optimized Condor Job_Router

machines remained the same, but the number of cores and thus the number of slots screen by the collector daemon increased from 700 to over 2600. To temporarily fix this problem, a larger port range has been opened on the central manager which roughly gives Condor two ports per slot; more machines have been requested to house collector daemons, which will lighten the load on the one collector/negotiator for the pool.

## 5.2   Condor Job_Router Speedup

We found that simple changes to the job_router routing table can make a large difference in throughput. The algorithm that the job_router uses to schedule the jobs begins with very high throughput but ends with a long tail of idle jobs. This asymptotic behavior makes sending a few small jobs impractical, so it is most useful for many long running jobs. The figure 5 solid line was created from information gathered by the Condor Router Log Parser (CROP) and shows the Condor job_router using the unaltered ReSS routing table to be unpredictable and ultimately resulting in a crash of the job_router daemon. We were able to test each site by submitting Condor jobs through the job_router and reviewing the job logs to see which sites never ran jobs. After we removed the sites that would not run jobs and the sites that were slow, we increased the number increase of idle jobs that could be at each site and resent the jobs, the result was a uniform graph (figure 5, broken line) that showed a marked improvement in submitted job throughput time as compared to other tests. ReSS returns some non-functional sites because when the OSG software stack is installed on a submit machine it automatically joins ReSS regardless of whether Condor has been properly configured. The process of testing and removing faulty sites from ReSS could be automated into a QoS system that runs test jobs from time to time and then

```
              Statistics Date    Total Run Time    Results Returned
              ------------------------------------------------------
                 11/11/08        2:283:21:19:32       3,661
                 10/19/08        3:150:17:17:06       4,612
Split Proj. ->    9/11/08        3:138:01:40:35       5,200
   All Labs ->    8/25/08        4:191:01:58:08       7,446   <- Summer
                  7/15/08        1:002:03:45:11         894
                  6/16/08        1:282:06:44:46       1,832
                  5/14/08        0:162:17:01:21         565
                  4/13/08        0:015:12:48:36          29
   Day One ->     3/29/08        0:000:13:06:38           1
```

Fig. 6. Sample Results for WCG, One Day A Month

updates the routing table with good sites, thus ensuring that new sites were
added to the table when they were properly configured.

## 5.3  BOINC Time Donated

Clemson University has donated over 450 years to humanitarian projects through
the World Community Grid (WCG) and has expanded project support to Ein-
stein@home and LHC@home. Figure 6 shows how the backfill system has grown
over the past year, starting from one test machine in March and moving to
the entire university by August, then slowly splitting more time between WCG,
Einstein@home, and LHC. The impact of users returning from Summer break
is noticeable from August to September, but is a good indicator that Condor is
correctly preempting BOINC for users. Clemson has been recognized in several
national and international venues such as International Science Grid This Week
[13] and the WCG News and Reports [15] as a top contributor to humanitarian
projects as a college, for both the United States and the world.

## 5.4  Power Consumed by the Pool

Conserving power has become a top environmental concern due to rising fuel
prices and a declining world economy. In response to the growing concern over
power conservation and cost, we monitored the power usage of a teaching lab with
stock Dell Optiplex 755's to determine how much extra power was being used by
the systems running Condor and BOINC as opposed to the control systems that
are not running either. We attached three randomly selected computers in the
teaching lab to Kill-A-Watt power monitoring strips and ran each in the following
states for approximately one week: idle with no operating system, Windows
Vista SP1 with Condor and BOINC, Windows Vista SP1 without Condor and
BOINC, and Windows Vista SP1 isolated with no lab user contact. The results,
which can been seen in Table 1, were disappointing but not unexpected when
we considered that an unused machine without Condor and BOINC goes into
sleep mode, which uses almost no power at all. Condor can be configured so

**Table 1.** Power Usage and Cost in a Teaching Lab at Clemson University per Computer

| State | Avg. KwH/Day | Cost per year (at $0.43/KH) |
|---|---|---|
| BOINC&Condor | 2.0534 | $322.38 |
| User Only | 0.4116 | $64.60 |
| Machine Isolated | 0.0552 | $8.66 |

that it only runs at particular times, which would limit power usage by BOINC, however we believe that the cost of running the backfill system in its current state is offset by the cross cultural impact of the humanitarian projects that benefit from the time Clemson donates to their causes. The following section will discuss several possible strategies that Clemson is considering to offset both the cost to the environment and the cost to the school.

### 5.5   Offsetting the Cost

The costs of running a backfill system can be measured in two ways: cost per kilowatt hour of backfill time minus cost per kilowatt hour of user time, and cost in carbon. We would like to address the cost in carbon. There have been studies that indicate storing carbon in trees may not be the best decision in the long run [10], but it can buy us time for now and is a viable way to offset the carbon generated by the production of electricity needed to run and cool the machines. We have estimated that the carbon generated by the backfill system at Clemson University could be offset by planting 19 trees [14] per year.

## 6   Future Expansion

The Windows Condor pool at Clemson University will soon be joined by the 6000-core Palmetto Cluster, composed of racked Linux machines. This pool has a separate Condor Collector and Central Manager, which will be connected to the Clemson University Condor pool via Condor flocking. This new expansion will give Clemson faculty and students a large Linux Condor pool along with the existing Windows Condor pool on the campus proper, creating new opportunities for research and education.

## 7   Conclusion

In this paper we discussed how to use Condor with BOINC Backfill to aggregate commodity machines into a usable grid service and make sure that almost no CPU cycles are wasted. A job_router was added to the pool to give us a computational cushion during peek need bursts. Statistics and experiments were presented to show where the Clemson Campus Grid is strong and where and how it can be improved. We identified ways that private institutions and companies as well as public institutions can help offset the cost of using a backfill system. With the proper motivation and social networking a institution can use preexisting technologies to create a fully functional Campus Grid that will not only meet the needs of the local users, but also provide a overhead of CPU time that can be donated to humanitarian projects around the world for the advancement of science and the benefit of man kind.

## Acknowledgments

The authors would like to acknowledge Nell Beaty Kennedy, Matt Rector and John Mark Smotherman for help and technical support with software deployment for the Clemson School of Computing and the university public labs, respectively. The authors would also like to thank Mike Murphy for Apache server administration. Our main Condor Team contact for troubleshooting Condor was Ben Burnett. This project was partially funded by an IBM Faculty Award and NSF grant OCI-753335 and in part by an NSF and DOE award to the Open Science Grid.

## References

1. Foster, I., Kesselman, C., Tuecke, S.: The Anatomy of the Grid: Enabling Scalable Virtual Organizations. International Journal of High Performance Computing Applications 15(3), 200–222 (2001)
2. Smith, P., Hacker, T., Song, C.X.: Implementing and Industrial-Strength Academic Cyberinfrastructure at Purdue University. In: Proc. IEEE International Symposium on Parallel and Distributed Processing IPDPS, pp. 1–7 (2008)
3. Gonzéalez, D., de Vega, F., Gil, G., Segal, B.: Centralized BOINC Resources Manager for Institutional Networks. In: Proc. IEEE International Symposium on Parallel and Distributed Processing IPDPS, vol. 14(18), pp. 1–8 (2008)
4. Litxkow, M.J., Livny, M., Mutka, M.W.: Condor: A Hunter of Idle Workstations. In: Proc. The International Conference on Distributed Computing Systems, pp. 104–111 (1988)
5. Anderson, D.P.: BOINC: A System For Public-Resource Computing and Storage. In: Proc. Fifth IEEE/ACM International Workshop on Grid Computing, pp. 4–10 (2004)
6. Livny, M., Basney, J., Raman, R., Tannenbaum, T.: Mechanisms for High Throughput Computing. SPEEDUP 11(1) (1997)
7. Sfiligoi, I., Quinn, G., Green, C., Thain, G.: Pilot Job Accounting and Auditing in Open Science Grid. In: Proc. 9th IEEE/ACM International Conference on Grid Computing, pp. 112–117 (2008)
8. Reed, D.A.: Grids, The TeraGrid and Beyond. Computer 36, 62–68 (2003)
9. Garzoglio, G., Levshina, T., Mhashilkar, P., Timm, S.: ReSS: A Resource Selection Service for the Open Science Grid. In: Grid Computing International Symposium on Grid Computing (ISGC) (2007)
10. Marland, G., Marland, S.: Should We Store Carbon In Trees? Water, Air, and Soil Pollution 64(18), 1–195 (1992)

11. The Condor Team, The Condor Manual version 6.8/7.0 (2008),
    http://www.cs.wisc.edu/Condor/manual/
12. Community, The Boinc Manual Wiki (2008),
    http://boinc.berkeley.edu/wiki/User_manual
13. Polowczuk, S., Heavey, A.: No Excuse For Under-Utilization: Clemson Back-Fills
    With BOINC, http://www.isgtw.org/?pid=1001404
14. Non-profit Community, Carbon Calculator,
    http://www.treefolks.org/prog_calculator.asp
15. News and Media, World Community Grid Interviews the Clemson School of Com-
    puting's Dr. Sebastien Goasguen,
    http://www.worldcommunitygrid.org/newsletter/08Q4/viewClemson.do

# Bicriteria Service Scheduling with Dynamic Instantiation for Workflow Execution on Grids

Luiz F. Bittencourt, Carlos R. Senna, and Edmundo R.M. Madeira

Institute of Computing - University of Campinas - UNICAMP
P.O. 6176, Campinas - São Paulo - Brazil
*{bit,crsenna,edmundo}@ic.unicamp.br

**Abstract.** Nowadays the grid is turning into a service-oriented environment. In this context, there exist solutions to the execution of workflows and most of them are web-service based. Additionally, services are considered to exist on a fixed host, limiting the resource alternatives when scheduling the workflow tasks. In this paper we address the problem of dynamic instantiation of grid services to schedule workflow applications. We propose an algorithm to select the best resources available to execute each task of the workflow on the already instantiated services or on services dynamically instantiated when necessary. The algorithm relies on the existence of a grid infrastructure which could provide dynamic service instantiation. Simulation results show that the scheduling algorithm associated with the dynamic service instantiation can bring more efficient workflow execution on the grid.

## 1 Introduction

A computational grid is a computing environment where heterogeneous resources are located on different administrative domains. The Open Grid Service Architecture (OGSA) [1] has moved grids to service-oriented computing (SOC) [2] based on Internet standards. Nevertheless, most grid solutions focus on the execution of task-based workflows [3], and only a few service-oriented grid environments provide dynamic service instantiation [4,5].

In a task-oriented grid environment, the workflow tasks can potentially be executed on any available resource. This led to the development of scheduling heuristics to distribute tasks over heterogeneous computing platforms [6,7]. On the other hand, in a service-oriented grid environment, the workflow execution is strongly dependent on the set of resources where services are already deployed. This can lead to overload on such resources, limiting the use of the grid resources according to the frequency of submissions of workflows using one or other type of service. Thus, powerful resources can be less used than middle-power ones, resulting in higher workflow execution times. To overcome this issue, we propose an algorithm to schedule services according to the incoming workflows.

---

* The authors would like to thank CAPES, FAPESP (05/59706-3) and CNPq (472810/2006-5 and 142574/2007-4) for the financial support.

N. Abdennadher and D. Petcu (Eds.): GPC 2009, LNCS 5529, pp. 177–188, 2009.

The algorithm relies on the existence of an infrastructure which provides both the execution of workflows composed of service-tasks and the dynamic instantiation of grid services [8]. The proposed algorithm considers service instantiation costs when selecting the resources to execute tasks of the submitted workflow. Therefore, we focus on the bicriteria scheduling problem of minimizing both the number of created services and the workflow execution time (makespan).

This paper is organized as follows. Section 2 shows a background on scheduling and defines the problem. Section 3 presents the proposed algorithm, while Section 4 shows the simulation results. Related works are overviewed in Section 5. Section 6 concludes the paper and presents a couple of future directions.

## 2   Service Scheduling

The task scheduling problem is NP-Complete in general [9]. In the traditional one-criterion scheduling problem, usually the goal is to minimize tasks execution time, consequently minimizing the overall workflow execution time (makespan). In the multicriteria scheduling the objective is to minimize (or maximize) more than one criterion at the same time, generally considering the execution time as the most important criterion [10]. With the emergence of utility computing, economic costs are also being considered as an optimization criterion [11].

In the multicriteria optimization problem the optimality definition depends on how we compare two possible solutions. Actually, more than one optimal solution can exist considering that two solutions cannot be compared straightforwardly when one solution is better than the other in a set of criteria, but worse in another one. In this sense, when optimizing a multicriteria objective function, we want to find the *Pareto set* of solutions, which is the set composed of all non-dominated solutions. A solution is said non-dominated if there is no other solution which optimizes one criterion without worsening another one.

In this paper we address the bicriteria scheduling problem where the two criteria to be optimized are the makespan and the number of created services. We approach this problem with a heuristic algorithm which uses the *as late as possible* (ALAP) concept [12]. Usually, heuristics are simple to implement, have low complexity and execution time, and give good results. There are other ways of dealing with bicriteria optimization. One way is to optimize only one criterion, maintaining the other one between fixed thresholds [11]. Building an aggregate objective function (AOF) is another technique, where both objectives are combined in only one function to be optimized [10]. A common AOF is the weighted linear sum of the objectives: $f(obj_1, obj_2) = \alpha \times obj_1 + (1 - \alpha) \times obj_2$, $\alpha \in [0, 1]$. Another technique, among others, is the Multiobjective Optimization Evolutionary Algorithms (MOEA) [13].

### 2.1   Problem Definition

We consider a set of heterogeneous autonomous resources $\mathcal{R} = \{r_1, r_2, ..., r_k\}$, with associated processing capacities $p_{r_i} \in \mathbb{R}^+$, connected by heterogeneous network links. Each resource $r_i$ has a set of links $\mathcal{L}_i = \{l_{i,1}, l_{i,2}, ..., l_{i,m}\}$, $1 \leq m \leq k$,

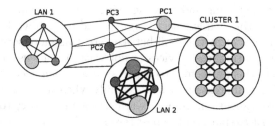

**Fig. 1.** Example of groups in the infrastructure

where $l_{i,j} \in \mathbb{R}^+$ is the available bandwidth in the link between resources $r_i$ and $r_j$, with $l_{i,i} = \infty$. The resources are arranged in groups, where each group can be a LAN or a cluster, for instance. Each group is autonomous, and all groups are connected by heterogeneous links. Resources inside the same group are considered to have links with the same bandwidth between them. Figure 1 shows an example of a resources pool. Nodes are resources and edges are communication links. Edges thickness represents bandwidth, while nodes radium represents processing capacities and gray tones represent different operating systems.

Let $\mathcal{S}$ be the set of all services instantiated on all resources. Each resource $r_i$ has a set of already instantiated services $\mathcal{S}_i = \{s_{i,1}, ..., s_{i,p}\} \in \mathcal{S}$, $p \geq 0$.

A workflow is represented by a directed acyclic graph (DAG) $\mathcal{G} = (\mathcal{V}, \mathcal{E})$ with $n$ nodes (or tasks), where $t_a \in \mathcal{V}$ is a workflow task with an associated computation cost (weight) $w_{t_a} \in \mathbb{R}^+$, and $e_{a,b} \in \mathcal{E}$, $1 \leq a \leq n$, $1 \leq b \leq n$, $a \neq b$, is a dependency between $t_a$ and $t_b$ with an associated communication cost $c_{a,b} \in \mathbb{R}^+$. Each task $t_a$ has a set of candidate services $\zeta_a \subseteq \mathcal{S}, \zeta_a \neq \varnothing$, which implement task $t_a$. Therefore, a task $t_a$ can be scheduled to a resource $r_i$ iff $\exists\, s_{i,p} \mid s_{i,p} \in \zeta_a$.

The task scheduling is a function $schedule_{DAG} : \mathcal{V} \mapsto \mathcal{S}$. Thus, each task $t_a \in \mathcal{V}$ is mapped to a service $s \in \mathcal{S}$.

# 3   Service Scheduling Algorithm

In order to minimize the workflow's makespan, we developed a scheduling algorithm which considers the instantiation (or creation) of new services in the resources set when scheduling tasks, instead of using only existing services. This way, the workflow execution time can be minimized by creating the necessary services on resources with high processing power. But, there are some issues which must be considered when developing such an algorithm. First, the algorithm must consider how much it costs to send and deploy a service into a new host. Note that, in a utility grid, the creation of a new service may have monetary costs, thus creating too many services can lead to an expensive workflow execution. Second, neglectfully creating services can lead to resources wastefulness, such as waste of bandwidth and processing. Furthermore, this can delay the execution of workflows already running, since processing time and bandwidth would be in constant use for transferring and creating new services abroad. Third, not creating services (or creating too less services) can lead to high workflow completion times. Thus, there is a clear trade-off between creating more services to speedup the execution, or creating less services to not waste resources (or money).

Our approach to this problem is to *create services when necessary*. This means that the algorithm will create new services only when not creating them would delay the workflow execution. To achieve this, it is mandatory to schedule tasks which are in the critical path on the best resources by creating services for them. For tasks which are not in the critical path, the algorithm uses the ALAP (as late as possible) to determine whether a service must be created. The scheduling is performed in a list-scheduling manner. At a glance, the steps of the algorithm are: select which task is the next to be scheduled; determine whether a service must be created for the selected task; and schedule the selected task on the best resource, given the service creation conditions. These three steps are repeated until all tasks are scheduled.

In the first step, the next task to be scheduled is the not scheduled one with the highest *blevel*. The *blevel* of a task $t_a$ is the length of the longest path from $t_a$ to a task with no successors (an exit node). We can assume, without loss of generality, that every workflow has one, and only one, exit task. This can be achieved by adding a costless task $t_{exit}$ and adding a set of costless edges $\{e_{a,exit} \ \forall \ t_a \in \mathcal{V} \mid t_a$ has no successors$\}$. On the other hand, the *tlevel* of a task $t_a$ is the length of the longest path from the entry node to $t_a$. These two attributes are known in the scheduling literature [14], and they are computed based on the costs of tasks and edges, on the capacity of the resources where they are scheduled, and on the links capacities. All these costs and capacities are previously known, as in most scheduling heuristics. For example, they can be obtained from a service repository with average costs and output sizes of the past executions, and from a resource repository, which can maintain the resources characteristics obtained from a resource monitor/discovery service.

The second step uses the ALAP of the task selected in the first step. Intuitively, the ALAP of a task is how much it can be delayed without increasing the schedule length, or by how much its *tlevel* can be increased. The ALAP of $t_a$ is computed by subtracting the *blevel* of $t_a$ from the length of the critical path. Thus, a task $t_{cp}$ in the critical path cannot be delayed, since its ALAP time is always equal to its *tlevel*. Therefore, tasks on the critical path will always be scheduled on the best available resource, and the necessary services will be created at that resource.

To determine if a service must be created to execute a task $t_a$, for each resource $r_i$ which already has the service to execute $t_a$, $t_a$ is inserted on $r_i$'s schedule, and $t_a$'s *tlevel* is computed. Let $tlevel_{t_a,r_i}$ be the *tlevel* of task $t_a$ on the schedule of resource $r_i$. If $\exists \ s_{i,p} \mid s_{i,p} \in \zeta_a, ALAP_{t_a} \leq tlevel_{t_a,r_i}$, then it is not necessary to create a new service for $t_a$, and $t_a$ is scheduled on the $r_i$ which has the smallest *tlevel* plus its execution time in that resource. Otherwise, $t_a$ is scheduled on the resource which has the smallest *tlevel* plus its execution time plus the costs of

**Algorithm 1.** Algorithm Overview

```
1:  compute blevel, tlevel and ALAP for each task
2:  while there are not scheduled tasks do
3:      t ← not scheduled task with highest blevel
4:      best_resource_t ← NULL
5:      best_time_t ← ∞
6:      R_t ← resources with services in ζ_t
7:      for all r_i ∈ R_t do
8:          calculate tlevel_t of r_i
9:          if (tlevel_t ≤ ALAP_t) AND (tlevel_t + exec_time_t < best_time_t) then
10:             best_resource_t ← r_i
11:             best_time_t ← tlevel_t + exec_time_t
12:         end if
13:     end for
14:     if best_resource_t == NULL then
15:         R ← all available resources
16:         for all r_i ∈ R do
17:             calculate tlevel_t of r_i
18:             if r_i does not have services in ζ_t then
19:                 costs_create_service_t ← cost_send_code_t + cost_deploy_t
20:                 tlevel_t ← tlevel_t + costs_create_service_t
21:             end if
22:             if tlevel_t + exec_time_t ≤ best_time_t then
23:                 best_resource_t ← r_i
24:                 best_time_t ← tlevel_t + exec_time_t
25:             end if
26:         end for
27:     end if
28:     schedule t in best_resource_t
29:     recompute tlevel and ALAP for each task
30: end while
```

creating the new service on the resources where it does not exist. Algorithm 1 gives an overview of these steps.

The first line of Algorithm 1 computes the task attributes (*blevel*, *tlevel*, and *ALAP*). This pre-calculation is done by assuming a homogeneous virtual system with unbounded number of resources, where each resource has the best capacity available on the real system. This is done to estimate the *ALAP* of each task on an ideal system, which will reflect in the flexibility when searching for a resource by reducing the acceptable delay for tasks not in the critical path. After that, an iteration to schedule each task is started (line 2). The next line selects the not scheduled task with the highest *blevel* to be scheduled, while lines 4 and 5 initialize two variables used through the algorithm. The set $R_t$, which contains the resources having a service able to execute task $t$, is created in line 6. After that, the iteration comprising lines 7 to 13 searches for the best resource that can execute task $t$ without surpassing the *ALAP* time of $t$. If none is found (line 14), then the algorithm starts the search for the best resource in the whole set of resources (line 15). If the current resource $r_i$ does not have the necessary service (line 18), the algorithm adds to the *tlevel* of $t$ both the inherent costs of creating a new service and of executing the task (lines 19, 20). Then, the algorithm verifies if the current resource has the best *tlevel + task's execution time* of every resource already tested (line 22). If so, it is elected as the current best resource (lines 23, 24). Before the outer loop iterates, the current task is scheduled on the best resource found (line 28), and the attributes are recomputed (line 29), since the new schedule can change the *tlevel* and ALAP values.

Note that the critical path is dynamically updated on every iteration of the outer loop. If a task $t$ not in the critical path can only be scheduled on a resource which has a *tlevel* bigger than its ALAP, then $t$ will be in the critical path in the next iteration. Also, the creation of new services can be biased by introducing a multiplier to the ALAP in line 9, which would give a control over the trade-off between service creation and makespan according to the target environment.

At execution time, the creation of a new service for a task $t$ is performed after all its predecessors finish. This policy aims at not using resources before the start of the task $t$ and its workflow, since it can delay the execution of other workflows running. Additionally, the creation of services at scheduling time can waste processing time and bandwidth if a target resource leaves the grid. Besides, if we consider the situation where creating a new service or using a resource has a monetary cost, creating too many services would lead to high costs.

## 4   Experimental Results

We compared the proposed algorithm with a HEFT-like (Heterogeneous Earliest Finish Time [6]) version, differing only in that, for each task, it only considers the set of resources which have the necessary service to execute it.

**Scenarios.** We varied the number of groups from 2 to 25, each with 2 to 10 resources with randomly generated capacities. Links between groups were randomly generated, as well as links between resources in the same group. For simulation purposes, links between groups never exceeded the capacities of links inside groups, since a machine inside a group cannot transmit faster than its link inside its group. Sixteen DAGs were taken for the simulations, where fifteen were randomly generated with number of nodes varying from 7 to 82, and the other one was a CSTEM DAG (Coupled Structural Thermal Electromagnetic Analysis and Tailoring of Graded Composite Structures), which weights were randomly generated but values proportional to those encountered in the original workflow [15]. All random numbers were taken from a uniform distribution.

One main parameter can influence the performance of the algorithm that does not create services: the number of services already in the resources. Let $P_{s_t,r_i} = \frac{\delta}{|\mathcal{R}|}$ be the probability of a service $s_t$, which can execute a task $t$ from the DAG, to exist in the resource $r_i$. We simulated $\delta$ varying from 1 to 5. A simulation with $\delta = 3$, for instance, means that $\forall\, t \in \mathcal{V} : E(|\zeta_t|) = 3$, i.e., it is expected that, for each task $t$ of the DAG, the number of resources which can execute $t$ is 3. We also simulated a hypothetical situation where all services existed in all resources, thus with $\delta = |\mathcal{R}|$. This aimed at evaluating if the ALAP policy would restrict the resources usage in a manner that would increase the makespan. Another characteristic that can influence the results is the capacity of the resources where the already existing services are on. Assuming that services are generally deployed on resources with good capacity, we also simulated scenarios where the already running services could only exist on a set of resources $\mathcal{R}_{50\%} = \{r_i \in \mathcal{R}|p_{r_i} \geq median\}$ where $median$ is the median of the set of processing capacities of all resources in $\mathcal{R}$. In other words, services could only exist on resources which have processing capacities higher or equal than the median of the capacities of all resources. On these scenarios, $P_{s_t,r_i} = \frac{\delta}{\lceil \mathcal{R}_{50\%} \rceil}$.

Each algorithm was executed 2000 times for each number of groups. On each execution a DAG was randomly chosen and costs of nodes and edges were randomly taken, both in the same interval. The costs of transferring and deploying a new service were randomly generated from a normal distribution according to the average size (250Kb) and standard deviation (120Kb) of the .gar files measured in our laboratory and file sizes found in the literature [16]. These files are called $grid$ $archives$ and each file has the source codes to deploy a service in the well known Globus Toolkit 4. The results show a confidence interval of 99%.

We compared the average makespan, average speedup and average schedule length ratio (SLR). The speedup means how many times faster is the achieved makespan when compared to the schedule of all tasks sequentially on the best resource (higher is better). The SLR means how many times larger is the makespan when compared to the execution of the critical path on the best resource (less is better). We also measured what was the percentage of services used by the proposed algorithm which were already existing services, represented by bars in the graphics (right axis). In the graphics, $\delta$ is the expected number of existing services for each task of the workflow. Labels $Exist$ are for the algorithm which does not create services (the HEFT-like approach), labels $Prop.$ are for the proposed algorithm, and labels with $50\%$ are for simulations where existing services could exist only on the 50% best resources.

**Schedule Length Ratio.** Figure 2 shows the average SLR for $\delta = 1$. Considering that existing services could be on all resources, the proposed algorithm outperforms the HEFT-like approach by around 43%, with 2 groups, and by around 53% when there are 25 groups. This is achieved with the proposed algorithm using existing services for 34% of the tasks for 2 groups and around 21% for 10 or more groups. When considering that existing services could be only on the 50% best resources, for 2 groups the SLR is decreased by around 34%, while for 25 groups the decrease is around 49%, respectively using existing services for 39% and around 21% of the tasks. Therefore, using the ALAP to decide when create new services improves the scheduling quality and allows the workflow to use many existing services, while creating the necessary ones.

We can observe the same pattern for $\delta = 2$ in the SLR results (Fig. 3), as well as in the speedup (Fig. 6) and makespan (Fig. 9) results, with a slightly better performance than for $\delta = 1$ when not creating new services. This is because the scheduler had more options for each task, improving the probability that a

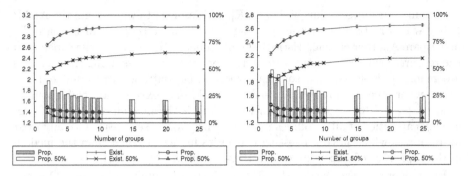

**Fig. 2.** Average SLR for $\delta = 1$       **Fig. 3.** Average SLR for $\delta = 2$

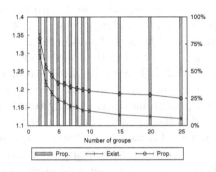

**Fig. 4.** Average SLR for $\delta = |\mathcal{R}|$

good resource would be chosen. When existing services were on any resource, the SLR for the proposed algorithm is 34% lower for 2 groups and 48% lower for 25 groups. This improvement was achieved using existing services for 44% and 23% of the tasks, respectively. When the existing services were only on the 50% best resources, the improvement varied from 27% for 2 groups, to 41% for 25 groups, using existing services for 49% and 24% of the tasks, respectively.

When $\delta = |R|$ we can observe that the proposed algorithm is slightly worse than HEFT[1]. The SLR difference ranges from 3% to 5% (Fig. 4). Note that this is a hypotetical situation, and having all services on all resources could lead to expensive workflow execution and resource squandering.

**Speedup.** For the average speedup with $\delta = 1$ (Fig. 5), the improvement is in a range from 74%, for 2 groups, to 113%, for 25 groups, with existing services on any resource. In the scenario where existing services could be only on the 50% best resources, these numbers are 50% and 92%, respectively. The speedup for $\delta = 2$ (Fig. 6) was improved by 48% for 2 groups and by 91% for 25 groups for existing services on any resource. These numbers are 32% and 68%, respectively,

---

[1] In this case the tasks could be scheduled on any resource, thus the algorithm used as comparison is the HEFT algorithm.

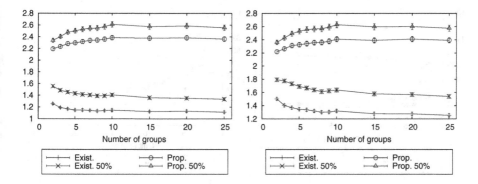

**Fig. 5.** Speedup for $\delta = 1$        **Fig. 6.** Speedup for $\delta = 2$

when the existing services were only on the 50% best resources. When $\delta = |R|$ (Fig. 7) the proposed algorithm is slightly worse than HEFT, and the difference between them ranges from 3% to 6%. Note that the higher the number of groups, the higher the difference between the proposed algorithm and the HEFT-like one. This is also observed in the SLR results, and it can be explained by the fact that the higher the number of resources, the higher the probability of good resources being not used by the workflow. Therefore, instantiating new services can use these resources, improving the workflow execution.

**Makespan.** Figure 8 shows the average makespan for $\delta = 1$. The average for the proposed algorithm was 44% lower for 2 groups and 55% lower for 25 groups in executions with existing services on any resource. For existing services only on the 50% best resources, the improvement was of 35% for 2 groups and 49% for 25 groups. The average makespan for $\delta = 2$ (Fig. 9) shows similar results. The improvement varies from 35% to 50% when existing services were on any resource, and it varies from 28% to 42% when existing services were on the 50% best resources. For $\delta = |R|$ we can observe that the proposed algorithm is slightly worse than HEFT, with the difference ranging from 3% to 6%.

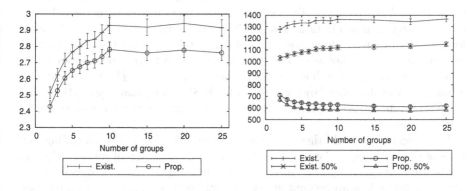

**Fig. 7.** Speedup for $\delta = |R|$        **Fig. 8.** Makespan for $\delta = 1$

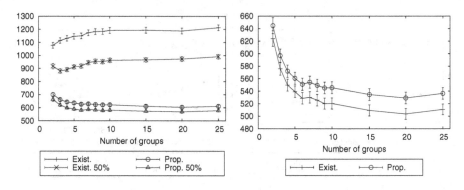

**Fig. 9.** Makespan for $\delta = 2$          **Fig. 10.** Makespan for $\delta = |R|$

The results for $\delta = 1$ and $\delta = 2$ show that the proposed algorithm can significantly improve the performance of the workflow scheduling on service-based grids. Simulations for $\delta$ varying from 3 to 5 suggests that the HEFT-like algorithm gives better results as higher is the $\delta$, however even for $\delta = 5$ the results of the proposed algorithm are still better than the results for the algorithm which does not create new services.

**Remarks.** The presented results show that the proposed algorithm can provide faster workflow execution by scheduling new services on resources with better performance. This is achieved by using many already existing services through the ALAP concept, determining which tasks need a new service to not delay the workflow execution. When compared to the usual execution of tasks on the existing services, the proposed strategy shows an improvement in the workflow execution by making better use of the best resources.

## 5   Related Work

While many grid middlewares focus on task-based workflows [3], others provide mechanisms for execution of workflows composed of tasks which execute on grid services [8]. The execution of workflows on grid services can be improved using dynamic service instantiation. The work described in [5] focus on mechanisms for provisioning dynamic instantiation of community services based on a highly available dynamic deployment infrastructure. However there is no mention to the necessity of a service scheduler to choose the best resources. The DynaGrid [4] is a framework for building large-scale Grid for WSRF-compliant applications that provides mechanisms to dynamic service deployment, but there is no mention to workflow support.

In the scheduling field there are works dealing with bicriteria scheduling, but none of them addresses the problem of dynamic instantiation of services, thus, to the best of our knowledge, the problem of minimizing the number of services created and the makespan was untouched. Additionally, in [11] there is no mention to approaches to this problem.

In [10] the authors deal with the bicriteria scheduling of workflows on grids by modeling it as an extension of the multiple-choice knapsack problem, giving good results when compared with algorithms that consider makespan and budget constraints. In [17] the authors address the multicriteria optimization problem using an integer programming model focusing on price, duration, availability and success rate. Robustness and makespan are the two criteria addressed in [13], while [15] deals with the trade-off between time and reliability. Also, many works focus on economic costs [11], which can also be extended to this work if we consider monetary costs on the creation of new services.

## 6    Conclusion

In this paper we propose an algorithm to schedule workflows on service-oriented grids. The proposed bicriteria scheduling algorithm relies on the existence of dynamic service instantiation to create new services, aiming at minimizing the final execution time (makespan). Additionally, the algorithm tries to minimize the number of created services by using the ALAP (as late as possible) concept, thus creating new services only when not creating them would delay the workflow execution. The minimization of the number of created services is important to avoid wasting resources as bandwidth and processing time, as well as to avoid high budgets when considering economic costs. The shown simulations suggest that the proposed algorithm can improve the workflows speedup by up to 113% using already existing services to execute around 25% of the tasks when there are 25 groups of resources, and can improve it by 74% using existing services to execute around 35% of the tasks when there are 2 groups of resources, thus complying with the biobjective minimization aims. Also, the instantiation of new services scheduled by the proposed algorithm can maximize the resources usage while balancing the load over the available resources when there are many requests to the same service.

As ongoing work, we are integrating the algorithm within a grid infrastructure which supports workflow orchestration [8]. This infrastructure can handle execution failures by raising exceptions. Thus, as future work, we plan to develop a task and service rescheduling algorithm integrated with the exception handling mechanism.

## References

1. Forum, G.G.: Open grid service architecture, version 1.0 (2002),
   http://www.gridforum.org/documents/gwd-i-e/gfd-i.030.pdf
2. Huhns, M.N., Singh, M.P.: Service-oriented computing: Key concepts and principles. IEEE Internet Computing 9(1), 75–81 (2005)
3. Dasgupta, G.B., Viswanathan, B.: Inform: integrated flow orchestration and meta-scheduling for managed grid systems. In: Middleware 2007: Proceedings of the 8th ACM/IFIP/USENIX international conference on Middleware, Newport Beach, California, USA, pp. 1–20 (2007)

4. Byun, E.K., Kim, J.S.: Dynagrid: A dynamic service deployment and resource migration framework for WSRF-compliant applications. Parallel Computing 33(4-5), 328–338 (2007)
5. Qi, L., Jin, H., Foster, I., Gawor, J.: Provisioning for dynamic instantiation of community services. IEEE Internet Computing 12(2), 29–36 (2008)
6. Topcuoglu, H., Hariri, S., Wu, M.Y.: Performance-effective and low-complexity task scheduling for heterogeneous computing. IEEE Trans. Parallel and Distributed Systems 13(3), 260–274 (2002)
7. Bittencourt, L.F., Madeira, E.R.M.: A performance oriented adaptive scheduler for dependent tasks on grids. Concurrency and Computation: Practice and Experience 20(9), 1029–1049 (2008)
8. Senna, C.R., Madeira, E.R.M.: A middleware for instrument and service orchestration in computational grids. In: Seventh IEEE International Symposium on Cluster Computing and the Grid (CCGRID 2007), Rio de Janeiro, Brazil. IEEE Computer Society Press, Los Alamitos (2007)
9. El-Rewini, H., Ali, H.H., Lewis, T.G.: Task scheduling in multiprocessing systems. IEEE Computer 28(12), 27–37 (1995)
10. Wieczorek, M., Podlipnig, S., Prodan, R., Fahringer, T.: Bi-criteria scheduling of scientific workflows for the grid. In: 8th IEEE International Symposium on Cluster Computing and the Grid (CCGrid 2008), Lyon, France, pp. 9–16. IEEE Computer Society, Los Alamitos (2008)
11. Yu, J., Buyya, R.: A taxonomy of scientific workflow systems for grid computing. SIGMOD Records 34(3), 44–49 (2005)
12. Simion, B., Leordeanu, C., Pop, F., Cristea, V.: A hybrid algorithm for scheduling workflow applications in grid environments (ICPDP). In: Meersman, R., Tari, Z. (eds.) OTM 2007, Part II. LNCS, vol. 4804, pp. 1331–1348. Springer, Heidelberg (2007)
13. Canon, L.C., Jeannot, E.: Scheduling strategies for the bicriteria optimization of the robustness and makespan. In: 11th International Workshop on Nature Inspired Distributed Computing (NIDISC 2008), Miami, Florida, USA (April 2008)
14. Yang, T., Gerasoulis, A.: Dsc: Scheduling parallel tasks on an unbounded number of processors. IEEE Trans. Parallel and Distributed Systems 5(9), 951–967 (1994)
15. Dogan, A., Özgüner, F.: Biobjective scheduling algorithms for execution time-reliability trade-off in heterogeneous computing systems. Computer Journal 48(3), 300–314 (2005)
16. Qi, L., Jin, H., Foster, I.T., Gawor, J.: Hand: Highly available dynamic deployment infrastructure for globus toolkit 4. In: 15th Euromicro IPDP, Naples, Italy, pp. 155–162. IEEE Computer Society, Los Alamitos (2007)
17. Zeng, L., Benatallah, B., Ngu, A.H.H., Dumas, M., Kalagnanam, J., Chang, H.: Qos-aware middleware for web services composition. IEEE Transactions on Software Engineering 30(5), 311–327 (2004)

# Ant Colony Inspired Microeconomic Based Resource Management in Ad Hoc Grids

Tariq Abdullah[1], Koen Bertels[1], and Luc Onana Alima[2]

[1]Computer Engineering Laboratory, EEMCS, Delft University of Technology,
Mekelweg 4, 2624 CD, Delft, The Netherlands
{m.t.abdullah,k.l.m.bertels}@tudelft.nl
[2]Distributed Systems Laboratory, University of Mons, Belgium
luc.onana@umh.ac.be

**Abstract.** Ad hoc grids are inherently complex and are dynamic systems. This is due to decentralized control, heterogeneity in resources of the participating nodes, variations in resource availability and user defined access and use polices for the resources. On the other hand, the universe is full of complex adaptive systems such as the immune system, sand dune ripples, and ant foraging etc. The participants in these systems apply simple local rules, resulting in robustness and self-organization. In this paper, we present an ant colony inspired, microeconomic based resource management system for ad hoc grids. The mechanism is based on the emergent behavior of the participating nodes and adapts itself to changes in the ad hoc grid environment. The mechanism enables the ad hoc grid to self-organize itself under varying workload of the participating nodes. Experiments are executed on PlanetLab to test the scalability and robustness of the proposed mechanism.

## 1 Introduction

The universe is full of Complex Adaptive Systems (CAS). The CAS are dynamic, highly decentralized networks and consist of many participating agents. The immune system, sand dune ripples and ant foraging are some examples of the natural CAS. These systems are characterized by decentralized control, emergent behavior, robustness and self-organization. The participating agents in these systems interact according to simple local rules which result in self-organization and complex behavior. Ad hoc grids and similar computational distributed systems are inherently dynamic and complex systems. Resource availability fluctuates over time in ad hoc grids. These changes require adaptation of the system to the new system state by applying some self-organization mechanism. Current scientific problems, like protein folding, weather prediction, particle physics experiments are complex, require huge computing power and storage space. These scientific problems can be solved by using ad hoc grids.

Ant Colony Systems (ACS) [1] are inspired by the colony of artificial ants cooperating in foraging behavior. Ant Colony Optimization (ACO) [2] is a heuristic algorithm that imitates the behavior of real ant colonies in nature. In ACO algorithms, ants drop a chemical, called pheromone, on their way from nest to the food source and vice versa, while they search for food source. Ants choose the path, from food source

N. Abdennadher and D. Petcu (Eds.): GPC 2009, LNCS 5529, pp. 189–198, 2009.

to their nest, with higher pheromone concentrations. The ant colony self-organizes by the local interactions of the individual ants.

In this paper, we apply ACO algorithm for micro-economic based resource management and self-organization in the local ad hoc grid. We assume that each consumer/producer is an ant and the resource manager (matchmaker) represents the food source. The proposed algorithm sends ants in search of resources/tasks to the matchmaker. All the experiments are executed on PlanetLab to test the scalability and robustness of the proposed algorithm.

The proposed system from user's point of view, can be viewed as a combination of centralized such as, Condor -for submitting and running arbitrary jobs- and a system such as BOINC or SETI@Home for distributing jobs from a server to a potentially very large collection of machines in a completely decentralized environment.

## 2   Related Work

Recently, some efforts have been invested in applying ACO for resource management and self-organization of large scale distributed systems. Cao [3] used simple ant-like self-organization mechanism to achieve overall load balancing in grids. The mechanism distributed jobs evenly among the available resources by a collection of simple local interactions. The number of ants and their (ants) steps are defined by the user and don't change during the load balancing process. This restriction is impractical for grid like environments. Messor [4] used Anthill framework [5]. In Messor, the ants can be in Search-Max or Search-Min states. An ant in Search-Max state wanders randomly in the environment until it finds an overloaded node. The same ant, then, changes its state to Search-Min and wanders randomly again in the environment, while looking for an underloaded node. After these state changes, the ant balances the underloaded and the overloaded node. However, considering the dynamism of grid environments, this information may cause erroneous load balancing decisions. Ritchie et al. [6] proposed a hybrid ant colony optimization algorithm to select the appropriate scheduler in a heterogeneous computing environment. The proposed approach was tested only for a scheduling problem in a static environment for independent jobs. Andrzejak et al. [7] compared different algorithms, including ant colony optimization algorithms, for self-organization and adaptive service placement in dynamic distributed environments. Fidanova et al. [8] attempted searching a best task scheduling for grid computing using ACO algorithm.

The main contributions of this paper are that it proposes an ant colony inspired, micro-economic based resource discovery mechanism in ad hoc grids. The results are compared with and without the load balancing factor on the proposed model. The proposed mechanism is tested on a planetary scale testbed, PlanetLab, to obtain results as closer to the real ad hoc grid environment as possible. We apply the following simplifying assumptions:

- The tasks are atomic and can't be sub-divided
- A participating node submits only one request/offer at any given time.
- The consumer, producer and the matchmaker agents are honest

The rest of the paper is organized as follows. Section-3 briefs about the necessary background knowledge to understand the proposed model. Section-4 describes the proposed architecture by describing our modified Ant Colony Optimization (ACO) algorithm. Experimental setup and discussion of experimental results is in Section-5. Whereas, Section-6 concludes the paper with some future research directions.

# 3    Background Knowledge

Before explaining the proposed model, first we explain the required necessary concepts to understand the proposed model and the experimental results.

## 3.1    Continuous Double Auction Based Resource Discovery

Double auctions are one of the many-to-many types of auctions. Continuous Double Auction (CDA) supports simultaneous participation of producer/consumer, observes resource/request deadlines and can accommodate the variations in resource availability. Consumer, Producer and Matchmaker are the three agents in each node of our ad hoc grid. A node can be a consumer or producer of resources at any given time. The consumers submit their computational needs in form of a resource request, called *bid*, to the matchmaker. A *bid* is represented by requested computational resource quantity, execution duration, validity period or Time-to-Live (TTL), and bid price. Whereas, producers submit their available resources in form of resource offers, called *ask*, to the matchmaker. An *ask* is represented by offered computational resource quantity, validity period (TTL), and ask price. The computational resource is expressed in terms of CPU cycles.

Auctioneer (matchmaker) collects bids/asks and matches them immediately on detecting a compatible bid/ask pair. A compatible bid/ask pair is a pair of a resource request and resource offer, where resource request constraints (such as resource quantity, time deadline, price) are satisfied. The auctioneer finds a match between buyer and seller by matching offers with requests. The matchmaker stores requests *(bids)* in descending order of bid prices and offers *(asks)* in ascending order of ask prices in its request/offer repositories respectively. When a task query is received by the matchmaker, the matchmaker searches all available resource offers and returns the best match. If no match is found, the bid/ask is stored in matchmaker repositories till the TTL for bids/asks is expired or a match is found. The consumers/producers do not have any global information about the supply and are not aware of the others' bids or asks. They submit their asks/bids based on their local knowledge. We refer to [9] for the details of our CDA based resource discovery approach.

## 3.2    Bid/Ask Price Calculation

The bid/ask price is the reflection of the value of each resource unit which the consumer or producer is willing to buy or sell. The consumer/producer joins the ad hoc grid with an initial bid/ask price and dynamically update the bid/ask price over time by using a history based dynamic pricing strategy. The pricing function is explained in our previous work [10]. An overview of the pricing function is given here. The agents perceive the demand and supply of the resources through their previous experiences and update their prices accordingly. Based on this strategy, ask and bid price at time interval $t$ are defined as:

$$P(t_2) = P(t_1) + \triangle P$$

Where $P(t_2)$ is the new bid/ask price at time $t_2$ and $P(t_1)$ denotes the previous bid/ask price at time $t_1$. $\triangle P$ represents the price change between time interval $t_1$ and $t_2$, such that $t_2 > t_1$. $\triangle P$ for seller and buyer is defined according to their resource/task utilization history. $\triangle P$ for seller:

$$\triangle P = \alpha * (\mu(t) - \mu_{thR}) * p(t_1)$$

$\triangle P$ for buyer:

$$\triangle P = \beta * (\mu_{thT} - \mu(t)) * p(t_1)$$

Where $\alpha$ and $\beta$ are the coefficients to control the price drift rate. In this paper $\alpha = \beta = 0.8$ is used. Whereas, $\mu_{thT}$ and $\mu_{thR}$ are task and resource utilization thresholds and $\mu_t$ is task/resource utilization of the individual node. $\mu_t$ is defined as:

$$\mu_t = \sum_{i=t_1}^{t_2} x(i) / \sum_{i=t_1}^{t_2} N(i)$$

Where $\sum_{i=t_0}^{t} x(i)$ is the sum of sold/purchased resources in time period $[t_1, t_2]$ and $\sum_{i=t_1}^{t_2} N(i)$ is the total number of offered/requested resources in time period $[t_1, t_2]$. The matchmaker calculates the transaction price as the average of the bid price and ask price of the matched pair. Note that the transaction price is the amount that a consumer will pay to the producer for consuming the producer's resources.

## 4    Proposed Architecture

In order to map ACS to ad hoc grid, first we explain their relationship. Each consumer/producer agent is considered as an *ant* and the matchmaker(s) are treated as *food sources*. The *pheromone value* indicates the weight of the matchmaker in the ant system. A matchmaker with higher pheromone value indicates that it has higher probability of finding a compatible resource offer for a submitted resource request and vice versa.

Each joining node, in our ad hoc grid, is under the responsibility of a matchmaker and sends its resource request/offer to its responsible matchmaker. The joining node gets the pheromone value(s) of the matchmaker(s) from its responsible matchmaker. The pheromone value of a matchmaker is updated for each received resource request/offer from a consumer/producer agent. The pheromone value of a matchmaker is computed according to the equations given in Section-4.1. All the matchmaker agents periodically exchange the pheromone value with each other. The updated pheromone value is sent to the consumer/producer node. Each consumer/producer maintains the pheromone values of the matchmakers and updates these pheromone values after receiving the updated pheromone values from its responsible matchmaker. The consumer/producer node uses the pheromone value as an indicator of matchmaker's matchmaking performance and send its next bid/ask message to the matchmaker with highest pheromone value. In this way, the matchmakers with low pheromone value are dropped out from matchmaker's list.

## 4.1  Ant Colony Optimization Algorithm

In this section, we describe our modified ant colony optimization algorithm for pheromone calculation. As mentioned earlier, consumer/producer agents represents *ants*, matchmakers are the *food sources* and pheromone value indicates the weight of a matchmaker. The pheromone value of a matchmaker is calculated periodically according to the following formula.

$$\tau_{new} = \begin{cases} \alpha * \tau_{old} + (1-\alpha) * \triangle\tau & if \ \triangle\tau > 0 \\ (1-\alpha) * \tau_{old} + \alpha * \triangle\tau & if \ \triangle\tau < 0 \end{cases} \tag{1}$$

The parameter $\alpha$ represents the pheromone evaporation rate. The value of $\alpha$ varies between 0 and 1. $\tau_{old}$ represents the pheromone value during time interval $T1 = [t_{s_1}, t_{e_1}]$. Whereas, $\triangle\tau$ is the change in pheromone value between time interval $T1 = [t_{s_1}, t_{e_1}]$ & $T2 = [t_{s_2}, t_{e_2}]$. The start time of both intervals is represented by $t_{s_1}$ & $t_{s_2}$ and $t_{e_1}$ & $t_{e_2}$ represent the end time of both time intervals, such that $T2 > T1$ & $t_{s_2} = t_{e_1}$. $\triangle\tau$ is calculated as:

$$\triangle\tau = \sum_{i=1}^{n} \tau(i)/N \tag{2}$$

$N$ is the total number of messages received by the matchmaker and $\tau(i)$ is the pheromone value contributed by an individual ant. The $\tau(i)$ for a consumer agent is calculated as:

$$\tau(i) = Perform(MM) * UPrice_{consumer} \tag{3}$$

$\tau(i)$ for a producer agent is calculated as:

$$\tau(i) = Perform(MM) * UPrice_{producer} \tag{4}$$

*Perform*(*MM*) represents the performance of a matchmaker and *UPrice* represents the unit price of a requested or offered computational resource by an ant. *Perform*(*MM*) is periodically calculated as:

$$Perform(MM) = Matched/N \tag{5}$$

*Matched* represents the number of matched pairs and *N* is the total number of messages processed by a matchmaker in time interval $T = [t_{start}, t_{end}]$. $t_{start}$ & $t_{end}$ represents the

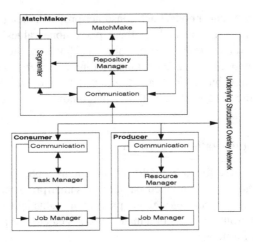

**Fig. 1.** System Architecture

start and end time, respectively, of time interval $T$. The $UPrice$ for each requested or offered computational resource by an ant is calculated as:

$$UPrice_{request} = (\frac{RQuantity_{request}}{BPrice}) * SMachine \qquad (6)$$

$$UPrice_{offer} = (\frac{RQuantity_{offer}}{APrice}) * SMachine \qquad (7)$$

$RQuantity_{request}$ & $RQuantity_{offer}$ represent the computational resource quantity of request and offer, respectively. $BPrice$ and $APrice$ represent the bid and ask price of the requested and offered computational resource, respectively. $SMachine$ represents a reference machine. The computational power of the reference machine is considered as $1GHz$. Figure-1 depicts different components and their interaction for our ant colony inspired, CDA based resource management approach. The Segmenter module in Figure-1 implements our ant colony optimization algorithm. We refer to [11] for the detailed description of the system architecture components.

### 4.2    Load Balancing Factor

In second set of experiments, we applied a load balancing factor to balance the work load among the participating matchmakers. This factor is required for distributing the resource discovery load among all the participating matchmakers. The load balancing factor ensures a minimum level of matchmaking efficiency and response time of a matchmaker. As soon as a matchmaker reaches the threshold of matchmaking efficiency and response time, the overloaded matchmaker transfers its excess workload to the closest matchmaker. In this way the overloaded matchmaker can maintain its minimum level of matchmaking. The overload threshold calculation details and excess workload sharing is described in [12], whereas, algorithms for locating the closest matchmaker and for redirecting nodes to other matchmaker(s) are described in [11]. We would like to point out that overload threshold calculation and matchmaker promotion and demotion mechanism proposed in [11,12], are not used to promote/demote matchmakers in this work. We used the overload threshold calculation mechanism only for load balancing among the matchmakers in this paper.

## 5   Experimental Setup and Results

The proposed model is implemented on top of Pastry [13] structured overlay network, for which an open source implementation (FreePastry) is available. However, in principle any other structured overlay network like Chord [14] or DKS [15] could have been applied. PlanetLab [16,17] is used as the experimental testbed.

The experiments are executed to evaluate the proposed model. The effecitveness of our microeconomic based resource discovery approach against a non microeconomic approach was studied in [9]. The matchmaking efficiency and the response time of the ad hoc grid for consumer requests and producer offers is computed and analyzed for analyzing the proposed model presented in this paper. The *matchmaking efficiency* is calculated as:

$$\left(\frac{MatchedMessage}{N}\right) * 100$$

*MatchedMessage* represents the count of matched messages and $N$ denotes the total number of messages processed by the matchmaker(s) in a unit time interval. The *response time* represents the time interval between receiving a request/offer message and finding a matching offer/request by the matchmaker. The experiments are executed in a balanced network condition, which means that the consumer-producer ratio is approximately $50 - 50$. The number of participating nodes is varied from $15 - 650$. The number of matchmakers is 5. The resource request and resource offer parameters like task execution time and resource quantity are randomly generated from a pre-specified range. The validity period (TTL) of request/offer message is set to 10000 milliseconds for accommodating delays observed in PlanetLab. The value of $\alpha$ (rate of pheromone evaporation) is set to 0.8 in these experiments.

### 5.1   Experimental Results

Figure-2 depicts matchmaking efficiency in different sets of experiments and Figure-3 represents the response time. The X-axis represents the work load (messages processed by the ad hoc grid per minute) in Figure-2 & 3, whereas, Y-axis represents the matchmaking efficiency in Figure-2 and response time in Figure-3.

The first set of experiments focused on pheromone calculation. It is observed that the matchmaker with the highest pheromone value, out of all participating matchmakers, received and processed all request and offer messages from all the participating consumer/producer nodes. This phenomenon is expected for an ant colony inspired resource management system. The higher pheromone of a matchmaker attracts more ants towards that matchmaker, which result in more workload for that matchmaker out of all participating matchmakers. Ultimately the matchmaker with highest pheromone value

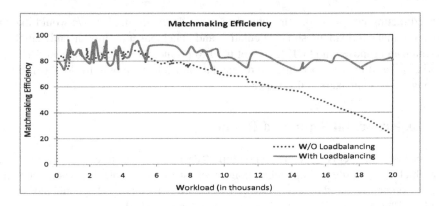

**Fig. 2.** Matchmaking Efficiency of the Ad Hoc Grid

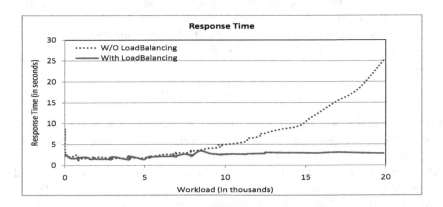

**Fig. 3.** Response Time of the Ad Hoc Grid

receives and processes the whole workload of the ad hoc grid. At the same time it is also observed that the matchmaking efficiency decreases and the response time of the system increases (Dotted line in Figure-2 & 3) with increasing workload of the matchmaker having highest pheromone value. However, the drop in matchmaking efficiency and increase in response time to the consumer/producer nodes is not desired. The drop in matchmaking efficiency means that the matchmaker is unable to find compatible request/offer pairs and the request/offer messages are being discarded by the matchmaker. The increased response time, with increasing workload of the matchmaker, depicts the increased processing time of the matchmaker. It is observed that the response time becomes higher than the validity period (TTL) of the request/offer messages with increased workload of a matchmaker.

In order to increase the matchmaking efficiency of the matchmaker(s) and to reduce the response time of request/offer message, due to increased workload of a matchmaker, we introduced a load balancing factor. The affects of load balancing factor is explained in the the next set of experiments. The load balancing factor is applied when the workload of a matchmaker approaches the threshold value. When a matchmaker reaches its threshold values for matchmaking efficiency, the excess workload is processed by the matchmaker with second highest pheromone value. We refer to [11,12] for the details of distributing excess workload among different matchmakers and threshold calculation, respectively. The load balancing factor results in increased matchmaking efficiency and decreased response time (Represented by the continuous line in Figure-2 & 3) for the same workload. It can be concluded from the above discussion that an ant colony inspired, microeconomic based approach to resource discovery in ad hoc grids the proposed approach gives a stable behavior of the system in resource management and shows a better load balancing.

# 6   Conclusion and Future Work

An ant colony inspired, microeconomic based resource management approach for ad hoc grids is presented in this paper. We used matchmaking performance as the basic factor for calculating the pheromone value. The pheromone value is periodically updated and communicated to consumer/producer nodes accordingly. We also applied load balancing factor for distributing work load among all participating matchmakers and for maintaining a minimum level of matchmaking efficiency. Experimental results indicate that the proposed mechanism gives a stable behavior of the system in resource management and shows a better load balancing. In future, we will look into associated issues with the resource management of multiple resources (such as disk storage, memory, network bandwidth, etc) demanded/offered by consumer/producer nodes in our ant colony inspired, CDA based resource management approach for ad hoc grids.

# References

1. Dorigo, M., Maniezzo, V., Colorni, A.: Ant system: Optimization by a colony of cooperating agents. IEEE Transactions on Systems, Man and Cybernetics-Part B 26(1), 29–41 (1996)
2. Dorigo, M., Blum, C.: Ant colony optimization theory: A survey. Theoretical Computer Science 344, 243–278 (2005)
3. Cao, J.: Self-organizing agents for grid load balancing. In: Proceedings of the 5th IEEE/ACM International Workshop on Grid Computing, GRID, pp. 388–395 (2004)
4. Montresor, A., Meling, H., Montresor, A.: Messor: Load-balancing through a swarm of autonomous agents. Technical report, University of Bologna (2002)
5. Babaoglu, Ö., Meling, H., Montresor, A.: Anthill: A framework for the development of agent-based peer-to-peer systems. In: Proceedings of the 22nd IEEE International Conference on Distributed Computing Systems, ICDCS 2002, pp. 15–22 (2002)
6. Ritchie, G., Levine, J.: A hybrid ant algorithm for scheduling independent jobs in heterogeneous computing environments. In: The Proceedings of the 23rd Workshop of the UK Planning and Scheduling Special Interest Group (2004)
7. Andrzejak, A., Graupner, S., Kotov, V., Trinks, H.: Algorithms for self-organization and adaptive service placement in dynamic distributed systems. Technical Report HPL-2002-259, HP laboratories Palo Alto (2002)
8. Fidanova, S., Durchova, M.: Ant algorithm for grid scheduling problem. In: Lirkov, I., Margenov, S., Waśniewski, J. (eds.) LSSC 2005. LNCS, vol. 3743, pp. 405–412. Springer, Heidelberg (2006)

9. Pourebrahimi, B., Bertels, K., Kandru, G., Vassiliadis, S.: Market-based resource allocation in grids. In: 2nd IEEE International Conference on e-Science & Grid Computing (2006)
10. Pourebrahimi, B., Bertels, K., Vassiliadis, S., Alima, L.O.: A dynamic pricing and bidding strategy for autonomous agents in grids. In: 6th International Workshop on Agents and P2P Computing (2007)
11. Abdullah, T., Alima, L.O., Sokolov, V., Calomme, D., Bertels, K.: Hybrid resource discovery mechanism in ad hoc grid using strucutred overlay. In: 22nd International Conference on Architecture of Computing Systems (March 2009)
12. Abdullah, T., Sokolov, V., Pourebrahimi, B., Bertels, K.: Self-organizing dynamic ad hoc grids. In: 2nd IEEE International Conference on Self-Adaptive and Self-Organizing Systems Workshops (October 2008)
13. Rowstron, A., Druschel, P.: Pastry: Scalable, decentralized object location, and routing for large-scale peer-to-peer systems. In: Guerraoui, R. (ed.) Middleware 2001. LNCS, vol. 2218, pp. 329–350. Springer, Heidelberg (2001)
14. Stoica, I., Morris, R., Karger, D., Kaashoek, M.F., Balakrishnan, H.: Chord: A scalable peer-to-peer lookup service for internet applications. In: Proceedings of the ACM SIGCOMM Conference, pp. 149–160 (2001)
15. Alima, L.O., El-Ansary, S., Brand, P., Haridi, S.: DKS(N, k, f): A family of low-communication, scalable and fault-tolerant infrastructures for P2P applications. In: Proceedings of the 3rd International workshop on Global and P2P Computing on Large Scale Distributed Systems, CCGRID (2003)
16. PlanetLab Online, https://www.planet-lab.org/
17. Peterson, L., Anderson, T., Culler, D., Roscoe, T.: A blueprint for introducing disruptive technology into the internet. In: 1st ACM Workshop on Hot Topics in Networks (2002)

# Dynamic Scheduling Algorithm for Heterogeneous Environments with Regular Task Input from Multiple Requests

Marc E. Frîncu

Institute e-Austria, Blvd. V. Parvan, Timisoara, 300223, Romania
mfrincu@info.uvt.ro

**Abstract.** Grids are very dynamic and their workload is impossible to predict. As a result systems using them need to offer mechanisms for adapting to the new configurations. To address this issue many scheduling policies have been created. In a Grid environment in which tasks needing to be scheduled arrive constantly it is costly to lend some computing resources to only one request consisting of jobs and postpone all others as long as the current one is executing. As a result a scheduling algorithm which minimizes each task's estimated execution time by considering the total waiting time of a task, the relocation to a faster resource once a threshold has been reached and the fact that it should not be physically relocated at each reassignment should be considered. This paper tries to offer a solution based on the above. To validate the model a comparison with other scheduling algorithms is performed.

## 1 Introduction

Due to the dynamic and unpredictable nature of the Grid, systems are required to implement and offer mechanisms for adapting themselves to the new configuration at any given moment. Most of the changes which could influence the execution time of a particular job appear either from changes in the workload or from availability of nodes or of network traffic. These problems are usually solved by implementing efficient Scheduling Algorithms (SAs). However many of these algorithms are static and do not take into account the unpredictable nature of the Grid. Dynamic algorithms on the other hand aim at providing solutions by periodically reschedule tasks based on future predictions or past configurations.

Resources are usually located on different nodes of a cluster or even on different clusters situated in different geographical areas. Therefore the time needed to transport the data from one resource to another needs to be optimized as much as possible. This is not an easy problem because the data packets are routed at the network level by routing algorithms. Besides transferring task data from one computing node to another, we need to choose the best possible solution for the destination of the data which exists at that particular point in time. This requires knowledge on current node workload, number of tasks waiting to be executing on that node, node resources in terms of memory, flops, disk, required

N. Abdennadher and D. Petcu (Eds.): GPC 2009, LNCS 5529, pp. 199–210, 2009.

software etc. Overall the aim of any good scheduling policy is to solve the problem of minimizing the time from the submission of the new task and the time it begins to execute. Also if possible it should maximize resource utilization such that no resource gets overused while others remain relatively free.

SAs usually handle jobs coming from batches of independent [9][1] tasks or workflows [16]. However in a Grid environment it is costly to lend some computing resources to only one request consisting of workflow or batch of jobs and postpone all others as long as this one is executing. Such a behaviour could lead to an unnecessary delay in the scheduling and execution of newer requests. As a result a dynamic SA in which all requests are given the same chance of competing for resources and every one of them has the smallest possible waiting time prior to the actual execution would be prefered. Other issues which should not be neglected are both the possibility of earlier completion by moving the job to another resource queue when the time spent on the current one reaches a given threshold and the fact that resources become available and unavailable in an unpredictable way. In order to reduce network traffic jobs should not be physically transported to new queues during rescheduling. Instead they should be only marked (assigned) as belonging to a new resource queue. The actual transport would take place at a moment depending on the time required for the transfer and the estimated start time of the task on the new resource. This is necessary as migrating tasks each time they get rescheduled on new resources would produce an undesired traffic overhead in the network.

This paper presents a dynamic SA based on the above and compares it with several classic SAs. The SA is studied in terms of convergence and existence of solution. The results show that while the overall makespan can be dramatically decreased using such an approach we can also obtain a good overall node workload and keep the execution time from increasing dramatically with the number of tasks to be scheduled as many of the studied SAs do.

As a whole the paper is structured as follows: Section 2 gives a brief overview on other SAs, Section 3 presents the proposed dynamic SA by defining the mathematical model and general characteristics, Section 4 details the main results of several tests and finally Section 5 outlines some conclusions and possible future directions of study.

## 2 Overview of Existing SAs

The problem of scheduling tasks in a Distributed Environment has been already addressed many times. Consequently, efficient SAs have been proposed. Many of the proposed SA are either static [1], [16], [9] or dynamic [6], [11], [7]. The first approach assumes that all the information about resources is priory known and that resources do not change over time, while the second takes into consideration the dynamics of the Grid. Since the cost for an assignment when dealing with dynamic scheduling is not available, a natural way to keep the whole system health is by balancing the loads of its resources. The advantage of dynamic load balancing over static scheduling is that the system does not need to be aware of the run-time behavior of the application before execution. It is useful in cases where the primary performance goal is maximizing resource utilization, rather than minimizing runtime for individual jobs. SAs [3] are usually heuristic or meta-heuristic based. Heuristic based algorithms include Myopic, Min-Min, Max-Min [9], Suffrage, XSuffrage [1], Minimum Execution Time, Backfilling [13], HEFT [16], etc. Meta-heuristic based algorithms comprise Genetic Algorithms, Simulated Annealing [15] and Greedy Randomized Adaptive Search Procedure (GRASP) [4].

Scheduling policies can try to provide a good schedule by working either at a macroscopic level where they seek to minimize the overall batch makespan or at microscopic level by minimizing the time until execution of each independent task in a dynamic manner everytime a reschedule is executed. The dynamic SA discussed in this paper combines both when building up the schedule.

## 3   A Dynamic Scheduling Policy with Regular Task Input from Multiple Requests

In what follows a scheduling policy for dynamically assigning tasks to resources will be discussed. The algorithm is based on a heuristic which aims at minimizing the total waiting time of each task in the schedule list by periodically reassigning tasks to new queues where they have a better chance of completing earlier. The decision to move the task is based on whether their waiting times on the currently assigned queue have reached or not certain thresholds. The algorithm's heuristic basically revolves around three main rules: **time** (when to move), **position** (where to move) and **force** (give priority to older tasks). Moreover it is assumed that tasks that need to be scheduled arrive periodically and are not restricted to the initial set. Each time a reschedule is started, there might be some new tasks which need to be scheduled for the first time. Tests that we have conducted have shown that it does not matter how these tasks are initially distributed on queues as it does not have an impact on the overall results of the schedule (as seen in Section 4).

### 3.1   Terms and Notion

The introduction of a couple of required terms is mandatory before proceeding with the description of the algorithm.

The *estimated completion time* (ect) is the estimated time when the task is completed. It is defined as in Equation (1):

$$ect = \max(itt, ewt, ist) + eet \tag{1}$$

where *itt* represents the *input transfer time* in seconds, *ewt* is the *estimated waiting* time until all tasks in front of the new one get executed, *ist* means the time needed for the start of the solver and *eet* stands for the *estimated execution time* of the task on the chosen resource. The reason for using *max* instead of *sum* is that the operations listed as arguments are supposed to start at the same moment rather than in a sequential manner. The *eet* is usually computed either by using previously known information related to tasks similar to the one in discussion or by using user given estimes. It may involve extrapolation functions, Genetic Algorithms or Neural Networks combined with a correction factor. Ideally however we could calculate the *eet*'s value exactly if we knew the number of instructions in each task and the current speed of the processors. In this case the *eet* becomes *execution time* (et). Unfortunately even though we can determine the processor speed, the number of instructions in a task is very hard to delineate. The *transfer cost* (tc) from one waiting queue to another is represented by Equation (2) and represents the time required by a task to move from the current queue to the new one. The SA which will be described in what follows relies rather on computational intensive than on data intensive tasks and as a result transfer costs are expected to be minimized as possible.

$$tc = \sum_{i}^{n}(lat_i + \frac{taskSize}{bw_i}) \tag{2}$$

where $n$ represents the number of links in the route between the old and new computing node, $bw_i$ and $lat_i$ stand for the latency and bandwidth offered by $link_i$ in the route. Their values can be determined by using either topology mapping tools or data extracted from an online platform catalogue.

Apart from these terms SAs also use some metrics which help establish their efficiency. The *makespan* is defined as the time required for all tasks to complete their execution. Generally the schedule refers to a single job composed of multiple tasks. Ordinarily, the goal of SAs is to find a good compromise between *makespan* and node workload. Still, when using this criterion we cannot find an optimal algorithm for scheduling, because of the fact the computing power of a grid varies over time depending on the workload. In contrast we can use the *Total Processor Cycle Consumption* (TPCC) [5] which represents the total computing power consumed by an application. Its advantage is that it can be little affected by the variance of resource performance. A schedule with a good *TPCC* is also a schedule with a good makespan.

The *compactness* of a SA is defined as the ratio between the queue with the smallest *ect* and the one with the largest one. As a result a SA is said to be ideal in terms of node workload if its *compactness* $\nearrow$ 1.

Given two SAs $SA_1$ and $SA_2$ the *gain* of $SA_2$ with respect to $SA_1$ is given by the ratio $\frac{makespan_{SA_1}}{makespan_{SA_2}} > 1$. The bigger the ratio the better the algorithm.

## 3.2   The Mathematical Model

Let $Q$ be the set of queues, $R$ the set of computing resources and $T$ the set of tasks (jobs). Every $q \in Q$ belongs to one $r \in R$ and is an ordered set (Remark 1) containing tasks. A schedule is a function $f : T \rightarrow R$ which maps every task $task \in T$ on a resource $r \in R$.

Given a $T_i^k \in q_k$ we define $lwt_i^k$ and $twt_i$ as the *local waiting time* of that task on $q_k$ respectively the *total waiting time* of the same task (the time since its submission). Furthermore $ect_i^k$ and $eet_i^k$ are defined as the *estimated completion time* respectively the *estimated execution time* of $T_i^k$ on $q_k$.

*Remark 1.* Queues are ordered sets such that $\forall q_k \in Q \forall t_i, t_j \in q_k (i > j \Rightarrow twt_i \leq twt_j)$.

The previous remark does not allow for younger tasks to be scheduled ahead of older ones. Its aim is not to allow the starvation of older tasks due to constant insertion of younger tasks with smaller $ect$ ahead of them. In case of batch jobs arriving at the same moment this remark will not influence in any way the scheduling decisions as all $twt_i$ would be equal. The three rules imposed on the algorithm and listed in Section 3 are as follows:

*Rule 1.* The time when a $T_i^j$ can be moved from $q_j$ is given by Equation (3):

$$e^{\sigma - lwt_i^j} \in \begin{cases} [0,1) & , move \\ [1,\infty) & , keep \end{cases} \tag{3}$$

where the value of $\sigma$ depends on how it is chosen. The previous equation simply sets a time threshold on the moment when a decision for moving a $T_i^j$ from queue $q_j$ to a new one should be made. There is no rule for chosing a proper value for $\sigma$ but tests (Section 4) have shown that the makespan is directly influenced by it. For example in the case in which we want to move $T_i$ to a new queue when its $lwt$ exceeded its $ect$ in the assumption that all tasks have the same $eet$ as it, we have a condition like the one in Relation 4:

$$\sigma = \begin{cases} eet_i^j \cdot (i-1) & , i > 0 \\ lwt_i^j & , i = 0 \end{cases} \tag{4}$$

Variants of $\sigma$ could use the smallest $eet$, the actual $ect$, a priority based approach (Relation 5) or simply reschedule tasks at each time interval equal with one time unit ($\sigma = 1$).

$$\sigma = \begin{cases} a \in (1,\infty) & , p_i = 1 \\ \frac{twt_i}{p_i} & , p_i > 1 \end{cases} \tag{5}$$

where $p_i$ is initially equal with 0 and increases with one unit each time the task is logically moved on another queue.

*Rule 2.* Let $ect_{q_j} = \sum_{l=0}^{l < |q_j|} eet_l^j$ be the *estimated completion time* of $q_j$ and $\theta_k = \frac{ect_i^j}{ect_i^k} \frac{1}{tc_i^{jk}}$. Choosing which is the new $q_k$ where to move $T_i^j$ means finding $k = \{i : \forall_{0 \leq j < n, j \neq i} (\theta_j \leq \theta_i)\}$ and satisfying the Relation (6):

$$\left[ ect_{q_j} - eet_{T_i^j}^j \geq ect_{q_k} + eet_{T_i^j}^k \right] \wedge \frac{ect_i^j}{ect_i^k} \geq 1 \tag{6}$$

where the first term ensures that the resulting $ect_{q_k}$ will be smaller than the remaining $ect_{q_j}$. The second term of the condition restricts us from moving a task to a queue $q_k$ where $ect_i^k \geq ect_i^j$. This situation may occur when $\forall q_k \in Q \setminus \{q_j\}(ect_i^k \geq ect_i^j)$ and $\theta_k$ is defined as follows:

*Remark 2.* Before computing the *ect* on a new queue a task is considered as being inserted at the position given by the ordering in Remark 1. Based on this position the *ect* value is then calculated.

*Remark 3.* New incomming tasks will be placed on a waiting queue. They will be moved on a queue assigned to a resource only if $\|T\|$ (Definitions 1 and 2) is smaller or equal with $\|T\|$ at the previous step. This is necessary to obey Definition 3.

*Rule 3.* The condition for executing tasks is given by $f_i = twt_i$. It is chosen such that in each $q_k$ tasks are executed in the descending order of their *twt*.

## 3.3   Convergence of the Solution

In order to establish whether our algorithm always produces augmented solutions or not, we need to study if its *makespan* always decreasingly converges to a limit. In this direction we introduce the following definitions:

**Definition 1.** *Given $Q$ the set of queues and $T$ the set of tasks we define a transition inside a schedule as the process of moving one task from a queue to another. More formally we can say that if $\exists q_j, q_k \in Q \exists T_i \in q_j (e^{\sigma - lwt_{T_i}^j} <$*

$1 \wedge \frac{ect_i^j}{ect_i^k} \geq 1) \wedge \left[ ect_{q_j} - eet_{T_i^j}^j \geq ect_{q_k} + eet_{T_i^j}^k \right]$ *where $k = \{i : \forall 0 \leq j < n, j \neq i \ (\theta_j \leq \theta_i)\}$, a transition $\mathcal{T}(T_i) : q_j \rightarrow q_k$ is defined by the following set of operations:*

$$\mathcal{T} = \begin{cases} q_j = q_j \setminus \{T_i\} \\ q_k = q_k \cup \{T_i\} \end{cases} \tag{7}$$

*where $\mathcal{T}(T_i)$ simply means taking $T_i$ from queue $q_j$ and placing it on queue $q_k$.*

**Definition 2.** *Let $s_m = \|T_m\| = \max(\sum_{l=0}^{l<|q_1|} eet_l^1, \sum_{l=0}^{l<|q_2|} eet_l^2, \ldots, \sum_{l=0}^{l<|q_n|} eet_l^n)$.*

**Definition 3.** *We say that the iterative process described by a dynamic SA is convergent if $s_m$ decreasingly converges to a limit.*

**Proposition 1.** *The SA presented in Section 3.2 is convergent.*

*Proof (of proposition).* From the rules defined in Section 3.2 we have that the sequence $s_m$ from Definition 2 is bounded by $\|T_0\|$ and 0. Furthermore it is a descending monotonic sequence. As a result the sequence has a limit and according to Definition 3 the SA is convergent.

Proposition 1 sustains that the envisioned SA always converges to a limit. Nevertheless there is an open issue concerning its *stability*. In order to find an answer to it we still need to solve two more problems concerning the experimental deduction of the $\sigma$ value which produces the best *makespan* and the study of that makespan's error with regard to the best possible one. These studies require however a large amount of space and time and will be dealt with in a future paper.

## 3.4  Physical Movement Condition for Tasks on New Queues

As mentioned in Section 1 physically moving tasks between queues as they get rescheduled implies an overhead in bandwidth usage and may lead to bottleneck problems. This is why tasks should be kept on their initial allocated queues until a certain threshold is reached and only then actually moved to the new queue. Each time a task is assigned to a new queue during rescheduling it is only logically marked as belonging to it without truly moving it there. The threshold should be chosen such that the chances of the task being executed on the new queue after movement is maximized. In this way we can assume that after a task has been moved it will not be rescheduled on a new queue before being executed. For this to happen no other task that could cause the task in discussion to delay its execution so that it gets rescheduled must exist after its physical relocation. Likewise the *ect* of the task at the moment of the physical relocation should be as close as possible to its *tc*. Formally this can be expressed as in Definition 4 and the interval which bounds it is defined in Proposition 2.

**Definition 4.** *We define the threshold value, $\phi$, for physically moving a $T_i$ to $q_k$ where it will execute as the moment $lwt_i^k$ when the following conditions are met: $e^{\sigma - lwt_i^k} \searrow 1$, $(ect_i^k - eet_i^k) \searrow tc_i$ and $\forall q_j \in Q \setminus \{q_k\}$ $\nexists task \in q_j (twt_{task} >$*

*$twt_{T_i} \wedge e^{\sigma - lwt_{task}^j} < 1 \wedge q_k = max_{q_k \in Q \setminus \{q_j\}}(\theta_k) \wedge \frac{ect_i^j}{ect_i^k} \geq 1) \wedge \left[ ect_{q_j} - eet_{T_i^j}^j \geq \right.$*

*$\left. ect_{q_k} + eet_{T_i^j}^k \right]$.*

**Proposition 2.** *The only admissible threshold values are located inside the interval $\phi \in (\sigma - \delta, \sigma)$ $\forall \delta > 0$ such that the relations in Definition 4 hold and $\phi$ is positive.*

*Proof (of proposition).* In what follows we will assume that we have a threshold $\phi$ as defined in Definition 4.

Let $f(x) = e^{g(x)}$, where $g(x) = \sigma - x$ and $x = \phi$. From Definition 4 we have that $\lim_{x \to \sigma} f(x) = 1$ and $f(x) \searrow 1$. These imply that $\lim_{x \to \sigma} g(x) = 0$ and $x < \sigma$.

From the $\epsilon$-$\delta$ definition of the limit we obtain $\sigma - \delta < x < \sigma + \delta$. As a result we can conclude that the threshold $\phi \in (\sigma - \delta, \sigma)$, $\forall \delta \in [0, \sigma]$ and the conditions from Definition 4 are met.

More generally Proposition 2 states two main facts. Firstly that a $T_i$ can be physically moved to its designated queue at any time between its assignment and the moment we need to relocate it again, if and only if there are no more tasks which could be added ahead of it; secondly, the time remaining until the start of its execution is almost equal with its transfer time.

## 3.5  Algorithm

Given the model described in Section 3.2 we can create an algorithm for a centralized dynamic SA. The algorithm will be based on user estimates for the value of *eet* which will be used when taking decisions to move one task from a queue to another. The envisioned algorithm was called *Dynamic Minimization of the Estimated Completion Time* (DMECT) and tries at each reschedule to minimize the *ect* of each task which violates the time condition expressed in Relation (3). As stated in the beginning of Section 3 the decision on where to assign new incoming tasks does not affect the overall schedule result. Therefore all new tasks will be assigned to random queues. This has no influence on the SA as all tasks which do not obbey the time condition will be reassigned according to the position condition expressed in Relation (6). Each time a processor/core on a queue is available the task with the smallest index value will be scheduled to run on it non-preemtively. The algorithm is described in the following lines:

```
while (exist tasks in T_list) do {
  foreach (task in T_list) do
    if (task is new) then
      assign task to random queue;
  foreach (queue in queue_list) do
    if (queue not sorted)
      sort tasks in current queue descending by twt;
  repeat {
    foreach (queue in queue_list) do
      foreach (task in current queue) do
        if (task exceeds time constraint) then {
          find new queue based on condition;
          find position to insert such that tasks
           remain ordered descending by twt;
          place task on new queue at the found position;
        }
  } until (not task has been moved)
}
```

## 3.6   Impact of the Value of EET in the SAs Overall Behaviour

Most of the SAs require some time execution estimates to be known prior to the actual scheduling. This information can be obtained either by using historical information and applying some learning mechanisms [12] or by using user given estimates. These estimates mostly concern the *eet* and, based on them, the SA takes decisions on how and where to schedule the task. Yet there are times when it is hard to predict them, as it is in the case of jobs which choose the algorithm for solving depending on the input data without the user's knowledge. These algorithms might have different complexities and run an unpredictable amount of time before producing any results. Consequently user estimates are not always useful as they could influence in a negative way the outcome of the applied heuristic [8]. However conclusions are divided as depending on various studies some SA might perform better [10] than when using exact run times, or even worse [2].

# 4   Test Results

Simulations conducted on *DMECT* using a value for $\sigma$ as described in Relation 4 have been accomplished on a sub-platform belonging to the Grid'5000[1] Grid consisting of 5 clusters (2 powerfull and 3 less powerfull) [14] with 10/272 (used/available) processors and a heterogeneity factor [14] of 100. Also four additional variations on $\sigma$ (based on those listed in *Rule 1* of the SA described in Section 3.2) have been tested in order to show how it influences the resulting makespan. *DMECT2* sets $\sigma = 1$, *DMECT3* uses a priority approach (Relation 5), *DMECT4* takes into consideration the minimum *eet* found in the current queue and *DMECT5* sets $\sigma$ to be equal with the tasks current *ect*. As stated in Section 3.6 the user estimate might influence in a smaller or greater amount the outcome of the SA. Thus a testing scenario in which tasks are divided into classes with each class having an average value for *eet* and a standard deviation which will be used for generating normalized random values has been envisioned. Each generated task will belong to a class $C_n$ and have an *eet* value corresponding to a normal distribution $N(\mu_{C_n}, \sigma_{C_n})$. To further refine the results tests were repeated for a number of 100 times and the average of their output was taken as the final result.

**Table 1.** Gain of *DMECT* with regard to other SAs

| No. tasks | Round Robin | Suffrage | Min-Min | Max-Min | MinQL |
|---|---|---|---|---|---|
| 10 | 1.19 | 0.90 | 0.93 | 1.10 | 1.09 |
| 50 | 1.84 | 1.59 | 1.75 | 1.89 | 1.81 |
| 100 | 2.44 | 1.93 | 2.33 | 2.44 | 2.40 |
| 150 | 2.47 | 1.92 | 2.40 | 2.51 | 2.44 |
| 200 | 2.60 | 1.93 | 2.54 | 2.59 | 2.58 |
| 250 | 2.68 | 1.86 | 2.61 | 2.65 | 2.63 |
| 300 | 2.98 | 2.00 | 2.94 | 2.99 | 2.95 |
| 350 | 3.22 | 2.07 | 3.16 | 3.20 | 3.18 |
| 400 | 3.19 | 1.94 | 3.14 | 3.16 | 3.14 |
| 450 | 2.91 | 1.70 | 2.87 | 2.89 | 2.88 |
| 500 | 3.27 | 1.81 | 3.23 | 3.25 | 3.22 |

For testing several characteristics of the SA such as *makespan* (Figure 1), *gain* (Table 1), *compactness* (Figure 2) and *schedule runtime* (Figure 3) were of interest. The five DMECT flavours were tested against dynamic versions of Min-Min, Max-Min, Suffrage, and Round Robin SAs. For makespan we also considered a dynamic SA (MinQL) which periodically rebalances the queues by moving tasks to faster resources and which does not consider the *eet* when taking decisions. The *DMECT* flavour performed better in all cases offering an average gain of 1.79 (Table 1) against the second best dynamic SA Suffrage. Regarding compactness (Figure 2) an average value of 0.6 was obtained for *DMECT* during

---

[1] https://www.grid5000.fr/

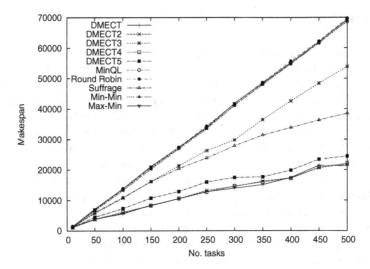

**Fig. 1.** Makespan of various DMECT flavours compared with other SAs

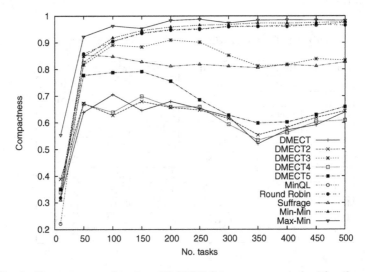

**Fig. 2.** Compactness of various DMECT flavours compared with other SAs

tests. This shows that the *DMECT* flavour tends to offer a solution at a time when its largest queue has an *ect* of almost the double size of its smallest queue in terms of *ect*. Out of all the DMECT flavours *DMECT3* performed best at these tests and offered an average value of 0.81. However this behavior still needs to be investigated as it may be connected to the threshold value used when deciding whether to move or not a task to a new queue. *DMECT* also performed well with regard to the overall time required for assigning all the tasks (Figure 3) as it gave the best schedule build time out of Suffrage, Min-Min and Max-Min.

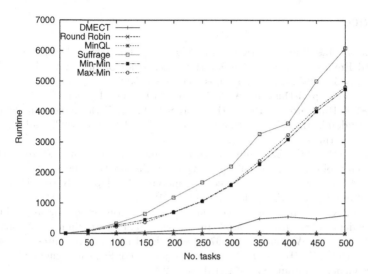

**Fig. 3.** Avg. schedule runtime of DMECT compared with other SAs

## 5  Conclusions and Future Work

In this paper we have presented a SA which reassigns periodically incoming tasks when their waiting time on a queue reaches a threshold and tries to relocate them on a queue with the best chance of completing them at the earliest possible time. Moreover due to the threshold existence tasks assigned to queues whose resources become unavailable will be reassigned. As tests have shown the SA which has been called DMECT gives good makespan and average compactness for batches consisting of large number of tasks. Also it has been outlined that the improvement of the makespan is related with the moment $\sigma$ chosen as threshold for moving the task to a new queue. The time needed to build a schedule is also smaller compared to other SAs.

As future enhancements more tests using different platforms with a wider range of heterogeneity are taken into consideration. Also scenarios in which tasks have a wider range of *eet* need to be considered. The purpose of these tests is to determine if the schedule is similar in all scenarios or is dependent on the platform configuration and task properties. The limit defined in Definition 3 and the *makespan* error related with it need to be tested experimentally. Moreover a value for $\sigma$ which produces the best schedule *makespan* needs, if possible, to be experimentally determined. Also a descentralized and parallel approach based on the fact that the SA is easily representable by using rules is under consideration.

**Acknowledgments.** This research is partially supported by European Union Framework 6 grant RII3-CT-2005-026133 SCIEnce: Symbolic Computing Infrastructure in Europe.

# References

1. Casanova, H., et al.: Heuristics for Scheduling Parameter Sweep Applications in Grid Environments. In: The 9th Heterogeneous Computing Workshop (HCW 2000), pp. 349–363. IEEE Press, Los Alamitos (2000)
2. Chiang, S., Arpaci-Dusseau, A.C., Vernon, M.K.: The Impact of More Accurate Requested Runtimes on Production Job Scheduling Performance. In: Feitelson, D.G., Rudolph, L., Schwiegelshohn, U. (eds.) JSSPP 2002. LNCS, vol. 2537, pp. 103–127. Springer, Heidelberg (2002)
3. Dong, F., Akl, S.G.: Scheduling algorithms for grid computing: State of the art and open problems. Technical report, Queen's University (2006)
4. Feo, T.A., Resende, M.G.C.: Greedy Randomized Adaptive Search Procedures. Journal of Global Optimization 6, 109–133 (1995)
5. Fujimoto, N., Hagihara, K.: A comparison among grid scheduling algorithms for independent coarse-grained tasks. In: International Symposium on Applications and the Internet Workshops, pp. 674–680. IEEE Press, Los Alamitos (2004)
6. Gao, Y., Rong, H., Huang, J.: Adaptive grid job scheduling with genetic algorithms. Future Gener. Comput. Syst. 21, 151–161 (2005)
7. Kurowski, K., et al.: Improving Grid Level Throughput Using Job Migration And Rescheduling. Scientific Programming 12(4), 263–273 (2004)
8. Lee, C., Schartzman, Y., Hardy, J., Snavely, A.: Are User Runtime Estimates Inherently Inaccurate? In: Feitelson, D.G., Rudolph, L., Schwiegelshohn, U. (eds.) JSSPP 2004. LNCS, vol. 3277, pp. 253–263. Springer, Heidelberg (2005)
9. Maheswaran, M., et al.: Dynamic Matching and Scheduling of a Class of Independent Tasks onto Heterogeneous Computing Systems. In: The 8th Heterogeneous Computing Workshop (HCW 1999), pp. 30–44. IEEE Press, Los Alamitos (1999)
10. Mu'alem, A.W., Feitelson, D.G.: Utilization, Predictability, Workloads, and User Runtime Estimates in Scheduling the IBM SP2 with Backfilling. IEEE Transactions in Parallel Distributed Systems 12(6), 529–543 (2001)
11. Sakellariou, R., Zhao, H.: A Low-Cost Rescheduling Policy for Efficient Mapping of Workflows on Grid Systems. Scientific Programming 12(4), 253–262 (2004)
12. Smith, W., Foster, I.T., Taylor, V.E.: Predicting Application Run Times Using Historical Information. In: Feitelson, D.G., Rudolph, L. (eds.) IPPS-WS 1998, SPDP-WS 1998, and JSSPP 1998. LNCS, vol. 1459, pp. 122–142. Springer, Heidelberg (1998)
13. Srinivasan, S., Kettimuthu, R., Subramani, V., Sadayappan, P.: Characterization of Backfilling Strategies for Parallel Job Scheduling. In: Proceedings of the 2002 International Conference on Parallel Processing Workshops, pp. 514–519. IEEE Press, Los Alamitos (2002)
14. Suter, F., Casanova, H.: Extracting Synthetic Multi-Cluster Platform Configurations from Grid 5000 for Driving Simulation Experiments, Tech. Rep. RT-0341, INRIA (2007)
15. YarKhan, A., Dongarra, J.J.: Experiments with Scheduling Using Simulated Annealing in a Grid Environment. In: Parashar, M. (ed.) GRID 2002. LNCS, vol. 2536, pp. 232–242. Springer, Heidelberg (2002)
16. Zhao, H., Sakellariou, R.: An Experimental Investigation Into the Rank Function of the Heterogeneous Earliest Finish Time Scheduling Algorithm. In: Kosch, H., Böszörményi, L., Hellwagner, H. (eds.) Euro-Par 2003. LNCS, vol. 2790, pp. 189–194. Springer, Heidelberg (2003)

# Balanced Scheduling Algorithm Considering Availability in Mobile Grid*

JongHyuk Lee[1], SungJin Song[1], JoonMin Gil[2], KwangSik Chung[3], Taeweon Suh[1], and HeonChang Yu[1,**]

[1] Dept. of Computer Science Education, Korea University
{spurt,white}@comedu.korea.ac.kr, {suhtw,yuhc}@korea.ac.kr
[2] Dept. of Computer Science Education, Catholic University of Dague
jmgil@cu.ac.kr
[3] Dept. of Computer Science, Korea National Open University
kchung0825@knou.ac.kr

**Abstract.** The emerging Grid is extending the scope of resources to mobile devices and sensors that are connected through unreliable networks. Nowadays the number of mobile device users is increasing dramatically and the mobile devices provide various capabilities such as location awareness that are not normally incorporated in fixed Grid resources. Nevertheless, mobile devices exhibit inferior characteristics such as poor performance, limited battery life, and unreliable communication, compared to fixed Grid resources. Therefore, the job scheduling and the load balancing are more challenging and sophisticated in mobile Grid environment. This paper presents a novel balanced scheduling algorithm in mobile Grid, taking into account the mobility and availability in scheduling. We analyzed users' mobility patterns to quantitatively measure the resource availability that is classified into three types: full availability, partial availability, and unavailability. We also propose a load balancing technique by classifying mobile devices into nine groups depending on availability. The experimental results show that our scheduling algorithm provides a superior performance in terms of execution times to one without considering availability and load-balancing.

**Keywords:** scheduling, load balancing, availability, mobile grid.

## 1 Introduction

Grid [1] is a large-scale virtual computing environment where geographically distributed resources collaboratively provide a computing infrastructure. It is used for solving computing-intensive and data-intensive problems that are not practically feasible to run in traditional distributed computing environments. The

* This work was supported by the Korea Research Foundation Grant funded by the Korean Government (MOEHRD) (KRF-2006-311-D00173).
** Corresponding author.

N. Abdennadher and D. Petcu (Eds.): GPC 2009, LNCS 5529, pp. 211–222, 2009.

early Grid was implemented mostly with physically fixed resources with high-performance, and the resources are connected through high speed and reliable networks.Emerging Grids [2] are extending a scope of resources to mobile devices and sensors that are connected through unreliable networks. Especially, a mobile Grid focuses on incorporating mobile devices by supporting new functionalities such as mobility.

A mobile device in mobile Grid can play roles as both a consumer and a provider. As a consumer it requests service to a Grid, and as a provider it actively participates in processing service requests. Compared to physically fixed Grid resources such as desktop computers, mobile devices tend to provide a relatively inferior performance in terms of CPU capability, amount of main memory, and storage capacity. They also have a limited battery life and are commonly connected to wireless networks that are not as reliable as wired networks. Due to the availability and reliability issues, it is not straightforward to use a mobile device as a Grid resource and there are skepticisms on using a mobile device as a provider. Nevertheless, mobile devices offer various capabilities such as location awareness that are not normally incorporated in fixed Grid resources. Nowadays the number of mobile device users is exploding and devices are rolled out equipped with a processor and large memory with advanced technology at an ever-faster pace. Considering the devices' capabilities and enormous number of gadgets, mobile devices have immense potential to serve as resource providers in mobile Grid environment.

The challenges in mobile Grid are job scheduling and load balancing issues under the unreliable communication environment. For example, the network link in mobile Grid could be broken while executing a job that may require data communication. Then, the job should wait until the connection is reestablished. This leads to performance degradation of the job. Without proper load balancing, all jobs may be allocated only to the stable resources such as physically fixed Grid components. It results in discriminating mobile devices with less performance but with the enormous number of population. It incurs not only the decrease of the Grid resources' utilization, but also the performance degradation due to the improper load-balancing.

This paper presents a novel balanced scheduling algorithm taking into account the mobility and availability in scheduling. We analyzed users' mobility patterns to quantitatively measure the resource availability that is classified into three types. We also propose a load balancing technique by dividing mobile devices into nine groups depending on availability and job type (computing-intensive and data-intensive).

The rest of the paper is organized as follows. Section 2 presents related work on scheduling algorithms in mobile Grid. Section 3 discusses challenges introduced by the mobile device's mobility. Section 4 demonstrates the system architecture of a mobile Grid and describes characteristics of users' mobility patterns, which are used to propose our load balancing algorithm in Section 5. Experimental results are presented in Section 6. Finally, we conclude our paper with future works in Section 7.

## 2    Related Work

Several studies have researched on scheduling issues in mobile Grid focusing on power efficiency, communication availability due to mobility, and job replication. From the power efficiency point of view, Chang-Qin Huang et al. [3] proposed a proxy based hierarchical scheduling model that takes into account mobility and power management in wireless environment. In this model, the scheduler is comprised of two levels (top level and proxy level) to efficiently utilize the energy of wireless node and to guarantee QoS at the same time.

There are several studies on the communication availability. Park et al. [4] proposed a scheduling algorithm with the processor and the communication availabilities. This algorithm confined communication scope and thus can be useable even when the network link is broken due to the mobile device's mobility. However, this algorithm has a shortcoming in that it is applicable to specific job types with no communication during a job execution. Farooq et al. [5] devised a generic mobility model to predict a time duration for which a user (and thus a device) will remain in a specific domain. It is based on learning from the user's behavior in the past. This model computes the average mobility and the time in range based on the user range parameter. Then, it calculates how many jobs a mobile device can execute. Ghosh et al. [6] proposed a scheduling algorithm that applies a pricing strategy to the job allocation problem and optimizes a total system cost. Since these algorithms do not consider the processor availability and load balancing, they have limitations on the scheduling optimization.

In job replication aspect, Litke et al. [7] proposed a method that estimates a number of job replications using the Weibull reliability function and maximizes the resource utilization for workloads caused by replication with the knapsack formulation.

## 3    Problem Statement

As opposed to a traditional Grid, the mobile Grid has a characteristic that Grid resources are changing their physical positions according to users' movement. When a mobile device crosses domains in wireless network, a mobile user demands the terminal mobility to maintain a session. Even when a mobile user opens a session on one device and moves to another device, the user still demands both user mobility and session mobility for the continuation of the service. Present mobile computing guarantees the terminal mobility and the session mobility through MIP and SIP. It is implemented in either network layer or its upper layer. When the network condition is stable, resource and job management techniques in traditional Grid are directly applicable to the mobile Grid. Nonetheless resources in mobile Grid may actively participate in a Grid or may be separated from the Grid, depending primarily on the network health. Therefore, the traditional techniques on resource and job managements are not pertinent to the mobile Grid environment. Especially a fault tolerance feature withstanding unstable network links should be incorporated in mobile Grid to achieve the performance goal.

The availability and reliability of the system is greatly influenced by device's mobility. Availability is defined as whether the user can use a system immediately at a specific time. On the other hand, Reliability is whether the user can utilize a resource without a failure. Thus the availability in mobile Grid can be defined as a ratio of the expected uptime (e.g. system power is on) to the sum of the expected values of uptime and downtime (e.g. system power is off).

$$Availability = \frac{T_{up}}{T_{up} + T_{down}} \tag{1}$$

where $T_{up}$ is uptime and $T_{down}$ is downtime.

The downtime is classified into a planned downtime and an unplanned downtime. For example, the rebooting caused by system configuration changes belong to the planned downtime. Unhandled exceptions and physical problems such as hardware failure belong to the unplanned downtime. Since the planned downtime is inevitable, we focus on reducing the unplanned downtime caused by power supply shortage and network link failure. There are four different combinations depending on power status and network link status. Especially, we pay a special attention to the case where the system power is on, but the network link is down. This case is an uptime from a job point of view if it does not require communication during execution via the network link. However, this case becomes a downtime in the opposite situation where the job does require communication. It means that the system availability becomes different according to the job characteristic. When a job should be executed for a relatively long time without suspension, the reliability plays an important role and the communication failure caused by device's mobility should be taken into account in the formula.

## 4    System Model

### 4.1    System Architecture

Mobile Grid is a convergence of wired and wireless computing environment to efficiently utilize fixed and mobile Grid resources. It typically consists of physically fixed devices, mobile devices, and proxies. Fig. 1 shows the system architecture of a mobile Grid. The proxy is a delegation system that delivers job requests to a Grid, so mobile devices requesting jobs do not have to be online all the time. The main functionalities of proxy are information service and job scheduling. The information service collects resource information through information providers such as Network Weather Service (NWS). The job scheduler chooses a suitable resource to execute a requested job according to a scheduling algorithm. Our scheduling algorithm takes into account user mobility and load balancing described in Section 4.2 and Section 5.

### 4.2    Characteristics of User Mobility

This section investigates characteristics of users' mobility patterns. We first discuss mobility parameters investigated in the prior research, and introduce new parameters suitable for the mobile Grid environment.

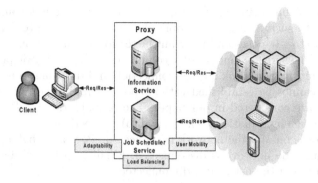

**Fig. 1.** System architecture of a mobile Grid

In computer networks, an Access Point (AP) is a device that allows wireless devices to connect to a wireless network. The mobile device user may freely move around APs and has access to a network. In a mobile environment with APs, all time ($T_{all}$) of a mobile device is divided into an uptime and a downtime. The uptime is further divided into a time duration ($T_{connected}$) during which a network is connected and a time duration ($T_{disconnected}$) during which a network is disconnected. In [8], two metrics are introduced to model the user mobility: AP prevalence and user persistence. These two metrics are defined as follows:

**Definition 1.** *AP Prevalence: a ratio of the time duration ($T_{ij}$) during which the $i^{th}$ user spends in the $j^{th}$ AP to the time duration ($T_{connected}$) during which the network is connected.*

$$Prev_{ij} = \frac{T_{ij}}{T^i_{connected}} \quad (2)$$

The more a user visits an AP and/or spends time at the AP, the AP prevalence becomes higher. In [8], each user is classified into one of five groups (stationary, occasionally mobile, regular, somewhat mobile, and highly mobile) based on the maximum prevalence and the median prevalence. Since the AP prevalence does not take into account users' mobility pattern of how a user maintains a session in AP, it is not able to represent the communication instability caused by user's frequent movements among APs. The user persistence complements this shortcoming.

**Definition 2.** *User Persistence: a time duration during which the $i^{th}$ user stays at the $j^{th}$ AP until the user moves to another AP or the network link is down.*

$$\sum_{k=1}^{n} Pres_{ijk} = T_{ij} \quad (3)$$

*where $n$ is the number of sessions.*

If the terminal mobility of mobile devices is guaranteed, a mobile device can continuously interact with a job requestor and the user persistence does not contribute to reliability. In mobile Grid, however, a network link could be down unexpectedly. In such a situation, mobile devices are not able to communicate with the requestor. It poses an important factor for job allocation.

As mentioned, there are four possible combinations depending on power status (on and off) and network link status (connection and disconnection). Since the network link cannot be established without power supply, the remaining three combinations are considered in our paper. The probabilities $P_c$, $P_p$, and $P_d$ of each case are given by Equations (4), (5), and (6), respectively. $P_c$ is a probability that the power is on and the network is connected. $P_p$ is a probability that the power is on and the network is disconnected. Finally, $P_d$ is a probability that the power is off and the network is disconnected.

$$P_c^i = \frac{\sum_{k=1}^n Pers_{ijk}}{T_{all}^i} = \frac{T_{ij}}{T_{all}^i} \tag{4}$$

$$P_p^i = \frac{T_{up}^i}{T_{all}^i} - P_c^i \tag{5}$$

$$P_d^i = 1 - (P_c^i + P_p^i) = \frac{T_{down}^i}{T_{all}^i} \tag{6}$$

Using the above three equations, we classify availability into three types: full availability, partial availability, and unavailability.

**Definition 3.** *Full Availability: a probability that a mobile device fully executes jobs and returns outcome via network link.*

$$A_c = \frac{P_c}{P_c + P_p + P_d} \tag{7}$$

**Definition 4.** *Partial Availability: a probability that a mobile device fully executes jobs but does not return outcome due to the network failure.*

$$A_p = \frac{P_p}{P_c + P_p + P_d} \tag{8}$$

**Definition 5.** *Unavailability: a probability that a mobile device does not execute jobs at all because the device is off.*

$$A_d = 1 - (A_c + A_p) \tag{9}$$

The job execution in a Grid consists of three phases: input transmission, computation, and outcome transmission. Data transmission may occur in the middle of computation, which is obviously possible only when a mobile device is connected to a network. We present the data transmission time in terms of the full availability and define communication unit time ($u_{cm}$) as a time to transmit data when the network condition is healthy. The expected transmission time $E_{cm}$ in terms of $u_{cm}$ is given by Eq. (10). A condition of whether the network link is established at the beginning of transmission is included in the formula.

$$E_{cm} = A_c * u_{cm} + (1 - A_c) * (u_{cm} + \frac{1}{A_c}) = u_{cm} + \frac{1}{A_c} - 1 \tag{10}$$

We define computation unit time ($u_{cp}$) as a time for computation when the computing resource is completely available. If an amount of communication ($mu_{cm}$) is required for the c number of times during the job execution, the expected computation time $E_{cp}$ in terms of $u_{cp}$ and $u_{cm}$ is given by

$$E_{cp} = (A_c + A_p) * u_{cp} + (1 - A_c - A_p) * (u_{cp} + \frac{1}{A_c + A_p}) + \sum_{i=1}^{c} E_{cm}(mu_{cm}^i)$$

$$= u_{cp} + mu_{cm} + \frac{1}{A_c + A_p} + \frac{c}{A_c} - c - 1 \qquad (11)$$

Therefore, the expected execution time $E$ is expressed as follows.

$$E = (su_{cm} + mu_{cm} + eu_{cm}) + u_{cp} + \frac{1}{A_c + A_p} + \frac{c+2}{A_c} - c - 3 \qquad (12)$$

where $su_{cm}$ is a time to transfer input data at the beginning and $eu_{cm}$ is a time for outcome transmission at the end of a job execution.

The first four terms ($su_{cm}$, $mu_{cm}$, $eu_{cm}$, $u_{cp}$) in Eq. (12) represent communication times spent in reliable wired network. The rest ($1/(A_c + A_p)$, $(c+2)/A_c$, $c$, 3) is mobile-computing specific factors. In other words, the expected execution time is increased by these three terms. Therefore, the parameters ($A_c$, $A_p$, $c$) should be used as criteria for choosing mobile devices as target Grid resources to minimize the overall execution time of workloads. Under a full availability condition like a traditional Grid, the expected computation time ($E_{cp}$) and the expected execution time ($E$) are reduced to Eqs (13) and (14) since $A_p$ becomes zero.

$$E_{cp} = A_c * u_{cp} + (1 - A_c) * (u_{cp} + \frac{1}{A_c}) + \sum_{i=1}^{c} E_{cm}(mu_{cm}^i)$$

$$= u_{cp} + mu_{cm} + \frac{1+c}{A_c} - c - 1 \qquad (13)$$

$$E = (su_{cm} + mu_{cm} + eu_{cm}) + u_{cp} + \frac{3+c}{A_c} - c - 3 \qquad (14)$$

The Eq. (14) is always higher than the Eq. (12). In other words, by means of utilizing devices of partial availability ($A_p$) in mobile Grid, the expected execution time is decreased at a maximum by $1/A_c - 1/(A_c + A_p)$. Therefore, to increase the performance in execution of workload, it is imperative for scheduling algorithm to consider both the full availability and the partial availability of the computing resources.

## 5   Balanced Scheduling Algorithm Considering Availability

In a Grid, a job is commonly classified into two types: computing-intensive job and communication-intensive job. Those have different resource requirements. In

**Table 1.** Nine groups based on the full availability and the partial availability

| $A_c$ \ $A_p$ | Low $A_p \in [0, \omega_{A_p})$ | Medium $A_p \in [\omega_{A_p}, o_{A_p})$ | High $A_p \in [o_{A_p}, 1]$ |
|---|---|---|---|
| Low $A_c \in [0, \omega_{A_c})$ | LL | LM | LH |
| Medium $A_c \in [\omega_{A_p}, o_{A_c})$ | ML | MM | MH |
| High $A_c \in [o_{A_c}, 1]$ | HL | HM | HH |

mobile Grid, it tends to provide a superior performance when a scheduler first assigns a job with a large amount of communication to a stable mobile device under healthy network condition. It is because the job execution could be delayed by unexpected network breakdowns in the middle of execution. Especially in mobile Grid, it is imperative to assign a job to a pertinent mobile device according to a job type. For the job allocation, we propose a multi-level queue scheduling algorithm with priority. The priority is determined based on the full availability and the partial availability.

Mobile devices are classified into nine groups based on the full availability and the partial availability as shown in Table 1, where $o$ and $\omega$ represent an upper bound and a lower bound, respectively, for the classification.

In practice, communication reliability of the groups HH, HM, and HL is preferable for executing jobs since the computing resource and network condition are relatively stable and healthy. However, it is wasteful to assign all jobs to devices from just three groups in terms of execution time and resource utilization. A job with no communication may be executed in a resource with a full and a partial availability ($A_c$ and $A_p$), resulting in a superior performance in overall execution. In the opposite case where communication is involved in execution, the number of transmissions ($c$) should be additionally considered. We propose the following scheduling algorithm according to the job type.

- A job with long communication interval is assigned to a mobile device with a higher $A_p$ even if $A_c$ is not high.
- A job with a large amount of communication is assigned to a mobile device with a higher $A_c$.
- Determine a priority level (high, middle, low) according to the communication interval of a job and select a queue corresponding to the level of $A_p$.
- Determine a priority level (high, middle, low) according to the amount of communication and select a queue corresponding to the level of $A_c$.

## 6   Experiments

### 6.1   Experimental Environment

We evaluated our scheduling algorithm using SimGrid toolkit [9] with a real-life trace: WLAN trace [10] of Dartmouth campus. After analyzing the trace, network information was extracted and it is supplied to the SimGrid platform. The trace is composed of the syslog records produced by APs from September 1,

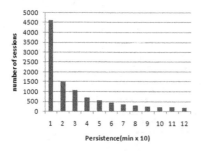

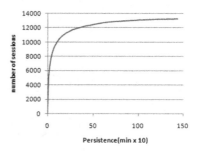

**Fig. 2.** Histogram of the number of sessions lasting less than 2 hours

**Fig. 3.** Cumulative density function of the number of sessions

2005 to October 4, 2006. The trace as of June 6, 2006 is chosen to create network information to provide input to the SimGrid platform. Fig. 2 shows a histogram of the number of sessions lasting less than 2 hours. Fig. 3 shows a cumulative density function of the number of sessions. The data shown in Fig. 3 includes sessions maintained for more than 24 hours. Due to the unstable communication environment, the number of the sessions maintained for less than 2 hours is about 80% of the trace. After fitting the probability density function to various statistic distributions, we found that the Pareto distribution fits best with the shape parameter 1.2602 and the scale parameter 3018.0. To provide the processor status information to SimGrid platform, we used the Weibull distribution since it effectively represents the machine availability [11]. We randomly extracted time durations by the inverse function of the Weibull distribution.

Based on the network information and the time durations, we created testvectors for full and partial availabilities. The network information from the WLAN trace is used as time slots for full availability. The time durations are used as the time slots for partial availability. Then the processor start time is calculated by padding time duration from the network information in front of processor time duration, and the processor completion time is calculated by padding time duration from the network information behind the processor time duration. In this way, the processor information is synchronized with network information. Fig. 4 shows a distribution of $A_c$ and $A_p$ for mobile devices. The dotted lines on the x and y axes indicate upper and lower bounds of $A_c$ and $A_p$, so it is classified into nine groups. Then we randomly created jobs with various computation and communication sizes and limited a number of data transmissions during the job execution to two.

### 6.2 Experimental Results

Our experiments investigated effects of two factors (*i.e.* user mobility and load balancing) on execution time. First, we experimented the effect of user mobility. Four methods are used as shown in Table 2. The method I-1 in Table 2,

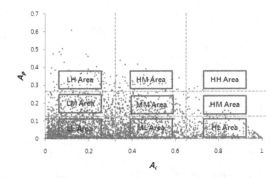

**Fig. 4.** Distribution of $A_c$ and $A_p$ for mobile devices

**Table 2.** Four methods to evaluate effects of user mobility on performance

| considerations | Methods | | | |
|---|---|---|---|---|
| | I-1 | I-2 | I-3 | I-4 |
| full availability | X | O | O | O |
| partial availability | X | X | O | O |
| data transmission in executing a job | X | X | X | O |

for example, means that it allocates jobs to resources without considering full availability, partial availability, and data transmission during job execution.

Fig. 5 shows average execution time of each method when 4,000 jobs are executed. As shown, the method I-4 reports the shortest execution time. Our algorithm provides a 10% performance improvement compared to a prior work [4], of which condition is reflected in the method I-3. Currently, our dynamic scheduling algorithm is not directly applicable to batch jobs. However, we expect that the performance of batch jobs would be greatly enhanced by applying min-min and max-min according to the job type.

Second, we investigated effects of the load balancing on execution time. Based on the method I-4, we experimented with the following three methods.

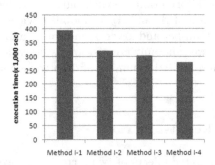

**Fig. 5.** Average execution time of Methods I-1, I-2, I-3, and I-4

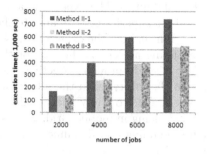
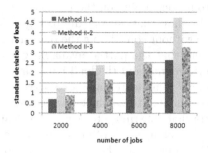

**Fig. 6.** Average execution time of Methods II-1, II-2, and II-3

**Fig. 7.** Standard deviation of load for Methods II-1, II-2, and II-3

- Method II-1: jobs are evenly allocated to mobile devices in a round robin fashion.
- Method II-2: mobile devices are classified into three groups according to the full availability, and a job is allocated to a group corresponding to a job type.
- Method II-3: mobile devices are classified into nine groups according to full availability and partial availability, and a job is allocated to a group corresponding to a job type.

Fig. 6 shows average execution time of each method and Fig. 7 shows standard deviations of the number of loads on Grid resources. We found that the method II-2 provides the best performance, yet marginally better than the method II-3. However, the method II-2 reports the worst load balancing. The method II-1 provides the best load balancing but the worst execution time. The method II-3 reports a medium standard deviation of loads and comparable execution time to the best. Consequently, it is not unreasonable to state that the method II-3 is suitable for job scheduling because it is satisfactory in terms of execution time and at the same time it provides a relatively low standard deviation of load distribution.

The average execution time and the degree of load balancing are influenced by the upper and the lower bounds. Because our scheduler determines a group according to job type, if many mobile devices belong to a group with a fewer jobs, the average execution time and the load balancing would get worsen. Therefore, it is imperative to determine the upper and the lower bounds dynamically.

# 7 Conclusions and Future Work

This paper presents a novel balanced scheduling algorithm in mobile Grid, considering mobility patterns of mobile device users. Our algorithm takes into account mobility and load balancing in scheduling. We analyzed user's mobility patterns to quantitatively measure the resource availability that is classified into three types: full availability, partial availability, unavailability. An adaptive load balancing technique is also proposed by classifying mobile devices into nine groups depending on the full and the partial availabilities. The experimental results show that our scheduling algorithm provides a superior performance to the one without considering the partial availability. Throughout the experiments, we found that the partial availability and the grouping are crucial factors for the performance and the load balancing. Overall, our study provides effective algorithms to allocate mobile resource according to the job type. In the future, we are planning to conduct a wider variety of experiments to study additional factors that contribute to performance and load balancing in mobile Grid. We also have a plan to apply methods such as batch scheduling and dynamic selection of the upper and the lower bounds to a mobile Grid.

# References

1. Foster, I., Kesselman, C.: The Grid 2: Blueprint for a New Computing Infrastructure. Morgan Kaufmann Publishers, San Francisco (2004)
2. Kurdi, H., Li, M., Al-Raweshidy, H.: A Classification of Emerging and Traditional Grid Systems. IEEE Distributed Systems Online 9(3) (2008)
3. Huang, C., Zhu, Z.T., Wu, Y.H., Xiao, Z.H.: Power-Aware Hierarchical Scheduling with Respect to Resource Intermittence in Wireless Grids. In: Proc. of the Fifth Int. Conf. on Machine Learning and Cybernetics (2006)
4. Park, S.M., Ko, Y.B., Kim, J.H.: Disconnected Operation Service in Mobile Grid Computing. In: Proc. of the Int. Conf. on Service Oriented Computing (2003)
5. Farooq, U., Khalil, W.: A Generic Mobility Model for Resource Prediction in Mobile Grids. In: Proc. of the Int. Symp. on Collaborative Technologies and Systems (2006)
6. Ghosh, P., Roy, N., Das, S.K.: Mobility-Aware Efficient Job Scheduling in Mobile Grids. In: Proc. of Cluster Computing and Grid (2007)
7. Litke, A., Skoutas, D., Tserpes, K., Varvarigou, T.: Efficient task replication and management for adaptive fault tolerance in Mobile Grid environments. Future Generation Computer Systems 23, 163–178 (2007)
8. Balazinska, M., Castro, P.: Characterizing Mobility and Network Usage in a Corporate Wireless Local-Area Network. In: ACM MobiSys. (2003)
9. Casanova, H.: Simgrid: A toolkit for the simulation of application scheduling. In: Proc. of 1st IEEE/ACM Int. Symp. on Cluster Computing and the Grid (2001)
10. Henderson, T., Kotz, D.: CRAWDAD trace dartmouth/campus/syslog/05_06 (v. 2007-02-08),
    http://crawdad.cs.dartmouth.edu/dartmouth/campus/syslog/05_06
11. Nurmi, D., Brevik, J., Wolski, R.: Modeling machine availability in enterprise and wide-area distributed computing environments, UCSB Computer Science Technical Report Number CS2003-28

# Bi-objective Optimization: An Online Algorithm for Job Assignment

Chien-Min Wang[1], Xiao-Wei Huang[1], and Chun-Chen Hsu[1,2]

[1] Institute of Information Science, Academia Sinica, Taipei, Taiwan
{cmwang,xwhuang,tk}@iis.sinica.edu.tw
[2] Department of Computer Science and Information Engineering,
National Taiwan University, Taipei, Taiwan
d95006@csie.ntu.edu.tw

**Abstract.** We study an online problem that occurs when the capacities of machines are heterogeneous and all jobs are identical. Each job is associated with a subset, called feasible set, of the machines that can be used to process it. The problem involves assigning each job to a single machine in its feasible set, i.e., to find a feasible assignment. The objective is to maximize the throughput, which is the sum of the bandwidths of the jobs; and minimize the total load, which is the sum of the loads of the machines. In the online setting, the jobs arrive one-by-one and an algorithm must make decisions based on the current state without knowledge of future states. By contrast, in the offline setting, all the jobs with their feasible sets are known in advance to an algorithm. Let $m$ denote the total number of machines, $\alpha$ denote the competitive ratio with respect to the throughput and $\beta$ denote the competitive ratio with respect to the total load. In this paper, our contribution is that we propose an online algorithm that finds a feasible assignment with a throughput-competitive upper bound $\alpha = O(\sqrt{m})$, and a total-load-competitive upper bound $\beta = O(\sqrt{m})$. We also show a lower bound $\alpha\beta = \Omega(\sqrt{m})$ of the problem in the offline setting, which implies a lower bound $\alpha\beta = \Omega(\sqrt{m})$ of the problem in the online setting.

**Keywords:** Online algorithms, job assignment, bi-objective optimization, throughput, load.

## 1 Introduction

In the scenario where a number of machines with different positive capacities are ready to provide services for a set of jobs, each job is associated with one non-negative unit weight and a subset, called the *feasible set*, of the machines that can be used to process it. The problem involves assigning each job to a single machine in its feasible set, i.e., to find a feasible assignment. The objective is to maximize the throughput, which is the sum of the bandwidths of the jobs; and minimize the total load, which is the sum of the loads of the machines. We consider the online problem in the following model. There are $m$ machines with different capacities, and $n$ jobs. Each job $i$ has the same weight and a feasible

N. Abdennadher and D. Petcu (Eds.): GPC 2009, LNCS 5529, pp. 223–234, 2009.

set $F_i$. In the online setting, the job arrives with its weight and its feasible set. An online algorithm must assign the job to a single machine in its feasible set without knowledge of future states and the decision cannot be revoked at a later stage. By contrast, in the offline setting, all the jobs and their feasible sets are known in advance to an algorithm.

Given a feasible assignment, which is a mapping from the jobs to the machines, the load on a machine in the assignment is the sum of the number of the jobs assigned to it divided by its capacity [1]. The amount of bandwidth allocated to a job in an assignment, which represents the quality of service, depends on the total weight of jobs that share the resource with it [6, 11]. Specifically, in our model, if $l$ jobs are assigned to the same machine with capacity $c$, then each one will be allocated a bandwidth of $c/l$, since all jobs have the same weight. We measure the assignment by the throughput as the utility, defined as the sum of the bandwidths of all jobs, and the total load as the congestion, defined as the sum of the loads of all machines. As mentioned earlier, our goal is to find a feasible assignment in order to simultaneously maximize the throughput and minimize the total load.

Our contribution in this paper is twofold. First we present an online algorithm for the online job assignment problem when considering the throughput and the total load. The algorithm has the throughput-competitive ratio $\alpha = O(\sqrt{m})$ and the total-load-competitive ratio $\beta = O(\sqrt{m})$, which will be equal to the ratio with respect to the average of the loads. Our second contribution is that we show a lower bound of this problem in the offline setting with $\alpha\beta = \Omega(\sqrt{m})$, where $\alpha$ is the competitive ratio with respect to the throughput and $\beta$ is the competitive ratio with respect to the total load. Note that the problem in the offline setting must be easier than or equivalent to the problem in the online setting.

The remainder of this paper is organized as follows. Section 2 contains a literature review. In Section 3, we define the problem formally. Section 4 presents the proposed online algorithm and its properties, and Section 5 shows a lower bound of the offline problem.

## 2   Related Work

Many approaches for measuring the quality of a job assignment have been proposed. For example, a popular measure that minimizes the maximum load [1, 3], measures for minimizing the $l_2$-norm or any other $l_p$-norm of the machine load vector [2, 8], measures that consider both fairness and balancing issues [6, 11], and some other quality measures are discussed in [16]. However, it is not always clear how to properly measure the quality of an assignment in general. Hence, it is desirable to find a solution that can approximate several measures simultaneously [2, 4, 6, 7, 9–11, 13, 18]. In this work, we focus on a measure that maximizes the throughput and minimizes the total load simultaneously.

In [1, 3], the authors studied the load balancing problem with the objective of minimizing the maximum load. The restricted assignment model was studied with respect to this measure in [3]. In the restricted assignment model, there are $m$ identical machines and $n$ jobs. Each job is associated with a non-negative weight and a feasible set of machines to which it can be assigned. It was showed that the maximum load generated by the greedy online strategy is within $O(\log m)$ factor of the optimal load.

Kleinberg et al. [14] studied fairness issues in several routing and load balancing models in an offline setting. They defined the notion of prefix competitiveness and a stronger notion of coordinate-wise competitiveness and considered several offline problems in terms of these measures.

In [11], the authors studied the $1 - \infty$ model in an online setting from the fairness and load balancing perspective. Under the $1 - \infty$ model, there are $m$ identical machines and $n$ jobs. Each job is associated with the same weight and with a feasible set of machines to which it can be assigned. The $1 - \infty$ model is a special case of the restricted model; the only difference is that in the $1 - \infty$ model, all jobs have the same (one unit) weight. Goel et al. [11] proved that the greedy strategy, which always assigns a job to the machine with the smallest load in its feasible set based on the current state is globally $O(\log n)$-fair and globally $O(\log m)$-balanced, where $m$ is the number of machines and $n$ is the number of jobs. They also showed that any online algorithm must be globally $\Omega(\log m)$-fair as well as globally $\Omega(\log m)$-balanced in [11]. Buchbinder and Naor [6] solved the open problem in [11] and proved that the greedy strategy is globally $O(\log m)$-fair and globally $O(\log m)$-balanced in the $1 - \infty$ model.

It is important to note that our model is different from the $1 - \infty$ model in [6, 11], since the machines in the $1 - \infty$ model must be identical and the machines in our model have different positive capacities. Clearly, the greedy strategy proposed in [6, 11], which always assigns a job to the least loaded machine in the feasible set, can not work well in our model. To illustrate this point, consider a simple setting with only two machines with capacities $c_1$ and $c_2$, where $c_1 \gg c_2$, and two jobs that can be processed by the both machines. After assigning the first job to one machine, the greedy strategy assigns the second job to the other machine whose loaded is zero and results in an assignment such that the total load is $\frac{1}{c_1} + \frac{1}{c_2}$. Since there exists another assignment such that the total load is $\frac{2}{c_1}$, we can see that the ratio is $\frac{1}{2} + \frac{c_1}{2c_2}$ and may be greater than any given constant if $c_1 \gg c_2$.

## 3    The Problem Definition

In this section, we formally define our job assignment problem.

**Definition 1 (A feasible assignment).** *Given the machines' index set $\mathcal{M} = \{1, \cdots, m\}$, the jobs' index set $\mathcal{J} = \{1, \cdots, n\}$ and the non-empty feasible set $F_i \subset \mathcal{M}$ of job $i$ for all $i \in \mathcal{J}$, a feasible assignment $\phi : \mathcal{J} \to \mathcal{M}$ is a mapping from $\mathcal{J} = \{1, \cdots, n\}$ to $\mathcal{M} = \{1, \cdots, m\}$ subject to $\phi(i) \in F_i$ for all $i \in \mathcal{J}$.*

Given a feasible assignment, the bandwidth allocated to a job in the assignment is the quality of service it gets depends on the total weight of jobs that share the resource together with it [6, 11]. In our model, there are $m$ machines with different capacities and $n$ jobs with the same (one unit) weight. Hence, the amount of bandwidth allocated to a job depends on the number of jobs that share the resource with it. We define the bandwidth vector of the feasible assignment as follows:

**Definition 2 (The bandwidth vector of a feasible assignment).** *Given $m$ machines with capacities $c_1, c_2, \cdots, c_m$, $n$ jobs with their feasible sets, and a feasible assignment $\phi : \mathcal{J} \to \mathcal{M}$, where $\mathcal{J}$ is the jobs' index set and $\mathcal{M}$ is the machines' index set, the bandwidth of job $i$ in the assignment is $b_i = \frac{c_{\phi(i)}}{|A^\phi(\phi(i))|}$, where $A^\phi(k)$ is the set of jobs assigned to machine $k$ in the assignment $\phi$. The bandwidth vector of the assignment $\boldsymbol{B}_\phi = (b_1, b_2, \cdots, b_n)$.*

The load on a machine in a feasible assignment is the sum of the number of jobs assigned to it divided by its capacity [1]. We define the load vector of the feasible assignment as follows:

**Definition 3 (The load vector of a feasible assignment).** *Given $m$ machines with capacities $c_1, c_2, \cdots, c_m$, $n$ jobs with their feasible sets, and a feasible assignment $\phi : \mathcal{J} \to \mathcal{M}$, where $\mathcal{J}$ is the jobs' index set and $\mathcal{M}$ is the machines' index set, the load of machine $j$ in the assignment is $l_j = \frac{|A^\phi(j)|}{c_j}$, where $A^\phi(k)$ is the set of jobs assigned to machine $k$ in the assignment $\phi$. The load vector of the assignment $\boldsymbol{L}_\phi = (l_1, l_2, \cdots, l_m)$.*

We measure a feasible assignment $\phi$ of the job assignment problem by taking the throughput as the utility function $U(\boldsymbol{B}_\phi) = \sum_{i=1}^n b_i$ and the total load as the congestion function $C(\boldsymbol{L}_\phi) = \sum_{i=1}^m l_i$ in the following model. Our goal is to find a feasible assignment in order to simultaneously maximize the throughput and minimize the total load. In multi-objective optimization problems, it is unlikely that the different objectives could be optimized simultaneously by the same alternative parameter choices, especially for some conflicting objectives. Hence, to ensure that a design is satisfactory, there must be a trade-off between the criteria.

**Definition 4.** *[The job assignment problem envloves maximize the throughput and minimize the total load in an offline setting] Given $m$ machines with capacities $c_1, c_2, \cdots, c_m$ and $n$ jobs with their feasible sets, the problem is to find a feasible assignment $\phi : \mathcal{J} \to \mathcal{M}$ such that*

$$\alpha U(\boldsymbol{B}_\phi) \geq U(\boldsymbol{B}_{\phi'}) \text{ for all other feasible assignmets } \phi',$$

*and*

$$C(\boldsymbol{L}_\phi) \leq \beta C(\boldsymbol{L}_{\phi''}) \text{ for all other feasible assignmets } \phi'',$$

*where the competitive ratio $\alpha, \beta$ are as small as possible simultaneously.*

In the online setting, jobs arrive with their feasible sets one-by-one and the algorithm must immediately assign job $i$ to machine $\phi(i)$ when job $i$ arrives. This contrasts with the offline setting, where all the jobs and feasible sets are given initially.

# 4   The Proposed Online Algorithm and Its Properties

In this section, we introduce the proposed online algorithm and its properties. We begin by introducing notations. Let $A(i,j)$ denote the set of the jobs assigned to machine $j$ when job $i$ arrives, and $A(i,j) \subseteq \{1, 2, \ldots, i-1\}$. Let $S_i$ denote the index set of machines which no job is assigned to when job $i$ arrives. Let $max(i)$ denote the index of the machine with the most capacity in the feasible set $F_i$ of job $i$, and $un(i)$ denote the index of the machine with the most capacity in $F_i \cap S_i$. In addition, let $\gamma_{k,i}$ denote the number of times that the machine $k$ is regarded as the most powerful machine in the feasible sets of the first $i$ jobs, i.e., $\gamma_{k,i} = |\{j|max(j) = k, 1 \le j \le i\}|$. Observing the problem, assigning jobs to the machine $un(i)$ can increase the throughput of the assignment. However, the total load objective provides a tradeoff to this. Hence, in order to maximize the throughput and minimize the total load simultaneously, the proposed online algorithm must avoid assigning jobs to the machine with low capacity. We find a threshold for the design of Algorithm 1 and analysis its performance. The proposed online algorithm is detailed in Algorithm 1.

---

**Algorithm 1.** The proposed online algorithm: When a job $i$ arrives, the algorithm assigns the job to a machine in its feasible set $F_i$.

$S_i := \{j | |A(i,j)| = 0, 1 \le j \le m\}$
if $max(i) \in S_i$ then
　assign job $i$ to machine $max(i)$
else if $max(i) \notin S_i$ and $S_i \cap F_i = \emptyset$ then
　assign job $i$ to machine $max(i)$
else if $max(i) \notin S_i$ and $S_i \cap F_i \ne \emptyset$ then
　if $\sqrt{\gamma_{max(i),i}} c_{un(i)} \le c_{max(i)}$ then
　　assign job $i$ to machine $max(i)$
　else if $\sqrt{\gamma_{max(i),i}} c_{un(i)} > c_{max(i)}$ then
　　assign job $i$ to machine $un(i)$
　end if
end if

---

Now, we give a simple example to explain how Algorithm 1 works. Consider 2 machines with capacity $c_1 = \sqrt{5}, c_2 = \sqrt{2}$ and 3 jobs arrive sequentially:

1. When job 1 arrives with $F_1 = \{1, 2\}$, Algorithm 1 will assign job 1 to the machine $max(1) = 1$ since $S_1 = \{1, 2\}$ and $max(1) = 1 \in S_1$.
2. When job 2 arrives with $F_2 = \{1, 2\}$, Algorithm 1 will compute $\gamma_{max(2),2} = \gamma_{1,2} = |\{j|max(j) = 1, 1 \le j \le 2\}| = 2$ since $max(2) = 1 \notin S_2$ and $S_2 \cap F_2 = \{2\} \ne \emptyset$. Then Algorithm 1 assigns job 2 to the machine $max(2) = 1$ according to $\sqrt{\gamma_{max(2),2}}\sqrt{2} = \sqrt{2}\sqrt{2} \le \sqrt{5}$.
3. When job 3 arrives with $F_3 = \{1, 2\}$, Algorithm 1 will compute $\gamma_{max(3),3} = \gamma_{1,3} = |\{j|max(j) = 1, 1 \le j \le 3\}| = 3$ since $max(3) \notin S_3$ and $S_3 \cap F_3 = \{2\} \ne \emptyset$. Then Algorithm 1 assigns job 3 to the machine $un(3) = 2$ according to $\sqrt{\gamma_{max(3),3}}\sqrt{2} = \sqrt{3}\sqrt{2} > \sqrt{5}$.

## 4.1  The $O(\sqrt{m})$-Competitive Ratio for the Total Load

**Lemma 1.** *Given a feasible assignment $\phi$, the total load is*

$$C(\boldsymbol{L_\phi}) = \sum_{k=1}^{m} l_k = \sum_{k=1}^{m} \sum_{i \in A^\phi(k)} \frac{1}{c_{\phi(i)}} = \sum_{i=1}^{n} \frac{1}{c_{\phi(i)}}.$$

*Proof.* Since the load of machine $k$ is $l_k = \frac{|A^\phi(k)|}{c_k} = \sum_{i \in A^\phi(k)} \frac{1}{c_k}$, we have

$$C(\boldsymbol{L_\phi}) = \sum_{k=1}^{m} l_k = \sum_{k=1}^{m} \sum_{i \in A^\phi(k)} \frac{1}{c_k}.$$

Note that $i \in A^\phi(k)$ means job $i$ is assigned to machine $k$ in the assignment $\phi$, i.e., $\phi(i) = k$. Hence,

$$C(\boldsymbol{L_\phi}) = \sum_{k=1}^{m} \sum_{i \in A^\phi(k)} \frac{1}{c_k} = \sum_{k=1}^{m} \sum_{i \in A^\phi(k)} \frac{1}{c_{\phi(i)}} = \sum_{i \in \bigcup_{k=1}^{m} A^\phi(k)} \frac{1}{c_{\phi(i)}}.$$

Moreover, all jobs in $\mathcal{J} = \{1, 2, \cdots, n\}$ must be assigned to some machine $k \in \mathcal{M}$ in the assignment $\phi$; thus, we can see that $\bigcup_{k=1}^{m} A^\phi(k) = \mathcal{J}$ and

$$C(\boldsymbol{L_\phi}) = \sum_{i \in \bigcup_{k=1}^{m} A^\phi(k)} \frac{1}{c_{\phi(i)}} = \sum_{i \in \mathcal{J}} \frac{1}{c_{\phi(i)}} = \sum_{i=1}^{n} \frac{1}{c_{\phi(i)}}. \qquad \square$$

According to Lemma 1, we can find an optimal assignment $\phi^L$ for the total load by assigning each job $i$ to machine $max(i)$. It is easy to see that $\phi^L$ has $\beta = 1$-competitive ratio for the total load. We refer to $\phi^L$ as the optimal assignment for the total load. In the following, Lemma 2 shows the proposed online algorithm has $\beta = O(\sqrt{m})$-competitive ratio for the total load.

**Lemma 2.** *The proposed online algorithm results in a feasible assignment $\phi$ with $\beta = O(\sqrt{m})$ such that $C(\boldsymbol{L_\phi}) \leq \beta C(\boldsymbol{L_{\phi^L}})$, where $\boldsymbol{L_\phi}$ is the load vector of the assignment $\phi$ derived by the proposed algorithm and $\boldsymbol{L_{\phi^L}}$ is the load vector of the optimal assignment $\phi^L$ for the total load.*

*Proof.* First of all, we evaluate the total load of the assignment $\phi^L$. By Lemma 1, we calculate the total load of the assignment $\phi^L$ as follows:

$$C(\boldsymbol{L_{\phi^L}}) = \sum_{k=1}^{m} \sum_{i \in A^{\phi^L}(k)} \frac{1}{c_{\phi^L(i)}} = \sum_{k=1}^{m} \frac{|A^{\phi^L}(k)|}{c_k}.$$

Then, we evaluate the total load of the assignment $\phi$ derived by the proposed online algorithm. Observe the load, which is $\frac{|A^\phi(k)|}{c_k}$, on the machine $k$ in the assignment $\phi$, we have that $|A^\phi(k)| - |A^{\phi^L}(k)| \leq 1$ for all $k$ according to the algorithm. Consider the upper bound of the ratio of the load on the machine $k$ for all $k$ in the cases of $|A^\phi(k)| - |A^{\phi^L}(k)| \leq 0$ and $|A^\phi(k)| - |A^{\phi^L}(k)| = 1$:

1. If $|A^\phi(k)| - |A^{\phi^L}(k)| \leq 0$, the load on the machine $k$ in the assignment $\phi$ is equal to or less than the load on the machine $k$ in the assignment $\phi^L$, i.e. $\frac{|A^\phi(k)|}{c_k} \leq \frac{|A^{\phi^L}(k)|}{c_k}$.

2. If $|A^\phi(k)| - |A^{\phi^L}(k)| = 1$ and $|A^{\phi^L}(k)| \geq 1$, we have the ratio

$$\frac{\frac{|A^\phi(k)|}{c_k}}{\frac{|A^{\phi^L}(k)|}{c_k}} = 1 + \frac{1}{|A^{\phi^L}(k)|} \leq 2.$$

3. If $|A^\phi(k)| - |A^{\phi^L}(k)| = 1$ and $|A^{\phi^L}(k)| = 0$, we can see that the unique job $i$, assigned to the machine $k$, in the set $A^\phi(k)$ must be assigned to some machine $k'$ such that $\sqrt{\gamma_{k',i}} \frac{1}{c_{k'}} > \frac{1}{c_k}$ in the assignment $\phi^L$. Hence, the ratio will be bounded by the load of the machine $k'$, i.e.

$$\frac{\frac{|A^\phi(k)|}{c_k}}{\frac{|A^{\phi^L}(k')|}{c_{k'}}} = \frac{\frac{1}{c_k}}{\frac{|A^{\phi^L}(k')|}{c_{k'}}} < \frac{\sqrt{\gamma_{k',i}}\frac{1}{c_{k'}}}{\frac{|A^{\phi^L}(k')|}{c_{k'}}} = \frac{\sqrt{\gamma_{k',i}}}{|A^{\phi^L}(k')|}.$$

Note that there are at most $m - 1$ jobs in this case since there are at most $m$ machines. Therefore, the ratio of the load of these machines in this case will be bounded by $\dfrac{\frac{1}{c_k}\sum_{i=|A^{\phi^L}(k)|-m+1}^{|A^{\phi^L}(k)|}\sqrt{i}}{\frac{|A^{\phi^L}(k)|}{c_k}}$, for some machine $k$.

Let $k^*$ denote the machine's index with

$$\max_{1\leq k\leq m}\left\{\frac{\frac{|A^{\phi^L}(k)|}{c_k} + \frac{|A^{\phi^L}(k)|+1}{c_k} + \frac{1}{c_k}\sum_{i=|A^{\phi^L}(k)|-m+1}^{|A^{\phi^L}(k)|}\sqrt{i}}{\frac{|A^{\phi^L}(k)|}{c_k}}\right\}.$$

We obtain that

$$\beta \leq \frac{C(L_\phi)}{C(L_{\phi^L})} = \frac{\sum_{k=1}^m\frac{|A^\phi(k)|}{c_k}}{\sum_{k=1}^m\frac{|A^{\phi^L}(k)|}{c_k}} \leq \frac{\frac{|A^{\phi^L}(k^*)|}{c_{k^*}} + \frac{|A^{\phi^L}(k^*)|+1}{c_{k^*}} + \frac{1}{c_{k^*}}\sum_{i=|A^{\phi^L}(k^*)|-m+1}^{|A^{\phi^L}(k^*)|}\sqrt{i}}{\frac{|A^{\phi^L}(k^*)|}{c_{k^*}}}$$

$$\leq 3 + \frac{1}{|A^{\phi^L}(k^*)|}\sum_{i=|A^{\phi^L}(k^*)|-m+1}^{|A^{\phi^L}(k^*)|}\sqrt{i}.$$

Consider the cases of that $|A^{\phi^L}(k^*)| \leq m$ and $|A^{\phi^L}(k^*)| > m$:

1. If $|A^{\phi^L}(k^*)| \leq m$, it follows that

$$\beta \leq 3 + \frac{1}{|A^{\phi^L}(k^*)|}\sum_{i=1}^{|A^{\phi^L}(k^*)|}\sqrt{i} \leq 3 + c\frac{|A^{\phi^L}(k^*)|^{\frac{3}{2}}}{|A^{\phi^L}(k^*)|} \leq 3 + c\sqrt{m} = O(\sqrt{m}),$$

where $c$ is a constant.

2. If $|A^{\phi^L}(k^*)| > m$, it follows that

$$\beta \leq 3 + \frac{1}{|A^{\phi^L}(k^*)|} \sum_{i=|A^{\phi^L}(k^*)|-m+1}^{|A^{\phi^L}(k^*)|} \sqrt{i} \leq 3 + \frac{m\sqrt{|A^{\phi^L}(k^*)|}}{|A^{\phi^L}(k^*)|} \leq 3 + \sqrt{m} = O(\sqrt{m}).$$

$\square$

## 4.2     The $O(\sqrt{m})$-Competitive Ratio for the throughput

In this subsection, we show our proposed algorithm has a $O(\sqrt{m})$-competitive ratio for the throughput by exploring the relation between our proposed algorithm and an online greedy assignment algorithm.

The online greedy assignment algorithm works as follows. It assigns job $i$ to machine $un(i)$ when $F_i \cap S_i \neq \emptyset$ and assigns job $i$ to machine $max(i)$ when $F_i \cap S_i = \emptyset$. We will show that the online greedy assignment algorithm has a 2-competitive ratio for the throughput in Lemma 4. Before introducing Lemma 4, we first introduce Lemma 3 used in Lemma 4.

Lemma 3 states that the throughput of an assignment $\phi$ can be calculated as the sum of the capacities of those machines which there is at least one job assigned to in the assignment $\phi$.

**Lemma 3.** *Given a feasible assignment $\phi$, we can calculate the throughput of $\phi$ as follows.*

$$U(\boldsymbol{B}_\phi) = \sum_{i=1}^{n} b_i = \sum_{k \in T} c_k,$$

*where $T$ denotes the set of machines with at least one job in the assignment $\phi$, i.e., $T = \{k||A^\phi(k)| > 0, 1 \leq k \leq m\}$,*

Due to lack of space, the proofs of Lemma 3 and Lemma 4 will be given in the full version of this paper [17].

Lemma 4 shows that the online greedy assignment algorithm results in a feasible assignment with a 2-competitive ratio for the throughput.

**Lemma 4.** *The online greedy assignment algorithm results in an assignment with $\alpha_1 = 2$ such that $\alpha_1 U(\boldsymbol{B}_g) \geq U(\boldsymbol{B}_{\phi^*})$, where $\boldsymbol{B}_g$ is the bandwidth vector of the assignment $g$ derived by the online greedy assignment algorithm and $\boldsymbol{B}_{\phi^*}$ is the bandwidth vector of the optimal assignment.*

In Lemma 5, we show our proposed algorithm has a $O(\sqrt{m})$-competitive ratio with respect to the throughput by exploring the relation between the proposed online algorithm and the online greedy assignment algorithm since the online greedy assignment algorithm results in a feasible assignment with a constant competitive ratio $\alpha_1 = 2$ with respect to the throughput.

**Lemma 5.** *The proposed online algorithm results in a feasible assignment $\phi$ with $\alpha_2 = O(\sqrt{m})$ such that $\alpha_2 U(\boldsymbol{B}_\phi) \geq U(\boldsymbol{B}_g)$, where $\boldsymbol{B}_\phi$ is the bandwidth vector of the assignment $\phi$ derived by the proposed algorithm and $\boldsymbol{B}_g$ is the bandwidth vector derived by the online greedy assignment algorithm.*

*Proof.* We begin by introducing notations. Let $\phi$ be the assignment derived by the proposed algorithm, and $g$ be the assignment derived by the online greedy assignment algorithm. Let $T$ denote the set of machines with at least one job in the assignment $\phi$, and $U$ denote the set of machines with at least one job in the assignment $g$. Let $V = \{max(i)|1 \leq i \leq n\}$. By Lemma 3, we have

$$\frac{U(B_g)}{U(B_\phi)} = \frac{\sum_{i=1}^n \frac{c_{g(i)}}{|A^g(g(i))|}}{\sum_{i=1}^n \frac{c_{\phi(i)}}{|A^\phi(\phi(i))|}} = \frac{\sum_{p \in U} c_p}{\sum_{k \in T} c_k}.$$

Note that $V \subset T$ and $U \subset T \cup (U\backslash T)$,

$$\frac{U(B_g)}{U(B_\phi)} = \frac{\sum_{p \in U} c_p}{\sum_{k \in T} c_k} \leq \frac{\sum_{p \in T} c_p + \sum_{p \in U\backslash T} c_p}{\sum_{k \in T} c_k} = 1 + \frac{\sum_{p \in U\backslash T} c_p}{\sum_{k \in T} c_k}.$$

For each job $p \in U\backslash T$, the proposed algorithm assigns no job to $p$ while the greedy assigns at least one job to $p$. Let $p$ be a machine in the set $U\backslash T$, and $i_p$ be a job in the set $A^g(p)$. Job $i_p$ is assigned to $p = un(i_p) \neq max(i_p)$ in the online greedy assignment algorithm due to $F_{i_p} \cap S_{i_p} \neq \emptyset$ while $i_p$ is assigned to $max(i_p)$ in the proposed algorithm due to $\sqrt{\gamma_{max(i_p),i_p}} c_p \leq c_{max(i_p)}$. Hence, $c_p \leq \frac{1}{\sqrt{\gamma_{k,i_p}}} c_k$ where $k = max(i_p)$ for some job $i_p \in A^g(p)$. Note that $\gamma_{max(i_p),i_p} \geq 2$ since $p = un(i_p) \neq max(i_p)$, which implies that machine $max(i_p)$ has been regarded as the most powerful machine in the feasible sets of at least two jobs when job $i_p$ arrives. We have

$$\frac{U(B_g)}{U(B_\phi)} \leq 1 + \frac{\sum_{p \in U\backslash T} c_p}{\sum_{k \in T} c_k} \leq 1 + \frac{\sum_{p \in U\backslash T} c_p}{\sum_{k \in V} c_k} \leq 1 + \frac{\sum_{p \in U\backslash T} \frac{1}{\sqrt{\gamma_{max(i_p),i_p}}} c_{max(i_p)}}{\sum_{k \in V} c_k}$$

$$\leq 1 + \frac{\sum_{k \in V} \sum_{i=2}^{\gamma_{k,n}} \frac{1}{\sqrt{i}} c_k}{\sum_{k \in V} c_k} = \frac{\sum_{k \in V} \sum_{i=1}^{\gamma_{k,n}} \frac{1}{\sqrt{i}} c_k}{\sum_{k \in V} c_k}.$$

Since there are only $m$ machines,

$$\frac{U(B_g)}{U(B_\phi)} \leq = \frac{\sum_{k \in V} \sum_{i=1}^{\gamma_{k,n}} \frac{1}{\sqrt{i}} c_k}{\sum_{k \in V} c_k} \leq \frac{\sum_{k \in V} \sum_{i=1}^m \frac{1}{\sqrt{i}} c_k}{\sum_{k \in V} c_k}.$$

Furthermore,

$$\frac{\sum_{i=1}^m \frac{1}{\sqrt{i}} c_k}{c_k} = \sum_{i=1}^m \frac{1}{\sqrt{i}} = O(\sqrt{m}), \text{ for all } k \in V.$$

That is, for all $k \in V$, there exist constant $\delta$, $n_0$ such that $\sum_{i=1}^{\gamma_{k,n}} \frac{1}{\sqrt{i}} c_k \leq \delta \sqrt{m} c_k$ for $m \geq m_0$. It follows that there exist constant $\delta' = \delta$, $m_0' = m_0$ such that

$$\frac{U(B_g)}{U(B_\phi)} \leq \frac{\sum_{k \in V} \sum_{i=1}^{\gamma_{k,n}} \frac{1}{\sqrt{i}} c_k}{\sum_{k \in V} c_k} \leq \frac{\sum_{k \in V} \delta \sqrt{m} c_k}{\sum_{k \in V} c_k} = \delta' \sqrt{m} \text{ for } m \geq m_0'.$$

Therefore, we conclude that $\frac{U(B_g)}{U(B_\phi)} = O(\sqrt{m})$. $\qquad\square$
   Finally, we can obtain Theorem 1.

**Theorem 1.** *The proposed online algorithm for our problem results in a feasible assignment $\phi$ with the bandwidth vector $\boldsymbol{B}_\phi$ and the load vector $\boldsymbol{L}_\phi$ such that $\alpha U(\boldsymbol{B}_\phi) \geq U(\boldsymbol{B}_{\phi'})$ for the bandwidth vector $\boldsymbol{B}_{\phi'}$ of all other feasible assignments $\phi'$ and $C(\boldsymbol{L}_\phi) \leq \beta C(\boldsymbol{L}_{\phi''})$ for the load vector $\boldsymbol{L}_{\phi''}$ of all other feasible assignments $\phi''$, where $\alpha = O(\sqrt{m})$ and $\beta = O(\sqrt{m})$.*

*Proof.* By Lemma 2, Lemma 4 and Lemma 5, we obtain Theorem 1.     □

## 5   Lower Bounds

We now show a lower bound of our problem in the offline setting , where an algorithm knows all the jobs with their feasible sets in advance. The problem in the offline setting must be easier than or equivalent to the problem in the online setting.

**Theorem 2.** *If an algorithm for this problem in the offline setting results in a feasible assignment $\phi$ with the bandwidth vector $\boldsymbol{B}_\phi$ and the load vector $\boldsymbol{L}_\phi$, such that $\alpha U(\boldsymbol{B}_\phi) \geq U(\boldsymbol{B}_{\phi'})$ for the bandwidth vector $\boldsymbol{B}_{\phi'}$ of all other feasible assignments $\phi'$, and $C(\boldsymbol{L}_\phi) \leq \beta C(\boldsymbol{L}_{\phi''})$ for the load vector $\boldsymbol{L}_{\phi''}$ of all other feasible assignments $\phi''$, then $\alpha\beta = \Omega(\sqrt{m})$.*

*Proof.* We first construct a problem instance $P$ as follows:

1. There are $n = m$ jobs with feasible sets $F_1 = \{1\}$ and $F_i = \{1, i\}$ for $2 \leq i \leq n$.
2. There are $m$ machines with capacity $c_1 = \sqrt{m}$ and $c_i = 1$ for $2 \leq i \leq m$.

Given an algorithm $D$ with $\alpha$-competitive ratio for throughput and $\beta$-competitive ratio for total load, let $\phi_D$ denote the assignment generated by algorithm $D$ for the constructed problem instance $P$, and $x$ denote the number of machines that are assigned at least one job in the assignment $\phi_D$, i.e., $x = |\{k||A^{\phi_D}(k)| > 0, 1 \leq k \leq m\}|$.
We obtain the throughput $U(\boldsymbol{B}_{\phi_D})$ and total load $C(\boldsymbol{L}_{\phi_D})$ of $\phi_D$ as follows:

$$U(\boldsymbol{B}_{\phi_D}) = \sqrt{m} + (x - 1) \text{ and } C(\boldsymbol{L}_{\phi_D}) \geq \frac{m - x + 1}{\sqrt{m}} + (x - 1).$$

We also construct two assignments, $\phi'$ and $\phi''$ as follows:

1. In $\phi'$, each job $i$ is assigned to machine $i$.
2. In $\phi''$, all jobs is assigned to machine 1.

The throughput $U(\boldsymbol{B}_{\phi'})$ of $\phi'$ and the total load $C(\boldsymbol{L}_{\phi''})$ of $\phi''$ are as follows:

$$U(\boldsymbol{B}_{\phi'}) = \sum_{i=1}^{n} c_i = \sqrt{m} + (m - 1) \text{ and } C(\boldsymbol{L}_{\phi''}) = \frac{m}{\sqrt{m}} = \sqrt{m}.$$

It follows that

$$\alpha \geq \frac{U(\boldsymbol{B}_{\phi'})}{U(\boldsymbol{B}_{\phi_D})} = \frac{\sqrt{m} + (m - 1)}{\sqrt{m} + (x - 1)}$$

and

$$\beta \geq \frac{C(L_{\phi_D})}{C(L_{\phi''})} \geq \frac{\frac{m-x+1}{\sqrt{m}} + (x-1)}{\sqrt{m}}$$

$$= \frac{m-x+1}{m} + \frac{(x-1)}{\sqrt{m}} = 1 - \frac{x}{m} + \frac{1}{m} + \frac{\sqrt{m}(x-1)}{m}$$

$$= 1 + \frac{\sqrt{m}x + 1 - x - \sqrt{m}}{m}.$$

Since $1 \leq x \leq m = n$, we consider two cases where $1 \leq x < \sqrt{m}$ and $\sqrt{m} \leq x \leq m$.

1. if $1 \leq x < \sqrt{m}$, we have

$$\alpha \geq \frac{\sqrt{m} + (m-1)}{\sqrt{m} + (x-1)} \geq \frac{\sqrt{m} + (m-1)}{2\sqrt{m} - 1} \geq \frac{m}{2\sqrt{m}} = \frac{\sqrt{m}}{2}$$

and

$$\beta \geq 1 + \frac{\sqrt{m}x + 1 - x - \sqrt{m}}{m} \geq 1,$$

which implies that $\alpha\beta = \Omega(\sqrt{m})$.

2. if $\sqrt{m} \leq x \leq m$, we have

$$\alpha \geq \frac{\sqrt{m} + (m-1)}{\sqrt{m} + (x-1)} \geq \frac{\sqrt{m} + (m-1)}{2x-1} \geq \frac{m}{2x}$$

and

$$\beta \geq 1 + \frac{\sqrt{m}x + 1 - x - \sqrt{m}}{m} \geq 1 + \frac{\sqrt{m}x + 1 - m - \sqrt{m}}{m} \geq \frac{\sqrt{m}x - \sqrt{m}}{m}.$$

Then

$$\alpha\beta \geq \frac{m}{2x} \frac{\sqrt{m}x - \sqrt{m}}{m} = \frac{\sqrt{m}}{2} - \frac{\sqrt{m}}{2x} \geq \frac{\sqrt{m}}{2} - \frac{1}{2},$$

which implies $\alpha\beta = \Omega(\sqrt{m})$ also.      □

Note that Theorem 2 also implies a lower bound $\alpha\beta = \Omega(\sqrt{m})$ of the problem in the online setting.

**Acknowledgements.** The authors would like to thank the anonymous referees for their helpful suggestions. This research was supported in part by National Science Council under Contract No. NSC97-2221-E-001-001-MY3 and No. NSC97-2221-E-001-002-MY3.

# References

1. Aspnes, J., Azar, Y., Fiat, A., Plotkin, S., Waarts, O.: On-line routing of virtual circuits with applications to load balancing and machine scheduling. Journal of the ACM 44(3), 486–504 (1997)

2. Azar, Y., Epstein, L., Richter, Y., Woeginger, G.J.: All-norm approximation algorithms. Journal of Algorithms 52(2), 120–133 (2004)
3. Azar, Y., Naor, J., Rom, R.: The competitiveness of on-line assignments. Journal of Algorithms 18(2), 221–237 (1995)
4. Aslam, J.A., Rasala, A., Stein, C., Young, N.: Improved bicriteria existence theorems for scheduling. In: Proceedings of the 10th annual ACM-SIAM Symposium on Discrete Algorithms, January 1999, pp. 846–847 (1999)
5. Bondy, J.A., Murty, U.S.R.: Graph Theory with Applications. Elsevier North-Holland, Amsterdam (1976)
6. Buchbinder, N., Naor, J.: Fair online load balancing. In: Proceedings of the 18th annual ACM Symposium on Parallelism in Algorithms and Architectures (2006)
7. Buchbinder, N., Naor, J.: Improved Bounds for Online Routing and Packing Via a Primal-Dual Approach. In: 47th Annual IEEE Symposium on Foundations of Computer Science (2006)
8. Caragiannis, I.: Better bounds for online load balancing on unrelated machines. In: Proceedings of the 19th annual ACM-SIAM Symposium on Discrete Algorithms (2008)
9. Cho, S., Goel, A.: Pricing for fairness: distributed resource allocation for multiple objectives. In: Proceedings of the 38th ACM Symposium on Theory of Computing, May 2006, pp. 197–204 (2006)
10. Goel, A., Meyerson, A.: Simultaneous optimization via approximate majorization for concave profits or convex costs. Algorithmica 44(4), 301–323 (2006)
11. Goel, A., Meyerson, A., Plotkin, S.: Approximate majorization and fair online load balancing. ACM Transactions on Algorithms 1(2), 338–349 (2005)
12. Goel, A., Meyerson, A., Plotkin, S.: Combining fairness with throughput: online routing with multiple objectives. Journal of Computer and System Sciences 63(1), 62–79 (2001)
13. Goel, A., Nazerzadeh, H.: Price based protocols for fair resource allocation: convergence time analysis and extension to Leontief utilities. In: Proceedings of the 19th Annual ACM-SIAM Symposium on Discrete Algorithms (2008)
14. Kleinberg, J., Tardos, E., Rabani, Y.: Fairness in routing and load balancing. In: Proceedings of the 40th Annual Symposium on Foundations of Computer Science (October 1999)
15. Kumar, A., Kleinberg, J.: Fairness measures for resource allocation. In: Proceedings of the 41st Annual Symposium on Foundations of Computer Science (November 2000)
16. Lain, R.K., Chiu, D.-M., Howe, W.: A quantitative measure of fairness and discrimination for resource allocation in shared systems. DEC Res. Rep. TR-301 (1984)
17. Wang, C.-M., Huang, X.-W., Hsu, C.-C.: Bi-objective Optimization: An Online Algorithm for Job Assignment. Technical Report TR-IIS-08-011, Institute of Information Science, Academia Sinica (2008), http://www.iis.sinica.edu.tw/page/library/TechReport/tr2008/tr08011.pdf
18. Stein, C., Wein, J.: On the existence of schedules that are near-optimal for both makespan and total weighted completion time. Technical Report TR96-295 (1996)

# Achieving Co-allocation through Virtualization in Grid Environment

Thamarai Selvi Somasundaram, Balachandar R. Amarnath, Balakrishnan Ponnuram,
Kumar Rangasamy, Rajendar Kandan, Rajiv Rajaian, Rajesh Britto Gnanapragasam,
Mahendran Ellappan, and Madusudhanan Bairappan

CARE, Department of Information Technology,
Madras Institute of Technology,
Anna University, Chennai, India
{thamaraiselvis,balachandar.ra,baskrish1977,rangasamykumarme,
k.rajendar,rajivece,briittoraj,mahendran.e,madhusona}@gmail.com

**Abstract.** A typical grid application requires several processors for execution that may not be fulfilled by single cluster at times. Co-allocation is the concept of aggregating computing resources from more than one cluster to facilitate application execution. It poses great difficulty in implementing as these resources are distributed and managed locally. In this paper, we propose a metascheduling framework that achieves co-allocation using the concept of virtualization. Our approach differs from earlier ones as we create virtual machines to meet the requirements of application thereby utilizing the resources to the fullest possible extent while preserving their autonomy. We used Deviation Based Resource Scheduling algorithm to initiate SLA negotiation with other resources for participating in resource co-allocation. It also supports SLA monitoring and enforcement. Our preliminary results show that this approach achieves greater throughput against conventional scheduling.

**Keywords:** Grid Computing, Virtualization, Resource Co-allocation.

## 1 Introduction

A computational grid is a parallel and distributed system with a collection of computers that enables the dynamic sharing, selection, aggregation and management of resources for collaborative problem solving [1]. The grid middleware provides protocols and functionalities to the customers and providers for grid computing. Recent developments in grid technologies resulted in large number of participating resources making grid resource management a difficult task. In such an environment, the role of grid metascheduler is very important for discovery of suitable resource for application execution, resource management and monitoring, and load balancing across grid resources. However, if a single cluster could not provide the required number of nodes for the application execution, there would be a need to aggregate resources from other clusters and it is called as resource co-allocation. The concept of resource co-allocation poses special challenges in implementing using existing resource brokers as the resource spans across organizational boundaries and managed locally. Further,

N. Abdennadher and D. Petcu (Eds.): GPC 2009, LNCS 5529, pp. 235–243, 2009.
© Springer-Verlag Berlin Heidelberg 2009

co-allocation typically requires that each of a set of resources be able to deliver a specified level of service at a specified time. In this situation, it is mandatory for advance booking of resources from several clusters to reduce the probability of resource unavailability while negotiating co-allocation with another cluster.

We address this issue with the concept of "resource leasing" proposed in [2] with the help of virtualization. Virtualization allows addressing multiple problems in grid systems, like coping with the heterogeneity of grid resources, the difference in software stacks, enhanced features in resource management like a more general check pointing or migration models. Further, it relieves the resource providers from selecting a fixed and limited execution environment and therefore increases the flexibility and system utilization. We argue that this technology also address the difficulty of implementing co-allocation of different cluster resources by creating virtual machines in one cluster and connecting it to another. The main contributions of this paper are:

- Proposing a scheduling strategy for virtualized grid environment.
- Aggregation of virtual machines from different clusters for meeting the requirement of application execution.

We also adopt Deviation based Resource Scheduling algorithm proposed in our earlier work to initiate SLA negotiation with remote clusters towards co-allocation. We compare our scheduling approach with conventional scheduling and the experimental results shows that our approach achieves greater throughput and schedules more number of jobs in a given time.

The rest of the paper is organized as follows:- Section 2 highlights some of related works from which we took inspiration. Section 3 describes co-allocation in our context and the architecture we propose to achieve our objective. We describe the implementation of the architecture and its various other components in section 4. We also present our experimental results in that section itself. We conclude our paper highlighting the advantages of our approach and further works in section 5.

## 2   Related Work

There have been many attempts to integrate the Virtualization technology with Grid. We took inspiration from the following research works in this field and identified their potential shortcomings which we overcome with our proposal in this paper.

K. Keahey et al [2] they integrated virtual machine provisioning models into the current site resource management infrastructure as seamlessly as possible. The authors proposed a two-level scheduling to integrate VM provisioning into existing job schedulers.

K. Keahey et al [3, 4] introduced the concept virtual workspace (VW). Virtual workspace aims to provide a customizable and controllable remote job execution environment for Grid. Virtual Workspaces supports unmanned installation of legacy applications, which can effectively reduce the deployment time. By allocating and enforcing resources required by jobs with different priorities, virtual machine can realize fine-grained resource provision, including CPU, memory and network bandwidth. T. Freeman et al [5] addressed the management issues arising from division of labor. The abstractions and tools that allow clients to dynamically configure deploy and manage required execution environments in application-independent ways as well as to negotiate enforceable resource allocations for the execution of these environments.

Xuehai Zhang et al [6] extended the virtual workspace to encompass the notation of a cluster. In this paper they described the extensions needed for workspace definition, architecture extensions and changes to grid services supporting workspace definition and deployment.

Borja Sotomayor et al [7] developed a model, in which a virtual workspace associated with a well-defined resource allocation, in particular its availability, can be procured by negotiating an agreement with the resource provider using WS-Agreement.

Rodrigo et al [8] developed RouteGA algorithm which mainly focus on load balancing with the help of neighboring resources. It used Genetic algorithm approaches while considering historical information on parallel application behavior.

Grid MPI [9] and DUROC [10] are various libraries that supports physical resource co-allocation but does not support advance reservation.

Our approach in this paper differs with these works as we concentrate on creating virtual machines (VMs) in a different cluster after establishing SLA towards co-allocation in order to meet application requirements. We make these virtual machines as a part of the target cluster and enable the scheduler to submit the job in it.

## 3   Co-allocation through Virtualization

Co-allocation is the terminology used in Cluster / Grid computing community to define the process of aggregating computing powers such as CPUs, electronic devices from different resources that spans across organizational and geographical boundaries. This is because of the fact that a typical grid application may require computational power to be aggregated from different resources to meet the requirements. In such situation, negotiating with other resources is a complex process as they are governed by their own local resource manager policies. Further, while negotiating co-allocation with another cluster, it is mandatory to "reserve" the available CPUs so that they shall not be considered for another job scheduling. Hence, a generic co-allocation architecture must include mechanisms for negotiation, advance reservation and resource co-allocation. Also, this component should be integrated with grid metascheduler. However, most of the existing metaschedulers does not posses this capability due to the complexity involved in managing co-allocated resources.

In this paper, we argue that the concept of virtual machines eases the implementation of resource co-allocation. To support our argument, we consider a scenario where an application requires 8 CPUs for execution while the grid has currently two free clusters (Cluster A and Cluster B) each with 5 CPUs in it. In such situation, most of the schedulers will not schedule jobs as the requirements are not met by both the clusters. However, with co-allocation it is possible to aggregate the computing powers of both the clusters with Cluster A contribute all its 5 CPUs while Cluster B give up 3 CPUs in order to meet the application requirement. The complexity of implementing this is that being in the different administrative domain, the clusters will have completely different software environment that may not allow the successful execution of the application.

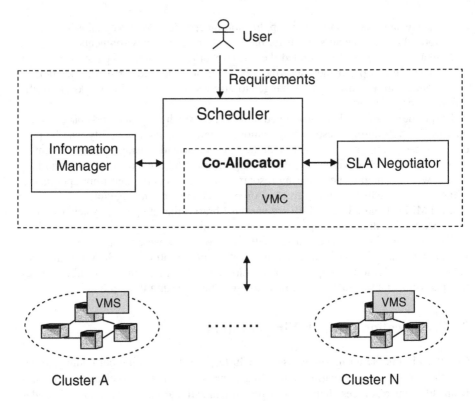

**Fig. 1.** Co-Allocation Architecture

We overcome this issue with the help of virtualization technology. Instead of leasing up 3 physical CPUs from cluster B, we create Virtual Machines in all the three CPUs, make necessary configuration as the target head node, that is, head node of the cluster A, and connecting to it with proper IP address assignment. Thus, three Virtual Machines will become execution nodes of the cluster A. Though the physical cluster B is managed locally, the VMs in it will be managed by Cluster A. At this point, the scheduler schedules the application to cluster A. Once the execution is completed, the VMs will be released to the cluster B. In this approach, the advance reservation must be done for the cluster A and not for cluster B since only a partition of it is going to be used for application execution. In addition to this, the malfunctioning of the virtual machine created in it will not affect the physical host characteristics. We developed a metascheduler (figure 1) that facilitates negotiation of co-allocation and supports creation of virtual machines in remote clusters for application execution.

The *scheduler* component receives application requirements from the user and discovers suitable resources matching the requirements and schedules the application to the selected resource. If the required number of nodes for application execution is not met by a single cluster, the scheduler refers the information manager and identifies free CPUs from other clusters participating in the grid.

The *SLA Negotiator* is invoked by the scheduler when resources are to be co-allocated. SLA negotiator is responsible to contact different clusters and establish an agreement for participating in resource co-allocation. It communicates the agreed resources to the scheduler to co-allocate those resources to meet the application requirements.

*Co-allocator* manages the process of virtual machine creation in the remote cluster and resource co-allocation. It receives remote resource ID and number of CPUs still required to meet the application requirement. It then invokes *negotiator* to initiate SLA negotiation with the remote resource and requesting it to participate in resource co-allocation. Once an agreement is formed, it invokes a component called *Virtual Machine Creator (VMC)*. VMC is a client software that invokes *Virtual Machine Service (VMS)* running in remote cluster that creates virtual machines in it to increase the number of nodes to meet the application requirements. This component is invoked as soon as a contract is established with the remote resource. At this point, it contacts the information manager for determining the IP address to be assigned for the virtual machines. This IP address will be in line with that of the target cluster so that the newly created VMs are in the same network as that of the target cluster. The VMC then invokes the VMS running in the head node of the remote cluster and sends the IP addresses, and number of CPUs to be created in it. VMC communicates the IP addresses to be assigned for the virtual machines to both the clusters. This information is needed by the target cluster's head node to configure the VMs as its execution nodes. Further, it monitors the job execution in the remote virtual machines and as soon as the execution finishes, it releases the virtual machines.

The *information manager* component contacts the available resources and aggregates physical resource information and stores in a database. It maintains a monitoring interval so that changes in the infrastructure are updated. It also keeps track of the application execution in a cluster and updates its status. It maintains a list of remote cluster resources in which virtual machines are created for application execution.

# 4 Implementation

We considered two clusters each with 4 CPUs and globus middlware was installed. The PBS resource manager was installed in both the clusters while operating system in them is RHEL 4.0. All the components of the architecture such as information manager, scheduler and virtual resource manager have been implemented in java. We took inspiration from Gridway Metascheduler [13] to implement portion of our architecture. The Middleware Access Driver modules of gridway are used for communicating with the underlying globus based grid resources while request handler of gridway was used to receive the application request. These modules were integrated with gridway metascheduler appropriately. However, the scheduling module of gridway does not support co-allocation, we have implemented our own scheduling strategy namely Deviation based Resource Scheduling which we proposed in our earlier work [11]. Hence, the flow of gridway has been slightly modified to suit our requirement.

## 4.1 Scheduler

In this paper, in order to determine whether an application requirement needs co-allocation, the Deviation based Resource Scheduling (DRS) algorithm is implemented.

The QoS requested by the application such as CPU_count, Free_memory and CPU_speed is matched with available resources and DRS algorithm determines three degrees of match viz exact, plug_in and subsume.

*Exact Match*: Here the QoS of the available resource (A) are exactly matches with that of request(R).

*Plug-in match*: This match occurs if A has greater capability than R requires.

*Subsume match*: This match occurs if A has lesser capability than R requires.

In exact and plug-in matches, single resource provider is sufficient to execute a job request. So there is no need of negotiation in these cases. But in the case of subsume match, it needs more than one resource provider in order to execute a job that leads to the formation of the VO on the fly by negotiating with the potential resource providers that have high matching percentage with job requirements. Such negotiations automatically lead to the agreement that specifies the terms and conditions imposed by each resource provider while executing a user job such as violation of this agreement, penalty and enforcement action.

In this paper, the subsume match will occur when the number of CPU requested by the application is not available in a singe cluster. Hence, this match leads to co-allocation of multiple resources. At this point, the scheduler figures out the target cluster (A) that provides maximum number of CPUs for application execution but still not enough to meet the requirement, say for instance, still two more CPUs are needed. Hence, the scheduler interacts with the information manager and determines free CPUs in other clusters to initiate SLA negotiation with them for co-allocation. For more information about DRS algorithm, refer [11].

### 4.2  SLA Negotiator

In order to co-allocate and co-ordinate multiple resources in grid environment to meet the application requirements it is mandatory to establish a contract between the users and the resource providers that clearly states the QoS required, restrictions on resource utilization and penalties while violation of the contract. In [12], we described an SLA management architecture shown in figure 2 that supports entire operations in SLA lifecycle such as negotiation, creation, monitoring, violation and enforcement.

We use this architecture for negotiation with remote resource to establish an SLA towards using a portion of that resource for creation of virtual machines in it. During SLA creation phase, the negotiator component contacts the selected remote resource and requests the number of virtual machines to be created in it. Once the remote resource agrees, the negotiator establishes a contract with it and invokes co-allocator component of the scheduler for creating VMs.

The co-allocation contract will be monitored by the SLA monitoring engine that notifies any violation of the contract to the enforcement engine to take appropriate actions.

### 4.3  Virtual Machine Service (VMS)

This service is to create virtual machines followed by necessary configuration and installation of required software running in the head node of every cluster. It is

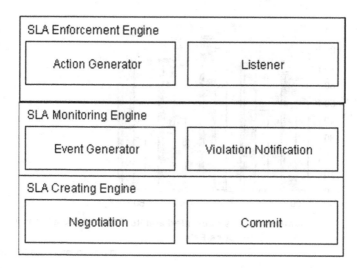

**Fig. 2.** SLA Negotiator

invoked by the VMC component of co-allocator with number of CPUs / VMs still required to meet the application requirement as input. It implements a script that automatically creates Xen based virtual machines in the execution nodes. In our implementation, the service assumes the number of CPUs corresponds to number of Virtual Machines to be created and hence assigns one CPU to each Virtual Machine. The creation of virtual machines is followed by the proper configuration of execution nodes to connect to target head node. For instance, if the target head node uses torque as its local resource manger, the VMS initiates appropriate script to assign the specified IP address and performs compute node configuration in the virtual machines. It then boots the virtual machines so as to connect to the target head node and sends a message to the VMC component of the metascheduler to initiate application scheduling. Further, in order to transfer required VM images to the selected node, NFS has been used in our experimentation. Currently, the concept of advance reservation is not implemented but it has been considered that the scheduler will consider an application scheduling only after the previous application has been scheduled. Hence, synchronization between arrivals of jobs to the scheduler is achieved and requirement of advance reservation is by-passed.

In our experimental setup, global IP addresses have been given to the clusters and it is 192.168.100.*. Hence, for five nodes, we used the address range 192.168.100.1 to 192.168.100.5. When this cluster is selected as target cluster, then the IP addresses for the VMs may start from 192.168.100.6 and one has to be careful in assigning this IP address to ensure all the nodes, both physical and virtual machines has been assigned unique IP address. This will be taken care by the co-allocator component.

The VMs have been created in the remote selected cluster on the fly by VMS provided the host machine possesses required RAM capacity. Then, the service does the client node configuration so that the VM becomes one of the client node of target cluster. This will be followed by LRM configuration in order to accept the job from the target cluster's head node. As soon as these processes are finished, it will return a

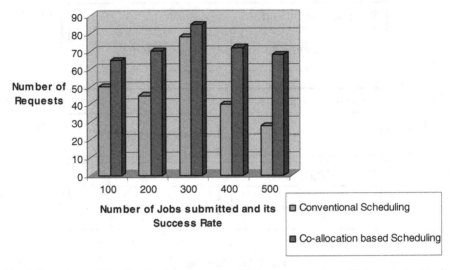

**Fig. 3.** Experimental Results showing 'throughput' when same number of job requests submitted to both conventional and co-allocation based scheduling approach

message to VMC which in turn enables the scheduler to submit job to the target cluster. With this approach, the scheduling process does not require to worry about the software environment but only the capability of the host resource to run a virtual machine in it.

The performance of co-allocation components such as negotiator, VMC and VMS integrated with gridway is being analyzed. There will be obvious overhead due to the invocation of these components and creation of virtual machines. However, this approach results in high throughput as application will be executed through co-allocation of different resources. Our preliminary simulation results shows that the application scheduling based on the proposed co-allocation approach is doing better as shown in figure 3 with respect to throughput against conventional scheduling approach found in gridway metascheduler.

## 4.4 Discussion

In our implementation of co-allocation, we create virtual machines in cluster B and adding it to cluster A as their execution nodes in order to deliver the number of CPUs requested by application. In this case, the virtual machines, though present in cluster B, will be managed by cluster A. Instead we shall also follow another approach that is, creating virtual machines in cluster B and let cluster B be their owner or using the free CPUs as it is in the cluster B, and using a traditional co-allocation tools such as GridMPI or DUROC to schedule application to them. This approach requires handling of resources that spans in two different domains leading to chaos in management. Our approach eliminates this drawback, makes management of co-allocated resources easy as it treats the resources spanning different clusters as a single cluster. Currently, we are in the verge of investigating the overhead of our approach against the conventional physical resource co-allocation.

# 5  Conclusion

In this paper, we proposed a scheduling architecture that supports resource co-allocation with the help of virtualization. It enables isolation of application execution and provides greater security to the participating resources. The SLA Negotiation component supports WS-Agreement based SLA negotiation and also it supports SLA enforcement and monitoring. Currently, the architecture is implemented such that the scheduler does not accept a new job until scheduling of first job finishes. However, since, advance reservation and co-allocation go hand in hand, the architecture still lack a mechanism for advance reservation which will be our concentration in future.

# References

1. Foster, I., Kesselman, C., Nick, J., Tuecke, S.: The Physiology of the Grid: An Open Grid Services Architecture for Distributed Systems Integration, Open Grid Service Infrastructure WG, Global Grid Forum (2002)
2. Freeman, T., Keahey, K.: Flying Low: Simple Leases with Workspace Pilot. In: Luque, E., Margalef, T., Benítez, D. (eds.) Euro-Par 2008. LNCS, vol. 5168, pp. 499–509. Springer, Heidelberg (2008)
3. Keahey, K., Foster, I., Freeman, T., Zhang, X., Galron, D.: Virtual Workspaces in the Grid. In: Cunha, J.C., Medeiros, P.D. (eds.) Euro-Par 2005. LNCS, vol. 3648, pp. 421–431. Springer, Heidelberg (2005)
4. Keahey, K., Foster, I., Freeman, T., Zhang, X.: Virtual Workspaces: Achieving Quality of Service and Quality of Life in the Grid. Scientific Programming Journal (2005)
5. Freeman, T., et al.: Division of Labor: Tools for Growing and Scaling Grids. In: SciDAC 2005 Conference, Boston, MA (June 2005)
6. Zhang, X., Foster, I., Freeman, T., Keahey, K., Scheftner, D., Sotomayor, B.: Virtual Clusters for Grid Communities. In: CCGRID 2006, Singapore (2006)
7. Sotomayor, B., et al.: A Resource Management Model for VM-Based Virtual Workspaces, Masters paper, University of Chicago (February 2007)
8. Rodrigo, et al.: Grid Job Scheduling using Route with Genetic Algorithm Support. Journal of Telecommunications, 147–160 (May 2008)
9. http://www.gridmpi.org
10. http://www.globus.org/toolkit/docs/2.4/duroc/
11. Thamarai Selvi, S., et al.: Service Level Agreement based Grid Scheduling. In: IEEE International Conference on Web Services (2008)
12. Thamarai Selvi, S., et al.: GSMA based Automated Negotiation Model for Grid Scheduling. In: IEEE International Conference on Services Computing (2008)
13. http://www.gridway.org

# MTS: Multiresolution Thread Selection for Parallel Workload Distribution

Chonglei Mei, Hai Jiang, and Jeff Jenness

Department of Computer Science, Arkansas State University,
Jonesboro, Arkansas 72467, USA
{chonglei.mei,hjiang,jeffj}@csm.astate.edu

**Abstract.** Computing workload distribution is indispensable for resource sharing, cycle stealing and other modes of interaction in distributed systems/Grids.
Computations should be arranged to adapt the capacity variation of system resources. Although computation migration is the essential mechanism to move
computing tasks around, the decision making of which task should be relocated is
even more critical, especially when multithreaded parallel programs are involved.
Multiple threads might be treated as partial workload and moved together. Based
on thread similarity, this paper proposes a novel Multiresolution Thread Grouping algorithm (MTG) to classify threads into hierarchical Thread Bundles (TB)
some of which can be picked by Multiresolution Thread Selection scheme (MTS)
for load distribution. During the process of MTG, global variables are reorded
so that one-time migration cost and post-migration communication volume and
frequency can be reduced. Experimental results demonstrate the effectiveness of
MTS for parallel workload distribution.

## 1 Introduction

From cluster computing to Internet computing and Grid computing, current computation technologies have caused more on collaboration, data sharing, cycle stealing, and
other modes of interaction among dynamic and geographically distributed organizations [1]. Distributed computing enables to spread workload across multiple machines.
Within each individual machine, parallel programming paradigm is employed to take
advantage of multicore/many-core or multiprocessor architectures. Local parallel workload should be able to be adjusted for load balancing, load sharing, fault resilience, and
data access locality. Thus, parallel workload scheduling is essential to application performance gain and system utilization efficiency.

As multithreading has been adopted by many applications, threads become the fine-
grained computation and migration units and thread migration approach is expected to
be widely adopted in the future. MigThread, a heterogeneous application-level thread
migration package is adopted for computation movement [2]. This paper intends to deploy the strategy to utilize the information collected by MigThread at compile time and
select proper threads for migration at run-time. The deployed migration policy strategy
is transparent to users so that programmers can write their code in parallel programming
mode whereas run-time systems dispatch threads to other machines for distributed/Grid
computing.

N. Abdennadher and D. Petcu (Eds.): GPC 2009, LNCS 5529, pp. 244–255, 2009.

Since possibly multiple threads are considered for migration, thread relationship plays a key role here. If closely related threads are separated, future interaction between them might slow down the overall execution. The cause of the interaction might be synchronization or data sharing activities which can be detected by analyzing the global data collected by MigThread's preprocessor at compile time. The ideal scenario is that migrating threads have no or few further interactions after migration and load re-distribution. Therefore, future communication volume and frequency will be reduced.

This paper makes three contributions. First, the Multiresolution Thread Grouping (MTG) algorithm is proposed based on thread similarity and data access pattern to group threads into Thread Bundles (TBs). The zoom-in/zoom-out feature with maps has been employed to identify TBs at multiple resolution-levels. Second, with support of MigThread, a data alignment scheme is applied during MTG process to place related global variables together to reduce possible synchronization volume and frequency when threads are separated. Third, the run-time scheduler adopts a Multiresolution Thread Selection (MTS) to detect proper combination of thread bundles from multiple resolution-layers so that one-time migration overhead and post-migration communication cost will be minimized.

The remainder of this paper is organized as follows: Section 2 gives an overview of related technologies for parallel workload distribution. Section 3 describes the design and implementation of MTS. In Section 4, performance analysis and experiment results are provided. Section 5 mentions some related work. Finally, our conclusion and future work are described in Section 6.

## 2   Techniques for Parallel Workload Distribution

In Grid and clusters environments, load imbalance is not only caused by the dynamic nature of applications, but also caused by the availability fluctuation of computing resources [3]. Whole or proper partial parallel computing workload needs to be relocated.

For computation mobility, a heterogeneous application-level thread migration package, MigThread [2], is adopted. MigThread consists of two parts: a preprocessor and a run-time support module. The preprocessor transforms user's source code, move the thread state out of its original location (libraries or kernels) and abstracts it up to the language level for platform-independence. All related information with regards to stack variables, function parameters, program counters, and dynamically allocated memory regions, is collected into certain pre-defined data structure so that the run-time support module can construct, transfer, and restore thread state promptly and dynamically [2].

Schedulers are employed to orchestrate computing parts distributed across multiple machines and decide when, where and who to migrate. For the migrating task, its run-time support module needs to decide how to split local parallel workload. Multithreaded applications have to determine a group of migrating threads whose associated data sets are small enough to minimize the one-time migration cost and post-migration communication cost for data sharing across machines. Both static and dynamic scheduling strategies can be applied to collect information and make decision at compile time or run-time.

Cluster algorithms aim to find natural groups in the unlabeled data of certain set and can be used to detect partial parallel workload. A general definition of clustering could be "the process to organize objects into groups whose members are similar." Members in one cluster are similar with respect to certain feature whereas the ones from different clusters might look quite different. Clustering can be based on object distance or difference between descriptive concepts.

# 3   Multiresolution Thread Grouping and Selection

In multithreaded parallel applications, threads are the basic computing units. Similarity is defined so that identical or similar threads can be grouped together for parallel workload distribution.

## 3.1   Multiresolution Thread Grouping (MTG)

At compile time, thread similarity can be defined by the sharing of global variables and used by runtime schedulers.

**Definition 1.** Thread weight: *the amount of data and synchronization variables the thread accesses.*

MigThread's preprocessor collects all global variables in predefined structures. Starting from the thread creation primitive, all functions referenced by the thread can be identified. By scanning these functions, the preprocessor can calculate the thread weight which should be considered for migration.

**Definition 2.** Thread similarity: *the rate of common (shared) data and synchronization variables among multiple threads.*

*Assuming that two threads, $T_1$ and $T_2$, access data sets $\{a_1, a_2, a_3, ..., a_{n_1}\}$ and $\{b_1, b_2, b_3, ..., b_{n_2}\}$, respectively, if the amount of common data accessed by both threads is $N_{comm}$, the similarity will be $N_{comm}/(n_1 + n_2 - N_{comm})$ where $n_1$ and $n_2$ are the numbers of data items.*

Thread similarity defines how similar two threads are. The higher the similarity, the more global variables they share. On the same machine, threads can share variables through the shared virtual address space whereas on different machines, communication has to be involved. Therefore, it is more efficient to keep highly similar threads on same machine to reduce communication overhead.

If there are $n$ threads, $\{T_1, T_2, T_3, ..., T_n\}$, in a program, the pair-wise thread similarity values can be represented as an $n \times n$ similarity matrix S where each entry, $S(i, j)$, stands for the similarity of certain pair of threads, $T_i$ and $T_j$. Along the diagonal, the values are always zeros since threads are not supposed to compare against themselves. One example of similarity matrix could be as follows:

$$\begin{bmatrix}
0.00 & 0.20 & 0.00 & 0.00 & 0.00 & 0.11 & 0.11 & 0.25 & 0.11 & 0.11 \\
0.20 & 0.00 & 0.00 & 0.00 & 0.00 & 0.23 & 0.33 & 0.23 & 0.23 & 0.23 \\
0.00 & 0.00 & 0.00 & 1.00 & 1.00 & 0.11 & 0.11 & 0.11 & 0.11 & 0.11 \\
0.00 & 0.00 & 1.00 & 0.00 & 1.00 & 0.11 & 0.11 & 0.11 & 0.11 & 0.11 \\
0.00 & 0.00 & 1.00 & 1.00 & 0.00 & 0.11 & 0.11 & 0.11 & 0.11 & 0.11 \\
0.11 & 0.00 & 0.11 & 0.11 & 0.11 & 0.00 & 0.75 & 0.75 & 0.75 & 0.75 \\
0.11 & 0.33 & 0.11 & 0.11 & 0.11 & 0.75 & 0.00 & 0.75 & 0.75 & 0.75 \\
0.25 & 0.23 & 0.11 & 0.11 & 0.11 & 0.75 & 0.75 & 0.00 & 0.75 & 0.75 \\
0.11 & 0.23 & 0.11 & 0.11 & 0.11 & 0.75 & 0.75 & 0.75 & 0.00 & 0.75 \\
0.11 & 0.23 & 0.11 & 0.11 & 0.11 & 0.75 & 0.75 & 0.75 & 0.75 & 0.00
\end{bmatrix}$$

**Definition 3.** Thread Bundle (TB): *a group of identical or similar threads with respect to certain feature.*

*During a finite period of time [0,T], there are N threads $\{T_0, T_1, T_2, ..., T_{N-1}\}$ running in a specific parallel or distributed system. Each thread $T_i (0 \leq i < N)$ has a finite life time $[t_{i,start}, t_{i,end}]$. A thread bundle B is a set of M threads $\{L_0, L_1, ..., L_{M-1}\}$, $L_j \in \{T_0, T_1, T_2, ..., T_{N-1}\}$, which have some common properties.*

The shared common data between any threads $T_i$ and $T_j$ in bundle $B_k$ can be expressed as $C_{in}(B_k, i, j)$. which is caused by the sharing of variables between. The shared data set between threads in bundles $B_{K1}$ and $B_{K2}$ can be $C_{out}(B_{k1}, B_{k2})$. Since normally threads in one bundle share more data than the ones from different bundles, there exists $C_{in} \gg C_{out}$. In other words, if some threads share more common variables than others, they are defined to be similar and should be put into one bundle which has few connections with other bundles.

Thread bundles are migration units since their threads share more common data. Most existing clustering algorithms use predefined distance or similarity thresholds to group items. Therefore, the clustering results are fixed. Multiresolution Thread Grouping (MTG) intends to loosely define the similarity thresholds and the whole grouping process is recorded. Without too high storage overhead, thread bundles can be defined, adjusted and retrieved. Thread bundles can merge and split until a proper combination is achieved. These bundles can be mapped onto different machines with minimized communication between them.

Multiresolution Thread Grouping is inspired by the zoom technology in maps. In distance, objects on maps might look together. When we get closer or zoom in, we can see their differences and objects are separate apart. When we zoom in/zoom out at different resolution levels, objects can be grouped in different ways. One extreme case is that we zoom in to the lowest level, we can see each individual object unless some of them are totally identical. Another extreme case is we zoom out to the infinite distance and all objects are blur and stay together.

With this multiresolution strategy, MTG initially treat each individual threads as bundles and then pull back/zoom out gradually. At each step, the most similar bundles are merged. Obviously, all identical threads will merge at the first step. By repeating this process, eventually only one bundle will be left. However, all bundle results at different resolution levels are kept with their corresponding data structures, called layers. Unlike most existing clustering algorithms whose results are normally on the same layer

```
Main grouping (S)          //S is original similarity matrix
1:     begin:
2:     While (number of bundles NB>1)
3:         max=FindMax(S)  //find maximum value in S
4:         SubGroup(max,S) //establish new layer of grouping tree
5:         UpdateBundle(S) //UpdateBunlde updates the similarity
                           //matrix and grouping tree
6:     end while
7:     end
```

**Fig. 1.** Main grouping process

[4], MTG can achieve the final result across multiple layers. So the results of MTG are hierarchical thread bundles.

The grouping process is shown in Fig. 1 where *NB* is the number of bundles for the current resolution and its original value is *n*, the number of threads. The parameter *S* is the current thread similarity matrix whose elements are meta-threads, i.e., thread bundles. As bundles merge, corresponding rows and columns combine and the new ones are defined based on data sharing. Function *FindMax* is called to find out the entries with the maximum value in the current similarity matrix. Function *SubGroup*, shown in Fig. 2, is used to merge thread bundles with the maximum value into bundles on a newly created layer. Function *UpdateGroup* is to update the similarity matrix to match the situation on the new layer. The updating process treats threads in one bundle as one meta-thread and then calculates the similarity of all meta-thread pairs. Thus, the size of the similarity matrix *S* is shrinking step by step until it turns into a 1 x 1 matrix.

Through this grouping process, identical or the most similar threads are glued together on the bottom layer first and eventually all thread bundles converge into one large bundle on the top layer. The convergence speed depends on how similar the threads are. With the above-mentioned similarity matrix, the convergence process can be represented by a grouping tree, shown in Fig. 3. Layers indicate resolution levels. Initially there are ten thread bundles staying on the bottom layer. As resolution decreases (zoom out), the number of bundles decreases and the sizes of some bundles increases. In the

```
SubGroup(max, S)
1:     begin:
2:     while(!endof(S))
3:         threadpair = find(max, S) // threadpair is the founded pair of
                                     // threads with similarity max
4:         if(only one of this pair is in one bundle)
5:             add the other one into this bundle
6:         else if (the two threads in separate bundles)
7:             join the two bundles
8:         else if (neither of the pair is in a bundle)
9:             establish a new bundle using this pair of threads
10:        end if
11:    end while
12:    end
```

**Fig. 2.** The SubGroup function to create new layers

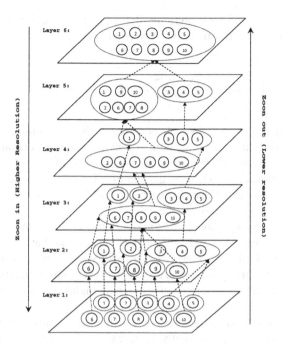

**Fig. 3.** Grouping tree of 10 threads

above example, there are two actual bundles, one with three threads and the other with five threads. As grouping process proceeds from bottom up, thread similarity becomes blur and the number of bundles is reduced .

### 3.2 Multiresolution Thread Selection (MTS)

**Thread Selection Criteria.** To distribute multithreaded parallel workload, two associated overheads are identified:

- *Migration cost*: To migrate a selected thread bundle, the weight summation of all thread members should be considered. If cut-through routing [5] is applied, the migration cost of the thread weight can be expressed as:

$$C_{mig}(n) = t_s + lt_h + t_w \sum_{i=0}^{N-1} m_i \tag{1}$$

where $N$ is the number of data to be transferred, $t_s$ is the startup time, $l$ is the maximum number of hops, $t_h$ is the per-hop time for the message header to travel, $t_w$ is the per-word transfer time, and $m_i$ is the size of datum $i$. Migration cost is a one-time issue and only happens during thread bundle migration unless this bundle needs to move again.

- *Communication cost*: After one thread bundle is migrated to a remote machine, it might still need to share global variables with other thread bundles on the original machine. Such post-migration sharing causes severe communication cost for synchronization at run-time. It can be expressed as:

$$C_{comm}(n) = \sum_{i=0}^{N-1} \sum_{j=0}^{F_i} (t_{s_{ij}} + t_{h_{ij}} l_{ij} + t_{w_{ij}} m_i) \qquad (2)$$

where $N$ is the number of global variables shared, $F_i$ is the communication frequency of datum i, $t_{s_{ij}}$ is the startup time of datum $i$ for the $j^{th}$ communication, $t_{h_{ij}}$ is the per-hop time of datum $i$ for the $j^{th}$ communication, $l_{ij}$ is the number of links for datum $i$ of the $j^{th}$ communication, $t_{w_{ij}}$ is per-word transfer time for $j^{th}$ communication of datum $i$, and $m_i$ is the size of datum $i$. If the channel bandwidth is $r$ words per second, then each word takes time $t_w = 1/r$ to traverse the link.

Obviously, the post-migration communication cost is a dynamic issue and dominant factor. Its actual value depends on both data volume and sharing frequency during the synchronization of different data copies distributed across multiple machines. Such communication is incurred by both data access and synchronization primitive use, such as barriers and locks. Since such frequency is always higher, i.e., $F_i \geq 1$, $C_{comm}$ could be much greater than $C_{mig}$.

The ideal selection of thread bundles is the ones with both minimum migration and communication costs. However, usually the thread bundles with least communication cost and ones with least migration cost do not overlap with each other. At most time, communication cost will be considered first. If migration cost complies the selection, the perfect solution is achieved. Otherwise, a relatively smaller migration cost selection will be taken.

## MTG-Based Thread Selection

The proposed thread selection scheme is based on hierarchical thread bundles acquired from MTG's Grouping Tree which indicates two pieces of significant information. One is that the threads are grouped based on similarity and on the same layers, threads in same bundles shares more global variables than those from different bundles. The other one is that during the top-down traversal of the grouping tree, the earlier the thread bundles are split apart, the less similar their thread members are.

To migration a certain number of threads, the idea of splitting a thread bundle is unacceptable since the communication between newly created bundles might not be clear. MTS adopts the hierarchical strategy to combine some bundles from different layers for the number of threads for migration. The grouping tree is traversed in top-down manner to detect the best thread bundle combination with possibly minimum communication overhead. The traversal stops on one layer $i$ where a bundle contains the closest number of threads, $m$, with $m \leq n$ ($n$ is the number of migrating threads provided by schedulers). The reason to stop at layer $i$ is that threads in bundles on upper layers have less similarity than the ones on layer $i$ or below. Then the $m$ threads from the selected bundle and $n-m$ threads from other bundles on the $i^{th}$ layer or lower layers form the bundle combination with the possibly least communication cost. This phase 1 of selection process is showed in Fig. 4.

```
Selection1(n, Gtree)          //Gtree is grouping tree
                              //n is number of threads to select
1:   begin:
2:   K = findLayer(n,Gtree)   //find layer k from top of Gtree on which there
                              //is a bundle B meeting (n-sizeof(B))≥ 0 and
                              //is minimum
3:   for i=k to 1
4:       candidate = NULL     //candidate used to store bundles whose
                              //size is smaller than n on layer i
5:       for j=0 to NB_k-1    //NB_k is number of thread bundles on layer i
6:           if (sizeof(bundle(j))≤ n )
7:               insert bundle(j) into candidate;
8:           end if;
9:       end for;
10:      if (existing n threads formed by the sizes of groups
             in candidate)
11:          return Result=FindLComm(n,candidate);
                              //FindLComm is to find n threads from
                              //candidate with lowest communication cost
12:      end if
13:  end for
14:  end
```

**Fig. 4.** Multiresolution Thread Selection - phase 1

However, sometimes the greedy algorithm in phase 1 of MTS cannot achieve the best results since it does not consider other combinations. Further tuning is provided by phase 2 as shown in Fig. 5. Some larger bundles might derive better results if their threads share few global variables. Therefore, their post-migration communication cost might be lower than the bundle combination based on the closest bundle acquired from MTS phase 1. However, although there are more larger bundles on upper layers, their thread similarity might be much lower. Therefore, the optimization in phase 2 only consider those larger bundles ($\geq n$) on the layer with the closest bundle ($k^{th}$ layer) or those layers below. Our experiments demonstrate the effectiveness of such optimization.

### 3.3    Data Realignment with Grouping Tree

There are two main costs in the threads migration: communication cost and migration cost. MTS intends to ensure that the communication cost is acceptably small. Since MigThread has collected global variables in predefined structures, variables shared by

```
Selection2(n, Gtree, result1)    //result is result of selecton1
1:   begin:
2:   result = result1;
3:   k = findLayer(n,Gtree)
4:   for i=k to 1
5:       for j = 0 to NB_k-1
6:           if(sizeof(bundle(j))> n )
7:               result2 = FindLComm(bundle(j))
8:               if(CommCost(result2)<CommCost(result))
9:                   result = result2
10:              end if
11:          end if;
12:      end for;
13:  end for;
14:  return result;
15:  end
```

**Fig. 5.** Tuning of MTS - phase 2

threads in the same bundles should be placed together to reduce possible migration and communication costs.

If shared data is distributed across multiple machines, future sharing will incur communication overhead. Normally, Distributed Shared Memory (DSM) systems are used widely to synchronize multiple copies distributed across several machines. Since most DSM systems [2] are page-based, it is better to reduce the total number of pages hosting the shared variables.

In MTS, threads are selected through bundles sitting on different layers in the grouping tree. Bundles on lower layers have more opportunities to be migrated to remote machines. If their shared global variables are stored continuously, the number of migrated or synchronized pages will decrease. MTS adopts the approach of realigning shared variables of threads in bundles from the penultimate layer up to the top layer until all the global data are realigned. Experimental results show that this method is effective.

## 4   Experimental Results

The experiment is conducted through a simulator which generates 20 threads and 25 global data variables with randomly assigned data types. Each thread can randomly access 5 to 12 variables to distinguish each other. To simulate a real situation, we assume that there are 5 bundles with single thread , one bundle with 3 threads, one bundle with 5 threads and one bundle with 7 threads. Within each bundle, 3/4 of data variables accessed by local threads are the same and the rests are different.

To evaluate MTS, up to half threads will be selected for migration because the symmetric case makes the other half exhibit the same performance. The MTS results will be compared against the optimal result acquired by checking all possibilities of thread selection. The ranking of MTS results indicates its effectiveness. With respect to different numbers of requested migrating threads, the simulation will be conducted 1000 times for the average ranks.

Naive Thread Selection scheme (NTS) is used for comparison. NTS selects threads with smallest communication cost one by one. To demonstrate the effectiveness of data realignment in MTS, we assume that the size of one page is 64, and the size of data can be 1, 2, 4, 8 and 32.

If three threads are selected for migration, the simulation results of MTS and NTS are showed in Fig.6. Part A shows that about 90% of MTS results rank top 10 of all the possible results in term of communication cost, and over 600 cases rank $1^{st}$ (with the least overhead). The vertical bars indicate all instances whereas the curve line dispicts the accumulation result. Part B shows that more than 80% of MTS results rank top 10 in term of migration cost, over 600 cases rank $1^{st}$. Part C illustrates that only 60% of NTS results rank top 10 and fewer than 400 cases rank $1^{st}$. Obviously, MTS outperforms NTS and most time MTS can select the optimal choices. Part D indicates that more than 60% of MTS results have reduced the number of data pages through data realignment.

For different numbers of migrating threads, the ranking results compared against the optimal solutions are shown in Fig.7. If only one thread needs to be selected, NTS outperforms MTS in term of communication cost because NTS always selects the ones

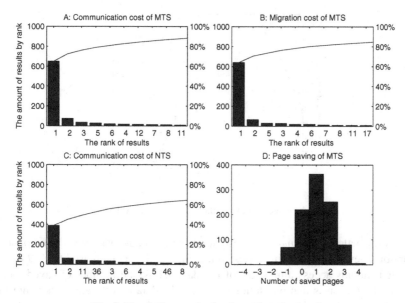

**Fig. 6.** Simulation results for three-thread migration

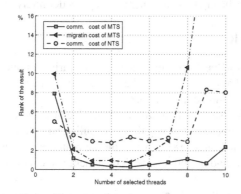

**Fig. 7.** Average ranking results with different numbers of migrating threads

with least communication overhead. As the number of selected threads increases, MTS performs much better than NTS in term of communication cost. From the migration cost line, it is clear that MTS performs well when the migrating number is between 2 and 7. However, when it is increased to 8, 9 and 10, the migration cost increases dramatically. This is because MTS gives communication cost higher priority. As communication frequency increases, the communication cost will dominate one-time migration time easily.

The effectiveness of data alignment in terms of the number of saved pages is shown in Fig. 8. When the number of selected threads is relatively small, less data will be accessed because of the simulation setting. Thus there are relatively more chances to

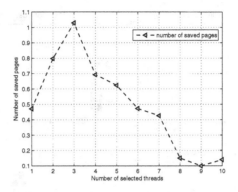

**Fig. 8.** Effectiveness of data alignment in MTS

save pages for better performance. As the number of threads increases, the number of data variable they access also increases. When the number is increased to 8, 9 or 10, the selected threads access almost all of the data. Thus, the number of saved pages decreases. The reason is that our simulation fixes the data access rate. This is not the actual scenario in the real world where the rate might be quite low. Then significant performance improvement in term of saved pages is expected. Without any negative results and much overhead, data alignment strategy is definitely effective.

## 5   Related Work

Computation migration has been implemented with variant granularity. Process migration can be deployed at application level as in the Tui system [6]. MigThread [2] supports both process and thread migration.

Job scheduling in distributed environments has been an active research topic for a long time. Cu *et al.* proposed a running time scheduling based on migration cost [3]. The scheduling strategy in Condor [8] is based on the match of the users' specification of their job requirements and preferences with the machines' characteristics, availabilities, and conditions.

Among clustering methods, K-means uses an iterative method to distributed n points into k (fixed number) clusters on a 2D plane. The Markov Cluster algorithm (MCL) [4] assumes that there are natural clusters in the given data set and intends to elaborate the data relations.

## 6   Conclusion and Future Work

This paper proposes a novel Multiresolution Thread Selection algorithm (MTS) to pick certain number of threads for parallel workload distribution. MTS defines thread bundles at different resolution levels and make a selection across them. Shared global variables are re-aligned in the process of MTS to reduce the possible migration/communication cost. Simulation results have demonstrated the effectiveness. The future work includes applying MTS on full-fledged dynamic schedulers and conducting experiments with real applications.

# References

1. Foster, I., Kesselman, C., Nick, J., Tuecke, S.: Grid services for distributed system intergration. Computer 35(6), 37–46 (2002)
2. Jiang, H., Chaudhary, V.: Thread migration and checkpointing in heterogeneous distributed systems. In: Proceedings of the 37th Annual Hawaii International Conference on System Science (2004)
3. Du, C., Sun, X., Wu, M.: Dynamic scheduling with process migration. In: Proceedings of the seventh IEEE International Symposium on Cluster Computing and the Grid, pp. 92–99 (2007)
4. van Dongen, S.: A cluster algorithm for graphs. PhD thesis, National Research Institute for Mathematics and Computer Science (CWI) (2000)
5. Grama, A., Gupta, A., Karypis, G., Kumar, V.: Introduction to Parallel Computing. Addison-Wesley, Reading (2003)
6. Smith, P., Hutchinson, N.: Heterogeneous process migration: the tui system. Technical Report 4, University of British Columbia (1996)
7. Dimitrov, B., Rego, V.: Arachne: A portable threads system supporting migrant threads on heterogeneous network farms. IEEE Transactions on Parallel and Distributed Systems, 459–469 (1998)
8. Lizkow, M., Livny, M., Tannenbaum, T.: Checkpointing and migraion of unix processes in the condor distributed environment. Technical Report 1346, Univ. of Wisconsin-Madision (1997)

# The gLite Workload Management System

Cecchi Marco[1], Capannini Fabio[1], Dorigo Alvise[1], Ghiselli Antonia[1],
Giacomini Francesco[1], Maraschini Alessandro[2], Marzolla Moreno[1],
Monforte Salvatore[1], Pacini Fabrizio[2], Petronzio Luca[2], and Prelz Francesco[1]

[1] I.N.F.N. - National Institute for Nuclear Physics - Viale Berti Pichat, 6/2 - Bologna, Italy
[2] Elsag-Datamat s.p.a. - Via Laurentina, 760 - Rome, Italy

**Abstract.** The gLite Workload Management System represents a key entry point
to high-end services available on a Grid. Being designed as part of the european
Grid within the six years long EU-funded EGEE project, now at its third phase,
the WMS is meant to provide reliable and efficient distribution and management
of end-user requests. This service basically translates user requirements and preferences into specific operations and decisions - dictated by the general status of
all other Grid services - while taking responsibility to bring requests to successful completion. The WMS has become a reference implementation of the "early
binding" approach to meta-scheduling as a neat, Grid-aware solution, able to optimise resource access and to satisfy requests for computation together with data.
Several added value features are provided for job submission, different job types
are supported from simple batch to a variety of compounds. In this paper we
outline what has been achieved to provide adequate workload and management
components, suitable to be deployed in a production-quality Grid, while covering
the design and development of the gLite WMS and focusing on the most recently
achieved results.

## 1 Introduction

Resource management and scheduling of distributed, data-driven applications in production Grid environments are challenging problems. The interested domains include
workload management, resource discovery, brokering, accounting, authorization and
authentication, resource access, reliability and dependability. Although significant results were achieved in the past few years, the development and the proper deployment
of generic, robust, reliable and standard components involving such huge scales and
factors as the ones a production Grid has to deal with, has brought out non trivial issues
requiring joint efforts with a strong degree of cooperation to be attained.

Grid computing technologies have been developed over the last decade to provide a
computing infrastructure for a disparate and ever growing number of e-Science applications. A first large scale production Grid infrastructure was deployed by the Enabling
Grids for E-SciencE (EGEE) [1] EU-funded project. Its operation was then further consolidated during its second phase (EGEE-II). The EGEE Grid infrastructure consists
of a set of middleware services deployed on a worldwide collection of computational
resources, with an extensive programme of middleware re-engineering that has resulted
in a consolidated software stack, gLite [2]. This long-standing project, now at its third

N. Abdennadher and D. Petcu (Eds.): GPC 2009, LNCS 5529, pp. 256–268, 2009.

phase (EGEE-III), will take further steps in moving Grids to dependable and sustainable production infrastructure while providing a continuous service to its expanding user base. EGEE-III will continue to develop gLite as its reference open-source middleware distribution.

In this paper we outline what has been achieved to provide adequate workload and management components, suitable to be deployed in a production-quality Grid, while covering the design and development of the gLite WMS, with particular respect to functionality and interoperability, focusing on the most recently achieved results.

## 2    The gLite WMS in a Nutshell

The gLite WMS represents a key entry point to high-end services available on a Grid. It has been designed with some fundamental principles in mind: first of all aiming at providing a dependable and reliable service, where primary importance is given to never losing track of jobs to be processed and always providing a prompt, responsive quality of service, yet keeping up with huge and even growing factors of scale. It is designed as part of a Service Oriented Architecture (SOA) complying with Web-Service Interoperability (WS-I) [3] specifications and strives to implement recommendations on web service foundations made by the Open Grid Forum (OGF) [4].

Fundamental to any Grid environment is the ability to discover, allocate and monitor the use of resources. The term "workload management" is commonly used to describe all those aspects that involve discovering the resources and selecting the most suitable ones, arranging for submission, monitoring and information gathering. In this respect, the WMS has to deal with a heterogeneous computing environment that in general encompasses different architectures and loss of centralized control, all this in presence of potential faults due to the distributed and diverse nature of the Grid environment, computers, networks and storage devices.

## 3    Functionality at Various Levels

The gLite Workload Management System (WMS) provides a service responsible for the distribution and management of tasks across resources available on a Grid, in such a way that applications are conveniently, efficiently and effectively executed. These tasks, which basically consist in execution requests, are usually referred to as "jobs". In a Grid environment the scope of such tasks/jobs needs to be extended to take into account other kinds of resources, such as storage or network capacity. The need for such a broader definition is basically due to the move from typical batch-like activity to applications with ever more demanding requirements in areas like data access or interactivity, both with the user and with other tasks. In this respect, the WMS does support different types of jobs:

- Single batch jobs.
- Work-flows: jobs with dependencies expressed as a direct acyclic graph (DAG).
- Collections: sets of jobs without dependencies grouped together and identified by a single handler.

- MPI: based on message passing interface - a widely-used library to allow for parallel programming within a single cluster (intra-cluster).
- Interactive: establishing a synchronous two way communication with the user on a socket stream.
- Parametric: allowing multiple jobs to be defined by a single description with attributes varying with a parameter.

The characteristics of a job are defined using a flexible and expressive formalism called Job Description Language (JDL) [5]. The JDL is based on Classified Advertisements or *ClassAds* [6], developed within the Condor project [7], which basically consist of a list of key/value pairs that represent the various characteristics of a job (input files, arguments, executable, etc.) as well as its requirements, constraints and preferences (physical and virtual memory, CPU, operating system, etc.). The user can then specify whatever attribute for the description of a request without incurring in formal errors, as ClassAds are not bound by any particular schema. Only a certain set of attributes are directly taken into account by the WMS on the base of documented semantics, the others will simply be passed on without specific processing. Also, the attributes used for describing high-end resources come from a common schema, the so called GLUE schema [8], born from a joint effort to standardize and facilitate interoperation between Grid infrastructures, e.g. the attribute "GlueCEStateFreeCPUs" will always indicate the number of free CPUs in all the resources making part of such a joint infrastructure.

Jobs are always associated with user proxy credentials and all job-dependent operations are performed on behalf of the user. gLite in general and the WMS in particular exploit experience and existing components from the Virtual Data Toolkit from Condor and Globus [9] (VDT). While Condor plays a significant role in the present architecture as a job submission and tracking layer (see later), the Globus Security Infrastructure (GSI) is used throughout for enabling secure authentication and communication. GSI provides in fact libraries and tools for authentication and message protection that use standard X.509 public key certificates, public key infrastructure (PKI), the SSL/TLS protocol, and X.509 Proxy Certificates, an extension defined for GSI to meet the dynamic delegation requirements of Grid communities. A specific service, called Proxy Renewal and conceived as be part of the WMS, is devoted to renewing credentials, automatically and securely, for long-running jobs. This is a desired feature not to propagate throughout the Grid proxy certificates of a significant duration, since they need to be reasonably longer than the expected duration of jobs, which in some cases can last for weeks, they are associated to. This scenario would obviously represent a security threat, but, on the other hand, working with short-lived certificates will cause long jobs to outlive the validity of their proxy and be consequentially aborted. To avoid this the WMS allows proxy certificates to be renewed automatically, when close to expiry, if the user allows the Proxy Renewal service to be enabled, this is done by specifying a MyProxy [10] server (the long-lived proxy keystore) in the job JDL. Another similar mechanism, implemented by the Job Submission Service (see later), is in place to forward freshly renewed certificates in the WMS instance to the Computing Element (CE, i.e. the Grid abstraction for a computing resource) where they will finally reach the Worker Node (WN, i.e. the machine where the job is actually executed).

The Grid is a complex system and things can go wrong at various stages of the so called submission chain. The WMS has been designed with the ability to recover from failures of the infrastructure by automatically resubmitting failed jobs, this is done at two levels. "Shallow" resubmission is utilized in those cases where an error occurs before the CE has started executing the job, in which case another CE can be tried immediately without any worry to compromise the results. This will also reduce the probability to have multiple instances of the same job over the Grid due to temporary loss of network contact. "Deep" resubmission happens whenever a job fails after it started running; this situation can be more problematic as the job may well have done a considerable amount of processing, producing output files or making other state changes, and may also have consumed a significant amount of (precious) CPU time. Users can therefore choose the number of times they will allow the job to be resubmitted in these two ways with two parameters of the JDL. If a job fails after having reached the maximum number of retries it will be terminally aborted.

Submitting a job actually means passing its responsibility to the WMS whose purpose is then finding the appropriate resource(s) matching user requirements, watching and directing the job on its way to completion, with particular attention to infrastructure failures requiring resubmission. The WMS will in the end forward the job to the selected set of CEs for execution. The decision about which resource is adequate to run the job is the outcome of a so called match-making process between the "demand", represented by the submission requirements and preferences, and the "offer", represented by the characteristics of the available resources. The availability of resources for a particular task depends not only on the actual state of the resources, but also on the utilization policies that the resource administrators and/or the administrator of the Virtual Organization (VO) the user belongs to have defined for each of their users. It can happen, not rarely, that none of the resources available on the Grid at a given time is able to satisfy some job's requirements, in suchcase the submission request is kept pending by the WMS and periodically retried, the retry period being a configuration parameter, until the request expires.

Besides request submission, the WMS also implements request management and control functionality such as cancellation and output retrieval. Another feature exists to list all the available resources matching a given job so that if a user (which can, by the way, also be represented by an automatic system) has no matching resources it can temporarily stop submitting. Request status follow-up can be achieved through the Logging&Bookeeping service (L&B) [11], another key service responsible for tracking jobs in terms of events (important points of job life, e.g. submission, transfer from a WMS component to another one, finding a matching CE, starting execution etc.) gathered from various WMS components as well as other Grid services. Each event type carries its specific attributes. The entire architecture is specialized for this purpose and is job-centric: any event is assigned to a unique Grid job identifier. The events are gathered from various WMS components by the L&B producer library, and passed on to the locallogger daemon, running physically close to avoid any sort of network problems in a store&forward fashion.

All the various job management tasks mentioned so far are accomplished by different components basically implemented (mostly in C++, with extensive usage of the Boost

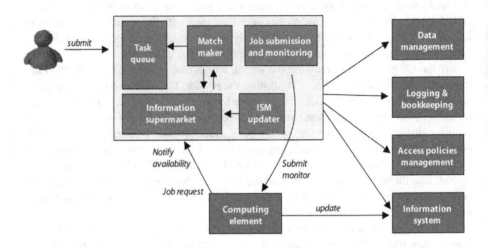

**Fig. 1.** A schetch of the gLite WMS internal architecture showing its interactions with other Grid Services

[12] libraries) as different processes or threads, all communicating via persistent data structures [Figure 1]. As anticipated, one core component is the Match-Maker which sorts out a list of resources satisfying the given requirements. These resources might even include Storage Elements (SE, i.e. the Grid abstraction for a storage resource) if the user requested to need manipulate data. Such returned list of suitable resources is ordered, given that more than one resource could match the specified requirements. The highest-ranked resource will typically be used. The ranking function is provided by the user in the JDL. Just a trivial example how a ranking expression would look like in the JDL:

$$Rank = -other.GlueCEEstimatedResponseTime; \qquad (1)$$

will indicate to send the job to the resource with the lowest estimated queue traversal time.

To avoid the top-ranked resource to be repeatedly chosen upon successively close in time requests, so becoming overrated, before the Local Batch System and the Information Systems could in turn update such dynamic information, a stochastic algorithm can be used to perform a smoothed selection among all the matching resources - weighted according to their actual rank - in such a way to prevent congestion for the initially best ranked resources.

Proper handling of massive data volumes is a very important aspect in production quality Grids (it is maybe worth noting that one of the projects from which EGEE originates was called "DataGrid"). The JDL allows the definition of requirements based on data through an attribute called "DataRequirements" which is structured in such a way to allow users to target experiment-specific catalogs for their jobs and to mix different input data types supported by different data catalogs in the same job description. Logical File Names (LFN), Grid Unique ID-entifiers (GUID), Logical Dataset (LDS) and/or generic queries can be used to retrieve data from SEs. All of them are used by the WMS to query the related Data Catalog for getting back a list of Physical File names (PFN) that are needed by the job as input for processing ([13] for more information). Output data can then be stored to a specified SE and registered to a catalog. While match-making is made between two entities - typically the job and the computing resource, another interesting feature relating data management, called gang-matching allows to take into account, besides CE information, also SEs in the process. A typical use case for gangmatching might be: a job has to run on a CE close to a SE with at least 300 Mb of available space. This translates into a JDL statement like the following:

$$Requirements = anyMatch(other.storage.CloseSEs, target.GlueSAStateAvailableSpace > 300); \quad (2)$$

Getting closer to the core business, one of the most important tasks performed by the WMS is, needless to say, scheduling (some would prefer call it planning, or meta-scheduling). More or less "eager" or "lazy" policies can be supported in this respect. At one extreme, eager scheduling dictates that a job is bound to a resource as soon as possible and, once the decision has been taken, the job is passed to the selected resource(s) for execution, where, very likely, it will end up in some queue. This mechanism is usually referred to as "push mode". At the other extreme, lazy scheduling foresees that the job is held by the WMS until a resource becomes available (hence requiring asyncronous communication with the Information Provider), at which point that resource is matched against the submitted jobs and the job that fits best is passed to the resource; this is called "pull mode". These two approaches are quite symmetrical indeed: eager scheduling implies matching a job against multiple resources, whereas lazy scheduling implies matching a resource against multiple jobs.

The WMS is potentially able, by design, to work with each of these two opposite modes. They both represent a neat grid-aware solution for job scheduling even if, in the course of time, the 'push-mode' emerged as the one and only method actually utilised in the production infrastructure (maybe due to the fact that pull-mode requires asynchronous Information Providers and that some care would be needed to handle notifications to more than just one WMS instance to allow for scalability and to prevent working with a single point of failure). For the record, other Grid meta-scheduling systems are able to enable late binding, apparently much like the pull-mode would behave. Actually such systems, sometimes referred to as "pilot-jobs" frameworks, implement sort of shortcut where a single VO-level scheduler submits "neutral" placeholder jobs - so keeping a constant pressure onto all the available resources - which, once running on the WN, are able to finally call forth end-user jobs. Of course such pilot jobs are seen (and accounted) by the Grid infrastructure as any other user job. A thorough analysis of the *pro et contra* of such emerging scheduling models would be out of the scope of this paper, nevertheless, other than being affected by security implications, they cannot really be considered as an alternative to the pull-mode, in any case, being just a custom layer built on top of the very same infrastructure. Apart from serious security implications which will not be addressed here, one way or the other pilots need to be scheduled within the Grid services and protocols, i.e. a Grid meta-scheduler (direct job submission cannot be considered at this level a Grid-aware solution).

Back to the WMS, the mechanism that allows for a flexible application of such different policies as the push or the pull mode is the decoupling between the collection of information about resources and its usage. This is enabled by a repository of cached resource information collected from the various supported Information Providers, called Information Super-market (ISM), which is available in read-only mode to the matchmaking engine and whose update can be the result of either the arrival of notifications or active polling on resources or some arbitrary combination of both from different source of Information Providers. The ISM represents one notable improvement in the WMS as inherited from the EDG and LCG projects where the information was collected in realtime - so contacting Information Providers for each single request, in a less efficient and reliable fashion.

Reflecting the demand-offer/job-resource symmetry, each single job request is kept in a event based priority queue (different request types have in fact different priority), which recently replaced a data structure called task-queue (TQ, inherited from Alien [14]). This allowed us to remove several locks throughout, once needed to keep the TQ synchronised, and now requests (coded as functors to be executed by a thread pool) line up as soon as they arrive waiting to be processed as stateless as possible, according to the specific situation and/or error condition, while preserving the ability to hold a submission request if no matching resources are immediately found. Such periodic activities (timed events) will in fact re-schedule themselves to show-up at a programmed later time in the priority queue.

Another interesting feature, which has been added quite recently, is represented by the so called "bulk match-making". This optimisation, enabled for collections, allows to perform the match-making for each subset of jobs sharing same characteristics instead of matching each single job. The original collection is partitioned into such subsets according to some significant attributes (JDL attribute "SignificantAttributes") which will identify by the equivalence classes. A typical use-case for specifying significant attributes could be, as an example, parting the original set on "Requirements", "DataRequirements" and "Rank".

Here is a summary of the more relevant functionalities implemented in the gLite WMS:

- Resubmission: shallow or deep
- Stochastic ranking
- Bulk-submission and bulk match-making
- Proxy renewal
- Support for MPI jobs even if the file system is not shared between CE and Worker Nodes (WN)
- Support for execution of all DAG nodes within a single CE - chosen by either user or by the WMS match-maker
- Support for file peeking to access files during job execution
- Load limiting mechanism to prevent system congestion based on machine's vital parameters
- Automatic sandbox files archiving/compression and sharing between jobs
- Match-making with data
- Gang-matching

# 4  Interoperability and Interfacing

Given the typically large number of different parties involved in a Grid infrastructure, interoperability plays a key role to facilitate establishing and coordinating agreements and interactions between all the involved entities. In this respect, the WMS, especially by virtue of his central, mediating role, has to deal with a wide variety of people, services, protocols and more, ranging from users - belonging to different VOs - to other services of the EGEE/gLite infrastructure and to other Grids as well.

For what concerns users, to be able to allow interaction adhering to the SOA model, a Simple Object Access Protocol (SOAP) Web Service has been implemented, its interface being described through a Web Service Description Language (WSDL) specification written in accordance to the WS-I profile, which defines a set of Web Services specifications to promote interoperability. This newly introduced Web Service based implementation replaced a legacy network interface based on a proprietary protocol.It manages user authentication/authorization and operation requests. It runs in an Apache [15] container extended with FastCGI [16] and Grid Site [17] modules. The Fast CGI module implements Common Gateway Interface (CGI) functionality along with some other specific features. The most important advantages of using FastCGI are its performance and persistence. FastCGI applications, in fact, are able to serve, in a multiprocessing fashion, multiple requests, where instances can be dynamically spawned or terminated according to the demand. In particular, an additional control mechanism over unpredictable error conditions such as undefinite hanging has been implemented to automatically terminate a serving process of the pool after a given configurable number of requests. Moreover, the Grid Site module provides an extension to the Apache Web Server for use within Grid frameworks by adding support for Grid Security Infrastructure (GSI), the Virtual Organization Membership Service (VOMS) [18] and file transfer over secure HTTP. It also provides a library for handling Grid Access Control Lists (GACL). The Web Service hosting framework provided by Apache, Grid Site and gSOAP has allowed the development of this front-end interoperable service in C++, giving continuity and consistency with the rest of the coding.

About interoperation with other Grid services, we need to describe in more detail how job management is accomplished by the WMS. A service called Job Submission Service (JSS) is responsible to actually establish an authenticated communication with the selected resource to forward the job and to monitor its execution. To implement such lower level layer Condor-G has been always adopted. A monitoring service, part of the JSS, is also responsible for watching the Condor log files intercepting interesting events concerning active jobs which affect the job state machine and trigger appropriate actions. Every CE supported by Condor-G is then implicitly supported by the WMS as well, in particular the LCG CE (pre-Web-Service Condor-G plus GRAM on the CE) and the gLite CE (pre-WS Condor-G plus Condor-C on the CE). Recently, with the advent of the newest WS-I/BES [19] CE called CREAM [20], a new component of the WMS suite, called Inteface to CREAM Environment (ICE), has been introduced as part of JSS for job management towards CREAM. ICE is a gSOAP/C++ layer which will securely manage job operations to CREAM CEs. In doing so, it subscribes to the gLite CEMon information system [21] in order to asynchronously receive notifications about job status changes. ICE also performs synchronous status polling for unresponsive jobs, in case some notifications are lost.

Interoperation with Information Providers is achieved either syncronously or asyncronously for those providers who support it. We actually do provide interfacing with the Berkely Database Information Index (BDII), support for other providers has been recently dismissed due to lack of use.

About formalisms for defining jobs, the WMS fully endorses the Job Submission Description Language (JSDL). This is an emerging OGF standard which aims at facilitating interoperability in heterogeneous environments, through the use of an XML based job description language that is free of platform and language bindings. JSDL contains a vocabulary and normative XML Schema that facilitate the expression of job requirements and preferences as a set of XML items. What happened in the past and still can happen is that several different organizations accommodate a variety of job management systems, where each system has its own language for describing job submission. This represents a severe obstacle for interoperability. In order to utilize such different systems altogether the involved organizations would have to prepare and maintain a number of different job submission documents, one for each system, basically all describing the same operations. The JSDL represent a significant effort toward unification and has semantics comparable to the current ClassAd-based JDL, its adoption as an OGF approved standard makes it a good candidate for support by the WMS.

On the front of Grid interoperability, having already set up a long-standing interaction with OSG, recent work has been done to enable interoperability with both NorduGrid [22], and its ARC CE, and UNICORE [23], with a contribution to the writing of the Grid Interoperation Now (GIN) [24] profile. More pragmatically, much of the issues concerning interoperability reflects in the way the WMS job-wrapper (the shell script generated by the WMS which surrounds the user job execution and performs basic setup and cleanup operations, downloading/uploading the sandbox, setting the execution environment, logging etc.) is engineered. Due to the diverse nature of resources belonging to one or more Grids, such script must be kept as simple and as robust as possible. The job-wrapper may in fact be running in an unfriendly WN environment where no or little assumption can be made on what is available. Again, due to the pivotal role of this script, a significant work has also been done to extend it in order to encompass all the different requirements expressed by the involved parties (users, VOs and resources) without losing functionality nor generality. To achieve this, a series of hooks is provided in the jobwrapper generation procedure, allowing specific customisations to be inserted by users, VO managers and site administrators. This approach reduces hard-coding, by decoupling general and specific operations, without limiting functionality. For users, prologue and epilogue scripts have been included - to be run before and after the job is executed - basically with the intent of setting and cleaning up the proper environment for "real" jobs; for VOs, a customisation point is foreseen mostly used to hook up the proper middleware version; for similar purposes resource managers are allowed to hook up their scripts throughout several strategic points of the job-wrapper.

Here is a summarized view of the functionality provided in the areas of integration with other services and interoperability:

- Backwards compatibility with LCG-2
- Automatic renewal of credentials
- GridFTP and HTTPS to handle secure file transfer for the sandbox
- Service Discovery for obtaining new serivice endpoints to be contacted
- Support of different mechanisms to populate the ISM from several sources (BDII, R-GMA, CeMon)
- Support for submission and monitoring for the LCG, gLite and CREAM CEs
- Support for Data management interfaces (DLI and StorageIndex)
- Support for JSDL
- Support for Grid Site delegation 2.0
- Interoperability with the american Open Science Grid (OSG), Nordugrid and UNICORE
- Integration with Grid accounting and autorization frameworks
- User prologue/epilogue scripts accompanying the job, more custom scripts allowed to be hooked for use by resource and VO administrators

## 5   Results and Future Developments

As of late 2008, the WMS has been deployed in a large number of multi-user and multi-VO scenarios. Thorough testing and intense troubleshooting have been accomplished during all these years, of course driven by the compelling needs of the LHC experiments. This has led to a significant level of service stability for the current production release. Much of this effort was accomplished using the development test-bed and the preview test-bed, which also includes new components not yet ready to be deployed in production, as it was the case for ICE. In addition, the concept of Experimental Service proved to be very effective: a development instance, attached to the production infrastructure, to be accessed by a selected number of users and immediately installed with the latest available patches.

Now that an acceptable level of sustained stability has been reached, work is being done to further target performance. In particular, after the (effective) introduction of collections, the average match-making time, performed on the full production BDII, has room to improve, especially for single jobs. The next to come release will be able to perform the match-making in parallel thanks to a re-design of the ISM that will be doubled in order to remove some locks with a huge scope at the moment necessary to keep the structure synchronised with readers and writers insisting on it. A read-only copy will be available for readers, the request handlers needing to perform the match-making, while another one will be created in background while purchasing. A pseudo-atomic swap between these two copies will occur periodically and timedly so that the ISM at the moment accessed by reader threads is disabled while, in the mean-time, the freshly purchased one, since then only accessed for writing, will then become available to the readers only. Two ISM instances will be contemporarily present in memory only for limited period - the time needed to carry out purchasing and to wait for the older threads, still pointing to that very copy, to complete - after which such instance can be definitely cleared. Such a design has already been stress tested in a prototypal

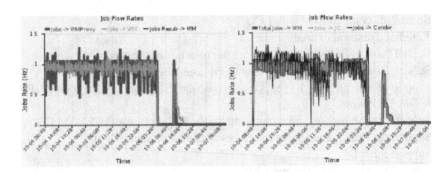

**Fig. 2.** Throughput of about 90.000 jobs/day (>1 Hertz rate as shown by the plot) over a period of more than two days on a stress test by CMS

instance installed as an experimental service, with the collaboration of the CMS experiment; a peak performance of about 100.000 jobs/day were reached for more than two consecutive days [Figure 2].

Also, one of the plus points of pilot-based job scheduling is the ability to match jobs to resources very quickly, as compared to our present gLite WMS. This can basically be done by virtue of the fact that the VO decides user prioritization in advance in such a way that as soon as a pilot on a resource signals its availabiliy to get new jobs, the VO scheduler just scans the job requests list, which is ordered according to a VO-wide policy, so that it can simply stop to the first job matching the requirements. Nothing prevents the gLite WMS to act in a similar way; in fact, the WMS allows each single user to specify a rank function to apply to his jobs, as we have already seen. This is a nice feature, nevertheless it requires matching against the whole ISM, not simply stopping to the first one. Provided a fixed rank (i. e. VO-based, much like pilot jobs frameworks work), the WMS could instead keep the ISM indexed accordingly so that the match-making could just stop to the first matching resource, which at that point will be also the highest ranked one. This will dramatically reduce the time for match-making (stochastic ranking could be done in any case truncating at the first n matching resources). This new model will represent a further step toward providing added value in such a way that, in a future scenario, the WMS will be even able to automatically find the best effective rank for its jobs, using some feed-back mechanism to rate resources according to their performance measured over the entire job's life-cycle (i.e. there is no feed-back at the moment about the quality of status information as published by the Information Provider).

Nonetheless, thanks to the modularity of its design, the present WMS architecture allows for scalability in a more flexible way than pilot submission frameworks. The VO pilot scheduler, in fact, other than being a single point of failure, needs to be able to manage the resource domain space in its entirety. Two different pilot schedulers would require parting the resource domain space to work together, with the consequence of fragmenting the computing offer into two separate sets. On the contrary, several gLite WMS instances can work together over the whole production infrastructure, the total throughput scaling up in an almost linear fashion. Stochastic ranking could be eventually utilised to minimise latencies coming from the Information System update rate.

In fact, this can be done, as compared to the pilot-based approach, right because each WMS instance would get status information by interoperating with a specific Grid service (the Information System, as said) and not directly from pilot jobs.

The next gLite WMS release (3.2), under preparation at the time of writing, will contain several improvements, as the result of the intense restructuring activity which took place during EGEE-II, not yet fully ported into the release branches. Among other things, this new release, aimed at providing a more lightweight and responsive service thanks to a significant redesign of its core component, will be instrumented with all the aforementioned parallel match-making, IPv6 compliancy, support for Grid Site delegation 2.0 and it will be Scientific Linux 5 ready. An official Web Site [25] and Twiki pages have been set up, being kept readily updated, for documentation and support about all the activity concerning the WMS.

# 6 Conclusions

The gLite WMS is designed and implemented to provide a dependable, robust and reliable service for efficient distribution and management of end-user requests for computation, storage, network, instruments and whatever resource may be shared across a production quality Grid. It comes with a fully-fledged set of added-value features to enhance low-level job submission. Thanks to the flexibility of a scalable, fault-tolerant and service-oriented architecture it has been deployed in a number of layouts and scenarios.

After seveal years of operation the WMS has reached sustained stability and a performance targeted at covering the current needs, coming in particular way from High Energy Physics and Bioinformatics. Development continues by supporting enhancements requests expressed by the increasing number of experiments and users of the EGEE community, keeping up with the standardization and definition of Grid services, compliancy to emerging formal and *de-facto* standards and protocols. We will also continue facing the challenge of reaching even higher levels of performance, scalability and reliability to find us prepared to meet the growing demand of the EGEE infrastructure.

# References

1. http://www.eu-egee.org/
2. http://glite.web.cern.ch/glite/
3. http://www.ws-i.org/
4. http://www.ogf.org/
5. JDL Attributes Specification, EGEE-JRA1-TEC-590869-JDL-Attributes-v0-4, https://edms.cern.ch/document/590869/1
6. http://www.cs.wisc.edu/condor/classad/
7. Litzkow, M.J., Livny, M., Mutka, M.W.: Condor-A hunter of idle workstations. In: Proceedings of the 8th International Conf. On Distributed Computing, San Jose, CA USA, pp. 104–111 (1988)
8. http://forge.gridforum.org/sf/projects/glue-wg
9. http://www.globus.org
10. Novotny, J., Tuecke, S., Welch, V.: An Online Credential Repository for the Grid: MyProxy. In: Proceedings of the Tenth International Symposium on High Performance Distributed Computing (HPDC-10). IEEE, Los Alamitos (2001)

11. Dvorak, F., Kouril, D., Krenek, A., Matyska, L., Mulac, M., Pospisil, J., Ruda, M., Salvet, Z., Sitera, J., Skrabal, J., Vocu, M., et al.: Services for Tracking and Archival of Grid Job Information. In: CGW 2005, Cracow - Poland, November 20 - 23 (2005)
12. http://www.boost.org
13. https://edms.cern.ch/document/487871
14. Bagnasco, S., Cerello, P., Barbera, R., Buncic, P., Carminati, F., Saiz, P.: AliEn - EDG interoperability in ALICE, CHEP-2003-TUCP005, p. 3 (June 2003)
15. http://www.apache.org
16. http://www.fastcgi.com
17. http://www.gridsite.org
18. Chiaschini, V., et al.: An Integrated Framework for VO-oriented Authorization, Policy-based Management and Accounting. In: Computing in High Energy and Nuclear Physics (CHEP 2006), T.I.F.R. Mumbai, India, February 13-17 (2006)
19. http://grid.pd.infn.it/NA5/bes-wg.html
20. Andreetto, P., Borgia, S.A., Dorigo, A., Gianelle, A., Marzolla, M., Mordacchini, M., Sgaravatto, M., Zangrando, L., et al.: CREAM: a simple, Grid-accessible, job management system for local computational resources. In: Computing in High Energy and Nuclear Physics (CHEP 2006), T.I.F.R. Mumbai, India, February 13-17 (2006)
21. CEMon, http://grid.pd.infn.it/cemon/field.php
22. http://www.nordugrid.org/
23. http://www.unicore.eu/
24. http://forge.ogf.org/sf/projects/gin
25. http://web.infn.it/gLiteWMS/

# On the Design of a Performance-Aware Load Balancing Mechanism for P2P Grid Systems

You-Fu Yu[1], Po-Jung Huang[1], Kuan-Chou Lai[1],
Chao-Tung Yang[2], and Kuan-Ching Li[3]

[1] Department of Computer and Information Science, National Taichung University,
Taichung, Taiwan, R.O.C.
kclai@mail.ntcu.edu.tw
[2] Department of Computer Science and Information Engineering, Tunghai University,
Taichung, Taiwan, R.O.C.
ctyang@thu.edu.tw
[3] Department of Computer Science and Information Engineering, Providence University,
Taichung, Taiwan, R.O.C.
kuancli@pu.edu.tw

**Abstract.** P2P grid computing systems integrate geographical computing resources across multiple administrative domains. In P2P grid systems, one of the
most important challenges is how to efficiently exploit the load balancing of
distributed computing resources. This paper proposes a performance-aware load
balancing mechanism in order to exploit distributed computing resources in P2P
grid computing systems. The performance-aware load balancing mechanism
supports the capabilities of resource information gathering, job migration and
load balancing. The resource information gathering uses the P2P technique to
collect distributed resource information; the job migration mechanism adopts
the P2P technique to improve the utilization of idle computing resources; and
the decentralized load balancing policy could dynamically adjust the load according to the system performance. We quantify the performance of our performance-aware load balancing mechanism. Experimental results show that our
proposed mechanism could efficiently distribute load in P2P Grid systems.

**Keywords:** Grid, P2P, Job Migration, Load Balancing.

## 1 Introduction

P2P networks and Grids share the same focus on harnessing distributed resources
across multiple administrative domains. Grid computing systems integrate distributed
resources into high-performance computing platforms for supporting transparent
services in virtual organizations; the P2P computing system has the similar objective
of the Grid system to coordinate large sets of distributed resources. Therefore, many
projects attempt to integrate these two complementary technologies to form an ideal
distributed computing system. A P2P Grid [13] is a grid system in which peers handle
the message exchange and the sharing of the distributed resources; and then, the P2P
model could help to ensure Grid scalability. The prototype of a P2P grid is shown in

N. Abdennadher and D. Petcu (Eds.): GPC 2009, LNCS 5529, pp. 269–280, 2009.
© Springer-Verlag Berlin Heidelberg 2009

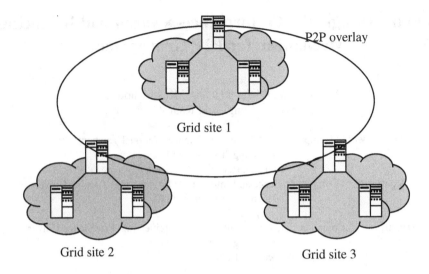

**Fig. 1.** Prototype of a P2P grid

Figure 1. With a multitude of distributed resources, an efficient load balancing across the P2P grid is required for improving the system performance. Due to uneven job arrival patterns and heterogeneous computing capabilities, the computing nodes in one site may be overloaded while others in different sites may be under-loaded. The dramatic load imbalances often waste system resources and cause poor system performance. Therefore, in these P2P grid systems, load balancing mechanism plays a critical role in achieving high utilization of distributed resources.

Load balancing algorithms could be classified as either static or dynamic. In general, dynamic load balancing outperforms static load balancing on the performance of improving load distribution with additional communication and computation overheads; and these additional overheads may be large for large heterogeneous distributed computing systems. Many research works in the literature focused on centralized dynamic load balancing strategies. However, the centralized strategy limits the scalability of the distributed computing systems. Therefore, we focus on the distributed dynamic load balancing approach in this paper.

The important issues in distributed dynamic load balancing mechanisms include the design of load migration mechanisms, the gathering of resource information, and the selection of dynamic load balancing policy. When a job is assigned to a computing node for execution, this job could not be re-scheduled to other computing nodes except that the load balancing mechanism supports the capability of job migration. Job migration represents transferring jobs between two computing nodes. When a job is considered to be migrated from one node to another node, the migration decision of the load balancing mechanism depends on the resource information of each candidate node. To understand the type and availability of distributed resources, the monitoring system collects some status of each node, such as system load, status of job queue, usage rate of CPU, usage status of memory, bandwidth of data transferring, and so on. Lack of knowledge about resources will hamper system performance. Therefore, after deciding the need to initiate load balancing across the system, the load balancing policy determines a suitably under-loaded node to receive load for improving the overall system performance. An effective load balancing policy ensures optimal use of the distributed resources whereby no node remains in an idle state while any other node is being utilized.

In this paper, we present a load balancing mechanism. Basing on the Globus Tool-kits (http://www.globus.org), we develop a prototype of the load balancing mechanism with JXTA technology. The load balancing mechanism consists of the resource monitoring, load balancing and job migration modules. Through the job migration mechanism, this study integrates distributed computing resources across virtual organizations, and improves the utilization of distributed computing resources. We also conduct experiments using a P2P grid environment to analyze the performance of the proposed mechanism. Experimental results confirm that our load balancing mechanism could achieve better performance.

The rest of the paper is organized as follows. In the section that follows, related works in the literature are briefly reviewed. Section 3 describes the load balancing mechanism. Section 4 evaluates the performance of the proposed mechanism. The paper concludes with Section 5.

## 2  Related Works

There are some projects which combine P2P technology with Grid systems. P-Grid [14] makes use of DHT overlays to perform lookups for tasks with an acceptable number of CPU cycles; and P3 [15] makes use of the concept of super-peers. The peers are responsible for mapping jobs to idle peers. Others include Jalapeno [11], SP2A [1], JNGI (http://jngi.jxta.org), and so on.

In this paper, we adopt JXTA technology (http://www.jxta.org) to implement the P2P functions for resource discovering. The JXTA is an open source platform developed by SUN. This platform defines the XML-based framework for message exchange and the network topology integration. JXTA framework could be divided into three layers: core layer, service layer and application layer. JXTA supports the following P2P services: peer discovery protocol, peer information protocol, peer resolver protocol, peer endpoint protocol, pipe binding protocol and rendezvous protocol.

Several research efforts have been focused on the design of dynamic load balancing techniques [6, 8] to optimize the performance of distributed computing systems. The load balancing policies could be broadly classified as sender initiated, receiver initiated, or symmetrically initiated [3, 9]. The dynamic load balancing policy uses the system information to make decision at run time. The general dynamic load balancing policies include Shortest Queue Policy, Never Queue Policy, Maximum Throughput Policy, and Adaptive Separable Policy [5].

Job migration is also an important issue on designing the load balancing mechanism. However, the process of job migration will incur extra system overhead for reserving resources for collecting and maintaining the information of system states [8]. In [9], the authors made the decisions of load balancing depending on the job arrival rates and the job response time. In [7], the authors only considered the CPU and memory state as the influence factors in load balancing. In [12], the author considered the deadline and the job migration cost to adjust load. There are many load indices explicitly or implicitly used in the literature [2, 4] to express the load, e.g., the CPU utilization, the job queue length, and more complicated equations consisting of these simple factors.

There are many resource monitoring systems to aggregate and index resource information. R-GMA[16] use a centralized server to monitor all resource information. Globus MDS2[17] and Ganglia[18] employ the hierarchical approach. Several P2P approaches, e.g., NodeWiz[19], also have been proposed to index and discover resources in a structured P2P network.

## 3   Performance-Aware Load Balancing Mechanism

In this section, we present the performance-aware load balancing mechanism for P2P grids in which each grid site consists of a superpeer and several general peers. Superpeers interact with other superpeers and exchange site information and load characteristics. When a certain site becomes overloaded, job migration can be used to utilize idle resources in remote sites.

To prevent from the disadvantage of the centralized system, our proposed mechanism adopts a loose decision-making approach to decide the job migration. The decentralized information discovery system in each superpeer gathers the resource information of all peers in the same site; and then the load balancing module in each superpeer makes the job migration decisions according to the resource information.

In this paper, we apply the sender-initiated policy to migrate jobs, which waiting in the job queue, from overloaded computing nodes to under-loaded computing nodes for reducing the job waiting time and improving the utilization of the computing resources.

We have implemented a preliminary prototype of our load balancing mechanism. Our system architecture follows the OSGA standard to be implemented by the JXTA environment. The components of the load balancing mechanism can be organized in a layered architecture as shown in Figure 2. The upper layer builds on the services offered by the lower layer in addition to interacting and cooperating with components on the same level. The upper layer consists of resource monitoring, load balancing and job migration; and the lower layer consists of configure service, file transfer, information service and execution management. The configure service module configures the basic setting and initialization of peers and peer-groups. The file transfer

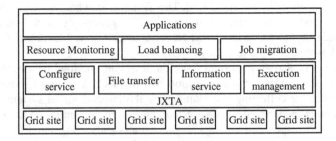

**Fig. 2.** Prototype of the load balancing mechanism

**Fig. 3.** Resource monitoring module

module adopts sockets to implement communication pipes for data, files and messages. The information service module supports the functions of computing resources discovery and integration. The execution management module handles the job execution and Condor job queues (http://www.cs.wisc.edu/condor/) by Condor Java APIs; and this module also supports the functions of the job status handling, job removing, and job submission.

In the upper layer, the resource monitoring module could gather information, for example, CPU speed, CPU type, memory size, memory free space, network bandwidth, and job queue length, across virtual organizations by using a decentralized approach, as shown in Figure 3. The superpeers in a site are responsible for the site resource collection periodically; and the general peers are responsible for supplying themselves information status to superpeers.

Security is an important issue in grid systems. Different virtual organizations require different certifications to ensure the system security. However, since the focus of this study is on the load balancing mechanism, we omit the security issue here.

In this paper, we propose a new load balancing policy: the modified minimal job turnaround time (MJRT) policy. The MJRT policy constructs the neighboring overlays according to the site's performance at first. The sites with the similar system performance would be contained in the same overlay. When the MJRT policy tries to migrate jobs, this policy searches the sites in the neighboring overlay. If there is a neighboring site with sufficient resources, the MJRT policy would migrate the jobs to this neighboring site. However, if there is no neighboring site with sufficient resources, the MJRT policy tries to find the site out of the neighboring overlay. If there is a site with sufficient resources, the MJRT policy would migrate the jobs to this site.

Let $Load_L$ be defined as the average load of the current local site, and $Load_R$ the average load of the current remote site. Let $Barrier_L$ be defined as the load barrier of the local site, and $Barrier_R$ the load barrier of remote sites. $Barrier_L$ and $Barrier_R$ are pre-set by the configure service in each grid site. The MJRT policy takes into account the resource heterogeneity, network bandwidth, job transfer cost, CPU capability and job queue length. When $Load_L \geq Barrier_L$, the load balancing mechanism starts to check the job queue for finding idle jobs. If there is any idle job, the load balancing mechanism would try to find a remote site where $Load_R$ is less than $Barrier_R$, and migrate this idle job to this remote site.

In this policy, the job response time (JRT) of each site is recorded. Assume that there are n jobs scheduled in the site, and then the average job response time is defined as follows:

$$JRT = \frac{1}{n}\sum_{i=1}^{n}(job_i \text{ finish time} - job_i \text{ start time}). \tag{1}$$

This policy also considers the transmission cost which is defined as the follows:

$$\text{Transmission cost} = (\text{code volume} + \text{data volume})/\text{average bandwidth}. \tag{2}$$

Here, we define the average job response time in local site as $JRT_L$, the number of idle jobs in the local job queue as $Idle_L$, and the number of running jobs in the local job queue as $Run_L$. Then, the time period of jobs waiting in the queue could be calculated as $Idle_L * JRT_L$, and the time period of finishing the execution of jobs in the CPU could be calculated as $Run_L*1/2*JRT_L$. Therefore, $Finish\_Time_L$ is defined as the time to finish the execution of a job waiting in the local queue.

$$Finish\_Time_L = JRT_L + Idle_L * JRT_L + \frac{1}{2}Run_L * JRT_L. \tag{3}$$

We also define the time finishing the execution of a job which is migrated to a remote site as $Finish\_Time_R$:

$$Finish\_Time_R = \text{Transmission cost} + JRT_R + Idle_R * JRT_R + \frac{1}{2}Run_R * JRT_R. \tag{4}$$

This MJRT policy would choose the remote site which has the minimal value of $Finish\_Time_R$ as the candidate site.

In the initial phase, the load balancing mechanism would set the load barrier of each site and setup the overlays of the neighboring sites. The steps of this MJRT policy are described as follows:

1. Set the load barrier ($Barrier_L$ and $Barrier_R$) of each site.
2. Construct the overlays of the neighboring sites.
3. When $Load_L \geq Barrier_L$, this site is overloaded; then, the load balancing mechanism starts to activate the job queue checking process.
4. The job migration mechanism checks whether there is any idle job waiting in the local job queue or not. If there is any idle job in the job queue, then step 5 is executed; else stop this policy.
5. The job migration mechanism starts to find the remote site in the neighboring sites, in which $Load_R$ is less than $Barrier_R$. If this site exists, then step 6 is executed; else go to step 7.
6. If there is a remote neighboring site whose $Finish\_Time_R$ is less than $Finish\_Time_L$, then the MJRT policy migrates this idle job to this remote site and stop this policy.
7. The job migration mechanism starts to find the remote site out of the neighboring sites, in which $Load_R$ is less than $Barrier_R$. If this site exists, then step 8 is executed; else stop this policy.

8. If there is a remote site whose Finish_Time$_R$ is less than Finish_Time$_L$, then the MJRT policy migrates this idle job to this remote site; else stop this policy.

The pseudo codes of the MJRT policy are described as follows.

```
Set the load barrier of each site and construct the overlay of the neighboring sites
if (LoadL ≧ BarrierL )
{
    Checking job queue
    if (exist.Job_idle)
    {
        if (LoadR in the neighboring sites < BarrierR)
        {
            if (Finish_TimeR in the neighboring sites < Finish_TimeL)
            {
                Migrating the idle job to the site with the minimal Finish_TimeR
            }
        }
        else
        {
            if (Finish_TimeR out of the neighboring sites < Finish_TimeL)
            {
                Migrating the idle job to the site with the minimal Finish_TimeR
            }
        }
    }
}
```

## 4 Preliminary Experimental Results

In the preliminary experiment, we adopt JXTA 2.5.1, Java 1.6.0, and Condor 6.7.20 to implement our load balancing mechanism in Taiwan Unigrid (www.unigrid.org.tw) for performance evaluation. In order to simplify the experimental environment, we assume that there are three sites, and that each site consists of one superpeer and 2 general peers. However, our approach could be extended to more complex systems. In this experiment, we assume that the sites 1 and 2 have better performance, and the site 3 has the worst performance. Table 1 shows the specification of our experimental platform, and host201 is in charge of job submission. Due to that site 1 and site 2 have the similar CPU speed and memory size, site 1 and site 2 are in the same neighboring overlay. However, we could elaborate the concept of the neighboring overlay on more performance indexes.

For the comparison of the performance of the MJRT policy, we also implement 2 policies: FIFO (First In First Out) and JRT (Job Turnaround Time) [10] policies. The

**Table 1.** Specification of our experimental platform

| Site | Hosts | Peer type | CPU Speed | Memory size | execution time per job |
|------|-------|-----------|-----------|-------------|------------------------|
| 1 | host201 | superpeer | Intel Pentium 4 3.40GHz X 2 | 512M | about 8 minutes |
| 1 | host204 | general peer | Intel Pentium D 2.80GHz X2 | 512M | about 9 minutes |
| 1 | host205 | general peer | Intel Pentium 4 3.40GHz X 2 | 512M | about 8 minutes |
| 2 | host206 | superpeer | Intel Pentium 4 3.40GHz X 2 | 512M | about 8 minutes |
| 2 | host207 | general peer | Intel Pentium 4 3.40GHz X 2 | 512M | about 8 minutes |
| 2 | host208 | general peer | Intel Pentium 4 3.40GHz X 2 | 512M | about 8 minutes |
| 3 | host221 | superpeer | Intel Pentium 4 2.00GHz | 256M | about 11 minutes |
| 3 | host222 | general peer | Intel Pentium 4 2.00GHz | 256M | about 11 minutes |
| 3 | host223 | general peer | Intel Pentium 4 2.00GHz | 256M | about 11 minutes |

FIFO policy migrates jobs whenever there is an under-load site, i.e., when a site is overloaded, it will try to find an under-loaded site to be the target site of job migration. In the FIFO policy, one overloaded site makes the migration decision only according to the load barrier. The JRT policy extends the FIFO policy by taking into account the resource heterogeneity, network bandwidth, job transfer cost, CPU capability and job queue length. In this policy, the job response time (JRT) of each site is recorded. This policy would choose the remote site which has the minimal value of Finish_Time$_R$ as the candidate site.

In this study, we focus on the efficiency of the load balancing mechanism. Therefore, in order to evaluate the performance influence by different load balancing policies, we adopt the jobs with similar execution time and transmission time behaviors. However, the heterogeneous jobs could be applied in this mechanism. All jobs are submitted from one site at the same time, and record the experimental data every 20 seconds. After submitting 50, 100, 150, and 200 jobs from host201, we record the total job response time and the status of the CPU loads. The experimental results are shown in Figure 4.

Figure 4 shows the experimental results for different numbers of jobs by three load balancing policies. We could observe that the FIFO policy wastes more time on waiting job migration. When the number of jobs increases, the performance decay becomes obvious by applying the FIFO policy. In general, MJRT policy outperforms

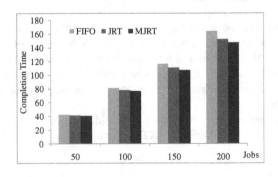

**Fig. 4.** Completion time by applying different policies

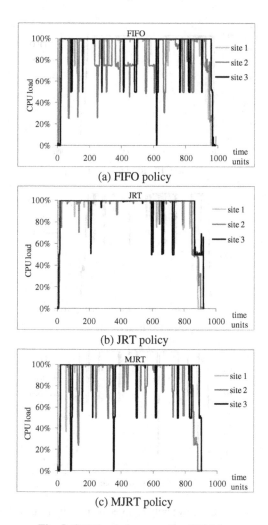

**Fig. 5.** CPU loads for executing 200 jobs

FIFO and JRT policies. It is reasonable that the MJRT policy would migrate the idle jobs to the neighboring sites in under-load. Due to that the FIFO policy migrates idle jobs from overloaded site to light-loaded sites depending on the CPU load; it is possible that jobs may be migrated to the site with poor computing ability. The FIFO policy could not ensure that the job migration will improve the system performance. However, the MJRT policy considers not only the load barrier but also the communication bandwidth and the computing capability. Therefore, the MJRT policy not only reduces the system idle time but also migrates jobs to the sites which have better execution performance.

Figure 5 shows that CPU loads for executing 200 jobs in three sites by different policies. When the system load of site 1 reaches to the maximal bound after submitting 200 jobs, the idle jobs are migrated from the site 1 to site 2 or site 3 by FIFO or

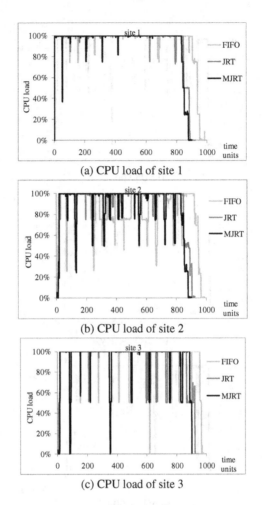

**Fig. 6.** CPU loads by applying three policies in distinct sites

JRT policies. However, due to that site 1 and site 2 are in the same neighboring over-lay, the MJRT policy would migrate the idle jobs from site 1 to site 2 at first till the CPU load of site 2 reaches the threshold, and then start to migrate the idle jobs from site 1 to site 3. In general, the finish time of 200 jobs' execution by adopting the MJRT policy is shorter than those by adopting the FIFO and JRT policies.

Figure 5(a) shows that CPU loads for executing 200 jobs in three sites by FIFO policy. When the site 2 or site 3 is idle, site 1 would migrate jobs to site 2 or site 3. Therefore, the status of the surges of CPU loads by applying the FIFO policy is more obvious than that by applying the JRT policy, i.e., the variation of the CPU load by applying JRT policy is more stable than that by applying FIFO policy, as shown in Figure 5(b).

Figure 6 shows that the CPU loads by applying three policies in distinct sites. From observing Figure 6, the MJRT policy outperforms FIFO and JRT policies. It is reasonable that the search burden of finding the target site for the overloaded job migration in the MJRT policy is less than that in the FIFO/JRT policies. Therefore, the site adopting the MJRT policy could spend more computing resources in the job execution. In Figure 6(a), the experimental results show that the occurrence of job migration in site 1 is comparatively less than that in site 2 or site 3. It is reasonable that the job submission starts from site 1; therefore, the site 1 would keep busy almost before finishing all jobs. The reason that the occurrence of job migration in site 2 appears more frequently is that the site 2 has the better performance, so that site 2 has a higher priority to receive jobs from other sites.

## 5 Conclusions

In this paper, we propose an efficient decentralized load balancing mechanism for the P2P Grid systems. In our experiment, there are two kinds of computing nodes: one is called the super-node and the other is called the general node. The super-peers are responsible for supporting the site information to the job migration mechanism, and the general peers are responsible for supporting the resource information of themselves to the super-peers. Therefore, the resource information system could be distributed efficiently. This proposed load balancing mechanism consists of resource monitoring, load balancing and job migration. It could use the decentralized resource monitoring system to gather the resource information. After obtaining the resource information of each site, the load balancing module could make the job migration decision according to the system performance.

The experimental results show that the load balancing mechanism indeed could balance the load of executing jobs. Therefore, the proposed load balancing mechanism is seen to be efficient and practical for the dynamic load balancing systems.

**Acknowledgments.** This study was sponsored by the National Science Council, Taiwan, Republic of China under contract number: NSC 97-2221-E-142 -001 -MY3.

## References

1. Amoretti, M., Zanichelli, F., Conte, G.: SP2A: a service-oriented framework for P2P-based Grids. In: Proceedings of the 3rd international workshop on Middleware for Grid computing (November 2005)
2. Ferrari, D., Zhou, S.: A load index for dynamic load balancing. In: Proceedings of 1986 ACM Fall Joint Computer Conference, pp. 684–690 (1986)
3. Eager, D.L., Lazowska, E.D., Zahorjan, J.: A comparison of receiver initiated and sender initiated adaptive load sharing. In: Performance Evaluation 1986, pp. 53–68 (1986)
4. Bosque Orero, J.L., Gil Marcos, D., Pastor, L.: Dynamic Load Balancing in Heterogeneous Clusters. In: Parallel and Distributed Computing and Networks (2004)
5. Koyama, K., Shimizu, K., Ashihara, H., Zhang, Y., Kameda, H.: Performance Evaluation of Adaptive Load Balancing Policies in Distributed Systems. In: Proceedings of the Singapore International Conference on Networks/ International Conference on Information Engineering 1993, pp. 606–611 (1993)
6. Yan, K.Q., Wang, S.C., Chang, C.P., Lin, J.S.: A hybrid load balancing policy underlying grid computing environment. Computer Standards & Interfaces 29, 161–173 (2007)

7. Lei, S., Yuyan, S., Lin, W.: Effect of Scheduling Discipline on CPU-MEM Load Sharing System. In: Sixth International Conference on Grid and Cooperative Computing, August 2007, pp. 242–249 (2007)
8. Dandamudi, S.P.: Sensitivity evaluation of dynamic load sharing in distributed systems. IEEE Concurrency 6(3), 62–72 (1998)
9. Shah, R., Veeravalli, B., Misra, M.: On the design of adaptive and decentralized load balancing algorithms with load estimation for computational Grid Environments. IEEE Transactions on Parallel and Distributed Systems (December 2007)
10. Lin, S.-J., Huang, M.-C., Lai, K.-C., Huang, K.-C.: Design and Implementation of Job Migration Policies in P2P Grid Systems. In: IEEE Asia-Pacific Services Computing Conference (2008)
11. Therning, N., Bengtsson, L.: Jalapeno: secentralized Grid computing using peer-to-peer technology. In: CF 2005: Proceedings of the 2nd conference on Computing Frontiers (May 2005)
12. Yang, C.T., Li, K.C., Chiang, W.C., Shih, P.C.: Design and Implementation of TIGER Grid: an Integrated Metropolitan-Scale Grid Environment, National Science Council, Taiwan (R.O.C.), under grants no. NSC93-2213-E-126-010 and NSC92-2218-E- 164-002
13. Briquet, C., et al.: Scheduling data-intensive bags of tasks in P2P grids with bittorrent-enabled data distribution. In: ACM Proceedings of the second workshop on Use of P2P, GRID and agents for the development of content networks, pp. 39–48 (2007)
14. Hauswirth, M., Schmidt, R.: An overlay network for resource discovery in Grids. In: Second International Workshop on Grid and Peer-to-Peer Computing Impacts on Large Scale Heterogeneous Distributed Database Systems (GLOBE 2005) (2005)
15. Oliveira, L., Lopes, L., Silva, F.: P3: Parallel peer to peer: An internet parallel programming environment. In: Proceedings of the International Workshop on Peer-to-Peer Computing; A workshop co-located with Networking 2002 (2002)
16. Cooke, A.W., et al.: The Relational Grid Monitoring Architecture: Mediating Information about the Grid. Journal of Grid Computing 2(4) (December 2004)
17. Czajkowski, S., Fitzgerald, K., Foster, I., Kesselman, C.: Grid Information Services for Distributed Resource Sharing. In: Proc. of HPDC (2001)
18. Massie, M.L., Chun, B.N., Culler, D.E.: Ganglia Distributed Monitoring System: Design, Implementation, and Experience. In: Parallel Computing, vol. 30, pp. 817–840 (2004)
19. Basu, S., Banerjee, S., Sharma, P., Lee, S.-J.: NodeWiz: Peer-to-Peer Resource Discovery for Grids. In: Proc. of Cluster Computing and the Grid (CCGrid) (2005)

# A Mediation Framework for the Implementation of Context-Aware Access Control in Pervasive Grid-Based Healthcare Systems

Vassiliki Koufi, Flora Malamateniou, and George Vassilacopoulos

University of Piraeus, Department of Digital Systems, 80, Karaoli & Dimitriou Str.,
18534 Piraeus, Greece
{vassok,flora,gvass}@unipi.gr

**Abstract.** Healthcare is an increasingly collaborative enterprise involving many individuals and organizations that coordinate their efforts toward promoting quality and efficient delivery of healthcare through the use of pervasive healthcare systems. In such systems, interoperability is highly demanded in all the levels including the service and data levels. This paper presents a distributed context-aware access control mechanism for pervasive process-based healthcare systems built on a Grid infrastructure. The system uses the Business Process Execution Language (BPEL) to automate healthcare processes on a Grid infrastructure. Client applications are portal-based, operate on mobile devices and can use radio frequency identification (RFID) technology for wireless capture of identification data. The proposed access control mechanism acts as a mediator between the clients and the underlying system and adheres to the least privilege principle by allowing authorized access to integrated data in a ubiquitous and pervasive manner. The mechanism is built on a software platform that exploits agent and workflow technology, thus providing robustness, high flexibility and fault tolerance in authorization procedures.

**Keywords:** Grid portal application, Business Process Execution Language, context-awareness, role-based access control, software agents, workflows.

## 1 Introduction

Healthcare delivery involves a broad range of in-patient, out-patient and emergency healthcare services, typically performed by a number of geographically distributed and organizationally disparate healthcare providers requiring increased collaboration and coordination of their activities in order to provide shared and integrated care when and where needed [1]. As healthcare providers are mostly hosting diverse information systems, promoting quality and efficient delivery of healthcare requires the use of interoperable healthcare information systems (HIS). With the advent of pervasive and ubiquitous computing technologies, the requirements for information technology to healthcare process alignment can be met with the least possible intervention from the participating parties. For example, an HIS architecture that places emphasis on supporting collaboration and coordination among various healthcare services can

N. Abdennadher and D. Petcu (Eds.): GPC 2009, LNCS 5529, pp. 281–292, 2009.

also fulfil the requirements to support internal mobility of healthcare professionals (e.g. during ward rounds) that may lead to a pervasive computing infrastructure. Thus, patient information which is scattered around disparate and geographically dispersed systems should be readily accessed in a pervasive manner by authorized users at the point of care. On these grounds, this paper describes a healthcare information system which is based on a service-oriented architecture (SOA) and is implemented in a Grid environment.

In the aforementioned system, healthcare processes are modeled using the Business Process Execution Language (BPEL) and are expressed as web services to enable integrated access to healthcare information which is scattered around disparate and geographically dispersed systems. These web services are high-level services that are created using Grid database services as the basic primitives. Grid database services offer capabilities such as data federation and distributed query processing and are generated by using Open Grid Services Architecture - Data Access and Integration (OGSA-DAI) [2], a middleware product which is part of the Globus Toolkit [3]. They are built as an extension to Web services and deliver added-value, high level data management functionality. For example, unlike traditional Web service solutions, OGSA-DAI supports dynamic creation of services which may combine and transform data from multiple distributed data resources (e.g. via a Distributed Query Processing service) in order to present an integrated or even derived view of the data [4]. In the remainder of this paper, we refer to web services that are defined, deployed and executed using these service-oriented Grid computing infrastructures as Grid services [5]. The healthcare processes modeled can be executed through personal digital assistants (PDAs) by means of a customized Grid portal application that complies with the restrictions imposed by PDA technology (e.g. limited display size). Moreover, radio frequency identification (RFID) technology is used for user identification and for accessing healthcare processes in a pervasive manner.

One important consideration during the development of such an HIS is fulfilling the requirement of protecting patient privacy by guaranteeing that patients fully control who sees any portion of their records, and to safeguard their information by adhering to the least privilege principle which requires a tight matching of permissions to actual usage and need. Hence, the enforcement of the least privilege principle requires continuous adjustments of the sets of user permissions to ensure that, at any time, users assume the minimum sets of permissions required for the execution of each task of a healthcare process. As access to patient information must be provided in a timely manner, the security framework employed in the HIS should meet the most stringent requirements for scalability, flexibility, performance and reliability.

Workflows and Agents Development Environment (WADE) is a common software platform suitable for the development of mission critical applications by exploiting agent and workflow technologies [6]. In this context, WADE constitutes a suitable platform for the development of an access control framework to be incorporated in the system described above. This framework is based on the role-based access control (RBAC) paradigm and is context-aware. As such, it incorporates the advantages of broad, role-based permission assignment and administration across object types, as in role-based access control (RBAC) [7], and yet provides the flexibility for adjusting role permissions on individual objects during a BPEL process enactment in accordance with the current context. During the execution of a process instance, changes in contextual information are sensed and user permissions are adapted to the minimum required for completing a job. Relevant access control policies are enforced at both the BPEL task level and the Grid database service level.

## 2   Using Agent and Workflow Technology for Access Control

During the last few years there has been a growing interest in the utilization of agent-based systems in a wide range of applications. Moreover, there has been a trend towards using agent technology in conjunction with workflow technology in the context of service-oriented architectures implemented in a grid environment [8][9][10][11] [12][13].

Healthcare applications often have life-or-death dimensions as a patient's life can hinge on the instant availability and accuracy of information. At the same time, data privacy and security issues are of paramount importance. Thus, appropriate safeguards of a technical nature should be used to secure personal information against unauthorized access, collection, use, disclosure or disposal. To this end, effective access control mechanisms should be employed that meet the most stringent security requirements while they comply with the requirements of high performance, reliability, robustness, high flexibility and fault tolerance. Making authorization decisions in such a distributed environment is a fairly complex task involving more than one healthcare provider of the health district. The conjunction of agent and workflow technologies provides the ability to execute such complex tasks and helps managing the complexity of the distribution in terms of both administration and fault tolerance. Hence, it can offer great benefits to the development of the aforementioned access control mechanisms.

WADE is essentially a middleware for the development of distributed agent-based applications exploiting the workflow metaphor for system logics definition. In WADE each workflow is expressed as a Java class with a well defined structure, thus combining the advantages of workflow technology with the power and flexibility of an actual programming language like Java. Although WADE can be used to target high level orchestration of services provided by different systems, it primarily targets at the implementation of the internal behavior of each single system. Thus, it is particularly suitable for applications that imply the execution of possibly long and fairly complex tasks such as those concerned with access control policy enforcement.

WADE is the main evolution of JADE, a popular Open Source framework that facilitates the development of interoperable multi-agent systems [14]. Furthermore, unlike the majority of existing workflow systems that provide a powerful centralized engine, in WADE each agent can embed a "micro workflow engine" and a complex process can be carried out by a set of cooperating agents each one executing a piece of the process [6].

## 3   Related Work

The trend towards an agent-oriented architectural approach to dealing with communications, system and application-level security is evident in the last few years [15][16]

[17][18]. However, they are not concerned with access control in the context of a pervasive, process-based healthcare system built on a Grid infrastructure. Such systems require a customized access control mechanism that will address the access control issues arising during BPEL process enactment. In particular, it will address the deficiencies of the access control mechanisms of the system's main components, namely BPEL and OGSA-DAI.

Security aspects, such as authentication and access control, are not standardized through BPEL, but are left to the implementation of BPEL compliant process engine [19][20][21]. In turn, grid middleware, namely Open Grid Services Architecture - Data Access and Integration (OGSA-DAI) [2], that facilitate data federation and distributed query processing through the use of grid database services provides relatively simple and static mechanisms regarding authorization and access control [22]. Hence, several studies have been conducted regarding both the enforcement of access control in BPEL [19][20][21][22] and the enhancement of access control mechanisms used by Grid middleware services [23][24]. Most of these studies argue that both BPEL and Grid middleware services can benefit from incorporating properly enhanced RBAC mechanisms [7].

In this paper a WADE based security mechanism is proposed for the realization of authorized access both to BPEL tasks and to Grid database services invoked by them at run time. The mechanism acts as a mediator between the clients and the underlying system and adheres to the least privilege principle by allowing authorized access to integrated data in a ubiquitous and pervasive manner.

## 4  Motivating Scenario

The basic motivation for this research stems from our involvement in a recent project concerned with defining and automating cross-organizational healthcare processes spanning a health district in order to implement a district-wide, process-oriented healthcare information system. The interoperability requirements and the stringent security needs of the system, where sensitive patient information is used, motivated this work and provided some of the background supportive information for developing the prototype presented in this paper.

Typically, a health district consists of one district general hospital (DGH) and a number of peripheral hospitals and health centers. As patient information is scattered around disparate and geographically dispersed systems and patient referrals are usually made among various healthcare providers within a district (e.g. for hospitalization, for outpatient consultation or for performing specialized medical procedures), there is a need to ensure that an interoperable environment is created and that authorized access to healthcare process tasks and to patient information required through the execution of these tasks is provided.

Suppose a healthcare process which is composed of the medical activities that may be performed during a physician's clinical ward round. Among others, this process involves assessing patient's condition, accessing the patient's medical record and issuing medical orders. As an example, consider the case where a patient's physician wishes to issue a radiological request for one of his/her patients. The request is sent to the radiology department of the hospital which schedules the radiological procedure

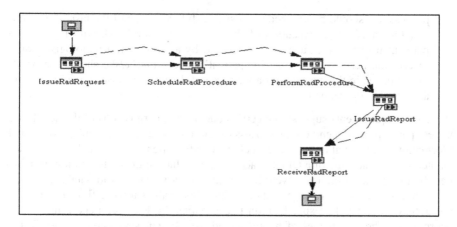

**Fig. 1.** Radiological request process model using IBM WebSphere Workflow

requested and sends a message to the requesting physician notifying him/her on the date and time scheduled. After performing the radiological procedure requested, the radiologist accesses the relevant part of the patient record, writes a radiological report and sends it to the requesting physician.

Figure 1 shows a high-level view of the healthcare sub-process concerned with radiology orders using the IBM WebSphere Workflow build-time tool [25]. In this business process two organizational units of the hospital are involved: the clinical department and the radiology department of a hospital. Two of the roles participating in the healthcare process are: clinical physician and radiologist. Table 1 shows an extract of authorization requirements regarding task execution and related data access privileges assigned to these roles, respectively. Similar requirements exist in many healthcare application fields where request-service situations occur [26].

From an authorization perspective, the healthcare process of Figure 1 surfaces several higher-level requirements with regard to task execution and, consequential, Grid database services invocation. These requirements include the following:

- Task execution – In certain circumstances the candidates for a task instance execution should be dynamically determined and be either a sub-group of the authorized users or only one, specific authorized user. For example, a certain radiological request (issued by a physician) should be routed only to the sub-group of radiologists who hold the relevant sub-specialty (e.g. CT or MRI) and the radiological report (issued by a radiologist) should be routed only to the requesting physician.

- Data access - Given that each role holder can execute certain tasks, he/she should be allowed to exercise a dynamically determined set of permissions on data objects, accrued from these tasks, under certain circumstances. For example, during the execution of the "IssueRadRequest" task, a physician is allowed to read patient record data and to issue (write, edit and send) radiological requests only for his/her patients while on duty and within the hospital premises.

- Permission propagation - Some role holders should receive additional permissions on certain data objects in order to effectively execute a task but these permissions should be revoked upon successful execution of the task. For example, for an effective execution of the "IssueRadReport" task with regard to a patient, in response to a request submitted by a physician, a radiologist should receive the permission to read the patient's record but he/she should not be allowed to retain this permission after successful task execution (i.e. after writing and sending the report).

The above requirements suggest that certain data access permissions of the healthcare process participants depend on the process execution context. In particular, contextual information available at access time, such as user-to-patient proximity, location of attempted access and time of attempted access, can influence the authorization decision regarding task execution and, given this permission, associated Grid database service invocation to access the relevant data objects. This enables a more flexible and precise access control policy specification that satisfies the least privilege principle by incorporating the advantages of having broad, role-based permissions across BPEL tasks and data object types, like RBAC, yet enhanced with the ability to simultaneously support the following features: (a) predicate-based access control, limiting user

**Table 1.** Extract of authorization requirements for the healthcare process of Figure 1 (Task execution and data access permissions)

| | Authorization Requirement |
|---|---|
| 1 | PHYSs may issue requests for radiological procedures on patients while on duty and within the hospital premises (IssueRadRequest). |
| 1.1 | PHYSs may write radiological requests for their current patients. |
| 1.2 | PHYSs may edit radiological requests for their current patients before sent. |
| 1.3 | PHYSs may send radiological requests for their current patients. |
| 1.4 | PHYSs may cancel radiological requests for their current patients after sent. |
| 1.5 | PHYSs may read patient records of their current patients. |
| 2 | RDDs holding a specific sub-specialty may perform only relevant radiological procedures on patients (PerformRadProcedure). |
| 3 | RDDs may issue patient-oriented radiological reports on request by physicians (IssueRadReport). |
| 3.1 | RDDs may read patient record data before sending their radiological reports. |
| 3.2 | RDDs may write patient-oriented radiological reports for their current patients. |
| 3.3 | RDDs may edit patient-oriented radiological reports for their current patients before sent. |
| 3.4 | RDDs may send patient-oriented radiological requests for their current patients. |
| 3.5 | RDDs may cancel patient-oriented radiological reports after sent. |
| 3.6 | RDDs may read past patient radiological reports prepared by them. |
| 4 | PHYSs may receive patient radiological reports issued by radiologists only if requested by them (ReceiveRadReport). |
| 4.1 | PHYSs may read the requested radiological reports on their patients. |
| 4.2 | PHYSs may read patient records of their patients. |

access to specific data objects, (b) a permission propagation function from one role holder to another in certain circumstances, and (c) determining qualified task performers during a process instance based not only on the role-to-task permission policy, specified at process build time, but also on application data processed during the process instance. In addition, the model should not incur any significant administrative overhead, should be self-administering to a great extent and meet strong requirements in terms of scalability, flexibility, high performance and fault tolerance.

## 5  Security Mediation Framework

Figure 2 illustrates a high-level view of the system architecture, which is described by a three-tier model, comprising the PDA client, the server site of the DGH and the Grid which, in turn, comprises remote data resources. The latter are heterogeneous and reside in geographically distributed and organizationally disparate healthcare providers within a health district.

Figure 3 illustrates a high-level view of the security mechanism incorporated into the system with the objective to enhance security of patient information by focusing on authorization and access control over the tasks comprising the BPEL processes and the underlying Grid database services. In essence, the mechanism is a distributed multi-agent security framework which serves as a mediation layer that handles access requests during client interactions with the underlying system. In particular, it mediates between subjects (healthcare professionals) and objects (BPEL tasks and Grid database services) to decide whether access of a given subject to given object should be permitted or denied by taking into account the current context.

In this mediation framework, agents are held in containers running on different servers which are distributed across healthcare organizations of a health district. In

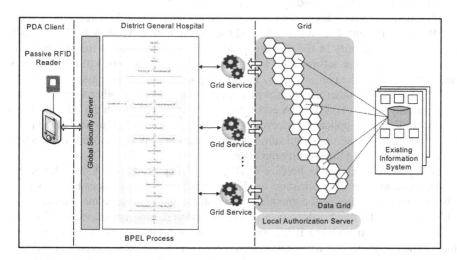

**Fig. 2.** Architecture of a pervasive process-based healthcare system

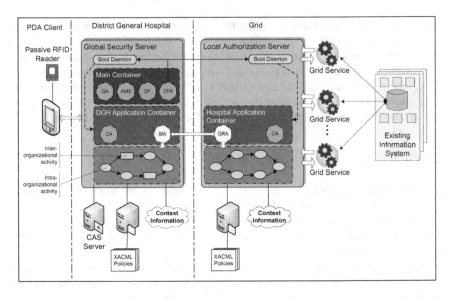

**Fig. 3.** Security architecture

this way, a distributed runtime environment is formed where agents process access requests and determine the requestors' access rights. Agents' tasks involved in this procedure are defined according to the workflow metaphor. The set of the aforementioned containers is called a platform. There is one main container which is deployed in a server at the DGH site and a number of peripheral containers deployed in servers residing at the healthcare organizations of the health district. The main container is the first one to start and all other containers register to it at bootstrap time. In each server, containers are activated by a BootDaemon process.

The main container holds three special agents, the Agent Management System (AMS), the Directory Facilitator (DF) and the Configuration Agent (CFA). The AMS represents the authority in the platform, namely it is the only agent that can activate platform management actions such as creating/killing other agents, killing containers and shutting down the platform [14]. The DF implements the yellow pages service by means of which the other agents advertise their services and find other agents offering services they need [14]. The CFA is responsible for interacting with the boot daemons and controlling the application lifecycle. A Gateway Agent (GA) also held at the main container, handles the communication between the client portal and the multi-agent system implementing the security mediator.

Each peripheral container holds a WADE-specific agent, namely Controller Agent (CA), and a number of application-specific agents. The CA is responsible for supervising activities in the local container and for all the fault tolerance mechanisms provided by WADE. Application-specific agents undertake the enforcement of access control policies on both the BPEL tasks and the Grid database services invoked by them. The logics of interactions that need to be carried out by the agents in order to ensure authorized access to the target objects are described as workflows. Thus, application-specific agents are designed to include a light workflow engine that will execute these workflows. In our environment, there are two kinds of application-specific agents, developed in WADE:

- Service Integration Agent (SIA): It is held in a container deployed on a server at the DGH site and manages user permissions on BPEL tasks.
- Grid Resource Agent (GRA): It is held in a container on a server at the site of each healthcare organization participating in a healthcare process and manages user permissions on Grid database services.

During user interaction with the system, application specific agents sense the context, collect contextual information and take appropriate actions according to the underlying security policies. The contextual information influencing authorization decisions is determined by a pre-defined set of attributes that may relate to the user (e.g. user roles, user/patient relationship), to the environment (e.g. client location and time of attempted access) and to the data resource provider (e.g. the healthcare organization's security policy). For example, the permissions of a physician accessing the system via his/her PDA, are adapted depending on his/her identity (included in his/her Community Authorization Service - CAS certificate), location and time of access as well as the security policy of each healthcare organization where a portion of the requested information is stored. Changes in user and environment context are sensed by both agents, whereas changes in resource context are sensed and dealt with by the GRA lying at each Grid node.

In order to validate the proposed architecture, an experimental, proof-of-concept system prototype has been developed that provides part of the functionality presented in the aforementioned motivating scenario. In the system prototype, CAS certificates are issued to healthcare professionals by a Community Authorization Service (CAS) server which has been set up at the DGH site. This server constitutes the Certificate Authority of the health district and is capable of managing policies and governing access to the health district's resources. However, for our purposes, its responsibility is confined to managing the users' role memberships. In particular, the CAS certificates issued to healthcare professionals specify only user-to-role assignments in the form of security assertions, expressed in Security Assertion Markup Language (SAML) [27][28]. The CAS certificate accompanies every request (either for task execution or Grid database service invocation) issued through the system front-end (i.e. the portal). The roles used in the certificate are functional and, hence, they remain unchanged until the certificate expires as they are independent of the constraints held at the time of attempted access.

The mapping of the aforementioned roles to the relevant permissions is performed by means of access control policies expressed by using the RBAC profile of eXtensible Access Control Markup Language (XACML) [28]. These policies are specified at the site where the target object (task or Grid database service) resides (tasks are hosted on the BPEL engine at the DGH site and Grid database services are hosted on the web servers at the hospital sites) and assist in the derivation of the exact permissions a subject should acquire for performing a task.

In particular, each time a request is issued for a task execution, the enforcement of a fine-grained, context-dependent access control policy involves a set of activities which are coordinated via a workflow. These are the following:

i.   *CAS certificate processing* - It involves extracting the user's roles from CAS certificate that accompanies the request.
ii.  *Context acquisition* - It involves collecting the relevant context information.
iii. *Task-related policy retrieval* - It involves specifying the relevant permissions regarding access to BPEL tasks using the file(s) where the XACML policies are stored. This file resides on the same server of the DGH site with the BPEL engine.
iv.  *Permission derivation (on BPEL tasks)* - It involves refining the policies retrieved during activity (iii) in order to adjust to the current state. Thus, task execution is initiated and the associated Grid service is invoked.
v.   *Permission derivation (on database services)* - It involves the derivation of permissions on the Grid database services, associated with the Grid service, that need to be executed in order to obtain the medical information requested. After the Grid database services have been identified, a request for their invocation is issued which is accompanied by the same CAS certificate. This triggers the execution of a fairly complex task that involves the concurrent execution of a number of workflow task instances distributed on the healthcare settings that hold portions of the medical information requested. The workflow from which the instances are generated consists of activities similar to the activities (i)-(iv) described above and aims at deriving the permissions a subject should acquire for the invocation of the relevant Grid database services. In particular, the roles extracted from this certificate are used in order to specify the relevant permissions regarding Grid database services using XACML policies stored in one file at each Grid node (i.e. healthcare organization) providing the portion of medical information requested. These permissions are also dynamically adapted by the constraints imposed by the current context.

Figure 4 illustrates a schematic view of the workflow coordinating the five activities using Workflow Lifecycle Management Environment (WOLF), a development environment for WADE-based applications [28].

Every workflow is implemented as a Java class and is executed by the relevant micro workflow engine which executes the workflow by just executing the compiled Java code implementing it rather than by using an interpreter of a workflow definition

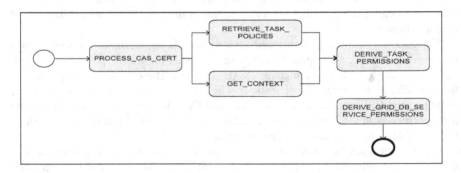

**Fig. 4.** Authorization workflow using Wolf

language. This improves significantly its performance which is a matter of prominent importance in the healthcare field.

## 6 Concluding Remarks

The development of pervasive, process-based systems that provide readily access to integrated healthcare information at the point of care contributes greatly to improving both the quality and safety of health care. Efficiency would also increase through, for example, the elimination of unnecessary duplicate tests and imaging procedures. Of course, any system of electronic medical records requires stringent privacy protections to prevent unauthorized access or use. In particular, the security risks with regard to authorization and access control which is introduced by the use of Grid technology to provide shared and coordinated use of diverse data resources should be confronted. Hence, relevant mechanisms must be in place that can conveniently regulate user access to information while providing confidence that security policies are faithfully and consistently enforced within and across organizations residing in a health district. To this end, a mediation framework has been developed to ensure authorized execution of BPEL tasks and invocation of relevant Grid database services in accordance with the current context. Thus, a tight matching of permissions to actual usage and need is ensured. To meet the requirements of scalability, flexibility, high performance and fault tolerance, the mediation framework presented in this paper is based on agent technology and describes the logics of the authorization procedures as workflows. Both the basic agent-related features and the ability to execute possibly long and complex tasks defined according to the workflow metaphor are provided to our framework by the WADE software platform.

## References

1. Malamateniou, F., Vassilacopoulos, G.: Developing a virtual patient record using XML and web-based workflow technologies. Int. J. Med. Inform. 70(2-3), 131–139 (2003)
2. Open Grid Services Architecture - Data Access and Integration (OGSA-DAI), http://www.ogsadai.org.uk/
3. The Globus Toolkit, http://www.globus.org/
4. Antonioletti, M., Hong, N.C., Hume, A., Jackson, M., Krause, A., Nowell, J.: Experiences designing and implementing Grid database services in the OGSA-DAI project. In: Designing and Building Grid Services Workshop, Global Grid Forum (2003)
5. Emmerich, W., Butchart, B., Chen, L., Wassermann, B., Price, S.: Grid Service Orchestration Using the Business Process Execution Language (BPEL). J. Grid Comp. 3, 283–304 (2006)
6. Caire, G., Gotta, D., Banzi, M.: WADE: A Software Platform to Develop Mission Critical Applications Exploiting Agents and Workflows. In: 7th International Conference on Autonomous Agents and Multiagent Systems - Industry and Applications Track, Estoril, Portugal, pp. 29–36 (2008)
7. National Institute of Standards and Technology (NIST) RBAC, http://csrc.nist.gov/groups/SNS/rbac/
8. Buhler, P.A., Vidal, J.M.: Towards Adaptive Workflow Enactment Using Multiagent Systems. J. Inf. Technol. Manag. 6(1), 61–87 (2005)

9. Poggi, A., Tomaiuolo, M., Turci, P.: An Agent-Based Service Oriented Architecture. In: WOA 2007, Genova (2007)
10. Foster, I., Jennings, N.R., Kesselman, C.: Brain Meets Brawn: Why Grid and Agents Need Each Other. In: Autonomous Agents and Multi Agent Systems, pp. 8–15 (2004)
11. Greenwood, D., Callisti, M.: Engineering Web Service-Agent Integration. In: IEEE Conference of Systems, Man and Cybernetics, The Hague (2004)
12. Savarimuthu, B.T.R., Purvis, M., Purvis, M., Cranefield, S.: Integrating Web services with agent based workflow management system (WfMS). In: 2005 IEEE/WIC/ACM International Conference on Web Intelligence, France (2005)
13. Negri, A., Poggi, A., Tomaiuolo, M., Turci, P.: Dynamic Grid Tasks Composition and Distribution through Agents. Concurr. Comp. - Pract. E 18(8), 875–885 (2006)
14. Java Agent Development Framework, http://jade.tilab.com/
15. Liu, Z., Naldurg, P., Yi, S., Qian, T., Campbell, R.H., Mickunas, M.D.: An Agent Based Architecture for Supporting Application Level Security. In: DARPA Information Survivability Conference and Exposition, Hilton Head Island, S.C. (2000)
16. Zhang, G., Parashar, M.: Context-aware Dynamic Access Control for Pervasive Applications. In: Communication Networks and Distributed Systems Modeling and Simulation Conference, San Diego (2004)
17. Pimentao, J.P., Sousal, P.A.C., Amaral, P., Steiger-Garcao, A.: Agent-based communication security. In: Lindemann, G., Denzinger, J., Timm, I.J., Unland, R. (eds.) MATES 2004. LNCS, vol. 3187, pp. 73–84. Springer, Heidelberg (2004)
18. Altiris Security Expressions Technology Overview: Agent-based and Agentless Vulnerability Management. Technical Report (2005)
19. Mendling, J., Strembeck, M., Stermsek, G., Neumann, G.: An Approach to Extract RBAC Models for BPEL4WS Processes. In: 13th IEEE International Workshops on Enabling Technologies: Infrastructure for Collaborative Enterprises, Modena (2004)
20. Thomas, J., Paci, F., Bertino, E., Eugster, P.: User Tasks and Access Control over Web Services. In: IEEE International Conference on Web Services, Utah (2007)
21. Bertino, E., Crampton, J., Paci, F.: Access Control and Authorization Constraints for WS-BPEL. In: IEEE International Conference on Web Services, Chicago (2006)
22. Dou, W., Cheung, S.C., Chen, G., Cai, S.: Certificate-Driven Grid Workflow Paradigm Based on Service Computing. In: Zhuge, H., Fox, G.C. (eds.) GCC 2005. LNCS, vol. 3795, pp. 155–160. Springer, Heidelberg (2005)
23. Adamski, M., Kulczewski, M., Kurowski, K., Nabrzyski, J., Hume, A.: Security and Performance Enhancements to OGSA-DAI for Grid Data Virtualization. Concurr. Comp. - Pract. E 19(16), 2171–2182 (2007)
24. Power, D., Slaymaker, M., Politou, E., Simpson, A.: A Secure Wrapper for OGSA-DAI. In: Sloot, P.M.A., Hoekstra, A.G., Priol, T., Reinefeld, A., Bubak, M. (eds.) EGC 2005. LNCS, vol. 3470, pp. 485–494. Springer, Heidelberg (2005)
25. IBM Corporation: IBM Websphere Workflow-Getting Started with Buildtime V. 3.6 (2005)
26. Polymenopoulou, M., Malamateniou, F., Vassilacopoulos, G.: Emergency Healthcare Process Automation using Workflow Technology and Web Services. Int. J. Med. Inform. 28(3), 195–207 (2005)
27. Pearlman, L., Welch, V., Foster, I., Kesselman, C., Tuecke, S.: A Community Authorization Service for Group Collaboration. In: 3rd IEEE International Workshop on Policies for Distributed Systems and Networks (2002)
28. OASIS Standards, http://www.oasis-open.org/
29. Caire, G., Porta, M., Quarantotto, M., Sacchi, G.: Wolf - an Eclipse Plug-In for WADE. In: ACEC, Canberra (2008)

# The Tiny Instrument Element

Francesco Lelli and Cesare Pautasso

Faculty of Informatics
University of Lugano
via Buffi 13
6900 Lugano, Switzerland
{firstname.lastname}@lu.unisi.ch

**Abstract.** In the past few years, the idea of extending the Grid to cover also the remote access, control, management of instrument devices has been explored in a few initiatives. Existing tools lack in generality and require advanced specialized computer science knowledge, thus making them difficult to be broadly adopted in the scientific community. In this paper we present a new open source initiative that is designed to overcome these problems. The Tiny Instrument Element project defines a high level architecture for plugging instruments into the Grid and provides the corresponding skeleton implementation. This lightweight approach, as opposed to existing middleware-based solutions, reduces the effort required to Gridify existing instruments. The paper evaluates the proposed abstraction with a case study from a pervasive computing scenario.

## 1 Introduction

The term Grid refers to a set of technologies for sharing and accessing storage space and computational power. Additionally, the desire to access, control, and acquire data from pervasive, widely-networked and distributed instruments reflects the need to include such scientific equipment as sensors and probes directly into the Grid. In previous works ([1], [2]) we defined the term Instrument Element (IE) as a set of services that provide the remote control and monitoring of physical instruments. In Grid terminology the words "instrument", "sensor", "actuator", and "device" are synonyms used to identify any piece of equipment that needs to be initialized, configured, calibrated, operated (with commands such as start, stop, standby, resume, reset), and monitored. Unlike the classical computing infrastructure composed of the Computing Element (CE) and the Storage Element (SE), the IE must be accessed using interactive computational job execution and usually requires a tightly coupled interaction with the users. In the past few years, the concept of Instrument Element and its definition has been adopted by few international cooperations (GridCC [3], RINGrid [4], DORII [5]). Not only complex instruments such as High Energy Physics experiments require a direct access to computational infrastructure. In this paper we consider additional use case scenarios where instruments:

N. Abdennadher and D. Petcu (Eds.): GPC 2009, LNCS 5529, pp. 293–304, 2009.

- are large in number.
- are widely distributed.
- have a highly dynamic behavior: for instance they often go on and off or can appear and disappear in a working net of sensors or probes.
- operate in embedded systems with low resources: for example FPGA based instrumentation.

Some example application domains that would require such widely sparse instrumentation are: (i) power grids, (ii) territory monitoring: to prevent geo-hazardous situations and detect forest fires, (iii) sea monitoring: for tsunami surveillance for example, (iv) distributed laboratories, (v) transportation remote control and monitoring.

Whereas in these applications a single device may not produce an amount of data comparable with the one produced by high-energy physics experiments, including such large collection of devices in the Grid can be very useful to run complex data processing and leverage the available distributed storage facilities. This way, the data produced by the sensor equipment may be directly and continuosly stored in a distributed storage system, making it possible to submit analysis jobs on the Grid as new data arrives.

In order to address the requirements of these usage scenarios, a new version of the Instrument Element is needed, since the complexity of the current middleware makes it very expensive and difficult to adopt by third party scientific institutions, end-users or programmers that have expressed an interested to use it for these applications. In this paper we present the Tiny Instrument Element project [6], which aims a developing a light-weight implementation of similar concepts. However, it uses a template-based approach based on widely adopted technology as opposed to a plug-in based middleware. Moreover, the project iself is developed according to the Web 2.0 open colleboration paradigm, in order to provide transparent access to the development and spur the growth of a large user and developer community. The Tiny Instrument Element Project [6] has started as a simplification of the code for the Run Control of the Compact Muon Solenoid (CMS) experiment at CERN [7] and now the first stable release is available for download. The rest of this paper is structured as follows: Section 2 presents a classification of related work and discusses its main limitations. Section 3 outlines the principles guiding the design of the Tiny Instrument Element. Section 4 introduces the architecture of the Tiny Instrument Element from a technical point of view. The case study presented in Section 5 is used to validate the present implementation. Section 6 concludes the paper with a discussion of the project roadmap.

## 2   Related Work

The goal is to produce a middleware that can act as glue between devices allowing their abstraction for making them accessible on the Grid. If we try to classify these efforts we can distinguish two levels of abstraction:

- **Low Level:** these provide general interfaces and mechanisms therefore they are very flexible but incomplete. A significant effort by developers is required in order to build an artifact design for a particular kind of instrument.
- **High Level:** these give management interfaces more specific to the domain of instrument control. However, they are less applicable to a large variety of instruments and they may require complex configuration. Still, less development effort is required in order to support a specific instrument.

In the first category (low level) we find the following: A WS-* based standard, WS-Notification [8], describes asynchronous publish/subscribe notification protocols that can be used for listening to remote service data element updates representing the state of a Grid-enabled instrument. The WSRF framework such as OGSA [9], [10], Apache-WSRF [11] and WSRF.NET [12] implement this standard. The Java Management Extensions (JMX) [13] technology is an open system for management and monitoring. Via its Instrumentation, Agent, and Distributed Services layers, this standard can be used for implementing management tools, and providing monitoring solutions. Jini [14] provides mechanisms to enable adding, removing, and locating devices and services on the network. The Java Message Service (JMS) define a common set of publish/subscribe APIs [15] that allow different peers of a distributed system to communicate using messages or data streams.

In category "high level" we find CIMA [16] and the Instrument Element (IE) [1], [2]. CIMA proposes a common instrument middleware based on Web Services using SOAP over HTTP as a communication layer and specific WSDL interfaces. The first reliable implementation of the IE has been provided by the GridCC project [3] and then few additional implementations have followed [17], [5]. Built on high level middleware that can fit in all possible use case, the integration of IE require not trivial efforts because each specific use case is not perfectly covered by the middleware itself.

In this paper we present another implementation of the Instrument Element concept. In the design of this version we tried to take the benefits of both high and low abstraction levels in order to create a transparent, open source project, independent from any particular initiative. As we will describe in the next section, instead of building yet another middleware framework, we propose to use a semi-finite artifact (i.e., a skeleton software) that can be extended, tailored, and customized in order meet the requirements of a specific use case. As we will show in our case study, this approach grants more flexibility and reusability than existing high level solutions. Also, it does not suffer from the generality of low level solutions, as it is designed around the instrument abstraction.

## 3   Design Principles

In this section we present how to integrate pervasive devices in the classical grid computing infrastructure. As outlined in the related work section many solutions have been proposed at a high and low level of abstraction, which require specialized expertise. In proposing this solution to a new community we can encounter a natural resistance from the people that have to learn how to use it. Moreover, high level solutions usually require the development of a plug-in and a deep knowledge of a complex and specialized middleware. Therefore even if some of the proposed solutions appear to be of general applicability they are hard to apply in practice due to the amount of time that has to be spent in learning how to use and extend them. Low level solutions instead require non-trivial computer programming expertise, because they are not designed targeting the Gridification of scientific instruments. Therefore solutions built starting from this abstraction level may be quite advanced but hard to reuse: customization to similar or other instruments may be performed only by experts.

To introduce our model for instruments Gridification, we take inspiration from modern Web development practices. For example, many Web 2.0 services, such as blogs, wikis, and social networking sites, target a variety of user categories:

- **End User:** definitely not a computer expert user, it has no understanding about the technology that he is using but he is able to use the functionality of a tool. For example, a blog writer may post his ideas on Web pages; a scientist may retrieve data from a pre-configured instrument.
- **Advanced User:** with some basic computer science knowledge, she is capable of following the instructions for the installation of the tool and for performing some simple customization. Advanced blog writers can create and customize the layout and appearance of their blog. Advanced scientists can setup and calibrate their instrument as they share it on the Grid.
- **API Developer:** thanks to their programming skills, these developers know how to develop applications using the API offered by the tool. Developer may write programs to retrieve and aggregate posts using the API of their favourite blogs. Scientist developers may extend the Tiny Instrument Element to support new kinds of instruments, as discussed in the case study.
- **Tool Programmer:** the builder of the tool itself, he has the ultimate knowledge on how to use, customize, and extend it for any application. Once the user community starts to grow, programmers should provide support to the users of the other categories and use their feedback to improve the tool.

From this classification we notice how many different groups of people can contribute to the success of a tool. We can also notice that non-specialized know-how is enough for performing simple adjustments. Therefore users may become familiar with the technology incrementally. This will foster the establishment of a community that will support the tool, contribute to its development, testing, extension, and application at the best of their knowledge. Interested users (and scientists in our case) will progress from simple user to more advanced ones as their familiarity of the tool increases, thus becoming able to apply a tool to more advanced and specialized use cases.

The Tiny Instrument Element project is centered around the previously described "gentle learning curve" principle. Additionally, the following guidelines are at the foundation of its design.

- **Skeleton Architecture:** the Tiny Instrument Element is a semifinal artifact that – used as a skeleton – can simplify and homogenize the construction
  of the final solution.
- **Technology Reuse:** we prefer to reuse existing and adopted technology as
  opposed to develop new middleware frameworks. This way, potential new developers may quickly contribute to the project by leveraging existing knowledge and skills.
- **Standard Packaging:** the project packaging follows a standard structure
  (e.g., the one of Maven) in order to be easy to understand by its users.
- **Template Customization:** several examples are given for common use
  cases to guide developers as they customize and extend the skeleton architecture to their needs.
- **Transparent Development:** the Tiny Instrument Element is an open
  source project driven by its user and developer community. Recent studies
  have shown that the adoption of these methodologies improves the quality
  of the software and reduces its development time [18].

Instead of presenting yet another complex middleware framework and showing
how to develop a new plug-in, we are focusing our attention on how the customization of existing code can be integrated in the given target application.
In [1] we showed with empirical evidence that different devices have different
needs even if they share similar functionalities. Therefore the development of a
single middleware for all the instruments results in a complex solution, which
is difficult to maintain and customize. This also hinders the creation of a large
user community.

In order to overcome such limitations we provide a well-defined modular architecture and we reduce the dependencies with external libraries. The goal is
to have new programmers become familiar with the project in a short time. In
addition, the adoption of Web based software deployment simplifies the installation procedure of the tool making it easy and convenient for scientists to access
its functionality through a Web-based interface.

## 4    Architecture and API Design

A Web service interface (WS) acts as front-end between external components
and the tiny Instrument Element (IE) itself. Using the Proxy/Wrapper pattern,
inside the IE one or more Control Manager (or Instrument Manager) map the
exposed WS to the actual devices. In the simplest scenario only one instrument
is controlled and the control manager acts just as a proxy for the information
contained in the device. Depending on the controlled equipment the control
manager could also perform fault tolerant and or autonomic control functionality.
A detailed technical documentation for the API can be found in the project Web
site [19]. Figure 1 summarizes the overall architecture of the system.

We describe the object-oriented design of the Tiny Instrument Architecture
following two common use cases. The first (detailed in Section 4.1) is about tailoring the framework to new kinds of instruments. The integration of an instrument

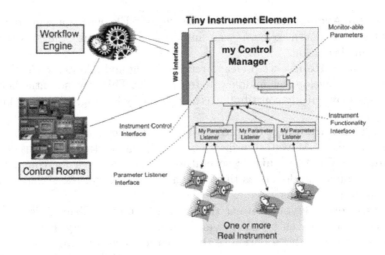

**Fig. 1.** Architecture of the Tiny Instrument Element

consists in the implementation of one or more interfaces that take care of the communication with the device. One or more instruments can be controlled using an object that implements the Parameter Listener interface. These objects present new events to the Control Manager using the Instrument Functionality interface. The proposed interfaces can support both stateless and stateful instruments, which can communicate both in a synchronous or asynchronous way.

The second use case concerns the remote access to the real instruments using the aforementioned Web service APIs (Section 4.2). External components like a control room or a workflow engine can access the controlled instrument(s) through the Web Service that retrieves the requested information via the instrument control interface.

### 4.1   How to Plug a New Instrument

From a conceptual point of view an Instrument Manager (IM) (i.e., an implementation of your control manager) is completely described by its parameters, attributes, commands, and a finite state machine:

- **Parameters** hold configuration information of the instrument.
- **Attributes** hold instrument variables (inputs and outputs).
- **Commands** hold actions that the device should perform.
- **Finite State Machine** specifies a state transition automata, used to constrain in which states can commands be executed.

This model is general enough to be applicable to different classes of instruments, since some of the elements are optional. Therefore we can have devices that, for instance, do not use the Finite State Machine because they only support one command, or that do not have input attributes.

As an example, consider an instrument manager for a simple Voltmeter (i.e., an instrument for measuring the voltage between two points in an electric circuit). Parameter are: Maximum Voltage, Minimum voltage. These characterize the instrument and do not change unless the given voltmeter provides the possibility to tune its measurement scale. Attributes: measured Voltage or set of measures. Commands: Perform a measure or Perform a set of measures. Finite State Machine: IM-Linked (the IM is connected the instrument), IM-Unlinked, Error.

From an practical point of view, developing a controller for a new kind of instrument involves implementing from 1 to 3 interfaces, depending on the control features supported by the device. In the simplest case, the instrument can be controlled by implementing the `InstrumentControl` interface, shown in Figure 2. This interface represents the abstraction of a generic instrument, and includes methods used for its remote control (such as `create()`, `destroy()`, `get/setParameters()`, `get/setAttributes()`, `executeCommand()`, `getStateMachine()`) and should be implemented by a controller that acts as a protocol adapter between the APIs and the actual instrument. In the UML diagram of Figure 2 the class `Command` represents a command while the class `Parameter` holds information about both attributes and parameters. Note also that commands can contain parameters and that parameters may contain arbitrarly typed objects. This design enables the instrument manager to execute complex command scripts to manage the instruments.

In more complex scenarios, additional interfaces `InstrumentFunctionality` and `ParameterListener` come into play, when the following assumptions do not hold:

- There is one controller for each instrument.
- The instrument does not send asynchronous messages.

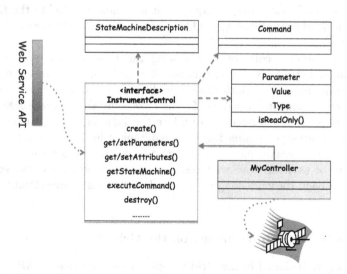

**Fig. 2.** How to Plug a New Instrument: Basic Functionality

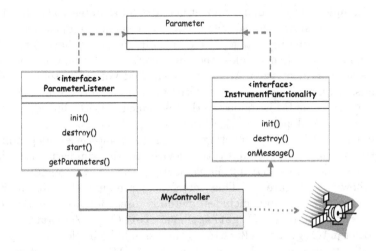

**Fig. 3.** How to Plug a New Instrument: Advanced Functionality

- The instrument can process commands in a short amount of time (less than one second).

Like the majority of control systems, the design supports instrument aggregation and grouping, as an Instrument Manager (IM) can bee also seen as an instrument. This is a very important feature for controlling a collection of instruments of similar kind through the same control instance.

More complex instruments require handling asynchronous inputs coming from other devices or subcomponents. The UML diagram in Figure 3 shows the additional interface that has to be implemented by a controller. Generic input like State changes or Errors from the equipment may be presented to the IM implementing the `InstrumentFunctionality` interface and the `ParameterListener` interface.

These two objects collaborate following the Observer pattern and add a method `onMessage()` to the `InstrumentControl` interface to support asynchronous communication. Both the method `init()` and `destroy()` come from the interface intrumentControl itself. Therefore only the method `onMessage()` has to be implemented in order to update the logic of the controller when an asynchronous message coming from the equipment has to be handled. On the other side of the observer pattern a `ParameterListener` interface can receive in synchronous or asynchronous way messages coming from the controlled devices and can call back the `onMessage()` method of the `instrumentFunctionality` interface.

### 4.2 How to Share Instruments on the Grid

Instruments are included in the Grid through a service-oriented API, providing the following operations:

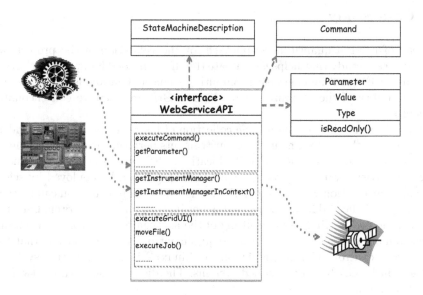

**Fig. 4.** Grid API design of an instrument element

- Monitor and control of one or more instruments.
- Access and retrieve an instrument configuration parameters and topology.
- Collect the current measurements performed by the instrument.
- Provide a set of APIs for the integration between instrument and Computational Infrastructure.

The API (shown in Figure 4) exposes a subset of the design elements introduced in the previous section. Following the principe presented in section 3, most of the Objects presented in section 4.1 have been reused in the Web Service APIs In in order to minimize the knowledge that potential new programmers should have in order to master the overall software.

The APIs take into account that more that an Instrument Element may contain more than one Instrument Manager and that IMs may be organized in certain topologies. Therefore graph navigation APIs have been provided like `getInstrumentManager()` and `getInstrumentManagerInContext()`. The Access to the computational infrastructure is provided by a wrapper around the Grid User Interface. Therefore the produced data can then be moved to a storage element using familiar commands sent to the instrument service via the `executeGridUI()` method or simplified methods like `moveFile()` or `submitjob()`. In the current stable release of Tiny Instrument Element, the Grid interface is only implemented using SOAP calls. We are currently extending it also to support a RESTful design to make it easier to invoke it from JavaScript applications.

## 5   Case Study

Instead of using a quantitative approach for the validation of the project, we present a case study that helps to evaluate the efforts needed for applying the tiny Instrument Element in a pervasive computing scenario. Our aim is to understand the reusability of the software where classical Grid middleware can encounter difficulties.

The case study is tracking a large collection of instruments, which are widely distributed in the environment. These instruments perform various kinds of measurements and data aquisition (GPS location, CPU usage, available memory, QoS properties, availability status, data traffic) and can be deployed by scientists at their location with minimal effort. The collected information can be then conveyed to dedicated instruments that act as information providers enabling the display, the geo-tagging and consulting of the aggregated data coming from different remote sources. An important requirement of the case study is that the instrument control software should run on Linux/Windows operating systems, but also in FPGA based embedded systems. The distribution of the software is handled in 3 different ways:

- Web Start Application (click a web link an the instrument element is installed to monitor your local machine).
- WAR Based Deployment (copy a file in the webapps folder of a Web application server and the instrument element service is ready to be invoked).
- Cross compilation and deployment script (run the instrument element on low resource systems such as FPGA).

Following the classification given in section 3 we can classify the people involved in the development as follow:

- **End User:** any user that want to perform the demo that is availlable at the web site.
- **Advanced User:** a small number of system administrators that deployed the software one expert that knows how to deploy application on FPGAs.
- **API Developers:** two expert programmers that have no previous knowledge of the given technology
- **Tool Programmer:** One of the people directly involved in the tiny IE project that was giving mail assistance in case of problems.

The result of this case study helps to support the claim that the Tiny Instrument Element can be extended in order to cover this pervasive computing application scenario with minimal effort. Also, it is important to point out that the case study demo [20] was built by two members of the project user community and not by its original authors. Using the Tiny Instrument Element as a starting point, the two programmers were able to apply it to 6 different kinds of instruments [21], extend it with a distributed index for data aggregation and complete it with a graphical user interface in less than two months. The feedback that was provided by these users was very positive, thus showing the potential of the

Tiny Instrument Element to cater for the needs of its user community. More in detail, the majority of the time was spent implementing a controller compatible with the `InstrumentControl` interface.

## 6 Conclusion

In this paper we present the Tiny Instrument Element project showing our proposed novel approach to the integration between instruments and the Grid. Instead of building a new middleware we propose to use a semifinite artifact (i.e., a skeleton software) that can be tailored to meet the requirements of a specific instrument characteristics. This approach not only provides an uniform access to the Gridified instruments but also leaves the flexibility to customize and tune the Tiny Instrument Element for optimal monitoring and control of the instruments. From the case study we have seen that none of the code included in the Tiny Instrument Element release was redundant and that the time required in order to gain a good understanding of the API and the corresponding skeleton was quite small. This supports the idea of template-based software development.

The Project has started full open source activities in September 2008. If we exclude our personal activity and the one performed by the case study participants, until the end of 2008, the project website attracted 304 unique visitors (7 Returning many times). The source code was downloaded 40 times and the authors were contacted with positive feedback by 2 users of the community. Whereas the project has been running for a relatively short time, these numbers are promising and show the benefit of a transparent development process to achieve wider dissemination of our research ideas.

In the future road map of the project, we plan to begin investigating a REST API for the remote access to the instruments, and the ability to publish instruments on different Grid/Cloud Middleware frameworks such as ARC [22] and Amazon EC2 [23] in order to prove the reusability of our proposed solution across different middleware. We also plan to embed the instrument control API into a scientific workflow system [24,25]

## Acknowledgements

We would like to thank Pietro Molini, Eric Frizziero and Silvano Squizzato for their participation in the Case Study.

## References

1. Lelli, F., Frizziero, E., Gulmini, M., Maron, G., Orlando, S., Petrucci, A., Squizzato, S.: The many faces of the integration of instruments and the grid. Int. J. Web Grid Serv. 3(3), 239–266 (2007)
2. Frizziero, E., Gulmini, M., Lelli, F., Maron, G., Oh, A., Orlando, S., Petrucci, A., Squizzato, S., Traldi, S.: Instrument Element: A New Grid component that Enables the Control of Remote Instrumentation. In: CCGRID 2006 (2006)

3. GridCC Project Web Site, http://www.gridcc.org/
4. RINGrid Project web site, http://www.ringrid.eu/
5. DORII Project web site, http://www.dorii.eu/
6. Tiny Instrument Element Project, http://instrumentelem.sourceforge.net/
7. The CMS Collaboration: The CMS experiment at the CERN LHC. Int. Journal of Instrumentation 3 (2008)
8. WS Notification specification, http://www-128.ibm.com/developerworks/webservices/library/specification/ws-notification/
9. Globus Open Grid Services Architecture, http://www.globus.org/ogsa/
10. Foster, I., Kesselman, C.: The Globus Toolkit. In: The Grid: Blueprint for a New Computing Infrastructure, pp. 259–278. Morgan Kaufmann Publishers, San Francisco (1999)
11. Apache WSRF Project, http://ws.apache.org/wsrf/
12. WSRF.NET Project, http://www.cs.virginia.edu/~gsw2c/wsrf.net.html
13. McManus, E.: JSR 160: JavaTM Management Extensions (JMX) Remote API 1.0 (2003)
14. Jini project, http://www.jini.org/
15. JMS standard API, http://java.sun.com/products/jms/
16. McMullen, D., Devadithya, T., Chiu, K.: Integrating Instruments and Sensors into the Grid with CIMA Web Services. In: Proc. of the 3rd APAC Conference on Advanced Computing, Grid Applications and e-Research (APAC 2005) (September 2005)
17. Vuerli, C., Taffoni, G., Coretti, I., Pasian, F., Santin, P., Pucillov, M.: Instruments in grid: The new instrument element. In: Grid Enabled Remote Instrumentation. Signals and Communication Technology. Springer, US (2008)
18. Jantunen, S., Smolander, K., Malinen, S., Virtanen, T., Kujala, S.: Utilizing Firm-Hosted Online Communities: Research Challenges and Needs. In: Proc. of 1st Int'l. Workshop on Social Software Engineering and Applications (September 2008)
19. InstrumentElement User Guide, http://instrumentelem.sourceforge.net/wiki/index.php/User_Guide
20. Case Study Demo, http://sadgw.lnl.infn.it:2002/MapsMonitor/
21. Released Instruments, http://sadgw.lnl.infn.it:2002/MapsMonitor/marker_guide.htm
22. Advanced Resource Connector ARC, http://www.nordugrid.org/middleware/
23. Amazon Elastic Compute Cloud EC2, http://aws.amazon.com/ec2/
24. Pautasso, C., Bausch, W., Alonso, G.: Autonomic computing for virtual laboratories. In: Kohlas, J., Meyer, B., Schiper, A. (eds.) Dependable Systems: Software, Computing, Networks. LNCS, vol. 4028, pp. 211–230. Springer, Heidelberg (2006)
25. Stirling, D., Welch, I., Komisarczuk, P.: Designing workflows for grid enabled internet instruments. In: CCGRID 2008, pp. 218–225 (2008)

# μOR – A Micro OWL DL Reasoner for Ambient Intelligent Devices*

Safdar Ali and Stephan Kiefer

Fraunhofer Institute for Biomedical Engineering,
Ensheimerstr. 48, 66386, St. Ingbert, Germany
{safdar.ali,stephan.kiefer}@ibmt.fraunhofer.de
http://www.ibmt.fraunhofer.de

**Abstract.** This paper describes the design, implementation and application of μOR, a lightweight micro **OWL** Description Logic **R**easoning
system developed for the resource-constrained devices to enrich them
with integrated *knowledge processing* and *reasoning* capabilities, and
leveraging them to the next generation Ambient Intelligent devices. We
have investigated the most commonly used reasoning systems and found
most of them infeasible to be used *solely* on the devices. μOR is based
on a subset of OWL-Lite entailments and the SCENTRA algorithm,
a simple *resolution* and *patterns matching* algorithm that we have
developed for resolving the queries and matching the knowledge base
triples.

**Keywords:** Semantic Web, Mobile Reasoning, Pervasive Computing,
Description Logics, Ambient Intelligent Devices.

## 1 Introduction and Related Work

The Semantic Web [1] initiative suggests standards, tools and languages to exploit the current Web to its full extent in different areas by *annotating* the
information through well-defined semantics and enabling it *processable* by machines. To achieve this goal, *ontologies* [2] play a key role as they are widely
used to represent knowledge by describing data in a formal way. The processing
of the knowledge represented through an ontology requires a *reasoning* system
to derive new information (*inferences*) from it. OWL [3] is a W3C standard for
creating and sharing ontologies on the Web and provides the means for ontology
definition and specifies formal semantics on how to derive inferences. Moreover,
in advanced Service Oriented Architectures (SOA), i.e. Semantic Web Services
[4], the services need to be well-defined with semantics to enable the peers to
perform (semi)automatic discovery, matching and invocation of these services.

The study of pervasive computing and ambient environments in different fields
of life [5][6] has introduced new research challenges. The entities that operate

---

* This work is partially supported by European Commission within the context
of SmartHEALTH IP Project, contract 016817, priority FP6-2004-IST-NMP-2
http://www.smarthealthip.com

N. Abdennadher and D. Petcu (Eds.): GPC 2009, LNCS 5529, pp. 305–316, 2009.
© Springer-Verlag Berlin Heidelberg 2009

in an ambient environment are expected to have different goals, experiences and they may use distinct ontologies to exhibit their capabilities. Due to the highly dynamic and open nature of the environment where various entities join and leave the environment at random times, they are not able to have *a priori* knowledge about all other entities that are present in the environment at a particular time instance. In addition to that, the need for *mobile reasoning* has been arisen with the advent of mobile Semantic Web Services in pervasive computing environments [7][8][9][10], although there exist various implementations [11][12] where the applications use an external reasoning system through DIG [13] or the native interfaces to fulfill the reasoning requirements. To cope with these challenges, the entities or more specifically the *devices* in a pervasive computing environment should have

- an integrated knowledge base, reasoning and querying system, which makes them autonomous.
- the ability to semantically discover and match the desired entities in a pure Peer-to-Peer (P2P) network, based on their physical and/or functional characteristics. The *physical* characteristics (i.e. device/sensor vendor, device/sensor group/type etc.) are exhibited using a device ontology, while the *functional* characteristics (i.e. what a semantic web service does, its methods and their semantic description etc.) are exhibited through service and domain/application ontologies.

This paper presents the design and implementation details of $\mu$**OR**, a powerful micro **OWL** Description Logic (DL) **R**easoning system that we have developed within the context of SmartHEALTH Project[1]. $\mu$OR is an integral part of *Semantic Medical Devices Space* (SMDS) [14] framework that we have developed for the development of next generation Ambient Intelligent (AmI) devices to cope with the afore-mentioned challenges. $\mu$OR is based on our own developed SCENTRA algorithm and a subset of OWL-Lite[2] [15] axioms. SCENTRA is a *variables' unification* and *patterns matching* algorithm designed to resolve the SCENT queries. Table 1 shows the constructs of OWL-Lite$^-$ that we have currently implemented for $\mu$OR, which gives us the following advantages.

- It does not produce *conflicts*.
- It avoids the complexities of *non-determinism*.
- It fulfills most of the requirements of pervasive computing scenarios.
- It is easier to be implemented for the resource-constrained devices.

## 1.1   SCENT: Semantic Device Language for N-Triples

In order to express the semantic queries, we need a query language, i.e. SPARQL[3] and further to process it, we require a query engine, i.e. SPARQL query engine[4],

---

[1] http://www.smarthealthip.com
[2] Hereafter referred as OWL-Lite$^-$.
[3] SPARQL Query Language for RDF, http://www.w3.org/TR/rdf-sparql-query/
[4] SPARQL Query Engine; http://sparql.sourceforge.net/

**Table 1.** OWL-Lite⁻ constructs currently implemented in $\mu$OR

| RDFS Features | (In)Equality | Properties | Header Info. | Datatypes |
|---|---|---|---|---|
| owl:Class<br>rdfs:subClassOf<br>rdf:Property<br>rdfs:subPropertyOf<br>rdfs:domain<br>rdfs:range | sameAs<br>differentFrom | ObjectProperty<br>DatatypeProperty<br>inverseOf<br>TransitiveProperty<br>SymmetricProperty<br>FunctionalProperty<br>InverseFunctionalProperty | Ontology<br>imports | xsd datatypes |

which is clearly not possible to run over a resource-constrained device. To cope with this problem, we have developed a simple alternative by modifying the EBNF (Extended Backus-Naur Form) of N-Triples[5], which is a line-based, plain text format and simple grammar to encode the basic standardized RDF notation. We call this extended version of N-Triple patterns language as SCENT (Semantic Device Language for N-Triples), which represents a subset of SPARQL expressiveness and its simplicity makes is possible to be processed by resource-constrained devices. Contrary to SPARQL, SCENT doesn't support PREFIX for the predicates and does not allow keywords, i.e. FILTER, OPTIONAL and other additional options. Table 2 shows a comparison between original N-Triples syntax and the SCENT language syntax specifications, where we modified the original subject and object productions with the inclusion of variable (starting with ? sign) which now allows to use variables together with absolute URIs at the places of subject or object of a triple.

**Table 2.** Comparison between N-Triples and SCENT Syntax Specifications

| Original N-Triples specification | Modified N-Triples specification |
|---|---|
| subject ::= uriref \| nodeID<br>object ::= uriref \| nodeID \| literal | subject ::= uriref \| nodeID \| variable<br>object ::= uriref \| nodeID \| literal \| variable<br>variable ::= '?' name |

Although there exist various implementations of OWL DL reasoners, i.e. Pellet [16], FaCT++ [17] and RacerPro [18], their memory requirements (installation/runtime) are quite high, restricting them to be used only on desktop systems or servers, but surely not on resource-constrained (mobile) devices. Such reasoners mostly implement *tableaux* algorithms that are developed for the expressive DL knowledge representation with high complexity. Bossam [19], a RETE-based [20] *forward chaining* production rule engine is another example of DL reasoner which takes comparatively less resources (750Kb of runtime-memory), but requires *namespace prefixing* to express knowledge/queries which is not supported by N-Triples, and hence not supported by our SCENT based semantic queries. To the best of our knowledge, Pocket KRHyper [21] is the only reasoner which

---

[5] W3C Recommendation, RDF Test Cases, 10 February 2004,<br>http://www.w3.org/TR/rdf-testcases/#ntriples

is targeted for mobile devices, thus most relevant to our work. It is a First Order Logic (FOL) theorem prover and model generator based on the *hyper tableau calculus* [22]. The drawback of Pocket KRHyper is that it works on a Set of *clauses* and does not support *direct* DL reasoning, rather it adds an additional layer for transforming all the DL expressions into *first order clausal logic* and the inference results back to DL expressions, which is clearly an overhead for small devices. Our aim is to make devices intelligent and autonomous w.r.t the capabilities of knowledge querying, processing and reasoning, all integrated *entirely* on devices, and to provide sufficient *expressiveness* and *extra-logical* features that we identified as requirement for effective OWL DL reasoning on mobile devices for pervasive computing scenarios.

The rest of the paper is organized as follows: Section 2 explains the architectural and algorithmic details of $\mu$OR. Section 3 explains the general applications of $\mu$OR, with the focus on a pervasive healthcare scenario. Section 4 gives the implementation details and the performance evaluation results. Finally, Section 5 gives the conclusions and direction for future work.

## 2   $\mu$OR: A Micro OWL DL Reasoner

Fig. 1 shows the overall architecture of a small but powerful querying and reasoning system that we have developed for resource-constrained Ambient Intelligent (AmI) devices. It consists of Query Processor, SCENTRA algorithm and $\mu$OR.

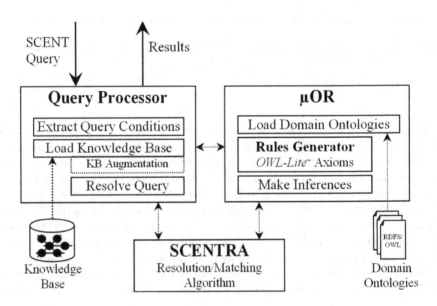

**Fig. 1.** Architecture of Semantic Query Processing & Reasoning System

```
1  ?d <http://www.w3.org/1999/02/22-rdf-syntax-ns#type>
                <http://www.ibmt.fhg.de/onto/2008/04/md#MedicalDevice> .
2  ?d <http://www.ibmt.fhg.de/onto/2008/04/md#hasGroup> ?g .
3  ?g <http://www.ibmt.fhg.de/onto/2008/04/md#deviceType>
                <http://www.ibmt.fhg.de/onto/2008/04/md#UrineAnalyzer> .
4  ?d <http://www.ibmt.fhg.de/onto/2008/04/smds#hasMeasurementOf> ?p .
5  ?p <http://www.ibmt.fhg.de/onto/2008/04/smds#patHisId> "23KD2008" .
```

**Fig. 2.** An example of a SCENT query

## 2.1 Query Processor (QP)

QP is responsible for processing the SCENT queries, which are described using
the syntax explained under Section 1. Fig. 2 shows an example of SCENT query[6]
that is composed of five *conditions/patterns*, where each condition involves *atleast*
one variable and terminated with '.'. This query is about finding device(s) (?d)
whose *type* is MedicalDevice and it belongs to the *group* (?g) of those devices
whose *category/type* is UrineAnalyzer, and it has performed the measurement of
a *patient* (?p) with the id 23KD2008. Such queries can be formulated using any
*domain/application* ontologies, which are used to exhibit the *physical* and/or
*functional* characteristics of the devices being used in that environment. In a
pervasive computing environment i.e. P2P unstructured network, such query
(embedded in the device discovery *request* message) is broadcasted from one
device to all other devices in the network, where the query processor running on
each device processes this query; and if matches are found, it returns back the
results (embedded in the device discovery *response* message) to the requesting
device. The complete structure of device discovery request and response messages
are not shown here because of the space limitation.

First of all, the QP *extracts* all the conditions/patterns from the SCENT
query, and adds them into a Set. Secondly, it *loads* the available knowledge base
(KB) triples stored on the device in a Set, and then it requests $\mu$OR to make
inferences on the given Set of KB, based on OWL-Lite$^-$ entailments. When
the QP gets back the inference results as a Set from $\mu$OR, it augments the
existing KB Set with these inferences using the Set *union* operation, and then
uses the SCENTRA algorithm (Fig. 3) to find the final results. When it gets back
the final results from SCENTRA algorithm, it formulates the results *only* for
the requested variable, e.g. in case of SCENT query presented in Fig. 2, only the
result for variable ?d will be returned.

## 2.2 SCENTRA: The SCENT Resolution Algorithm

Fig. 3 shows the SCENTRA algorithm, a simple variables' *unification algorithm*
that we have developed for the SCENT conditions/patterns matching and resolu-
tion. SCENTRA takes a Set $\mathbb{K}$ of knowledge base triples and a Set $\mathbb{C}$ of conditions

---

[6] Apparent line breaks are due to the space (width) limitation.

```
Input: A Set ℂ of conditions' triples where ℂ = {c₁, c₂, ..., cₘ}, and a Set 𝕂 of
       knowledge base triples where 𝕂 = {k₁, k₂, ..., kₙ}
Output: A Subset 𝕄 of matched triples
1 begin
2 │  Initialize(𝕀)   /* A set of sets for intermediate results */
3 │  Initialize(𝕄)   /* A set of sets for matched results */
4 │  𝕍 ← ExtractVariables(ℂ)  /* 𝕍 = {v₁, v₂, ..., vₚ} */
5 │  for c ∈ ℂ do
6 │  │  for k ∈ 𝕂 do
7 │  │  │  if Matches(cₘ, kₙ) = true then
8 │  │  │  │  for v ∈ 𝕍 do
9 │  │  │  │  │  /* Extract the value of vₚ for cₘ from kₙ */
10│  │  │  │  │  if temp ← ExtractValue(cₘ, kₙ, vₚ) ≠ null then
11│  │  │  │  │  │  /* Add temp into vₚ set of 𝕀 at index m */
12│  │  │  │  │  │  AddIntoSet(𝕀, m, vₚ, temp)

13│  for v ∈ 𝕍 do
   │                m
14 │  │  𝕄_{vₚ} ←₊ ⋂ 𝕀_{m vₚ}  /* zero matches found if 𝕄 = ∅ */
   │                1
15 end
```

**Fig. 3.** The SCENTRA Algorithm

```
Input: A Set ℂ of conditions' triples, where ℂ = {c₁, c₂, ..., cₘ}
Output: A Set 𝕍 of variables used in ℂ, where 𝕍 = {v₁, v₂, ..., vₚ}
1 begin
2 │  Initialize(𝕍)    /* A Set for variables used in ℂ */
3 │  for c ∈ ℂ do
4 │  │  if cₘ.subject is a variable then
5 │  │  │  𝕍 ←₊ cₘ.subject    /* Add the subject variable in Set */
6 │  │  if cₘ.object is a variable then
7 │  │  │  𝕍 ←₊ cₘ.object    /* Add the object variable in Set */
8 │  return 𝕍
9 end
```

**Fig. 4.** The *ExtractVariables* function

as *input* from QP or $\mu$OR, and returns a subset $\mathbb{M}$ of the *matched* triples that fulfills the conditions of Set $\mathbb{C}$. In case of QP, the Set $\mathbb{C}$ consists of the conditions made from SCENT query, while in case of $\mu$OR, the Set $\mathbb{C}$ consists of the conditions made from OWL-Lite⁻ entailments and the domain/application ontologies (The *Rules Generator* algorithm is not presented here because of lack of space).

SCENTRA extracts the variables from Set $\mathbb{C}$ by using *ExtractVariables* function shown in Fig. 4, and resolves each of the *variables* of Set $\mathbb{V}$. It applies

---

**Input**: A condition triple $c$ and a knowledge base triple $k$
**Output**: *true* if $k$ matches with $c$ ; else *false*

```
 1  begin
 2  │   let isMatched ← false
 3  │   if c.subject ∉ V then
 4  │   │   if c.subject = k.subject then
 5  │   │   └   isMatched ← true
 6  │   if c.predicate ∉ V then
 7  │   │   if c.predicate = k.predicate then
 8  │   │   └   isMatched ← true
 9  │   if c.object ∉ V then
10  │   │   if c.object = k.object then
11  │   │   └   isMatched ← true
12  │   return isMatched
13  end
```

**Fig. 5.** The *Matches* function

*Matches* function, shown in Fig. 5, to each triple of the Set $\mathbb{K}$ for each condition of Set $\mathbb{C}$. If a match is found, the value for each variable in Set $\mathbb{V}$ is *extracted* and stored in a temporary Set $\mathbb{I}$ at appropriate index. Finally, the *intersection* of Sets is taken for the found values of all variables used in each condition, and then *added* in the final Set $\mathbb{M}$. The symbol $\longleftarrow_+$ means the addition of elements (value of each variable) from a temporary Set $\mathbb{I}$ to the final Set $\mathbb{M}$ of results, where each element of $\mathbb{M}$ is a Set containing the values of variables used in a condition. The number of elements of Set $\mathbb{M}$ will always be equal to the number of elements of Set $\mathbb{V}$ if matches are found, otherwise $\mathbb{M}$ would be an empty Set.

**Complexity Analysis.** The overall complexity of SCENTRA algorithm, as shown in Eq. 1, would be $O(m.n.p)$ where $m$ is the total number of conditions in Set $\mathbb{C}$, $n$ is the total number of KB triples in Set $\mathbb{K}$, and $p$ is the total number of variables in Set $\mathbb{V}$. The complexity of *Matches* function (Line 7) and *retrieval/addition* operations (Line 10,12) on HashSet is of *constant* time, which can be ignored. Similarly, the complexity of *ExtractVariables* function ($O(m)$) on Line 4, and the complexity of HashSet *intersection* operation ($O(m.n)$) on Lines 13,14 can be ignored.

$$O(m) + O(1) + O(m.n.p) + O(m.n) \implies O(m.n.p) \qquad (1)$$

## 2.3  $\mu$OR

This section describes the details about $\mu$OR and its inference process using SCENTRA Algorithm. $\mu$OR loads all the available domain ontologies in RDF triples form, and if required, it generates the *implicit rules* based on the OWL-Lite$^-$ entailments, as mentioned in Table 1. Once the implicit rules are created, they are stored locally on each device and this process is not repeated, unless the domain ontology(ies) are changed. Every implicit rule contains two sets, one for *preconditions* and one for *postconditions*. The preconditions Set of each rule is matched with the available Set $\mathbb{K}$ of knowledge base triples using SCENTRA Algorithm, and if the matches are found, it creates new facts (triples) by *substituting* the variables of the *postconditions* Set with these matches. The resultant Set of new facts (*inferences*) is then returned back to the Query Processor.

## 3   Applications of $\mu$OR

$\mu$OR can be used in various pervasive computing applications where semantic knowledge processing and reasoning is required on mobiles/devices side. For example, it can be used

- for developing personal health systems where plug-n-play like *semantic* interoperability is required.
- for developing *intelligent health kiosks*, where the persons health and fitness status is assessed by dynamically connecting with his/her bio-sensors.
- for semantic *discovery/tracking* of assets/samples in hospitals/laboratories.
- for developing solutions for *ambient assisted living* scenarios, i.e. home monitoring for elderly people.
- for developing *smart* operation theaters, intensive care units etc.

### 3.1   Neuroblastoma Screening - An Application Scenario

In this section, we describe a laboratory healthcare scenario within the context of SmartHEALTH project for the screening/diagnosis of Pheochromocytoma and/or Neuroblastoma cancer, where the mobile semantic reasoning helps to realize the vision of semantic coordination among Ambient Intelligent medical devices [23]. Fig. 6 shows the complete interaction of the AmI medical devices and the forwarding of final results to the remote SmartHEALTH Information System (SIS). The SmartHEALTH Cancer Markers Analyzer (CMA) processes the blood sample of a patient and for the completion of the screening/diagnosis, it requires the urinary catecholamines levels of that patient. In order to do this, the CMA searches the network by broadcasting a query q, as shown in Fig. 2, which specifies the discrete conditions for the desired urine analyzer. Although, there are two other medical devices in the environment, but only that urine analyzer responds to the query of CMA, as it has performed the urine analysis of the patient with the id 23KD2008. In the second step, the CMA calls the Semantic Web Service of the urine analyzer to retrieve the urine analysis results of that patient and then computes the overall status of the tumor by comparing the both blood & urine analyses.

After computing the results and making a higher level of interpretation, the CMA searches the local network for a *gateway* device, which offers a Semantic Web Service to forward the final results to the SIS. The CMA now broadcasts the second query about a device having a 3G internet connection with the SIS, in the

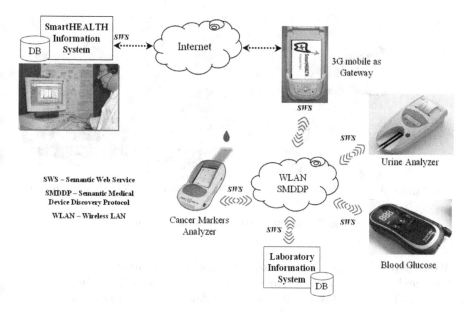

**Fig. 6.** Gateway Scenario - Semantic Coordination of AmI medical devices

similar way as it was broadcasted at first stage for the urine analyzer. As a result, the matched mobile gateway device responds to the CMA with its URI, and the CMA downloads the sawsdl file from gateway device, extracts the method name using SAWSDL API [24], calls that method by sending the encrypted measurement results. The mobile gateway device further calls the Semantic Web Service of SIS to send the measurement results. After the interpreted results are received on SIS side, the responsible health professional is informed in case of emergency (through an automatic alert, i.e. SMS/fax) about these results, so that s/he could login to the web portal of SIS site from his/her clinic (or even from home) and could view the measurement results along with a higher level of interpretation made by the server side analysis methods.

## 4   Implementation and Performance Evaluation

We developed the complete $\mu$OR system using Java™ programming language. For *filtering* and *parsing* of RDF information, we used small-sized (**12Kb**) Megginson's RDF Filter [25] and one of the fastest *SAX2* compliant Piccolo [26] XML parser respectively. Fig. 7(b) shows the hardware platform, the Gumstix[7] XL6P motherboard with wireless network card, Embedded Linux OS and Java Virtual Machine (JamVM), which we chose to deploy and test the $\mu$OR. All the medical devices used in the application scenario were attached with the Gumstix modules, one of them is shown in Fig. 7(a) with the Roche Urine Analyzer[8].

---

[7] Gumstix Miniature Computers; http://www.gumstix.com
[8] http://www.roche.com/prod_diag_urisys.htm

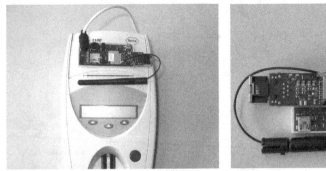
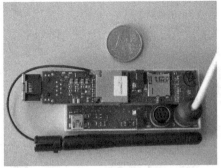

(a) Urine Analyzer from Roche®          (b) Gumstix with XL6P motherboard

**Fig. 7.** Implementation Platform for $\mu$OR

We have tested the performance of our semantic query processing and reasoning system in comparison with a couple of other small reasoning systems, namely Pocket KRHyper and Bossam. We used a Windows XP system with Pentium® 4, Intel® 2.40 GHz processor, 1.5Gb RAM to perform 10 different tests of loading different domain ontologies with varying sized knowledge bases. Fig. 8(a) shows the runtime memory size (**24Kb**) of complete $\mu$OR, which is far less than the memory sizes of Bossam (**750Kb**) and Pocket KRHyper (**245Kb**). Similarly, Fig. 8(b), Fig. 8(c), and Fig. 8(d) show the comparison of times taken for ontology loading/conversion, knowledge base loading and overall reasoning respectively. Because the Gumstix has Marvell® PXA270 processor with 600MHz speed, which is a ratio of 4:1 to 2.40 GHz processor, so all the times calculated for $\mu$OR

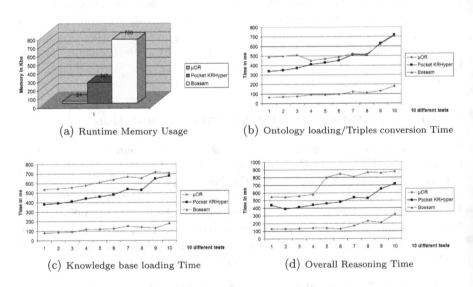

(a) Runtime Memory Usage          (b) Ontology loading/Triples conversion Time

(c) Knowledge base loading Time          (d) Overall Reasoning Time

**Fig. 8.** Performance Evaluation of $\mu$OR compared to Bossam and Pocket KRHyper

on PC would be of 1:4 ratio to Gumstix platform. In the light of above performance/memory results, we believe that the computing/memory requirements of $\mu$OR are lower enough to be used on small/mobile devices.

## 5  Conclusions and Future Work

We have developed a small but powerful OWL DL reasoning system, namely $\mu$OR for resource-constrained mobile devices. We have not implemented the *tableaux calculus*, rather we have developed a simple *variables' unification* algorithm for the reasoning process which does not demand higher memory/computing resources. Secondly, the current version of $\mu$OR supports CDC compliant devices only, because of using java.util.HashSet and java.util.HashMap classes for better performance, which are missing from the specifications of CLDC[9] and MIDP[10] compliant devices. However, we will provide a substitutional version in future which will support both CLDC and MIDP devices as well.

Currently, $\mu$OR supports the generation of implicit rules only, which are defined in the ontologies, but in future, we will add support for defining *explicit* rules in one of the widely adopted rules defining languages, i.e. SWRL[11]. Secondly, although we have compared the performance of $\mu$OR with two other reasoners using a Set of our own queries, but to evaluate its performance on some benchmark issues, we will continue to work using the available benchmarking systems, i.e. LUBM[12]. Last, but not the least, we will optimize the SCENTRA algorithm and implement the remaining axioms of OWL-Lite, if needed as per the requirements of our new pervasive computing scenarios.

## References

1. Lee, T.B., Hendler, J., Lassila, O.: The Semantic Web. Scientific American (2001)
2. Gruber, T.R.: A translation approach to portable ontologies. Knowledge Acquisition 5(2), 199–220 (1993)
3. Web Ontology Language (OWL), http://www.w3.org/2004/OWL/
4. McIlraith, S.A., et al.: Semantic Web Services. In: Proc. of IEEE Intelligent Systems (2001)
5. Finin, T., et al.: A Pervasive Computing System for the Operating Room of the Future. Mobile Networks and Applications 12(2-3) (March 2007)
6. Ossowski, S., et al.: Agent-Based Semantic Service Discovery for Healthcare: An Organizational Approach. IEEE Intelligent Systems 21(6), 11–20 (2006)
7. Helin, H., et al.: CASCOM - Context-Aware Health-Care Service Co-ordination in Mobile Computing Environments. ERCIM News num. 60

---

[9] http://java.sun.com/products/cldc/
[10] http://java.sun.com/products/midp/
[11] http://www.w3.org/Submission/SWRL/
[12] http://swat.cse.lehigh.edu/projects/lubm/

8. Ali, S., Uribarren, A., Parra, J.: Applications of Ambient Intelligence in medical devices and clinical environments. In: IEEE international conference of E-Medical Systems, Morocco (2007) ISBN: 9954-8905-0-5
9. Wahlster, W.: SmartWeb: Mobile Applications of the Semantic Web. In: Biundo, S., Frühwirth, T., Palm, G. (eds.) KI 2004. LNCS, vol. 3238, pp. 50–51. Springer, Heidelberg (2004)
10. Kleemann, T., Sinner, A.: Semantic user profiles and their application in a mobile environment. In: Proc. of Artificial Intelligence in Mobile Systems (2004)
11. Luther, M., Fukazawa, Y., et al.: lassification-based Situational Reasoning for Task-oriented Mobile Service Recommendation. The Knowledge Engineering Review 23(1), 7–19
12. Ejigu, D., Scuturici, M., Brunie, L.: An Ontology-Based Approach to Context Modeling and Reasoning in Pervasive Computing. In: Proceedings of the Fifth IEEE International Conference on Pervasive Computing and Communications Workshops (2007)
13. Bechhofer, S., Moller, R., Crowther, P.: The DIG Description Interface. In: Proc. Int'l. Workshop Description Logics 2003 (2003)
14. Ali, S., Kiefer, S.: Semantic Medical Devices Space, An Infrastructure for the interoperability of Ambient Intelligent Medical Devices. In: Proceedings of IEEE-ITAB Conference in Ioannina, Greece (October 2006)
15. OWL Web Ontology Language Overview, W3C Recommendation (2004), http://www.w3.org/TR/owl-features/
16. Sirin, E., Parsia, B., et al.: Pellet: A Practical OWL DL Reasoner. Int'l. Journal of Web Semantics (2007)
17. Horrocks, I., Tsarkov, D.: FaCT++ Description Logic Reasoner: System Description. In: Proc. Third Int'l. Joint Conference of Automated Reasoning 2006 (IJCAR 2006) (2006)
18. Möller, R., Harrslev, V.: Racer: A Core Inference Engine for the Semantic Web. In: Proc. 2nd Int'l. Workshop Evaluation of Ontology Based Tools, pp. 27–36 (2003)
19. Minsu, J., Sohn, J.: Bossam: An extended rule engine for OWL Inferencing. In: Antoniou, G., Boley, H. (eds.) RuleML 2004. LNCS, vol. 3323, pp. 128–138. Springer, Heidelberg (2004)
20. Forgy, C.L.: Rete: A Fast Algorithm for the Many Pattern/Many Object Pattern Match Problem. Artificial Intelligence 19, 17–37 (1982)
21. Kleemann, T., Sinner, A.: KRHyper - In Your Pocket. In: Nieuwenhuis, R. (ed.) CADE 2005. LNCS (LNAI), vol. 3632, pp. 452–457. Springer, Heidelberg (2005)
22. Baumgartner, P.: Hyper Tableaux - The Next Generation; Technical Report 32-97, Universität Koblenz-Landau (1997)
23. Ali, S., Kiefer, S.: Neuroblastoma Screening through Semantic Coordination of Ambient Intelligent Medical Devices. In: First International Research Workshop of The Internet of Things and Services, France (2008)
24. W3C SAWSDL, A mechanism to semantically annotate the Web Service Description Language files, http://www.w3.org/-2002/ws/sawsdl/
25. RDF Filter, http://rdf-filter.sourceforge.net/
26. Piccolo XML Parser for Java, http://piccolo.sourceforge.net/

# Sensor-Actuator Networks with TBox Snippets

Tomasz Rybicki and Jarosław Domaszewicz

Institute of Telecommunications, Warsaw University of Technology,
Warsaw, Poland
{trybicki,domaszew}@tele.pw.edu.pl

**Abstract.** Wireless sensor and actuator networks (WSAN) consist of many
nodes with limited computing resources. The nodes in such networks may provide different services, which gives rise to the possibility to compose the services at runtime. In order to fully exploit the power of such a service-oriented
approach, the services need to be properly described. We present a novel approach to service-oriented architectures for networks of resource-constrained
nodes. The services are described ontologically. Each node carries a tiny piece
of a full domain ontology, needed to describe the node's service. The descriptions of services available in the environment are merged at runtime. This leads
to a lean, runtime version of the domain ontology, suitable for resource-
constrained nodes. The runtime ontology is then processed to answer queries
about available composite services.

**Keywords:** wireless sensor and actuator networks, ad hoc networks, middlewares, resource management and runtime environments, service oriented computing, semantic grid and ontologies.

## 1 Introduction

Wireless sensor and actuator networks (WSAN) are the next generation of wireless
sensor networks (WSN) [1]. WSN consist of small, resource-constrained nodes capable of limited computation, wireless communication, and sensing the environment.
WSAN, by enriching the nodes with actuators, are able not only to observe the state
of the environment, but also to change it; for instance, fire detected by smoke and
temperature sensors might be put down by extinguisher actuators.

Nodes in WSAN might be divided into two overlapping groups: those that provide
a service (e.g., a wireless thermometer that provides body temperature readings) and
those that consume a service (e.g. a small display showing the patient's body temperature). This gives rise to node cooperation (service composition). When the membership in the network is dynamic, the node cooperation should be performed in an opportunistic manner; a node should not assume the presence of another node (e.g. the
display should not rely on certain thermometer but should be able to display readings
of any wireless body thermometer present nearby). Annotating services with coherent
descriptions facilitates service composition (e.g., since both body and room ther-
mometers provide temperature data, the display should be able to show outputs of
either of them). Annotating services with ontological descriptions allows even better

N. Abdennadher and D. Petcu (Eds.): GPC 2009, LNCS 5529, pp. 317–327, 2009.
© Springer-Verlag Berlin Heidelberg 2009

service composition, since it allows exploiting semantic relationships between service descriptions (e.g., since temperature is a numerical value, the display is able to show other kinds of a numerical value, like room air humidity).

A semantic, service-oriented approach to WSAN requires some additional infrastructure to be provided by a middleware (e.g. a common ontology, runtime descriptions of node services, service directory, etc.). This in turn raises the amount of computing resources required of the nodes hosting the middleware.

In this paper, we propose a semantic, service-oriented middleware for wireless sensor and actuator networks, which facilitates service composition and serendipitous cooperation between nodes in the network. The main contribution of this work are a technique of decomposing big domain ontologies into small ones that might be processed (at runtime) on resource-constrained nodes, as well as a technique of runtime processing of ontologies for the purpose of serendipitous service composition. The structure of this paper is as follows. In section 2, we present related work. In section 3, we outline our approach. The methods of decomposing the ontologies and annotating nodes with semantic descriptions are presented in section 4. Section 5 contains the discussion of the runtime processing of the descriptions. Section 6 summarizes the paper.

## 2   Related Work

The most notable example of service description is the web services architecture [2]. The services are described using WSDL (Web Services Description Language). WSDL is able to express only the syntax of services. WSDL-S [3] extends it with the ability to express semantic information. However, both WSDL and WSDL-S lack efficient solutions for resource-constrained devices. In order to overcome that, another effort was started – DPWS [4] (Device Profile for Web Services). Unfortunately, sensors and actuators are still beyond its reach [5]. Recently, a proxy-based architecture was proposed [6]; however, it lacks the ability to express and exploit semantic information.

Another proxy-based approach is presented in SONGS [7]. Sensors are connected to field servers, which act as proxies between them and the rest of the system. Ontologies are not used. Instead, services are described with Prolog facts. Service composition is performed by calculating Prolog rules.

The idea of describing a node's resources with ontologies and distributing the descriptions over a network is presented in [8]. Nodes are homogeneous, and each of them holds a part of the ontology that describes resources available in the whole network. The drawback of such an approach is the necessity to re-align the ontology upon node arrival or departure, which might require considerable number of messages to be sent, thus shortening the network lifetime.

Recent research recognizes the advantages of service oriented architecture in WSAN. TinySOA [9] is a prototype of service-oriented WSAN built on top of TinyOS. The approach features a query model, where both task queries (service invocations) and event queries (receiving notifications) are possible. TinySOA employs service-driven routing; they do not exploit advantages of the possible relations between service types.

Ontologies are used to describe a node's services in Common Instrument Middleware Architecture (CIMA) [10]. The primary goal of the approach is to enable self-descriptiveness of nodes and auto-configuration of application.

An ontology-based discovery is described in [11]. A node's services and service requests are described with ontologies, and matchmaking that exploits semantic relationships is possible. The solution, however, is targeted at high-end Bluetooth-enabled mobile devices, and as such does not deal with issues related to efficient ontology processing.

## 3   The Overview

We treat nodes of the network as independent entities that provide atomic services. Each node is characterized by the type of the service it provides and the types of the service's inputs and outputs. For example, the thermometer node shown in Fig. 1a) provides a `Thermometer` service which has no inputs and delivers one output of type `Temperature`. Fig. 1b) shows a `FireDetector` service that takes `Temperature` and `SmokeAlert` and outputs `FireAlert`.

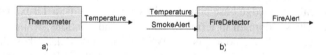

**Fig. 1.** Thermometer (a) and FireDetector (b) services

The atomic services might be invoked individually, but they may also be composed into complex services. The inputs of a complex service are all the inputs of its atomic services that are not connected to the outputs of its atomic services. Similarly, the outputs of a complex service are all the non-connected outputs of its atomic services. A complex service shown in Fig. 2 is used to detect fire. It consists of three atomic services: `Thermometer`, `SmokeSensor`, and `FireDetector`. The outputs of `Thermometer` and `SmokeSensor` are used as inputs to `FireDetector`. This way a complex service is created whose sole output is `FireAlert`.

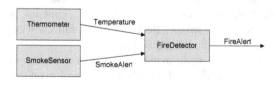

**Fig. 2.** A complex service example

Each atomic service has an ontological description built with concepts from a common domain ontology. The concepts in the ontology are grouped in two hierarchies: a hierarchy of service types (e.g. `SmokeSensor`, `Thermometer`, `FireDetector`) and

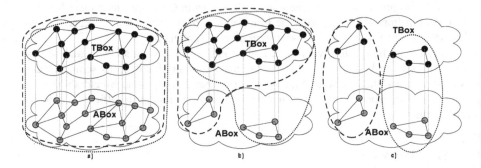

**Fig. 3.** (a) A straightforward approach is to embed full knowledge base in each node. (b) A more realistic scenario is to reduce the ABox to assertions concerning the node. (c) In our approach, both the TBox and ABox parts embedded in a node contain only statements concerning the node.

a hierarchy of service parameter[1] types (e.g. `Temperature`, `SmokeAlert`, `FireAlert`). The hierarchies are linked by axioms that define relationships between individual services and their parameters.

An ontological knowledge base consists of two components: a TBox and an ABox. The TBox describes a domain in terms of concepts and relations, while the ABox in terms of instances of those concepts. In WSAN, the TBox describes the types of nodes (services) and relations between the types, and the ABox represents actual nodes. A straightforward approach to handle an ontological knowledge base is to store information about all the types and all the instances on each node (Fig. 3a). Such an approach is unrealistic, if only due to network reconfiguration problems: a new node arrival would require updating the ABox assertions in all nodes. Another scenario is to store on a node only those ABox assertions that are related to this specific node (Fig. 3b). Such a solution, although more efficient, still has a severe drawback – since the TBox may consist of hundreds of concepts[2], its size may still be significant. In our approach, we not only reduce the size of the ABox; we also considerably lessen the size of the TBox. We use a so-called TBox snippets that, along with ABox assertions, constitute node descriptions used at runtime (Fig. 3c). A TBox snippet consists only of concepts and relations directly relevant to the node being described. This way a node contains only the information about itself, and the combined knowledge base, composed of all descriptions embedded in a network, contains information about available nodes only. Its size is smaller than that of the full knowledge base, and it is easier to process on resource-constrained nodes.

During the design time, the node manufacturer uses a domain ontology to create the description of a node's service and installs the description on the node. A description is created by "cutting out" concepts and relations that describe the type of the

---

[1] In the spirit of OWL-S, we use the term 'parameter' to refer to both inputs and outputs of a service.

[2] For instance, the OntoSensor ontology of sensors and actuators  consists of 439 classes (http://www.engr.memphis.edu/eece/cas/OntoSensor/OntoSensor).

node's service and its parameters from the TBox, and adding ABox statements about the specific node (e.g., id or manufacturer).

At runtime, one of the nodes is elected as the ontology composer. It gathers descriptions of all neighbouring nodes and composes a so-called runtime ontology. The composer then becomes a directory service; it resolves service queries by processing the runtime ontology. Such a query might refer to a particular type of a service (*give me a* Thermometer-*type service*) or a service that has parameters of particular types (*give me a service that returns* Temperature).

The runtime ontology has the same structure as the full, design time ontology, but it consists only of the concepts that are related to services available in the environment. This makes it smaller than the design time ontology, and more amenable to processing on resource-constrained nodes.

## 4 Design Time

The ontology used at design time consists of two layers: an upper level ontology and a domain ontology. The first one is domain-neutral and covers core concepts required for the system to function properly, the latter deals with concepts describing a specific domain of interest.

The upper ontology (shown in Fig. 4) describes entities from a service-oriented perspective. It contains a concept that denotes atomic services (AtomicService) and one that denotes their parameters (ServiceParameter). The domain ontology subclasses of the former represent actual service types (e.g., Thermometer), while the domain ontology subclasses of the latter represent data types used as service parameters (e.g., Temperature). The hasInput and hasOutput relations are used to link a service type with the types of its parameters. This ontology is extended by a domain ontology that contains actual service and parameter types. However, only the upper ontology is hardwired into the middleware; as a result, the middleware stays domain-agnostic.

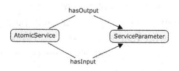

**Fig. 4.** The upper ontology

The domain ontology is created by a domain-responsible entity and made available to all interested parties (e.g., node manufacturers or third-party node-software providers). The domain ontology consists of three parts: a service types hierarchy, a service parameter types hierarchy, and axioms linking the hierarchies. Service types must be subsumed by AtomicService; service parameter types must be subsumed by ServiceParameter.

The upper ontology extended with a domain ontology forms a design time ontology. Fig. 5 shows an example of a simple design time ontology for the domain of

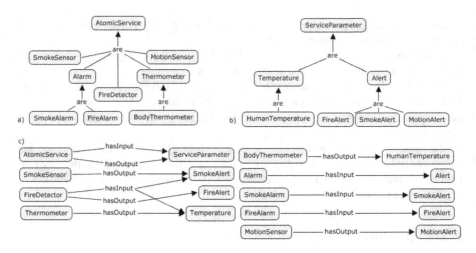

**Fig. 5.** An example of design time ontology

"home automation." The ontology contains eight service types: (1) a smoke sensor, (2) a "generic" alarm, (3) a "smoke detected" alarm, (4) a "fire detected" alarm, (5) a fire detector unit that based on temperature in the room and presence of smoke decides whether to signal a fire alert, (6) a generic temperature sensor, (7) a human body thermometer and (8) a motion sensor. Fig. 5a) shows a hierarchy of ontological concepts representing those service types: SmokeSensor, Alarm, SmokeAlarm, FireAlarm, FireDetector, MotionSensor, Thermometer and BodyThermometer. SmokeAlarm and FireAlarm are kinds of the Alarm service and so are subsumed by it. Similarly, BodyThermometer is subsumed by the Thermometer service type. Fig. 5b) shows the service parameter type hierarchy. It contains the following concepts, each representing a service's input or output: Temperature, Alert, HumanTemperature, FireAlert, SmokeAlert and MotionAlert. Again, HumanTemperature is a subtype of Temperature, and FireAlert, SmokeAlert, and MotionAlert are subtypes of Alert.

The relationships between service types and their parameter types are shown in Fig. 5c). For instance, it shows that FireDetector takes Temperature as input (indicated by the hasInput relation), and Thermometer outputs it (indicated by the hasOutput relation).

In order to simplify processing of the runtime ontology (reasoning), a number of pre-processing operations should be performed on the design time ontology. One of them is making implicit subsumptions explicit. This simplifies the processing, as it allows checking only direct subsumption of service and parameter type concepts (as opposed to traversing the whole hierarchy).

### 4.1 Describing Services with TBox Snippets

The service description consists of a set of concepts related to the service and extracted from the design time ontology (a so-called TBox snippet), as well as a "grounding" information (in the form of ABox assertions), which links the snippet

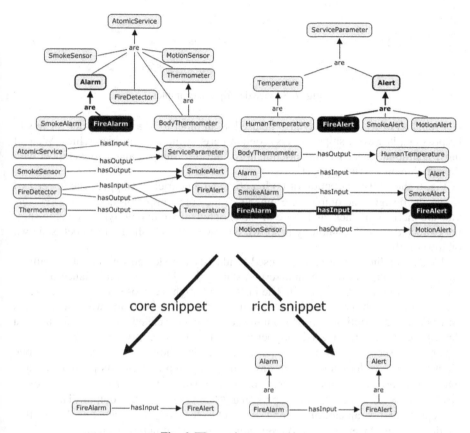

**Fig. 6.** TBox snippet extraction

with a specific instance of the service, running on a specific node. The design time ontology can be looked at as consisting of many, possibly overlapping TBox snippets.

We treat ontologies as directed graphs with concepts as vertexes and relations as edges. Using this approach, the problem of extracting a snippet from the design time ontology is reduced to finding a subgraph (the snippet) in a graph (the ontology).

A minimal TBox snippet consists of the concept representing the service type and one or more concepts representing the types of the service's parameters. We call such a snippet a 'core snippet'.

In order enable serendipitous service discovery and composition, it is essential for the snippets corresponding to different services to "overlap". The simplest case is when the same concept is used as a service parameter type of two different services. This is the case of Temperature, which is used in both Thermometer and FireDetector (see Fig. 5c), in the former as output, in the latter as input. A more elaborate scenario involves subsumption of concepts – this is the case of Alert, which is the input to Alarm and which subsumes SmokeAlert, FireAlert, and MotionAlert. These in turn are other services' outputs. The information on relationships between those concepts is used at runtime to detect service opportunities. Since SmokeAlert

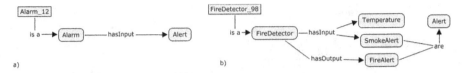

**Fig. 7.** Service description examples

is a subclass of `Alert`, it may also be used as an input to `Alarm`[3]. In order for this to be possible, however, snippets must contain parts of the concept hierarchies. We call those additional concepts "an enrichment" of the core snippet, and a core snippet with the enrichment – a rich snippet[4].

Fig. 6 shows the extraction of both a core and an enriched snippet. The upper part shows the design time ontology. Elements of the core snippet of the `FireAlarm` service are marked in black, and those of the enrichment are in bold type. The core snippet extracted from the ontology is shown on lower left, and the rich snippet is shown on lower right.

The "grounding" information is used to identify a node and link the node with its snippet. It is introduced with an assertion stating that the node is an instance of a service concept in the TBox snippet. The instance id might be chosen by the node manufacturer, or it might be generated at runtime (as long as it is unique within the node's network[5]). A description created from the core snippet is called the core description; a description created from a rich snippet is called a rich description. Fig. 7 shows two examples of service descriptions. The `Alarm` service shown in Fig. 7a) has only one input (`Alert`). It does not contain any concept not representing its parameters, and thus it is a core description. The `FireDetector` shown in Fig. 7b) takes `Temperature` and `SmokeAlert` as the inputs and `FireAlert` as the output. The `Alert` concept is not a parameter of `FireAlert`, and so the snippet is a rich one. Notice that the descriptions "overlap" – the `Alert` concept is present in both of them.

# 5   Runtime

At runtime, the system consists of a number of nodes, each node having its own service description. In order for the system to answer queries regarding available services, an ontology composer is elected. The ontology composer is a device that is most appropriate for processing the descriptions, either because of its computing power, available bandwidth, or location. The composer gathers all the descriptions and constructs a runtime ontology. All queries about available services are then forwarded to the ontology composer, which resolves them and sends the results back to the original query issuer. The latter contacts the desired service(s) directly.

## 5.1   The Runtime Ontology

The runtime ontology is created by merging the descriptions of services. Since the descriptions were parts of the design time ontology, the runtime ontology becomes a

---

[3] In section 5.2. we present the rules, according to which such inferences are performed.
[4] Note that the level of "richness" depends on the number of additional concepts.
[5] This might be achieved e.g. by using UUID number generator.

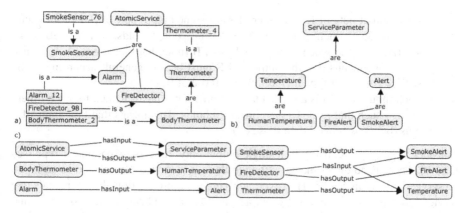

**Fig. 8.** Runtime ontology

subset of the design time ontology, extended with ABox assertions. The absence of concepts representing services that are not present in the environment makes the knowledge base lightweight and thus easier to be processed on resource-constrained nodes.

An example of a runtime ontology is presented in Fig. 8. It consists of descriptions of SmokeSensor, Alarm, FireDetector, BodyThermometer, and Thermometer services. Fig. 8a) shows the service type hierarchy, along with instances of service concepts. The instance identifiers represent the nodes the services run on. Fig. 8b) contains the hierarchy of service parameter types. Fig. 8c) depicts the relations that link services with their parameters. Notice that a rich snippet, when merged with a core snippet, may hide the lack of additional concepts in the latter one. For example, if the relation between HumanTemperature and Temperature is present in a rich Thermometer description, then merging with the core BodyThermometer description yields the same result as merging with a rich BodyThermometer description containing the above relation.

### 5.2 Service Query Resolution

There are two kinds of service queries: parameter-based queries and service-based queries. The former asks for a service that has specific (or matching) parameters, and the latter asks for a specific (or matching) service type. Both types of queries consist of concepts from the design time ontology, belonging either to the service type or service parameter type hierarchy.

The parameter-based query contains a list of parameter types that the requested service should take and return. A service matching the query must provide all of the desired outputs and must not require any other inputs[6]. Also, its parameters must be ontologically related to the parameters in the request. Specifically, we say that a service S matches a query R whenever:

---

[6] Notice that while a service that offers more outputs than specified in the query matches the request, a service that requires more inputs than specified in the query does not.

- Each output $out_R$ of R is a super-class of some output $out_S$ of S, i.e., for each $i$ there exists $j$ such that `subclassOf(out`$_{Sj}$`,out`$_{Ri}$`)` holds, where `subclassOf(A,B)` is true when A is a subclass of B (note that `subclass(A,A)` is also true). This means that the outputs of S must be less general (according to the service parameter type hierarchy) than those of R.
- Each input $in_S$ of S is a super-class of some input $in_R$ of R, i.e., for each $i$ there exists $j$ such that `subclassOf(in`$_{Rj}$`,in`$_{Si}$`)` holds. This means that the inputs of S must be more general than those of R.

Consider a query that consists of a single output only: the `Alert` parameter type (see Fig. 8). There is no direct match; although there is a service that takes it as an input, no service returns an `Alert`. However, applying the aforementioned rules reveals two services that match the query by outputting `Alert`'s subclasses (`FireAlert` and `SmokeAlert`). Those are `SmokeSensor` and `FireDetector`.

In some situations no atomic service matches the query. Consider a query for a service that outputs `FireAlert` and takes `Temperature` as input. Only one service outputs `FireAlert` (namely `FireDetector`), but it requires additional input, `SmokeAlert`. This is where the service composition comes into picture. A service that outputs `SmokeAlert` is found (`SmokeSensor`), and the two atomic services are composed into a complex one. The complex service that consists of `FireDetector` and `SmokeSensor` and that outputs `FireAlert` is returned as the result.

Another scenario of service composition is the case where no single service is able to deliver requested outputs. Consider the query consisting of `SmokeAlert` and `Temperature` as outputs. The only matching service is the complex one, consisting of `SmokeSensor` and `Thermometer`.

The other kind of a query is the service-based one. It contains the ontological concept denoting the type of service the requestor is looking for. Again, the ontology composer resolves it using the subsumption relationship. We say that a service S matches the query R whenever:

- The type of service S, $srv_S$, is a subclass of the type of service R, $srv_R$, i.e., `subclassOf(srv`$_S$`, srv`$_R$`)` holds. For example, a query with the `Thermometer` service type has two results: `Thermometer` and `BodyThermometer` (since the latter is a subclass of the query service type).

## 6  Summary and Future Work

This paper presents a novel approach to providing semantic services in resource-constrained environments. We use ontology decomposition and optimization techniques to create a lightweight, runtime-processable version of the domain ontology. The ontology is then used on resource-constrained nodes in service discovery and composition.

Currently, we are implementing a prototype running on handheld devices. Our target, however, are MicaZ-class WSAN networks. The preliminary results of our research indicate that achieving this target is possible.

# References

1. Akyildiz, I.F., Kasimoglu, I.H.: Wireless sensor and actor networks: research challenges. Ad Hoc Networks Journal 2(4), 351–367 (2004)
2. Chinnici, R., et al.: Web Services Description Language (WSDL) Version 2.0 Part 1: Core Language (2004)
3. Miller, J., et al.: WSDL-S: Adding Semantics to WSDL-White Paper, Technical report, Large Scale Distributed Information Systems (2004)
4. Jammes, F., Mensch, A., Smit, H.: Service-oriented device communications using the devices profile for web services. In: 3rd International Workshop on Middleware for Pervasive and Ad-Hoc Computing (MPAC 2005) at the 6th International Middleware Conference (2005)
5. Jammes, F., Smit, H.: Service-oriented architectures for devices-the SIRENA view. In: 3rd IEEE International Conference on Industrial Informatics (2005)
6. Leguay, J., et al.: An efficient service oriented architecture for heterogeneous and dynamic wireless sensor networks. In: 33rd IEEE Conference on Local Computer Networks (2008)
7. Liu, J., Zhao, F.: Towards semantic services for sensor-rich information systems. In: 2nd International Conference on Broadband Networks (2005)
8. Heine, F., Hovestadt, M., Kao, O.: Towards ontology-driven P2P grid resource discovery. In: 5th IEEE/ACM International Workshop on Grid Computing (2004)
9. Rezgui, A., Eltoweissy, M.: Service-oriented sensor-actuator networks: Promises, challenges, and the road ahead. In: Computer Communications, pp. 2627–2648. Elsevier, Amsterdam (2007)
10. McMullen, D.F., Devadithya, T., Chiu, K.: Integrating Instruments and Sensors into the Grid with CIMA Web Services. In: 3rd APAC Conference and Exhibition Advanced Computing, Grid Computing, Grid Applications and e-Research (2005)
11. Ruta, M., Di Noia, T., Di Sciascio, E., Piscitelli, G.: Ontology Driven Resource Discovery in Bluetooth Based M-Marketplace. In: 8th IEEE International Conference on E-Commerce Technology and The 3rd IEEE International onference on Enterprise Computing, E-Commerce and E-Services (2006)

# Prediction Based Mobile Data Aggregation in Wireless Sensor Network

Sangbin Lee, Songmin Kim, Doohyun Ko, Sungjun Kim, and Sunshin An

Department of Electronics and Computer Engineering,
Korea University, Seoul, Korea
{kulsbin,minkim,dhko,sjunii,sunshin}@dsys.korea.ac.kr

**Abstract.** A wireless sensor network consists of many energy-autonomous micro-sensors distributed throughout an area of interest. Each node has a limited energy supply and generates information that needs to be communicated to a sink node. To reduce costs, the data sent via intermediate sensors to a sink, are often aggregated. The existing energy-efficient approaches to in-network aggregation in sensor networks can be classified into two categories, the centralized and distributed approaches, each having its unique strengths and weaknesses. In this paper, we introduce PMDA (Prediction based Mobile Data Aggregation) scheme which uses a novel data aggregation scheme to utilize the knowledge of the mobile node and the infrastructure (static node tree) in gathering the data from the mobile node. This knowledge (geo-location and transmission range of the mobile node) is useful for gathering the data of the mobile node. Hence, the sensor nodes can construct a near-optimal aggregation tree by itself, using the knowledge of the mobile node, which is a similar process to forming the centralized aggregation tree. We show that the PMDA is a near-optimal data aggregation scheme with mobility support, achieving energy and delay efficiency. This data aggregation scheme is proven to outperform the other general data aggregation schemes by our experimental results.

**Keywords:** Data Aggregation, Mobility, Prediction, Wireless Sensor Networks.

## 1 Introduction

In sensor networks, the communication cost is often several orders of magnitude higher than the computation cost. In order to optimize the communication cost, in-network data aggregation is considered an effective technique. The inherent redundancy in the raw data collected from the sensors can often be eliminated by in-network data aggregation. In addition, such operations are also useful for extracting application specific information from the raw data. To conserve energy for a longer network lifetime, it is critical for the network to support a high incidence of in-network data aggregation. Optimal aggregation can be defined in terms of the total energy consumption for transporting the collected information

N. Abdennadher and D. Petcu (Eds.): GPC 2009, LNCS 5529, pp. 328–339, 2009.
© Springer-Verlag Berlin Heidelberg 2009

from the sensor nodes to the sink. Based on the topology of the network, the location of sources, and the aggregation function, an optimal aggregation tree can be constructed. Existing energy-efficient approaches to in-network aggregation in sensor networks can be classified into two categories, the centralized and distributed approaches, with each having its unique strengths and weaknesses. Various centralized approaches [2,9,11] have been proposed for aggregation in data gathering applications, where all nodes periodically report to the sink. Due to their unchanging traffic pattern, centralized approaches incur low maintenance overhead and are therefore suited for such applications. Various distributed approaches have been proposed for event-based applications [4,5,6,12]. However previous aggregation techniques for event based applications have several limitations. First, for dynamic scenarios, the overhead associated with the construction and maintenance of the structure may outweigh the benefits of data aggregation. Second, some distributed approaches such as [12] assume that there is a well defined center of the event and that the measured strength of the sensed signal is an indicator of the distance to the center of the event. For applications with amorphous events, such as biological hazards, chemical hazards, or fire detection, the absence of an explicit center or any evident point for optimal aggregation makes such approaches inapplicable. Third, centralized approaches that centrally compute the aggregation tree [11] are not practical for dynamic scenarios due to excessive communication overhead for centralized computation. The goal of our work is to design techniques and protocols that lead to efficient data aggregation. Combining a partially centralized approach with a distributed approach to further improve the performance is the goal of this paper. In this paper, we consider a wireless sensor network consisting of Mobile Nodes and Static Nodes. Moreover we propose a prediction based mobile data aggregation scheme to use the knowledge of the mobile node and the infrastructure (static node tree) in gathering data of the mobile node. This knowledge (geo-location, transmission range of the mobile node) is useful for gathering the data of the mobile node. The data of the mobile node has the properties similar to those of event-based applications (i.e. receiving the data from the mobile node ≈ sensing the event). However, the mobile node can inform static nodes of their transmission range and the present location whereas static nodes cannot know the region in which an event takes place in other event-based applications. A static node receiving data from a mobile node can predict which other static nodes may receive data from this mobile node by making use of these properties. Therefore, the sensor nodes construct the aggregation tree by itself and schedule the transmission in such a way as to minimize the energy consumption and gathering delay, which is a similar process to forming the centralized aggregation tree. The remainder of this paper is organized as follows: In Section 2, we summarize related work. Section 3 describes the system model (network, energy, data aggregation model). Section 4 presents the PMDA scheme. Section 5 provides a performance comparison between PMDA and other algorithms through simulations. Finally, Section 6 concludes this paper.

## 2   Related Works

Data aggregation has been an active research area in sensor networks because of its ability to reduce the energy consumption. Some works focus on how to aggregate data from different nodes [1], some focus on how to construct and maintain a structure to facilitate data aggregation [2,3,4]. In [2], the authors propose the LEACH protocol to cluster sensor nodes and let the cluster-heads aggregate data. The cluster-heads then communicate directly with the base station. PEGASIS [10] extends LEACH by organizing all nodes in a chain and letting nodes be the cluster-head in turn. [3] extends PEGASIS by allowing simultaneous transmission so as to balances the energy and delay cost for data gathering. Both LEACH and PEGASIS assume that any node in the network can reach the base-station directly in one-hop, which limits the size of the network for which they are applicable. GIT [13] uses a different approach as compared to LEACH. GIT is built on top of a routing protocol, Directed Diffusion [1], which is one of the earliest proposed attribute-based routing protocols. In Directed Diffusion, data can be aggregated opportunistically when they meet at any intermediate node. Based on Directed Diffusion, the Greedy Incremental Tree establishes an energy-efficient tree by attaching all sources greedily onto an established energy-efficient path and pruning less energy efficient paths. However due to the overhead of pruning branches, GIT might lead to high cost in moving event scenarios. In [12], the authors propose DCTC, Dynamic Convoy Tree-Based Collaboration, to reduce the overhead of tree migration in mobile event scenarios. DCTC assumes that the distance to the event is known to each sensor and uses the node near the center of the event as the root to construct and maintain the aggregation tree dynamically. However, it involves heavy message exchange which might offset the benefit of aggregation in large-scale networks. From the simulation results in [12], the energy consumption of tree expansion, pruning and reconfiguration is about 33% of the data collection. In [14], the authors propose an aggregation tree construction algorithm to simultaneously approximate the optimum trees for all non-decreasing and concave aggregation functions. The algorithm uses a simple min-cost perfect matching to construct the tree. Other works, such as SMT (Steiner Minimum Tree) and MST (Multiple Shared Tree) for multicast algorithms which can be used in data aggregation [15] build a structure in advance for data aggregation. In addition to their complexity and overhead, they are only suitable for networks where the sources are known in advance. Therefore, they are not suitable for networks with mobile events.

## 3   System Model

In this section, we present the preliminary system model for the design of our scheme. We state our assumptions and model and introduce some notations to be used. A summary list of the notation used in this paper is given in Table 1.

### 3.1   Network Model

We consider a multi-hop wireless network with $n$ nodes. The nodes communicate with each other via wireless links. A node can either send or receive data

**Table 1.** List of Notation

| Notation | Description |
|---|---|
| $\alpha$ | Path loss ($2 \leq \alpha \leq 5$) |
| $\beta$ | Constant $[Joule/(bits \cdot m^{\alpha})]$ |
| $L_p$ | length of packets $[bits]$ |
| $v_i$ | $i$-th static node |
| $r_i$ | Transmission range of $v_i$ |
| $l_e$ | Longest Edge in sensor network |
| $p_i(v_i)$ | The number of $p_i$-nodes of node $v_i$ when its range is $r_i$ |
| $M(r_m)$ | Region in $r_m$ from Mobile node |
| $V(r_m)$ | The set of the nodes in $M(r_m)$ |
| $\tau$ | The number of $V(r_m)$ |
| $N(r_i)$ | The number of neighbors of node $v_i$ when its range is $r_i$ |
| $t_{dc}$ | Delay constraint $[sec]$ |
| $p_i$-node | Node near the sink than $v_i$ |

at one time, and it can receive data correctly only if exactly one of its neighbors is transmitting at that moment. The main task of the sensor nodes is to collect data and transmit them back to the sink, and the data can be aggregated all the way to the sink. In other words, if a node receives one packet from its neighbor before its scheduled transmission time, then it can merge this packet with its own data packet and simply sends this merged packet later. Aggregation at an internal node is performed only after all input information is available at the node - either received from its children, or generated by receiving packet from the mobile node. The aggregated data is then transmitted to the parent node. Let $T_m = (V(r_m), E(r_m))$ denote the data gathering tree in the specific area $M(r_m)$, where $V(r_m)$ denotes the set of $\tau$ static nodes in $M(r_m)$, $V(r_m) = \{v_1, v_2, \ldots, v_\tau\}$, and $E(r_m)$ denotes the set of directed communication links between the members of $V(r_m)$. where $M(r_m)$ is the area in which the static nodes receive the packets from the mobile node. Every link in $E(r_m)$ is represented as a a pair $(i, j)$, implying that $v_j$ is the parent of $v_i$. Raw data is generated by $V(r_m)$. Data aggregation is performed by all non-sink and non-leaf nodes (referred to as internal nodes). Aggregation at an internal node is performed only after all input information is available at the node - either received from its children, or generated by receiving packet from the mobile node. The aggregated data is then transmitted to the parent node. As in a previous work [6], we make the simplistic assumption that an intermediate node can aggregate multiple incoming packets into a single outgoing packet. A data aggregation schedule can be thought of as a sequence of senders $\{S_1, S_2, \ldots\}$ (in which $S_i \subset V, \forall i$ ) satisfying the data aggregation property. This sequence represents the situation where all nodes in $S_1$ transmit in the first time slot, followed by all nodes in $S_2$ transmitting in the second time slot and so on and so forth. The data aggregation property simply means that after $S_1$ transmits its data, this data will be aggregated from $V$ to $V - S_1$ and after $S_2$ transmits its data, this data will be further aggregated from $V - S_1$ to $V - S_1 \cup S_2$. If we continue this process, finally all of the data will be aggregated to one single node, which is the sink. The property of single transmission is essentially equivalent to all $S_i$'s being disjoint. Now, the minimum data aggregation time problem can be formulated as follows. Given a graph $T_m = (V(r_m), E(r_m))$ and a sink $\in V$, find a data aggregation schedule with minimum delay. This problem is proven to be NP-hard even for unit disk graphs [8].

## 3.2   Energy Model

We assume that each node has a battery with a finite, non-replaceable energy. Whenever a node transmits or receives a data packet, it consumes some energy from its battery. However, the sink has an unlimited amount of energy available to it. The model for the energy consumption per bit at the physical layer is (As in [2]),

$$E = E_{ctrans} + E_{crec} + E_{aggre} + \beta d_{ij}^{\alpha} \tag{1}$$

where $E_{ctrans}$ is the energy utilized by the transmitter circuits (PLLs, bias currents, etc.) and digital processing. This energy is independent of distance; $E_{crec}$ is the energy consumed by the receiver circuits, $E_{caggre}$ is the energy consumed by data aggregation, and $\beta d_{ij}^{\alpha}$ accounts for the radiated power necessary to transmit over a distance $d_{ij}$ between node $v_i$ and node $v_j$. We assume that $E_{ctrans} = E_{crec} = E_{circuit}$. According to this link metric, the aggregation cost for node $v_i$ is expressed as

$$C_i^{Aggre}(r_i) = L_p \left[ (E_{circuit} + E_{caggre}) p_i(v_i) + E_{circuit} + \beta r_i^{\alpha} \right] \tag{2}$$

The expression $\beta r_i^{\alpha}$ represents the energy needed to transmit one bit over a distance $r_i$; thus $L_p(E_{circuit} + \beta r_i^{\alpha})$ is the energy needed for node $v_i$ to transmit the packet in its range, whereas the $p_i$-nodes in range of $v_i$ expends only $L_p \cdot (E_{circuit} + E_{caggre}) \cdot p_i(v_i)$ to receive and aggregate the packets. By adding these two components, we obtain the Eq.2.

# 4   Proposed Scheme

## 4.1   Transmission Range of Mobile Node

If $R$ is a unit square and n static nodes are distributed uniformly at random in $R$, the Eq.3, which refers to [7], denotes the transmission radius for $k$-connectivity, $r_n(k)$,

$$r_n(k) = \sqrt{\frac{\log n + (2k - 1) \log \log n + \xi}{\pi n}} \leq \max r, \tag{3}$$

where

$$\xi = \begin{cases} -2 \log \left( \sqrt{e^{-c} + \frac{\pi}{4}} - \frac{\sqrt{\pi}}{2} \right) & \text{if } k = 1 \\ 2 \log \frac{\sqrt{\pi}}{2(k-1)k!} + 2c & \text{if } k > 1 \end{cases}$$

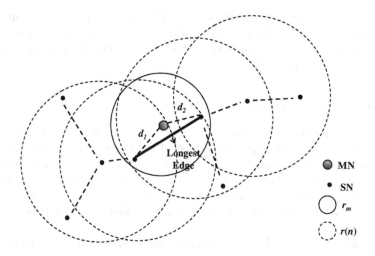

**Fig. 1.** Deciding the transmission range of mobile node from longest edge in wireless sensor network

As shown in Fig.1, if $d_1+d_2 \geq$ longest edge , the mobile node can be connected to the static nodes larger than one static node. Since $d_1 \leq r_m$ and $d_2 \leq r_m$,

$$\text{longest edge}(l_e) \leq d_1 + d_2 \leq 2\dot{r}_m \qquad (4)$$

Therefore,

$$r_m \geq \frac{l_e}{2} \qquad (5)$$

Moreover, the longest edge is related to $r_n(k)$ [7,9]. By Eq.5 and relation between $r_n(k)$ and $l_e$ , when $r_m$ is larger than $\frac{r_n(k)}{2}$, the mobile node may be connected to the static nodes with high probability. If the range of the mobile node is $r_m$, the longest distance among $V(r_m)$ must be shorter than $2r_m$. Therefore, when $r_m \leq \frac{\max r_i}{2}$, the members of $V(r_m)$ can know the information of all other members. In this case, the members of $V(r_m)$ can construct an aggregation tree distributedly and at the same time schedule their transmission time heuristically by using the table of their one hop neighbors because each member of $V(r_m)$ can predict the rest members and $\tau$. $r_m$ is decided according to application properties, as in Eq. 6.

$$\frac{r_n(k)}{2} < r_m \leq \frac{\max r_i}{2} \qquad (6)$$

After $r_m$ is determined, the mobile node transmits the data including its location and the value of $r_m$. The whole process described throughout this section eventually leads $\tau$ to be $\lim_{n \to \infty} P(\tau \geq 1) = 1$. In other words, probability of connectivity converges to one as $n \to \infty$. The delay is directly proportional to $\tau$, because the interference among the members of $V(r_m)$ prevents them from transmitting their packets simultaneously. Therefore, $\tau$ equals the number of TDMA slots in $M(r_m)$. When an application requires a specific delay constraint $(t_{dc})$, the mobile node determines the value of $r_m$ for the given delay constraint $(t_{dc} = \tau \approx k)$ by applying Eq.6.

## 4.2   Construction Aggregation Tree

We assign the numbers to each member of $V(r_m)$ for the purpose of scheduling and constructing the aggregation tree. If the static nodes maintain a table with information about their neighbors (node id, location, etc.), each member of $V(r_m)$ can predict the other members of $V(r_m)$ from the mobile node's location and transmission range $(r_m)$. In other words, if $d_{mj} \leq r_m$, $v_i$ knows that $v_j$ is a member of $V(r_m)$, where $d_{mj}$ is the distance between the mobile node and its neighbor $v_j$.

Since each member of $V(r_m)$ is aware of all other members, they can assign their own number as follows. As it gets farther from sink, it is assigned with a smaller number. (i.e. $v_1$ is the farthest node from the sink whereas $v_\tau$ is the closest). It is done so, since the distance of the nodes from the sink is the most important factor for deciding the hierarchical level. Sub-aggregation Tree rooted at $v_\tau$ in $M(r_m)$ is constructed considering the energy consumption and delay. Each member of $V(r_m)$ sets its range of transmission based on the following LP (Linear Programming) problem.

Objective :

$$\min E_{sub} = \sum_{i:v_i} C_i^{Aggre}(r_i), \qquad p_i(r_i) > 0 \qquad (7)$$

Clearly, $p_i(r_i)$ is reduced as $r_i$ is reduced. Therefore when $p_i(r_i) = 1$, $E_{sub}$ is minimized, meaning that each node decides the its range so that $p_i(r_i) = 1$ Hence, the Aggregation Tree is constructed as shown in Fig.2.

## 4.3   TDMA Scheduling

TDMA(Time Division Multiple Access) schemes have been proposed wherein the slot is optimally assigned according to the routing requirements, while minimizing the total energy consumption across the network. In particular, during the time slot assigned by the TDMA scheme, the corresponding node works in active mode. After finishing its data transmission, it turns off all of its circuits and enters sleep mode. In this way, the energy consumption can be minimized. A data aggregation schedule specifies how the data packets from all of the members of $V(r_m)$ are collected and transmitted to the sink. Deterministically assigning the TDMA slot to the nodes such that those closer to the sink wait longer can schedule the tree efficiently. The members of $V(r_m)$ receive the knowledge of the location and transmission range of mobile node (i.e. they can compute the area in which nodes are triggered by the mobile node), and know their location and their relative position compared to the other members of $V(r_m)$, and their distance to the sink. Therefore it can set the slot order inversely proportional to

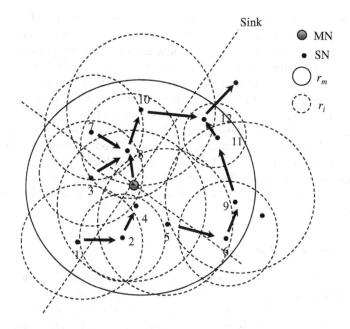

**Fig. 2.** Deciding the transmission range → Constructing the Aggregation Tree → TDMA slot allocation

its distance to the sink (In figure 1, $v_1$ transmits the packet in the first slot, while $v_{12}$ transmits in the 12-th slot). The latency will be proportional to the range of the mobile node. Therefore, each member of $V(r_m)$ delays its transmission according to the slot that it should select, from 0 to $\tau$, where $\tau$ is the maximum delay. In figure 2, if $v_{10}$ chooses a higher delay than $v_1$ and $v_4$, $v_1$ and $v_4$'s packets may be aggregated at $v_{10}$. Therefore, the slot length must longer than the aggregation time (transmission time + sampling time). The optimum value of the slot length depends on $\tau$ and the time required to transmit a packet. If the application is not delay tolerant, a low value of $\tau$ is required which can not reap the benefits of this approach. Since the nodes are able to know the size of the event ($r_m$), they can know the optimal value of the delay and aggregation tree.

## 5  Simulation

In this section we evaluate and compare the performance of PMDA with that of other protocols (Randomized Waiting aggregation (RW) [5], and Optimal Aggregation Tree (OAT) [6] ). We use the ns-2 network simulator to evaluate the protocols in a 200m x 200m network with uniformly random node separation. We assume that the data rate of the radio is $38.4Kbps$, the maximum transmission range of the nodes is $40m$ and the sink is located at (0,0). In our simulation, we set $\alpha = 2$, $\beta = 100pJ/bit/m^\alpha$, $E_{circuit} = 50pJ/bit$ and $E_{caggre} = 100pJ/bit$

for the power consumption model. We set the data packet size, $L_P = 1000bits$. We are particularly interested in the typical scenarios encountered in sensor networks applications. The model depends on several input parameters and on the appropriate choice of these parameters which are highly dependent on the technology and on the target application. We vary these parameters in order to study their relevant effects on the network performance. Moreover, we believe that the realistic tuning of these parameters must be aided by the real hardware implementation of the considered protocols. A mobile node moves in the network using the random way-point mobility model at a speed of $10m/s$ for 400 seconds. The nodes triggered by the mobile node will send packets every five seconds to the sink located at (0,0). The aggregation function evaluated here is perfect aggregation (i.e. all packets can be aggregated into one packet without increasing the packet size).

## 5.1   Impact of Nodes

We evaluate the total energy consumption and gathering delay for these protocols for different numbers of nodes. Fig.3 shows a comparison of the energy consumption of the different protocols. RW show the worst energy performance when the number of nodes is small since its aggregation is opportunistic. PMDA has the best performance amongst the various protocols because of its ability to perfectly aggregate packets at nodes closer to the source and, thus, it reduces the cost of forwarding packets from the sources to the sink and the interference of the nodes. The energy consumption of PMDA is shown to be sharply lower than that of the other protocols when the number of nodes increases. Thus, as the number of nodes increases, PMDA has higher performance than the other protocols. Fig.4 shows the total data gathering delay as a function of the number of nodes. RW show the worst delay performance since its wating time is randomly selected. The gathering delay of PMDA is lower than that of the other protocols,

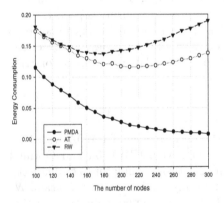

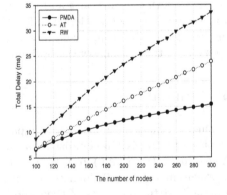

**Fig. 3.** Energy consumption according to the number of nodes

**Fig. 4.** Total gathering delay according to the number of nodes

due to its ability to aggregate packets early and scatter them away from each other to reduce contention. Also, the data gathering delay of PMDA is shown to be slightly higher than that of the other protocols when the number of nodes increases. Thus, as the number of nodes increases, PMDA exhibits higher data gathering delay performance than the other protocols.

## 5.2   Impact of $r_m$

We evaluate the total energy consumption and gathering delay for these protocols for different transmission ranges of the mobile nodes $(r_m)$. We calculate the range of $r_m$ from Eq. 6. If we assume that the number of nodes is 200 and $k = 1$, than $r_{200}(1)$ is 0.149. Since the simulation area is 200 x 200, 14.9 < $r_m \leq 20$. Therefore, we evaluate the total energy consumption and gathering delay on $14 < r_m \leq 20$. Fig.5 shows a comparison of the energy consumption of different protocols. RW shows the worst energy performance since its aggregation is opportunistic. PMDA has the best performance amongst the protocols because of its ability to perfectly aggregate the packets at nodes closer to the source and, thus, it reduces the cost of forwarding packets from the sources to the sink and the interference of the nodes. The energy consumption of PMDA is shown to be mostly uniform when the range of the mobile nodes increases. However, the energy consumption of the other protocols is sharply increases when the range of the mobile nodes increases. Thus, as the range of the mobile nodes increase, PMDA has higher performance than the other protocols. Fig.6 shows the total data gathering delay as a function of the range of the mobile nodes. RW also shows the worst delay performance since its wating time is randomly selected. The gathering delay of PMDA is lower than that of other protocols, due to its ability to aggregate packets early and scatter them away from each other to reduce contention. Also, the data gathering delay of PMDA is shown to be slightly higher than that of the other protocols (RW, OAT) when the number of

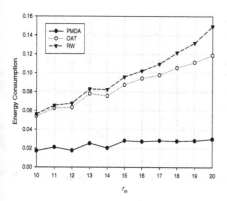

**Fig. 5.** Energy consumption according to $r_m$

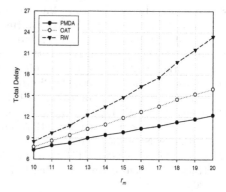

**Fig. 6.** Total gathering delay according to $r_m$

nodes increases. Thus, as the number of nodes increases, PMDA exhibits higher data gathering delay performance than the other protocols (RW, OAT).

## 6  Conclusion

In this paper, we propose a data aggregation protocol which supports the mobility of sensor nodes, schedules their transmission times and constructs the optimal aggregation tree. Furthermore, we showed that this protocol outperforms the other data aggregation protocols according to our simulation results. In the future, we will consider the transmissions of multiple mobile nodes.

## References

1. Intanagonwiwat, C., Govindan, R., Estrin, D., Heidemann, J., Silva, F.: Directed Diffusion for Wireless Sensor Networking. IEEE/ACM Transactions on Networking 11 (2003)
2. Heinzelman, W.B., Chandrakasan, A.P., Balakrishnan, H.: An Application-Specific Protocol Architecture for Wireless Microsensor Networks. IEEE Transactions on Wireless Communications 1(4) (2002)
3. Lindsey, S., Raghavendra, C., Sivalingam, K.M.: Data Gathering Algorithms in Sensor Networks Using Energy Metrics. IEEE Transactions on Parallel and Distributed Systems 13 (2002)
4. Zhang, W., Cao, G.: Optimizing Tree Reconfiguration for Mobile Target Tracking in Sensor Networks. In: Proceedings of INFOCOM 2004, vol. 4 (2004)
5. Fan, K.W., Liu, S., Sinha, P.: Structure-free Data Aggregation in Sensor Networks. IEEE Transactions on Mobile Computing 6 (2007)
6. Fan, K.W., Liu, S., Sinha, P.: Scalable Data Aggregation for Dynamic Events in Sensor Networks. In: Proceedings of ACM SenSys. 2006, Boulder, Colorado, USA (2006)
7. Wan, J., Yi, C.W.: Asymptotic Critical Transmission Radius and Critical Neighbor Number for k-Connectivity in Wireless Ad Hoc Networks. In: Proceedings of ACM MobiHoc 2004, Roppongi, Japan (2004)
8. Chen, X., Hu, X., Zhu, J.: Minimum data aggregation time problem in wireless sensor networks. In: Jia, X., Wu, J., He, Y. (eds.) MSN 2005. LNCS, vol. 3794, pp. 133–142. Springer, Heidelberg (2005)
9. Santi, P.: The Critical Transmitting Range for Connectivity in Mobile Ad Hoc Networks. IEEE Transaction on Mobile Computing 4(3) (2005)
10. Lindsey, S., Raghavendra, C.: PEGASIS: Power-efficient gathering in sensor information systems. In: Proceedings of IEEE Aerospace Conference, vol. 3 (2002)
11. Wong, J., Jafari, R., Potkonjak, M.: Gateway placement for latency and energy efficient data aggregation. In: 29th Annual IEEE International Conference on Local Computer Networks (2004)
12. Zhang, W., Cao, G.: DCTC: Dynamic Convoy Tree-based Collaboration for Target Tracking in Sensor Networks. IEEE Transactions on Wireless Communications 3 (2004)
13. Intanagonwiwat, C., Estrin, D., Goviindan, R.: Impact of Network Density on Data Aggregation in Wireless Sensor Networks. Technical Report 01-750, University of Southern California (2001)

14. Goel, A., Estrin, D.: Simultaneous Optimization for Concave Costs: Single Sink Aggregation or Single Source Buy-at-Bulk. In: Proceedings of the 14th Annual ACM-SIAM Symposium on Discrete Algorithms (2003)
15. Salama, H.F., Reeves, D.S., Viniotis, Y.: Evaluation of Multicast Routing Algorithms for Real-time Communication on High-speed Networks. IEEE Journal on Selected Area in Communications 15 (1997)

# A Distributed Architecture of Sensing Web for Sharing Open Sensor Nodes

Ryo Kanbayashi and Mitsuhisa Sato

Graduate School of Science and Engineering, University of Tsukuba,
1-1-1 Tennodai, Tsukuba, Ibaraki 305-8573, Japan
{kanbayashi,msato}@hpcs.cs.tsukuba.ac.jp

**Abstract.** Today, sensor devices such as video cameras are being installed at several places. It is a promising technology to make use of
these sensors connected with the network. Sensing Web is a conceptual
framework to shares sensors open in wide-area network with keeping privacy. While previous sensor grids target small and simple data such as
the temperature and humidity data, Sensing Web targets relatively large
data such as image data or voice data, which may include privacy information. In this paper, we propose a architecture named SW-agent to
realize the idea of Sensing Web SW-agent protects privacy information
with elimination of privacy information and appropriate access control.
The elimination of privacy is done with data processing by remote execution program shipped to a node near a sensor. SW-agent reduces the
amount of communication with elimination of useless data in a similar
way. We examined the basic performance of remote execution program.
We found that SW-agent can execute remote execution program with up
to 7% overhead in performance comparing its direct execution.

## 1 Introduction

Today, the need for real-world information is increasing rapidly. For example,
services such as *Google Street View* [1] enable people to see selected street views
on a web map without physically going to that street.

At the same time sensor devices such as video cameras, infrared sensors and
microphones are being installed in buildings on roads and in station yards. Therefore, *Ubiquitous Sensor Networks*(USNs) are a promising technology for making
use of these sensors. So far, however, only the owners of USN's have implemented
major applications, and these closed networks are generally available only to the
owners. For example, these are applications such as surveillance cameras in stores
or cameras showing traffic flow with fixed point cameras, but the sensor data is
available only to the respective owners and selected employees.

A concept called *Sensing Web*[2] is to enable people to share sensors openly
in a wide-area network. The goal of the Sensing Web is to allow people to access
actual sensor data in the same way they access the World Wide Web (WWW).
In the Sensing Web, new applications or services using sensors can be created
for implementation on both open and closed systems. Consider that you loses an

N. Abdennadher and D. Petcu (Eds.): GPC 2009, LNCS 5529, pp. 340–352, 2009.

object, a lost property finder service accessible with the Web browser through the Sensing Web might be used to find the missing object.

Different from existing sensor grids[3], Sensing Web is a open system. In addition, target data and target application are different. Most important requirement of Sensing Web is privacy protection[4]. Previous sensor grids target simple data such as the temperature and humidity data, which don't include privacy. In contrast, Sensing Web targets data such as image data or voice data, which includes many privacy information. Transmission of data including privacy information puts the information in danger. Therefore, an appropriate privacy protection method is needed. Handling data in network for acquisition of sensor data is also a important requirement. The data such as image data or voice data may be large, although the required information in the data may often be small. Transmission of all sensor data consumes network resources excessively. A method for acquisition of sensor data which consumes little network resources is needed. In addition, consideration of problems arise from several privileges of sensors and machines managing the sensors is needed. Since, unlike sensor grids, these resources of Sensing Web is offered by general public. Administration policies of these are also different from sensor grids.

We propose a distributed architecture named SW-agent as a prototype system of Sensing Web Protection of privacy can be realized with elimination of privacy information and a access control mechanism. Elimination of privacy is done with data processing by remote execution program shipped to a node near a sensor. Reduction of communication traffic can also be done with elimination of useless data in a similar way.

Contribution of our research is following: First of all, we reveal issues of design for sharing sensor data on open systems, which will emerge in the future. We have designed and implemented a system called SW-agent. We developa a prototype of SW-agent and report its basic performance.

Remainder of the paper describes SW-agent and is organized as follows. Section 2 presents an overview of the Sensing WebSection 3 presents the design of SW-agent, which is composed of program shipping facility, privacy protection model, and authorization for access control. Section 4 presents prototyping of SW-agent. Section 5 describes an overview of related work. Our conclusions and future work are discussed in Section 7.

## 2   Sensing Web Project

The Sensing Web Project[2] is a three-year project launched in the fall of 2007. Goal of the project is to develop information technologies necessary for sharing the data of USNs spreading across society openly like current WWW.

However, natures of information handled on the WWW and the Sensing Web differ. On the WWW, privacy information can be removed or otherwise protected because most of the information is entered by humans. In contrast, it can not be removed because the information is actual sensor data automatically collected by sensors. Existing sensor usage, including sensor grids, need not to consider privacy protection because these are closed system. However, privacy protection should be considered on Sensing Web because it is open system. Focusing on handling of privacy information is a notable characteristic of Sensing Web.

Realization of following elemental technologies is important on the Sensing Web.

- Sharing Sensor Data through Service/Request Matching: The information user requested is offered by matching the request and sensor data.
- Privacy Information Management in Sensor Data Acquisition: data. When sensor data is acquired, it is handled in symbolized form including no privacy information, which protects privacy information from leaking the information to malicious people.
- Information Integration for Presenting the Real World Information: Actual sensor data acquired from real world is integrated and offered to users as appropriate applications.

Our research develops a system, which realizes Sensing Web. Especially, solution to privacy information management in sensor data acquisition is offered.

## 3    Design of SW-Agent

In this section, we present the design of SW-agent as a distributed architecture to realize the concept of Sensing Web. SW-agent is composed of two elements: program shipping facility, privacy protection model.

### 3.1    Architecture for Sensing Web

Figure 1 shows a typical environment of the Sensing Web, which currently is composed of closed sensor networks and standalone sensors such as Web cameras. Because these sensors are managed by several PCs connected to the Internet, these sensors are accessible through the Internet.

From the design's point of view, the Sensing Web is characterized by two property: privacy information and large sensing data. Although several sensor grids[3] were already proposed, it targets simple data such as the temperature and humidity data, which don't include privacy. The Sensing Web targets image data and human voice data, which may include many privacy information[4]. The size of data acquired by intelligent sensors such as video cameras may be large and often include many useless information.

To realize the concept of Sensing Web, we propose SW-agents as a distributed architecture for Sensing Web. The SW-agent is an agent program installed near to the sensor to execute applications handling the sensor data. The system administrator sets up the SW-agent near to the sensor. At a minimum, directory service providing information about a sensor's location, user authentication and user authorization are needed for access to sensors.

The application developer uploads his or hers application handling the sensor data to the SW-agent by *Program Shipping Facility*. The client application communicates with its shipped application program to provide a service.

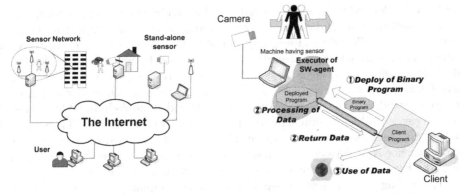

**Fig. 1.** A typical environment          **Fig. 2.** Program Shipping Facility

The SW-agent provides several methods to protect privacy information by monitoring the access to the device and the traffic to the client through the network.

Prior to the use of sensor data, sensor data were typically accumulated in storage and then accessed in sensor grids. However, as stated above, the required information in the sensor data is relatively small and confidential in comparison with the total amount of sensor data. Transmission of whole data consumes network resources excessively because the amount of whole data, such as images from video cameras, is large. Furthermore, the people captured in images may not prefer accumulation of the sensor data out of concern for the leaking of privacy information. Therefore, the Sensing Web handles requested data only by data processing near sensors without accumulating and storing data to storages.

### 3.2   Program Shipping Facility

The *Program Shipping Facility* allows an application binary program to be deployed near a sensor, shown in Figure 2. We describe the deployment as "program shipping". Program shipping has following advantages:

- Flexible data processing: Users can process sensor data flexibly through familiar program languages. The flexible data processing extract useful information out of a large amount of sensor data.
- Utilization of existing code: A program using a sensor can be used with little change. This advantage is important because most users will have their own application using a sensor in a diffusion process of the Sensing Web.
- Usability: Users can use languages familiar to them. That is, users do not need to learn a special language.

A binary program is deployed through a procedure of web services, which make flexible deployment such as automatic deployment based on the algorithms possible.

Sensor information from the shipped program can be acquired by two means. The first is acquisition of data by web services. Users can acquire the data through pre-defined web service procedures. This technique is useful for acquisition of small amounts of data, such as the coordinate data from the lost property finder service. A flexible and user-customizable data access interface can be realized because an arbitrary procedure can be defined by web services. Flexible data access interface bridges the gap between sensor data and request of user, which was mentioned in section 2. In addition, the use of a web service enhances the compatibility of the Sensing Web with the World Wide Web. In addition, use of web service enhance compatibility of Sensing Web between Web. The second way is to use stream communication. If the size of processed data is large or data transfer is performed continuously, stream communication should be used because the overhead of remote procedure calls becomes a problem.

The SW-agent also performs sandboxing for the shipping program. Although shipping is performed by authorized users only, the machines managing the sensors used by the shipping program need ready protection from possible malicious users. Otherwise, the sensors and machines for shipping are not protected by the owner. Therefore, sandboxing is important for the Sensing Web.

SW-agent also provides virtual devices abstracting the sensor devices. Consequently, users can acquire sensor data with a unified procedure using a virtual device without concern for the differences between environments.

### 3.3   Privacy Protection Model

The SW-agent protects privacy by running the remote execution program near sensors. Users can access all sensor data by deployment of a program near sensors, but users also are obligated to eliminate privacy information before sending data to a client through a network. The elimination is achieved through symbolization of sensor data. For example, we show protection on an application that surveys people passing on a road. The protection is achieved by following.

1. Authorization of User: A user who wants to deploy a program must acquire authorization from an access control service of the SW-agent.
2. Deployment of Program: The user deploys a binary program to a machine near a sensor, which manages the sensor. Then, the deployed binary program is started by the executor of SW-agent.
3. Elimination of Privacy Information: The program applies image processing to the image data acquired from the surveillance camera and outputs the number of passages per unit time.
4. Access to Privacy Eliminated Data: The user uses the processed information, which does not include privacy information.

In this application, video data from the surveillance camera may include confidential information, such as images of pedestrians' faces. However, this information is eliminated with symbolization by the shipping program. Therefore, the proposed model can enable a user to get sensor data while protecting the privacy of the sensor data.

However, if an inconsiderate user is authorized, data including privacy information may be sent to to the general public because the proposed model allows an authorized user to acquire all sensor data. Therefore, proper authorization is important in the SW-agent.

## 3.4   Authorization for Access Control

First of all, it is important who have the authority of access control for privacy information. Naturally, captured person, who privacy information belongs to, should be able to authorize. However, authorization by captured people is difficult, which needs the people to carry a special device, which notice sensor authorized users, or interaction between the people and sensors. Therefore, in SW-agent, owners of sensors authorize the accesses instead of captured people. For the representation, SW-agent targets sensors whose owner can represents captured people such as cameras on home.

Appropriate authorization model is also needed. Authorization model for Sensing Web should satisfy followings;

– Performance: Processing costs needed for the model should not be large.
– Management Costs: Management costs for the model should not be high.
– Usability for Users and Owners: Both users and sensor owners should be able to apply for authorization without encountering problems.
– Transparent Use of Sensors Scattered across Different Organizations: Sensors used in the Sensing Web are scattered across different organizations. Users should be able to use these sensors transparently.

In the Sensing Web, sensors are classified into the following two units.

– Sensor Network: Sensors belonging together, which are managed as a sensor network. Typically, the sensors are owned by an organization such as a research institute or a company.
– Standalone Sensor: A sensor exists singularly. Typically, these sensors are owned by an individual.

*Virtual Organization* (VO) [5] is a promising model for the management of resources by grouping the resources needed by users. Grouping sensor networks by VO enables users to use sensors scattered across different organizations transparently. However, VO can't be applied to standalone sensors because there is no administrator for standalone sensors. Each standalone sensor is managed by an individual not interested in the Sensing Web. Therefore, separate authorization is needed for each standalone sensor.

Authorization for standalone sensors may lead to much extra work for users. For example, if a user needs to acquire authorization from each site in order to run an application, which uses hundreds of sensors, the user has to send e-mails to hundreds of administrators or access hundreds of web portals to create an account. Therefore, an authorization model with few or no manual steps is needed for standalone sensors.

For realization of separate authorizations which need only a few manual steps, the *Policy Based Model* and *Chain of Trust Model* can be used. The Policy Based

Model authorizes users by matching the policies of sensors with the attributes of users. The authorization is performed without any extra procedures by the user. However, the expressiveness of the policy is limited by the expressiveness of the attributes of the users, but a listing of attributes which allow arbitrary policy decisions is difficult. The Policy Based Model is suitable for authorization which needs a broad level of permission control, but it is not suitable for a precise level of control.

The Chain of Trust Model authorizes users by a chain of trusts based on the following rule: "friends of my friend are trustworthy." A representative model of the Chain of Trust is *Pretty Good Privacy* (PGP) [6], which can authenticate users by a chain of trusts. For example, a user who has been allowed to access sensor-$A$ on a building can access sensor-$B$ on the same building. However, the effectiveness of the Chain of Trust Model depends on the activity level of owners of the sensor.

The models described above can be used simultaneously in a mutually complementary manner. In the future, we are planning the simultaneous use of multiple models based on the needs of the community.

# 4   Implementation of SW-Agent

We implemented a prototype system of the SW-agent. Primarily, the execution functionality for program shipping is implemented. Figure 3 shows an overview of the execution environment.

The prototype is implemented based on BEE[7]. BEE emulates system calls in different operating systems (OSs) such as Linux and Windows, which enables a user to run a Linux binary on a different OS. Together, BEE and the mechanism for deployment of an execution binary enable the operation of program shipping. However, the prototype does not have a deployment mechanism and can only run on Linux at this time. Using dynamic class loading and the sandboxing

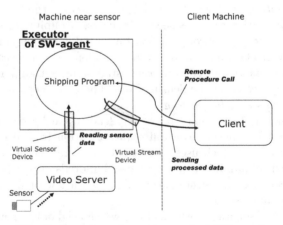

**Fig. 3.** Overview of executor part of SW-agent

mechanism of Java may be used for realization of remote execution. However, Java programs consumes more memory, thus limiting the scalability of the Sensing Web, which runs many processes on a machine. In addition, useful native code libraries such as *Open Computer Vision Library* (OpenCV) [8] cannot be used with implementations constructed with Java.

In the following sections, we describe our implementation of the SW-agent in more detail.

## 4.1 Sandboxing for Secure Execution

Sandboxing is achieved by hooking system calls using the *ptrace* system call in Linux. SW-agent changes the system call handler by *ptrace*, and forces system calls to be handled by the modified call handler by modification of the stack data. The modified handler determine whether each call is permitted with predefined policies. If a call is permitted, the handler calls the original system call using passed arguments. Otherwise, the handler blocks the request and returns a error code. Currently, SW-agent supports *open* system call.

## 4.2 Virtual Devices

The prototype has two virtual devices: a *Virtual Sensor Device* and a *Virtual Stream Device*. Virtual devices are realized by system call emulation, which changes the system call handler with *ptrace*, as in sandboxing. We implemented only the essential system calls: *open, read, write, close, ioctl*.

Virtual Sensor Device enables the user to access a sensor device transparently. The prototype supports emulation of a video device. We implemented the essentials of the video4linux [9] API interface, which is a standard interface for accessing video devices. For supporting video4linux interfaces, we implemented emulations of *ioctl*. Virtual Sensor Device is exported as *"/dev/sensor."* A program can read data by calling the *read* function for *"/dev/sensor."* Virtual Sensor Device acquires sensor data from a video server. The video server provides sensor data read from a real video device to Virtual Sensor Device through interprocess communication. The video server is implemented as a process separate from the executor. While normal device access uses a video device exclusively, our implementation enable users to share a sensor device simultaneously.

Virtual Stream Device realizes easy and efficient data sending to multiple clients. Virtual Stream Device abstracts the stream channel to clients and is exported as *"/dev/client."* Currently, the prototype supports sending data to a clients only.

Unlike the specification of web services for stream data such as MTOM/XOP [10][11], a user can set socket parameters for the Virtual Sensor Device. This capability means communication can be adopted to a network environment. Furthermore, flexible transfer such as third-party transfer is possible by switching transfer destinations.

### 4.3    Remote Procedure Call Interface

We used *Simple Object Access Protocol* (SOAP) for realization of remote procedure call. SOAP supports not only primitive numeric values but also arrays and structured data as the arguments and return values, which enables flexible data access. Most codes for realizing remote procedure calls can be generated by our generation tools. Users only have to write the definitions and implementations of the procedures. We used the gSoap [12] for implementation. The code generation tools invokes tools of gSoap internally.

### 4.4    User Scenario

In this section, we present the user scenario of SW-agent. An execution binary for shipping is created by the following steps.

1. Describe Procedure Definition: A user describes the definition of a remote procedure call of web services with the description format of gSoap. In gSoap, a definition is described as a prototype definition on a header file.
2. Generation of Skelton Code: The user generates the skeleton code of a remote procedure call with the generation tool of gSoap.
3. Implementation of Procedure: The user writes the implementation of the generated skeleton code.
4. Generation of Execution Binary: The user makes an execution binary by linking the object file generated from the implemented code and our offering object file. Our offering object file includes the main function and something. Linking should be static due to the constraints of BEE.

Deployment of the execution binary is also performed through a remote procedure call of the web service. Currently, the prototype does not support deployment of an execution binary. We are planning to offer a client-side tool that deploys an execution binary through SOAP.

## 5    Performance Evaluation and Experiment

In this section, we report the results of an experiment and a performance evaluation of the SW-agent. The objective of this evaluation and experiment is to examine availability and especially performance characteristic of shipping program facility. First, we examined the basic performance of shipping program facility. Second, we conducted a sandboxing experiment.

● **Basic Performance of System Call Emulation:** SW-agent executes most of a codes directly on processors, except for system calls. Therefore, although a program which does not have a system call is executed without overhead, a program which has a system call is executed with the overhead of the system call hooking.

First, we examined the overhead of system call hooking. The overhead is the average execution time acquired by measuring the time of the *getuid* system call.

We calculated the average execution time by executing the system call 10,000 times on and not on SW-agent. Machine used for evaluation had Core2Duo 2.4GHz and 2GB memory, and ran Linux Kernel 2.6.24.

As a result, the direct execution time was approximately 0.25 $\mu$sec. The execution time of SW-agent was approximately 15 $\mu$sec. This result means that overhead of SW-agent is approximately 15 $\mu$sec. The impact of this overhead on applications is examined in the following evaluations.

• **Performance of Virtual Sensor Device:** We have examined performance of Virtual Sensor Device. The performance is the average time calculated by measuring the time required to acquire 10,000 frames. We measured the execution time by using both the real sensor device directly and the Virtual Sensor Device. The frame size was 640x480. Machine used for evaluation was same as prior evaluation. Capturing board attached to the machine is Buffalo CBP-AV, whose frame-rate is 30fps and resolution is 640x480.

As a result of the experiment, the execution time required to acquire frame data was approximately 33375 $\mu$sec by direct access and approximately 33376 $\mu$sec by the Virtual Sensor Device. This result means that the overhead of the Virtual Sensor Device is approximately 1 $\mu$sec. This overhead is because of system call hooking by *ptrace* and inter-process communication between the video server and the executor part of the SW-agent. This overhead is smaller than that of a former evaluation. We assume that this decrease occurs because the Virtual Sensor Device omits some device calls which the direct access needs, such as the order of starting capture. The overhead of the Virtual Sensor Device is sufficiently small.

• **Performance of Remote Procedure Call:** We examined the performance decline of the remote procedure call resulting from system call emulation. We measured the execution time on and not on SW-agent, as well as the execution time on the three transition paths shown in Figure 1. In the evaluation, we used two procedures: procedure-A, procedure-B. Procedure-A has no arguments and returns an integer value. Procedure-B has no arguments and returns 900 Kbytes of data, equivalent to video frame data whose size is 640x480. The communication data between the shipping program and the client is base64 encoded and then transmitted as XML messages using the HTTP protocol. For examination of average execution times, we executed procedure-A 10,000 times and procedure-B 100,000 times. The network latency on the WAN was approximately 2 msec. For the examination, we used two machines: Machine-A, Machine-B. Machine-A had Core2Duo 2.2GHz, 2GB memory, and Gigabit Ethernet, and ran Linux Kernel 2.6.24. Machine-B had Xeon 3.0GHz, 2GB memory, and Gigabit Ethernet, and ran Linux Kernel 2.6.9. gSoap library used for implementation of web service is version 2.7.

Table 2 shows the execution time of each configuration and the ratios of the overhead. The result shows that the overhead of procedure-A is greater than that of procedure-B. This is because the system call dominates a larger part of the total execution time in procedure-A. The result also shows that a larger network environment has smaller overhead with both procedures. This is because

**Table 1.** Evaluation Configurations

| Name | Machine | Network |
|------|---------|---------|
| Local | Machine-B to Machine-B | omni.hpcc.jp |
| LAN | Machine-A to Machine-B | omni.hpcc.jp |
| WAN | Machine-A to Machine-B | hpcs.cs.tsukuba.ac.jp to omni.hpcc.jp |

**Table 2.** Execution Time of Remote Procedure Calls

| Network | Procedure | Native | SW-agent | Overhead |
|---------|-----------|--------|----------|----------|
| Local | Procedure-A | 31 $\mu$sec | 1117 $\mu$sec | 351% |
|  | Procedure-B | 35 msec | 37 msec | 107% |
| LAN | Procedure-A | 1103 $\mu$sec | 1449 $\mu$sec | 131% |
|  | Procedure-B | 36 msec | 38 msec | 106% |
| WAN | Procedure-A | 6903 $\mu$sec | 7396 $\mu$sec | 107% |
|  | Procedure-B | 78 msec | 79 msec | 102% |

the overhead of system call hooking becomes smaller as the data transition time increases. The WAN performance is important in the Sensing Web, which shares sensors on the Internet. The overhead on WAN is sufficiently small.

• **Basic Performance of Stream Data Transmission:** We evaluated the stream data transmission between the shipping program and client. The performance of stream data transmission is dependent on the data transmission bandwidth. We measured the bandwidth of the Virtual Stream Device and MTOM/XOP on LAN and WAN.

On burst transfer through a raw socket, the max bandwidth for LAN was approximately 871 Mbps and approximately 134 Mbps for WAN. As a result of the measure, the max bandwidth of the Virtual Stream Device for LAN was approximately 876 Mbps and approximately 134 Mbps for WAN. The max bandwidth of MTOM/XOP for LAN was approximately 860 Mbps and approximately 128 Mbps for WAN. This result shows that the performance of both stream transmissions was almost equivalent to a normal raw socket.

# 6   Related Work

There has already been a proposal to utilize the data acquired from sensors installed in the real world. Open Geospatial Consortium (OGC) proposed *Sensor Web Enablement* (SWE) [13], which is embraced in several projects. Buyya et al. proposed *Open Sensor Web Architecture* (OSWA) in [3] and implemented it in [14]. SWE cannot process stream data efficiently because SWE acquires sensor data by query language with expressiveness that is poor for processing stream data. Therefore, SWE cannot avoid sending all the data to a client. In addition, OSWA does not consider privacy. In contrast, SW-agent can process stream data efficiently with remote execution program and has a mechanism for protecting privacy.

Some systems can already realize remote program deployment [15]. However, most of these can run a system-specific binary only. Users are forced to learn a system-specific rule to prepare the program. Therefore, these cannot be used for realization of the Sensing Web, which is targeted toward sharing by people who do not have a high level of computer skills.

Issues of privacy information in pervasive computing are discussed on [4].

## 7   Conclusion and Future Work

In this paper, we described an overview of Sensing Web and presented that the research issues for realizing it are privacy protection and consumption of communication resources. We proposed a architecture named SW-agent. SW-agent can resolve the issues by shipping a program, which eliminates privacy information and needless data, into the node near a sensor and with access control based on the authentication mechanism.

We implemented a prototype system, tested the sandboxing function and then evaluated the basic performance. The results of our examination showed that SW-agent can execute remote execution program with up to 7% overhead in performance comparing direct execution, which is acceptable for Sensing Web.

In the future, we intend to work on the following:

- Currently our prototype has no authorization system and deployment system. Therefore, we plan to construct an appropriate authorization model based on the needs of a community and implement an authorization system based on it. In addition, we plan to implement a deployment service.
- Mutual use of processed information between shipping programs may achieve more flexible and efficient sensor use in terms of both usability and network resource consumption. We plan to investigate it with a work-flow model on mutually connected shipping programs.

## Acknowledgment

We would like to thank Dr.Yuich Ota and Dr.Itaru Kitahara, and Takashi Tsushima (Graduate School of Systems and Information Engineering in University of Tsukuba) for technical advices and supports. The authors achnowledges the contribution of all the members of the Sensing Web Project. The present study was supported by Effective and Efficient Promotion of the Coodination Program of Science and Technology Projects in the Special Coodination Funds for Promoting Science and Technology, which is conducted by MEXT of Japan, and Japan Science and Technology Agency(JST).

## References

1. Google Street View: http://www.google.com/help/maps/streetview/
2. Minoh, M., et al.: Sensing Web Project - How to handle privacy information in sensor data (June 2008)

3. Tham, C.k., Buyya, R.: SensorGrid: Integrating Sensor Networks and Grid Computing. Special Issue on Grid Computing (July 2005)
4. Bhaskar, P., Ahamed, S.I.: Privacy in Pervasive Computing and Open Issues (2007)
5. Foster, I., et al.: Physiology of the Grid: Making the Global Infrastructure a Reality, pp. 863–869. Wiley, Chichester (2003)
6. Open PGP: http://www.openpgp.org/
7. Uemura, Y., Nakajima, Y., Sato, M.: Direct Execution of Linux Binary on Windows for Grid RPC workers (March 2007)
8. Open Computer Vision Library: http://sourceforge.net/projects/opencvlibrary
9. video4linux: http://linux.bytesex.org/v4l2/
10. SOAP Message Transmission Optimization: http://www.w3.org/TR/soap12-mtom/
11. XML-binary Optimized Packaging: http://www.w3.org/TR/xop10/
12. The gSOAP Toolkit for SOAP Web Services and XML-Based Applications: http://www.cs.fsu.edu/~engelen/soap.html
13. Percivall, G., Reed, C.: OGC Sensor Web Enablement Standard. Sensors & Transducers, vol. 9, pp. 698–706 (September 2006)
14. Chu, X.: Open Sensor Web Architecture: Core Service (December 2005)
15. Brown, S., Sreenan, C.J.: Updating software in wireless sensor networks: A survey. Tech. rep. ucc-cs-2006-13-07, Dept. of Computer Science, University College Cork, Ireland (2006)

# Efficient Parallelized Network Coding
# for P2P File Sharing Applications

Karam Park[1], Joon-Sang Park[2], and Won W. Ro[1]

[1] School of Electrical and Electronic Engineering
Yonsei University, Seoul, Korea
{riopark,wro}@yonsei.ac.kr
[2] Department of Computer Engineering
Hongik University, Seoul, Korea
jsp@hongik.ac.kr

**Abstract.** In this paper, we investigate parallel implementation techniques for network coding to enhance the performance of Peer-to-Peer (P2P) file sharing applications. It is known that network coding mitigates peer/piece selection problems in P2P file sharing systems; however, due to the decoding complexity of network coding, there have been concerns about adoption of network coding in P2P file sharing systems and to improve the decoding speed the exploitation of parallelism has been proposed previously. In this paper, we argue that naive parallelization strategies of network coding may result in unbalanced workload distribution and thus limiting performance improvements. We further argue that higher performance enhancement can be achieved through load balancing in parallelized network coding and propose new parallelization techniques for network coding. Our experiments show that, on a quad-core processor system, proposed algorithms exhibit up to 30% of speed-up compared to an existing approach using 1 Mbytes data with 2048×2048 coefficient matrix size.

**Keywords:** Network coding, parallelization, random linear coding.

## 1 Introduction

Multi-core systems nowadays are prevalent; they are found in a wide spectrum of systems, from high performance servers to special purpose embedded systems. Recently, the trend has been embedding more and more cores in a processor rather than increasing clock frequency rate to boost processors' performance [1]. In this paper, we propose new implementation techniques that can enhance the performance of network coding [2] by fully exploiting parallelism on the multi-core systems.

Network coding which is generally due to Ahlswede *et al.* [2] is a method that can be used to enhance network throughput and reliability. In addition, it has been shown that network coding benefits peer-to-peer (P2P) file sharing [3], especially so-called file swarming type systems. In file swarming systems, a file is divided into multiple pieces and pieces are exchanged among peers. To download a file, a peer must collect all the pieces comprising the file. If a peer downloads multiple pieces simultaneously from peers, it dramatically reduces downloading delay, which is the main advantage

N. Abdennadher and D. Petcu (Eds.): GPC 2009, LNCS 5529, pp. 353–363, 2009.

of using the file swarming technique. However, the selection of peers and pieces to download has a big impact on the overall performance, which is generally referred to as the *piece selection problem*. The use of network coding mitigates this problem in P2P file swarming systems [3]. In network coded systems, the data are "encoded" into packets such that the packets are equally important, i.e., no difference exists among the packets being exchanged, and thus a peer is only suppose to collect a specific number of equally important packets.

One pitfall of network coding is computational overhead. Original data are coded before exchanging and downloaded packets are to be decoded to recover the original information. The decoding process is implemented usually as a variation of Gaussian elimination which has $O(n^3)$ computational complexity. This complexity is quite pricy in fact especially when the size of the file is huge. It is probable that the time spent for decoding may actually cancel out all the benefit of reduced transmission time. Thus, it is critical for network coded P2P systems to have a fast enough decoder. To provide fast decoding speed, Shojania *et al.* has suggested *Parallelized Progressive Network Coding (PPNC)* [4]. However, due to its unbalanced workload on each parallel task (or thread), their algorithms cannot take full advantage of parallelism.

In this paper, we propose parallel implementations of network coding that in nature balance workload among parallel tasks. Via real machine experiments, we show that our new techniques allow meaningful reduction of execution time compared to *PPNC*. On a quad core system for example, we achieve speed-up of 3.25 compared with a serial implementation and 30% of performance improvement over *PPNC* algorithm with 1Mbytes data and the coefficient matrix size of 2048×2048.

## 2  Background

In this section, we present an introduction of network coding and related work.

### 2.1  Principles of Network Coding

Fig. 1 depicts a directed graph representing a simple communication network; the edges represent pathways for information transfer and the node $S$ is the source, and the node $D$ and $E$ represent receivers. The other remaining nodes represent intermediate points in the routing paths.

In this example, network coding enables us to multicast two bits per unit time assuming that each link conveys a bit per unit time, which cannot be achieved without

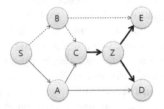

**Fig. 1.** A Communication Networks for Network Coding

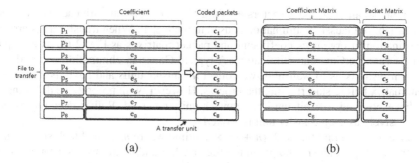

**Fig. 2.** Encoding Concept and Received Data Structure

network coding, i.e., through traditional routing. Suppose we generate data bits $a$ and $b$ at source $S$ and want to send the data to both $D$ and $E$. We send data $a$ through path $SAC$, $SAD$, and data $b$ through $SBC$, $SBE$. With the routing, we can only send either $a$ or $b$ but not both, from $C$ to $Z$. Suppose we send data $a$ to $Z$. Then $D$ would receive $a$ twice from $A$ and $Z$, and would not get $b$. Sending $b$ instead would also raise the same problem for $E$. Therefore, routing is insufficient as it cannot send both data $a$ and $b$ to both $D$ and $E$ simultaneously. Using network coding, on the other hand, we could encode the data $a$ and $b$ received in $C$ and send the encoded version to $CZ$. Say we use bitwise xor for encoding. Then, $a$ and $b$ are encoded to '$a$ xor $b$'. The encoded data is sent along on the path $CZD$ and $CZE$. Node $D$ receives data $a$ and '$a$ xor $b$', so it can decode $b$ from them. It is the same for node $E$, where it receives data $b$ and '$a$ xor $b$'.

However, to assume the increased throughput that network coding allows, the encoding/decoding process must not be the bottleneck. The encoding/decoding process depends on the coding solution to be used and there are several ways to find out an optimal coding solution given a network. In this paper we restrict ourselves to the random linear coding [6][7], since it is the most widely used coding solution which is asymptotically optimal in any network. Now we explain how encoding and decoding works in random linear coding.

Let us assume that an application transfers a file. Then the file is divided into a specific *number of blocks* as shown in Fig. 2-(a) where $\mathbf{p}_k$ denotes $k^{th}$ block. A coded packet $\mathbf{c}_i$ is a linear combination of the blocks constituting the file. That is $\mathbf{c}_i = \sum_{k=1}^{n} \mathbf{e}_k \mathbf{p}_k$, where $n$ is the number of blocks and the coefficient $\mathbf{e}_k$ is a certain element randomly chosen in a certain finite field $\mathbf{F}$. Every arithmetic operation is over the field $\mathbf{F}$. The coded packet $\mathbf{c}_i$ is broadcasted to other destination nodes along with the coefficient vector, $[\mathbf{e}_1, ..., \mathbf{e}_n]$, stored in the header. This "transfer unit" is shown in Fig. 2-(a).

On reception of coded packets, nodes in the path to the destinations re-encode the coded packets and send them to downstream nodes. When a coded packet reaches a destination node it has to be stored in the local memory. For the destination node to decode the packets and recover the original file, it needs to get $n$ transfer units with independent coefficient vectors. Let say a receiver has collected $n$ transfer units and let $\mathbf{E}^T = [\mathbf{e}_1^T ... \mathbf{e}_n^T]$, $\mathbf{C}^T = [\mathbf{c}_1^T ... \mathbf{c}_n^T]$ and $\mathbf{P}^T = [\mathbf{p}_1^T ... \mathbf{p}_n^T]$ where superscript $T$ stands for the transpose operation. As the coded packet was calculated as $\mathbf{C} = \mathbf{EP}$, we can recover the original file $\mathbf{P}$ from $\mathbf{C}$ by $\mathbf{P} = \mathbf{E}^{-1}\mathbf{C}$. Note that $\mathbf{E}$ needs to be invertible, so all coefficient vectors $e_k$'s must be independent with each other. Usually a variant of Gaussian elimination is used to recover $P$. When transfer units arrive to a destination, it organizes coefficient and packet matrixes as Fig. 2-(b) as a preparation for running Gaussian elimination. A typical Gaussian elimination or LU decomposition restricts us to wait until we collect $n$ transfer units and have the $n \times n$ coefficient matrix before start running the process. However, with progressive decoding [6], we have no need to wait until all transfer units received. Rather decoding is done progressively as each transfer unit is arrived.

Since the decoding takes $O( (n + m) \times n^2)$ time where $m$ is the block size, $m$ and $n$ are important parameters and given the file size l, $n$ and $m$ are inverse proportional to each other since $l = n * m$. In the file swarming scenarios, the bigger $n$ enables the greater downloading delay reduction, since a peer can receive at most $n$ simultaneous block transfers reducing the downloading delay by $n$. But since the decoding delay which might cancel out the downloading delay benefit increases proportional to $n^3$, fast decoding implementation is a key to get the benefit comes with a large $n$. In other words, given a fast decoding algorithm, a larger $n$ allows a bigger performance gain.

## 2.2  Related Works

Ahlswede *et al.* first introduced the network coding and showed the usefulness of network coding [2]. Koetter and Medard proved later that in a network, the maximum throughput can be achieved with linear network codes [5]. With these backgrounds, Chou *et al.* in [6] and Ho *et al.* in [7] suggested random linear network coding, which is our target and is conceived to be the most practical scheme for single multicast flow cases. Lun *et al.* showed the utility of network coding on wireless network systems in [8], until then, researches of network coding were focused on wired networks. Katti *et al.* proposed practical solutions for wireless networks with multiple unicast flows in [9] and Park *et al.* suggested a practical protocol based on network coding for ad hoc multicasting networks and showed improvements of reliability of ad hoc network systems by network coding in [10]. In addition, using network coding in P2P was first proposed in [11] and recent feasibility studies on network coding in real testbeds have been done in [12] and Lee *et al.* showed the utility of network coding in mobile P2P systems [13]. Gkantsidis *et al.* also showed that network coding allows smooth, fast downloads and efficient server utilization on a P2P setting [3].

Shojania *et al.* suggested parallelization of network coding in [4]. They employed hardware acceleration into the network coding and used a multi-threaded design to take advantages of multi-core systems. There are some other performance enhancement techniques (e.g. [14], [15]). Their work is different from our work in that their focus is reducing the computational complexity of encoding/decoding operation and ours focuses on improving decoding performance via parallelization.

There are many researches such as parallelization of matrix inversion [16], parallel LU decomposition [17], and parallelization of Gauss-Jordan elimination with block-based algorithms [18]. In fact, those existing parallel algorithms could be used to decode received packets of network coding. However, these algorithms need to receive the entire matrix before starting decoding operations.

In network coded systems, waiting for the entire matrix to be formed is not an optimal solution. In P2P settings, transfer units are delivered one by one and the time

**Table 1.** Operation of Each Stage in Progressive Decoding [4]

| Stages | Task Descriptions |
|--------|-------------------|
| A | Using the former coefficients rows, reduce the leading coefficients in the new coefficient row to 0. |
| B | Find the first non-zero coefficient in the new coefficient row |
| C | Check for linear independence with existing coefficient rows |
| D | Reduce the leading non-zero entry of the new row to 1, such that result in REF |
| E | Reduce the coefficient matrix to the reduced row-echelon form |

gap between the arrivals of transfer units can be large. Thus, instead of waiting all the packets to arrive, partial decoding is performed on reception of each transfer unit hence the name of "progressive" decoding [4]. Our focus is on this type of progressive decoding.

To enhance the performance of the progressive decoding, *Parallelized Progressive Network Coding (PPNC)* is proposed [4]. It is basically a variant of the Gauss-Jordan elimination algorithm. A simple description of Gauss-Jordan elimination borrowed from [4] is presented in Table 1.

To enable progressive decoding, the stages of *PPNC* start operating when the destination receives a transfer unit containing coded packet and coefficient, that means a new row is added to matrix. On each transfer unit's arriving, the operations from *Stage A* to *Stage E* operate on the coefficient and packet matrixes to form the reduced row-echelon form. In these stages, *Stage A* and *E* are dominant procedures. According to [4], *Stage A* has 50.05%, and *Stage E* has 49.5% of decoding workload. So the parallelization is focused on *Stage A* and *E*.

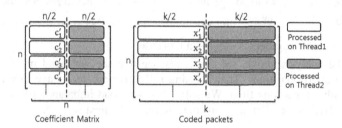

**Fig. 3.** Concept of Thread Dividing in *PPNC*

The main concept of the parallelization is to divide the coefficient matrix and packet matrix into a limited number of operational regions each of which is fed to parallel tasks (or threads). The regions are divided by vertically and equally as Fig. 3 with *PPNC*. Since dependency between threads exists, at start and end of each stage, synchronization between threads is needed.

# 3 Algorithms for Parallelization of Network Coding

In this section, the proposed parallelized network coding algorithms are discussed. We present an arithmetic analysis on the workload balancing problem of the parallel progressive decoding algorithm and propose three new parallelization methods to improve the performance.

## 3.1 Arithmetic Analysis of Thread Balancing

The best way to divide overall workload in parallel algorithms is to allocate same amount of load to each parallel task so that all the tasks can start and end simultaneously. If the workload is unbalanced, the benefit of parallelism diminishes, which limits the performance of *PPNC* proposed in [4]. Our algorithms have been developed mainly focusing on paralleling the *E* stage of *PPNC*.

To illustrate the problem, let us assume that the size of coefficient matrix is $n{\times}n$. The *Stage E* operations start with all threads, but later, when index of decoding go to row of $\frac{n}{number\ of\ threads}$, the first thread has no work during coefficient matrix operation on *Stage E*. The region for that thread is already filled with 0 and 1, and no additional operation is needed. If there are two threads, the first thread has no operation after $\frac{n}{2}$ row's operation. In case of 4 threads, first thread has no operation after $\frac{n}{4}$ row's operation. The more threads are added, the more inefficiency occurs.

To compute the workload of each thread, we define a sequence of a subtraction after a multiplication on a spot of matrix which operates in *Stage E*, to a unit operation. With arithmetical approach, in case of 2 threads, the first thread operates $\frac{n^3+6n^2+8n}{48}$ unit operations and the second thread operates $\frac{n^3+6n^2+8n}{48}+\frac{n^3+2n^2}{8}$ operations. The gap between two threads' numbers of operations is $\frac{n^3+2n^2}{8}$, and it is bigger than first thread's whole operation numbers. In case of 4 threads, the gap between the threads is getting larger. The first thread operates $\frac{3n^3+6n^2+16n}{192}$ unit operations, and the last thread operates $\frac{3n^3+6n^2+16n}{192}+\frac{3n^3+6n^2}{32}$ unit operations. The gap between the first and the last thread's operation numbers is $\frac{3n^3+6n^2}{32}$ in this case.

From the analysis above, we can easily see that the workload imbalance gap of *PPNC* is proportional to $n^3$. That is, using PPNC threads may have to wait for other treads possibly for a long time. We solve this workload imbalance problem and suggest more efficient parallel decoding algorithms in the next section.

## 3.2 DOA: Dynamic Operation Assignment for Balanced Workload

We suggest three different methods for efficient parallelization of the network coding. The first two methods are based on the horizontal division of matrix in order to balance the task separation. The easiest way of horizontal dividing is *round robin (RR)* method, which means a row is assigned to a thread, and the next row is assigned to the next thread, and continues as Fig. 4-(a). However, when two threads are assigned to any odd numbers of rows, the last row is always assigned to the first thread unevenly. Therefore, the first thread has the heavier workload, and unbalanced work distribution is made. More efficient horizontal dividing is *backward round robin (BRR)* after round robin as Fig. 4-(b). In this way, the thread of heaviest workload is changing, but also in case of operations on rows with odd numbers, perfect load balancing is not possible. Moreover, this method needs more complex arithmetic

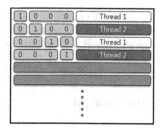
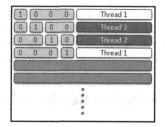

(a) *RR - Round Robin* Method          (b) *BRR – Backward Round Robin* Method

**Fig. 4.** Concept of Horizontal Separation for Balanced Task Partitioning

operations to find the row to operate than *round robin* and need more time for that. So we expect there exist some trade-offs; we will discuss this matters with the experimental results of two algorithms on real machines in Section 4.

In case of round robin, the first thread, which has the maximum workload, would take $\frac{2n^3+9n^2+10n}{24}$ unit operations on 2 threads, and $\frac{2n^3+17n^2+30n}{48}$ on 4 threads. On the other hand, last thread which has the minimum load would take $\frac{2n^3+3n^2-2n}{24}$ on 2 threads and $\frac{2n^3-n^2}{48}$ operations on 4 threads. The gaps between threads are $\frac{n^2+2n}{4}$ with 2 threads and $\frac{3n^2+5n}{8}$ with 4 threads. Compared to the gap calculated with *PPNC*, we can find out that *round robin* is much more efficient.

The third method is to use dynamic vertical separation of operation area which is named *DOA (Dynamic Operation Assignment)*. In this method, the dividing point is dynamically varied for each row operations as illustrated in Fig. 5. When the first row is to be handled as shown in the left most diagram, each thread is assigned $\frac{n-1}{2}$ columns, and when working on the second row and the third row shown in the next two diagrams, each thread works on area of $\frac{n-2}{2}$ and $\frac{n-3}{2}$ columns, respectively. If the number of columns to be assigned is not the multiples of the number of threads, the remaining columns are assigned unevenly.

As the algorithms progress, the region assigned to each thread is getting narrower and deeper. In this way, we can easily achieve fair balancing of workloads among

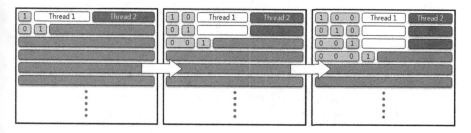

**Fig. 5.** Concept of Dynamic Thread Separation on Operation Area

threads. Imbalanced distribution happens when the number of remaining columns is not a multiple of $k$ (where $k$ denotes the number of threads). However, that kind of imbalance is negligible especially when $k$ is smaller compared to $n$ and the *DOA* is an efficient algorithm for parallelization of *Stage E*.

## 4   Experimental Results and Performance Analysis

In this section, we evaluate the proposed three algorithms via extensive experiments on real multi-core machines. The specification of the machines we have used for our experiments is described in Table 2.

**Table 2.** Experimental Environment

|  | Dual-Core | Quad-Core |
|---|---|---|
| CPU | Intel Core 2 Duo E6750 | AMD *Phenom-X4* 9550 |
| CPU Clock | 2.66GHz | 2.2GHz |
| RAM | 2GByte | 4GByte |
| Cache Configuration | 2x32KByte L1 cache<br>4MByte Shared L2 cache | 4 x 128KByte L1 cache<br>4 x 512KByte L2 cache<br>2MByte Shared L3Cache |
| Operating Systems | Fedora Linux Core 8 | Fedora Linux Core 8 |

### 4.1   Performance Evaluation Considering *Stage E* Only

The first set of experiments is carried on in order to see the performance of Gauss-Jordan elimination only with the coefficient matrix; which means we exclude the execution time spent on the packet matrix.

Fig. 6-(a) shows the execution time spent only on *Stage E* of the coefficient matrix operation for four different algorithms: *PPNC, RR, BRR,* and *DOA*. Fig. 6-(b) presents the speed-up of *RR, BRR,* and *DOA* compared to *PPNC*. The size of the file used is 1MB. From the figures, we notice that *DOA* shows the best performance. The speed-up factor ranges from 2 to 2.4 compared to *PPNC* (again, when considering only *Stage E* of the coefficient matrix operation). We also notice that the execution time of

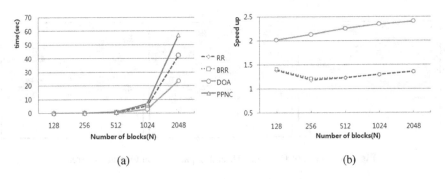

**Fig. 6.** Execution Time on *Stage E* and Speed-up (Coefficient Matrix Operation Only)

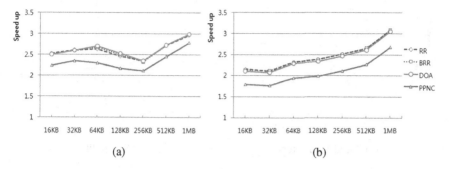

(a)                                    (b)

**Fig. 7.** Decoding Process Speed-up with Varying the Data Size

*round robin (RR)* and *backward round robin (BRR)* are very similar. This is due to the fact that the advantages/disadvantages of two different thread assignment methods diminish in the real implementation.

### 4.2 Speed-Up Comparison on Dual-Core Systems

In this part, the speed-up factor of total decoding time considering a whole file is measured. We have calculated the speed-up factors compared to sequential algorithms for various experimental scenarios. In Fig. 7, we can find out the speed-up factors of decoding process with four proposed algorithms on a dual-core processor. Fig. 7-(a) and (b) show speed-ups with $n = 1024$ and $n = 2048$ on a dual-core processor. On the dual-core processor, *RR*, *BRR*, and *DOA* do not show sharp improvement on speed-up while showing a better performance compared to *PPNC*. These results prove that our proposed algorithms are more efficient than *PPNC*.

### 4.3 Total Decoding Time Comparison

In this part, the total execution time on process is measured. In Fig. 8, we can find out the decoding time of the various file sizes. Fig. 8 presents the execution time in case with $n = 1024$ at (a), and $n = 2048$ at (b). Due to the *PPNC*'s unbalanced parallel workload distribution, the *PPNC* approach results in the longest decoding time

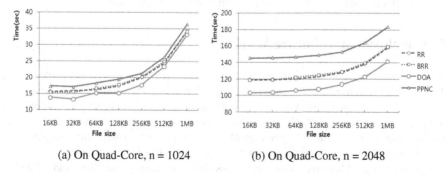

(a) On Quad-Core, n = 1024              (b) On Quad-Core, n = 2048

**Fig. 8.** Decoding Execution Time (in sec) with Different Data Sizes on Quad-core

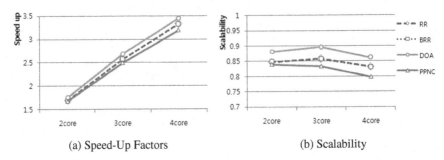

(a) Speed-Up Factors                    (b) Scalability

**Fig. 9.** Speed-up Factors and Scalability of Each Algorithm (2MB Data, $n=1024$)

compared to the other three algorithms in the whole decoding process. In fact, the operations in the remaining stages but *Stage E* in our algorithms are very similar to those operations in PPNC. In other words, the speed up in Stage E is a dominant factor.

Ratio of execution time on coefficient matrix increases with larger coefficient matrix size, therefore *DOA, RR,* and *BRR* show better performance results on whole decoding process with large $n$. It is very important finding since the performance improvement in large sizes is crucial for file swarming as mentioned in Section 2.1. As indicated in [4], the task of coding more than 128 blocks is challenging and should be addressed. We claim that our approach can provide a better solution for the network coding with large numbers of blocks.

### 4.4  Scalability Comparison

We measure the speed-up factors and scalability using various numbers of cores to verify the efficiency of each algorithm. The scalability means the capability to accelerate the operation speed with the addition of cores. In this section, the results on scalability are derived with the speed-up divided by the number of cores. All the results are calculated considering the execution time of a sequential program on a single core. Fig. 9-(a) shows the speed-up factors of each algorithm with using various numbers of cores. We can find out the *DOA* shows the best performance over other three algorithms. Fig. 9-(b) shows the scalability calculated from the results shown on Fig. 9-(a). It is also demonstrated that the *DOA* algorithms show the best scalability and these results prove the efficiency of *DOA* in multi-core environments.

## 5  Conclusion and Future Work

This paper introduced efficient parallel algorithms for the random network coding. To be more specific, we proposed "balanced" parallel algorithms. We showed via analysis that our algorithms have less workload difference between tasks compared to the previously proposed *PPNC* algorithm. Via real machine experiments, we showed that our algorithms achieved speed-up of 3.05 compared to a sequential implementation. Compared to *PPNC*, our approach showed 14~30% improvement in the decoding performance. Moreover, our algorithms showed better scalability than *PPNC* on the number of processing units (e.g., processor cores). We expect that our work can be applied to further enhance the performance of various network coding applications such as peer-to-peer file sharing systems.

## Acknowledgement

This work was supported by the Korea Research Foundation Grant funded by the Korean Government (KRF-2008-313-D00871).

## References

1. Geer, D.: Industry trends: Chip makers turn to multi-core processors. Computer 38(5), 11–13 (2005)
2. Ahlswede, R., Cai, N., Li, S.-Y.R., Yeung, R.W.: Network information flow. IEEE Trans. Inform. Theory 46(4), 1204–1216 (2000)
3. Gkantsidis, C., Rodriguez, P.: Comprehensive View of a Live Network Coding P2P System. In: IMC 2006, Rio de Janeiro (2006)
4. Shojania, H., Li, B.: Baochun Li: Parallelized Progressive Network Coding With Hardware Acceleration. In: 15th IEEE International Workshop on Quality of Service, pp. 47–55 (2007)
5. Koetter, R., M'edard, M.: An algebraic approach to network coding. IEEE/ACM Trans. Networking 11(5), 782–795 (2003)
6. Chou, P., Wu, Y., Jain, K.: Practical Network Coding. In: 51st Allerton Conf. Commun., Control and Computing (2004)
7. Ho, T., M'edard, M., Koetter, R., Karger, D.R., Effros, M., Shi, J., Leong, B.: A Random Linear Network Coding Approach to Multicast. IEEE Trans. Information Theory 52(10), 4413–4430
8. Lun, D.S., Ratnakar, N., M'edard, M., Koetter, R., Karger, D.R., Ho, T., Ahmed, E., Zhao, F.: Minimum-cost multicast over coded packet networks. IEEE Trans. Inform. Theory 52(6), 2608–2623 (2006)
9. Katti, S., Rahul, H., Hu, W., Katabi, D., M'edard, M., Crowcroft, J.: XORs in the Air - Practical Wireless Network Coding. IEEE/ACM Transactions on Networking 16(3), 497–510 (2008)
10. Park, J.-S., Gerla, M., Lun, D.S., Yi, Y., M'edard, M.: Codecast: a network coding based ad hoc multicast protocol. IEEE Wireless Communications 13(5), 76–81 (2006)
11. Gkantsidis, C., Rodriguez, P.R.: Network coding for large scale content distribution. In: 24th Annual Joint Conference of the IEEE Computer and Communications Societies, vol. 4, pp. 2235–2245 (2005)
12. Wang, M., Li, B.: Lava: A Reality Check of Network Coding in Peer-to-Peer Live Streaming. In: INFOCOM 2007. 26th IEEE International Conference on Computer Communications, pp. 1082–1090. IEEE, Los Alamitos (2007)
13. Lee, U., Park, J.-S., Yeh, J., Pau, G., Gerla, M.: CodeTorrent: Content Distribution using Network Coding in VANETs. In: 1st international Workshop on Decentralized Resource Sharing in Mobile Computing and Networking. MobiShare 2006. ACM, New York (2006)
14. Ma, G., Xu, Y., Lin, M., Xuan, Y.: A content distribution system based on sparse linear network coding. In: NetCod 2007, 3rd Workshop on Network Coding, Miami (2007)
15. Maymounkov, P., Harvey, N.J.A., Lun, D.S.: Methods for efficient network coding. Allerton, Monticello (2006)
16. Csánky, L.: Fast Parallel Matrix Inversion Algorithms. SIAM J. Computing 5, 618–623 (1976)
17. Bisseling, R.H., Van de Vorst, J.G.G.: Parallel LU decomposition on a transputer network. LNCS, vol. 384, pp. 61–77. Springer, Heidelberg (1989)
18. Melab, N., Talbi, E.-G., Petiton, S.: A Parallel Adaptive Gauss-Jordan Algorithm. The Journal of Supercomputing 17(2), 167–185 (2000)

# Scheduling Strategy of P2P Based High Performance Computing Platform Base on Session Time Prediction*

Hao Zhang, Hai Jin, and Qin Zhang

Services Computing Technology and System Lab
Cluster and Grid Computing Lab
School of Computer Science and Technology
Huazhong University of Science and Technology, Wuhan, 430074, China
hjin@hust.edu.cn

**Abstract.** P2P based *high performance computing* (HPC) system introduces many new and interesting problems. P2P environment is heterogeneous and asynchronous. At the same time, P2P platform is not stable. The joining and leaving of peers are random. These characteristics make the P2P based HPC platform have great difference to the traditional HPC platform and the global computing project. To achieve effective job scheduling on P2P based platform, this paper introduces a DHT based monitor and task management scheme. Further, we propose a data structure of distributed bidirectional *Skiplist* to keep the prediction session time. Our scheme distributes the task to the nodes which have longer online session time. With such scheme, we can reduce the migration of tasks among different nodes and improve the resource utilization of computing nodes. Finally, we use a real trace to demonstrate the efficiency of our algorithms and scheduling schemes.

**Keywords:** High Performance Computing, Peer to Peer, Scheduling, Distributed Hash Table.

## 1 Introduction

P2P technology is widely used in file sharing. Technologies such as BitTorrent, eMule, Gnutella have taken advantage of the bandwidth and resources over internet. While, for many researchers in academia and industry, P2P has another attraction: the widely distributed idle computing resource over internet. Although the global computing projects, such as SETI@Home [1], Stanford Folding [2], have achieved success in some fields. But such type of model usually requests central server to dispatch the tasks and deal with the results returned from volunteers. The global computing model does not take full advantage of the characteristics of P2P network, and many different kinds of applications could not be deployed with such a model.

---

* This paper is supported by ChinaGrid project from Ministry of Education of China, the National High-Tech Research and Development Plan of China under grant No.2006AA01A115, and National Science Foundation of China under grant No.90412010, No.60433040 and NSFC/RGC Joint Research Foundation under grant No.60731160630.

N. Abdennadher and D. Petcu (Eds.): GPC 2009, LNCS 5529, pp. 364–375, 2009.

The structured P2P network based on *Distributed Hash Table* (DHT) [7][8][9][10] is a significant improvement to traditional P2P network. Many characteristics which the unstructured P2P network does not have are introduced. The improvement has provided more possibilities to HPC under P2P environments. Tasks can be better organized running under the DHT based P2P network. DHT characterizes the network with better distribution, better scalability and better fault tolerance. Such characteristics have created favorable foundation for HPC.

Churn is an important characteristic of P2P network. Many nodes may enter the P2P network simultaneously, while at the same time many other nodes may leave the network. For the tasks running on the nodes, when the nodes leave the network, those computation tasks should be suspended and migrate to another node to continue the computation process. However, the costs of the migration of tasks on the internet are large. Thus, the adaptive scheduling strategy is to place one task onto the node which has longer online session time. In this way, the frequency of the task migration will be reduced. Our research is based on such ideas: in P2P network, although the entering and leaving of a certain node is hard to predict, but when a large number nodes do the same thing many times, their behavior will show some statistical characteristics. On the other hand, for a single node, its session time for a certain landing is hard to predict. However, it is possible to speculate according to its running habit within a long term. Thus, computation task can be dispatch onto the node whose predicted online session time is closely consistent with the time needed to complete the task. In principle, this model can optimize task scheduling, and shorten the time needed to complete the task.

The rest of the paper is organized as follows. In section 2, we will introduce the different scheduling strategy of global computing and parallel system, and then compare them with the strategy introduced in this paper. Section 3 will explore the resource management model and task scheduling strategies of HPC platform based on P2P. Section 4 will evaluate the scheduling algorithm. In the end, our work and contributions are summarized.

## 2  Related Work

SETI@Home [1] is the first global computing projects running over internet. It aims to make use of the large amount of computing resources over internet. When the resources are idle, the server dispatches tasks onto those computers and run computation on them. When one volunteer completes the sub-task it got, it returns the result to central server. The architecture of such models is a typical client/server model, in which every volunteer accepts task from the central server, and return results to the central server. Besides, because there are huge amount of tasks, almost every volunteer can receive one relevant portion of task. Thereby, the scheduling of such tasks is relatively easy---the tasks are divided on the server beforehand, then allocated to volunteers when they request for tasks.

Boinc [3] aims to excavate the general scheme of global computing, and provides them a uniform platform. Many global computing projects are all migrated to the platform. Boinc is also one form of the client/server model, but it takes uniform control of the volunteers working for different projects. The scheduling strategy is as follows: when one Boinc client remains idle for a certain time, it will send out a scheduling request to the server which keeps the tasks and data of a project, and then the server dispatches a sub-task to the client. Boinc collects the credit of the clients by the history running record of the tasks the client got. The dispatcher is prone to allocate tasks to the nodes with better credit.

CCOF [4] and WaveGrid [5] are all desktop grid systems developed in recent years. They adopt the scheduling strategy based on the time zone of the nodes in the platform. When the resource of one node is busy, the scheduler dispatches some of the HPC tasks run on the node to the night-time zone nodes whose resource is often unoccupied. In such a way, HPC tasks can find nodes on the whole internet to complete the computation tasks more efficiently. However, the scheduling strategy based on time zone is coarse on the whole. When tasks on the internet are migrated according to this scheduling policy, too many tasks may be migrated at the same time, which is a heavy burden for the system.

Task scheduling is also an important issue for the parallel machine and is widely studied. Optimal scheduling of parallel tasks with some precedence relationship on a heterogeneous parallel machine is known to be NP-complete. To solve this problem, many researchers have developed heuristic algorithms to get polynomial time optimized solutions [6]. The scheduling algorithm on heterogeneous parallel machine often considers many situations: whether the number of processors is limited or unlimited, the communication latency between nodes, the time of data exchange between nodes and etc. The introduction or ignoring of a parameter would lead different algorithms. But almost all these algorithms can not be used in P2P based HPC platform directly as P2P network does not have stable nodes. However, these scheduling strategies have provided good reference for the dispatch strategy under P2P condition.

## 3   Problem Analysis

The objective of scheduling is to complete HPC projects as soon as possible. To achieve effective scheduling in P2P based HPC platform, the specifics of P2P environment should be first discussed. Then we analyze the way to handle the information in P2P based HPC platform---basic data structure to handle nodes' session time is introduced. With the new designed data structure, the details of the scheduling strategy are discussed.

### 3.1   Environment of P2P Based HPC Platform

P2P network is not a stable environment. When a task is dispatched to a certain nodes, the scheduler assumes that the task could not complete on the node *with high probability* (whp). The scheduler should always prepare to re-dispatch the task to the other nodes to resume the computation. But data exchange between peers in internet is costly. For many case, scheduling strategy with many task migration is unwise. However P2P based HPC platform can support the scheduling of tasks with some precedence relationship rather than the single scheduling model in the global computing. Such platform can be extended to more fields.

Compare with the client/server model, P2P has some inherent characteristics: 1) P2P network is scalable, the peers can serve to each other and peers can take part in the network without the limitations of the central server. 2) Resource discovery is much hard than traditional global computing model. To support HPC, P2P network needs efficient techniques to achieve the resource discovery and management.

Based on the discussion, the design of the P2P based HPC platform should meet the following qualifications: 1) Take full advantage of the scalability of P2P network to reduce or eliminate the function of central server. 2) The management of nodes and discovery of resources in the system are distributed. The information of nodes is preserved in the system with distributed way. If needed, nodes in system can obtain enough information to schedule tasks to appropriate nodes.

## 3.2  The Platform Model

To satisfy the above requirements, P2P network adopts a structural network, namely a P2P overlay based on DHT. We choose Chord as the basic protocol for overlay of the platform in this paper. Chord has a ring-based architecture. For every pair of *Key* and *Value*, the system uses the same hash function for the *Key*. With the result of the hash function, the <*Key, Value*> is stored on the nearest node in the clock-wise direction. Every node stores the information of its previous node and successor node. Meanwhile, Chord has a finger table to store more routing information.

Traditional DHT model is unable to meet the demand that the scheduling program searches nodes within a certain range in the whole P2P environment. Under the DHT model, many models have been developed to support range queries [13][14]. Nevertheless, those models are designed for specific application and cannot be widely applied. The scheduling algorithm discussed in this paper needs to preserve the predicted value of the left online session time for every online node. Such values will change as time passes, and are preserved in another distributed data structure which will be thoroughly discussed in the following section.

## 3.3  Basic Data Structure for Session Time

Every node in the system will publish its information on the platform. The nodes taking care of preserving such information also monitor those nodes and update their information to make sure that such information can be used right at that time. At the same time, the monitoring nodes record the online time and offline time for the monitored nodes. Such information is preserved on the monitoring nodes, and serves as the basic data for the following scheduling algorithm.

Many different types of data exist in the system, such as information of nodes, tasks and program data, which are distinguished according to *Type Id*. As shown in Fig.1, the node **N12** combines the *Type Id* and *Node Id* into one key, while the characteristic is preserved as value on the node **N38**. The monitoring module on node **N38** will inquire the node **N12** periodically to obtain the updated data.

When the monitoring module monitors other nodes, it will record the online time and offline time for the node. Two values are chosen to represent predicted online

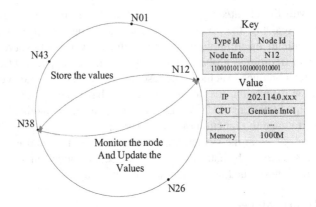

**Fig. 1.** Preserving of nodes information and monitoring among nodes

session time for a node in the system. One is the *mean value* of previous session time. The other is the *median value* of previous session time.

The elapsed online time of the node is defined as $T_{ela}$, the expected session time is defined as $T_{exp}$, and the expected left online time is defined as $T_{left}$. Then:

$$T_{left} = T_{exp} - T_{ela} \tag{1}$$

When scheduling tasks, the node will inquire the value of $T_{left}$ to decide which node is best suited for a certain task. Therefore, the values of $T_{left}$ should be preserved in system in advance.

P2P is usually regarded as one heterogeneous and asynchronous system. There is not a uniform clock to confirm the predicted lifetime for every node. Although without a uniform reference frame, for every node the time unit is the same. Besides, during every landing, the expected session time is maintained unchanged. Meanwhile, the changes of elapsed time are the same for every node. Therefore, although the left life-time ($T_{left}$) is changing every second, the order relationship of $T_{left}$ for nodes is stable.

We use the distributed bidirectional Skiplist [12] to preserve such order relation-ship of $T_{left}$ of nodes in the network so as to support the range query for the node's left online session time. The distributed bidirectional Skiplist is similar to Skipnet [11]. However, it is not applied in DHT, but only used to preserve the order relationship of several parameters of nodes.

Fig.2(a) is the table stored in the monitoring node's module recording the expected left session time of the monitored nodes. Besides, the system also preserves two route sub-lists for every node: the left route sub-list and right route sub-list. The expected left session time($T_{left}$) of the nodes in the left sub routing table is no less than that of local node, while expected left session time ($T_{left}$) of the nodes in the right sub routing table is shorter than that of local node. The nodes closest to local node are preserved on the top layer of the route sub table according to the order relationship. Then, it stores the information of the node that is $2^x$ ($x = 0, 1...$) far away. The first item in the sub routing table is the node with the closest value to the local $T_{left}$. The other items are to optimize the queries. In the worst case, adding a set of data needs *logN* steps to find the right position. In the best case, only one step is required. Fig.2(b) is the global view of connection of the data in the system.

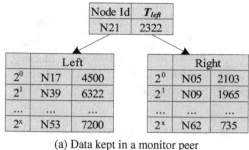

| Node Id | $T_{left}$ |
|---------|------------|
| N21     | 2322       |

| Left | | | | Right | | |
|------|-----|------|--|-------|-----|------|
| $2^0$ | N17 | 4500 | | $2^0$ | N05 | 2103 |
| $2^1$ | N39 | 6322 | | $2^1$ | N09 | 1965 |
| ... | ... | ... | | ... | ... | ... |
| $2^x$ | N53 | 7200 | | $2^x$ | N62 | 735 |

(a) Data kept in a monitor peer

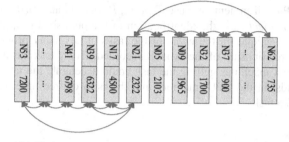

(b) Global view of the distributed bidirectional Skiplist

**Fig. 2.** Order relationship of $T_{left}$ kept in distributed bidirectional Skiplist

### 3.4 The Expression of Tasks

*Directed Acyclic Graph* (DAG) is the usual way to express tasks in the high performance computing. In DAG, every node indicates a sub task, and the lines among nodes
and the arrows represent the relationship of sub-tasks. Fig.3 is an example of DAG. In
the system, a task is published by a user. The expression of these tasks is converted
into the corresponding data and stored in the P2P network.

Clients generate tasks based on a project. Every sub-task and the corresponding
data are stored as *<Key, Value>* pairs. It distributes *<Key, Value>* pairs on different

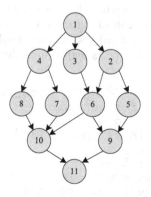

**Fig. 3.** Example of *Directed Acyclic Graph* (DAG)

| | Value | |
|---|---|---|
| | Code | P001 .jar |
| | Time | 2793 |
| | Memory | 1000M |
| | Parents | 8,7,6 |
| | Children | 11 |
| | ... | ... |

| Key | | |
|---|---|---|
| Type Id | Project Id | Task Id |
| Task Info | p001 .gird.hust.edu.cn | 10 |
| 100011001010010010100010 | | |

**Fig. 4.** <Key, Value> expression of a sub-task

nodes in the P2P environment. We use *Type Id*, *Project Id* and *Task Id* as the properties of the *Key*. *Project Id* is the identification of the published project. In the whole network, the *Id* is unique. In the *value* of the tasks, it has many properties of a task. The precedence relationship of the tasks is recorded. Every task has a standard process time. Different machines getting the task could accelerate the task. The acceleration ratio depends on the CPU, memory and the ratio of free time. Fig.4 shows the *<Key, Value>* of a task.

### 3.5 Scheduling

The objective of scheduling is to rationally distribute tasks on a proper node, and finish the task as soon as possible. Our scheduling is based on the nodes' expected online session time. With the limited resources, system will dispatch the task on the nodes that has longer online session time. Meanwhile, every task has redundancy. That means for every task, there are **K** backup copies running on other nodes. In such case, the redundancy of the task is defined to **K**. When the original copy or any other copy is done, the scheduling module will inform other copies to stop.

When a task running on a certain node, if the node leaves while the task is still running, it needs to send the interim results to the scheduler. After the scheduler gets the interim results and the related information, it will reschedule the task.

The node storing the task information is responsible for scheduling the related tasks. The following code describes the range queries process of a certain node. The query deploys on the data structure of distributed bidirectional Skiplist. The algorithm always expects to find out nodes whose left session time ($T_{left}$) is suitable for the time the task needs. If the system cannot get the enough nodes within the expected left session time ($T_{left}$), the expected left session time would reduce to its half and continue the search. Such process repeats until it finds the result or there are no enough free nodes.

```
INPUT : Project_Id, Task_Id, Type_Id
INPUT : K     // k for redundancy
//get the information of a task
Task_Value = get (Key(TypeId, ProjectId, TaskId));
int Number_of_node = 0;
For (int i = 1 ; ; i++){
//find nodes whose expect left session time >
//(Task_value.Expect_complete_time/i)
Node_list=
```

```
FindNodes(Task_value.Get(Expect_complete_time/i));
If (Node_list.size >= K+1)
// Descending sort by expect left online time
      Sort ( Node_list);
      Send (Task, Node_list[0~K] );
      break;
Else
      If (Number_of_node == Node_list.size() )
         break;
      Else
         Number_of_node = Node_list.size()
         contitnue;
End If
End If
End For
```

When a sub-task is completed, the scheduler would notify the nodes keeping the next level sub-tasks. When all of the upper sub-tasks finish, the scheduler will schedule the following tasks. Every running task has a *Copy Id* to identify different tasks. The *Copy Id* of the original copy is 0, and the *Copy Id* of the nth copy is *n*. The task with the smaller *Copy Id* has larger priority.

## 4  Performance Evaluation

In this section, we will evaluate the above algorithm. The trace for the evaluation is from http://www.cs.berkeley.edu/~pbg/availability/. The trace is collected by ping a mount of PCs once an hour. We randomly select a set of nodes from 51,662 computers. We use the session data for 51,662 PCs of 35 days from July 6, 1999. We construct a corresponding P2P network with those nodes.

Fig.5 is the evaluation for the randomly selected 1,000 nodes. To show the discipline of node history session time more clearly, we sort the node id in ascending order by the mean value of session time.

Fig.5(a) is the distribution of the session time of 1000 nodes in 35 days. It shows that on the left down corner, there is a condense distribution. That is to say, for most of the nodes, the change of session time is not huge. Fig.5(b) is the comparison of the mean value and median value of the session time. The nodes representing median value are lower than the nodes for the mean value. But the difference is small. That means it is conservative to use median value as the expected session time than mean value. Fig.5(c) shows the variance of expected session time based on mean value and median value. From the figure, we can see that the variance of most of nodes around 0 or the variance is small. That is to say, in most cases, using the average value to predict the session time is reasonable. Either using the median value or the mean value as the expected session time does not make much difference. For convenience, Fig.5(b) and Fig.5(c) are generated based on selecting 250 nodes from the 1000 nodes uniformly. Fig.5(d) is the number of active nodes in 35 days. We can see that the number of nodes has a repeated fluctuation. The fluctuation period is about 7 days (604800sec). The reason could be some nodes left at weekend.

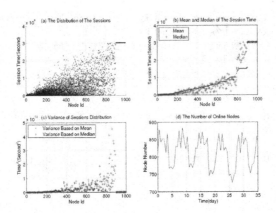

**Fig. 5.** The distribution of nodes and node's session time

## 4.1 Simulation Metrics and Parameters

**Task Size:** The size of task is defined by its standard running time. The larger standard running time means larger size.

**Average Number of Migrations per Task:** The running tasks could be migrated to other nodes because of nodes' leaving. This parameter is used to measure the number of migrations of tasks. A larger task usually needs several migrations to be finished. More migrations mean the less performance.

**Redundancy:** Every task has relative redundant copies. Redundancy indicates the number of backup copies for each task when it is running.

**Task Start Time:** After the system running for a period of time, the history session time of a node can be used to predict its online session time, and the efficiency of the algorithm begins to take effect.

## 4.2 Simulation Results

In following figures, every point indicates average results of 10 times simulation. In following experiments, the network contains 2,000 nodes chosen randomly from the 51,662 nodes in the record of the trace document.

In the simulation shown in Fig.6, 300 tasks of the same size are set to run 26 times with different start time. At the very beginning, none of the nodes have historical record, and the scheduler uses the default value to predict the session time for all nodes (3024000 sec).

From the result we can get that the average of migration times for each task whose nodes' expected online session time is predicted by mean or median value is much smaller than those with random schedule strategy. The overlap ratio of the curves below is rather high, which suggests that the use of mean or median of historical session data has little influence on the final result of our experiment. The three curves all

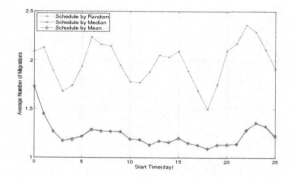

**Fig. 6.** The influence of different task start time on the efficiency of scheduling (Task Size = 259200sec, Redundancy = 1)

show a certain degree of periodicity. Compared with Fig.5(d), that time is the time when the number of nodes in system begins to decrease.

To test the influence of task size on the average migrations times, we use tasks with 30 different sizes, from 1 hour to 88 hours, and fix the task start time to the 15th day (the 1728000th second). For each task size, 300 tasks of the same size are dispatched to 2,000 node P2P network. In Fig.7, the curves show that for random scheduling strategy, the average migration times of tasks increase rapidly as the task size increases. While for the simulations using scheduling algorithm, the average migration times of tasks increase comparatively quite slowly.

The third simulation tests the impact of different redundancy on the average migration times of scheduling algorithm. As one copy accomplishes its computation, the left copies are notified to stop. It can be observed from Fig.8 that the use of certain amount of redundancy does reduce the average migration times of tasks, thus reduces the time to complete tasks and promotes computation efficiency.

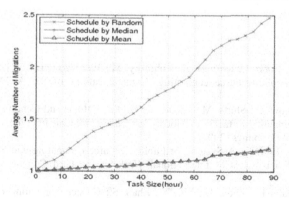

**Fig. 7.** The influence of different task size (Task Start Time = 1728000th sec, Redundancy = 1)

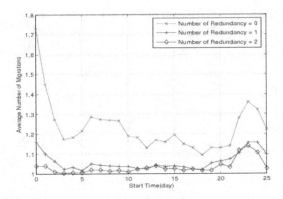

**Fig. 8.** The influence of redundancy number (Task size = 259200 sec)

## 5 Conclusions

Deploying high performance computing on P2P system is an interesting research work. This paper utilizes DHT to organize and manage tasks and worldwide computing resources. Further, we establish a new data structure supporting range queries: distributed bidirectional Skiplist. As large quantity of online sessions on numerous nodes show statistical regularity, current online time for a certain node could be predicted by historical record and is stored on the distributed bidirectional Skiplist dynamically. Our new HPC platform provides a scheduling strategy right based on that session time prediction which dispatches tasks onto the nodes with most suitable life duration according to their sizes. With less migration from node to node, much higher computing efficiency is gained.

The results of simulation with real nodes' session data demonstrates our protocol—using predicted nodes' session time could improve task scheduling performance and reduce task migration times.

## References

1. Anderson, D., Cobb, J., Korpela, E., Lebofsky, M., Werthimer, D.: SETI@home: an experiment in public-resource computing. Communications of the ACM 45(11), 56–61 (2002)
2. Larson, S., Snow, C., Shirts, M., Pande, V.: Folding@Home and Genome@Home: Using distributed computing to tackle previously intractable problems in computational biology. Computational Genomics (2002)
3. Anderson, D.: BOINC: A System for Public-Resource Computing and Storage. In: Proceedings of 5th IEEE/ACM International Workshop on Grid Computing, pp. 365–372 (2004)
4. Lo, V., Zappala, D., Zhou, D., Liu, Y., Zhao, S.: Cluster Computing on the Fly: P2P Scheduling of Idle Cycles in the Internet. In: Voelker, G.M., Shenker, S. (eds.) IPTPS 2004. LNCS, vol. 3279, pp. 227–236. Springer, Heidelberg (2005)

5. Zhou, D., Lo, V.: WaveGrid: a Scalable Fast-turnaround Heterogeneous Peerbased Desktop Grid System. In: Proceedings of the 20th International Parallel & Distributed Processing Symposium (2006)
6. Bajaj, R., Agrawal, D.: Improving Scheduling of Tasks in a Heterogeneous Environment. IEEE Transaction on Parallel and Distributed Systems, 107–118 (2004)
7. Stoica, I., Morris, R., Karger, D., Kaashoek, M., Balakrishnan, H.: Chord: A scalable peer-to-peer lookup service for internet applications. In: Proceedings of the 2001 SIGCOMM conference, vol. 31(4), pp. 149–160 (2001)
8. Rowstron, A., Druschel, P.: Pastry: Scalable, Decentralized Object Location, and Routing for Large-Scale Peer-to-Peer Systems. In: Guerraoui, R. (ed.) Middleware 2001. LNCS, vol. 2218, pp. 329–350. Springer, Heidelberg (2001)
9. Ratnasamy, S., Francis, P., Handley, M., Karp, R.: A Scalable Content-Addressable Network (CAN). In: Proceedings of ACM SIGCOMM (2001)
10. Zhao, B., Huang, L., Stribling, J., Rhea, S., Joseph, A., Kubiatowicz, J.: Tapestry: A global-scale overlay for rapid service deployment. IEEE Journal on Selected Areas in Communications (2003)
11. Harvey, N., Jones, M., Saroiu, S., Theimer, M., Wolman, A.: SkipNet: a scalable overlay network with practical locality properties. In: Proceedings of the 4th Conference on USENIX Symposium on Internet Technologies and Systems, p. 9 (2003)
12. Pugh, W.: Skip Lists: A Probabilistic Alternative to Balanced Trees. In: Proceedings of Workshop on Algorithms and Data Structures, pp. 437–449 (1989)
13. Zheng, C., Shen, G., Li, S., Shenker, S.: Distributed Segment Tree: Support of Range Query and Cover Query over DHT. In: Proceedings of IPTPS 2006 (2006)
14. Ramabhadran, S., Ratnasamy, S., Hellerstein, J., Shenker, S.: Prefix Hash Tree: An Indexing Data Structure over Distributed Hash Tables. IRB Technical Report (2004)

# An Activeness-Based Seed Choking Algorithm for Enhancing BitTorrent's Robustness

Kun Huang[1], Dafang Zhang[2], and Li'e Wang[3]

[1] School of Computer and Communication, [2] School of Software,
Hunan University, Changsha, Hunan Province 410082, P.R. China
{huangkun,dfzhang}@hunu.edu.cn
[3] College of Computer Science and Information Technology,
Guangxi Normal University, Guilin, Guangxi Province 541004, P.R. China
wle3@163.com

**Abstract.** BitTorrent suffers from the free-riding problem induced by selfish peers, hurting the system robustness. Existing research studies have focused on the fairness, performance, and robustness of BitTorrent, resulting from the Tit-For-Tat (TFT) choking algorithm, while very few studies have considered the effect of the seed choking algorithm. This paper experimentally analyzes the impact of the free riding of selfish peers on BitTorrent's performance and robustness, and proposes an activeness-based seed choking algorithm, where according to the activeness values of request peers, which are the ratios of the available download bandwidth to the available upload bandwidth, a seed preferentially uploads to five request peers with the highest activeness values, without any explicit reputation management system. Our simulation experiments show that compared to existing seed choking algorithms, the activeness-based seed choking algorithm not only restrains the free riding of selfish peers but also improves the performance of benign peers, enhancing BitTorrent's robustness.

## 1 Introduction

BitTorrent is a large-scale Peer-to-Peer (P2P) content distribution system, which has recently become one of the most important applications in the Internet [1]. In essence, BitTorrent organizes peers interested in a shared file into a collaborative P2P overlay network, where the file is divided into a number of equal-sized independent blocks and each peer exchanges blocks with each other. Moreover, BitTorrent exploits the uplink bandwidths of all peers to improve the performance and scalability when the number of participants increases [2].

To ensure the performance and scalability, BitTorrent adopts the sound core mechanisms, including Tit-For-Tat (TFT) choking algorithm and Optimistic Unchoke (OU) algorithm [3]. The TFT algorithm is employed to preferentially upload to four request peers with the highest upload rates, while the OU algorithm is to randomly upload to one of other request peers. The purpose of the TFT algorithm is to motivate peers to contribute their resources to the system, guarantee the fairness of blocks exchange between peers, and deter the free-riding problem [4, 18], where a peer

N. Abdennadher and D. Petcu (Eds.): GPC 2009, LNCS 5529, pp. 376–387, 2009.

eagerly downloads blocks from others but does not contribute to others. The OU algorithm is to avoid the first block problem to bootstrap new peers and allow each peer to explore other peers with the potential higher upload rates.

However, BitTorrent suffers from the free riding induced by selfish peers. Unlike leechers who employ the TFT algorithm and OU algorithm to reciprocate, seeds employ a choking algorithm based on available download bandwidth to upload to request peers. The seed choking algorithm is purposed to quickly distribute blocks among all peers and speed up the download process of the overall system. But there are opportunities for the free riding of selfish peers, who exploit the reciprocation protocols of BitTorrent to download more blocks without uploading any block, in BitTorrent's incentive mechanisms. First, since the OU algorithm is an altruistic strategy, selfish peers can exploit the OU algorithm to download blocks from benign leechers. Second, since seeds are altruistic peers, selfish peers can exploit the seed choking algorithm to download blocks from seeds. Finally, after completing all the blocks, selfish peers immediately leave the system, never to contribute to others. Therefore, BitTorrent is faced with the free riding of selfish peers, which incurs the performance degradation of benign peers and hurts BitTorrent's robustness.

A large number of research studies have focused on analytical models, measurements, system designs, and incentive mechanisms of BitTorrent. Studies of analytical models and measurements [2, 5-11] show that the TFT algorithm is effective and fair, and the seeding capacity has a great impact on the file availability and system stability. According to studies of system designs and incentive mechanisms [12-23], the TFT algorithm is not sufficient to effectively prevent the free riding of selfish peers, and there are several modified free-riding BitTorrent clients running in real torrents, which can exploit BitTorrent's incentive mechanisms to complete all the blocks with uploading no or a few blocks, threatening the fairness of BitTorrent. These existing research studies have focused on the fairness, performance, and robustness of BitTorrent, resulting from the TFT algorithm, while very few studies have considered the impact of the seed choking algorithm on BitTorrent's robustness.

This paper explores the impact of the seed choking algorithm on the performance of both benign peers and selfish peers, and then proposes a modified seed choking algorithm to improve BitTorrent's robustness. The main contributions of this paper are as follows. First, we experimentally analyze the free riding of selfish peers, indicating that the free riding of selfish peers incurs the performance degradation of benign peers and overloads the initial seeds. Second, we propose an activeness-based seed choking algorithm, where a seed preferentially uploads to five request peers with the highest activeness values which are the ratios of the available download bandwidth to the available upload bandwidth, without any explicit reputation management system. Finally, we conduct extensive simulation experiments to validate that the activeness-based seed choking algorithm is a simple and effective scheme, which not only restrains the free riding of selfish peers but also improves the performance of benign peers, enhancing BitTorrent's robustness.

The rest of this paper is organized as follows. Section 2 presents an overview of BitTorrent. Section 3 introduces related work. In Section 4, we analyze the free riding of selfish peers using simulation experiments. The activeness-based seed choking algorithm is described in detailed in Section 5 and experimental results are given to validate our proposed algorithm in Section 6. Section 7 concludes this paper.

## 2  BitTorrent Overview

In recent years, BitTorrent has become the popular large-scale P2P content distribution system in the Internet. The key idea of BitTorrent is that a shared file is divided into a number of equal-sized independent blocks (typically 256KB in size) and each peer simultaneously downloads and uploads multiple blocks [3]. The tracker is a unique centralized component of BitTorrent, which keeps track of the global information of each torrent.

The file download process of BitTorrent is as follows. First, a user downloads a metadata file of a shared file from a Web site, and starts the BitTorrent client to join as a new peer. Second, the new peer registers on the tracker, which responds to it with a list of randomly chosen 40 active peers possessing blocks, and then attempts to establish connections with these peers as its neighbor peers. Finally, the new peer begins to exchange blocks with its neighbor peers in a cooperative manner, and when completing all the blocks, a leecher turns into a seed and leaves the system. The flash crowd stage [15], when an amount of new peers burstly join in the system and don't leave the system until they complete all the blocks, is the most challenging for BitTorrent's performance and robustness. So this paper mainly focuses on the flash crowd stage of BitTorrent.

When downloading a block, a leecher employs the LRF algorithm [3] as the block selection strategy. The key idea of the LRF algorithm is that a leecher preferentially downloads the missing blocks that is least replicated among its neighbor peers. The LRF algorithm is a local optimized block download strategy, purposed to uniformly distribute all the blocks among all peers and avoid the last block problem. When uploading a block, a leecher employs the TFT algorithm and OU algorithm [3] as the peer selection strategy which is how to upload to which peer. The key idea of the TFT algorithm is that a leecher preferentially uploads to four request peers who upload blocks to it with the highest rates every 10 seconds, while the key idea of the OU algorithm is that a leecher randomly uploads to one of other request peers every 30 seconds. In fact, the TFT algorithm is a reciprocal scheme to ensure the fairness of blocks exchange and avoid the free riding problem, while the OU algorithm is an altruistic scheme to complement the TFT algorithm, which is purposed to bootstrap new peers for free, and avoid the first block problem.

Unlike leechers, a seed employs the choking algorithm based on available download bandwidth to preferentially upload to five request peers with the highest available download bandwidths every 10 second. The purpose of the seed choking algorithm is to quickly distribute all the blocks in the system, startup the block exchanges between peers, or speed up the block download process of the overall system. Although the new version of BitTorrent protocol specification advises a random seed choking algorithm, yet current mainline BitTorrent clients do not implement the new seed choking algorithm. So this paper mainly explores the original seed choking algorithm based on available download bandwidth.

## 3  Related Work

BitTorrent is the successful large-scale P2P content distribution system in the Internet, which has recently attracted considerable research interest. There are a large number of research studies on analytical models [2, 5-7], measurements [9-11], system designs [12-17], and incentive mechanisms [4, 18-24] of BitTorrent.

Several incentive mechanism studies have been performed to understand and improve BitTorrent's fairness and robustness. Jun et al. [18] argue that due to the lack of reward and punishment, the TFT algorithm is not sufficient to prevent the free riding, and propose a deficit-based TFT algorithm to enforce BitTorrent's fairness. Liogkas et al. [19] design and implement three exploits that allow selfish peers to maintain high download rates without contribution, and indicate that although such selfish peers can obtain more bandwidth, there is no considerable degradation of the overall system's quality of service. Locher et al. [20] design and implement a free-riding BitTorrent client, called BitThief, illustrate that the selfish peer can achieve high download rates, even in the absence of seeds. Sirivianos et al. [21] explore the large view exploit based on maintaining a larger than normal view of the torrent, and indicate that as the number of selfish peers increases, both selfish peers and benign peers suffer from substantial performance degradation. Piatek et al. [22] observe that high-capacity peers typically provide low-capacity peers with an unfair block exchange, and design and implement a selfish BitTorrent client, called BitTyant, for high-capacity peers to maximize the peer download rates, but degrading the performance of other low-capacity peers. Dhungel et al. [23] analyze two anit-P2P network attacks on the leechers of BitTorrent. Levin et al. [4] present an auction-based model to reveal new strategic manipulation, and propose a proportional-share auction based choking algorithm to achieve the fairness and robustness of BitTorrent.

Since these existing research studies indicate that the TFT algorithm is not sufficient to prevent the free riding induced by selfish peers, they predominately explore the free riding that exploits the OU algorithm, while very few studies have considered the impact of the seed choking algorithm on BitTorrent's performance and robustness, and how to prevent the free riding that exploits the seed choking algorithm. Recently related to our work, Chow et al. [24] explore how to utilize the seeding capacity to discourage the free riding of selfish peers and at the same time improve the performance of benign peers, and then propose two simple and scalable schemes, including the sort-based and threshold-based seed choking algorithm. The key idea of the sort-based seed choking algorithm is that a seed preferentially upload to request peers that have furthest from the middle of all blocks, while the key idea of the threshold-based seed choking algorithms is that a seed preferentially upload request peers whose percentages fall in either $[0 \cdots K / 2]\%$ or $[(100 - K / 2) \cdots 100]\%$. Our later experimental results show that when selfish peers camouflage new peers by cheating, both the sort-based and threshold-based algorithms are not able to effectively prevent the free riding of selfish peers, even incurring the significant degradation of benign peers' performance. Unlike above seed choking algorithms, we propose an activeness-based seed choking algorithm, which enables to not only restrain the free riding of selfish peers but also improve the performance of benign peers.

# 4  Analyzing Free Riding

This section analyzes the impact of the free riding on the performance of both benign peers and selfish peers using simulation experiments. The free riding of selfish peers

**Table 1.** BitTorrent simulation parameters

| Num. of total peers | 1001 | Num. of neighbor peers | 10-40 |
|---|---|---|---|
| Uplink bandwidth | 400KBps | Downlink bandwidth | 1500KBps |
| Num. of initial seeds | 1 | Peer arrival time | Poisson |
| Seed staying time | Uniform | Size of shared file | 100MB |
| Size of block | 256KB | Num. of blocks | 400 |
| Upload quotas | 5 | TFT period | 10 Second |
| OU period | 30 Second | Seed choking period | 10 Second |

refers to the following strategic manipulation. First, selfish peers camouflage new peers using the cheating strategy, where selfish peers deceive the tracker and its neighbor peers. Second, selfish peers frequently contact the tracker to request a list of new neighbor peers every 30 seconds. Finally, selfish peers immediately leave the system after completing all the blocks. We do not consider the complicated exploits, such as faked upload blocks [19] and Sybil attacks [27], since recent studies [20, 22] have indicated that these exploits can be easily identified and prevented.

### 4.1 Methodology

We examine the main metrics of BitTorrent's performance are the download time, the upload quota utility ratio, and the upload/download ratio. The download time and the upload quota utility ratio characterize the efficiency of BitTorrent, while the upload/download ratio characterizes the fairness of BitTorrent. We design and implement a discrete event driven simulator for BitTorrent. Table 1 shows the simulation parameters of BitTorrent.

### 4.2 Analyzing Results

Figure 1 depicts the download time of the first block. As shown in Figure 1(a), when the percentage of selfish peers increases, the average download time of the first block increases. Figure 1(b) shows that compared to selfish peers, benign peers have the less increase of the average download time of the first block. For example, in the scenarios of 10%-50% selfish peers, the average download times of the first block of benign peer and selfish peer increase by a factor of 0.8-8.3 and 15.0-17.0 respectively.

Figure 2 depicts the download time of the last block. As shown in Figure 2(a), when the percentage of selfish peers increases, the average download time of the last block decreases. Figure 2(b) shows that the average download time of the last block of benign peer increases, while that of selfish peer decreases. For example, in the scenarios of 10%-50% selfish peers, the average download time of the last block of benign peer increases by a factor of 0.4-2.3, while that of selfish peer decreases by 38%-92%.

Figure 3 depicts the download time of all blocks. As shown in Figure 3(a), when the percentage of selfish peers increases, the average download time of all blocks increases. Figure 3(b) shows that compared to selfish peers, benign peers have the less increase of the average download time of all blocks. For example, in the scenarios of 10%-50% selfish peers, the average download times of all blocks of benign peer and selfish peer increase by a factor of 0.2-1.9 and 2.1-8.3 respectively. Figure 3 shows

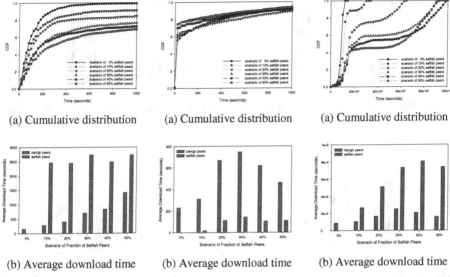

(a) Cumulative distribution      (a) Cumulative distribution      (a) Cumulative distribution

(b) Average download time      (b) Average download time      (b) Average download time

**Fig. 1.** First block          **Fig. 2.** Last block          **Fig. 3.** All blocks

that the TFT algorithm is effective and fair, guaranteeing the fairness and performance of BitTorrent, but selfish peers can exploit the OU algorithm and seed choking algorithm to download blocks without uploading any block.

Figure 4 shows that benign peers almost keep the upload quota utility ratios constant, but have the low upload quota utility ratios with the average values of less than 10% and the max values of less than 50%. In order to improve the upload quota utility ratio, Huang et al. [16] proposes a dynamic quota-based adaptive peer strategy to ultimately improve the download time of the overall system. As show in Figure 5, when the percentage of selfish peers increases, the number of upload blocks of benign peers slowly increases. For example, in the scenarios of 10%-50% selfish peers, benign peers increase the average upload blocks by 6-25 and the maximal upload blocks by 12%-223%. Also, Figure 5 shows that selfish peers can exploit the OU algorithm to free ride, resulting in that benign peers have to upload more blocks.

As shown in Figure 6, when the percentage of selfish peers increases, the number of the fair peers fluctuates, while the number of the generous peers increases. For example, in the scenarios of 10%-50% selfish peers, the percentage of the generous peers increases from 20% to 24%. As shown in Figure 7, when the percentage of selfish peers increases, the number of upload blocks of the initial seed quickly increases. For example, in the scenarios of 10%-50% selfish peers, the number of upload blocks of the initial seed increases by a factor of 1.7-9.1. Figure 7 shows that from the single peer view, compared to each benign peer, the initial seed has to upload enormously more blocks to selfish peers.

Therefore, these above experimental results motivate this paper. On one hand, the TFT algorithm is effective and fair, which reduces the performance of selfish peers and ensures the robustness of BitTorrent. On the other hand, selfish peers can exploit

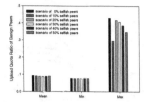

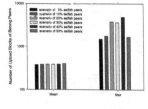

**Fig. 4.** Upload quota utility ratio of benign peers

**Fig. 5.** Number of upload blocks of benign peers

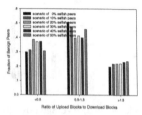

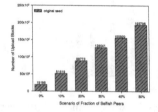

**Fig. 6.** Upload/download ratio of benign peers

**Fig. 7.** Number of upload blocks of initial seed

the OU algorithm and seed choking algorithm to free ride. So a good seed choking algorithm is the key to appropriately utilizing the seeding capacity, which not only prevents the free riding of selfish peers, but also improves the performance and robustness of BitTorrent.

# 5  Activeness-Based Choking Algorithm

To enhance BitTorrent's robustness, this paper proposes an activeness-based seed choking algorithm, where according to the activeness values of request peers, a seed preferentially uploads five request peers with the highest activeness values. The purpose of the activeness-based seed choking algorithm is twofold. First, it is to quickly distribute all the blocks among all peers and accelerate the file download process by selecting the request peer with the maximal available download bandwidth. Second, it is to fairly distribute all the blocks in the system and deter the free riding of selfish peers by selecting the request peer with the minimal available upload bandwidth.

In essence, the activeness-based seed choking algorithm is to preferentially upload to the request peer with the maximal available download bandwidth and the minimal available upload bandwidth. For each request peer, the available download bandwidth is used to characterize its capacity, while the available upload bandwidth is used to characterize its contribution. Unlike the original seed choking algorithm which considers only the capacity of a request peer, our proposed activeness-based seed choking algorithm considers both the capacity and contribution of a request peer so as to preferentially upload to the request peer with the highest capacity and largest contribution.

We assume that a request peer $p$ has the available download bandwidth $D_p$ and the available upload bandwidth $U_p$, then the activeness value of $p$ is $A_p = D_p / U_p$. When BitTorrent is under homogeneous environment, where all leecher have the same maximal available upload/download bandwidths, when a benign peer $b$ is a new peer with the maximal available upload bandwidth $U_{max\,b}$ and maximal available download bandwidth $D_{max\,b}$, then the activeness value $A_b$ of $b$ is $A_b = D_{max\,b} / U_{max\,b}$. Similarly, when a selfish peer $s$ camouflages a new peer with the available download bandwidth $D_s$ and available upload bandwidth $U_s$, then the activeness value $A_s$ of $s$ is $A_s = D_s / U_s = D_s / U_{max\,s}$. Since benign peer $b$ and selfish peer $s$ are homogeneous, $D_s$ is less than or equal to $U_{max\,b}$, then $A_b \geq A_s$. Hence, when both a benign peer and a selfish peer simultaneously request a seed for a block under homogeneous environment, the seed utilizes the activeness-based seed choking algorithm to preferentially upload to the benign seed, which not only decreases the download time of benign peers but also increases the download time of selfish peers.

When BitTorrent is under heterogonous environment, where each leecher has the different maximal available upload/download bandwidth, the activeness value of a request peer $p$ is normalized by $\overline{A_p} = (D_p / D_{max\,p}) / (U_p / U_{max\,p})$, where $D_{max\,b}$ and $U_{max\,b}$ is the maximal available download and available maximal upload bandwidth of $p$. When a benign peer $b$ is a new peer with the maximal available upload bandwidth $U_{max\,b}$ and maximal available download bandwidth $D_{max\,b}$, then the normalized activeness value $\overline{A_b}$ of $b$ is $\overline{A_b} = (D_b / D_{max\,b}) / (U_b / U_{max\,b}) = 1$. When a selfish peer $s$ camouflages a new peer with the available download bandwidth $D_s$ and available upload bandwidth $U_s = U_{max\,s}$, then the normalized activeness value $\overline{A_s}$ of $s$ is $\overline{A_s} = (D_s / D_{max\,s}) / (U_s / U_{max\,s}) = D_s / D_{max\,s} \leq 1$. Hence, when both a benign peer and a selfish peer simultaneously request a seed for a block under heterogonous environment, the seed utilizes the activeness-based seed choking algorithm to preferentially upload to the benign seed, which not only decreases the download time of benign peers but also increases the download time of selfish peers.

To accurately and quickly estimate the available upload/download bandwidth of a request peer, we adopt either the packet-pair based available bandwidth estimation scheme [12] or the capacity estimation tool MultiQ [28] for each seed in BitTorrent. Since both the packet-pair scheme and MultiQ are a lightweight albeit approximate scheme, they incur much less overhead and delay than a full block transfer. So we neglect the overhead and delay of available bandwidth estimation, and effectively simulate idealized bandwidth estimation on every request peer in our experiments.

The activeness-based seed choking algorithm is a simple and effective scheme, suitable for real BitTorrent. On one side, since a selfish peer can not camouflage or fake its available upload/download bandwidth, both the packet-pair scheme and MultiQ can quickly and accurately estimate the available bandwidth of every request peer by active probing. On the other side, a seed can not identify the selfish peer by its available upload/download bandwidth estimation. Moreover, our proposed activeness-based seed choking algorithm does not need any explicit reputation management system, such as EigenTrust [29] and PeerTrust [30]. Such reputation systems are either too complex or unrealistic, or very easy to be circumvented, especially not suitable for the scalability, dynamics, and heterogeneity of real BitTorrent.

# 6   Experimental Evaluation

To evaluate the activeness-based choking algorithm, we conduct a serial of experiments in both the uncooperative and cooperative peering scenarios. The uncooperative peering scenario is that each leecher downloads all blocks from the initial seeds, without blocks exchange between peers, while the cooperative peering scenario is that each leecher not only downloads blocks from the initial seeds, but also exchanges blocks with each other.

## 6.1   Uncooperative Peering Scenario

Figure 8 shows that compared to existing seed choking algorithms, our activeness-based seed choking algorithm not only increases the average download time of all blocks of selfish peer, but also decreases the average download time of all blocks of benign peer. As seen in Figure 8(a), compared to the original seed choking algorithm, the activeness-based seed choking algorithm decreases the average download time of all blocks of benign peer by 37% and increases the average download time of all blocks of selfish peer by 56%. As seen in Figure 8(b), compared to the original seed choking algorithm, the activeness-based seed choking algorithm decreases the average download time of all blocks of fast benign peer by 6%, decreases the average download time of all blocks of slow benign peer by 55%, and increase the average download time of all blocks of slow selfish peer by 128%. Therefore, our activeness-based seed choking algorithm not only restrains the free riding of selfish peers but also improve the performance of benign peers. Also, Figure 8 shows that both the sort-based and threshold-based seed choking algorithms are not suitable for real BitTorrent.

## 6.2   Cooperative Peering Scenario

Figure 9 shows that our activeness-based choking algorithm has the more improve of the average download time of the first block of benign peers than that of selfish peers.

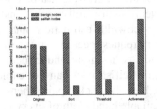
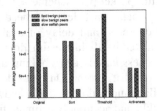

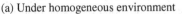

(a) Under homogeneous environment    (b) Under heterogeneous environment

**Fig. 8.** Comparison of average download time of all blocks under different environments

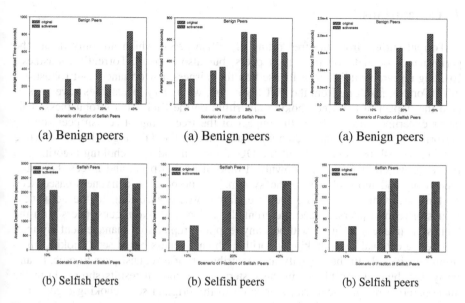

(a) Benign peers            (a) Benign peers            (a) Benign peers

(b) Selfish peers           (b) Selfish peers           (b) Selfish peers

**Fig. 9.** Download time of    **Fig. 10.** Download time of    **Fig. 11.** Download time of all
first block                     last block                      blocks

For example, in the scenario of 10%, 20%, and 40% selfish peers, compared to the
original seed choking algorithm, the activeness-based seed choking algorithm increases the average download time of the first block of benign peer by 40%, 45%, and
28% respectively, and decreases the average download time of the first block of selfish peer by 16%, 18%, and 7% respectively.

Figure 10 shows that our activeness-based choking algorithm decreases the average download time of the last block of benign peers, while it increases the average
download time of the last block of selfish peers. For example, in the scenario of 10%,
20%, and 40% selfish peers, compared to the original seed choking algorithm, the
activeness-based seed choking algorithm separately increases 11%, decreases 3% and
22% of the average download time of the last block of benign peer, and increases the
average download time of the last block of selfish peer by 153%, 22%, and 25% respectively.

Figure 11 shows that our activeness-based seed choking algorithm has the more
improve of the average download time of all blocks of benign peers than that of selfish peers. For example, in the scenario of 10%, 20%, and 40% selfish peers, compared
to the original seed choking algorithm, the activeness-based seed choking algorithm
separately increases 5%, decreases 24% and 28% of the average download time of all
blocks of benign peers, and increases 5%, decreases 9% and 19% of the average
download time of all blocks of selfish peers. Figure 11 shows that the activeness-
based seed choking algorithm improves the average download time of benign peers,
which increases the number of benign peers exploited by selfish peers, so that it also
decreases the average download time of selfish peers.

# 7 Conclusions

BitTorrent suffers from the free riding of selfish peers, which not only incurs the performance degradation of benign peers, but also hurts BitTorrent's robustness. Existing research studies have focused on the fairness, performance, and robustness of BitTorrent, resulting from the TFT algorithm, while very few studies have considered the impact of the seed choking algorithm on the BitTorrent's robustness. This paper experimentally analyzes the impact of the free riding of selfish peers on the performance of BitTorrent, indicating that although the TFT algorithm is effective and fair, selfish peers can exploit the OU algorithm and seed choking algorithm to free ride, which increases the download time of benign peers and forces the initial seed to upload more blocks to the system. We propose an activeness-based seed choking algorithm to mitigate the free riding, where according to the activeness values of request peers, a seed preferentially uploads to five request peers with the highest activeness values, without any explicit reputation management system. Unlike the original seed choking algorithm, the activeness-based seed choking algorithm considers both the capacity and contribution of a request peer to quickly and fairly distribute all the blocks in the system. Experimental results show: (1) in the uncooperative peering scenario, compared to the original seed choking algorithms, the activeness-based seed choking algorithm not only decreases the average download time of all blocks of benign peer, but also increases that of selfish peer; (2) in the cooperative peering scenario, the activeness-based seed choking algorithm decreases more the average download time of all blocks of benign peer than that of selfish peer, and selfish peers have more the average download time of all blocks than benign peers by several factors.

## Acknowledgment

This work is supported by the National Science Foundation of China under grant No.60673155 and No.90718008.

## References

1. The True Picture of Peer-to-Peer File Sharing, http://www.cachelogic.com
2. Yang, X., Veciana, G.: Service Capacity of Peer-to-Peer Networks. In: Proc. of IEEE INFOCOM, pp. 2242–2252 (2004)
3. Cohen, B.: Incentives Build Robustness in BitTorrent. In: Proc. of the Workshop on Economics of Peer-to-Peer Systems (2003)
4. Levin, D., LaCurts, K., Spring, N., et al.: BitTorrent is an Auction: Analyzing and Improving BitTorrent's Incentives. In: Proc. of ACM SIGCOMM, pp. 243–254 (2008)
5. Qiu, D., Srikant, R.: Modeling and Performance Analysis of BitTorrent-like Peer-to-Peer Networks. In: Proc. of ACM SIGCOMM, pp. 367–378 (2004)
6. Massoulie, L., Vojnovic, M.: Coupon Replication Systems. In: Proc. of ACM SIGMETRICS, pp. 2–13 (2005)
7. Fan, B., Chiu, D.M., Lui, J.C.: The Delicate Tradeoffs in BitTorrent-like File Sharing Protocol Design. In: Proc. of IEEE ICNP, pp. 239–248 (2006)

8. Izal, M., Urvoy-Keller, G., Biersack, E.W., et al.: Dissecting BitTorrent: Five Months in a Torrent's Lifetime. In: Proc. of Passive & Active Measurement Workshop, pp. 1–11 (2004)
9. Pouwelse, J., Garbacki, P., Epema, D., et al.: The BitTorrent P2P File-Sharing System: Measurements and Analysis. In: Castro, M., van Renesse, R. (eds.) IPTPS 2005. LNCS, vol. 3640, pp. 205–216. Springer, Heidelberg (2005)
10. Guo, L., Chen, S., Xiao, Z., et al.: Measurement, Analysis, and Modeling of BitTorrent-like Systems. In: Proc. of IMC, pp. 35–48 (2005)
11. Legout, A., Urvoy-Keller, G., Michiardi, P.: Rarest First and Choke Algorithms are Enough. In: Proc. of IMC, pp. 203–216 (2006)
12. Bharambe, A.R., Herley, C., Padmanabhan, V.N.: Analyzing and Improving a BitTorrent Network's Performance Mechanisms. In: Proc. of IEEE INFOCOM, pp. 1–12 (2006)
13. Tian, Y., Wu, D., Ng, K.W.: Modeling, Analysis, and Improvement for BitTorre-like File Sharing Networks. In: Proc. of IEEE INFOCOM, pp. 1–11 (2006)
14. Bindal, R., Cao, P., Chan, W., et al.: Improving Traffic Locality in BitTorrent via Biased Neighbor Selection. In: Proc. of IEEE ICDCS, pp. 66–77 (2006)
15. Legout, A., Liogkas, N., Kohler, E., et al.: Clustering and Sharing Incentives in BitTorrent Systems. In: Proc. of ACM SIGMETRICS, pp. 301–312 (2007)
16. Huang, K., Wang, L., Zhang, D., et al.: Optimizing the BitTorrent Performance Using Adaptive Peer Selection Strategy. Future Generation Computer Systems 24(7), 621–630 (2008)
17. Marciniak, P., Liogkas, N., Legout, A., et al.: Small is Not Always Beautiful. In: Proc. of IPTPS (2008)
18. Jun, S., Ahamad, M.: Incentives in BitTorrent Induce Free Riding. In: Proc. of the Workshop on Economics of Peer-to-Peer Systems (2005)
19. Ligokas, N., Nelson, R., Kohler, E., et al.: Exploiting BitTorrent for Fun (But Not Profit). In: Proc. of IPTPS (2006)
20. Locher, T., Moor, P., Schmid, S., et al.: Free Riding in BitTorrent is Cheap. In: Proc. of HotNets (2006)
21. Sirivianos, M., Park, J.H., Chen, R., et al.: Free-riding in BitTorrent Networks with the Large View Exploit. In: Proc. of IPTPS (2007)
22. Piatek, M., Isdal, T., Anderson, T., et al.: Do Incentives Build Robustness in BitTorrent? In: Proc. of NSDI, pp. 1–14 (2007)
23. Dhungel, P., Wu, D., Schonhorst, B., et al.: A Measurement Study of Attacks on BitTorrent Leechers. In: Proc. of IPTPS (2008)
24. Chow, A.L., Golubchik, L., Misra, V.: Improving BitTorrent: A Simple Approach. In: Proc. of IPTPS (2008)
25. Strauss, J., Katabi, D., Kaashoek, F.: A Measurement Study of Available Bandwidth Estimation Tools. In: Proc. of IMC, pp. 39–44 (2003)
26. BitTorrent, http://www.bittorrent.com/
27. Douceur, J.R.: The Sybil Attack. In: Druschel, P., Kaashoek, M.F., Rowstron, A. (eds.) IPTPS 2002. LNCS, vol. 2429, p. 251. Springer, Heidelberg (2002)
28. Katti, S., Katabi, D., Blake, C., et al.: MultiQ: Automated Detection of Multiple Bottleneck Capacities Along a Path. In: Proc. of IMC, pp. 245–250 (2004)
29. Kamvar, S., Schlosser, M., Garcia-Molina, H.: The EigenTrust Algorithm for Reputation Management in P2P Networks. In: Proc. of WWW, pp. 640–651 (2003)
30. Xiong, L., Liu, L.: PeerTrust: Supporting Reputation-Based Trust for Peer-to-Peer Electronic Communities. IEEE Transactions on Knowledge and Data Engineering 16(7), 843–857 (2004)

# Resource Aggregation Effectiveness in Peer-to-Peer Architectures

Mircea Moca and Gheorghe Cosmin Silaghi

Babeș-Bolyai University, Str. Theodor Mihali 58-60, 400599, Cluj-Napoca, Romania
{Mircea.Moca,Gheorghe.Silaghi}@econ.ubbcluj.ro

**Abstract.** As service-oriented systems emerge toward a fully decentralized collaborative environment, resource aggregation becomes one of the important features to study. In this paper we investigate the effectiveness of resource aggregation in a peer-to-peer architecture with autonomous nodes that can either supply or consume services. We consider various setups concerning the initial endowment of the system with resources, the load with service requests, the intrinsic capability of the system for resource discovery and the subjective valuation of peers concerning the delivered services. We show that for high loads of the system with service requests, the performance of the resource supply does not degrade in the long run and for low loads the resource discovery method combined with the partner selection algorithm succeeds to deliver a better performance.

## 1 Introduction

As the grid emerges toward fully distributed P2P networks [1], service oriented architectures need to adapt to the new peer-to-peer networked environment. To make the P2P-based SOA pervasive, the challenge is to let all the nodes in the system to play both roles: consumers and producers of services. Such an ideal system should be able to discover and aggregate the suitable resources to supply a consumer query.

Therefore, a system designer faces several major challenges when building such a system: which is the suitable underlying structure of the P2P network, which mechanism to employ for resource discovery, what model to apply in order to select the proper providers or whether the designed mechanisms can lead to scalable, stable and reliable SOA environments.

On the other hand, agent research contributes with resource allocation mechanisms [2], emphasizing on various issues on interest like agent preferences, production of the social welfare, complexity, negotiation, algorithm and mechanism design etc. But, up to now, very few research concerns whether those conceptual models are effective in fully distributed P2P networked environments.

In this paper we investigate the effectiveness of resource aggregation in unstructured P2P networks with autonomous nodes. By resource aggregation we understand the process of gathering quantities of the same resource from many providers. We let each node to be either a service consumer or resource provider,

N. Abdennadher and D. Petcu (Eds.): GPC 2009, LNCS 5529, pp. 388–399, 2009.

to be equipped with some decision making model and to have different prefer-ences over the decision criteria employed for partner selection. We want to draw out some conclusions about how the global performance of the aggregation is affected by the network topology and size, the demand load and the power of the resource discovery mechanism. Further, we investigate whether a consumer-tailored subjective decision making model can bring global gains on the system.

The paper is organized as follows. In section 2 we describe P2P system model, the decision making algorithms employed and the measures used to evaluate the effectiveness of the resource aggregation scheme. Section 3 presents our simu-lations and describes the results. Section 4 briefs related work while section 5 concludes the paper.

## 2   Background

### 2.1   The P2P System Architecture

We present in this section the system architecture and the aggregation mecha-nisms employed in our setting.

The discussed system comprises a set of $N$ participants, organized in a un-structured peer-to-peer architecture. Each peer owns a certain quantity of re-sources and it is linked to a subset of other peers, called neighbors. Consequently, our system is a connected graph. This structure is established a-priori, in the sense that it remains stable during one round of experiments. Thus, before each run, we randomly build the graph structure of the system architecture by select-ing the neighbors of each peer.

Each peer $p_i$ owns a quantity $q_i$ from some resource $R$. The resource $R$ (which might be a service) is defined by a set of issues (properties) $\{is_1, ..., is_k\}$ that characterize the resource. These issues might be the price, the resource quality etc. and can hold numerical values $\{v_{i,1}, v_{i,2}, ..., v_{i,k}\}$, specific for the resource provider $p_i$. For the sake of simplicity, as the goal of this paper is to investigate resource aggregation, we endow the system with only one sort of resource $R$ and we vary the issues values.

In our experiments we consider various endowments of the system with re-sources. Thus, the wealth can be uniformly distributed among the peers or they might be unequally equipped with resources (e.g. some peers might own a big quantity and ask for a higher price in contrast with other peers that can supply only with a small quantity of resource).

Upon this peer-to-peer infrastructure we construct the resource aggregation functionality employing two mechanisms: resource discovery and service compo-sition. During resource discovery, the process starts at a node - called *initiator* - that demands a quantity $Q_d$ of the resource $R$ for $T_d$ units of time. We assume the network is equipped with some resource discovery mechanism that search network in order to discover potential resource providers [3]. The resource dis-covery mechanism has some intrinsic discovery power in the sense that it is able to investigate a fraction $f$ of the total number of peers. Later in this paper, we will address the models for resource discovery. The resource discovery process returns a list of potential providers.

Next, the service composition mechanism is applied after resource discovery. During service composition, the initiator selects the proper peers to aggregate resources from, by filtering the list returned by the resource discovery mechanism. In section 2.2 we describe the procedure applied in the service composition phase in order to select the best peers for a resource demand. If the initiator can not aggregate the entire demanded quantity, the query fails.

The time $T_d$ related with a resource demand indicates the duration in time units for which the initiator occupies the selected resource during service consumption. Thus, if a provider $p_i$ enters a transaction for a resource demand with $T_d$, during those time units the provider will not be able to commit the resource for another query, thus eliminating the possibility of distributed deadlocks in the system. For simplicity, we assume that each initiator can estimate the time $T_d$ for a resource demand, and if $T_d$ is not enough to supply the initiator's needs, the initiator will launch a new query for the additional required duration.

Models for resource discovery in peer-to-peer architectures are presented in [3]. Among them, we can consider message broadcasting. With message broadcasting, each resource query is broadcasted by the initiator in the network with a time-to-live parameter TTL. The TTL is strongly related with the connection degree of the network. They determine the number of nodes reached by the search - the query horizon. The bigger the TTL, the further the message is delivered in the network, and the query horizon of the resource discovery mechanism increases. The theoretical query horizon can be deduced out of the network size, topology and TTL. The actual horizon is the total number of distinct nodes that actually respond the queries. The theoretical horizon calculation is often irrelevant [4] since it does not take into account graph cycles and variable connection degree at different hops. Hence, we employ in our study the actual horizon, and for simplicity refer with horizon. Being tracked and reported by the system, this value is accurate.

For our experiments, we employed the deterministic simple-flooding broadcasting protocol [5]. Broadcasting is very suitable for our needs because there is a direct relation between the query horizon and the size of the TTL parameter.

In this paragraph we describe the experimentation setup employed in our study. A round of experiments consists of multiple resource demands, each being delivered at individual time units on the time scale. For a resource demand, a peer $p_i$ is randomly selected and it initiates a query for $Q_d$ quantity of resources with $T_d$. The resource discovery mechanism retrieves a list of potential providers. Next, the initiator applies some decision model in order to select the peers to aggregate resources from. The efficacy of the selection is evaluated and next, the transaction happens in the sense that the selected peers will have the selected quantity of resource unavailable for the next $T_d$ units of time. This resource demand scenario is applied several times and at the end, we report the total efficacy achieved.

During experimentation (section 3) we change various inputs and we report and conclude about how effective the resource aggregation procedure described above is. Next, we describe the decision models used for service composition and the metrics employed to evaluate the efficacy.

## 2.2  Decision Models for Resource Aggregation

In this section we describe the decision models employed for service composition.

As indicated by the decision making literature [6,7], decision makers take action based on various criteria and on their preference among them. Criteria can be qualitative and quantitative and the decision models are parametric or non-parametric as they employ rankings of the alternatives based on the values ordering or they fully employ the values scored by the criteria in some complicated computations.

For the scope of this paper we only need a simple decision making algorithm that has variants emphasizing or not some decision criteria. We do not intend to search the best possible decision making model. Thus, we selected a non-parametric model named Onicescu, presented in [8], developed by the Romanian mathematician Octav Onicescu, which is applicable in the same initial conditions of the ELECTRE method [6]. The key requirements of the method are:

- the decision makers include more criteria in the model;
- actions are evaluated on an ordinal scale;
- a strong heterogeneity related to the nature of the evaluations exists among criteria;
- compensation of the loss on a given criterion by the gain on another may not be acceptable for the decision maker.

The Onicescu algorithm assigns a score to each alternative and ranks the alternatives based on the scores. The score is an evaluation of the decision maker's preference for the evaluated alternative. We present below two variants of the Onicescu's decision criteria algorithm.

Given the set of alternatives $V = \{v_i\}$, $i = \overline{1, n}$, the decision maker uses a set of criteria $C = \{c_j\}$, $j = \overline{1, k}$ to evaluate the alternatives. In our case, potential providers represent the alternatives, and the price and quantity proposed by peers, as well as other issues are the criteria.

The Onicescu algorithm starts with a matrix $A$ of size $n \times k$ having a line for each alternative and a column for each decision criteria. Value $a_{i,j}$ represents the actual values of the $i$th alternative for the $j$th criterion. Next, the algorithm builds a matrix $B$ of size $n \times k$ where the value $b_{i,j}$ represents the rank of value $a_{i,j}$ among the values on the column $j$ of $A$. Hence, the $b_{i,j}$ represents the ranking of alternative $v_i$ on criterion $c_j$.

In the objective version of the Onicescu's algorithm, from $B$, we further build a new matrix $C$ of size $n \times n$, where $c_{i,j}$ represents the count of rank $j$ for the alternative $v_i$ on all values on line $i$ of $B$. Thus, matrix $C$ depicts how many times alternative $v_i$ ranked first, second, third etc. among all decision criteria. Equation 1 gives the score for an alternative $v_i$ computed out of C:

$$SC_1(v_i) = \sum_{j=1}^{n} c_{i,j} \frac{1}{2^j} \qquad (1)$$

Next, each alternative is ranked according with the score $SC_1$, the first one being the one that scores highest.

The subjective version of Onicescu's algorithm takes as input the matrix $B$ containing all rankings of alternatives $v_i$ for all criteria. This version allows the decision maker to assign importance weights to each criterion. Assuming that the $k$ criteria are ordered according with the preference of the decision maker (criterion 1 being the most preferred one, next criterion 2 and so on), eq. 2 presents a possible weighting scheme that puts on each criterion twice as much importance than the next positioned one:

$$W = \{w_j, \ w_j = \frac{1}{2^j}, \ j = \overline{1,k}\} \qquad (2)$$

With this weighting, the subjective Onicescu's score for each decision alternative is presented in eq. 3:

$$SC_2(v_i) = \sum_{j=1}^{k} w_j \frac{1}{2^{b_{i,j}}} \qquad (3)$$

The variants of Onicescu differ only on the score assigned to the decision alternatives. We note that the subjective variant of Onicescu personalizes the decision making process. Each decision maker can have another preference order among criteria and this preference order might vary from a resource demand to another. More, the decision maker can use other weighting schemes instead the one described in eq. 2 and recommended in [8]. The subjective approach was envisaged as more realistic, coming close to the real-world decision problems.

Another issue in the above-presented decision making scheme is the existence of a ranking method for each decision criteria. The algorithm assumes that the decision maker is able to crystal-clear decide which values for a criterion are better than others. This is equivalent with assuming that each criterion is equipped with an ordering relation on its values.

In our experiments, for the sake of simplicity, we considered only two decision criteria: the price and the quantity and both Onicescu's scores. More criteria can be added like real-life issues for a particular resource (which are related with the QoS parameters for the resource). In the subjective approach, we considered quantity being more preferred than price. Thus, we model a consumer searching for a specific resource rather than searching for the cheapest one. Such a consumer will be more happy to directly deal with a small number of providers to aggregate a big quantity of resources than to fragment the demand in many shipments.

The ranking produced by the decision making algorithm is valuable in the case when no single provider can deliver the demanded quantity. Thus, the provider will have a mean to select the top-ranked potential providers in order to aggregate the demanded quantity. If one provider can supply the demand, the initiator will select the first-ranked potential provider.

## 2.3 Evaluating the Quality of Resource Discovery

In this section we present the evaluation criteria to assess the effectiveness of the resource aggregation process.

Evaluation should be done individually at the level of each resource demand and globally at the level of all resource demands covered is a experimentation run.

At the end of the resource aggregation process the initiator holds an optimal list with partners as the result of the query injected into the system. As available resources permanently fluctuate in the system in terms of provider and quantity, consecutive demand queries would provide different results. Thus, at the resource demand level, we evaluate the utility perceived by the initiator concerning the result delivered by the system in response to its query. A selected result consists in a number $N_p$ of selected partners, the total prices $P_i$, $i = \overline{1, N_p}$ paid by each partner and the quantities $Q_i$ delivered for the prices $P_i$. Initiators are interested in:

- aggregating all the demanded quantity $Q_d$
- minimizing the payments
- minimizing the risks associated with the transaction delivery. In our case, risks increase with the number of partners per transaction.

Eq. 4 describes the individual 'utility' associated with a query.

$$U_d = \frac{1}{N_p} \times \frac{1}{\sum_{i=1}^{N_p} P_i} \times \frac{1}{\sum_{i=1}^{N_p} Q_i} \tag{4}$$

The bigger the utility scored by a demand $d$, the better. Utilities can be aggregated over all demands in a run of experiments to obtain the global utility $U_g$ of a system setup. The global utility $U_g$ characterizes the social welfare concept, presented in [2].

Besides the above-described utility, we also count the number of failures to supply the entire demanded quantity and the total payments. From the consumers' point of view, the objective is to minimize the payments. From the providers' point of view, the objective is to maximize the payments.

## 3  Experiments and Results

In this section we describe the experiments and comment on the results of our study. The experimentation is performed on a message-based simulator for a P2P network, implemented at the Faculté Polytechnique de Mons Belgium[1] and modified to accommodate the resource aggregation.

---

[1] We thank Sebastien Noel from Faculté Polytechnique de Mons Belgium for letting us to use the initial version of the P2P network simulator and for support during the development.

We employ the P2P system architecture described in section 2.1 with the broadcasting protocol for resource discovery. Next, we present the set with the main system parameters that drive our experiments:

- the TTL of the broadcasting mechanism employed for resource discovery,
- the connection degree ($D_c$), representing the number of neighbors of a node;
- the query horizon ($H_d$), meaning the number of potential providers that an initiator discovers; this is the practical achieved value for the parameter $f$ - the coverage factor of the resource discovery mechanism
- the number of selected providers ($N_p$ - as in previous section),
- the initial endowment $q_i$ of a node,
- the total number of request messages ($N_m$) broadcasted for a particular resource demand. This is a cost measure for the resource discovery mechanism;
- the demanded quantity $Q_d$ for a query; might be (i) low, (ii) high or can uniformly vary between the low and the high value. Each fulfilled query will hold the committed resources busy for the next $T_d$ queries, with $T_d$ being set up to a random number from 2 to 10. The demanded quantity is in fact the load factor of the network, as employed in [9].
- and the failure rate ($R_f$), which is the number of queries that fail within the running of a scenario. A query is considered failed when the initiator ends the resource aggregation procedure without fulfilling all the requested quantity $Q_d$.

We experiment on three different sorts of networks regarding the distribution of $q_i$. If $QN$ is the total quantity of the resource available in the system, we experiment with networks where:

- $q_i \sim \frac{1}{QN}$ (uniform distribution),
- $q_i \sim Pois(1)$ (Poisson distribution with parameter $\lambda = 1$) - where very few nodes hold large quantities of resources, and
- $q_i \sim Pois(4)$ (Poisson distribution with parameter $\lambda = 4$) distribution, where the majority own the average quantity $\frac{1}{QN}$ and only few nodes own large or small quantities.

For the rest of our discussion, a scenario (or a run of experiments) is a set of 100 queries initiated by participants randomly chosen from a network of 500 nodes. The results we present below scales proportionally with the network size and the load in queries, by maintaining the same network topology.

We first inspect how TTL influences the global utility since a higher value would lead to a broader horizon. Thus, for fixed values of $D_c$ and $Q_d$ we run scenarios for a range of TTL values. The total utility $U_g$ increases with the TTL, as depicted in figure 1a. Figure 1b depicts the failure rate $R_f$ decreasing with increasing TTL. We identify three 'stages' for the progress of $U_g$ as we modify TTL. First, for very low values of TTL, $U_g$ is 0, since $R_f$ is 100%. It means the horizon is insufficient for the initiator to discover enough nodes to fulfill $Q_d$. Starting from a certain TTL, the $U_g$ rises and then becomes stable, while $R_f$ decreases.

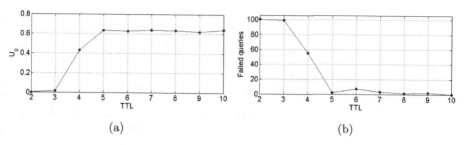

**Fig. 1.** a) Total utility $U_g$ as a function of TTL; b) The failure rate $R_f$

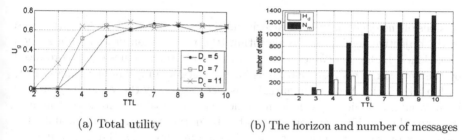

(a) Total utility          (b) The horizon and number of messages

**Fig. 2.** Gains and costs as a function of TTL, for various connection degrees

Keeping the same setting, we ran scenarios with different values for $Q_d$. The pattern followed by the global utility vs. TTL holds as in figure 1a. However, for high values of $Q_d$, $U_g$ begins to increase only with a higher TTL.

The connection degree is another parameter that determines the horizon's ampleness. Thus, for the same scenarios as before: a range of TTL values and fixed $Q_d$, we inspect $U_g$ while modifying the connection degree $D_c$. Figure 2a show the total utility curve $U_g$ for three distinct values of $D_c$; $Q_d$ being fixed. We observe that a greater $D_c$ improves $U_g$, in the sense that stages of increasing and stabilizing emerge sooner, thus for lower values of TTL.

A more detailed analysis of $U_g$ from the communication costs' perspective, conveys us to the assertion that both $D_c$ and TTL are worth increasing up to a certain level. That is, after $U_g$ converged to its upper limit for the given network setup, increasing $D_c$ and TTL lead only to higher costs, without improving the total utility. Figure 2b depicts the horizon $H_d$ as it flattens with a certain TTL, although the number of messages continue to increase with TTL. We also note that this behavior holds in scenarios with different values of $Q_d$ and $D_c$. More, if we simultaneously look at how $U_g$ and $H_d$ modify, we observe that they converge for the same values of TTL and $D_c$. Consequently, when designing a real system, $D_c$ and TTL should be adjusted to values that maximize $U_g$ and still avoid useless retransmission.

In settings with dynamic values of $Q_d$ we identify different levels of utility for different ranges of $Q_d$. In figure 3 we depict total utility lines for setups with low, high and uniformly distributed values of demanded quantities. We run both

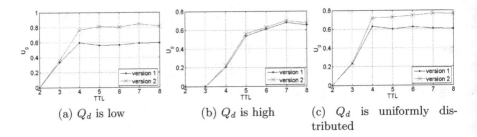

(a) $Q_d$ is low    (b) $Q_d$ is high    (c) $Q_d$ is uniformly distributed

**Fig. 3.** Total utility curves for different values of $Q_d$, for both versions of the decision making algorithm

versions of the decision making algorithm, the lines with solid circles correspond to the objective version of the algorithm (the first version described in section 2.2). Hence, higher $Q_d$ values are, lower the total utility values $U_g$ are produced by the network. This assertion holds both for static and dynamic values of $Q_d$ within a scenario. Another remarkable aspect implied by the value of $Q_d$ is that both variants of Onicescu's algorithm tend to produce same $U_g$ for high demands. It means that within a system dominated by initiators with high demands, the preference over a certain variant of the decision making algorithm is not an issue of performance. However, within scenarios with uniformly distributed $Q_d$, the two versions of Onicescu's algorithm perform differently in terms of $U_g$, as shown in figure 3c.

Figures 4a - 4c show the numbers of providers selected by both versions of Onicescu's algorithm as a function of TTL and $Q_d$. As presented in section 2.1, the discovery of nodes with available resources is performed by the

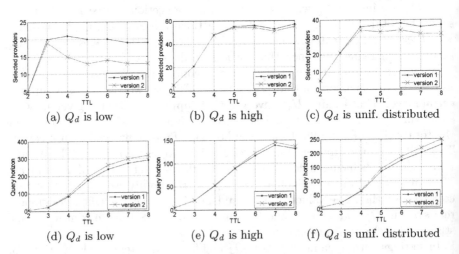

(a) $Q_d$ is low    (b) $Q_d$ is high    (c) $Q_d$ is unif. distributed

(d) $Q_d$ is low    (e) $Q_d$ is high    (f) $Q_d$ is unif. distributed

**Fig. 4.** Number of selected providers providers and query horizon for both versions of Onicescu's algorithm, as a function of TTL and for different values of $Q_d$

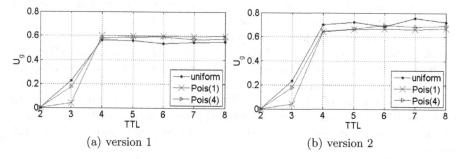

(a) version 1                                  (b) version 2

**Fig. 5.** $U_g$ for different distributions of $q_i$ and for both versions of decision making algorithm

broadcasting mechanism in the first phase of the resource aggregation process. After the run of a query within a scenario, the resources of certain nodes (the selected providers) are occupied by the initiator of the respective query. As we experiment with both versions of Onicescu's algorighm, we observe that they perform differently in terms of total selected providers. Since the second version ranks better the nodes with higher values of the initial endowment $q_i$, it minimizes the number of selected providers for a given $Q_d$. Consequently, at the end of an aggregation process, the second version of Onicescu's algorithm would occupy less nodes (as compared to the first version) from within the horizon. More, this leads to horizons of different extents within experiments for the distinct versions of Onicescu's algorithm. As depicted in figures 4d - 4f, the second version of Onicescu's algorithm decides on a broader horizon, for low, high and uniformly distributed values of $Q_d$.

The distribution of the wealth ($q_i$) on the network has a great impact on global utility. Hence, we inspect $U_g$ in experiments with the distributions mentioned at the beginning of this section. Figure 5 depicts the utility for these distributions, where we observe that subjective *Onicescu* (figure 5b) yields a better utility for all distributions of $q_i$. We also note (figure 5b) that the subjective version of the Onicescu's decision making algorithm is able to take advantage from the heterogeneity in the endowment of the peers. Thus, the utility scored for the network with uniformly distributed wealth is higher than the remaining cases. This is exactly converse in the objective version of the Onicescu's algorithm with favors the most homogeneous structure. We can conclude that a decision making algorithm that reflects closer the preference of the users between various decision criteria is most suitable for heterogeneous environments and can take advantage from the heterogeneity.

## 4   Related Works

Figueira et al. [6] presents various decision making models. The ELECTRE model is employed in managerial decisions similar with the one considered in this paper, but with more than one decision maker. Other alternatives are the PROMETHEE method or the multi-attribute utility theory.

Resource allocation is widely studied in multi-agent systems [2]. They present various issues of interest we should consider when designing a resource allocation mechanism. Such mechanism are employed in grid systems for job scheduling [9]. X.Y. Li et al. [10] is concerned in designing mechanisms that provide more trust in intermediate nodes of a transaction. They treat the "moral hazard" (as called in economics) problem in networks with multi-hop routing and design incentive schemes for nodes to eliminate hidden information that stands between end-points of a transaction.

Service composition in the sense of finding the proper instantiation for an orchestration is approached in [11] by employing genetic algorithms. The authors propose a slower (than integer programming) but scalable solution that deals with generic QoS attributes.

Emerging cooperative behavior in P2P networks is mostly based on developing incentive techniques, like the one presented in [12] to confront the problem of "free riding" (lack of cooperation). The basis of their techniques consist in the Generalized Prisoner's Dilemma and the Reciprocative decision function. Jurca & Faltings [13] propose a reputation model to stand as an incentive mechanism.

## 5 Conclusion

In this paper we investigated the effectiveness of resource aggregation over a P2P networked infrastructure. Resource aggregation is viewed as the process of collecting quantities from the same resource from various providers.

We concluded that unstructured P2P networks equipped with resource discovery mechanisms with a given horizon are able to properly fulfill the consumers' queries. By experimentation, one can find the proper parameters for the network connectivity and for the resource discovery mechanism. Increasing the connectivity or the power of the resource discovery mechanism more than an optimum will not lead to more satisfaction among consumers. We investigated two variants of the decision making algorithm that put equal emphasis on the decision criteria or consider the decision maker's preference among them. We noticed that when the wealth is heterogeneously distributed on the environment, the variant of the decision making algorithm that differences between the criteria can bring more global welfare.

As a future work we intend to evaluate other decision making algorithms, including parametric ones. Besides aggregation we intend to consider the more sophisticated bundling of resources, where a bundle can comprise quantities from several sorts. Also, reputation of nodes can help as an additional decision criterion during both resource discovery and service composition. The resource discovery costs can be reduced by properly selecting the nodes. Another issue to consider is the budget limitation of the initiators, thus, the demand might be bounded.

**Acknowledgements.** This work is supported by the Romanian Authority for Scientific Research under doctoral scholarship no. 399/2008 and project IDEI_2452.

# References

1. Foster, I.T., Iamnitchi, A.: On death, taxes, and the convergence of peer-to-peer and grid computing. In: Kaashoek, M.F., Stoica, I. (eds.) IPTPS 2003. LNCS, vol. 2735, pp. 118–128. Springer, Heidelberg (2003)
2. Chevaleyre, Y., Dunne, P.E., Endriss, U., Lang, J., Lemaître, M., Maudet, N., Padget, J., Phelps, S., Rodríguez-aguilar, J.A., Sousa, P.: Issues in multiagent resource allocation. Informatica 30(1), 3–31 (2006)
3. Trunfio, P., Talia, D., Papadakis, H., Fragopoulou, P., Mordacchini, M., Pennanen, M., Popov, K., Vlassov, V., Haridi, S.: Peer-to-peer resource discovery in grids: Models and systems. Future Generation Computer Systems 23(7), 864–878 (2007)
4. Fisk, A.: Gnutella Dynamic Query Protocol v0.1. LimeWire LLC (2003), http://www9.limewire.com/developer/dynamic_query.html
5. Mkwawa, I.H., Kouvatsos, D.: Broadcasting methods in mobile ad hoc networks: An overview. In: Technical Proc. of the Third Intl. Working Conf. HET-NETs, Networks UK, T9/1–14 (2005)
6. Figueira, J., Greco, S., Ehrgott, M.: Multiple Criteria Decision Analysis: State of the Art Surveys. Springer, Heidelberg (2005)
7. Abdellaoui, M., Hey, J.D.: Advances in Decision Making Under Risk and Uncertainty. Springer, Heidelberg (2008)
8. Ilies, L., Mortan, M., Lungescu, D., Lazar, I., Popa, M., Veres, V.: Handbook of Management (in Romanian). Risoprint (2006)
9. Chunlin, L., Layuan, L.: Multi economic agent interaction for optimizing the aggregate utility of grid users in computational grid. Applied Intelligence 25(2), 147–158 (2006)
10. Li, X.Y., Wu, Y., Xu, P., Chen, G., Li, M.: Hidden information and actions in multi-hop wireless ad hoc networks. In: MobiHoc 2008: Proc. of the 9th ACM Intl. Symposium on Mobile Ad Hoc Networking and Computing, pp. 283–292. ACM, New York (2008)
11. Canfora, G., Penta, M.D., Esposito, R., Villani, M.L.: An approach for qos-aware service composition based on genetic algorithms. In: GECCO 2005: Proc. of the 2005 Conf. on Genetic and Evolutionary Computation, pp. 1069–1075. ACM, New York (2005)
12. Feldman, M., Lai, K., Stoica, I., Chuang, J.: Robust incentive techniques for peer-to-peer networks. In: Proc. of the 5th ACM Conf. on Electronic Commerce, New York, NY, USA, pp. 102–111 (2004)
13. Jurca, R., Faltings, B.: Reputation-based pricing of p2p services. In: P2PECON 2005: Proc. of the 2005 ACM SIGCOMM Workshop on Economics of Peer-to-Peer Systems, pp. 144–149. ACM, New York (2005)

# Web Services for Deeply Embedded Extra Low-Cost Devices*

David Villa, Felix Jesús Villanueva, Francisco Moya, Fernando Rincón,
Jesús Barba, and Juan Carlos López

Dept. of Technology and Information Systems
University of Castilla-La Mancha
School of Computer Science. 13071 - Ciudad Real. Spain
{David.Villa,Felix.Villanueva,Francisco.Moya,Fernando.Rincon,
Jesus.Barba,JuanCarlos.Lopez}@uclm.es

**Abstract.** This paper describes a new approach to implement Web Services in embedded devices connected to Wireless Sensor Networks. The sensor/actuator node is able to process standard requests (XML-RPC and SOAP), perform an action and generate a valid response.

These stand-alone nodes show good interoperability with standard Web Services using just a transport protocol gateway.

## 1 Introduction

While interoperability may be achieved by means of low cost TCP/IP implementations, interoperability at the application layer continues to be a key problem [4].

Web Services emerge as an interoperable, language and platform independent solution to access sensor services thought Internet. Being able to introduce Web Services directly in the WSN devices would allow deploying application independent gateways. This implies a set of interesting advantages as we will show below.

Obviously, the use of SOAP [5] in wireless sensor networks introduces considerable overhead compared to most binary protocols. Therefore it may not always be appropriate in some application domains where power consumption or latency are critical. Our prototype implementation was focused on emergency light control, which shows a number of characteristics compatible with this approach:

- Nodes do not have power supply problems because they are attached to the power line.
- Nodes are static. There are no mobile nodes in the network.
- Interaction across the WSN is quite limited. In fact, the nodes will only provide autochecking notifications on request so that delay and bandwidth are not major bottlenecks.

---

* This work was supported by ERDF, the Regional Government of Castilla-La Mancha, and the Spanish Ministry of Science and Innovation under grants PAI08-0234-8083 (RGrid), TEC2008-06553 (DAMA), and Hesperia CENIT.

N. Abdennadher and D. Petcu (Eds.): GPC 2009, LNCS 5529, pp. 400–409, 2009.

– The configuration procedure should be as simple as possible in order to reduce installation cost. We initially aim at per-node remote configuration. Global configuration would be handled as an external system-wide service.

In this case, or any other field with similar properties, Web Services seem to be a good approach to solve the problem of interoperability at the application layer.

## 2   Related Work

Most of the former approaches take the raw data from wireless sensor networks using proprietary protocols and export them through Web Services residing in a gateway [1,3]. The web service is actually running in the gateway and not in the WSN device. Each new application would require specific developments, and each web service becomes a wrapper or a facade for the binary protocols used in the WSN.

Our approach, as we will see later, uses generic gateways (independent of the wireless sensor network devices deployed) and reduces configuration procedures required to describe and publish the WSN nodes to a specific network. We aim at removing the need of an intermediate application-level proxy such as the Sensor Collection Service described in [1].

In [2] a framework has been developed to facilitate the use of SOAP in WSN focusing on reducing the overhead (e.g reducing the number of messages) on the network by means of data aggregation techniques. Their implementation is done in the NS2 network simulator and we are not aware of any implementation for actual devices.

Other approaches [8] try to embed the Web Services architecture in low-cost devices reducing the size of the protocol stack (TCP/IP, XML and SOAP processor, etc.). These low-cost devices exceed the average capacity of many wireless sensor networks devices.

In this paper we propose a different way to embed a minimun web service in a WSN device which follows the general principles described in [11]. Instead of reducing existing implementations of the Web Services protocol stack, we are going to define the smallest feature set that a web service needs to provide and build it up from there.

## 3   Embedding Web Services, a Bottom-Up Approach

Although it is important that each device looks like a web service, it is not essential that they are real Web Services. If devices are able to generate coherent replies when they receive predefined request messages then the system will work as expected. For a given WSDL [7] specification these request and reply messages are completely specified by the communication protocol (SOAP or XML-RPC).

Let us analyze an HTTP embedded SOAP request and the corresponding reply for a very simple interaction (e.g. get the status of an emergency light). We will show the full SOAP messages to make it easier to follow the behavior of the automaton of figure 1.

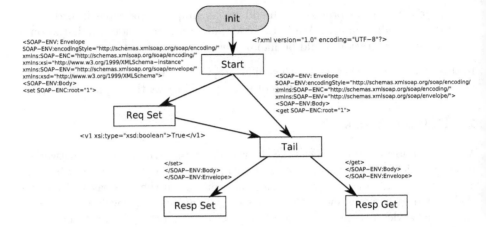

**Fig. 1.** Finite state machine for **get()** and **set()** SOAP messages

```
POST / HTTP/1.0
Host: localhost:8080
User-agent: SOAPpy 0.12.0 (pywebsvcs.sf.net)
Content-type: text/xml; charset="UTF-8"
Content-length: 336
SOAPAction: "get"

<?xml version="1.0" encoding="UTF-8"?>
<SOAP-ENV:Envelope
  SOAP-ENV:encodingStyle="http://schemas.xmlsoap.org/soap/encoding/"
  xmlns:SOAP-ENC="http://schemas.xmlsoap.org/soap/encoding/"
  xmlns:SOAP-ENV="http://schemas.xmlsoap.org/soap/envelope/">
<SOAP-ENV:Body>
<get SOAP-ENC:root="1">
</get>
</SOAP-ENV:Body>
</SOAP-ENV:Envelope>
```

It seems clear that SOAP is a verbose protocol where most of the information is in the Body part of the message. This message can be obtained from the WSDL specification:

```
[...]
 <message name="getRequest">
 </message>

 <message name="getResponse">
   <part name="retval" type="xs:boolean" />
 </message>
[...]
<operation name="get">
     <input message="getRequest" />
     <output message="getResponse" />
</operation>
[...]
```

We implement an ad-hoc parser from the WSDL specification which recognizes the request and builds, in a dynamic way, an appropriate answer to such a request:

```
HTTP/1.0 200 OK
Server: <a href="http://pywebsvcs.sf.net">SOAPpy 0.12.0</a> (Python 2.5.2)
Date: Fri, 21 Nov 2008 10:52:17 GMT
Content-type: text/xml; charset="UTF-8"
Content-length: 501

<?xml version="1.0" encoding="UTF-8"?>
<SOAP-ENV:Envelope
  SOAP-ENV:encodingStyle="http://schemas.xmlsoap.org/soap/encoding/"
  xmlns:SOAP-ENC="http://schemas.xmlsoap.org/soap/encoding/"
  xmlns:xsi="http://www.w3.org/1999/XMLSchema-instance"
  xmlns:SOAP-ENV="http://schemas.xmlsoap.org/soap/envelope/"
  xmlns:xsd="http://www.w3.org/1999/XMLSchema">
<SOAP-ENV:Body>
<getResponse SOAP-ENC:root="1">
<Result xsi:type="xsd:boolean">False</Result>
</getResponse>
</SOAP-ENV:Body>
</SOAP-ENV:Envelope>
```

Typical sensors usually expose a very simple interaction model. Therefore we propose a set of very simple WSDL interfaces to access the data provided by the nodes. We define a get/set interface that may be used by the clients to obtain the current value of a sensor (**get**) or manipulate and actuator (**set**). Of course, the approach is not limited to this interface, but it illustrates perfectly the proposed solution.

We focus on minimizing the amount of memory required to parse the messages in order to be able use WSAN devices with limited resources. To achieve this, we use several techniques:

- We implement an ad-hoc finite state machine in order to recognize a request and build up the answer. The parser removes redundant whitespace, and XML comments in order to feed a canonical XML stream into the automaton.
- Instead of saving and comparing all possible tags that a request message can have, we calculate a CRC using the CCITT-CRC 16 bit algorithm [10]. In the parser, we only compare CRC values of the XML tags with the precalculated CRC for each request available in the WSDL specification.
- We do not store whole messages. Each message is parsed incrementally as it is being received, much like a SAX parser, but using an ad-hoc parser to reduce overall resource consumption.

For example, for the request message shown above, we implement the finite state machine shown in figure 1. Basically, we calculate the CRC for each XML tag (delimited by '<>'). From the **Init** state, we start to parse the input data ignoring the HTML header. This header does not include relevant information from the point of view of the WSAN devices.

The parser ignores all incoming data until the tag `<?xml version="1.0" encoding="UTF-8"?>` is recognized (the calculated CRC matches the expected CRC for this tag). This event triggers the transition to the **Start** state, which will discriminate among the available operations. Input data will include some encoding tags inmediately followed by the operation being invoked, which helps us to recognize whether the request is a valid verb (*set* or *get* in our example). Depending on the CRC calculated at the expected positions of the incoming data stream there will be a transition to the state where the corresponding arguments are read. Operations without arguments will lead to a transition to the `Tail` state which validates the remaining of the request message.

Operations with parameters will go through intermediate parameter parsing states. In our example, in the `Req Set` state, the automaton will parse the parameter attached to the *set* operation and then it will trigger a transition to the `Tail` state. Finally, after a completely validated request is received we build up the response message specifically for each request. Note that there is no need to store which method is being invoked since the tail of each request is different and may be used to discriminate among the response generators.

In each of the response generation states (`Resp Set` and `Resp Get` in our example), the user needs to provide an appropriate routine which executes the validated request and builds the appropriate response.

Although not explicitly stated in figure 1 (for the sake of clarity) whenever the incoming tags do not match any of the expected CRCs the state machine is reset to the initial state `Init` and the connection is closed. This provides a reasonable protection against faulty clients.

### 3.1  Compiler

The design and implementation of the finite state machine is a tedious and error prone task. Therefore we are building a compiler that takes a WSDL specification and a service definition and automatically generates the appropriate finite state machine for the corresponding messages from the interfaces defined in the WSDL file.

The compiler (see figure 2) takes four files as inputs:

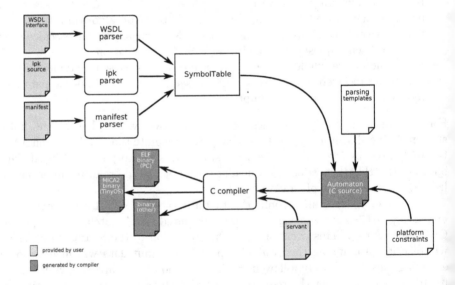

**Fig. 2.** Compiler block diagram

- The WSDL interface declaration. The services provided by the WSN node must adhere to the interfaces specified in this file.
- The servant (method implementation). This file contains the application specific code. Usually this includes code to access to the underlying hardware and read or write a physical transducer.
- Service definition. The programmer defines in this file which concrete services the node holds and the interface (**portType**) exposed by each sensor or actuator in the node. We use a very simple syntax defining services and basic interaction events. The following listing shows a little example.

```
uses "DUORW.wsdl";

local myLocalEP("xbow -h 0x0001") {
    DUOIBoolRW_Service svc1;
}

remote myRemoteEP("xbow -h 0x0002") {
    DUOIBoolRW_Service svc2;
}

repeat(5) {
    svc2.set(svc1.status(), svc1.endpoint);
}
```

This example defines both a local and a remote web service endpoint. It also states that a periodic request must be done in the remote service sending the status and the endpoint of the local service.

- A manifest file which contains the interfaces for user-provided procedures, such as the procedures to read hardware sensors. The *status* procedure of the listing above is one such example:

```
private DUOIBoolRW status(11) {
    output = bool;
};
```

The compiler is able to generate generic parsers that may be compiled on several platforms. This include support for the MICA2 (Crossbow) on the TinyOS [13] operating system, and also for OS-less implementations for general purpose microcontrolers such as ATMega128, 8051 or even mid-range Microchip devices.

## 4   Network Architecture

In our application field (emergency lighting), a control center usually manages and monitors several buildings distributed in a large geographical area. Buildings with hundreds or even thousands of emergency lights are quite common (airports, museums, etc.). Each installation is connected to an external network (e.g. Internet) by means of one or more gateways (figure 3).

Each gateway performs three main tasks:

- It encapsulates SOAP messages from Internet transport protocol (typically TCP protocol) in the WSN transport protocol. The reverse process is also needed for outgoing messages (encapsulation of SOAP messages from WSN transport protocol to Internet). This task is shown in figure 4.

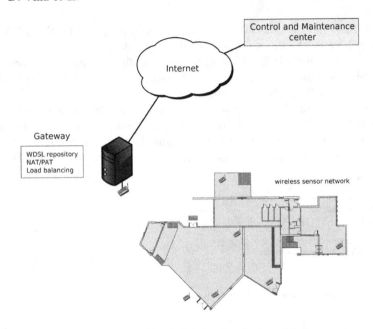

**Fig. 3.** Physical network topology

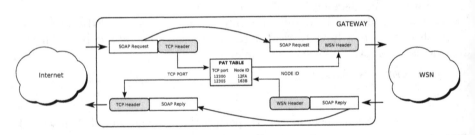

**Fig. 4.** Simplified gateway process

– It must implement a bidirectional correspondence between TCP ports and node IDs. This is a crucial aspect for avoiding hand-made configuration procedures. When we install a WSN node, the gateway must assign a TCP port to its node ID.

The association established between the TCP port and the node ID must be represented in the WSDL. A WSDL file represents the interface for users of the service and also some properties of that service, for example, its location (endpoint).

We embed both the WSN location and the TCP port assigned in the WSDL tag `soap:address`, as shown below. The gateway needs to know the WSN node ID of each WSN device available in the network and it generates the corresponding WSDL file. This task may be accomplished without human intervention using a modification of ASDF [12] (our service discovery protocol for WSN).

When a WSN node is attached to the network it sends an advertisement with the name of the interfaces that it implements and its node ID. The gateway builds a WSDL file from a template which contains the service interface and the service implementation. In the service implementation section we may include some common information about the environment such as human readable location, node ID, etc.

Here is an example:

```
[...]
<!-- Service to export -->
  <service name="ExitDoor_Service">
    <port name="IBoolRW_Port" binding="IBoolRW_Binding">
      <soap:address location="http://example.com:7890"/>
    </port>
  </service>
[...]
```

With this WSDL file, the services may also be located by means of UDDI protocol. The process of publishing any Web Service associated to a WSN device in a UDDI registry is similar to any other Web Service, namely, the web service interface like UDDI t-model structure and the Web Service implementation like a UDDI business Service.

Additionally, it is possible to install more advanced services in the gateway to provide additional features such as logging, authorization, etc.

The gateway may be able to generate the associated WSDL file from a set of templates for each of the interfaces implemented by nodes in the network. There are two possible solutions:

- Templates for each interfaces are stored in the gateways. Whenever new nodes are installed in the WSN their interfaces must be added to the template repository of the gateways (if they where not already there). This situation introduces coupling between gateways and applications deployed in the SAN, but do not affect nodes themselves.
- When a node is advertised through the network, the gateway may request the template of the interfaces implemented in the node. This is easily achieved with a small modification of ASDF storing the WSDL template in the node and implementing an operation to retrieve the template. This is more expensive for the nodes in terms of the amount of required FLASH/ROM, but it allows simpler gateways, fully independent of the application.

## 5   Prototypes

Using the strategies and policies described so far we developed a set of prototypes on widespread WSN hardware.

Probably one of the most used microcontrollers in WSN platforms is the Atmel ATMega128 with the TinyOS operating system. OS-less devices are also quite common.

We compare here the size of different Web Services implementations. In a first step, we implement a basic get/set service (see section 3), using two lightweight

**Table 1.** Size of the implementation (in bytes) of a simple emergency light controller as described in section 3

| Software | Platform | Middleware | Binary size | Other |
|---|---|---|---|---|
| C-SOAP | x86 | SOAP | 1,731,508 | OS |
| libXML-RPC | | XML-RPC | 768,536 | OS |
| Embedded WS | x86 | SOAP | 507,676 | OS |
| | | XML-RPC | 504,772 | OS |
| | TinyOS | SOAP | 35,150 | |
| | | XML-RPC | 11,216 | |
| | AVR | SOAP | 1,068 | ZigBee (4.261) |
| | | XML-RPC | 1,182 | ZigBee (4.261) |

general-purpose libraries: `csoap` [14] and `libxml-rpc` [15]. Then we implement the same service using our approach on three platforms: a PC, a MICA2 running TinyOS and on an OS-less AVR microcontroller. The size of the resulting binaries are shown in the table 1. Notice that:

- All the x86 prototypes are statically linked and they run on a conventional PC with Debian GNU/Linux. All of them require an operating system whose size is not taken into account.
- The x86 Embedded WS prototypes are pure C programs with standard socket support.
- The TinyOS and AVR prototypes include all the required components. The data refers to the binary file we install in the device. The AVR prototype does not use an operating system but just a simple cyclic executive runtime, much smaller than TinyOS although it lacks most of TinyOS features.

The source code for all these tests is available in our EWS webpage [16]. The current reference implementations and other useful data may be found there.

## 6   Conclusions

In this paper we presented a very low-footprint implementation of web services for wireless sensor actuator networks. As far as the authors know this is the most reduced implementation of this type of architecture in WSAN.

Introducing web services directly in the WSAN devices allows building generic and application independent gateways. In this way, we enable the deployment on WSAN devices with minimun configuration procedures.

Some prototypes for SOAP and XML-RPC have been implemented showing the feasibility of our approach. Our current efforts are focused on improving and testing the compiler to allow the generation of complete ready-to-use sensor nodes.

## References

1. Kobialka, T., Buyya, R., Leckie, C.: Open Sensor Web Architecture: Stateful Web Services. In: Proceedings of the Third International Conference on Intelligent Sensors, Sensor Networks and Information Processing (ISSNIP)(2007)

2. Al-Yasiri, A., Sunley, A.: Data aggregation and middleware in wireless sensor networks. In: Sensor and theory applicatios XIV (SENSOR 2007), Journal of Physics: Conference Series, vol. 76 (2007)
3. Arch Rock Corporation. Arch Rock Primer Pack product gateway datasheet. Product Catalog (2007)
4. Priyantha, B., Kansal, A., Goraczko, M., Zhao, F.: Tiny Web Services for Sensor Device Interoperability. In: International Conference on Information Processing in Sensor Networks (IPSN) (2008)
5. Gudgin, M., Hadley, M., Mendelsohn, N., Moreau, J., Nielsen, H.F.: SOAP Version 1.2 Part 1: Messaging Framework.W3C Recommendation (2003), http://www.w3.org
6. Winer, D.: XML-RPC Specification. UserLand Software, Inc. (2003), http://www.xmlrpc.com/
7. Winer, D.: WSDL Specification. World Wide Web Consortium (2001), http://www.w3.org/TR/wsdl
8. Helander, J., Xiong, Y.: Secure Web services for low-cost devices. In: Eighth IEEE International Symposium on Object-Oriented Real-Time Distributed Computing (2005)
9. Helander, J.: Deeply Embedded XML Communication, Towards an Interoperable and Seamless World. In: EMSOFT (2005)
10. Koopman, P., Chakravarty, T.: Cyclic Redundancy Code (CRC) Polynomial Selection For Embedded Networks. In: Dependable Systems and Networks (2004)
11. Villa, D., Villanueva, F.J., Moya, F., Rincón, F., Barba, J., López, J.C.: Embedding a general purpose middleware for seamless interoperability of networked hardware and software components. In: Chung, Y.-C., Moreira, J.E. (eds.) GPC 2006. LNCS, vol. 3947, pp. 567–576. Springer, Heidelberg (2006)
12. Villa, D., Villanueva, F.J., Moya, F., Rincón, F., Barba, J., López, J.C.: Minimalist Object Oriented Service Discovery Protocol for Wireless Sensor Networks. In: Cérin, C., Li, K.-C. (eds.) GPC 2007. LNCS, vol. 4459, pp. 472–483. Springer, Heidelberg (2007)
13. Hill, J., Szewczyk, R., Woo, A., Hollar, S., Culler, D., Pister, K.: System Architecture Directions for Networked Sensors. In: Proceedings of Ninth International Conference on Architectural Support for Programming Languages and Operating Systems (ASPLOS) (2000)
14. csoap client/server SOAP library in pure C, http://csoap.sourceforge.net/
15. XML-RPC for C and C++, A lightweight RPC library based on XML and HTTP, http://xmlrpc-c.sourceforge.net/
16. EWS Webpage, http://arco.esi.uclm.es/en/ews

# A Group-Based Reputation Mechanism for Mobile P2P Networks

Xu Wu[1], Jingsha He[2], and Fei Xu[1]

[1] College of Computer Science and Technology, Beijing University of Technology,
Beijing 100124, China
{wuxu,xfei}@emails.bjut.edu.cn
[2] School of Software Engineering, Beijing University of Technology, Beijing 100124, China
jhe@bjut.edu.cn

**Abstract.** This paper presents a group-based reputation mechanism and gives a distributed implementation method for mobile p2p networks. In the proposed mechanism peers with similar mobility are clustered into a set of groups, where there are two different kinds of peers: Mobile and Power peers. Mathematic analyses and simulations show that the adoption of group avoids the communication overload in global trust computation, and the benefits of trust evaluation are maintained by managing trust in the groups. Compared to the current p2p reputation mechanisms, the proposed mechanism is slightly affected by the dynamic joining and departing of peers. Additionally, it effectively encourages new peers to take part in the systems actively and friendly.

**Keywords:** reputation, trust, P2P networks, mobility.

## 1 Introduction

Peer-to-Peer systems have gained tremendous attention of many researchers and companies. Each peer in a P2P system is presumed to have the equivalent functionality and is willing to share resources. Because of its ability to pool together and harness the large volume of resources, P2P systems' features include scalability, service availability, self-organization, fault tolerance, and load balancing. However, most P2P systems assume peers are using fixed Internet instead of wireless networks. Here we consider a mobile P2P network is an infrastructure designed to support mobile devices and wireless networks.

Mobile p2p Networks are also organized according to the P2P principle, they are autonomous (independent of any infrastructure), self-organized and decentralized. A mobile p2p network is a set of moving objects that communicate with each other via unregulated, short-range wireless technologies such as IEEE 802.11, Bluetooth, or Ultra Wide Band (UWB) [1]. No fixed infrastructure is assumed or relied upon. It is also an abstract, logical network called an overlay network which builds on basic communication network, because there is no control of peers joining or leaving the network, a lot of drawbacks of the real mobile P2P systems have been disclosed. In P2P applications, Free-Riding is a typical problem. According to the Gnutella file

N. Abdennadher and D. Petcu (Eds.): GPC 2009, LNCS 5529, pp. 410–421, 2009.

trace [2] approximately 25 percent of the clients do not share data at all, and totally about 75 percent of the hosts share less than 100 unique files. On the other hand, roughly 5 percent of the peers share 99 percent of all files. Similar challenges can be anticipated in the MP2P system, too. The major reason is lacking of the effective cooperation mechanism inherently in the P2P systems, so not all participators can be encouraged to take part in the systems actively and friendly.

Normally the P2P applications give computers or devices access to other peers' resources, e.g. hard drives, but there exist some security problems in the mobile p2p network. For example when a user tries using smart phone to download a file from another user's one, he may worry about the virus or attack embedded in that file; the mobile user shares resources with others but who do not; and so on [3]. All of these risks limit the applications build in the mobile P2P network. It is an effective solution to construct the reputation mechanism in the networks to build up the trust among the mobile users.

The idea is motivated from existing human societies in the world. Embedded in every social network is a web of trust; with a link representing the trustworthiness between two individuals. When faced with uncertainty, individuals seek the opinions of those they trust. The intent is to develop a similar reputation mechanism for mobile p2p Networks, where mobile peers maintain reputation for other peers. This reputation is used to evaluate the trustworthiness of other peers. This establishes a web of trust in the network, which is then used as an inherent aspect in predicting the future behavior of peers in the network.

In the P2P environment, the users can reenter the network system by changing their network identities to get new reputation values to avoid the penalty imposed on them, which can't be identified from the fresh users to the network. This greatly hampers the implementation of the practical reputation system. So others [6] advise conservatively trusting nobody initially at the beginning of users' participating to the network, which impose the serious penalty on the malicious peers. But in reality, the useful behaviors of newcomers have also been unfairly restricted in the case of this strategy. It will take new peers very long time to cumulate enough reputation values to take part in the cooperation in the network, which decreases the network efficiency seriously in the case of mobile peers joining and departing the network with high frequency. Although the security objectives in mobile peer-to-peer networks and fixed peer-to-peer networks are considered the same, the realization of reputation mechanism in mobile p2p networks is quite different due to some characteristics of mobile environment such as high mobility of the peers, limited-range as well as unreliability of wireless links, which indicates the trust between participants can not be set up simply on the traditional reputation mechanism.

Therefore, in the paper we present a group-based reputation mechanism and give a distributed implementation method for mobile p2p networks. As we will show, the proposed mechanism is fit in such a mobile environment. By managing trust in the groups, the benefits of trust evaluation are maintained and the communication overload in global trust computation is avoided. In addition, it effectively encourages participators to take part in the systems actively and friendly.

The remainder of this paper is organized as following: Section 2 presents the related work. The section 3 describes the proposed group-based reputation mechanism in detail, which is organized into two subsections named group-based reputation architecture and distributed implementation method respectively. Theoretical analysis and simulation results to the performance of the new reputation mechanism are given in section 4. Finally, section 5 concludes the paper.

## 2 Related Work

Trust-management approach for distributed systems security was first introduced in the context of Internet as an answer to the inadequacy of traditional cryptographic mechanisms. Some of the notable earlier works in this domain have been trust-management engines. Since then, reputation-based frameworks based on the approach of trust management have been extensively studied in many contexts and equally diverse domains such as human social networks, e-commerce, 802.11 networks, peer-to-peer networks etc. In this paper, we study the applicability of this approach in developing high integrity mobile p2p networks.

The proposed mechanism does borrow some design features from several existing works in literature but as a complete system differs from all the existing methods or schemes.

Lance, et al. studied trust from a number of influencing factors from the engineering and psychological points of view and tried to combine these factors in order to provide a comprehensive model [4].

EigenTrust [5] model is designed for the reputation management of P2P systems. The global reputation of peer $i$ is marked by the local trust values assigned to peer $i$ by other peers, which reflects the experience of other peers with it. The core of the model is that a special normalization process where the trust rating held by a peer is normalized to have their sum equal to 1. The shortcoming is that the normalization could cause the loss of important trust information.

Runfang Zhou and Kai Hwang [6] proposed a power-law distribution in user feedbacks and a computational model, i.e., PowerTrust, to leverage the power-law feedback characteristics. The paper used a trust overlay network (TON) to model the trust relationships among peers. PowerTrust can greatly improves global reputation accuracy and aggregation speed, but it can't avoid the communication overhead in global trust computation.

John Chuang [7] designs an incentive mechanism for p2p systems, the proposed methods radically to trust all the users initially when they enter the network, so every peer can trade with others rapidly and extensively.

Thomas Repantis and Vana Kalogeraki [8] propose a decentralized trust management middleware for ad-hoc, peer-to-peer networks, based on reputation. In the work, the middleware's protocols take advantage of the unstructured nature of the network to render malicious behavior, and the reputation information of each peer is stored in its neighbors and piggy-backed on its replies.

A new trust model based on recommendation evidence (RETM) is proposed for P2P Networks by Tian Chun Qi etc [9]. The proposed model has advantages in modeling dynamic trust relationship and aggregating recommendation information. It filters out noisy recommendation information.

Mobile p2p networks are self-organized among the mobile peers. Research work on providing a relatively stable layer of network on top of flat ad hoc network routing forms a major research focus, and in the context of group-based paradigm, mobile peer clustering in the network into sets of groups. Popular schemes proposed include lowest-id and highest degree heuristics [10].

Those works also proposed different techniques for group management. Group management involves the mechanisms for maintaining the membership of mobile hosts in the groups, including procedures for handling the join and leave events of mobile hosts with respect to a group. Our basic join procedure in the proposed mechanism takes on a similar approach as the one in [11].

# 3  The Group-Based Reputation Mechanism

We proposed a group-based reputation mechanism in the paper. The motivation is taken from observing the evolution of existing social networks in the world. Embedded in every social network is a web of trust with a link representing the amount of trust between two individuals. Let us analyze the integrated role of "reputation" and "trust" in these networks. Trust can simply be defined as the expectation of one person about the actions of others. It is used by the first person to make a choice, when an action must be taken before the actions of others are known. Reputation is defined as the perception that a person has of another's intentions. When facing uncertainty, individuals tend to trust those which have a reputation for being trustworthy. The proposed mechanism is a similar framework where mobile peers maintain reputation for other peers in the network.

In the section, we describe the proposed group-based reputation mechanism in detail, which is organized into two subsections named group-based reputation architecture and distributed implementation method respectively.

## 3.1  Group-Based Reputation Architecture

The logical group-based reputation architecture is shown in Fig. 1. We consider mobile peers with similar mobility are clustered into a set of groups. A group is a natural collection of mobile peers that can communicate with one another and that move together in an aggregated manner. A member of a group should be at most a distance of $r$ away from the position of the group. A group is defined based on the stable connectivity of mobile peers. In our scheme, the stable connectivity indicates relative stability in distance over time. In the group we have two different kinds of peers: Mobile and Power peers.

Mobile peers can consist of any kind of mobile devices. Peers in the same group can exchange files and data directly between each other over the wireless link. Connections between Mobile and Power peers are carried over the cellular or WLAN networks. All mobile peers are connected to one Power peer in the same group, which is most reputable in the group and also interacts with rest of the world.

A Power peer is elected by the mobile agent [14] running in the MP2P network from a group to act on behalf of the group, which has multiple tasks. To start with, each mobile peer has in a Power peer a cache memory, eq. a mirror page, that provides an efficient reputation information anchor to the MP2P, and even further, to

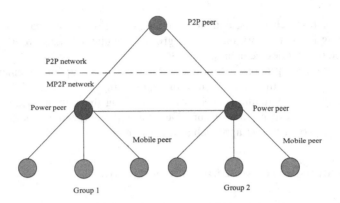

**Fig. 1.** The logical group-based reputation architecture

the wired P2P networks. A cache acts as a virtual storage meaning that reputation information can be offered from the cache, instead of the mobile peer itself, when a mobile peer is switched off or out of coverage. Here reputation information is about the reputation table of a mobile peer, which is depicted in the 3.2.2 section.

A Power peer can provide functions, such as routing, service discovery, security and network topology management tasks. A Power peer acts as a firewall against malicious and this power peer can fetch interesting trust information on behalf of the mobile peer from other MP2P and P2P networks. In this situation a Power peer acts as a P2P Proxy towards the P2P networks.

The architecture is formed on top of the mobile, cellular and fixed networks. All peers are connected to each other but the routes are controlled by the Power peer, except when the mobiles are communicating in the same group. A peer monitors the behavior of other peers in the same group based on which it builds up their reputation over time. It uses this reputation to evaluate their trustworthiness and in predicting their future behavior. At the time of collaboration, a peer only cooperates with those peers that it trusts.

## 3.2 Distributed Implementation Method

When a peer moves to another cluster, topology mismatching problem will occur. A distributed implementation method is developed within the group-based reputation architecture. This dynamic deployment method overcomes this problem. The method works as follows.

(a) A power peer communicates with its peers periodically.
(b) A mobile peer selects to join a group based on a join procedure before establishing trust relationship.
(c) If a mobile peer leaves, the power peer will update its index file of reputation table to reflect the fact that a mobile peer has left.
(d) If a power peer dies, leaves, or disappears abnormally, the mobile peers in the same group will find this out after a certain period of time (e.g. using timeout), and a new power peer will be elected by the mobile agent.

### 3.2.1  Group Joining Process

In the group-based reputation architecture, each mobile peer $p$ is assumed to possess a simple device for keeping track of its existing location and its movement information such as a GPS sensor etc.

The current location of $p$ is denoted by $(x_p, y_p)$, while the movement information is maintained and represented as a vector $\overrightarrow{V}_p = (v_{x_p}, v_{y_p})$, being resolved into the $x$ and $y$ components. A single group has only one member in the group. It will search periodically another group or another mobile peer based on a predefined period $\sigma_s$. The group finding process will end until another group is found or another peer considers joining this single group. Every member within a group has a similar mobility. Degree of affinity is used to measure the movement similarity between mobile peers or groups.

The degree of affinity, $u_{i,k}$, between two mobile domains, $i$ and $k$, is defined by the equation:

$$u_{i,k} = \alpha(1 - \frac{dist(i,k)}{r}) + \beta(1 - \frac{\sqrt{(v_{xi} - v_{xk})^2 + (v_{yi} - v_{yk})^2}}{\sqrt{v_{xi}^2 + v_{yi}^2} + \sqrt{v_{xk}^2 + v_{yk}^2}}) \qquad (1)$$

Where $\alpha + \beta = 1$ and $dist(i,k)$ is the Euclidean distance between two mobile units $i$ and $k$.

Before establishing trust relationship, a mobile peer selects to join a group based on a join procedure. In the join procedure, a mobile host (group seeker) needs to find an appropriate group so that the impact on the stability of the target group can be minimized. It interacts with neighbors from other groups in order to gather group information and makes a group joining decision. Our basic join procedure in the proposed mechanism takes on a similar approach as the one in [11]. The step of basic join procedure is depicted in the following.

Basic Join Procedure

1. Group seeker m obtains all the related group information by broadcasting a "FIND_GROUP"message to its neighbors

2. A neighbor that receives the "FIND_GROUP"message replies with a "GROUP_INFO"message to m with its group information

3. Group seeker m receives group information from neighbors

4. For each group G discovered, add G to the set of potential groups if dist (m,G) < r and dist (mr,Gr) < r.

5. if the set of potential groups is not NULL then send a "join"message to the leader of the group G* with the highest degree of affinity, Sm, G* store the group leader and group location and movement information

6. else // no group is available for this moment create a new group and set itself to be the leader

### 3.2.2  Trust Computing

In the mechanism, the trust of a peer is related to its reputation. We use mathematical method to represent the reputation of a peer, and continuously update it based on new direct/indirect observations. An enhanced trust model based on reputation [12] is used to evaluate the trustworthiness of peers. In the trust model, a peer's trustworthiness is defined by an evaluation of the peer in terms of the level of reputation it receives in interacting with other peers in the past. In order to effectively evaluate the trustworthiness of peers and to address various malicious behaviors in a p2p network, seven trust factors are identified in evaluating trustworthiness of peers.

This trust model has two types of trust: direct trust and recommendation trust. Direct trust is used to evaluate trustworthiness when a peer has enough interacting experience with another peer. On the other hand, recommendation trust is used when a peer has little interacting experience with another one.

We assume that peer $j$ and $i$ are in the same group. Direct trust of peer $j$ computed by peer $i$ is given by:

$$T_i(j) = \alpha * \sum_{i=0}^{N(j)} \left( \frac{S(i,j)*M(i,j)*Z}{N(j)} + pen(m)\frac{1}{1+e^{-n}} \right) + \beta Risk(j) \qquad (2)$$

$\alpha, \beta$: weighting factors. $\alpha$ and $\beta$ are weighting factors that satisfy the condition $\alpha + \beta = 1$.

$N(j)$: total number of interactions

$S(i,j)$: peer satisfaction degree of interaction. Satisfaction and dissatisfaction degrees express how well and how poor this peer has performed in the interaction, respectively. Satisfaction or dissatisfaction degree can encourage interacting sides to behave well during interactions.

$M(i,j)$: ratio of the interaction size. Some peers have a higher interaction frequency than some other peers due to a skewed interaction distribution. A peer will be more familiar with other peers by increasing the number of interactions. This factor is related to the interaction authority.

$Z$: time factor. We introduce time factor to reflect this decay, that is, the most recent interaction usually has the biggest time factor.

$pen(m)$: punishment function. Punishment should be involved by decreasing its trust degree according to the amount of malicious behaviors. Therefore we introduce the punishment factor in our model to be used to fight against subtle malicious attacks.

$\frac{1}{1+e^{-n}}$ : acceleration factor. $\frac{1}{1+e^{-n}}$ is the acceleration factor where $n$ denotes the number of failures. It can make trust value drop fast when an interaction fails. As this factor increases with $n$, it helps avoid heavy penalty simply because of a few unintentional cheats.

$Risk(y)$: risk factor. Every peer has its own security defense ability which is reflected by risk factor, such as the ability to detect vulnerabilities, the ability to address any viruses and to defend against intrusions.

Peers' recommendation is received through a polling protocol according the trust model. The recommendation trust of a peer is impacted by the polling results from other peers, the total number of transactions a peer performs, and the credibility of the polling sources. Let $k$ denotes a voting peer, then

$$DT_k(j) = \sum_{k=1}^{N(j)} \left( \frac{S(k,j) * M(k,j) * Z}{N_k(j)} + pen(m) \frac{1}{1+e^{-n}} \right) \tag{3}$$

where $DT_k(j)$ is the poll value of $k$ in $j$. The more details of the model can be found in [12].

Peer $i$ has Reputation table $RT_i$. It is related to every peer $j$ for which peer $i$ maintains a reputation. Index file of reputation table of mobile peer $i$ is storaged at its Power peer, which is easily updated in the Power Peer keeping the system simple to manage.

When the mobile peer wants to interact with others, it firstly checks their reputation values through the proposed mechanism, and then determines whether to do. Consider the situation where a peer $i$ wants to interact with another peer $j$ in order to accomplish a certain task. Peer $i$ will not interact unless it is sure that peer $j$ is trustworthy. In order to find out whether peer $j$ is trustworthy or not, peer $i$ calculates a reputation value for peer $j$. If two peers are in same group, peer $i$ can get the trust value of $j$ through its Power peer; otherwise if two peers are in different groups, peer $i$ must search for $j$'s group and retrieves its reputation value from its Power peer. Peer $j$ does the same as $i$.

At the end of interaction, peer $i(j)$ updates the $j(i)$'s reputation value in its reputation table according to the following reputation adjusting principle.

1. The reputation of a peer should be increased as the probability of its normal action, in order to avoid that newcomers take very long time to cumulate enough reputation values to take part in the interaction in the network.

2. When the peer behaves well, its reputation should be increased with small span in order to prevent that the malicious peer can reenter the network system by changing its network identities to get good reputation values.

3. When the peer behaves badly, its reputation should be decreased in large span in order to prevent the networks from the attacks of malicious peers.

The principle can efficiently encourage participators to take part in the systems actively and friendly.

# 4  Experimental Study

We have evaluated the group-based reputation mechanism. The simulation software used is PlanetSim version 3.0 [13], which is written in Java, and is a simulation software for P2P network. A P2P file sharing network is simulated with PlanetSim version 3.0. The environments of the network are as follows. We assume that mobile peers are distributed at the area whose size is 5000m x 5000m. Each peer is located at a random position. Communicating range of a mobile device is 70m. In this analysis, all mobile peers are assumed to have a same amount of battery power.

The first experiment evaluates the communication efficiency of global reputation by the comparison of computing time. We collect 3000 transaction data of mobile peers and let peers' feedback rates from {-1, 0, 1} to {0, 0.5, 1}. Table1 shows the data description. The error between computing result and actual feedback rating are used as metric to measure the value of trust model.

**Table 1.** Comparison of computing time

| Number of peers | EigenTrust Model | | PowerTrust Model | | Group-based reputation mechanism | |
|---|---|---|---|---|---|---|
| | Computing times | time | Computing times | time | Computing times | time |
| 100 | 2650 | $2.86 \times 10^{-6}$ | 2520 | $1.82 \times 10^{-7}$ | 2417 | $1.26 \times 10^{-8}$ |
| 300 | 21254 | $3.54 \times 10^{-6}$ | 20174 | $2.03 \times 10^{-6}$ | 20589 | $0.96 \times 10^{-6}$ |
| 500 | 43347 | 84.53 | 43189 | 44.01 | 52128 | 23.15 |
| 700 | $4.41 \times 10^{30}$ | $5.31 \times 10^{23}$ | $4.43 \times 10^{30}$ | $4.34 \times 10^{23}$ | $5.67 \times 10^{30}$ | $2.25 \times 10^{23}$ |

As table 1 shows, comparing with EigenTrust [5] and PowerTrust Model [6], the group-based reputation mechanism gets more efficient. Because of the adoption of group, the communication overload is avoided in global trust computation, and the benefits of trust evaluation are maintained by managing trust in the groups.

The second experiment examines the cooperation success rate of new peer. Cooperation success rate presents the ratio between the number of new peers' successful interactions and the total number of new peers' interactions. We set the total number of new peers to 1500 in the P2P file sharing network. The reputation of each peer in the network is computed separately with our reputation mechanism and PowerTrust. Fig. 2 presents a number of interesting observations. First, we see an obvious gain of the cooperation success rate in the network where the reputation of each peer is computed with our reputation mechanism. Second, PowerTrust Model [6] is not as effective as our reputation mechanism. Third, it is also interesting to observe that the cooperation success rate reaches 90% after 7h in the network with our reputation mechanism and then stays fairly stable.

The experiment results show that our mechanism can effectively deal with new peer reputation problem, compared to PowerTrust where the reputation value of new peers is get based on feedback scores from their neighbors. It is because in reality the useful behaviors of newcomers have also been unfairly restricted in the case of feedback-based strategy. The PowerTrust approach gets reputation value of new peers based on feedback scores from their neighbors. Since a new peer hasn't any interacting experience with its neighbors, it is endowed the lowest trust value. It will take new peers very long time to cumulate enough reputation values to take part in the cooperation in the network, which decreases the network efficiency seriously in the case of mobile peers joining and departing the network with high frequency. However, the group-based reputation mechanism can adjusts the peer initial reputation according to its behavior based on a flexible reputation adjusting principle expressed in section 3.

The third experiment shows that our proposed reputation mechanism is slightly affected by the dynamic joining and departing of peers. The dynamic joining and leaving process is simulated by processing random joining or leaving of each individual node. The probability of joining and leaving of a node equals to 0.5. This means that

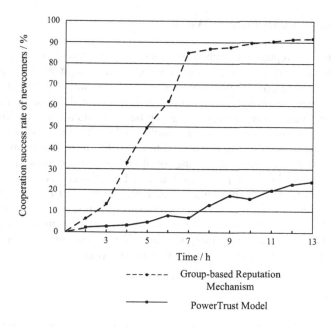

**Fig. 2.** Cooperation success rate of newcomers

nodes' leaving and joining are of the same chance. We examined the network performance at each 250 interval and get the results as shown in fig. 3. The whole process ended
when network has experienced 3000 times joining/leaving actions. The simulation is
conducted on a network with size n=10,000 and n=6,000. Compared with the network
of size 6000, the performance is basically the same. We can see that the network performance actually has little change. Fig. 3 represents the experiment result which clearly
shows that our reputation mechanism is very robust in a dynamic environment.

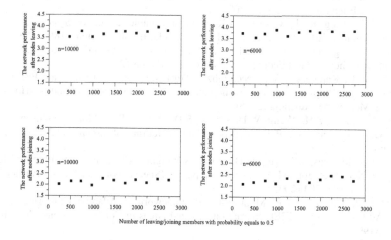

**Fig. 3.** The network performance after nodes leaving or joining

# 5 Conclusion and Future Work

The realization of reputation mechanism in mobile p2p networks is quite different due to some characteristics of mobile environment such as high mobility of the peers, limited-range as well as unreliability of wireless links, which indicates the trust between participants can not be set up simply on the traditional reputation mechanism.

Therefore, in the paper we present a group-based reputation mechanism and give a distributed implementation method for mobile p2p networks. We consider mobile peers with similar mobility are clustered into a set of groups. The motivation is taken from observing the evolution of existing social networks in the world. In the group we have two different kinds of peers: Mobile and Power peers. As we will show, the proposed mechanism is fit in such a mobile environment. Our mechanism deals with the fundamental reputation management problem, it can serve as the building block for higher level security solutions such as key management mechanisms or secure routing protocols. In the near future, we would like to test our mechanism into more real mobile p2p systems and analyze the system performances.

# References

1. Wolfson, O., Xu, B., Yin, H., Cao, H.: Search-and-Discover in Mobile P2P Network Databases. In: 26th IEEE International Conference on Distributed Computing Systems (2006)
2. Saroiu, S., Gummadi, P.K., Gribble, S.D.: A Measurement Study of Peer-to-Peer File Sharing Systems. In: Multimedia Computing and Networking (MMCN 2002), California, USA, pp. 156–170 (2002)
3. Yan, Z., Zhang, P.: Trust Collaboration in P2P Systems Based on Trusted Computing Platforms. WSEAS Transactions on Information Science and Applications 3(2), 275–282 (2006)
4. Lance, J., Hoffman, L.J., Kim, L.J., Blum, J.: Trust Beyond Security: an Expanded Trust Model. Communications of the ACM 49(7), 94–101 (2006)
5. Kamvar, S.D., Schlosser, M.T., Molina, H.G.: The EigenTrust Algorithm for Reputation Management in P2P Networks. In: 12th International Conference on Word Wide Web, Budapest, Bulgaria, pp. 640–651 (2003)
6. Zhou, R., Hwang, K.: PowerTrust: A Robust and Scalable Reputation System for Trusted P2P Computing. IEEE Transactions on Parallel and Distributed Systems 18(5) (2007)
7. John, C.: Designing Incentive Mechanisms for Peer-to-Peer Systems. In: 1st IEEE International Workshop on Grid Economics and Business Models (2004)
8. Repantis, T., Kalogeraki, V.: Decentralized Trust Management for Ad-hoc Peer-to-Peer Networks. In: 4th international workshop on Middleware for Pervasive and Ad-Hoc Computing, Melbourne, Australia (2006)
9. Tian, C.Q., Zou, S.H., Wang, W.D., Cheng, S.D.: A New Trust Model Based on Recommendation Evidence for P2P Networks. Chinese Journal of Computers 31(2), 271–281 (2008)
10. Chatterjee, M., Das, S.K., Turgut, D.: WCA: A Weighted Clustering Algorithm for Mobile Ad hoc Networks. Journal of Cluster Computing (Special Issue on Mobile Ad hoc Networks) 5(2), 193–204 (2002)
11. McDonald, A.B., Znat, T.F.: Mobility-based Framework for Adaptive Clustering in Wireless Ad hoc Networks. IEEE Journal on Selected Areas in Communications 17(8), 1466–1487 (1999)

12. Xu, W., He, J.S., Fei, X.: An Enhanced Trust Model Based on Reputation. In: IEEE International Conference on Sensor Networks, Ubiquitous, and Trustworthy Computing, Taichung, Taiwan, pp. 67–73 (2008)
13. http://planet.urv.es/planetsim/
14. Yan, P., Wang, F.C., Liu, F.: Distributed Integrating Method for Enterprise Information Based on Peer-to-Peer Network. Computer Integrated Manufacturing Systems 10(5), 492–496+555 (2004)

# A Partition-Based Broadcast Algorithm over DHT for Large-Scale Computing Infrastructures

Kun Huang[1] and Dafang Zhang[2]

[1] School of Computer and Communication, [2] School of Software,
Hunan University, Changsha, Hunan Province 410082, P.R. China
{huangkun,dfzhang}@hunu.edu.cn

**Abstract.** Scalable and efficient broadcast is essential to the large-scale computing infrastructures such as PlanetLab and Grids. Existing DHT-based broadcast algorithms suffer from the limitations of scalability and load balancing, incurring high-overhead construction and maintenance of a distributed broadcast tree (DBT). This paper proposes a partition-based broadcast algorithm over DHT for the large-scale computing infrastructures, where each node hierarchically partitions its identifier space into two subspaces and selects the agent nodes in the subspaces as its children in a top-down approach. Our theoretical analysis and experimental results demonstrate that the partition-based broadcast algorithm can construct and maintain a balanced DBT with low overhead, where the branching factors of each node are at most two, and the tree height is $O(\log n)$ in a Chord of $n$ nodes, without any extra storage space for each node and explicit maintenance overhead for the parent-child membership in the DBT.

## 1 Introduction

The federated planet-scale computing infrastructures such as PlanetLab [1] and Grids [2] have become increasingly important for developing and deploying many emerging distributed applications such as content distribution networks, peer-to-peer systems, and scientific computing. These computing infrastructures typically consist of large numbers of personal workstations and dedicated servers scattered around the world. As the size of the computing infrastructures continues to grow, it is very challenging for administrators to efficiently manage such large-scale dynamic distributed systems.

Distributed information management systems [3-6] have been extensively used in the large-scale computing infrastructures for a broad range of network services such as network monitor and management, resource management, and content distribution. Distributed broadcast is one of the fundamental primitive operations of distributed information management systems to disseminate information on a global scale. For example, in PlanetLab, researchers replicate their programs, along with the corresponding execution environment, on tens of thousands of nodes before launching a distributed application. In recent years, the Peer-to-Peer (P2P) based broadcast algorithms have been proposed to perform scalable content distribution across the large-scale computing infrastructures in a decentralized fashion. There are two design principles for a P2P-based broadcast algorithm according to overlay structures: tree-based and mesh-based approaches. The tree-based approach constructs a tree overlay rooted at the source node as the content delivering structure, such as ESM [16], NICE

N. Abdennadher and D. Petcu (Eds.): GPC 2009, LNCS 5529, pp. 422–433, 2009.

[17], Scribe [8], and Bayeux [18]. Since the single tree structure is vulnerable to the failure of an interior node, the multiple-tree approach such as SplitStream [9] and CoopNet [10] is proposed to improve the resilience, where each sub-stream of content is delivered along one of multiple disjoint trees. The mesh-based approach such as Bullet [11], FastReplica [12], Bullet' [13], BitTorrent [19], and CoBlitz [15] constructs a data-driven mesh overlay as a swarm system, where each node has a small set of neighbors to exchange data. Despite of these arguments [20-21] against the two approaches, the tree-based approach is more suitable for the large-scale computing infrastructures with a large fraction of relatively stable dedicated nodes due to its simplicity and controlled overhead.

DHT-based broadcast algorithms [4-10, 15, 18, 28-31] have been recently proposed to support efficient broadcast on large scale. These broadcast algorithms utilize the routing mechanisms of DHT to build up an overlay routing path between a source node and each destination node, and then construct a DBT rooted at the source node by merging all the routing paths. The DHT-based broadcast algorithms have two approaches for constructing a DBT: top-down and bottom-up approaches. For example, the k-ary search based broadcast algorithm [30] constructs a DBT over DHT in a top-down approach, while the reverse-path forwarding based broadcast algorithm [8] constructs a DBT over DHT in a bottom-up approach. However, existing DHT-based broadcast algorithms suffer from the limitations of scalability and load balancing. First, DHT is a greedy routing algorithm, where each node always forwards a searched key to the closest preceding node in its finger table, whose identifier is closer to the key in the identifier space. The greedy essence of DHT would result in that existing DHT-based broadcast algorithms such as the k-ary search based broadcast algorithm [30] and the reverse-path forwarding based broadcast algorithm [8] construct a flat and unbalanced DBT either in a top-down approach or in a bottom-up approach. Second, existing DHT-based broadcast algorithms have high construction and maintenance overhead of a DBT with respect to a large number of participating nodes. For example, the reverse-path forwarding based broadcast algorithm [8] requires interior nodes to consume extra storage space to contain its children for reverse forwarding, which leads to high overhead of maintaining these children. Moreover, although existing DHT-based broadcast algorithms often adopt the pushdown and anycast methods [8-9] to tackle the overloading of nodes by adjusting the branching factors between nodes in a DBT, Bharambe et al. [32] indicated that these adjustment methods would result in a significant number of non-DHT links that are present in the DBT but are not part of the routing links of DHT, which not only restricts the scalability of DBT but also incurs higher maintenance overhead of these non-DHT links due to the dynamic nodes [22-23].

To address the above limitations, this paper proposes a partition-based broadcast algorithm over DHT for scalability and load balancing in the large-scale computing infrastructures, where a balanced DBT is implicitly constructed from the novel routing paths of DHT such as Chord, without explicit parent-child membership maintenance. The key idea of the partition-based broadcast algorithm is that by leveraging the topology and routing mechanisms of Chord, each node hierarchically partitions its identifier space into two subspaces and selects the agent nodes in the subspaces as its children in a top-down approach. Our theoretical analysis and experimental results show that the partition-based broadcast algorithm can construct and maintain a scalable and balanced DBT, where the branching factors of each node are at most two, and the tree height is $O(\log n)$ in a Chord of $n$ nodes, without any extra storage space for each node and explicit maintenance overhead for the parent-child membership in the DBT.

The rest of the paper is organized as follows. Section 2 overviews the Chord network. In Section 3, we present in details the partition-based algorithm. Section 4 gives the experimental results. Related work is introduced in Section 5 and Section 6 concludes the paper.

## 2  Chord Overview

The Chord network is modeled as an undirected graph $G = (V, E)$, where the vertex set $V$ contains $n$ nodes and $E$ is the set of overlay links between nodes. According to the identifiers of nodes, Chord organizes nodes as a ring topology in the circular space. An object's identifier $k$ is assigned to the first node whose identifier is equal to or follows $k$ in the identifier space of Chord. This node is called the successor node of the identifier $k$, denoted by $Succ(k)$. In Chord, $Pred(u)$ refers to the immediate predecessor of a node $u$, while $Succ(u)$ refers to the immediate successor of a node $u$. Besides its immediate predecessor and successor, each node $u$ also maintains a set of $m$ finger nodes that are spaced exponentially in the identifier space of Chord. The $i^{th}$ finger node of a node $u$, denoted by $Finger(u, i)$, is the first node that succeeds $u$ by at least $2^i$ in the identifier space, that is $Finger(u, i) = Succ((u + 2^i) \bmod 2^m)$, where $0 \le i \le m - 1$.

Chord adopts a greedy finger routing algorithm [24] to recursively (or iteratively) forward a query message with an object's identifier $k$ to its successor node $Succ(k)$ that maintains a pair $(k, v)$, where $v$ is the object's value. When a node $u$ want to lookup an object's identifier $k$, it forwards a query message with the identifier $k$ to its finger node $Finger(u, j)$, which is closest to the successor node $Succ(k)$ in the circular identifier space, satisfying $Finger(u, j) \in (u, Succ(k)]$ and $Min\{Dist(Finger(u, j), k), 0 \le j \le m - 1\}$, where $Dist(u_1, u_2)$ is the numeric distance between two identifiers $u_1$ and $u_2$, that is $Dist(u_1, u_2) = (u_1 - u_2 + 2^m) \bmod 2^m$. And then the finger node $Finger(u, j)$ continues to forward the query message to the next node using the similar routing algorithm, until to the successor node $Succ(k)$. Therefore, the finger routing algorithm of Chord is a scalable and efficient lookup algorithm, with average routing path length of $O(\log n)$ and average node state space of $O(\log n)$ in a Chord of $n$ nodes.

## 3  Partition-Based Broadcast Algorithm

We propose a partition-based broadcast algorithm over DHT to achieve the scalability and load balancing, where each node hierarchically partitions its identifier space into

```
1:   // receive (P, R, Limit) represents that node P receives
       a broadcast message from source node R with subspace Limit.
       T he initial value of Limit is R, when starting to broadcast
2:   // Select right child for broadcasting
3:   for j←m-1 to 0 do
4:     if Finger(P, j)∈ (P, Limit) then
5:       Right←Finger(P, j);
6:     else
7:       Right←Null;
8:     endif
9:   endfor
10:  if Right=Null then
11:    exit(0);
12:  endif
13:  // Select left child for broadcasting
14:  for i←0 to m-1 do
15:    if Finger(P, i)∈ (P, Right) then
16:      Left ← Finger(P, i);
17:    else
18:      Left ← Null;
19:    endif
20:  endfor
21:  // Eliminate redundant child and set new limit for subspace
22:  if (Left ≠Null) and (Left≠Right) then
23:    NewLimit←Right;
24:    send (Left, R, NewLimit);
25:  endif
26:  send (Right, R, Limit);
```

**Fig. 1.** Pseduo-codes of partition-based broadcast algorithm

two subspaces, and selects the agent nodes in the subspaces as its children, and then a balanced DBT rooted at the source node is constructed in a top-down approach. The balanced DBT construction process of the partition-based broadcast algorithm is as follows.

First, on receiving a broadcast message with a limitation value $l$ of identifier space, each node $N_i$ partitions its limited identifier space $(N_i, l)$ into two subspaces $(N_i, Finger(N_i, j))$ and $[Finger(N_i, j), l)$, where $Finger(N_i, j)$ is the closest finger node to the limitation value $l$ in the circular identifier space. Second, the node $N_i$ selects the agent node $Finger(N_i, k)$ in $(N_i, Finger(N_i, j))$ as its left child, where $Finger(N_i, k)$ is the farthest finger node from $Finger(N_i, j)$, and selects the agent node $Finger(N_i, j)$ in $[Finger(N_i, j), l)$ as its right child. Finally, the node $N_i$ forwards the broadcast message with the limitation value $Finger(N_i, j)$ to its left child $Finger(N_i, k)$ and the broadcast message with the limitation value $l$ to its right child $Finger(N_i, j)$, until no any child is selected. When initiating a broadcast message with a limitation value $l$, the source node $N_s$ sets the limitation value $l = N_s$, which means that its identifier space $(N_s, N_s)$ is the whole identifier space. When a node $N_d$ selects its left child $N_l$ and right child $N_r$, if $N_l = N_r$, then the broadcast message is only forwarded to its right child $N_r$. The pseudo-codes of the partition-based broadcast algorithm are illustrated in Figure 1.

Figure 2 depicts an example of the balanced DBT construction using the partition-based broadcast algorithm in an 11-node Chord. In Figure 2(a), the source node $N_0$ sets the limitation value $l = N_0$, and partitions the whole identifier

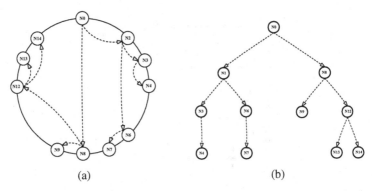

(a)                                                    (b)

**Fig. 2.** Balanced DBT construction using partition-based broadcast algorithm in an 11-node Chord: (a) Finger routing paths rooted at $N_0$; (b) Constructed balanced DBT rooted at $N_0$

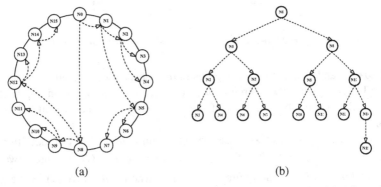

(a)                                                    (b)

**Fig. 3.** Balanced DBT construction using partition-based broadcast algorithm in a 16-node Chord: (a) Finger routing paths rooted at $N_0$; (b) Constructed balanced DBT rooted at $N_0$

space $(N_0, N_0)$ into two subspaces $(N_0, N_8)$ and $[N_8, N_0)$, where $N_8$ is the closest finger node to the limitation value $l = N_0$, and selects the agent node $N_2$ in $(N_0, N_8)$ as its left child and the agent node $N_8$ in $[N_8, N_0)$ as its right node, and then forwards the broadcast message with the limitation value $N_8$ to $N_2$ and the broadcast message with the limitation value $N_0$ to $N_8$; similarly, when receiving the broadcast message with the limitation value, $N_2$ and $N_8$ further partition their identifier space into two subspace respectively, and then continue to forward the broadcast message to their children until no any child is selected. Figure 2(b) shows the corresponding balanced DBT rooted at $N_0$ constructed from the finger routing paths in Figure 2(a). As seen in Figure 2, the partition-based broadcast algorithm constructs a balanced DBT, where the branching factors of each node are at most two, and the tree height is $3 < \lceil \log_2 n \rceil = 4$, in which $n = 11$ is the number of nodes in Chord.

Also, the partition-based broadcast algorithm is adapted to construct a scalable and balanced DBT for broadcasting in a Chord with the uniform identifier space. For example, Figure 3(a) depicts an example of the balanced DBT construction using partition-based broadcast algorithm in a 16-node Chord, where there is the uniform identifier space. Figure 3(b) shows the corresponding balanced DBT rooted at $N_0$ constructed from the finger routing paths in Figure 3(a). As seen in Figure 3, the partition-based broadcast algorithm also constructs a scalable and balanced DBT, where the branching factors of each node are at most two and the tree height is $\lceil \log_2 n \rceil = 4$, in which $n = 16$ is the number of nodes in Chord.

### 3.1 Algorithm Analysis

The essence of the partition-based broadcast algorithm is that the identifier space of each node is hierarchically partitioned into two subspaces to construct a binary partition tree. Thus it is guaranteed by the novel binary partition of the partition-based algorithm that a DBT is balanced and all the destination nodes are hierarchically covered. Figure 4 illustrates the properties of the partition-based broadcast algorithm in an 11-node Chord. As seen in Figure 4(a), the source nod $N_0$ partitions the whole identifier space into two subspaces, each of which is further partitioned into two subspaces, until the identifier subspace contains only one node, so that a balanced partition tree rooted at $N_0$ is constructed by the hierarchical binary partition. As seen in Figure 4(b), when the source node $N_0$ forwards a broadcast message, each node $i$ partitions its identifier space into two subspace $(i, i + 2^j)$ and $[i + 2^j, Limit)$, and selects the finger node $i + 2^0$ as its left child and $i + 2^j$ as its right child, and then forwards the broadcast message to its children, until all the destination nodes $N_2, N_3 \cdots N_{14}$ are covers in a hierarchical approach to construct a balanced DBT root at $N_0$.

A DBT constructed by the partition-based broadcast algorithm is scalable, where the tree height is $O(\log n)$, in which $n$ is the number of nodes in Chord. We assume that Chord has the identifier space $[0, 2^m)$, and the $i^{th}$ binary partition divides the whole identifier space into $2^i$ subspaces, each of which has the size of $2^m / 2^i$, where $1 \le i \le h$ and $h$ is the tree height of DBT. After the $h^{th}$ binary partition, since each subspace contains only one node, which means that it is $\lceil n / 2^h \rceil = 1$, we deduce that it is $h = \lceil \log_2 n \rceil$ in which $n$ is the number of nodes in Chord. Hence, we prove that the tree height is $O(\log n)$ and the DBT is scalable.

Moreover, the partition-based broadcast algorithm needs no explicit construction and maintenance overhead of a balanced DBT. First, since the partition-based broadcast algorithm hierarchically selects the children by partitioning the identifier space into two parts in a top-down approach, each parent does not need extra storage space for its children, so that a balanced DBT is implicitly constructed from the finger routing paths of Chord. Second, due to the finger stabilization algorithm [24] of Chord, besides periodically updating the finger tables of nodes, the partition-based algorithm does not need extra cost to repair the parent-child membership in the DBT, which significantly reduces the maintenance overhead of the balanced DBT. Therefore, a

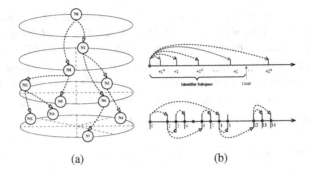

(a)                 (b)

**Fig. 4.** Properties of partition-based broadcast algorithm in an 11-node Chord: (a) Hierarchical binary partition of the node identifier space from $N_0$; (b) Alternately covering all the destination nodes to construct balanced DBT rooted at $N_0$

DBT constructed by the partition-based broadcast algorithm has no any extra storage cost and explicit maintenance overhead of each node.

## 4  Experimental Evaluation

This section presents the simulation experiments to validate the performance of our partition-based broadcast algorithm. The performance metrics of a DHT-based broadcast algorithm include branching factor, path length, message overhead, and message imbalance factor. Message imbalance factor refers to the ratio between the maximal number of messages and average number of messages on each node in a DBT. In the experiments, we implement the k-ary search based broadcast algorithm, the reverse-path forwarding based broadcast algorithm, and the partition-based broadcast algorithm, and simulate from 200 to 2000 nodes of Chord to examine the performance metrics of above three DHT-based broadcast algorithms.

Figure 5 depicts the comparison of branching factor. As seen in Figure 5(a), the partition-based algorithm keeps the constant maximal branching factor, while the

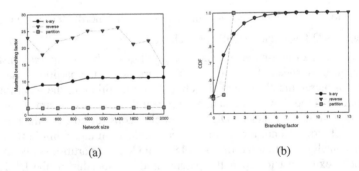

(a)                 (b)

**Fig. 5.** Branching factor: (a) Maximal branching factor; (b) Cumulative distribution function in a 2000-node Chord

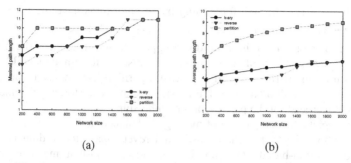

(a)                                      (b)

**Fig. 6.** Path length: (a) Maximal path length; (b) Average path length

maximal branching factor of both the k-ary search based and reverse-path forwarding based algorithms fluctuates with various network sizes. For example, the partition-based algorithm has the constant maximal branching factor of 2, whereas the k-ary search based algorithm has the maximal branching factor of about 11 and the reverse-path forwarding based algorithm has the maximal branching factor varying from 14 to 26. As seen in Figure 5(b), both the k-ary search based and reverse-path forwarding based algorithms construct a skewed DBT, while the partition-based algorithm constructs a balanced DBT. For example, about 88% of nodes in the DBT constructed by both the k-ary search based and reverse-path forwarding based algorithms has the branching factor of equal to or less than 2, while about 50% of nodes of the DBT constructed by the partition-based algorithm have the branching factor of 2.

Figure 6 depicts the comparison of path length. As seen in Figure 6(a), the maximal path length of the partition-based algorithm is larger than that of both the k-ary search based and reverse-path forwarding based algorithms. For example, when Chord has no more than 1400 nodes, the maximal path length of the partition-based algorithm is kept 10, while the maximal path length of both k-ary search based and reverse-path forwarding based algorithms varies with different network sizes, but not beyond 10. As seen in Figure 6(b), compared to both k-ary search based and reverse-path forwarding based algorithms, the partition-based algorithm separately increase 55%~68% and 58%~100% of the average path length. Therefore, the partition-based broadcast algorithm constructs a scalable DBT, where the tree height is $O(\log n)$ in which $n$ is the number of nodes in Chord.

Figure 7 depicts the comparison of message overhead. As seen in Figure 7, both the k-ary search based and partition-based algorithms have the same messages

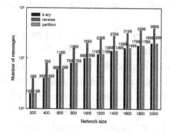

**Fig. 7.** Message overhead

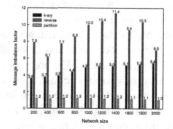

**Fig. 8.** Message imbalance factor

of $n-1$, while the reverse-path forwarding based algorithms have the message overhead of $2(n-1)$. The reason is that both the k-ary search based and partition-based algorithms construct a DBT in a top-down approach, which reduces the number of broadcast messages and results in no extra storage space for a node's children in the DBT. Therefore, the partition-based broadcast algorithm has low-overhead construction and maintenance of a balanced DBT, without any extra storage cost and explicit maintenance overhead for the parent-child membership.

Figure 8 depicts the comparison of message imbalance factor. As seen in Figure 8, compared to both the k-ary search based and reverse-path forwarding based algorithms, the partition-based algorithm has the lower constant message imbalance factor. For example, in a 2000-node Chord, the partition-based algorithm has the message imbalance factor of 1.0, while both the k-ary search based and reverse-path forwarding based algorithms have the message imbalance factor of 5.4 and 6.9 respectively. Therefore, compared to both the k-ary search based and reverse-path forwarding based algorithms, the partition-based broadcast algorithm separately reduces 67%~81% and 81%~90% of the message imbalance factor, further indicating that a DBT constructed by the partition-based algorithm is balanced.

## 5  Related Work

There have been many research efforts on multicast and broadcast in past decades. In general, broadcast is a special case of multicast. In recent years, application-level multicast and broadcast algorithms are categorized into tree-based and mesh-based approaches as follows.

In the tree-based approach, a tree overlay rooted at a source node is constructed as the content delivering structure. For example, ESM [16] is a classic application-layer multicast system towards small-sized groups for audio and video conferencing applications. NICE [17] is proposed to support a larger number of participating nodes using a hierarchical clustering approach. Bayeux [18] is proposed to construct a scalable and fault-tolerant application-layer multicast system by replicating root nodes and clustering receivers via identifier on top of Tapestry [27]. Since the single tree structure is vulnerable to node dynamics, the multiple-tree approach has been proposed, where a forest with multiple disjoint sub-trees is constructed and each substream of the content is delivered along each sub-tree. For example, SplitStream [9] is proposed to construct an interior-node disjoint forest of multiple Scribe [8] trees on top of Pastry [26]. CoopNet [10] is proposed to compute locally random or node-disjoint forests of trees in a manner similar to SplitStream, primarily designed for resilience to node departures.

In the mesh-based approach, a data-driven mesh overlay is constructed as a swarm system, where each node has a small of neighbors to exchange data. For example, Bullet [11] and Bullet' [13] are proposed for large-file distribution in the wide area, where a overlay mesh is constructed over any overlay tree and each node transmits a disjoint set of data to its children in order to maintain uniform distribution of each data and achieve high throughput. BitTorrent [19, 33] is one of the most popular P2P content distribution systems, where a file is divided into multiple equal-sized blocks and all participating nodes upload and download blocks in parallel. These mesh-based swarm systems can mitigate link stresses and the performance bottleneck of the origin, but can incur enormous traffic stresses on the Internet Service Providers (ISP).

Moreover, distributed aggregation is also one of the fundamental primitive operations to recursively computing the global information by applying an aggregate function such as min, max, count, and sum on a set of local status in the large-scale computing infrastructures. DHT-based aggregation algorithms for global resource monitor and discovery related to our work have been recently proposed. For example, Astrolabe [3] is a DNS-like distributed management service by organizing the resources into a hierarchy of domains, specifying an aggregation tree between domains, and exchanging information across domains using an unstructured gossip protocol. SDIMS [4] is a scalable distribution information system, where each attribute is hashed to a key and the aggregation tree rooted at the key is built upon the routing mechanisms of Plaxton. Other algorithms also include SOMO [28], Willow [29], and DAT [7]. The DHT-based aggregation algorithms are designed to provide a scalable all-to-one operation for collecting global information, while on the contrary the DHT-based broadcast algorithms are proposed to provide a scalable one-to-all operation for disseminating global information.

# 6  Conclusions

It is very challenging to support scalable and efficient broadcast in the large-scale computing infrastructures such as PlanetLab and Grids. Although most DHT-based broadcast algorithms have been recently proposed, by exploiting the greedy routing mechanisms of DHT, they suffer from the limitations of scalability and load balancing, incurring high construction and maintenance overhead of a DBT. This paper proposes a partition-based broadcast algorithm over DHT for the large-scale computing infrastructures, where each node hierarchically partitions its identifier space into two subspaces and selects the agent nodes in the subspaces as its children. We leverage the topology and routing mechanisms of Chord to select the appropriate children of each node from its finger table in a top-down approach, so that a balanced DBT is implicitly constructed from the novel routing paths of Chord, without explicit parent-child membership maintenance. Our experimental results show that the partition-based broadcast algorithms construct a scalable and balanced DBT, where the branching factor of each node is at most 2, and the tree height is $O(\log n)$, without any extra storage space for the children of each node and explicit maintenance overhead for the parent-childe membership in the DBT; compared to both the k-ary search based and reverse-path forwarding based broadcast algorithms, the partition-based broadcast algorithm separately reduces 67%~81% and 81%~90% of the message imbalance factor. Therefore, our partition-based broadcast algorithm would be widely adopted to support scalable and efficient information management in the large-scale computing infrastructures.

# Acknowledgment

This work is supported by the National Science Foundation of China under grant No.60673155 and No.90718008.

# References

1. Bavier, A., Bowman, M., Chun, B., et al.: Operating System Support for Planetary-Scale Network Services. In: Proc. of NSDI, pp. 253–266 (2004)
2. Foster, I., Kesselman, C., Tuecke, S.: The Anatomy of the Grid: Enabling Scalable Virtual Organizations. International Journal of Supercomputer Applications 15(3), 200–222 (2001)
3. Renesse, R.V., Birman, K.P., Vogels, W.: Astrolabe: A Robust and Scalable Technology for Distributed System Monitoring, Management, and Data Mining. ACM Transaction on Computer Systems 21(2), 164–206 (2003)
4. Yalagandula, P., Dahlin, M.: A Scalable Distributed Information Management System. In: Proc. of ACM SIGCOMM, pp. 379–390 (2004)
5. Oppenheimer, D., Albrecht, J., Patterson, D., Vahdat, A.: Design and Implementation Tradeoffs for Wide-Area Resource Discovery. ACM Transactions on Internet Technology 8(2), 1–40 (2008)
6. Jain, N., Kit, D., Mahajan, P., Yalagandula, P., Dahlin, M., Zhang, Y.: STAR: Self-Tuning Aggregation for Scalable Monitoring. In: Proc. of VLDB, pp. 962–973 (2007)
7. Cai, M., Hwang, K.: Distributed Aggregation Algorithms with Load-Balancing for Scalable Grid Resource Monitoring. In: Proc. of IPDPS, Long Beach, California (2007)
8. Castro, M., Druschel, P., Kermarrec, A.-M., Rowstron, A.: SCRIBE: A Large-Scale and Decentralized Application-Level Multicast Infrastructure. IEEE Journal on Selected Areas in Communication 20(8), 1489–1499 (2002)
9. Castro, M., Druschel, P., Kermarrec, A., Nandi, A., Rowstron, A., Singh, A.: Splitstream: High-bandwidth Multicast in Cooperative Environments. In: Proc. of SOSP, pp. 298–313 (2003)
10. Padmanbhan, V.N., Wang, H.J., Chou, P.A., Sripanid-Kuchai, K.: Distributed Streaming Media Content Using Cooperative Networking. In: Proc. of ACM NOSSDAV, pp. 177–186 (2002)
11. Kostic, D., Rodriguez, A., Albrecht, J., Vahdat, A.: Bullet: High Bandwidth Data Dissemination Using an Overlay Mesh. In: Proc. of SOSP, pp. 282–297 (2003)
12. Cherkasova, L., Lee, J.: FastReplica: Efficient Large File Distribution within Content Delivery Networks. In: Proc. of USITS (2003)
13. Kostic, D., Braud, R., Killian, C., VandeKieft, E., Anderson, J.W., Snoeren, A.C., Vahdat, A.: Maintaining High Bandwidth under Dynamic Network Conditions. In: Proc. of USENIX Annual Technical Conference, pp. 193–208 (2005)
14. Ganguly, S., Saxena, A., Bhatnagar, S., Banerjee, S.: Fast Replication in Content Distribution Overlays. In: Proc. of IEEE INFOCOM, pp. 2246–2256 (2005)
15. Park, K., Pai, V.S.: Scale and Performance in the CoBlitz Large-File Distribution Service. In: Proc. of NSDI, pp. 29–44 (2006)
16. Chu, Y., Rao, S.G., Seshan, S., Zhang, H.: A Case for End System Multicast. IEEE Journal on Selected Areas in Communication, Special Issue on Networking Support for Multicast 20(8), 1456–1471 (2002)
17. Baerjee, S., Bhattacharjee, B., Kommareddy, C.: Scalable Application Layer Multicast. In: Proc. of ACM SIGCOMM, pp. 205–217 (2002)
18. Zhuang, S., Zhao, B., Joseph, A., Katz, R., Kubiatowicz, J.: Bayeux: An Architecture for Scalable and Fault-tolerant. Wide-area Data Dissemination. In: Proc. of ACM NOSSDAV, pp. 11–20 (2001)
19. Cohen, B.: Incentives Build Robustness in BitTorrent. In: Proc. of Workshop on Economics of Peer-to-Peer Systems (2003)

20. Venkataraman, V., Yoshida, K., Fancis, P.: Chunkyspread: Heterogeneous Unstructured End System Multicast. In: Proc. of IEEE ICNP, pp. 2–11 (2006)
21. Wang, F., Xiong, Y., Liu, J.: mTreebone: A Hybrid Tree/Mesh Overlay for Application-Layer Live Video Multicast. In: Proc. of IEEE ICDCS (2007)
22. Rhea, S., Geels, D., Roscoe, T., Kubiatowicz, J.: Handling Churn in a DHT. In: Proc. of USENIX Technical Conference, pp. 127–140 (2004)
23. Godfrey, P.B., Shenker, S., Stoica, I.: Minimizing Churn in Distributed Systems. In: Proc. of ACM SIGCOMM, pp. 147–158 (2006)
24. Stoica, I., Morris, R., Karger, D., Kaashoek, F., Balakrishnan, H.: Chord: A Scalable Peer-to-Peer Lookup Service for Internet Applications. In: Proc. of ACM SIGCOMM, pp. 149–160 (2001)
25. Ratnasamy, S., Francis, P., Handley, M., Karp, R., Shenker, S.: A Scalable Content Addressable Network. In: Proc. of ACM SIGCOMM, pp. 161–172 (2001)
26. Rowstron, A., Druschel, P.: Pastry: Scalable, Decentralized Object Location, and Routing for Large-scale Peer-to-Peer Systems. In: Guerraoui, R. (ed.) Middleware 2001. LNCS, vol. 2218, pp. 329–351. Springer, Heidelberg (2001)
27. Zhao, B., Kubiatowicz, J., Joseph, A.: Tapestry: a Fault-tolerant Wide-area Application Infrastructure. ACM Computer Communication Review 32(1), 81 (2002)
28. Zhang, Z., Shi, S.-M., Zhu, J.: SOMO: Self-organized Metadata Overlay for Resource Management in P2P DHT. In: Kaashoek, M.F., Stoica, I. (eds.) IPTPS 2003. LNCS, vol. 2735. Springer, Heidelberg (2003)
29. Renesse, R.V., Bozdog, A.: Willow: DHT, Aggregation, and Publish/Subscribe in One Protocol. In: Voelker, G.M., Shenker, S. (eds.) IPTPS 2004. LNCS, vol. 3279, pp. 173–183. Springer, Heidelberg (2005)
30. El-Ansary, S., Alima, L.O., Brand, P., Haridi, S.: Efficient Broadcast in Structured P2P Networks. In: Kaashoek, M.F., Stoica, I. (eds.) IPTPS 2003. LNCS, vol. 2735. Springer, Heidelberg (2003)
31. Ratnasamy, S., Handley, M., Karp, R., Shenker, S.: Application-level Multicast Using Content-Addressable Networks. In: Proc. of International Workshop on Networked Group Communicaion, pp. 14–29 (2001)
32. Bharambe, A.R., Rao, S.G., Padmanabhan, V.N., Seshan, S., Zhang, H.: The Impact of Heterogeneous Bandwidth Constraints on DHT-Based Multicast Protocols. In: Castro, M., van Renesse, R. (eds.) IPTPS 2005. LNCS, vol. 3640, pp. 115–126. Springer, Heidelberg (2005)
33. Huang, K., Wang, L., Zhang, D., Liu, Y.: Optimizing the BitTorrent Performance Using Adaptive Peer Selection Strategy. Future Generation Computer Systems 24(7), 621–630 (2008)

# Novel Crash Recovery Approach for Concurrent Failures in Cluster Federation

Bidyut Gupta and Shahram Rahimi

Department of Computer Science
Southern Illinois University
Carbondale, IL 62901, USA
{bidyut, rahimi}@cs.siu.edu

**Abstract.** In this paper, we have proposed a simple and efficient approach for check pointing and recovery in cluster computing environment. The recovery scheme deals with both orphan and lost intra and inter cluster messages. This check pointing scheme ensures that after the system recovers from failures, all processes in different clusters can restart from their respective recent check-points; thus avoiding any domino effect. That is, the recent check points always form a consistent recovery line of the cluster federation. The main features of our work are: it uses selective message logging which enables the initiator process in each cluster to log the minimum number of messages, the recovery scheme is domino effect free and is executed simultaneously by all clusters in the cluster federation, it considers concurrent failures, message complexities in each cluster for both check pointing and recovery schemes are just $O(n)$, where n is the number of processes in a cluster. These features make our algorithm superior to the existing works.

## 1 Introduction

Cluster federation is a union of clusters, where each cluster contains a certain number of processes. A Cluster may be defined as an independent computer combined into a unified system through software and networking. Cluster computing environments have provided a cost-effective solution to many distributed computing problems by investing inexpensive hardware [2], [3], [15]. With the growing importance of cluster computing, its fault-tolerant aspect deserves significant attention. It is known that check pointing and rollback recovery are widely used techniques that allows a system to progress in spite of a failure [1]. The basic idea is to periodically record the system state as a checkpoint during normal system operation and upon detection of faults, to restore one of the checkpoints and restart the system from there [4]-[7], [10]-[12], [16]. It may be noted that a distributed system / cluster federation is said to be consistent, if there is no message which is recorded in the state of its receiver but not recorded in the state of its sender [1]-[7]. But if such a message exists, then it is known as orphan message. Such a consistent state of the system is also referred to as a recovery line which in effect consists of one checkpoint per process of the system. It is the responsibility of each cluster to determine its consistent checkpoint set that consists of

N. Abdennadher and D. Petcu (Eds.): GPC 2009, LNCS 5529, pp. 434–445, 2009.
© Springer-Verlag Berlin Heidelberg 2009

one checkpoint from each process present in it. But this consistent checkpoint set of one cluster may not be consistent with the other clusters' consistent checkpoint sets, because clusters interact through inter cluster messages which may result in dependencies among the clusters, meaning thereby that some such inter cluster messages may become orphan messages. Therefore, a collection of consistent checkpoint sets, one from each cluster in the federation, does not necessarily produce a consistent federation level checkpoint (also known as federation level recovery line). Consequently, rollback of one failed process in a cluster may force some other processes in the other clusters to rollback in order to maintain consistency of operation by the cluster federation. In the worst case, consistency requirement may force the system to rollback to the initial state of the system, losing all the work performed before a failure. This uncontrolled propagation of rollback is known as domino-effect [1]. Besides, for correct computation of the underlying distributed computation after the system recovers from failures, a recovery scheme must ensure that all lost messages are identified and replayed to the appropriate processes when they restart.

**Problem Formulation:** The main objective of this work is three fold. First, it must take care of both orphan messages during the check pointing phase itself unlike the existing works [2],[3],[13],[14]. For this purpose we will consider designing a single phase non blocking check pointing scheme that must take care of both intra and inter cluster orphan messages. Second, it must identify all intra and inter cluster lost messages in an efficient way at the time of recovery. Third, recovery schemes in the different clusters must have to be executed simultaneously and the processes must restart from their respective recent (latest) checkpoints, thereby avoiding the domino effect.

This paper is organized as follows. In Section 2 we have presented the different data structures. In Section 3 we have presented the check pointing algorithm and its performance. Section 4 contains the recovery scheme along with its performance. Section 5 draws the conclusion.

## 2   Relevant Data Structures and System Model

### 2.1   System Model

We assume that processes are deterministic in the sense that from the same state, if given the same inputs, a process executes the same sequence of instructions. We also assume that processes are fail stop. It means that upon failure, a process does not perform any incorrect actions and simply ceases to function.

### 2.2   Notations and Relevant Data Structures

The proposed recovery approach needs the following data structures to be maintained in each cluster.

The $k^{th}$ cluster of the cluster federation is denoted as $C^K$. The $i^{th}$ process in $C^K$ is denoted as $P_i^K$. The $x^{th}$ checkpoint taken by the $i^{th}$ process $P_i^K$ in the $k^{th}$ cluster is denoted as $CP^{i,K}_x$. An intra cluster message from $P_i^K$ is denoted as $m_s^i$, where s is the message sequence number assigned by the sender $P_i^K$. We term this sequence number as the primary sequence number (PSN). An inter cluster message from the $i^{th}$ process

$P_i^K$ ($\in C^K$) is denoted as $M_s^{K(i)}$, where s is the PSN of the message. We assume that every cluster has an initiator process which has a two-fold responsibility; first, it is responsible for invoking the check pointing algorithm in this cluster and second, it determines the lost messages in this cluster in the event of failures. For the $k^{th}$ cluster $P^k$ represents the initiator process. In order to identify lost messages in the event of a failure, we assume that for every cluster all intra and inter cluster messages are routed through its initiator process on their way to the respective destinations. Thus in a cluster $C^K$ any message communication between any two application processes takes place via the initiator $P^K$. To every message (including both intra and inter cluster ones) to be delivered to a process, say $P_i^K$, the initiator process $P^K$ assigns a new sequence number, termed as the secondary sequence number (SSN) following its order of arrival at the initiator. Each such message is then delivered along with its SSN to the destination process $P_i^K$. This destination process in its recent checkpoint just remembers only the maximum SSN in $SEQ_{i(max)}$. Note that these SSNs (in ascending order) actually create the total order of the messages sent to a receiving process. In each cluster its initiator process maintains a message log for each process belonging to this cluster. Thus in cluster $C^K$ the initiator process $P^K$ maintains a message log, MESG-LOG$_i$ for each process $P_i^K$. This log stores copies of the messages to be delivered to the $i^{th}$ process following their order of arrival at the initiator. $P^K$ saves the maximum SSN found in the message log for process $P_i^K$ in $SSN_{i(max)}$. As an example, assume that $P^K$ has received first an intra cluster message $m_2^r$, followed by another one, $m_6^t$ from the $r^{th}$ and $t^{th}$ processes respectively for the destination $P_i^K$. After that it receives an inter cluster message $M_4^{Q(n)}$ coming from the $n^{th}$ process $P_n^Q$ of the $q^{th}$ cluster $C^Q$ for the same destination $P_i^K$. Note that the three PSNs of the messages are 2, 6, and 4 respectively. However the initiator process $P^K$ now assigns the secondary sequence numbers 1, 2, and 3 to these messages following their order of arrival at it. Now $SSN_{i(max)}$ contains 3. The message log for process $P_i^K$ is stated below along with the messages' respective SSNs appearing in brackets.

$$\text{MESG-LOG}_i^K = [m_2^r\,(1),\ m_6^t\,(2),\ M_4^{Q(n)}\,(3)]$$

## 2.3 Check Pointing Interval and Selective Message Logging

As in [14], we assume that the value of the common check pointing interval T used in all the clusters is just larger than the maximum message (considering both intra and inter cluster messages) passing time between any two processes of the cluster federation. In the following discussion we have used some of the idea reported in [14]. We now state the benefits for such an assumption. It is known that message logging [17] is used to take care of lost and delayed messages. So naturally the question arises for how long a process will go on logging the messages it has sent before a failure (if at all) occurs. We have shown below that because of the above mentioned value of the common check pointing interval T, a process $P_i^K$ in cluster $C^K$ needs to save in its recent checkpoint $CP_x^{i,K}$ only all the messages it has sent in the recent check pointing interval $(CP_x^{i,K} - CP_{x-1}^{i,K})$. In other words, we are able to use as little information related to the lost and delayed messages as possible for consistent operation after the system restarts.

Consider the situation shown in Fig. 1. For simplicity we will explain using a single cluster, say $C^K$ with only two processes and with intra cluster messages only. Let

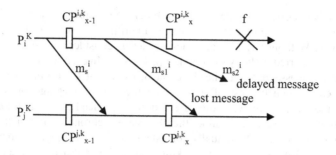

**Fig. 1.** Messages $m_{s1}{}^i$ and $m_{s2}{}^i$ are lost messages

the processes be $P_i{}^K$ and $P_j{}^K$. The observation is true for clusters consisting of any number of processes as well as for inter cluster messages as well. Observe that because of our assumed value of T, the duration of the check pointing interval, any message $m_s{}^i$ sent by process $P_i{}^K$ during its check pointing interval $(CP^{i,K}{}_{x-1} - CP^{i,K}{}_{x-2})$ always arrives before the recent checkpoint $CP^{j,K}{}_x$ of process $P_j{}^K$. Now assume the presence of a failure f as shown in the figure. Also assume that after recovery, the two processes restart from their recent $x^{th}$ checkpoints. Observe that any such message $m_s{}^i$ does not need to be resent as it is processed by the receiving process $P_j{}^K$ before its recent checkpoint $C^{j,K}{}_x$. So it is obvious that such a message $m_s{}^i$ can not be either a lost or a delayed message. Therefore, there is no need to log such messages by the initiator process $P^K$. However, messages, such as $m_{s1}{}^i$ and $m_{s2}{}^i$, sent by process $P_i{}^K$ in the interval $(CP^{i,K}{}_x - CP^{i,K}{}_{x-1})$ may be lost or delayed. So in the event of a failure f, in order to avoid any inconsistency in the computation after the system restarts from the recent checkpoints, we need to log only such sent messages at the initiator so that they can be resent after the processes restart. Observe that in the event of a failure, any delayed message, such as message $m_{s2}{}^i$, is essentially a lost message as well. Hence, in our approach, we consider only the recent checkpoints of the processes and the messages logged at the initiator process are the ones sent only in the recent check pointing interval. From now on, by 'lost message' we will mean both lost and delayed message. Observe that without such an assumption about the value of the common check pointing interval T, the above mentioned selective message logging is not possible; rather without such an assumption the messages logged may include not only the ones which a process $P_i{}^K$ has sent in its current interval $(CP^{i,K}{}_x - CP^{i,K}{}_{x-1})$, but also those which $P_i{}^K$ sent in the previous intervals as well.

## 3  The Check Pointing Algorithm

It is known that the classical synchronous check pointing scheme for distributed systems has three phases: first an initiator process sends a request to all processes to take checkpoints; second the processes take temporary check points and reply back to the initiator process; third the initiator process asks them to convert the temporary check points to permanent ones. Only after that processes can resume their normal computation. In between every two consecutive phases processes remain blocked. In this work our objective is to design a single phase non-blocking synchronous approach as in [12] in each cluster. The proposed check pointing algorithm in every cluster works in the following way. Without any loss of generality let us consider a cluster $C^K$. The algorithm is invoked periodically by the initiator process $P^K$. In each invocation the initiator sends a request message $M_c$ to the different processes of $C^K$ asking them to take a checkpoint each. Each process after receiving the request message $M_c$ will take its checkpoint independent of what others are doing. As in [12], no additional control message exchange is necessary unlike the classical synchronous approach for making individual recent checkpoints mutually consistent. However the present approach faces similar problem as in [12] regarding making checkpoints consistent. We explain first the problem considering the cluster $C^K$ only and then we will state a solution which is similarly applicable to other clusters as well. Assume that the check pointing algorithm has been initiated by the initiator process $P^K$ and it has sent a request message $M_c$ to the processes of the cluster $C^K$. Also assume that it is the $x^{th}$ execution of the algorithm. Suppose that after receiving $M_c$ the $i^{th}$ process $P_i^K$ takes its $x^{th}$ checkpoint $CP^{i,K}_x$ and immediately then sends an intra cluster application message $m_s^i$ to the $j^{th}$ process $P_j^K$. Note that in our approach all processes act independently after receiving $M_c$. Suppose at time $(t + \epsilon)$, where $\epsilon$ is very small with respect to t, process $P_j^K$ receives the message $m_s^i$. Also suppose that $P_j^K$ has not yet received $M_c$ from the initiator process. So, it processes the message. Now the request message $M_c$ arrives at $P_j^K$. Process $P_j^K$ now takes its checkpoint $CP^{j,K}_x$. We find that message $m_s^i$ has become an orphan due to the checkpoint $CP^{j,K}_x$. Hence, the checkpoints $CP^{i,K}_x$ and $CP^{j,K}_x$ cannot be consistent.

To avoid this problem we propose the following simple solution. Every sending process $P_i^K$ piggybacks a flag, say \$, only with its first application message, say $m_s^i$, sent (after it has taken its checkpoint for the current execution of the check pointing algorithm and before its next participation in the algorithm) to any other process $P_j^K$ in the cluster. Process $P_j^K$ after receiving the piggybacked application message learns immediately that the check pointing algorithm has already been invoked; so instead of waiting for the request it takes its checkpoint first, then processes the message $m_s^i$ and later it ignores the current request when that arrives. Observe that the above solution holds good for all inter cluster messages also. The reason is that the $x^{th}$ execution of the check pointing algorithm takes place simultaneously in the different clusters. Note that in our check pointing approach each initiator process interacts with the other processes in its cluster only once via the control message $M_c$. After receiving $M_c$ each such process, independent of what others are doing, just takes its checkpoint and resumes normal computation. That is why we term it as a single phase non-blocking algorithm. Below we describe the algorithm. Assume that it is the $x^{th}$ invocation of the check pointing algorithm.

### 3.1 Algorithm Non-blocking

For each cluster $C^K$

At each process $P_i^K$ ($\in C^K$)

if    $P_i^K$ receives $M_c$
      takes checkpoint $CP^{i,K}_x$ ;
      continues its normal operation;

else if $P_i^K$ receives a piggybacked application message $< m_s^j / M_s^{Q(t)}$ , $\$>$ && $P_i^K$ has not yet received $M_c$ for the current execution of the check pointing algorithm, it takes checkpoint $CP_x^{i,K}$ without waiting for $M_c$; continues its normal operation;
// processes the received intra cluster message $m_s^i$ / inter cluster message $M_s^{Q(t)}$ and ignores $M_c$, when received later

**Proof of Correctness:** In the 'if' block every process $P_i^K$ takes its $x^{th}$ checkpoint $CP_x^{i,K}$ when it receives the request message $M_c$. That is, none of the intra / inter cluster messages it has sent before this checkpoint can be an orphan. In the 'else if' block, a receiving process $P_i^K$ takes its $x^{th}$ checkpoint $CP_x^{i,K}$ before processing any intra / inter cluster application message $m_s^j / M_s^{Q(t)}$ , sent by a process which took its $x^{th}$ checkpoint first before sending the message to $P_i^K$. Therefore the message $m_s^j / M_s^{Q(t)}$ can not be an orphan as well. Since this is true for all the processes, hence all recent $x^{th}$ checkpoints in cluster $C^K$ are mutually consistent.    •

**Theorem 1.** The $x^{th}$ checkpoints of all processes in the cluster federation are mutually consistent.

**Proof.** Without any loss of generality let us consider two clusters $C^K$ and $C^L$ and we assume that it is the $x^{th}$ invocation of the check pointing algorithm. Observe that the same check pointing interval is used by the respective initiator processes $P^K$ and $P^L$ in these two clusters. Suppose that the $i^{th}$ process $P_i^K$ ($\in C^K$) has just taken its $x^{th}$ checkpoint $CP_x^{i,K}$ and immediately after that it sends an inter cluster application message $M_s^{K(i)}$ to the $j^{th}$ process $P_j^L$ ($\in C^L$). According to our proposed solution this message is piggybacked with the flag $\$$.

Now assume that process $P_j^L$ receives this application message before it receives the request message $M_c$ corresponding to the $x^{th}$ execution of the algorithm from its initiator $P^L$. If process $P_j^L$ has not yet received any other piggybacked application message yet, whether it is intra or inter cluster, then instead of waiting for the request to come from its initiator $P^L$, it first takes its $x^{th}$ checkpoint $CP_x^{j,L}$, then processes the message $M_s^{K(i)}$ and later it ignores the current request when that arrives. Now observe that the message $M_s^{K(i)}$ cannot be an orphan. Hence the two checkpoints $CP_x^{i,K}$ and $CP_x^{j,L}$ are mutually consistent. Now assume that process $P_j^L$ receives this piggybacked application message after it receives the request message $M_c$ corresponding to the $x^{th}$ execution of the algorithm from its initiator $P^L$. This means that process $P_j^L$ has received the inter cluster message after taking its $x^{th}$ checkpoint $CP_x^{j,L}$. So obviously the message $M_s^{K(i)}$ cannot be an orphan and hence the two checkpoints $CP_x^{i,K}$ and $CP_x^{j,L}$ are mutually consistent.

Since the above observation is true for any two checkpoints belonging to different clusters in the cluster federation and also Algorithm Non-blocking guarantees that the checkpoints inside a cluster are mutually consistent, therefore all checkpoints in the cluster federation are mutually consistent.    •

### 3.2 Performance

The algorithm is a synchronous one. However it differs from the classical synchronous approach in the following sense; it is just a single phase one unlike the three phase classical approach, it does not need any exchange of additional (control) messages except only the request message $M_c$, there is no synchronization delay, and finally it is non-blocking. However it enjoys the main advantage of the three phase classical approach in that the recent checkpoints are always consistent; so processes after recovery from failures can restart from these checkpoints (i.e. domino-effect free recovery). Therefore, it offers the advantages of both synchronous and asynchronous check pointing approach while avoiding their main drawbacks, such as blocking, synchronization delay, and domino effect. About message complexity in each cluster the initiator process broadcasts $M_c$ only once. So the message complexity is $O(n)$ for an n-process cluster. Also note that it is simultaneously executed in all the clusters.

Since a cluster is nothing but an individual distributed system, so we compare the proposed algorithm used in each cluster with some noted check pointing algorithms.

**Comparisons with Some Existing Works.** We use the following notations (and some of the analysis from [7]) to compare our algorithm with some of the most notable check pointing algorithms [1], [6], and [7]. The analytical comparison is given in Table 1. In this Table:

$C_{air}$ is average cost of sending a message from one process to another process;
$C_{broad}$ is cost of broadcasting a message to all processes; Note that we assume IP broadcasting.
$n_{min}$ is the number of processes that need to take checkpoints.
n is the total number of processes in the system;
$n_{dep}$ is the average number of processes on which a process depends;
$T_{ch}$ is the check pointing time;

**Table 1.** System Performance

| Algorithm | Blocking time | Messages | Distributed |
|-----------|---------------|----------|-------------|
| Alg. [1]  | $n_{min} * T_{ch}$ | $3 * n_{min} * n_{dep} * C_{air}$ | Yes |
| Alg. [6]  | 0 | $2 * C_{broad} + n * C_{air}$ | No |
| Alg. [7]  | 0 | $\approx 2 * n_{min} * C_{air} + min(n_{min} * C_{air}, C_{broad})$ | Yes |
| Our Alg.  | 0 | $C_{broad}$ | Yes |

Fig. 2 illustrates how the number of control messages (system messages) sent and received by processes is affected by the increase in the number of the processes in the distributed system (cluster). In Fig. 2, the $n_{dep}$ factor is considered being 5% of the total number of processes in the system and $C_{broad}$ is equal to $n*C_{air}$. We observe that the number of control messages does increase in our approach with the number of processes, but it stays smaller compared to other approaches when the number of the processes is higher than 7 (which is the case most of the time).

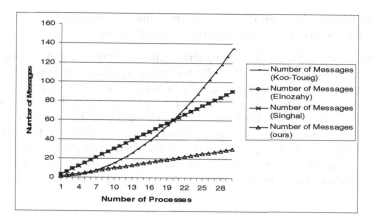

**Fig. 2.** Number of messages vs. number of processes for four different approaches

# 4 Recovery Scheme

Our recovery approach is independent of the number of processes that may fail concurrently. In order to identify lost messages in the event of a failure, we assume that for every cluster all intra and inter cluster messages are routed through the initiator process (s) on their way to their respective destinations. Also, in each cluster, say $C^K$, the messages sent to the $i^{th}$ process $P_i^K$ in the cluster are logged at its initiator process $P^K$ according to the order of their arrival at the initiator. The message log for $P_i^K$ is denoted as MESG-LOG$_i^K$.

## 4.1 Algorithm Recovery

The following recovery algorithm is executed simultaneously in all clusters. It works for any number of concurrent failures.

For each cluster $C^K$

At each process $P_i^K$ ($\in C^K$):

$P_i^K$ sends its SEQ$_{i(max)}$ to $P^K$;

At the initiator process $P^K$:

if    SSN$_{i(max)}$ > SEQ$_{i(max)}$

$P^K$ replays to $P_i^K$ the messages with sequence numbers from SEQ$_{i(max)}$ + 1 to SSN$_{i(max)}$;
// Lost messages are resent to $P_i^K$ following their total order
$P_i^K$ restarts computation;

else  $P_i^K$ restarts computation;
// no lost message to $P_i^K$ exists

**Theorem 2.** Algorithm Non-blocking together with the recovery scheme results in correct computation of the underlying distributed application.

**Proof:** According to the check pointing algorithm and Theorem 1 there does not exist any orphan message with respect to the recent checkpoints of the processes in the cluster federation. Also, in each cluster $C^K$, its initiator process $P^K$ identifies the lost messages, if any, with respect to the recent local checkpoints of the processes in the cluster and the recovery approach ensures through the use of the secondary sequence numbers that the lost messages are resent following their total order to the appropriate destinations in the cluster after the system restarts. Therefore there does not exist any orphan or lost message with respect to the recent checkpoints of the processes in the cluster federation. Hence the correctness of the underlying distributed computation is ensured.                                                                                      ●

### 4.2  Performance

The following are the salient features of our approach. First of all, processes restart from their respective recent checkpoints; that is there is no further rollback (i.e. domino effect free recovery). It also means that processes save only their recent checkpoints replacing their previous ones. Second, the choice of the value of the common check pointing interval T enables to use as little information related to the lost messages as possible for consistent operation after the system restarts. Third, our work is independent of, if it is a single failure or concurrent failures. Fourth, the recovery approach needs just one control message from each of the processes of a cluster, which carries the $SEQ_{(max)}$. Therefore it needs only n control messages for an n-process cluster and so the message complexity is $O(n)$ in each cluster. Besides, it takes care of both orphan and lost messages. Finally, the recovery scheme is executed simultaneously by all clusters in the cluster federation.

### 4.3  Comparison

Since a cluster is nothing but an individual distributed system, so first we compare the proposed recovery scheme used in each cluster with some noted recovery algorithms existing in the area of distributed computing.

Comparison with noted recovery approaches in distributed systems: In [5] the message overhead is $O(F)$, where F is the number of recovery lines established, where as in our work it is absent. Note that by 'message overhead' it is meant the size of the control information that is piggybacked with each application message which are exchanged during normal computation. Another important difference is that the work in [5] will establish a recovery line for each failure and then establish a consistent recovery line for the distributed system after the occurrence of concurrent failures. It is not needed in our work, because in our work it does not depend on if it is a single failure or concurrent failures; our recovery line always consists of the recent checkpoints of the individual processes of the system independent of single or concurrent failures. In the classical work reported in [8] there is always an extra control message for each application message, i.e. it requires receive sequence number (RSN) and acknowledgement messages in addition to the application message. We don't require it. Besides, we handle both single and concurrent failures where as it is only single failures

**Table 2.** Brief Summary of Comparisons

| Algorithm | Required Message ordering | Maximum rollbacks Per failure | Message Overhead | Message Complexity | Number of concurrent Failures |
|-----------|--------------------------|-------------------------------|------------------|--------------------|-------------------------------|
| [5] | None | 1 | $O(F)$ | $O(n^2)$ | n |
| [8] | None | 1 | $O(1)$ | $O(n)$ | 1 |
| [11] | None | 1 | $O(1)$ | $O(n^2)$ | n |
| [9] | None | 1 | $O(n)$ | $O(n^2)$ | n |
| Our Alg. | None | DEF | None | $O(n)$ | n |

in [8]. Below in Table 2 we state a brief summery of comparisons of some important features of the different check pointing / recovery approaches. Note that 'DEF' in the 3rd column denotes 'domino effect free'. In the proposed solution of [9], fault-tolerant vector clock has been used to track causal dependencies in spite of failures. In order to determine a consistent state after failure, it uses checkpointing along with a history mechanism that helps to detect orphan and obsolete messages. In [11], an optimistic recovery algorithm has been proposed that uses $O(n^2)$ messages in arbitrary networks. Each application message is appended with information of size $O(1)$.

Comparisons with recovery approaches in cluster federation: We will now compare our approach with some existing works that deal with recovery in cluster federations. The work in [2] has considered a very restricted architecture in which multiple coordinated checkpointing subsystems are connected with a single independent checkpointing subsystem and the multiple coordinated subsystems can not communicate directly with each other; rather they do it via the independent subsystem. The assumed restricted architecture is the main short coming of this work. In the proposed solution of [3], whenever a cluster fails, it broadcasts an alert message after recovering. Each time there is a rollback, the rolled back cluster further broadcasts the alert message triggering the next iteration of the algorithm. The algorithm terminates when there is no more any alert message. The main drawbacks of the algorithm are: it suffers from domino effect; if all clusters have to roll back except the failed cluster, then it may result in a message storm of the alert messages; it does not consider lost messages and concurrent failures. We have none of these drawbacks. The work in [13] considers communication-induced check pointing scheme. Although it does not suffer from any message storm unlike in [3] and it has a better message complexity than in [3], however, it also suffers from domino effect and it considers only single failures and orphan messages. We don't have any such drawback. The work in [14] offers advantages similar to ours. However, its message complexity is $O(N^2)$, where N is the total number of processes in the cluster federation; where as in our work it is $O(N)$ because the message complexity in an n-process cluster is just $O(n)$. Also in [14] authors have used quite complex data structures, for example, each process maintains two vectors of size equal to the number of clusters to handle inter cluster lost messages. Also to handle intra cluster lost messages each process in a cluster maintains two more vectors of size equal to the number of processes inside the cluster. In our work each process maintains just one simple data structure SEQ(max) to save the maximum SSN. In Table 3 we have summarized the comparisons.

**Table 3.** Comparison Summary. $N$ = Number of processes in the cluster federation, $N_1$ = Number of clusters in the cluster federation, and $K$ = Number of iterations of the recovery algorithm.

| Criteria | Our Approach | Alg [14] | Alg [3] | Alg [13] |
|---|---|---|---|---|
| Architecture Dependent | Yes | No | No | No |
| Domino – Effect Free | Yes | Yes | No | No |
| Concurrent Failures | Yes | Yes | No | No |
| Inter – Cluster Lost Messages | Yes | Yes | No | No |
| No. of checkpoints / process | 1 | 1 | >> 1 | >> 1 |
| Message complexity | $O(N)$ | $O(N^2)$ | $O(KN_1)$ | $O(KN_1^2)$ |

## 5 Conclusion

In this work, we have proposed a single phase non-blocking check pointing approach free from any synchronization delay and domino effect. The proposed value of the common check pointing interval T enables to use as little information related to the lost messages as possible for consistent operation. Also, it is independent of the number of processes that may fail concurrently. The message complexity of the check pointing algorithm as well as the recovery approach is just $O(n)$ for an n process cluster. Both the check pointing and recovery schemes are executed simultaneously in all clusters. The proposed schemes are independent of the effect of any clock drift on the respective sequence numbers of the recent checkpoints of the processes, Finally, it should be noted that since existing tools are not sufficient to implement the algorithm, a large amount of additional work is required for its implementation.

## References

1. Koo, R., Toueg, S.: Checkpointing and Rollback-Recovery for Distributed Systems. IEEE Trans. Software Engineering, SE-13(1) 1, 23–31 (1987)
2. Cao, J., Chen, Y., Zhang, K., He, Y.: Checkpointing in Hybrid Distributed Systems. In: Proceedings of the 7th International Symposium on Parallel Architectures, Algorithms and Networks (ISPAN 2004), Hong Kong, China, pp. 136–141 (2004)
3. Monnet, S., Morin, C., Badrinath, R.: Hybrid Checkpointing for Parallel Applications in cluster Federations. In: Proceedings of the 4th IEEE/ACM International Symposium on Cluster Computing and the Grid, Chicago, IL, USA, pp. 773–782 (2004)
4. Gupta, B., Rahimi, S., Liu, Z.: A Novel Low-Overhead Roll-Forward Recovery Scheme for Distributed Systems. IET Computers and Digital Techniques 1(4), 397–404 (2007)
5. Manivannan, D., Singhal, M.: Asynchronous Recovery without using vector timestamps. Journal of Parallel and Distributed Computing 62, 1695–1728 (2002)
6. Elnozahy, E.N., Johnson, D.B., Zwaenepoel, W.: The Performance of Consistent Check pointing. In: Proceedings of the 11th Symp. Reliable Distributed Systems, pp. 86–95 (1992)
7. Cao, G., Singhal, M.: Mutable Checkpoints. A New Checkpointing Approach for Mobile Computing Systems. IEEE Transactions on Parallel and Distributed Systems 12(2), 157–172 (2001)

8. Johnson, D.B., Zwaenepoel, W.: Sender-Based Message Logging. In: Proceedings of the 17th Fault-Tolerant Computing Symposium, Pittsburgh, pp. 14–19 (1987)
9. Damini, O.P., Garg, V.K.: How to Recover Efficiently and Asynchronously When Optimism Fails. In: Proceedings of the 16th International Conference on Distributed Computing Systems, pp. 108–115 (1996)
10. Venkatesan, S., Juang, T., Alagar, S.: Optimistic Crash Recovery Without Changing Application Messages. IEEE Trans. Parallel and Distributed Systems 8(3), 263–271 (1997)
11. Juang, T., Venkatesan, S.: Efficient Algorithm for Crash Recovery in Distributed Systems. In: Proceedings of the 10th Conference on Foundations on Software Technology and Theoretical Computer Science, pp. 349–361 (1990)
12. Gupta, B., Rahimi, S., Rias, R.A., Bangalore, G.: A Low-Overhead Non-Blocking Checkpointing Algorithm for Mobile Computing Environment. In: Chung, Y.-C., Moreira, J.E. (eds.) GPC 2006. LNCS, vol. 3947, pp. 597–608. Springer, Heidelberg (2006)
13. Gupta, B., Rahimi, S., Ahmad, R., Chirra, R.: A Novel Recovery approach for Cluster Federations. In: Cérin, C., Li, K.-C. (eds.) GPC 2007. LNCS, vol. 4459, pp. 519–530. Springer, Heidelberg (2007)
14. Gupta, B., Rahimi, S., Allam, V., Jupally, V.: Domino-Effect Free Crash Recovery for Concurrent Failures in Cluster Federation. In: Wu, S., Yang, L.T., Xu, T.L. (eds.) GPC 2008. LNCS, vol. 5036, pp. 4–17. Springer, Heidelberg (2008)
15. Qi, X., Parmer, G., West, R.: An Efficient End-Host Architecture for Cluster Communication. In: Proceedings of the 2004 IEEE Intl. Conf. on Cluster Computing, San Diego, California, pp. 83–92 (2004)
16. Shrivastava, S.K., Mancini, L.V., Randell, B.: The Duality of Fault- Tolerant System Structures. Software-Practice and Experience 23(7), 73–798 (1993)
17. Alvisi, L., Marzullo, K.: Message Logging: Pessimistic, Optimistic, and Causal. In: Proc. 15th IEEE Int. Conf. on Distributed Computing Systems, pp. 229–236 (1995)

# JACEP2P-V2: A Fully Decentralized and Fault Tolerant Environment for Executing Parallel Iterative Asynchronous Applications on Volatile Distributed Architectures

Jean-Claude Charr, Raphaël Couturier, and David Laiymani

Laboratory of computer sciences, University of Franche-Comté (LIFC)
IUT de Belfort-Montbéliard, Rue Engel Gros, BP 527, 90016 Belfort, France
Tel: +33-3-84587781
{jean-claude.charr,raphael.couturier,david.laiymani}@univ-fcomte.fr

**Abstract.** This article presents JACEP2P-V2, a Java environment dedicated to designing parallel iterative asynchronous algorithms (with direct communications between nodes) and executing them on global computing architectures or distributed clusters composed by a large number of volatile heterogeneous distant computing nodes. This platform is fault tolerant, multi-threaded and completely decentralized. In this paper, we describe the different components of JACEP2P-V2 and the various mechanisms used for scalability and fault tolerance purposes. We also evaluate the performance of this platform and we compare it to JACEP2P by implementing a parallel iterative asynchronous application and by executing it on a volatile distributed architecture using both platforms.

**Keywords:** Decentralized global Convergence, Peer-to-Peer architectures, Distributed clusters, Parallel iterative asynchronous algorithms.

## 1 Introduction

The simulation of natural and nuclear reactions (like climate change or nuclear fusion) requires solving very large and complex numerical problems and necessitates computing very large data in order to obtain precise and reliable results. These problems cannot be solved using a single computing unit because most of the time, the numerical problems are so huge that a single computing unit does not have enough memory nor computing power to store the application and to solve it. These problems could only be solved using simultaneously many computing resources. With the development of new reliable network equipments and the emergence of cheap and fast desktops, scientists are able nowadays to create distributed architectures using only these simple low cost devices. Most of the time, these distributed architectures tends to replace equally powerful but more expensive supercomputers. In numerical computing we can distinguish three kinds of distributed architectures:

N. Abdennadher and D. Petcu (Eds.): GPC 2009, LNCS 5529, pp. 446–458, 2009.

1. **Local clusters** are composed of similar workstations connected via a local network with low latency and large bandwidth.
2. **Distributed clusters** are composed of many distant clusters with heterogeneous computing units that are connected via heterogeneous networks with high latency and large bandwidth.
3. **Global computing architectures** are mainly composed of public unused heterogeneous workstations connected to Internet. These architectures offer free and unlimited computing power but suffer from the volatility of the nodes and from the slowness of communications.

Most of the time, the local cluster architecture does not have enough computing power to solve very large numerical problems. Therefore, in this paper, we are only interested in distributed clusters and global computing architectures. Using one of these parallel architectures, developers have to parallelize the method that solves the numerical problem in order to execute a subsystem of the problem on each computing unit. However, to use these architectures, the developer needs to manage carefully the exchange of data between the different computing units, especially when using high latency networks with heterogeneous and volatile nodes.

There are two classes of methods to solve numerical problems:

- **Direct methods** give the exact solution of a numerical problem after executing a finite number of operations. However, they are not really suited to distributed clusters and global computing architectures because they require several synchronizations.
- **Iterative methods** iterate many times the same block of instructions until obtaining a good approximation of the solution (e.g., Jacobi or Conjugate Gradient algorithms [1]). An iterative method converges when the "residual vector" (there is many methods to evaluate the value of the residue, for example $Residue = max_i(|x_i^{k+1} - x_i^k|)$ where $x_i^k$ denotes the value of the component $i$ at iteration $k$) is inferior to the precision ($\epsilon$) requested by the user. Iterative methods are well adapted for very large problems.

Since we would like to solve very large numerical problems, in the rest of this paper we only focus on iterative methods. Now, from a parallel point of view, there are two models of parallel iterative algorithms:

- **The synchronous iteration model.** Using this model, as shown in figure 1, after each iteration (represented by a filled rectangle in the figure), a node sends its dependencies to its neighbors and waits for the reception of all the dependency messages from all its neighbors. Then all the nodes must synchronize to test if the system has globally converged. This results in large periods of idle time (represented by white spaces between the rectangles). These synchronizations can drastically penalize the overall performances in the case of large scale heterogeneous platforms. Moreover, if a dependency message is lost, the receiver will wait forever for that message and the application will be blocked. In the same way, if a computing node is dead,

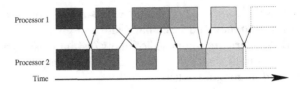

**Fig. 1.** Two processors using the synchronous iteration model

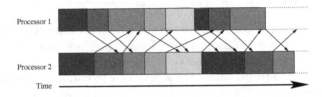

**Fig. 2.** Two processors using the asynchronous iteration model

all the rest of the nodes will be blocked until the dead node is replaced. In conclusion, this model is not well suited for large scale volatile computing environments.

- **The asynchronous iteration model** [2]. Using this model, as shown in figure 2, after each iteration, a computing node sends its dependencies to its neighbors and begins the next iteration using the last received dependency data. The node does not have to wait for the reception of the dependencies messages from its neighbors, consequently, there is no idle time anymore (no white spaces between iterations). The sending and the receiving mechanisms are asynchronous and the computing nodes tolerate the loss of data messages. Even if a node dies, the rest of the nodes can continue the computation process using the last dependency message sent by the dead node. In conclusion, the asynchronous iteration model is well adapted for volatile environments like peer-to-peer architectures or distributed clusters.

To tackle the specificities of the asynchronous iteration model on distributed clusters or global computing architectures, we have developed JACEP2P-V2, a new and improved version of JACEP2P [3]. JACEP2P-V2 is a fully decentralized and fault tolerant platform dedicated to designing and executing parallel iterative asynchronous algorithms on volatile architectures. The aim of this paper is to present the design and the features of this new platform.

The rest of this paper is organized as follows: in the next section we present some existing platforms related to our work. These platforms are briefly described and the differences between our work and these platforms are emphasized. In the third section, we present JACEP2P's architecture and its limits. Then, we introduce JACEP2P-V2 and we describe in details its mechanisms and functionalities. In the fourth section, we present the experiments conducted on the Grid5000[4] testbed using JACEP2P-V2 to solve a numerical problem. Finally, we end this paper with a conclusion and some perspectives.

## 2   Related Work

Recently, many middlewares for distributed clusters and global computing platforms have been developed. However, most of them are not well adapted for large numerical computing. Here are some examples:

- **Seti@home [5]:** The amazing success that this platform has achieved, helped the creation of generalized environments like Xtrem Web [6] and Boinc [7]. They are independent of the application and fault tolerant. The user creates a parallel application and executes it using the "workers". However, in these platforms, the clients cannot communicate with each others. So they cannot execute a parallel computing application with dependencies between nodes.
- **JXTA [8]:** It is an open-source project, composed of a set of peer-to-peer protocols that allows any connected device (cell phone to PDA, PC to server) on the network to communicate and collaborate. However, JXTA is a low level platform and offers a lot of general functionalities that are not well adapted for executing complex computing applications.
- **ProActive [9]:** It is an Open Source Java library for parallel, distributed, and multi-threaded computing. Although this environment provides direct communications between nodes using the RMI technology, when two nodes communicate, they must be synchronized (even if the concept of future objects exists). Moreover ProActive uses a global checkpointing mechanism [10] that requires synchronizing all the nodes in case of failures. In consequence, the asynchronous iteration model cannot simply be used on this platform.
- **JACE [11]:** "Java Asynchronous Computation Environment" is a multi-thre- aded Java based library designed to build asynchronous iterative algorithms and execute them in a Grid environment. In JACE, two nodes exchange data (synchronously or asynchronously) using either Sockets, RMI or NIO (New Input/Output). However, this platform is not fault tolerant, so it cannot be used in large scale volatile environments.

## 3   JACEP2P-V2

### 3.1   JACEP2P

JACEP2P is a distributed platform implemented using the Java programming language and dedicated to developing and executing parallel iterative asynchronous applications. JACEP2P executes parallel iterative asynchronous applications with dependencies between computing nodes. On the other hand, JACEP2P is fault tolerant which allows it to execute parallel applications over volatile environments and even for stable environments like local clusters and grids, it offers a safer and crash free platform.

**JACEP2P's architecture.** Figure 3, presents the architecture of JACEP2P and the various components that form the platform:

– The first entity is the "super-node" (represented by a big circle in figure 3). Each super-node stores in its register the identifiers (IP address) of all the computing nodes that are connected to it and are not executing an application. The super-node regularly receives heartbeat messages (represented by doted lines in figure 3) from the computing nodes connected to it. If the super-node does not receive a heartbeat message from a computing node included in its register for a given period of time, it declares that this computing node is dead and deletes its identifier from the register.

– The second entity is the "spawner" (represented by a square in figure 3). When a user wants to execute a parallel application, he or she launches a spawner with the required parameters which contacts a super-node to reserve the required computing nodes. The super-node reserves the demanded daemons (see next paragraph) which are removed from the super-node's register and returns to the spawner a register containing the identifiers of the reserved computing nodes. When the spawner receives the register, it creates a task for each computing node and starts the execution of the tasks on the respective daemons. The spawner has to send its register to all the computing nodes in order for them to be able to communicate with each others. Moreover, the spawner is responsible for detecting the disconnection of a computing node. Indeed, when the computing nodes are reserved by the spawner, they start sending their heartbeat messages to the spawner. If the spawner detects that a computing node has not sent to it a heartbeat message for a while, it declares that this computing node is dead. Then, it fetches a new one from the super-node in order to replace the dead one. The spawner initializes the new daemon, which retrieves the last backup of the dead node and continues the computing task from that checkpoint. Finally, the spawner is also responsible for detecting the global convergence of the parallel iterative application. When a subsystem converges locally, the computing node executing it sends a convergence message to the spawner. If the spawner receives a convergence message from all the computing nodes, it declares that the parallel iterative application has globally converged.

– The third entity is the "daemon" or the computing node (represented in figure 3 by a hashed small circle if it is free and by a white small circle if it is executing an application). Once launched, it connects to a super-node and

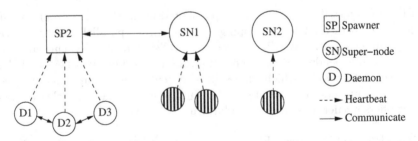

**Fig. 3.** JACEP2P's architecture and the different components

waits for a task to execute. During the execution of the parallel application, the daemons can communicate with each others and they regularly save their state on their neighbors. At the end of a task, the daemons reconnect to the super-node.

To be able to execute asynchronous iterative applications, JACEP2P has an asynchronous messaging mechanism (for more details interested readers can refer to [3]) and to resist to daemons' failures, it implements a distributed backup mechanism called the uncoordinated distributed transparent checkpointing [12]. This method allows daemons to save their data on neighboring daemons without any user intervention. The asynchronous nature of the application allows two daemons to execute two different iterations, thus each daemon saves its status without synchronizing with other daemons. This decentralized procedure allows the platform to be very scalable, with no weak points and does not require a secure and stable station for backups. Moreover, if a daemon dies, the other computing nodes continue their tasks and they are not affected by this failure.

**JACEP2P's limitations.** In [13], the experiments' results proved that the first version of JACEP2P performs very well and presents a relatively small overhead. Nevertheless, this version has some important limits:

- JACEP2P is not fully fault tolerant. Indeed, in this version, spawners' crashes are not tolerated. Moreover, while executing the global convergence process, the platform does not resist well to the disconnection of daemons.
- JACEP2P has a centralized failure detection. The spawner receives heartbeat messages from all the daemons and detects if a daemon is dead. If the application is being executed by a large number of daemons, the spawner will be overloaded with heartbeat messages. This will delay the detection of a dead daemon and could even lead to a false crash detection. Moreover, if many daemons die successively and there is only one spawner to handle the dead daemons, then the spawner will take a lot of time to replace them. This may reduce the performance of the platform.
- JACEP2P has a centralized global convergence detection mechanism which is not well adapted for executing asynchronous parallel iterative algorithms on volatile architectures. The daemons executing such applications do not receive dependencies messages from their neighbors at each iteration. This may lead to a false local convergence and thus result to false global convergence detection. Furthermore, the spawner could be overloaded by convergence messages, if many daemons converge locally at the same time.
- JACEP2P has many centralized mechanisms like launching the application, detecting the global convergence and detecting the dead nodes. These centralizations limit the scalability of JACEP2P.
- In JACEP2P, each daemon receives the whole register which contains the identifiers of all the daemons executing the application. If a daemon crashes and is replaced by a new one, the spawner has to notify the modifications to all the daemons in order to update their registers. This could overload the spawner and increase the congestion of messages in the network.

To remedy these problems we present JACEP2P-V2 a fully decentralized and fault tolerant platform. In the next subsection, we will describe in details the functionalities and characteristics of the new platform.

## 3.2   JACEP2P-V2's Architecture

Figure 4 shows the architecture of JACEP2P-V2 where we notice that there are two spawners handling the execution of a single application and each group of entities (spawners, daemons and super-nodes) forms a circular network. JACEP2P-V2 has similar entities as JACEP2P but with different functionalities:

- **Super-nodes.** They form a circular network now and store in an equally distributed manner the identifiers of all the computing nodes that are connected to the platform and that are not executing any application. Each super-node has a status table containing the number of connected computing nodes to each super-node and all the super-nodes share a "token" that is passed successively from a super-node to the next one. Once a super-node has the token, it computes the average number of computing nodes connected to a super-node ($avg$) using the status table. If $avg$ is lower than the number of computing nodes connected to it, then it sends the identifiers of the extra computing nodes to the super-nodes that have the number of computing nodes connected to them less than $avg$. If the number of computing nodes connected to it has changed, it broadcasts the information to all the super-nodes in the platform. Finally, it passes the token to the next super node. This distribution reduces the overload of the super-nodes.
- **Spawners.** When a user wants to execute a parallel application that requires $N$ computing nodes, he or she launches a spawner. The spawner contacts a super-node to reserve the $N$ computing nodes plus some extra nodes in order to transform them into spawners. When the spawner receives the register from the super-node, it transforms the extra daemons into spawners and stores the identifiers of the rest of the daemons in its own register. Once

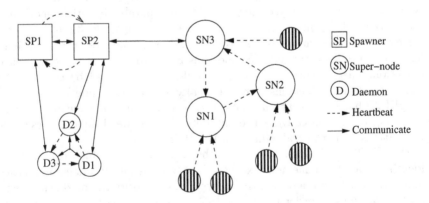

**Fig. 4.** JACEP2P-V2's architecture and different components

the extra nodes are transformed into spawners, they form a circular network and they receive the register containing the identifiers of the computing nodes. Then each spawner becomes responsible for a subgroup of computing nodes, starts the tasks on the computing nodes under its command and sends a specified register to them. So each computing node receives a specified register that only contains the identifiers of the daemons it interacts with and that depends on the application being executed. These specified registers reduce the number of messages sent by the spawners to update the register of the daemons after a daemon crashes because usually a small number of daemons is affected by this crash.

- **Daemons.** Once they begin executing an application they form a circular network which is only used in the failure detection mechanism. Each daemon can communicate directly with the daemons whose identifiers it has in its register.

### 3.3    JACEP2P-V2 Functionalities and Characteristics

After describing quickly the modifications made on the architecture of JACEP2P-V2, in this section we present in details the different new functionalities and characteristics implemented in JACEP2P-V2:

- **Completely decentralized.** JACEP2P-V2 is completely decentralized. In fact, all the tasks are divided between the entities of the same type. For example, a daemon can be connected to any super-node and the group of super nodes shares equally the control of the free daemons connected to the super-node network. The spawners are also decentralized: once a spawner is launched to execute an application, it quickly duplicates itself into several spawners (depending on the number of daemons required to execute the parallel application) by transforming some daemons into spawners. Each spawner becomes responsible for starting the application on a subgroup of daemons and handling the needs of that subgroup. For the computing nodes, each one executes a part of the application and the sum of their work gives the solution of the global problem. This distribution of tasks, allows JACEP2P-V2 to solve very large problems and thus to become very scalable with theoretically no limiting conditions.
- **Completely fault tolerant.** We have implemented many mechanisms to make the three entities that form the core of JACEP2P-V2 fault tolerant. An important concept available for the three entities is the decentralized crash detection mechanism. It enables the neighbors of a node to detect if it is dead or alive. Each group of entities forms a circular network. This organization is needed to apply the decentralized crash detection mechanism we have implemented. Each entity has a "heartbeat thread" that signals regularly to the next node in the circular network that the sender is still alive and another thread, the "scan thread", that tests at each iteration if the previous node in the circular network has recently sent a heartbeat message. If for a given period of time the node does not receive a heartbeat message from

the previous one, the scan thread detects that the previous node is probably dead. Depending on the type of the dead node, the disconnection is handled. In fact, each entity has a restoring mechanism which is also dependent on the saving mechanism used for each type of entity.

- For daemons we use the distributed backup mechanism described before and we have implemented two types of backup in JACEP2P-V2. The first backup contains all the information concerning the state of a node (convergence data) and its computing process (solution vector). This backup is saved each $N$ iterations ($N$ given by the user and usually depends of the length of an iteration) on a different neighbor using the "round-robin" strategy. On the other hand, the second backup only contains the status data. This backup has a smaller size and it is saved when the status of a daemon has changed, especially when it concerns the global convergence detection mechanism. This backup is saved on all the backup neighbors simultaneously. Once a daemon detects that the previous daemon is dead, the daemon signals it to the spawner responsible for it. The spawner contacts a super-node and acquires a new daemon. The new daemon replaces the dead one and retrieves the last status backup and the last data backup. Once it has the backups, it continues the task from that last checkpoint. During all this operation, all the other daemons continue their tasks normally.

- For spawners, we use the duplication mechanism. The spawner is duplicated into many spawners. All the spawners have all the information concerning all the daemons and each one manages only a subgroup of daemons. If a spawner dies, the next spawner detects it (using the same scheme described before). Then, that spawner contacts a super-node, gets a new daemon and transforms it into a spawner. Once it becomes a spawner, it receives the register containing the identifiers of all the daemons executing the application, it identifies its subgroup of daemons, it informs them that it is the new spawner and it is reintegrated into the circular spawner network.

- For super-nodes, there is no saving mechanism, they do not contain very valuable information. When a dead super-node is detected by the next super-node, it is rejected from the circular super-node network. All the daemons that were connected to the dead super-node will reconnect onto another super-node.

- **Multi-threaded.** JACEP2P-V2 is multi-threaded. The computing process is never blocked by the exchange of data messages between daemons. Each functionality (communicating, detecting crashes, saving and computing) has its own thread.

- **Decentralized global convergence detection algorithm:** JACEP2P-V2 has implemented this algorithm to detect efficiently the global convergence of the asynchronous iterative parallel algorithms executed on the platform. It consists of two phases: the detection phase and the verification phase. This algorithm is presented in details in these papers [2,13].

- **Acknowledge mechanism:** JACEP2P-V2 tolerates the loss of data messages when it executes parallel asynchronous iterative algorithms. However, it has to ensure the right reception of the convergence messages by the receivers in order to ensure a coherent system. Therefore, we had to implement an acknowledge mechanism dedicated to the convergence messages. When a computing node sends a convergence message to another one, the receiver handles the received message (this usually changes the state of the receiver) then it saves its new state on its backup neighbors and next it returns an acknowledge message to the sender. Once the sender receives the acknowledge message, it knows that the receiver has received the convergence message and then it saves its state on its backup neighbors so it does not send the convergence message again. On the other hand, if the sender does not receive the acknowledge message, it knows that the message did not reach its destination and that it has to send the convergence message all over again.

## 4   Experiments

In order to evaluate the benefits of the improvements that have been implemented in JACEP2P-V2, we have conducted two sets of experiments on Grid'5000 French national grid. The same experiments were realized using JACEP2P and JACEP2P-V2 in order to compare both platforms. Both sets of experiments were realized on two different architectures. During these tests, both platforms had to execute a parallel iterative application that solves a three dimensional advection-diffusion equations system. This system represents mathematically the transport processes of pollutants, salinity, and so on, combined with their bio-chemical interactions.

### 4.1   Mathematical Description

A system of 3D advection-diffusion-reaction equations has the following form:

$$\frac{\partial c}{\partial t} + A\left(c, a\right) = D\left(c, d\right) + R\left(c, t\right) \tag{1}$$

where $c$ denotes the vector of unknown species concentrations, of length $m$, and the two vectors $A(c, a) = [\mathbf{J}(c)] * a^T$ and $D(c, d) = [\mathbf{J}(c)] * d * \nabla^T$ respectively define the advection and diffusion processes ($\mathbf{J}(c)$ denotes the Jacobian of $c$ with respect to $(x, y, z)$). The local fluid velocities $u$, $v$ and $w$ of the field $a = (u, v, w)$ and the diffusion coefficients matrix $d$ are supposed to be known in advance. A simulation of pollution evolution in shallow seas is obtained if $a$ is provided by a hydro-dynamical model. The chemical species dynamic transport is defined by both advection and diffusion processes, whereas the term $R$ includes interspecies chemical reactions and emissions or absorption from sources. For more details, readers can refer to [14].

**Table 1.** Execution time with 3 random crashes every $n$ seconds

| n | ∞ | 90 | 60 | 30 |
|---|---|---|---|---|
| Execution time for JACEP2P | 522s | 873s | 1003s | 1611s |
| Total number of crashes for JACEP2P | 0 | 30 | 51 | 159 |
| Execution time for JACEP2P-V2 | 495s | 565s | 595s | 744s |
| Total number of crashes for JACEP2P-V2 | 0 | 18 | 28 | 68 |

## 4.2   First Experiment: Local Cluster

In this experiment, we compare JACEP2P to JACEP2P-V2 while executing the same application on a single site. This application solves a system containing 405.224.000 components and that simulates a 90 seconds time interval. 252 bi-processors computing units, located in Orsay, were used to run this application. The computing nodes were equipped with 2 AMD Opteron 246 2.0GHz or 250 2.4GHz processors. To prove that the two platforms are fault tolerant, we used a shell script that randomly kills three computing nodes each $n$ seconds.

The results for this set of experiments are presented in table1. It shows the execution times taken by JACEP2P and JACEP2P-V2 to solve the problem with various frequencies of nodes crashes. It is obvious that JACEP2P-V2 outperforms JACEP2P in each category. We also notice that JACEP2P-V2 is less affected than JACEP2P by the disconnection of computing nodes. Indeed, when the computing nodes disconnect frequently, JACEP2P suffers a lot because of the centralized nature of some of its components. On the other hand, with the JACEP2P-V2's decentralized dead nodes detection, the dead nodes are detected faster by their neighbors and thus they are replaced quickly by new ones to continue their tasks. These mechanisms reduce the influence of the crashes on the performance of JACEP2P-V2 platform.

## 4.3   2nd Experiment: Distributed Clusters

In this second set of experiments, we aimed at simulating a global computing architecture which has the following characteristics: large number of heterogeneous computing units, high latency communications and volatile nodes. So, we used the same number of computing nodes but this time we have chosen them from three distant sites in order to have heterogeneous computing nodes. Moreover, the latency between two nodes from distinct sites is superior to the one between two nodes located on the same site, thus the latency of the communications is also heterogeneous. The computing nodes were selected from the following sites: Nancy where each station is equipped with 2 double cores 1.6 GHz Intel Xeon 5110, Sophia where each station is equipped with 2 processors AMD Opteron 246 2.0GHz and Orsay which is described in the first experiment. We executed the same application as in the first experiment using JACEP2P and JACEP2P-V2. We have also simulated the volatility of the computing nodes by using the same perturbator script. However in this experiment, the script killed one daemon on each site each $n$ seconds. The results for this set of experiments are presented in

**Table 2.** Execution time with one crash every $n$ seconds at each site

| n | ∞ | 90 | 60 | 50 |
|---|---|---|---|---|
| **Execution time for JACEP2P** | 565s | 1438s | 2008s | 2050s |
| **Total number of crashes JACEP2P** | 0 | 48 | 100 | 122 |
| **Execution time for JACEP2P-V2** | 581s | 624s | 632s | 663s |
| **Total number of crashes JACEP2P-V2** | 0 | 19 | 30 | 38 |

table 2. As in the previous experiment, JACEP2P-V2 outperforms JACEP2P, in particular when the environment is highly volatile. Moreover, the crashes overhead is totally acceptable in JACEP2P-V2. These experiments prove that the modifications implemented in JACEP2P improve its performance on volatile architectures that suffer from high latency between computing nodes.

## 5  Conclusion and Perspectives

In this paper we have presented the new version of JACEP2P, called JACEP2P-V2. This parallel platform is dedicated for designing and executing parallel asynchronous iterative applications in volatile environments. This new version is fully fault tolerant which makes it able to resist the failure of any node in the platform, especially the ones executing an application. We have also implemented a decentralized mechanism for detecting dead nodes in order to replace them. We also conducted two sets of experiments using two different architectures. In all these tests JACEP2P-V2 outperformed JACEP2P.

In the near future, we want to test JACEP2P-V2 using more computing units. We also would like to test it on a real global computing architecture, using unused public computing units connected via Internet. Finally, we want to implement many types of iterative asynchronous applications on JACEP2P-V2 to show the benefits of this platform and its general utility.

## References

1. Saad, Y.: Iterative Methods for Sparse Linear Systems. PWS publishing (1996)
2. Bahi, J., Contassot-Vivier, S., Couturier, R.: Parallel Iterative Algorithms: from sequential to grid computing. Numerical Analysis & Scientific Computating, vol. 1. Chapman & Hall/CRC, Boca Raton (2007)
3. Bahi, J., Couturier, R., Vuillemin, P.: JACEP2P: an environment for asynchronous computations on peer-to-peer networks. In: Cluster 2006, pp. 1–10 (2006)
4. grid 5000, http://grid5000.fr
5. Seti@home, http://www.setiathome.berkley.edu/
6. Cappello, F., Djilali, S., Fedak, G., Herault, T., Magniette, F., Néri, V., Lodygensky, O.: Computing on large-scale distributed systems: XtremWeb architecture, programming models, security, tests and convergence with grid. Future Generation Computer Systems 21(3), 417–437 (2005)
7. BOINC, http://www.boinc.berkley.edu/
8. JXTA, http://www.jxta.org/

9. ProActive, http://www.proactive.inria.fr/
10. Cao, G., Singhal, M.: On coordinated checkpointing in distributed systems. IEEE Transactions on PDS-9 (12), 1213–1225 (1998)
11. Bahi, J., Domas, S., Mazouzi, K.: Jace: a java environment for distributed asynchronous iterative computations. In: PDP 2004, Spain, February 2004, pp. 350–357 (2004)
12. Plank, J.S., Beck, M., Kingsley, G., Li, K.: Libckpt: Transparent checkpointing under UNIX. In: USENIX Winter, pp. 213–224 (1995)
13. Charr, J.C., Couturier, R., Laiymani, D.: A decentralized convergence detection algorithm for asynchronous iterative algorithms in volatile environments (submitted, 2008)
14. Bahi, J., Couturier, R., Mazouzi, K., Salomon, M.: Synchronous and asynchronous solution of a 3D transport model in a grid computing environment. Applied Mathematical Modelling 30(7), 616–628 (2006)

# Performance Evaluation of Scheduling Mechanism with Checkpoint Sharing and Task Duplication in P2P-Based PC Grid Computing*

Joon-Min Gil[1], Ui-Sung Song[2], and Heon-Chang Yu[3]

[1] Dept. of Computer Science Education, Catholic University of Dague
330 Geumnak, Hayang-eup, Gyeongsan-si, Gyeongbuk 712-701, Korea
jmgil@cu.ac.kr
[2] Dept. of Computer Science Education, Busan National University of Education
37 Gyodae-ro, Yeonje-gu, Busan 611-736, Korea
ussong@bnue.ac.kr
[3] Dept. of Computer Science Education, Korea University
5-1 Anam-dong, Sungbuk-gu, Seoul 136-701, Korea
yuhc@comedu.korea.ac.kr

**Abstract.** An important issue in the PC grid computing environment that is characterized by volatility and heterogeneity is the minimization of execution time for all tasks. This paper proposes a scheduling mechanism to reduce such execution time by means of both checkpoint sharing and task duplication under a peer-to-peer (P2P) architecture. In the mechanism, the checkpoint executed by an individual peer (*i.e.*, a desktop PC) is used as an intermediate result and executed in other peers via its duplication and transmission. As a result, as the checkpoint is close to a final result, the reduction of execution time for each task becomes higher. Ultimately, turnaround time can be reduced. Moreover, an analytical model with an embedded Markov chain is presented to evaluate the transmission cost and execution time of our scheduling mechanism. The performance of our scheduling mechanism is also compared with that of the existing mechanism operating on client-server architecture. The analytical results show that our scheduling mechanism is superior to the existing mechanism with respect to the reduction of execution time.

**Keywords:** P2P-based PC Grid Computing, Checkpoint Sharing, Task Duplication, Embedded Markov Chain.

## 1 Introduction

One performance factor of a PC grid computing environment is the minimization of the execution time of all tasks [1]. Unexpected failures can be considered

---

* This work was supported by the Korea Research Foundation Grant funded by the Korean Government (KRF-2008-331-D0447).

N. Abdennadher and D. Petcu (Eds.): GPC 2009, LNCS 5529, pp. 459–470, 2009.

degrading factors in the minimization of the execution time, which can be partially addressed with the use of a checkpointing method in application level. Another method of minimizing the execution time is to share all the checkpoints performed on each PC [5]. The sharing of checkpoints is a method of reusing the checkpoint, which was recently performed on a local PC, in other PCs; i.e., the intermediate result of a task is relayed to other PCs so that task execution from the last checkpoint position would be restated. Ultimately, the purpose of this method is to reduce the execution time, compared to the execution of each task from the beginning.

Most PC grid computing systems, however, has used a client-server model as their main architecture [2,4,6]. Although this model is simple in architecture as well as in control of resources and tasks, it concentrates all functions on the central server, which heightens the bottleneck phenomenon in the server. Moreover, in the client-server model, checkpoint sharing is based on a method of storing checkpoints into a central stable storage [5]. However, the checkpoints of all PCs are also concentrated on the central stable storage, which again brings about the bottleneck phenomenon in the central stable storage. To overcome this shortcomings of the client-server model in a PC grid computing environment, this paper utilizes the peer-to-peer (P2P) model [3] as a fundamental architecture, which has been widely used in Internet services, such as file sharing or content delivery. Compared to the client-server model that completely depends on the central server, the P2P-based PC grid computing environment used in this paper is based on a three-layered structure (central server, peer groups, and peers). In this structure, the central server controls only peer groups, and a representative peer in a peer group controls the peers that belong to the corresponding group so as to disperse the functions of the central server and ultimately, to reduce the bottleneck phenomenon in the central server.

To cope with peer failures in a P2P-based PC grid computing environment, each peer performs checkpointing on its local disk at a periodic cycle. The intermediate result, which is stored in a peer as a checkpoint, is transmitted to another peer requesting a task. Then the peer continuously executes the intermediate result beginning from the last checkpoint position. This checkpoint sharing leads to the reduction of the execution time. In order to deal with peer volatility and heterogeneity, this paper uses a task duplication method along with the checkpoint sharing method; when a peer requests a task, an intermediate result with the last checkpoint among replicas for the task is allocated to the peer. The requesting peer successively executes the task, utilizing the intermediate result. Therefore, it is expected that our scheduling mechanism will more significantly reduce the execution time than the existing mechanism, where the duplicated tasks are executed from the beginning.

Eventually, this paper aims to devise a scheduling mechanism of reducing execution time per task using checkpoint sharing and task duplication methods in a P2P-based PC grid computing computing environment, and ultimately, of providing large-scale applications with fast turnaround time. Contrary to the existing mechanism which is based on a client-server model, our scheduling mechanism performs checkpoint sharing and task duplication on the basis of a P2P architecture. Thus, our mechanism can highly distribute the load of central server. As for checkpoint sharing, it does not need any central storage. Instead, checkpoints in each peer are autonomously transmitted to other peers by the mediation of a specific peer in a peer group. To show the superiority of our scheduling mechanism, this paper presents a mathematical analysis model with an embedded Markov chain. Based on the model, we compare our mechanism with the existing one, in terms of message/data transmission cost and the reduction of execution time.

The rest of this paper is organized as follows: In Section 2, we provide a system model for a P2P-based PC grid computing environment. This section also describe checkpoint sharing and task duplication processes in our system model. Section 3 presents an analytical model for our scheduling mechanism and analyzes the performance of our scheduling mechanism from the viewpoint of message/data transmission cost and the reduction of execution time. Section 4 provides the performance evaluation of our scheduling mechanism. Finally, the conclusion of this paper is given in Section 5.

# 2   P2P-Based PC Grid Computing Environment

## 2.1   System Model

Fig. 1 shows a system model for the P2P-based PC grid computing environment that this paper assumes. This system model is based on the three-layered structure that consists of a central server, peer groups, and peers. The central server operates minimum functions, such as peer group management, peer authentication management, and metadata management for tasks and peers, instead of all kinds of managements for peers and tasks. The peer groups (PGs) consist of peers with identical characteristics under certain conditions. A unique peer within a peer group becomes a representative peer (RP) of the peer group, and the other peers become member peers (MPs) of the peer group.

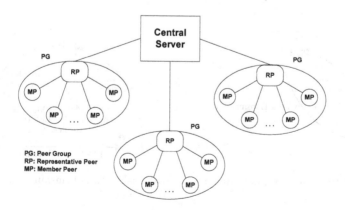

**Fig. 1.** System Model

Generally, a large-scale application in a PC grid computing environment is divided into hundreds and millions of unit tasks, each of them should be suitable to be executed in a peer (or a PC). These unit tasks are also structured in such a way that there is no dependency among unit tasks [1].

In our system model, an RP keeps a list of tasks, $W_g = \{w_1, w_2, \cdots, w_m, \cdots, w_M\}$, to manage the tasks to be allocated to the MPs that belong to its PG. Here, $g$ is an index for distinguishing a PG, and $M$ is the number of tasks. An element of the list, $w_m$, has the following data structure: $w_m = \{w_{id}, w_d, w_c\}$ $(1 \leq m \leq M)$, where $w_{id}$ is a unique identifier for a task. For task duplication, each task $w_m$ should recognize how many replicas are being executed on different MPs. The $w_m$ keeps the current number of replicas $w_d$ which has one of the following values: $\{0, 1, \cdots, D\}$, where $D$ is the maximum number of duplications. The $w_c$ represents the largest number of checkpoints among those of the duplicated tasks. This information is also used for the RP to duplicate the intermediate result that has the largest number of checkpoints when an identical task is being duplicated.

Meanwhile, a member peer in a PG, $MP_l$, has the following data structure: $MP_l = \{MP_{id}, PG_g, w_{id}, MP_c\}$, where $MP_{id}$ and $PG_g$ are the identifier of the MP and that of the PG to which $MP_{id}$ belongs, respectively; $w_{id}$ is the identifier of the task allocated from the RP; and $MP_c$ represents the checkpoint status of the task, which has one of the following values: $\{0, 1, \cdots, C\}$, where $C$ represents the maximum number of checkpoints. If $MP_c = 0$, it means the status that has not yet taken a checkpoint; i.e., it means either a stand-by status or a status of having executed a task just before being taken the first checkpoint. If $MP_c$ has a value of $c$ $(1 \leq c < C)$, it means the status that has taken the $c$th checkpoint and executed a task just before being taken the $(c+1)$th checkpoint. If $MP_c = C$, it means task execution has ended.

## 2.2   Checkpointing and Task Duplication

Figs. 2 and 3 show the duplication process and the checkpointing process between RP and MP, respectively. The process of task duplication (Fig. 2) is as follows:

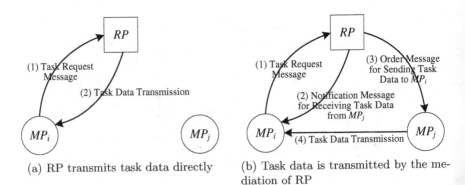

(a) RP transmits task data directly

(b) Task data is transmitted by the mediation of RP

**Fig. 2.** Duplication Process between RP and MP

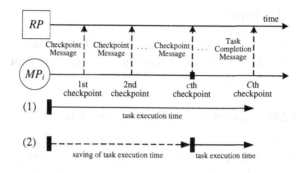

**Fig. 3.** Checkpointing Process Between RP and MP

First, if $MP_i$ sends a task request message to $RP$ [(1) in Fig. 2 (a) and (b)], $RP$ searches for the task with the smallest number of duplications from the task list it keeps. Assume that this task is $w_m$. By examining the $w_d$ value of $w_m$, $RP$ can know how many member peers execute $w_m$ in duplication. If $w_d$ is 0, it means $w_m$ has not been duplicated yet, and therefore, $RP$ directly transmits the task data of $w_m$ to $MP_i$ [(2) in Fig. 2 (a)]. If $w_m$ has the $w_d$ value larger than 1, $RP$ recognizes an MP (or MPs) to which $w_m$ has been already allocated (let the MP be $MP_j$). At this point, $RP$ sends $MP_i$ the notification message that task data would be transmitted from $MP_j$ [(2) in Fig. 2 (b)]. Then $RP$ sends an order message to $MP_j$ so that $MP_j$ would transmit task data to $MP_i$ [(3) in Fig. 2 (b)]. On receiving this message, $MP_j$ sends $MP_i$ its last checkpoint as task data. In other words, it sends the intermediate result, which was produced by checkpointing, to $MP_i$ [(4) in Fig. 2 (b)].

Fig. 3 shows the checkpointing process. As the intermediate result of a task, each checkpoint is saved in the local disk of an MP at a periodic cycle ($MP_i$ in Fig. 3). Right after checkpointing is performed, $MP_i$ notifies $RP$ that its checkpoint has been taken. Since checkpointing is performed at a periodic cycle, $MP_i$ sends the $RP$ the checkpoint messages of total $C$ times, from the beginning to the end of a task ((1) in Fig. 3). Meanwhile, by checkpoint sharing, $MP_i$ can receive a checkpoint as an intermediate result from another MP. If the checkpoint transmitted to $MP_i$ has been performed up to the $c$th checkpoint, $MP_i$ will send the checkpoint messages of $C - c$ times to $RP$ until the task is completed. ((2) in Fig. 3). At this time, task execution time can be also reduced because $MP_i$ executes a task from the $c$th checkpoint time, not from the beginning.

Having received from $MP_i$ a checkpoint message for the task $w_m$, $RP$ updates the $w_c$ value of $w_m$ in the task list. At this point, $w_c$ is compared to the $MP_c$ of $MP_i$, which is included in the checkpoint message; and if $w_c < MP_c$, $w_c$ is replaced with $MP_c$. This case indicates that in a state where the task $w_m$ is being executed on several MPs in duplication, the $MP_i$ with the largest number of checkpoints sends its checkpoint message to $RP$. If $w_c \geq MP_c$, $w_c$ is kept without any change. Meanwhile, if $RP$ receives a task completion message from $MP_i$, it confirms that task execution has been completed. Then $RP$ receives a final result from $MP_i$.

# 3   Analytical Model

The proposed mechanism in this paper is modeled by embedded Markov chain and analyzed from the viewpoint of message/data transmission cost and the reduction of execution time.

## 3.1   Analysis Modeling with Embedded Markov Chain

The proposed mechanism is analyzed with embedded Markov chain model. Fig. 4 shows the state transition diagram established when MPs execute at most two checkpoints ($C = 2$) until completing each replica, permitting three duplications per task ($D = 3$). As shown in Fig. 4, when $D = 3$ and $C = 2$, each state is expressed as a state vector $(a, c_1, c_2, c_3, r)$. The first element $a$ ($0 \le a \le D$) represents the number of replicas for the task $w_m$. The second to the fourth elements $c_1$, $c_2$, $c_3$ come in the order of the number of checkpoints of the MPs executing the task, which is $0 \le c_3 \le c_2 \le c_1 < C$. That is, $c_1$ is the number of checkpoints of the MP that has the largest number of checkpoints among the MPs executing the task. On the other hand, $c_3$ is the number of checkpoints of the MP that has the smallest number of checkpoints. Because the checkpoint status for all the MPs executing the task should be expressed in the state vector, the total number of $c_i$ elements is required as many as $D$ (*i.e.*, the number of duplications). The last element $r$ represents the number of the completed tasks among the duplicated ones.

In this paper, it is assumed that task request and checkpoint report follow the Poisson process [7] with the ratio of $\lambda_1$ and $\lambda_2$, respectively. $\lambda_1$ indicates the mean number of events generated for unit time when the RP receives a task request from an MP and allocates a task to the MP, and $\lambda_2$ indicates the mean number of events generated for unit time when the MP executing a task performs checkpointing and reports to the RP that it has taken the checkpoint. From Fig. 4, we can observe that the state transition of a task by checkpoint sharing and task duplication is caused by an MP's task request or

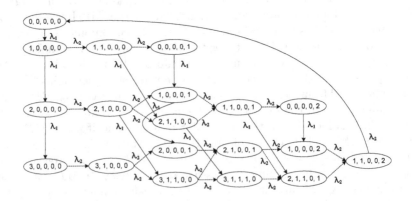

**Fig. 4.** State Transition Diagram ($D = 3$, $C = 2$)

checkpoint report. Whenever either a task request event or a checkpoint event occurs in an MP, the RP receives messages for the event from the MP. Thus, if such the messages are observed on the RP, the state transition of a task can be modeled. Let $p_{(a,c_1,c_2,c_3,r),(a',c_1',c_2',c_3',r')}$ be the one-stop transition probability from a state $(a,c_1,c_2,c_3,r)$ to a state $(a',c_1',c_2',c_3',r')$. It can be calculated based on the state transition shown in Fig. 4. The one-step transition matrix $P = (p_{(a,c_1,c_2,c_3,r),(a',c_1',c_2',c_3',r')})$ can be expressed as follows:

$$
P = \frac{1}{L}
\begin{pmatrix}
0 & L & 0 & 0 & 0 & 0 & 0 & 0 & 0 & 0 & 0 & 0 & 0 & 0 & 0 & 0 & 0 & 0 & 0 & 0 \\
0 & 0 & \lambda_1 & 0 & \lambda_2 & 0 & 0 & 0 & 0 & 0 & 0 & 0 & 0 & 0 & 0 & 0 & 0 & 0 & 0 & 0 \\
0 & 0 & 0 & \lambda_1 & 0 & \lambda_2 & 0 & 0 & 0 & 0 & 0 & 0 & 0 & 0 & 0 & 0 & 0 & 0 & 0 & 0 \\
0 & 0 & 0 & 0 & 0 & L & 0 & 0 & 0 & 0 & 0 & 0 & 0 & 0 & 0 & 0 & 0 & 0 & 0 & 0 \\
0 & 0 & 0 & 0 & 0 & 0 & 0 & \lambda_2 & 0 & \lambda_1 & 0 & 0 & 0 & 0 & 0 & 0 & 0 & 0 & 0 & 0 \\
0 & 0 & 0 & 0 & 0 & 0 & 0 & \tfrac{1}{2}\lambda_2 & \tfrac{1}{2}\lambda_2 & 0 & \lambda_1 & 0 & 0 & 0 & 0 & 0 & 0 & 0 & 0 & 0 \\
0 & 0 & 0 & 0 & 0 & 0 & 0 & 0 & 0 & \tfrac{1}{2}L & \tfrac{1}{2}L & 0 & 0 & 0 & 0 & 0 & 0 & 0 & 0 & 0 \\
0 & 0 & 0 & 0 & 0 & 0 & 0 & L & 0 & 0 & 0 & 0 & 0 & 0 & 0 & 0 & 0 & 0 & 0 & 0 \\
0 & 0 & 0 & 0 & 0 & 0 & 0 & 0 & 0 & \lambda_1 & 0 & \lambda_2 & 0 & 0 & 0 & 0 & 0 & 0 & 0 & 0 \\
0 & 0 & 0 & 0 & 0 & 0 & 0 & 0 & 0 & 0 & 0 & \lambda_2 & 0 & \lambda_1 & 0 & 0 & 0 & 0 & 0 & 0 \\
0 & 0 & 0 & 0 & 0 & 0 & 0 & 0 & 0 & 0 & 0 & 0 & L & 0 & 0 & 0 & 0 & 0 & 0 & 0 \\
0 & 0 & 0 & 0 & 0 & 0 & 0 & 0 & 0 & 0 & 0 & 0 & 0 & \tfrac{1}{2}L & \tfrac{1}{2}L & 0 & 0 & 0 & 0 & 0 \\
0 & 0 & 0 & 0 & 0 & 0 & 0 & 0 & 0 & 0 & 0 & 0 & 0 & 0 & 0 & \lambda_2 & 0 & \lambda_1 & 0 & 0 \\
0 & 0 & 0 & 0 & 0 & 0 & 0 & 0 & 0 & 0 & 0 & 0 & 0 & 0 & 0 & \tfrac{1}{2}L & \tfrac{1}{2}L & 0 & 0 & 0 \\
0 & 0 & 0 & 0 & 0 & 0 & 0 & 0 & 0 & 0 & 0 & 0 & 0 & 0 & 0 & 0 & 0 & L & 0 & 0 \\
0 & 0 & 0 & 0 & 0 & 0 & 0 & 0 & 0 & 0 & 0 & 0 & 0 & 0 & 0 & 0 & 0 & 0 & L & 0 \\
0 & 0 & 0 & 0 & 0 & 0 & 0 & 0 & 0 & 0 & 0 & 0 & 0 & 0 & 0 & 0 & 0 & 0 & 0 & L \\
0 & 0 & 0 & 0 & 0 & 0 & 0 & 0 & 0 & 0 & 0 & 0 & 0 & 0 & 0 & 0 & 0 & L & 0 & 0 \\
0 & 0 & 0 & 0 & 0 & 0 & 0 & 0 & 0 & 0 & 0 & 0 & 0 & 0 & 0 & 0 & 0 & 0 & 0 & L \\
L & 0 & 0 & 0 & 0 & 0 & 0 & 0 & 0 & 0 & 0 & 0 & 0 & 0 & 0 & 0 & 0 & 0 & 0 & 0 \\
\end{pmatrix}
$$

In this transition matrix, $\lambda_1$ and $\lambda_2$ indicate the task request rate and the checkpoint arrival rate per unit time, respectively, and $L = \lambda_1 + \lambda_2$. In the above transition matrix, the elements of each column and row are listed in the following $(a,c_1,c_2,c_3,r)$ order: $(0,0,0,0,0)$, $(1,0,0,0,0)$, $(2,0,0,0,0)$, $(3,0,0,0,0)$, $\cdots$, $(0,0,0,0,2)$, $(1,0,0,0,2)$, $(2,1,1,0,2)$, and $(1,1,0,0,2)$.

Next, let $N$ be the total number of states and $\pi_{(a,c_1,c_2,c_3,r)}$ be the steady-state probability of a state $(a,c_1,c_2,c_3,r)$. The unique steady-state probability distribution vector $\pi$ for these states can be obtained from the following formula [7]:

$$
\pi = e(I + E - P)^{-1} \tag{1}
$$

where, $E$ and $e$ are the matrix $(N \times N)$ and the row $(1 \times N)$, whose element has a value of 1, respectively. Eq. (1), a variation of $\pi = \pi P$, is used very significantly for the numerical calculation; and using this formula, we can compute each $\pi_{(a,c_1,c_2,c_3,r)}$.

## 3.2   Analysis of Transmission Cost

Now, we describe the transmission cost required by task requests and checkpointing when $D = 3$ and $C = 2$. Firstly, consider the transmission cost related to task requests. Let the message cost and the data cost be expressed as $m_r$ and $d_r$, respectively. If it is assumed that initial task data and intermediate result data have the same size, the transmission cost for the two data would also be identical; i.e., the transmission cost for each data is $d_r$. Then the unit cost required by a task request event can be calculated by

$$
RU_1 = m_r + d_r \tag{2}
$$
$$
RU_2 = 3 \cdot m_r + d_r
$$

where, $RU_1$ is the unit cost made when the RP directly transmits task data, and $RU_2$ is the unit cost made when task data is transmitted by the mediation of the RP. Using Eq (2) and the transition probability for task request, the total cost $R_c$ required by a task request event is calculated by

$$R_c = R_1 \cdot RU_1 + R_2 \cdot RU_2 \tag{3}$$

$$R_1 = \sum_{i=0}^{D-1} \pi_{(0,0,0,0,i)} + \left( \sum_{i=1}^{D-1} \pi_{(i,0,0,0,0)} + \pi_{(1,0,0,0,1)} \right) \cdot \left( \frac{\lambda_1}{\lambda_1 + \lambda_2} \right)$$

$$R_2 = \left( \sum_{i=0}^{D-2} \pi_{(1,1,0,0,i)} + \sum_{j=0}^{C-1} \pi_{(2,1,j,0,0)} \right) \cdot \left( \frac{\lambda_1}{\lambda_1 + \lambda_2} \right)$$

where, $R_1$ is the total sum of the transition probabilities that the RP directly sends task data to an MP for a task request, and $R_2$ is the total sum of the transition probabilities that the checkpoint of another MP as task data is sent the MP making a task request by the mediation of the RP.

Secondly, consider the transmission cost related to checkpointing. Let message cost and data cost for checkpointing be expressed as $m_c$ and $d_c$, respectively. The cost of one checkpoint message is incurred only when the notification of the checkpoint acquisition is made. However, there is an exception when an RP is notified of the completion of a task. In this case, the transmission costs of both task completion message and final result data are incurred each once. Also, if the checkpoint message and the task completion message have the same cost, the unit cost required by a checkpoint event can be calculated by

$$CU_1 = m_c \tag{4}$$
$$CU_2 = m_c + d_c$$

where, $CU_1$ represents the unit cost required when an MP notifies the RP that it has acquired a checkpoint, and $CU_2$ represents the unit cost required when the MP notifies the RP that it has completed the allocated task. Using Eq (4) and the transition probability for checkpointing, the total cost of a checkpoint event can be calculated by

$$C_c = C_1 \cdot CU_1 + C_2 \cdot CU_2 \tag{5}$$

$$C_1 = \left( \sum_{i=0}^{D-2} \pi_{(1,0,0,0,i)} + \pi_{(2,0,0,0,0)} + \frac{1}{2} \cdot \pi_{(2,1,0,0,0)} \right) \cdot \left( \frac{\lambda_2}{\lambda_1 + \lambda_2} \right) +$$

$$\sum_{i=0}^{D-1} \pi_{(D-i,0,0,0,i)} + \frac{1}{2} \cdot \left( \pi_{(2,1,0,0,1)} + \sum_{j=0}^{C-1} \pi_{(3,1,j,0,0)} \right)$$

$$C_2 = \left( \sum_{i=0}^{D-2} \pi_{(1,1,0,0,i)} + \pi_{(2,1,1,0,0)} + \frac{1}{2} \cdot \pi_{(2,1,0,0,0)} \right) \cdot \left( \frac{\lambda_2}{\lambda_1 + \lambda_2} \right) +$$

$$\pi_{3,1,1,1,0} + \pi_{2,1,1,0,1} + \pi_{1,1,0,0,2} + \frac{1}{2} \cdot \left( \pi_{(2,1,0,0,1)} + \sum_{j=0}^{C-1} \pi_{(3,1,j,0,0)} \right)$$

where, $C_1$ is the total sum of the transition probabilities that an MP notifies the RP of the execution of checkpointing, and $C_2$ is the total sum of the transition probabilities that the final result of the completed task is transmitted to the RP.

So far, using Eqs. (3) and (5), we have calculated the average cost for one task request event and one checkpoint report event. Until a task is completed going through checkpoint sharing and task duplication, on the average, $D$ times of task request reports and $D \cdot C$ times of checkpoint reports occur. Thus, the total cost of our scheduling mechanism, $TC$, is the sum of the task request cost and the checkpoint report cost, as follows: $TC = D \cdot R_c + (D \cdot C) \cdot C_c$.

### 3.3  Analysis of Execution Time Reduction Cost

Here, we examine how much execution time our mechanism can reduce as compared to the client-server model. The average execution time ($\overline{ET}$) reduced per task request in our scheduling mechanism can be calculated by

$$\overline{ET} = \left( \sum_{i=0}^{D-2} \pi_{(1,1,0,0,i)} + \sum_{j=0}^{C-1} \pi_{(2,1,j,0,0)} \right) \cdot \left( \frac{1}{C} \cdot T \right) \cdot \left( \frac{\lambda_1}{\lambda_1 + \lambda_2} \right) \quad (6)$$

where, $T$ is the execution time required when one task is performed from the beginning to the end without the use of the intermediate result, and $C$ is the total number of checkpoints. For analytical convenience, it is assumed that all MPs have the same performance. Accordingly, all checkpoints will be taken at a periodic cycle. Then we can see that a mean execution time between two consecutive checkpoints is $\frac{1}{C} \cdot T$. The reduction of the execution time is determined by how few checkpointing the MP has performed after it receives an intermediate result from another MP; i.e., as a checkpoint in an intermediate result is close to a final result, the execution time becomes less, as much as any times of $\frac{1}{C} \cdot T$. On the other hand, tasks in the client-server model are not executed utilizing an intermediate result; rather, even replica is executed from the beginning. As a result, in the client-server model, if a task is duplicated $D$ times, the total execution time becomes $D \cdot T$. Therefore, the execution time reduction ratio (ETRR) of our scheduling mechanism to the client-server model is as follows:

$$ETRR = \frac{D \cdot \overline{ET}}{D \cdot T} = \frac{\overline{ET}}{T} \quad (7)$$

## 4  Performance Evaluation

In this section, the performance of our scheduling mechanism is compared to that of the scheduling mechanism based on the client-server model. Using the analytical model described in the previous section, the total cost generated by the task request and checkpoint events for one task were calculated. For analytical convenience, it was assumed that the messages cost generated in the task request and checkpoint events is identical and that the data cost in the two events is

**Table 1.** Parameters

| Parameter Description | Values |
|---|---|
| The number of duplications per task ($D$) | 2, 4, 6 |
| The number of checkpoints per task ($C$) | 3, 4, 5 |
| The ratio of message transmission cost to data transmission cost ($\alpha$) | 1:100 |
| The ratio between the proposed mechanism and the client-server model for message/data transmission cost | 1:2 |
| The ratio of task request and checkpoint report ($\rho$) | $0.1, 0.2, \cdots, 6.0$ |

also identical; *i.e.*, $m_r = m_c$ and $d_r = d_c$. Generally, data transmission needs more cost than message transmission, so we define a relation between two costs as the following formula: $d_r = \alpha \cdot m_r$ ($\alpha \geq 1$).

In the proposed mechanism, an RP can be located either in the identical network where each peer is located, or in a network not far away from each peer; message/data transmission is performed within one hop on the average because an RP is located in between central server and MPs. On the other hand, since there is no a special peer such as an RP in the client-server model, more than two hops are needed to be transmitted message or data. Thus, it is assumed that message/data transmission of the client-server model costs twice as much as that of the proposed mechanism. Table 1 shows the parameters used for our performance evaluation.

The effect of $D$ and $C$ on total costs is now examined. Towards this end, $D$ and $C$ were divided into three cases ($D = 2, 4, 6$ and $C = 3, 4, 5$), respectively. The total costs for the nine cases based on all the combinations of $D$ and $C$ were calculated and compared.

Fig. 5 shows a relative cost for message/data transmission between two mechanisms. The relative cost is defined as the ratio of the message/data transmission cost of the proposed mechanism to that of the client-server model. A relative cost of more than 1.0 means that the proposed mechanism costs less than the client-server model. From Fig. 5, we can observe that in all combinations of $D$ and $C$, the relative cost is larger than 1.0. This result signifies that the message/data transmission cost of the proposed mechanism is relatively lower than that of the client-server model. As a result, the proposed mechanism can distribute the load of message/data transmission as compared to the client-server model.

The effect of the relative cost is now examined based on the ratio $\rho$ of the task request ratio $\lambda_1$ to the checkpoint report ratio $\lambda_2$. Fig. 5 shows that for all cases of $C$, the relative cost rapidly declined in a region where $\rho \leq \kappa$. Here, $\kappa$ represents the lowest relative cost in each graph of Fig. 5. For $C = 3, 4, 5$, $\kappa$ has 1.1, 1.5, 1.8, respectively. This sharply decline is because the number of task requests is relatively more than that of checkpoint reports. Since few MPs receive intermediate results when they request the task to be executed, most task executions are performed from the beginning; there is a high probability that MPs perform lots of checkpointing without the reduction of the number of checkpoint reports. As a result, the increase in the checkpoint reports causes

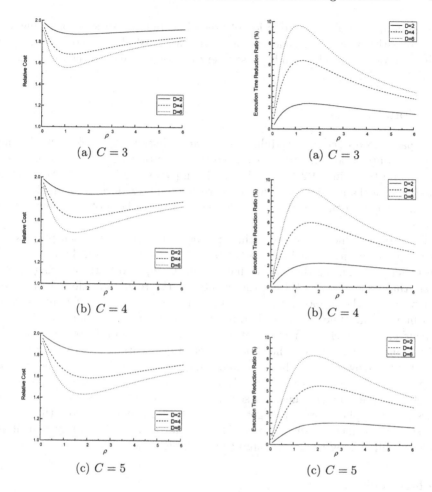

(a) $C = 3$   (a) $C = 3$

(b) $C = 4$   (b) $C = 4$

(c) $C = 5$   (c) $C = 5$

**Fig. 5.** Message/Data Transmission Cost    **Fig. 6.** Execution Time Reduction Ratio

transmission cost to increase. On the other hand, in the region where $\rho > \kappa$, the relative cost gradually increases. In this region, the number of checkpoint reports is relatively more than that of task requests, and most MPs receive intermediate results from other MPs when they request the task to be executed. Accordingly, the MPs can perform checkpoint reports fewer than $C$ times; and therefore, message cost in this region are lower than that in the remaining region.

Fig. 6 shows the ETRR (Execution Time Reduction Ratio) according to the variations of $D$ and $C$. From this figure, we can observe that as $D$ increases in relation to each $C$, the ETRR becomes higher. When $D = 6$ for each $C$, the execution time of the proposed mechanism is reduced as much as about 9-10%, compared to that of the client-server model. This is because when an MP requests a task, the frequency of task executions based on the checkpoint of other MPs becomes more as $D$ increases. It should be noted that as the checkpoint is more close to a final result, the reduction of execution time per task becomes higher. Consequently, by means of checkpoint sharing and task duplication, we can see that the proposed mechanism has a shorter execution time than the client-server model.

## 5 Conclusions

This paper proposed a scheduling mechanism based on checkpoint sharing and task duplication in order to reduce the execution time of all tasks (*i.e.*, turnaround time) in a P2P-based PC grid computing environment. Also, using a mathematical analysis model, we compared and analyzed the transmission cost and the execution time of the proposed mechanism to those of the client-server model.

The proposed mechanism uses the checkpoint performed by each peer as an intermediate result, and when another peer requests for a task, duplicates and executes the task using the intermediate result. Compared to the existing mechanism that executes a task from the beginning, the reduction effect of the execution time in the proposed mechanism is heightened as the checkpoint is close to a final result. The analysis of transmission cost and execution time by the embedded Markov chain showed that the transmission cost of the proposed mechanism somewhat increases when the number of duplications per task increases. However, it showed that when checkpointing is executed more and more, the proposed mechanism can considerably reduce the execution time compared to the client-server model. Thus, our scheduling mechanism can reduce the time it takes for an application user to get a final task result. It is expected that when our scheduling mechanism is implemented in an actual PC grid system, it is useful in minimizing the turnaround time of large-scale applications.

## References

1. Abbas, A.: Grid Computing: A Practical Guide to Technology and Applications. Charles River Media Inc., Massachusetts (2004)
2. Anderson, D.: BOINC: A System for Public-Resource Computing and Storage. In: 5th IEEE/ACM Int. Workshop on Grid Computing, pp. 4–10 (2004)
3. Barkai, D.: Peer-to-Peer Computing: Technologies for Sharing and Collaborating on the Net. Intel Press (2002)
4. Chien, A., Calder, B., Elbert, S., Bhatia, K.: Entropia: Architecture and Performance of an Enterprise Desktop Grid System. J. Parallel and Distributed Computing 63, 597–610 (2003)
5. Domingus, P., Silva, J.G., Silva, L.: Sharing Checkpoints to Improve Turnaround Time in Desktop Grid Computing. In: 20th Int. Conf. on Advanced Information Networking and Applications, pp. 6–11 (2006)
6. Fedak, C., Germain, V., Neri, V., Cappello, F.: XtremWeb: A Generic Global Computing Systems. In: 1st Int. Symp. on Cluster Computing and the Grid, pp. 582–587 (2001)
7. Minh, D.L.: Applied Probability Models. Brooks/Cole Publishing Co. (2001)

# A Probabilistic Fault-Tolerant Recovery Mechanism for Task and Result Certification of Large-Scale Distributed Applications

Rim Chayeh[1], Christophe Cerin[2], and Mohamed Jemni[1]

[1] Ecole Supérieure des Sciences et Techniques de Tunis, Unité de recherche UTIC
5, Av. Taha Hussein, B.P. 56, Bab Mnara, Tunis, Tunisia
Tel.: (+216) 71 496 066; Fax: (+216) 71 391 166
rim.chayeh@utic.rnu.tn, mohamed.jemni@fst.rnu.tn
[2] LIPN-UMR CNRS 7030, Institut Galilée – Université Paris-Nord
99, avenue Jean-Baptiste Clément, 93430 Villetaneuse, France
Tel.: +33-(0)1.49.40.35.78; Fax: +33-(0)1.48.26.07.12
christophe.cerin@lipn.univ-paris13.fr

**Abstract.** This paper deals with fault tolerant recovery mechanisms and probabilistic results certification issues on large scale architectures. The related works in the result certification domain are based on a total or a partial duplication of the application. However, they are limited to independent tasks executions. In the present work, we extend these mechanisms to dependant tasks applications. First of all we propose an approach, based on an abstract representation of a parallel execution called macro-dataflow graph. Second we introduce probabilistic certification algorithms that avoid the re-execution of the program, allowing for recovery on different platforms under different number of processors. We also sketch how to simulate our framework according to state of the art, modeling workloads and fault injection tools.

**Keywords:** Meta-computing, Distributed systems, Probabilistic certification, Recovery, Result checking, Fault-Tolerance by value.

## 1 Introduction

Grid and cluster architectures are gaining in popularity for scientific computing applications. The distributed computations, as well as their underlying infrastructure consisting of a large number of computers, storage and networking devices, pose challenges in overcoming the effects of node failures. In this unbounded environment one should consider possible malicious acts that may result in massive attacks against the whole global computation. This is supported by an exponentially increasing number of reported incidents [1]. Usually, global computations are expected to tolerate certain rates of faults [2, 3], e.g. small number of isolated intrusions. However, in order to ensure correctness of the computed results, one should detect if the global computation has been the victim of a massive attack resulting in an error rate larger than what can be tolerated by the application. In order to eliminate any assumption on

N. Abdennadher and D. Petcu (Eds.): GPC 2009, LNCS 5529, pp. 471–482, 2009.

the attack and the distribution of errors in the context of a general parallel computation with dependencies, we propose to adopt a view directly inspired by probabilistic
algorithms. Specifically, given the results of a global computation with task dependencies, we attempt to detect if the execution contains faulty results, and try to throw
an efficient process of recovery when a fault is discovered. Probabilistic algorithms
are presented that make random choices and determine whether the execution is correct or faulty. Since the detection is probabilistic, its output may be wrong. However,
contrary to previous approaches, the probability of certification error is not related to
the application, i.e. the global computation, but only to the unlucky random choices
associated with task selection for verification.

This work is motivated by Desktop Grid applications, for instance philogenetic application [6] studied with the help of the XtremWebCH[14] (**XWCH**) tool under
**GTRS**[15] platform. The probabilistic certification and recovering algorithms introduced in this paper can detect if these computations have been subjected to a massive
attack with a so-called attack ratio greater than or equal to $q < 1$. If the presence of an
error is confirmed during the certification phase, we throw a recovery process, only
on the infected parts of the application. The bound on the error is not related to q, but
to the minimum number of so-called initiator tasks.

This paper is organized as following, in section 2, we present definitions and notations adopted in this work. Our contributions are explained in sections 3 and 4: we
present a set of optimized algorithms for detecting and recovering faults in applications with independent and dependant tasks. In section 5, we present our work in
progress for simulating our framework which is a challenging task in itself with the
current technologies. In section 6, we review related works on probabilistic certification of tasks, and we demonstrate the difference between them and our approach.

## 2  Definitions and Assumptions

We assume that applications are executed on the global computing platform such as the
one presented in [4]. A user initiates a computation, represented by a directed acyclic
graph G, that is then executed on (a potentially large number of) unreliable workers. In
order to verify the correctness of the results of the execution, verifiers, implemented by
reliable resources that know graph G, re-execute selected tasks. Communication between workers and verifiers is through a checkpoint server containing computations
submitted by workers [4]. Whereas any attack can occur on the worker or between the
worker and the checkpoint server, the checkpoint server and verifiers are considered
secure. Let us recall the important definitions as they appear in [4]. A data-flow graph is
a directed graph $G = (V, \varepsilon)$, where V is a finite set of vertices and $\varepsilon$ is a set of edges. The
total number of tasks $T_j$ in G is n. E denotes the execution of a workload represented by
G with a set $\hat{I}$ of initial inputs on a set of unreliable resources.

Each task T in E executes with inputs i(T,E) and creates output o(T,E). The inputs
of a task $T_j$ are composed of either inputs from $\hat{I}$ or outputs of other tasks $T_k$, i.e.
$o(T_k,E)$. $\hat{E}$ denotes the execution of the program on a verifier, i.e. a reliable resource.
If $E = \hat{E}$, i.e. if every task in E uses the same inputs and computes the same outputs as
those in $\hat{E}$, then E is said to be "correct". Conversely, if $E \neq \hat{E}$, then at least one task
in E produced a wrong result and the execution is said to have "failed".

i(T,E) denotes the input of T in E and î(T, Ê) the input of T in Ê. Furthermore, o(T,E) denotes the output of T on the client, ô(T,E) the output of T on the verifier based on inputs from E, and ô(T, Ê ) the output of T on the verifier based on inputs from Ê . Note that the notations ô(T,E) and ô(T, Ê ) differ. We consider probabilistic certification based on a probabilistic algorithm that uses randomization in order to state if E has failed or not. Given an execution E, a Monte Carlo certification is defined as a randomized algorithm that takes an arbitrary $\varepsilon$, $0 < \varepsilon \leq 1$, as input and delivers (a) either CORRECT or (b) FAILED, together with a proof that E has failed. The probabilistic certification is said to be with error $\varepsilon$ if the probability of the answer CORRECT, when E has actually failed, is less than or equal to $\varepsilon$. For instance, a Monte Carlo certification may consist of re-executing randomly chosen tasks in G on a verifier, comparing results to those obtained in E.

If the results differ, E has failed. Otherwise, E may be correct or failed. However, if E has failed, a probabilistic certification with error $\varepsilon$ ensures that the probability of non-detection of failure (based on randomly selecting tasks in G for re-execution) is less than or equal to $\varepsilon$. Authors in [4] introduce a Monte Carlo certification approach against massive attacks. In the sequel, we denote the number of forged tasks in G by $n_F$. We are considering the two scenarios where either all tasks execute correctly, i.e. $n_F = 0$, or $n_F$ is large, corresponding to a massive attack. A massive attack with attack ratio q consists of falsifying the execution of at least $n_q = \lceil q \cdot n \rceil \leq n_F$ tasks. E is said to be "attacked with ratio q" and $(n_F / n) \geq q$. It should be noted that q is assumed relatively large, resulting from massive attacks such as caused by a virus.

The objective is to provide a probabilistic Monte Carlo certification against such massive attacks and try to recover, when errors are detected, during the certification phase. Note that detection of small attacks, e.g. single intrusions, is not the scope of this work. As indicated in Section 1, global computations are expected to tolerate certain fault rates.

# 3 Applications with Independent Tasks

We first consider the case where all tasks in G are independent. In this case, certification of tasks is equivalent to certification of results. The following algorithm TestI [12], based on task re-execution on a verifier, will be used to detect if execution E contains forged tasks.

This certification method costs better  than $\mathcal{O}(-)$ (naive duplication).

## 3.1 Certification

| Algorithm 1 [4,12] : TestI (T, E) |
|---|
| // Re-execute T on a verifier, using inputs from E, i.e. i(T,E), to get output ô(T,E). |
| ô(T,E) ← **ReexecuteOnControler**(T, i(T,E)); |
| If o(T,E) $\neq$ ô(T,E) then  // it means that T is failed |
| Return 1 ; // we return 1, to say that E contains forged tasks. |
| Else   Return 0 // it means that T is correct |
| End If |
| End **TestI** |

Since all tasks in G are independent we always have i(T,E) = î(T, Ê), (We note that in case of dependencies between tasks, this assumption about the inputs does not hold anymore, as we will see later ).

If Algorithm TestI selects a forged task, then one knows that the execution E has failed. However, if TestI returns CORRECT, then one can only make conclusions based on the probabilities of randomly selecting a falsified or non-falsified task. The following lemma addresses these probabilities.

**Lemma 1.** Let E be an execution with n independent tasks, $n_F$ of that have been forged. The probability that TestI returns FAILED is $(n_F /n)$ and the probability that it returns CORRECT is $1 - (n_F /n) \leq 1 - q$.

**Theorem 1 [12].** Let E be an execution with only independent tasks and assume that E is either correct or massively attacked with ratio q. For a given $\varepsilon$, the number of independent executions of algorithm TestI necessary to achieve a certification of E with probability of error less than or equal to $\varepsilon$ is $N \geq \left\lceil \dfrac{\log \varepsilon}{\log( 1 - q )} \right\rceil$.

The N calls to TestI, is explained as follows into algorithm 2 (Verify).

| **Algorithm 2 : Verify** (E) |
|---|
| {Tcertified}← Ø // { Tcertified } contains correct tasks, that has been already verified,  (in the beginning {Tcertified } is empty , because all the tasks must be candidates for the test) |
| $N\varepsilon,q \leftarrow \left\lceil \dfrac{\log \varepsilon}{\log( 1 - q )} \right\rceil$ |
| For i=1 to N$\varepsilon$,q do |
| Choose one task  T, randomly  from G – { Tcertified } |
| If (**TestI**(T, E) = =1) then  Return **FALSIFIED** |
| Else // T is correct |
| { Tcertified } ← { Tcertified } U T |
| End If |
| End For |
| Return **CORRECT** |
| **End verify** |

**Proof (Theorem1).** Consider N executions of Algorithm TestI. If during any of the N executions TestI selects a forged task, the execution has failed. Therefore, assume that only non-forged tasks are selected. According to Lemma 1 the probability of TestI selecting a non-forged task is $(n -n_F) / n \leq 1 - q$. Then N independent applications of TestI lead to a Monte-Carlo certification with a probability of error bound by $\varepsilon \leq (1-q)^N$. For a given $\varepsilon$, it is thus sufficient to select $N \geq \left\lceil \dfrac{\log \varepsilon}{\log( 1 - q )} \right\rceil$ tasks.

So the Total cost is: $O\left(\dfrac{\log \varepsilon}{\log( 1 - q )}\right)$ quickly negligible, with a probability of error $\leq \varepsilon$.

## 3.2 Recovery

Before describing the recovery process that we are adopting, we indicate here that this part is makes the difference with the related works (see Section 6) and is the basis for allowing checkpointing in a heterogeneous environment with the flexibility of recovery on any type or number of processors.

For our recovery step we apply a local recovery principle (not a global one) and it implies that only the roll-back of the falsified tasks is necessary, so we do not need to stop the execution of the dataflow nor obliging the application to save its global state of execution regularly.

In this first case, where we have graphs without independencies between tasks, we run the following steps:

_We replace the falsified output of the forged task by the correct outputs in E.
_We isolate the machine that has executed the forged task T.
_We put this machine (M) in the black list, so we do not reuse it in the future.
_We locate all the tasks (other then T) that has been executed by M, then we put them in a suspicious list ({LTSuspect}), to be r-executed later on reliable machines.

---

**Algorithm 3 Recover** (T : falsified task , G)

**Replace** (o(T,E),ô(T,E)) // we replace the falsified output of the forged task T by the correct outputs in E.
{ Tcertified }← { Tcertified } U T // after correcting T in E, we can add this task to the list of certified tasks ({Tcertified})
M ← **Research** ( T , MachineList) // we get the machine (from MachinList) witch executed T
**Blacklist** (M) // we put M in the black list
{LTSuspect} ← **Localize** (MachineList , M ) - { Tcertified } // we locate all the tasks (other then T) witch has been executed by M, then we put them in a suspicious list ({LTSuspect})
**ReExecution** ({LTSuspect}) // re-execute all the suspicious tasks (executed by M) on reliable machines.
{ Tcertified }← { Tcertified } U {LTSuspect} //after re-executing {LTSuspect}, we can add them to certified tasks
**End Recover**

---

## 4 Certification in the Presence of Task Dependencies

In the previous section there is no difference between certification of tasks and their respective results. If one allows for dependencies among tasks the certification of the results of tasks is more difficult. The problem lies in the way a reliable resource has to determine the validity of results. Any measure of validity of a task's result based on the comparison to the results obtained by re-executing the same task on a reliable resource depends on the validity of the inputs the reliable resource uses for re-execution. The fact that the outputs of a task execution and its re-execution on a reliable resource produce identical results does not provide more information about

the validity of that result, since in the assumed deterministic computing environment the same faulty input will produce identical faulty output. Thus, in the presence of dependencies, $o(T,E) = ô(T,E)$ only indicates that the results are the same,
but not that they are correct. It should be noted that correctness would imply that
$o(T,E) = ô(T, Ê)$.

## 4.1 Faulty Tasks and the Concept of Initiators

The randomized testing used in Section 3 is only valid for result certification of
independent tasks. If we were to apply the same reasoning in the presence of dependencies, certification based on repeated application of Algorithm TestI would
only certify results if $o(T,E) \neq ô(T,E)$ for each falsified T selected by TestI. However, this assumption is too restrictive since it would assume that a re-execution with
some (perhaps incorrect) input values would always expose the forgery. This weak
assumption could be easily exploited by an attacker. Suppose Algorithm TestI is
used. If $o(T,E) \neq ô(T,E)$ then E has failed. However, $o(T,E) = ô(T,E)$ indicates a
correct output only if the inputs are correct, i.e. $î(T, Ê )$. This implies that T has no
forged predecessors. In the following discussion, falsified tasks that have no falsified
predecessors will be called **initiators** [12]. The probabilities associated with randomly selecting initiators will be the basis for result certification. It should be noted
that it is difficult to speculate on the capabilities of detecting incorrect results of
falsified tasks that are not initiators. Pathological attacks may be derived where the
output of one falsified task may be custom tailored to produce results for other falsified tasks that do not differ from their re-executions (with the forged inputs) on reliable resources.

## 4.2 Certification

Result certification is directly related to the probability of the certification algorithm
selecting initiators. Let $n_I$ denote the number of initiators in G. Note that the determination of $n_I$ depends on the graph and on the nodes that have been falsified. The following lemma and theorem, modified from Lemma 1 and Theorem 1, can be stated.

**Lemma 2.** Let E be an execution with n tasks with dependencies. Furthermore, let $n_F$
and $n_I$ be the number of forged tasks and initiators respectively, $n_I \leq n_F$. The probability that TestI returns FAILED is at least $(n_I /n)$ and the probability that it returns
CORRECT is less than or equal to $1 - (n_I /n)$ .

Since re-execution of a task with incorrect inputs may still result in $o(T,E) = ô(T,E)$
one has to consider the limitations induced by the inputs.

Note that it is similar to Algorithm TestI, except that it contains forecasting operations to verify all predecessors for the task T selected for verification. Thus, it effectively verifies $G \leq (T)$.

Algorithm **Test** for **Dependant** tasks (**TestD₁**)[12,4], for this algorithm we proposed two other different versions called **TestD2** and **TestD3**, in witch we tried to
optimize it by adding additional tests and hypothesis to make the certification step
more efficient, then we proposed a recovery model when an error is detected.

| Algorithm 4: TestD$_1$ (T, E) |
|---|
| For all Tj in G$\leq$T, that have not been verified yet and $\notin$ { Tcertified } do<br>ô(T$_j$,E) $\leftarrow$ **ReexecuteOnControler**(T$_j$, i(T$_j$,E));<br>If o(T$_j$,E) $\neq$ ô(T$_j$,E) then // T$_j$ is an initiator<br>return j ; // we return the index of the initiator task T$_j$<br>End If<br>End For<br>{ Tcertified }$\leftarrow$ { Tcertified } U G$\leq$T<br>Return 0 // 0 means that the certification of G$\leq$T is correct |
| End TestD$_1$ |

**Theorem 2.[12]:** For a single execution of Algorithms TestD the probability of error is

$e_E \leq 1 - q$. The average cost in terms of verification, i.e. the expected number of

verifications, is $C = \dfrac{\sum_{Ti \in G} |G \leq Ti|}{n}$ . (1)

**Proof.** A pathological attacker who knows that uniform random task selection is used and that all predecessor tasks are verified can minimize detection by falsifying tasks in such a way as to minimize error propagation, thereby minimizing the total number of tasks affected by falsifications. In other words, in the worst case $n_q$ falsified tasks in G are distributed so that the number of T whose G$\leq$(T) contain falsified tasks is minimized. This can be achieved in any scenario that attacks the $n_q$ tasks T$_i$ with the smallest successor graph G$\geq$(i), e.g. first attack only leaf tasks, then tasks at the second level, etc... until $n_q$ tasks have been attacked. Finally, the error $e_E$ is 1 minus the probability of G$\leq$(T) containing a faulty task. In the worst case, described above, this leads to $e_E \leq 1 - (n_q / n) \leq 1 - q$.

The average number of verifications is simply the average number of tasks in the predecessor graph verified in TestD. Note that once T is selected, the cost can be specified exactly as |G$\leq$(T)|.

So the average cost TestD is : $O \left( \dfrac{\sum_{Ti \in G} |G \leq Ti|}{n} \right)$.

We implemented two other optimized versions of the algorithm TestD, called **TestD2** and **TestD3**, and this is the most important contribution and it makes the difference with related works (see section 6).

In **TestD2**, we proposed to order the sub-graph of predecessors of a task T (G$\leq$(T)) by runtime decreasing, in order to maximize the probability of finding initiators (if the execution is falsified) in a short time.

For the third version of our algorithm **TestD3**, we tried to optimize the certification test by including the concept of certificated machines into the verification of G$\leq$T.

We consider that machines have stable states into each sub_graph, so if we find a correct task Ti $\in$ G$\leq$T, executed by a machine M, we adopt that this machine is reliable into G$\leq$T, thus we exclude the verification of all Tj $\in$ G$\leq$T executed by M.

| |
|---|
| **Algorithm 5: TestD$_3$ (T, E)** |
| For all Tj in G$\leq$T, that have not been verified yet and $\notin$ {Tcertified, LTsures } do<br>ô(T$_j$,E) $\leftarrow$ ReexecuteOnControler(T$_j$, i(T$_j$,E));<br>    ➤ If o(T$_j$,E) $\neq$ ô(T$_j$,E) then  // T$_j$ is an initiator<br>      • return j ; // we return the index of the initiator task T$_j$<br>    ➤ Else<br>      • M $\leftarrow$ **Research** (Tj, MachineList) // research returns the worker who executed Tj from the set of machines participating on the computation.<br>      • {LTsure} $\leftarrow$ **LocalizeT** (MachineList, M)  U {LTsure} // localizeT locates the set of tasks executed by M into G$\leq$T.<br>    ➤ End If<br>End For<br>{ Tcertified } $\leftarrow$ { Tcertified } U G$\leq$T<br>Return 0; |
|    **End TestD$_3$** |

Algorithm Verify is rewriting as follows:

| |
|---|
| **Algorithm 6: Verify**(E) |
| {LTsure}$\leftarrow$ Ø // this list contains tasks yet executed by certificated machines.<br><br>{ Tcertified }$\leftarrow$ Ø ,and N$_{\varepsilon,q}$ $\leftarrow$ $\left\lceil \dfrac{\log \varepsilon}{\log(1-q)} \right\rceil$<br><br>**For** i = 1 to N$_{\varepsilon,q}$ do<br>Choose one task  T, randomly  from G – { Tcertified, LTsure }<br>j $\leftarrow$ **TestD** (T , E)<br>**If** (j $\neq$ 0) // it means that an error was detected, so j contains the index of the initiator  of this error, later we will recover from the task who has the index j<br>Return **Falsified**<br>**End If**<br>**End For**<br>Return **Correct** |
| End **Verify** |

## 4.3  Recovery

The overhead associated with fault-free execution is the penalty one pays for having a recovery mechanism. It remains to show how much overhead is associated with recovery as the result of a fault and how much execution time can be lost under different strategies. The overhead associated with recovery is due to loading and rebuilding G. This can be effectively achieved by loading the sub-graph Gi of the affected tasks. The time depends on the size of Gi and is dominated by the size of the data representing the tasks inputs.

The main difference with the case of applications with independent tasks is that an error in one task can affect different parts of the dataflow graph, so we should detect and recover all the affected parts of G.

Thus the overhead of this recovery process depends on the size of the graph that needs to be loaded and rebuilt.

As soon as a fault is detected in a task denoted Tj (initiator), many alternatives should be left aside: first we have to stop the execution of the sub-graph of successors of Tj : G≥Tj, then we blacklist the failing machine M that has executed Tj, next we try to locate all the tasks has been executed by M, and we put them in a suspicious list. Finally, we look for the smallest common ancestor (denoted CA) for all these suspicious tasks, then, we re-execute the sub-graph with vertex CA.

The flexibility of macro dataflow graphs has been exploited to allow for a platform-independent the description of the application state. This description resulted in flexible and portable recovery strategies, allowing for rollback at lowest level of granularity, with a maximal computation loss of one task. However, its overhead was sensitive to the size of the application graph, i.e. the number of tasks.

| **Algorithm 7: Recover ($T_i$ : initiator , G)** |
|---|
| ➢ **StopExecution(G≥Tj)** // we stop the execution of the sub-graph G≥Tj |
| ➢ M ← **Research** ( $T_j$, MachineList) |
| ➢ **Blacklist** (M) // we put M in the black list |
| {LTSuspect} ← **Localize** (MachineList , M ) - { Tcertified } // we locate all the tasks (other then T) wish has been executed by M, then we put them in a suspicious list |
| ➢ CA ← **ResearchCA** ( {LTSuspect}, G ) // we try to get the smallest common ancestor (CA) of the set {LTSuspect}(see [13] ) |
| ➢ **ReExecution**( G≥CA) // re-execute the sub-graph with vertex CA |
| ➢ { Tcertified }← { Tcertified } U **G≥CA** |
| End **recover** |

# 5  Results

The purpose of this section is to present some results about simulating our fault tolerant algorithms under the grid GTRS [15]. We have injected errors into the workloads to simulate a fault by value.

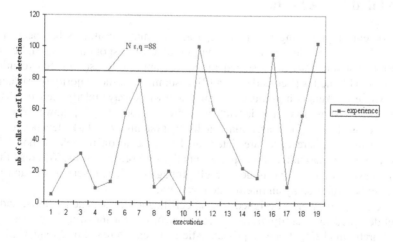

**Fig. 1.** Evaluations of the algorithm TestI and verif

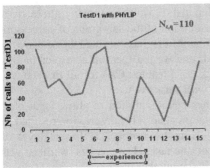
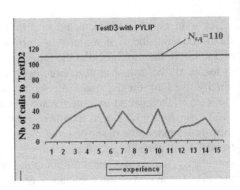
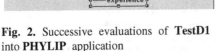

Fig. 2. Successive evaluations of **TestD1** into **PHYLIP** application

Fig. 3. Evaluations of **TestD3** with **PHYLIP**

The figure 3 evaluates the number of calls to TestI before detecting and recovering the massive attack of an execution E, with n=106 tasks, q = 10% and $\varepsilon=10^{-4}$. Moreover, when this number is superior to $N_{\varepsilon,q}$ = 88, the algorithm verif() gives a wrong result. This experience shows that the verification of $N_{\varepsilon,q}$ tasks, leads to a wrong result in 0,008% of cases, witch is lower than $\varepsilon$. The different executions demonstrate that in average, our fault tolerant process allows to certificate and to recover an application with a rate of error $\leq \varepsilon$.

To validate our fault tolerance process for dependant tasks we considered the philogenetic application "PHYLIP"[6], with n=144 tasks, q=0,1 and $\varepsilon$ =$10^{-5}$.The figure 2 shows that we can detect and *recover* the massive attack in more than 98% of cases before achieving the N$\varepsilon$,q calls to TestD1. This allows certification and recovering in a reasonable time, and with an acceptable degree of certification. The figure 3 shows the impact of adopting the concept of certificated machines in TestD3 in order accelerate the verification and recovering process.

# 6 Related Work Section

The problem of protecting a computation against massive attacks has been mainly addressed for independent tasks. The analysis of voting, spot-checking and credibility-based fault tolerance is presented in [3]. An approach based on re-execution of tasks on reliable nodes is considered in [2], assuming that the majority of workers are honest while workers compromised by an attack will always falsify their results. Under the same assumption, task dependencies are considered in [4], however, dependencies are used only for correction. Faults in systems with task dependencies are addressed in [5] where tasks are determined to execute on reliable or non-reliable nodes in order to maximize the expected number of correct results. Whereas the approach considers the critical issue of fault propagation, it is deterministic and therefore could be exploited by an intelligent adversary.

There are a few works designed for the certification of dependant tasks, and they are not designed for identifying the source of error nor for throwing a recovery process. S.Varette in [12,4] studied a probabilistic certification based on Monte Carlo Test (MCT) to verify if the global computation has been the victim of a massive attack or not, but his probabilistic approach does not make any assumptions about the attack nor her initiator or the procedure to throw for correcting them.

We use a similar MCT approach to certify the execution, but we tried to optimize it by adding additional tests and hypothesis to make the certification step more efficient, and we proposed a recovery model when an error is detected.

# 7 Conclusion

This paper discussed certification and recovery of large distributed applications executing in hostile environments, where tasks or data may be subject to attacks. Unlike previous work based on independent tasks, and do not reach the recovery phase, we considered fault propagation occurring in applications with dependent tasks. We present a set of certification probabilistic and recovering algorithms that avoid the total re-execution of the program and launch thereafter a recovery process if necessary. The certification is done with a low additional number of tasks re-executed compared to a total duplication. Furthermore, our fault tolerant approach is based on the following principle: when an error is detected during the execution of an application, we try to confine this error to prevent its spread to other parts of the application and make a recovery in order to make the program able to provide a correct result. In other words, our contribution in the field of integrity is related to the correctness of certification for distributed executions through result checking. Using an abstract representation of a parallel execution called macro-dataflow graph, partial duplication mechanisms are extended to provide probabilistic certification algorithms that are very efficient.

# References

1. CERT/CC Statistics 1988-2004, CERT Coordination Center,
   http://www.cert.org/stats/cert_stats.html
2. Germain, C., Playez, N.: Result Checking in Global Computing Systems. In: Proceedings of the 17th Annual ACM International Conference on Supercomputing (ICS 2003), SanFrancisco, California, 23-26 June, pp. 218–227 (2003)
3. Sarmenta, L.F.G.: Sabotage-Tolerance Mechanisms for Volunteer Computing Systems. Future Generation Computer Systems 18(4), 561–572 (2002)
4. Jafar, S., Varrette, S., Roch, J.-L.: Using Data-Flow Analysis for Resilence and Result Checking in Peer to Peer Computations. In: Proceedings of the 15th International Workshop on Database and Expert Systems Applications (DEXA 2004), Zaragoza, Espagne (2004)
5. Gao, L., Malewicz, G.: Internet computing of tasks with dependencies using unreliable workers. In: Higashino, T. (ed.) OPODIS 2004. LNCS, vol. 3544, pp. 443–458. Springer, Heidelberg (2005)
6. http://www.xtremwebch.net/doc/falsh.pdf
7. Tixeuil, S., Silva, L.M., Hoarau, W.: An Overview of Existing Tools for Fault-Injection and Dependability Benchmarking in Grids. In: Proc. of the Springer-Verlag, 2nd CoreGRID Workshop on Grid and Peer To Peer Systems Architecture (January 2006)
8. Tixeuil, S., Silva, L.M., Hoarau, W.: Fault-Injection and Dependability Benchmarking for Grid Computing Middleware. In: Proc. of the Springer-Verlag, Workshop of Integrated Research in Grid Computing, Pisa, Italy (November 2005)

9. Silva, L.M.: Reputation-based trust management systems and their applicability to grids, CoreGRID Technical Report, TR-0064 (February 2007)
10. Kondo, D., Araujo, F., Malecot, P., Domingues, P., Silva, L.M., Fedak, G., Capello, F.: Characterizing Result Errors in Internet Desktop Grids. In: Kermarrec, A.-M., Bougé, L., Priol, T. (eds.) Euro-Par 2007. LNCS, vol. 4641, pp. 361–371. Springer, Heidelberg (2007)
11. Kondo, D., Araujo, F., Silva, L.M., Domingues, P.: Result Error Detection on Heterogeneous and Volatile Resources via Intermediate Checkpointing. In: CoreGRID Workshop on Grid Programming Model/Grid and P2P Systems Architecture/Grid Systems, Tools and Environments, Heraklion, Greece (June 2007)
12. Varrette, S., Roch, J.-L., Leprevost, F.: FlowCert: Probabilistic Certification for Peer-to-Peer Computations. In: Proceedings of the 16th Symposium on Computer Architecture and High Performance Computing, IEEE SBAC-PAD 2004, Foz do Iguaçu, Bresil, pp. 108–115. IEEE, Los Alamitos (2004)
13. http://www.absoluteastronomy.com/topics/Most_recent_common_a ncestor
14. http://www.xtremwebch.net/
15. The Tunisian Research Grid GTRS (Grille Tunisienne pour la Recherche Scientifique), http://www.utic.rnu.tn/gtrs/index.htm

# Author Index